DATE DUE

~~OC 22~~ '97			

Right Turn

This book is printed on acid-free paper that meets the American National Standard for Permanence of Paper for Printed Library Materials.

Library of Congress Catalog Number: 96-21485
ISBN: 1-56000-257-3
Printed in the United States of America

Library of Congress Cataloging-in-Publication Data

Wolters, Raymond, 1938–
Right turn : William Bradford Reynolds, the Reagan administration, and Black civil rights / Raymond Wolters.
p. cm.
Includes bibliographical references and index.
ISBN 1-56000-257-3
1. Afro-Americans—Civil rights—History. 2. Reynolds, William Bradford. 3. Attorneys general—United States—Biography. 4. United States—Politics and government—1981–1989. I. Title.
KF4757.W65 1996
342.73'085'092—dc20 96-21485
[347.30285092] CIP

Right Turn

Right Turn

William Bradford Reynolds, the Reagan Administration, and Black Civil Rights

Raymond Wolters

Transaction Publishers

New Brunswick (U.S.A.) and London (U.K.)

This book is printed on acid-free paper that meets the American National Standard for Permanence of Paper for Printed Library Materials.

Library of Congress Catalog Number: 96-21485
ISBN: 1-56000-257-3
Printed in the United States of America

Library of Congress Cataloging-in-Publication Data

Wolters, Raymond, 1938–
Right turn : William Bradford Reynolds, the Reagan administration, and Black civil rights / Raymond Wolters.
p. cm.
Includes bibliographical references and index.
ISBN 1-56000-257-3
1. Afro-Americans—Civil rights—History. 2. Reynolds, William Bradford. 3. Attorneys general—United States—Biography. 4. United States—Politics and government—1981–1989. I. Title.
KF4757.W65 1996
342.73'085'092—dc20 96-21485
[347.30285092] CIP

For Jeff, Kevin, and Tom

Contents

Acknowledgments

This book was written the old fashioned way—without any foundation-subsidized time off and while teaching five courses and between 300 and 400 students each year; that is to say, this book was written during summer vacations. I had not planned it that way. In the past I had received fellowships that made it easier to write other books, but this time my applications for released time were unavailing. Perhaps, it was a blessing in disguise. It allowed me to proceed at my own pace and to discover the pleasure of being more actively engaged with students. I am grateful to the University of Delaware for a sabbatical leave and to the Earhart Foundation for funds that defrayed research expenses.

As an historian, I was trained to regard documents as better sources than interviews. For that reason, I am grateful to Jill Eastland for providing me with duplicate copies of speeches, memoranda, and correspondence from the files of William Bradford Reynolds. These records were then supplemented with the enormous quantity of documents that are available in the court records of several civil rights cases.

I am especially indebted to William Bradford Reynolds for cooperating with me on this project and for giving me complete freedom with respect to the method and the substance of the book. My notes mention a number of "interviews" with Reynolds, but they were a peculiar sort of interview. Before meeting with Reynolds, I would write chapters that were based almost entirely on written sources. Reynolds would then read those chapters, and we would get together for a few hours to discuss the text. Reynolds offered comments and suggestions, but I made the final decision on every point.

Another special debt is to my family and to our summer house at Long Point on the Bohemia River. After spending four or five hours writing each morning, I could walk out the door, climb on a boat, and patrol the waters of the Chesapeake Bay. As in the past, my wife Mary has been a tremendous source of support, companionship, and love. This book is dedicated to our three sons.

Introduction

When I first thought about a book on the civil rights policies of the Reagan administration, I had in mind a biographical study of William Bradford Reynolds, the assistant attorney general who was the principal architect of the administration's civil rights policies. At the time I had not met Reynolds, but from press reports I had the impression that he combined a good legal mind with opposition to every sort of racial discrimination. I wanted to write about a principled conservative who worked intelligently and persistently and, in the end, made a difference.

As it turned out, however, this book is less a biography than a study of legal policy in three important areas of civil rights law. After some introductory comments about Ronald Reagan and William Bradford Reynolds, the book proceeds to an analysis of their policies on voting rights, affirmative action, and school desegregation.

My major concern is with a series of what can be called "second-generation civil rights problems"—problems that usually are not discussed in accounts of the civil rights movement. The familiar emphasis is on segregation and discrimination against blacks, but by the 1980s another set of questions had come to the fore.

In the 1950s and early 1960s, most civil rights activists said that race and color were irrelevant to the proper consideration of a person's worth. They sought the advancement of blacks but assumed this could be accomplished if the government and private employers treated citizens as individuals, without regard to race, color, creed, or national origin. The Civil Rights Act of 1964 and the Voting Rights Act of 1965 called for nondiscrimination.

Later in the 1960s, new ideas gained currency. To make amends for the invidious discrimination of the past, some people called for benign discrimination to give blacks a special boost. In business and government this could be done if affirmative action was redefined to require racial preferences or quotas. In public education it could be accomplished by taking race into account when assigning students to school. In politics more could be done than ensure that each person had the right to vote; district lines could also be drawn to maximize the likelihood that African-Americans would actually be elected to office. "To get past racism," it was said, "we must first take account of race."[1]

During the 1970s the administrations of Richard Nixon and Jimmy Carter moved from color-blindness toward color consciousness, from nondiscrimination and the rights of individuals to affirmative discrimination and group rights. School desegregation turned into court-ordered busing for racial balance. "No discrimination" in employment came to signify opposition to policies (like testing or requiring educational credentials) that affected blacks adversely. "Voting rights" became a euphemism for affirmative gerrymandering.

By 1980 the course of civil rights had reached a crossroads. The nation had to choose between individual rights and group representation, between equality of opportunity and equality of results. This book maintains that Ronald Reagan made the *right turn*, not only when he opposed both quotas and forced busing but also when he questioned and limited the use of racial considerations in drawing electoral boundaries. The book also shows that the Reagan administration enjoyed considerable success in reviving within the judiciary (as well as reinforcing within the country) the conviction that rights inhere in individuals and that *all* people are entitled to the equal protection of the laws. In a speech to the American Bar Association, Reagan sounded the keynote of this policy:

> The promise in the Declaration of Independence, that we are endowed by our creator with certain inalienable rights, was meant for all of us. It was not meant to be limited or perverted by special privilege, or by double standards that favor one group over another.[2]

In response, critics of the administration said that Reagan wanted to "turn back the clock" on civil rights. They said that legal notions of color-blind impartiality sounded fair but actually served to prolong injustice. They depicted nondiscrimination as an obstacle to the compensatory racial preferences that were needed to improve the overall position of African-Americans. They said Reagan was a racist.

William F. Gibson, the chairman of the Board of Directors of the National Association for the Advancement of Colored People (NAACP), was one of the people who made this charge. Reagan was "basically a reactionary and a racist," Gibson declared. Benjamin J. Hooks, the executive director of the NAACP, was only slightly more charitable. When asked whether he thought Reagan was racially prejudiced, Hooks answered: "If he doesn't have a discriminatory bone in his body, somebody around him does."[3]

Several black journalists concurred. Carl T. Rowan wrote that Reagan's policies were "neither fair nor humane, but cruelty covered up by glib cliches." Manning Marable characterized Reagan's policies as "nonracist racism," and Roger Wilkins declared that an "insidious racism" pervaded "the entire Reagan domestic program." The key to Reagan's political success,

Wilkins said, was that Reagan had "found a way to make racism palatable and politically potent again."[4]

Three of the nation's most prominent African-Americans seemed to agree. Supreme Court Justice Thurgood Marshall said Reagan was "the worst" president of modern times; William T. Coleman, Jr., a black Republican who once served as secretary of Transportation, said the civil rights policies of the Reagan administration were "just about 100 percent wrong and despicable;" and historian John Hope Franklin asserted that Reagan "shared the views...that blacks lacked the qualities by which they could 'make it' in the way others made it." A *Washington Post* poll in 1986 indicated that 56 percent of blacks regarded Reagan as a racist.[5]

Reagan bristled when he heard allegations of racism. That charge "strikes at my heart every time I hear it," he said. "No matter how you slice it, that's just plain baloney."[6]

Reagan said he had worked for civil rights "before they used the term." When he was a sports announcer in the 1930s, Reagan recalled, he was "one among a handful in the country who opposed the banning of blacks from organized baseball." He also remembered that he took a black college teammate into his home as an overnight guest rather than patronize a segregated hotel. Reagan said he had been reared "in a household in which the only intolerance I was taught was the intolerance of bigotry." He said his father would not allow him and his brother to see the movie *Birth of a Nation* because it glorified the Ku Klux Klan. He remembered that his mother taught him to judge people as individuals, not by their creed or color.[7]

In 1948 Reagan campaigned enthusiastically for Harry Truman and apparently favored civil rights as liberal Democrats of that time conceived of them. In the 1960s, however, Reagan's support for the civil rights movement cooled. In 1965 he said the Civil Rights Act of 1964 should be "enforced at gunpoint, if necessary." But eight months later Reagan questioned the constitutionality of parts of the legislation and said he would have voted against it if he had been a member of Congress. Reagan also opposed the Voting Rights Act of 1965 (which he thought invaded rights that had been reserved to the states) and the Fair Housing Act of 1968 (which he considered to be violative of property rights).[8]

As Reagan saw it, the civil rights laws of the 1960s, although questionable for constitutional reasons, were enacted to bring an end to discrimination. These laws were the product of a national consensus that held that official racial classifications were morally wrong and ought not to be tolerated. Reagan recalled that Senator Hubert Humphrey, the chief sponsor of the Civil Rights Act of 1964, had said he would eat the bill's pages "one after another" if the new law contained language requiring racial preferences.[9]

Nevertheless, Reagan said, judges, government bureaucrats, and civil rights activists had "turned our civil rights laws on their head, claiming they mean exactly the opposite of what they say." "These people tell us that the government should enforce discrimination in favor of some groups." In 1985 Reagan said that "if Senator Humphrey saw how some people today are interpreting [the civil rights laws], he'd get a severe case of indigestion."[10]

Numerous examples could be cited to substantiate Reagan's point. By the 1980s most selective colleges and universities had double standards for admission, with black students, on average, scoring about 180 points lower than whites on the Scholastic Aptitude Test (SAT). This led to resentment, and not just among white students. Donald H. Werner, the headmaster of a private prep school, complained about the decision the University of California, Berkeley, made with respect to two California residents who had graduated from his school. "Student A was ranked in the top third of his class, student B in the bottom third.... Student A had SAT scores totaling 1290; student B's scores totaled 890. Student A had a record of good citizenship; student B was expelled...for breaking a series of major rules. Student A was white; student B was black. Berkeley rejected student A and accepted B."[11]

Nor were such instances limited to academia. By the 1980s, affirmative discrimination was common in the work place as well. Nevertheless, most Americans, when responding to Gallup polls, consistently expressed strong opposition to racial preferences.

> Q. Some people say that to make up for past discrimination, women and minorities should be given preferential treatment in getting jobs and places in college. Others say that ability, as determined by test scores, should be the main consideration. Which point of view comes closer to how you feel on the subject?[12]

Year	Give Preference	Ability
1977	10%	83%
1980	10%	83%
1984	10%	84%
1989	10%	84%

The results were similar when the Leadership Conference on Civil Rights sponsored a poll of its own. By the Reagan years, it seemed, many whites no longer regarded the civil rights movement as working to make sure that all citizens enjoyed equality of opportunity. Instead, they had come to regard the movement as a special-interest lobby that used rhetoric about "racial justice," while it pursued the interests of its own constituents at the expense of others. The results were so devastating that the Leadership Conference tried to suppress the findings of its own poll.[13]

Even before he became president, Reagan recognized that Democrats and liberals were vulnerable because they had abandoned their earlier opposition to racial discrimination and instead had come to support affirmative racial preferences to achieve equal outcomes. Reagan knew that some of the opposition to racial preferences stemmed from racism. But he also recognized that, in one of the ironies of history, many whites had come to favor the standard that the civil rights movement had upheld in the past—color-blind opposition to all forms of official discrimination. Reagan recognized that by campaigning for equality of opportunity and rejecting equality of results, Republicans could win the support of many white people who had previously voted Democratic.[14]

In a 1977 speech to the American Conservative Union, Reagan argued that Republicans should take advantage of the opportunity to create a new political coalition. They could maintain the support of the Republican base by continuing to favor lower taxes and less government regulation of business. And they could also use "the so-called social issues—law and order, abortion, busing, [and] quota systems"—to appeal to millions of other Americans "who may never have thought of joining our party before." Reagan wanted to reach out for "the man and woman in the factories, for the farmer, for the cop on the beat." His goal was "to combine the two major segments of contemporary American conservatism into one politically effective whole."[15]

Consequently, during the presidential campaign of 1980, Reagan criticized his Democratic opponent, Jimmy Carter, for supporting both busing for racial balance and racial preferences for jobs and admission to selective schools and programs. Reagan noted that the Carter administration had even defended the use of an explicit quota at the medical school of the University of California. On one occasion Carter said, "If I didn't have to get Senate confirmation of appointees, I could just tell you that 12 percent of all my judicial appointees would be blacks, 3 percent would be Spanish-speaking, 40 percent would be women, and so forth."[16]

Reagan rejected the idea of a society ordered along racial lines. Instead of proportional representation and equality of results, Reagan stood for individual rights and equality of opportunity. He also said he would appoint officials who would "carry out my policies...the policies that reflect our best principles as a nation." When it came to civil rights, Reagan said, the principle that would guide him "and the one embodied in the law, is one of nondiscrimination."[17]

In William Bradford Reynolds, Reagan found a like-minded assistant attorney general to head the Civil Rights Division in the Department of Justice. Reynolds was not a 50 percent civil righter who fought discrimination against blacks only. He was against all racial discrimination. His goal was to see that in areas covered by the law, no one suffered, and no one especially benefited, because of the color of his or her skin. At his first official appearance before a congressional committee, Reynolds said he was personally committed to the view that every person should be free "to pursue his or her goals in an environment of racial and sexual neutrality." The great lesson of contemporary history, Reynolds said, was that "discrimination on the basis of race is illegal, immoral, unconstitutional, inherently wrong, and destructive of democratic society."[18]

Reynolds also said that racial preferences were a "quick fix" that would have little curative effect. They did not address (and in fact diverted attention away from) the most serious problems that beset blacks—joblessness, family dissolution, indifference to schoolwork, and the destruction of neighborhoods by crime and drug trafficking. Rejecting the idea that race-conscious plans were an appropriate way to abolish the legacy of racism, Reynolds insisted that the United States could not "get beyond racism by borrowing the tools of the racist." If the government wanted to end racial discrimination, Reynolds said, it should do just that.[19]

Reynolds also maintained that preferences were dangerous because they created "a kind of racial spoils system in America" and fostered "competition not only among individual members of contending groups, but among the groups themselves." He noted that the United States was becoming a multiracial society and said that racial preferences, in addition to polarizing blacks and whites, would pit one minority against another. In the end, Reynolds predicted, preferences would foster, not soothe, resentments.[20]

From the outset of his tenure as chief of the Civil Rights Division, Reynolds declared his dedication "to the principled path of color-blindness, where the right to be free from government-imposed discrimination (no matter how benign the motive) inheres in *all* individuals." Reynolds did not say that U.S. society had become blind to racial differences, but he insisted that the government should not try to remedy historical discrimination with race-conscious affirmative discrimination.[21]

Reynolds was born in 1942 and was a direct descendant and namesake of Governor William Bradford, the Puritan leader who traveled to the New World on the *Mayflower*, wrote the classic history *Of Plymouth Plantation*, and served as governor of the colony nearly every year from 1621 until his death in 1657. Reynolds's mother, Nancy Bradford du Pont, was a scion of the prominent business family, and his maternal grandfather, Eugene (Popsey) du Pont, was an important industrialist who owned a vast estate where Reynolds as a youth spent several weeks each year hunting and fishing. Reynolds's father, William Glasgow (Scotty) Reynolds, was the head patent and trademark lawyer at the Du Pont Company, and his paternal grandfather, John Lacey Reynolds, was a Tennessee lawyer and county judge.

As a youth, Reynolds was educated at the private Tower Hill School and at Phillips Andover Academy. He then attended Yale University and the Vanderbilt University School of Law, where he graduated with the second-highest grades in his class and was editor-in-chief of the *Vanderbilt Law Review*. After graduation, Reynolds spent three years with a prominent New York Law firm and another three years on the staff of Erwin Griswold, the solicitor general of the United States. While employed by the solicitor general, Reynolds argued eleven cases before the Supreme Court and wrote some forty legal briefs that were submitted to the justices. Then, at the age of thirty-two, Reynolds became a partner in the Washington firm of Shaw, Pittman, Potts and Trowbridge, where he earned in excess of $200,000 a year specializing in commercial litigation. One of his cases involved the defense of the Metropolitan Edison Company after a much-publicized nuclear-power accident at Three Mile Island. When he joined the Reagan administration in 1981, Reynolds possessed securities valued at $1.7 million. His family owned much more.[22]

Attorney General William French Smith first heard of Reynolds from Griswold, whom Smith had come to know as a fellow trustee of the University of California. Griswold had already recommended Reynolds to head the division of the Department of Justice that handled civil litigation, but he said Reynolds could also do well with civil rights. In the years immediately prior to this, Reynolds had concentrated on commercial lawsuits, but Griswold recalled that when Reynolds had worked in the solicitor general's office he had worked on cases that involved school desegregation and voting rights.[23]

Smith immediately recognized the possibilities. Because Smith and President Reagan were on record as opposed to forced busing and racial preferences, the established civil rights leaders were certain to look with suspicion on anyone the Reagan administration nominated to head the Civil Rights Division. To minimize the opposition of such groups, it made sense to appoint someone who had worked on the staff of Erwin Griswold, a solicitor general whom the established civil rights leaders frequently praised.[24]

Smith also regarded it as an advantage that Reynolds would assume office with a working knowledge of civil rights law. This was important because the new assistant attorney general would have to control approximately 170 staff lawyers who were already employed in the Civil Rights Division. As Smith saw it, many of these lawyers were fired by a sense of mission. To advance the interests of blacks, they would manipulate, and even invert, the civil rights laws. They saw no problem if the inversions discriminated against nonblacks.[25]

To control his staff Reynolds put in prodigious hours, often staying up until the early morning and working on weekends as well. He did so to review and modify the legal briefs prepared by the staff lawyers, making sure that "equal rights" had not been twisted into "special preferences." Reynolds also assigned the important cases to a handful of top deputies. He later said that the struggle within the administration was just as significant as the more visible and publicized struggle with outside critics.[26]

Although Reynolds was personally committed to the principle of color-blind nondiscrimination, as a lawyer he knew that in the U.S. legal system the law includes not only statutes but judicial interpretations of the statutes. He recognized that although the civil rights laws of the 1960s had called for nondiscrimination, subsequent court rulings had countenanced a certain amount of compensatory discrimination. In the courtroom, as an attorney arguing specific cases for the U. S. government, Reynolds maintained that restrictions should be placed on compensatory discrimination. In public, as the chief spokesperson for the civil rights policies of the Reagan administration, he maintained that the national policy should be one of color-blind nondiscrimination.

In taking these positions, Reynolds scandalized people who thought the assistant attorney general for civil rights should function as part of the civil rights establishment. In a conversation with Reynolds in 1981, Maryland Senator Charles McC. Mathias made this point when he said, "I think you must be the advocate—the advocate—of all those people whom the civil rights laws had been designed to protect." Reynolds then answered, "No, Senator. As the assistant attorney general for the Civil Rights Division, my job will be to enforce the law."[27]

This response pointed to Reynolds's bedrock principles. As a matter of personal opinion, he favored policies that were color-blind and nondiscriminatory. And, as a matter of legal history, he thought the civil rights laws of the 1960s required nondiscrimination. One of his friends said that Reynolds reminded him of "a seventeenth-century lawyer. He gets ideas into his head that this is the way the law is, and then, by God, it's like that." Another friend explained that Reynolds had "a sense of the importance of principles that in some ways is out of tune with the more expedient ways of the 20th century." Yet another friend said that Reynolds became "a demi-god in the conservative movement because...he stands for something."[28]

Supreme Court Justice Clarence Thomas, then the chairman of the Equal Employment Opportunity Commission (EEOC), summarized the "something." Reynolds "zeroed in on an expansive reading of the law by the prior administration," Thomas said. "He doesn't want to undercut the law; he wants to roll back the law into a reasonable context. He does not want to discriminate against blacks, and he doesn't want to discriminate for blacks." Zebbie King, a black administrative assistant in the Civil Rights Division, agreed. She said Reynolds was "just trying to set the record straight so when the government works to stop discrimination against blacks, it does not allow discrimination against whites."[29]

Critics offered a different assessment. Instead of praising Reynolds for opposing all sorts of racial discrimination, they disparaged him as a headstrong ideologue. In the U.S. Senate, Arlen Specter of Pennsylvania criticized Reynolds for elevating "[his] own legal judgment over the judgment of the courts," while Howard Metzenbaum of Ohio found fault with Reynolds for "zealously pursuing [his] own interpretation of the law, rather than the law as enacted by Congress and as interpreted by the courts." Within the Department of Justice, career attorneys in the Civil Rights Division often clashed with Reynolds, and Solicitors General Rex E. Lee and Charles Fried sometimes found Reynolds a bit rigid and self-righteous.[30]

Some of the criticism was phrased in strong language. William Raspberry of the *Washington Post* depicted Reynolds as an "infiltrator" who had "transform[ed] his office into the opposite of what it was designed to be." According to Raspberry, the Civil Rights Division had been established to protect and promote the interests of African-Americans, but Reynolds was using the civil rights laws for the unanticipated purpose of making sure that efforts to advance blacks did not subject whites to reverse racial discrimination.[31]

Mary Frances Berry, a black historian and a member of the U.S. Commission on Civil Rights, made a similar point in more theoretical language. As Berry saw it, the civil rights laws were intended to give special benefits to minorities that had been disfavored in the past. They were not enacted to protect those whose interests were already protected and sustained by an economic and social structure that allegedly had been put in place to benefit white men. Thus, according to Berry, it was a violation of the civil rights laws to discriminate against blacks or women, but not illegal to discriminate against white men.

> Civil rights laws were not passed to give civil rights protections to all Americans.... Instead, they were passed out of a recognition that some Americans already had protection because they belonged to a favored group; and others, including blacks, Hispanics, and women of all races, did not because they belonged to disfavored groups.[32]

Some of Reynolds's critics complained that Reynolds had unilaterally revised the law. They said that if Congress had objected to affirmative racial preferences, it could have changed the law—in essence telling those who had developed or sanctioned preferences that they had misunderstood the intention of Congress. The critics said that Congress' failure to do so should be understood as an endorsement of benign discrimination. Robert Drinan, a congressman from Massachusetts, explained that if the Reagan administration was convinced that racial preferences were wrong, "it could, of course, ask Congress to make that clear." According to Drinan, the administration had not done so because it knew Congress was "not likely" to insist on racial impartiality. Congress would not do so because most members thought "the existence of pervasive discrimination based on race can be corrected only by sophisticated techniques of recognizing race for benign purposes."[33]

This argument seemed worthy, but actually was deceptive. Under the U.S. system of government, a bill can become a law only if it surmounts a host of obstacles that have been deliberately embedded in the structure of the Constitution. But the racial preferences of the 1970s, unlike the nondiscrimination of the civil rights laws of the 1960s, had become a social policy without ever having been subjected to the conventional legislative process.

The critics were demanding that Reynolds do more to repeal racial preferences and forced busing than the initiators of the policies had done in the 1970s. The policies had been created administratively and judicially, but the critics were saying that to change things the Reagan administration should surmount the checks and balances associated with the usual legislative process. This tilted the playing field for, as Richard E. Morgan has noted, the same set of interest groups that are

> insufficient to persuade Congress to adopt a policy in the first place, may be quite sufficient, if the policy can be put in place judicially or bureaucratically, to keep the legislature from disestablishing it.[34]

The nub of the critics' complaint was that Reynolds opposed the race-conscious policies that most civil rights groups had favored in the recent past. The National Conference of Black Mayors declared that "race- and sex-conscious measures" were "the most successful remedy in reducing racial and sexual discrimination." Mickey Leland, a leader of the Congressional Black Caucus, affirmed that his group was "united" in its view that "aggressive affirmative action" was needed "to eradicate, once and for all, the wholesale discrimination against groups in our society." The *Nation* accused Reynolds of "dismantling the apparatus previous administrations had built to facilitate the redress of grievances regarding discrimination." The *New York Times* faulted Reynolds for opposing "decades of hard-won advances."[35]

The criticism of Reynolds culminated in June 1985, when the Senate Judiciary Committee rejected President Reagan's nomination to promote Reynolds to the third-highest position in the Department of Justice, associate attorney general. The rejection came as a surprise, since Republicans at the time outnumbered Democrats on the committee, 10 to 8. The Democrats on the committee, almost all of whom depended on the support of groups that favored racial preferences and busing for racial balance, were expected to vote against Reynolds, but the final vote went against Reynolds because the Democrats remained united while two Republicans switched sides. The swing votes were cast by Senators Arlen Specter of Pennsylvania and Charles McC. Mathias of Maryland, who both favored the sort of affirmative action that the Reagan administration opposed.[36]

The Senate hearings on Reynolds's nomination for associate attorney general provided a dramatic forum for assessing the civil rights policies of the Reagan administration. At these hearings, civil rights activists took particular exception to Reagan and Reynolds's approach to voting rights, affirmative action, and school desegregation. They said the administration's policies in these areas were so misguided as to disqualify Reynolds for the promotion. One of the major purposes of this book has been to assess the evidence that was presented at the Senate hearings.

Reynolds's critics rejoiced when the promotion was defeated, but they were mistaken if they thought the rejection would prompt Reynolds to resign. Instead of prompting a return to private life, the failed promotion increased Reynolds's determination to continue as assistant attorney general for civil rights. Ronald Reagan reinforced this determination by telling Reynolds, "Don't you go anywhere. I'm counting on you to stay." In a radio address to the country, Reagan said that "Reynolds's civil rights views reflect my own," that "the policies he pursued are the policies of this administration, and...will remain our policies as long as I am president."[37]

Reynolds also stayed on because, despite the rebuff by the Senate Judiciary Committee, he never lost the confidence of Attorneys General William French Smith and Edwin Meese. Some observers speculated that Meese, who had his own bruising confirmation battle with the Senate Judiciary Committee, felt a kinship born of adversity. In any case, after Reynolds's rejection for associate attorney general, Meese vowed that Reynolds would receive "important new duties."[38]

Meese kept his word. Before long, Reynolds, while remaining in charge of the Civil Rights Division, also had influence in almost every important policy issue at the Department of Justice. He helped choose a new director of the FBI, and he advised the attorney general on matters as diverse as the strategy for combating pornography and the legal arguments that should be presented with respect to abortion and church-state relations. Reynolds was one of three Justice Department officials who conducted the initial fact-finding inquiry into the Iran-Contra affair. He also was the chairman of the Strategic Planning Board, a group of senior officials who planned Department of Justice policy at breakfast meetings every other Thursday.[39]

Reynolds eventually became Meese's most trusted advisor and confidant. Reynolds conveyed something of the nature of his relationship with Meese when he said, "Whenever [Meese] is in town, and sometimes when he's out of town, I'm with him. If he's in by 7 A.M., generally I'm in at 7. If he's in at 8,

I'm in at 8, and I see him from the beginning of the day right through the day on a whole raft of things. It really is a very close, one-to-one relationship." Reynolds said he visited Meese's office three or four times a day, "maybe more than that."[40]

Reynolds also worked closely with the solicitor general and his staff of elite lawyers who represented the government in the Supreme Court—so closely that one critic characterized Reynolds as the "Shadow Solicitor." Solicitor General Charles Fried later observed that although Reynolds's "official title gave him a quite limited role, in fact he was ubiquitous."[41]

In 1987 Reynolds received a second title, counselor to the attorney general, a designation that did not require approval by the Senate Judiciary Committee. One reporter characterized this appointment as "a brassy act of defiance," since Reynolds had in effect received "the job the...Senate denied him in 1985, plus additional power and control the Senate had not contemplated." Senator Joseph Biden of Delaware complained that the Reagan administration was "doing indirectly what it could not accomplish directly." Senator Edward Kennedy of Massachusetts accused the administration of making "an end run" around the Senate.[42]

Reynolds's influence continued to grow after Attorney General Meese became preoccupied with the Iran-Contra matter and distracted by the death of a grandson and an investigation of the Wedtech Corporation. In October 1987, one official who admired Reynolds flatly stated that Reynolds had become "the real head of the department." *New York Times* reporter Kenneth B. Noble wrote that by then Reynolds was "the department's most important official." Juan Williams of the *Washington Post* wrote that "a case could be made that Meese had allowed Reynolds to become the de facto attorney general."[43]

Thus ensconced at the Department of Justice, Reynolds proceeded on two fronts. In legal briefs and arguments presented to the appellate courts, he continued to make the case for the administration's civil rights policies. And he took special care to see that sympathetic judges were appointed to the federal courts. "There's no way we could have accomplished our goals," he later said, "without appointing judges who understood our philosophy. Fortunately, both [Attorneys General] Bill Smith and Ed Meese asked me to play a major role in choosing judges during that eight-year period."[44]

Smith and Meese turned to Reynolds because Reynolds had a plan. He calculated that by 1988 President Reagan would be able to appoint three or more Supreme Court justices and something like one-half of all federal judges. He thought the Reagan judges could check liberal misinterpretations and assert sound constitutional principles without endangering the prospects for a Republican successor to Reagan. The successor could then continue the work by appointing more conservative judges to roll back the tide of affirmative discrimination.[45]

Reynolds recognized that this strategy would work only if the Reagan administration departed from the approach of previous Republican administrations. Past Republican presidents had appointed federal judges primarily on the basis of party membership and recommendations from bar associations. Reynolds, however, insisted that the Reagan administration should pay attention to the legal philosophy as well as the technical, professional competence of prospective judges.[46]

Reynolds played the key role in 1986 in choosing Associate Justice William H. Rehnquist as the successor to the retiring Chief Justice Warren E. Burger. Attorney General Meese and President Reagan barely knew Rehnquist personally, although they were aware of Rehnquist's reputation as the Court's most conservative justice. Reynolds, on the other hand, had known Rehnquist since the early 1970s, when they had offices on the same hall in the Department of Justice. Reynolds drew on that familiarity to convince Meese and Reagan that Rehnquist had the personal qualities that were needed to become an effective chief justice.[47]

The harder decision concerned the nomination for the seat that was then vacant on the Court. At the top of the administration's short list stood the names of two Reagan-appointed judges on the U.S. Court of Appeals in Washington: Robert H. Bork and Antonin Scalia. Both were good writers and brilliant legal theorists, and they were thought to be equally conservative. But Reynolds and Meese favored Scalia because they feared that the combination of Rehnquist and Bork would provoke a huge confirmation fight in the Senate. "If we put the two of them [Rehnquist and Bork] up there together, they would have made a big target," Reynolds said. Reynolds thought Bork should be nominated for the next vacancy on the Court.[48]

White House counsel Peter Wallison favored a different approach. He recommended that Bork be chosen for the first vacancy, on the grounds that Rehnquist would shield Bork because most of the criticism probably would be directed at Rehnquist. If the administration postponed Bork's nomination, Wallison predicted, feminist and civil rights groups would gang up on him.[49]

It turned out that Wallison was right. But as Reagan listened to the discussion, his attention focused on the fact that Scalia would be the first Italian-American to sit on the Supreme Court. It was noted, too, that at age fifty Scalia was nine years younger than Bork and that Bork was overweight and a heavy smoker. In the end, Reagan sided with Reynolds and chose Scalia.[50]

In 1987 Reagan endorsed two more of Reynolds's recommendations for appointments to the Supreme Court. When Justice Lewis H. Powell retired that summer, Reynolds and Meese had no difficulty persuading Reagan that the time had come to put Bork on the Court. By 1987, however, the Democrats had gained control of the Senate, and Bork's nomination was eventually rejected by a vote of 58 to 42.[51]

After Bork's defeat, two names rose to the top of the list of candidates to succeed Justice Powell: Anthony M. Kennedy and Douglas H. Ginsburg. Reynolds thought well of Kennedy, who since 1975 had been a judge of the Ninth Circuit Court of Appeals in California. If Kennedy were put on the Supreme Court, Reynolds said, he would probably decide "the right way 99 out of 100 times." Yet Reynolds detected notes of caution in some of Kennedy's previous judicial opinions. There was a slight chance, Reynolds came to fear, that a Justice Kennedy would equivocate and perhaps even endorse some liberal misinterpretations of the Constitution.[52]

Reynolds therefore supported the candidacy of Douglas H. Ginsburg of the appeals court in Washington. Reynolds did so because he knew Ginsburg personally and was confident that Ginsburg could be trusted to support the administration's positions on abortion, affirmative action, and antitrust law. "I knew it for a fact," Reynolds said. "Doug and I were very good friends. We went back a long way. We had had discussions."[53]

Reynolds then rallied Attorney General Meese and President Reagan to support Ginsburg. In this instance, however, the nomination became a disaster almost as soon as it was announced. It turned out that Ginsburg had run a computerized dating service as a college student and that his second wife, a doctor, had performed abortions. In addition, it was learned that during the 1970s, when he had been a law professor at Harvard, Ginsburg had smoked marijuana at parties. Taking everything into account, Ginsburg did not measure up to the standards expected of a conservative justice. Finally, only two weeks after the nomination had been announced, Reynolds called Ginsburg at his home and told him he must withdraw.[54]

Attorney General Meese then informed Kennedy that he would be nominated for the Supreme Court. "Sometimes the Lord works in mysterious ways," Meese said. Kennedy was quickly confirmed, by a vote of 97 to 0.[55]

With Kennedy and Scalia as justices of the Supreme Court, and with Rehnquist as chief justice, the Court changed its approach to proportional representation, affirmative racial preferences, and busing for racial balance. These three justices, together with Byron White and Sandra Day O'Connor and others who would be appointed when George Bush succeeded Ronald Reagan as president, made up a Supreme Court that eventually endorsed much of Reagan and Reynolds's approach to civil rights.

These cases and opinions of the Supreme Court will be described in the body of this book. Three opinions that came down in 1989 were especially important. In one case from Richmond, Virginia, the Supreme Court placed strict limitations on state agencies that wished to reserve or set aside positions or contracts for members of minority groups. In a case from Alaska, the Court said that people who made allegations of employment discrimination must satisfy a more demanding burden of proof than that to which they had been accustomed. And in a case from Birmingham, the Court affirmed that white workers were entitled to bring lawsuits alleging reverse discrimination.[56]

Two years later the Court endorsed Reagan and Reynolds's key points on school desegregation. In a case from Oklahoma City, the Court said that busing for racial balance was intended as a temporary measure to remedy past discrimination, and it allowed for a return to neighborhood schools even if that led to racially imbalanced enrollments.[57]

Then, in 1992 and 1993, the Court handed down two rulings that endorsed Reagan and Reynolds's approach to voting rights. In a case from Alabama it ruled that the voting rights act did not require the federal government to approve changes in the authority of state and local officials; and in a case from North Carolina it placed limits on the measures that could be taken to promote the proportional representation of blacks.[58]

Reynolds felt vindicated by these decisions. "I think our effort succeeded," he said. "We wanted to get rid of group entitlement and equal results and move toward equal opportunity. I think that's been accomplished." Reynolds noted that the Supreme Court had said "that if you charge discrimination, you have to prove discrimination.... And the remedies better be narrowly tailored, and they better be careful that they don't discriminate against anyone else." "As a practical matter," Reynolds said, "that's the whole ball game."[59]

For once, the leaders of the civil rights lobby agreed with Reynolds. Ralph Neas of the Leadership Conference conceded that "some elements of the Reagan Administration's Justice Department's views have found favor in the Supreme Court." Benjamin Hooks of the NAACP declaimed, "Night has fallen on the Court as far as civil rights are concerned." Hooks said the Supreme Court had become "more dangerous to this nation than any Bull Connor with a fire hose; than any Jim Clark with a billyclub; more dangerous than Ross Barnett standing, saying 'they shall not pass'; more dangerous than George Wallace proclaiming, 'Segregation today, segregation tomorrow, segregation forever.'" By 1990, civil rights activists were demanding that Congress take action to curb an errant Supreme Court.[60]

Despite the successes with the Supreme Court, Reagan and Reynolds were denied some of their victory because the administrations of George Bush and Bill Clinton backed away from enforcing the Supreme Court's new rulings on voting rights, affirmative action, and school desegregation. This led one despairing scholar, Abigail M. Thernstrom, to complain that affirmative discrimination had become "so institutionalized that court decisions will have the most marginal effect.... [It] almost doesn't matter what the Supreme Court does." Writing at the end of the Reagan administration, Robert B. Hawkins, the president of the Institute for Contemporary Studies, similarly noted that "preferential policies remained"; and Robert R. Detlefsen, a professor at Hollins College, concluded that "the administration was unable substantially to redirect civil rights policy."[61]

In the long run, however, what the Supreme Court says is likely to matter. This is especially so when the point at issue concerns the widely popular principle that citizens should not be disadvantaged because of their race or ancestry. My guess is that color-blind nondiscrimination eventually will predominate and that Reynolds's effort to coax the Supreme Court back to the principle of the 1964 Civil Rights Act will be regarded as one of the most significant developments of the Reagan years.

Yet, as the following text will show, Reynolds's success did not come easily. He had to return to the Supreme Court again and again and again. In the end, Reynolds made a difference, but only because he was tenacious in challenging the idea that broad racial preferences were required to make amends for racial discrimination.

Principle and tenacity. These were the qualities that characterized Reynolds. They also were qualities that endeared him to many of the conservative activists who followed Ronald Reagan to Washington. By the end of the Reagan years, Reynolds was regarded as a much more than a good soldier with an upper-class pedigree. He had become a paradigm of the conservative lawyer on active service with the government. The humorist Russell Baker even reported that "ninety-seven Young Fogies out of one hundred" had taken to wearing wire-rim glasses as a way of "showing respect for William Bradford Reynolds, whom they always refer to as 'Brad,' whether they know him or not."[62]

This book explains why many conservatives regarded Reynolds as one of the heroes of the Reagan revolution. It does so by describing and assessing Reagan and Reynolds's policies with respect to voting rights, affirmative action, and school desegregation.

Notes

In a book with so many quotations, some difficult decisions had to be made with respect to documentation. The notes contain references to all sources that were quoted directly or paraphrased closely, but to save space I have consolidated the citations into a single note for each paragraph in the text. I have also mentioned some books and articles that influenced my thought greatly, but I decided against using the notes as a bibliography of the already vast and steadily increasing literature on the Reagan administration, the civil rights movement, and civil rights law.

1. Statement of Justice Harry Blackmun, University of California v. Bakke, 438 U.S. 265 (1978), 407.
2. *New York Times*, 2 August 1983, 14:1.

3. *Washington Post*, 18 May 1985, A4a; *Los Angeles Times*, 24 February 1982, 17:1.
4. Carl T. Rowan, *Breaking Barriers* (Boston: Little Brown and Company, 1991), 326, 315; *Greene County Democrat*, 4 January 1989; 11 January 1989; 1 February 1989; *Nation* (3 November 1984): 437. Marable was a black scholar who wrote a syndicated column that appeared in several black newspapers.
5. Carl T. Rowan, *Breaking Barriers*, 326, 315, 318; *Washington Post*, 22 July 1984, Bld; 9 September 1987, A8e; *Nation* (3 November 1984): 437; *New York Times*, 9 July 1984, 10:1.
6. *Washington Post*, 16 September 1982, Alb; *New York Times*, 16 September 1982, 1:1; 1 July 1982, IV, 21:1.
7. *Wilmington News Journal*, 9 June 1985; *New York Times*, 26 July 1981, IV, 4:3; Ronnie Dugger, *On Reagan* (New York: McGraw-Hill, 1983), 196; Ronald Reagan, *An American Life* (New York: Simon and Schuster, 1990), 30, 52.
8. Ronnie Dugger, *On Reagan*, 197–8.
9. *Congressional Record*, 12723, 7420 (1964).
10. *New York Times*, 16 June 1985, 25:1; *Los Angeles Times*, 16 June 1985, 5:2.
11. *New York Times*, 4 June 1988, 27:1. For the median SAT scores of blacks, whites, and Asians at 26 selective colleges, see Richard J. Herrnstein and Charles Murray, *The Bell Curve* (New York: The Free Press, 1994), 452.
12. The Gallup Polls have been conveniently summarized by Ben Wattenberg, *The First Universal Nation* (New York: The Free Press, 1991), 67.
13. *Wall Street Journal*, 18 March 1991, A14:1 and A14:6.
14. For a good discussion of this point, see Thomas Byrne Edsall and Mary D. Edsall, *Chain Reaction* (New York: W. W. Norton and Company, 1991), passim.
15. Ronald Reagan, *A Time for Choosing* (Chicago: Regnery Gateway, 1983), 184, 189, 185.
16. Jimmy Carter, quoted by Theodore H. White, *America In Search of Itself* (New York: Harper & Row, Publishers, 1981), 215.
17. *New York Times*, 16 June 1985, 25:1; *Los Angeles Times*, 16 June 1985, 5:2.
18. James J. Kilpatrick, "Some Remarkable Ironies," *Wilmington News Journal*, 4 June 1985; WBR, statement to House Committee on Education and Labor, 23 September 1981, quoting Alexander M. Bickel, WBR Papers.
19. WBR, remarks at Chautaqua Institute, 30 June 1987, WBR Papers; *New York Times*, 10 August 1982, 17:6; 30 May 198 , 6:1.
20. *Los Angeles Times*, 13 February 1982, 6:1; *New York Times*, 30 April 1983, 7:4; WBR, remarks at Amherst College, 29 April 1983, WBR Papers; Paul A. Gigot, "Lone Wolf's Work," *Wall Street Journal*, 16 June 1989, 6:3.
21. WBR, remarks to Bureau of National Affairs, 14 June 1984, WBR Papers; *Time*, 13 May 1985, 58.
22. *Current Biography Yearbook* (1988): 476.
23. Interview with WBR, 11 January 1991.
24. Ibid.
25. Ibid.
26. Ibid.
27. Nomination of William Bradford Reynolds to be Associate Attorney General, *Hearings before the Senate Judiciary Committee*, 97th Congress, 1st Session, June 1985, 130 (cited hereafter as 1985 Senate Hearings).
28. *Washington Post Magazine* (10 January 1988): 13, 15; Lincoln Caplan, *The Tenth Justice* (New York: Alfred A. Knopf, 1987), 84.

29. Juan Williams, "William Bradford Reynolds" *Washington Post Magazine* (10 January 1988): 13.
30. *1985 Senate Hearings*, 9; *Los Angeles Times*, 19 June 1985, 8:1; 28 June 1985, 1:4.
31. *Washington Post*, 13 December 1984, A19a; 28 June 1985, A25e; *Wilmington News Journal*, 7 June 1985. In response, Reynolds pointed to statistics that indicated that during his tenure 90% of the work of the Civil Rights Division was on behalf of minorities and women.
32. *Toward an Understanding of Stotts* (U.S. Commission on Civil Rights: Clearinghouse Publication 85, January 1985), 63.
33. *America* (24 September 1983): 144–47; Melvin I. Urofsky, *A Conflict of Rights: The Supreme Court and Affirmative Action* (New York: Charles Scribner's Sons, 1991), 171.
34. Richard E. Morgan, *Disabling America: The 'Rights Industry' in Our Time* (New York: Basic Books, 1984), 187.
35. *1985 Senate Hearings*, 146, 815–16; *Nation* (29 June 1985): 1; *New York Times*, 7 November 1985, 35:1; 19 June 1985, 21:1.
36. *1985 Senate Hearings*, passim. For press coverage, see the stories in the *New York Times* and the *Washington Post*, June 1985.
37. Interview with WBR, 11 January 1991; *National Review* (12 July 1985): 18–19.
38. *New York Times*, 3 October 1985, II, 8:3.
39. Ibid.; Charles Fried, *Order and Law* (New York: Simon & Schuster, 1991), 43.
40. *New York Times*, 20 October 1987, 32:3.
41. Lincoln Caplan, *The Tenth Justice*, 81; Charles Fried, *Order and Law*, 41.
42. *U.S. News* (23 November 1987): 23–24; *Washington Post Magazine*, 10 January 1988, 15; *Washington Post*, 19 May 1987, A17d.
43. *New York Times*, 20 October 1987, 32:3; *Washington Post Magazine*, 10 January 1988, 17.
44. Interview with WBR, 13 November 1991.
45. Ibid.; William Kristol, "The Constitution: Standing Tall on Realignment," *American Spectator* (February 1985): 20–21.
46. Ibid.
47. David G. Savage, *Turning Right: The Making of the Rehnquist Supreme Court* (New York: John Wiley & Sons, 1992), 8–9.
48. Ibid., 17.
49. Ibid., 18.
50. Ibid., p. 17.
51. Ibid., 133–46. Also see Robert H. Bork, *The Tempting of America* (New York: The Free Press, 1990); and Ethan Bronner, *Battle for Justice* (New York: W. W. Norton & Company, 1989).
52. David G. Savage, *Turning Right*, 177. Reynolds was haunted by the specter of Harry Blackmun. Blackmun was an obscure appeals court judge who had been a compromise choice after the Senate rejected two of Richard Nixon's earlier nominees. Blackmun had been considered a conservative when he was appointed to the Supreme Court, but he later embraced much of the liberal agenda. He upheld the legality of affirmative racial preferences, opposed any form of school prayer, and wrote the controversial opinion on abortion, *Roe v. Wade*.
53. Ibid., 176.
54. *Human Events*, 14 and 21 November 1987; David G. Savage, *Turning Right*, 180.

55. David G. Savage, *Turning Right*, 180; *New York Times*, 4 February 1988, 18:1.
56. Richmond v. Croson, 488 U.S. 469 (1989); Wards Cove v. Atonio, 109 S.Ct. 2115 (1989); Martin v. Wilks, 490 U.S. 755 (1989).
57. Oklahoma City v. Dowell, 111 S.Ct. 630 (1991).
58. Presley v. Etowah County Commission, 60 LW 4135 (1992); Shaw v. Reno, 61 LW 4818 (1993).
59. *Wall Street Journal*, 16 June 1989, 6:3; interview with WBR, 13 November 1992.
60. *New York Times*, 13 June 1989, II, 5:1 and 5:3; 10 July 1989, 14:1.
61. Abigail M. Thernstrom, "Permafirm Action," *New Republic* (31 July 1989): 19, 17; Robert B. Hawkins, Introduction to Robert R. Detlefsen, *Civil Rights Under Reagan* (San Francisco: Institute for Contemporary Studies, 1991), ix, 4.
62. *National Review* (12 July 1985): 18–19; *New York Times Magazine* (3 August 1986): 12.

Part I

Voting Rights

Introduction to Part I

In 1965 President Lyndon B. Johnson ordered his staff to prepare the "goddamndest, toughest voting rights bill" they could devise. The ensuing Voting Rights Act turned out to be more far-reaching than Johnson had recognized at the time. The new law quickly achieved its original objective—guaranteeing blacks the right to register and vote. Subsequently, as a result of twenty years of interpretation, revision, and implementation, the law was turned into an affirmative action program for black politicians. By the 1980s the United States had reached a point almost no one had envisioned in 1965. Allegations of racial discrimination in voting rarely involved access to the polls; they involved, instead, charges that local governments had failed to arrange electoral boundaries to facilitate the election of blacks.[1]

Voting rights activists vigorously criticized William Bradford Reynolds and the policies of the Reagan administration. The activists initially faulted Reynolds and Reagan for opposing a 1982 proposal that Reynolds said amounted to a quota system for black politicians. Then, after an amended version of the proposal became law, voting rights activists faulted Reynolds for not insisting that local governments must create the maximum number of districts that were safe for black candidates (that is, districts where blacks made up about 65 percent of the voters). Asserting that Reynolds was dragging his feet on affirmative gerrymandering, the activists accused the administration of disrespect for the established law.[2]

At the same time, other critics paradoxically found fault with the Reagan administration for going too far on voting rights. Although conceding that Reynolds had parted company with voting rights activists in some instances, these critics said Reynolds generally sided with the civil rights organizations on voting rights—but that he did so as part of a scheme to use voting rights to boost the fortunes of the Republican Party.[3]

The allegations were grave. But were they well-founded? To answer, it is necessary to review the course of voting rights since 1965.

Notes

1. Abigail M. Thernstrom, *Whose Votes Count? Affirmative Action and Minority Voting Rights* (Cambridge: Harvard University Press, 1987), 15; Steven R.

Lawson, *Black Ballots: Voting Rights in the South, 1964–1969* (New York: Columbia University Press, 1976); Lawson, *In Pursuit of Power: Southern Blacks and Electoral Politics, 1965–1982* (New York: Columbia University Press, 1985).

2. Frank R. Parker has offered this explanation of what is sometimes called the "65 percent rule": "[S]tatistics confirm that not only must districts be majority-black for black voters to elect candidates of their choice, but generally the districts must be at least 65 percent black in population and 60 percent black in voting-age population, a standard recognized...as the '65 percent rule.' This figure reflects the realities of black political participation that, because of socioeconomic differences and past discrimination, blacks generally constitute a smaller proportion of the voting-age population than of the total population, are registered to vote at lower rates than whites, and turn out to vote at lower rates than whites. Consequently, the black population percentage of a given election district must be augmented 5 percent for voting-age disparities, 5 percent for registration disparities, and 5 percent for turnout disparities, so that at 65 percent, black voters will have a chance of electing candidates of their choice." *Black Votes Count* (Chapel Hill: University of North Carolina Press, 1990), 138–39.
3. For examples, see the articles by Matthew Cooper and Abigail M. Thernstrom, cited below in chapter 7, notes 3 and 4.

1

Preclearance

The Voting Rights Act of 1965 gave the federal government powerful weapons for fighting racial discrimination in nine southern states. In theory, these states had been singled out for special treatment because they met two criteria—they had used literacy tests, and fewer than 50 percent of their adults had voted in the 1964 presidential elections. In fact, they had been singled out because racial discrimination was known to be especially prevalent in certain states and counties.[1]

The Voting Rights Act targeted these areas. In addition to banning racial discrimination, it suspended literacy tests, authorized the federal government to dispatch officials to register voters and to observe the casting and counting of ballots, and required the "covered" jurisdictions to seek approval or "preclearance" from either the attorney general of the United States or from the District Court for the District of Columbia for any electoral changes that were made after 1 November 1964.[2]

The ban on racial discrimination was permanent. It did not need periodic extensions. But because preclearance was at odds with dual federalism and states' rights, the Voting Rights Act established preclearance for only five years. In 1970 the practice was extended for another five years, and in 1975 there was a second extension until 6 August 1982. A "bailout" provision stated that, at that time, districts that had not used any discriminatory devices since 1965 would be released from preclearance.[3]

Preclearance was considered necessary because prior to 1965 discrimination against blacks had continued despite the Fifteenth Amendment's guarantee that the right to vote should not be denied or abridged on account of race. In 1960, only 29.1 percent of all voting age blacks were registered to vote in eleven southern states, compared with 61.1 percent of whites.[4]

To insure that the Fifteenth Amendment was enforced across the land, voting rights activists said it was necessary to go beyond a 1957 law that gave the Department of Justice the power to bring lawsuits against racial discrimination in voting. They demanded close federal supervision of southern elections, even if this supervision infringed upon rights that had been reserved to the states. Jack Greenberg, a lawyer for the NAACP, recalled instances in the past where electoral arrangements were struck down by courts as discriminatory but replaced with other devices that accomplished the same end. A requirement that voters must have "good character" might be substituted for the literacy test, or a complicated residency requirement might be devised. Some laws were enacted with knowledge that they would affect blacks disproportionately. One Louisiana law, for example, disfranchised seven categories of people, including partners in common-law marriages and parents of illegitimate children.[5]

Some southern officials boasted about this. In 1960 Mississippi governor James Coleman candidly acknowledged that elected officials were using ingenious laws to prevent blacks from voting. "Any legislature can pass a law faster than the Supreme Court can erase it," Coleman observed.[6]

To protect the voting rights of minorities, the Voting Rights Act of 1965 required states with a past record of discrimination to seek federal approval of any change that touched on voting. If they thought at all about the system of federalism, voting rights activists apparently regarded states' rights as existing in a category akin to constitutional guarantees suspended in wartime. They said the southern states had forfeited the right to control their elections. "Preclearance did not just happen," explained Herbert O. Reid, a lawyer for the NAACP. "It resulted from the 'hard knocks' of experience."[7]

In 1965 Ronald Reagan saw things differently. He stressed that Article I of the Constitution authorized states to set their own qualifications for voting. The Fifteenth Amendment limited states' rights—by giving the federal government the power to make sure that states did not discriminate racially. But restricting the franchise on the basis of literacy was not the same as restricting because of race. Some states and districts had invited federal regulation because they had used literacy tests to camouflage racial discrimination, but other areas were using literacy tests impartially because they thought the ability to read and write promoted an intelligent use of the ballot. According to Reagan, the Fifteenth Amendment did not give anyone the right to vote. It allowed states to set qualifications for voting as long as they did not abridge or deny the right to vote because of race, color, or previous condition of servitude. It allowed states to have literacy tests as long as the tests were not used to disguise racial discrimination.

Guilty districts could be prosecuted under existing laws, Reagan maintained. But the fact that some areas were guilty was no excuse for piling one constitutional wrong upon another. Reagan thought the Voting Rights Act was a bad bill because it sought to remedy a violation of one part of the Constitution, the Fifteenth Amendment, by assaulting the very foundation of the Constitution, the principle of federalism. Reagan said he was "in complete sympathy" with the goals and purposes of the Voting Rights Act, but nevertheless opposed the legislation because it was, "in my view, unconstitutional."[8]

Reagan's position should have appealed to William Bradford Reynolds. Like Reagan, Reynolds believed that the genius of U.S. constitutional government lay in its division of sovereignty, its separation of powers. Under the system designed by the nation's founders, Reynolds said, there were guarantees of states' rights and limits on the power of the national government. Reynolds was opposed to what he called "a radical enlargement of the national government's powers...over the legitimate authority of the States." Reynolds thought the dispersion of power, and the autonomy of the states, had played a key role in protecting individual liberties. He considered it "tragic" that by the 1980s "the framers' original commitment to limited and decentralized government...ha[d] all but disappeared."[9]

Yet despite his agreement with Reagan on the theory of federalism, Reynolds never opposed the Voting Rights Act. In 1965, when he was a law student, Reynolds viewed the legislation as necessary. He continued to believe the Voting Rights Act was a useful tool to combat voting discrimination in the 1980s.[10]

However, Reynolds did have some misgivings. He knew it was arbitrary to have a 50 percent test to determine which districts could have a literacy test. Under the terms of the 1965 Voting Rights Act, for example, Hyde County, North Carolina, was "covered" and could no longer use a literacy test, because only 49.7 percent of the voting age population had cast ballots in 1964; but in New York City, Manhattan was not covered because 51.3 percent had voted there.[11]

The arbitrariness was especially galling because by 1969 blacks were more likely to be voting in the covered states than elsewhere. By 1980, 72.2 percent of adult blacks were registered to vote in Mississippi, as compared with 46.5 percent in New York, 48.9 percent in New Jersey, and 52.4 percent in Washington, D.C. But, because of past sins, the southern states had been singled out for preclearance, while no such sanction was applied to the District of Columbia, New Jersey, and most of New York. Because of preclearance, every time a southern jurisdiction made an electoral change—every time it moved a polling place or changed the hours for registration—the jurisdiction had to have prior approval from the attorney general in Washington.[12]

The preclearance feature of the act was scheduled to end in 1982 if it was not renewed by Congress. Many southerners regarded the continuation of preclearance as an unfair form of regional discrimination. Former North Carolina Senator Sam Ervin even said that voting rights activists "harbored prejudices against Southerners akin to those they professed to be desirous of eradicating from Southern minds." Senator Thad Cochran of Mississippi complained that because of preclearance local officials had to "go to Washington, get on their knees, kiss the ring, and tug their forelock to third-rate bureaucrats."[13]

Emory Folmar, the mayor of Montgomery, Alabama, expressed the complaint of many white Southerners. Since there had not been a "sustained complaint" against his city since 1965, Folmar said it was unfair to require Montgomery to prove its innocence "before some faraway tribunal." Folmar noted that preclearance "presupposes guilt." "Treat us as equals," he pleaded. "If we do something wrong, right the wrong." But under the U.S. legal system, people were not supposed to be incarcerated "just to keep them honest. No, we must have proof of guilt before judge and jury, before even the most unsavory character can be removed from society."[14]

Yet when the constitutionality of preclearance was challenged, only one member of the Supreme Court agreed with Mayor Folmar's position. Under preclearance, Justice Hugo Black wrote, the Southern states were being treated like "conquered provinces." They were required "to submit in advance any proposed legislation" and then send local officials "hundreds of miles away to beg federal authorities" for approval. Black thought it "inconceivable...that such a radical degradation of state power was intended in any of the provisions of the Constitution."[15]

The majority of the Court, however, held that preclearance was a constitutionally valid way to implement the Fifteenth Amendment and to "banish the blight of discrimination in voting." Chief Justice Earl Warren acknowledged that preclearance was "an uncommon exercise of congressional power," but Warren noted that "exceptional conditions can justify measures not otherwise appropriate." Preclearance should be "judged with reference to the historical experience which it reflects." Because the South had been ingenious in devising methods "to bar Negroes from the polls," it was appropriate for federal authorities to review any new proposals "to determine whether their use would perpetuate voting discrimination."[16]

For the next two decades, this would remain the standard defense of preclearance. In 1984 Justice John Paul Stevens reiterated that Congress had established preclearance as a response to the "'unremitting and ingenious' defiance of the command of the Fifteenth Amendment for nearly a century in certain parts of the nation." The basis for preclearance, Stevens wrote, "was a presumption that jurisdictions which had 'resorted to the extraordinary stratagem of contriving new rules of various kinds for the sole purpose of perpetuating voting discrimination in the face of adverse federal court decrees' would be likely to engage in 'similar maneuvers in the future.'"[17]

While proponents of preclearance stressed these dangers, critics noted that the gap between black and white voter participation had closed appreciably, and said it was unfair to continue to single out the South for special treatment. Whereas only 29.1 percent of blacks had been registered to vote in the eleven states of the former Confederacy in 1960, as compared with 61.1 percent of whites, by 1975 the differential had shrunk to only 4.8 percent (63.1 percent as compared with 67.9 percent).[18]

Many Southerners insisted that their states had reformed. South Carolina Senator Strom Thurmond spoke for them when he said it was time either to suspend federal supervision of local elections or to apply the supervision nationwide. Former Attorney General Griffin Bell, a native of Georgia, bluntly declared, "You still need to protect the right to vote, but the preclearance argument is poppycock.... The Voting Rights Act is no longer required in that area."[19]

Ronald Reagan had long regarded the selective application of the Voting Rights Act as "humiliating to the South," and during the campaign of 1980, he had advocated that the law be applied to all fifty states. During the campaign Reagan had also promised, in Mississippi, that he would "restore to state and local governments the power that properly belongs to them." He said, further, that federalism and states' rights would be guiding principles during his administration.[20]

This rhetoric irritated blacks. "For black people, states' rights has mainly been states' wrongs," Jesse Jackson observed. Moreover, because of mounting criticism of affirmative action and because of the Reagan administration's proposed cuts in social and welfare programs, the civil rights movement seemed to be in retreat. To counter this impression, black leaders were determined to oppose any dilution of the Voting Rights Act. Parren Mitchell, a black Congressman from Maryland, explained that because of "the climate we find ourselves in," any dilution of the Voting Rights Act would be of "enormous significance." It would augment "a fear that was already pervading the black community." "This is going to be one of the toughest civil rights fights of all time," said civil rights lawyer Joseph Rauh.[21]

Civil rights activists rejected the suggestion that preclearance should be applied to all fifty states. They said that if minorities outside the South received the same sort of federal protection, the limited budget of voting rights enforcers would be stretched too thin. If preclearance were extended nationwide, "it would be strengthened to death." Voting rights activists insisted that preclearance should continue to be focused on the South.[22]

The strength of the black commitment to preclearance created a problem for the Reagan administration. Reagan did not wish to antagonize blacks and felt he could not afford a bloody battle over voting rights at the same time he was pushing for painful budget cuts. But philosophically preclearance was at odds with Reagan's belief in states' rights, and the president also wanted to take a position that would maintain the support of Southern whites.

Fortunately for the administration, it turned out that by 1981 the question of regional discrimination had become passé for many whites. Southern officials routinely complained about preclearance, but they had learned to live with the Voting Rights Act. Preclearance was no longer regarded as a call to arms; it had become simply a "burdensome" but "trivial" administrative procedure, one city attorney explained. Besides, most proposals eventually were approved (all but 695 of 39,000 submitted between 1965 and 1980, as it turned out).[23]

Consequently, the administration intentionally dropped any plans to alter preclearance. When specific proposals were made to ease the burden of federal supervision of Southern elections, they did not come from the White House or the Department of Justice. They issued instead from the office of Henry Hyde, a Republican Congressman from Illinois. And Hyde proceeded without cooperation from the Reagan administration.[24]

By 1982 Hyde thought the time had arrived to release reformed jurisdictions from the burden of preclearance. "A handful of southern states have been in the penalty box for 17 years," Hyde declared. Many districts could honestly say they had lived up to the law, that they had not had a single complaint of racial discrimination in voting, and that they had not used any subtle schemes to deny any citizen the right to register or vote. Hyde implied that preclearance was similar to a curfew imposed after a riot—an emergency measure that should be lifted as soon as conditions allowed. He further believed the Southern states had reformed and were entitled to be treated like states elsewhere in the country. He thought it was time to end the requirement that electoral changes in the South must be approved by the attorney general. Specifically, Hyde proposed to shift the burden of proof. Localities that wanted to change voting policies would no longer have to prove that changes were not discriminatory; instead, complaining parties would have to prove they were.[25]

Hyde was a states' righter who said the "sovereign states are important entities" that "ought to be treated alike." He also had reservations about the administrative process of preclearance. Because many Southern communities before 1965 had compiled what Hyde called "a pretty tragic, shabby record" in voting rights, the region had been denied the presumption of innocence, saddled with the burden of proof, and deprived of control over its elections. This reminded Hyde of preventive detention. It was similar to saying that those who came from groups with "a profile of criminality" should forfeit the presumption of innocence. This might prevent crimes, but at the cost of violating basic precepts of justice. It was time, Hyde said, to restore due process to the South. If a Southern state or district manipulated electoral changes to practice racial discrimination in voting, the wrong could be righted through the courts. If a district was found guilty in court, that district could fairly be subjected to preclearance. But Hyde thought it was no longer necessary to assume guilt, no longer necessary to make the South prove its innocence in a distant, bureaucratic tribunal. Hyde explained,

> I have a preference for court proceedings, where the rights and rules of evidence and burdens of proof have full play. I think more justice for both sides is available there. Yes, you can get quick justice in an administrative proceeding with one man sitting behind the desk, but...we have a court system to adjudicate rights under the rule of law.[26]

Most black leaders rejected the suggestion that preclearance had outlived its usefulness and now represented nothing more than unwarranted federal intrusion in local elections. Harold E. Ford, a black Congressman from Tennessee, expressed a prevailing view when he said "the Voting Rights Act...has worked well for 17 years. I don't think we are totally ready to say that it is...no longer necessary or that the burden of proof of discrimination should be on the complaining party. This is not the time to retreat."[27]

Some black leaders added psychological arguments. After noting that blacks had benefited disproportionately from some programs that the Reagan administration proposed to curtail, Ralph Abernathy of the Southern Christian Leadership Conference warned that the mood of blacks might become ugly if "in addition to being thrown off the welfare rolls, we are now placed at the mercy...of state governments on so fundamental a right as voting." Eddie N. Williams of the Joint Center for Political Studies said that if social programs were cut back, "the only real safety net that minorities and the poor can rely on is their own capacity to influence the political system."[28]

Several officials of the NAACP insisted that preclearance was still needed to insure the right to vote. Benjamin Hooks said the Southern states had not so completely redeemed themselves that the need for preclearance no longer existed. Elaine Jones said that "any weakening" of preclearance would be "totally unacceptable" and would "send us back to the period before 1965." Michael Brown feared that Hyde's proposal would embolden "the 'good ole boys' to turn back the clock and the calendar to the 'good old days' which were dark days for blacks." Aaron Henry declared, "We must not risk a return to the conditions that we struggled so long to change."[29]

Some whites concurred. Without preclearance, they predicted, some Southern districts would refuse to locate polling places in black neighborhoods, and other jurisdictions would shape electoral boundaries to the disadvantage of black candidates. Historian J. Morgan Kousser said that nineteenth-century white southerners had destroyed black political power after Reconstruction by using "at least sixteen different techniques," many of which were "facially neutral and might even be upheld by courts today." Kousser warned that if preclearance were ended, white Southerners might use "sophisticated means of abridging black political power." Historian C. Vann Woodward also warned that "a weakening of...the preclearance clause will open the door to a rash of measures to abridge, diminish, and dilute if not emasculate the power of the black vote in the southern states."[30]

When Henry Hyde presented legislation to end preclearance, California Congressman Don Edwards, the chairman of the House Judiciary Subcommittee on Civil and Constitutional Rights, arranged for hearings in Washington and elsewhere. Edwards instructed his staff to work closely with the major civil rights groups, and as a result only 13 of the 156 witnesses who appeared before the House committee supported Hyde's legislation. In part this was because Hyde called only a few witnesses. Later he explained that he did not wish to subject his supporters to the "intimidating style of lobbying" that civil rights groups employed. Hyde maintained that sincere critics of preclearance should not have their motives challenged, stating that "no one wishes to be the target of racist characterization."[31]

Hyde's comments smacked of rationalization and excuse. Nevertheless, some of those who supported Hyde's proposal at the congressional hearings were treated rudely—or worse. One congressman insinuated that the testimony of Robert Brinson, the city attorney of Rome, Georgia, should not be believed because in the past there had been wrongdoing in his region. Another complained about the way University of Georgia professor A. B. Saye used the word "Negro." Abigail M. Thernstrom, a scholar who was then writing a book on the Voting Rights Act, withdrew as a witness after learning that civil rights leaders would deny interviews and otherwise refuse to assist her research if she did not back out of the hearings. Wilber O. Colom, a black lawyer from Mississippi, said that voting rights activists resorted to unfair tactics when they tried to persuade him not to testify. "It stopped being pressure and started being intimidation at some point," Colom recalled. "My father said that he had never heard such vicious things about his son."[32]

Civil rights activists were doing whatever was necessary to defeat Hyde's proposal. One congressional aide privately explained, "The ends justify the means, and we'll do whatever we have to do." A Senate Judiciary Subcommittee later reported that it was "remarkable that so little opportunity...was afforded to those individuals" who supported Hyde's bill.[33]

The lobbying against Hyde's bill was conducted by the Leadership Conference on Civil Rights. This organization had been established in 1950, and over the years the original black, labor, and Jewish groups had been joined by Hispanic, Asian, Chicano, and women's groups. In 1981 the Leadership Conference was made up of 165 groups.[34]

Critical journalists characterized the Leadership Conference and its executive director, Ralph Neas, as "mountebanks" who were able "to bully politicians" who desperately wanted to avoid "being labelled racist or sexist." In an essay for the *Wall Street Journal*, political scientist John Bunzel, a former president of San Jose State University, characterized the civil rights movement as "a good cause" with "a lot of justice on its side." But, Bunzel wrote that "no one invited to testify before Congress should have to bow to this sort of pressure."[35]

More sympathetic observers praised Neas for holding the Leadership Conference together, for shaping the way the media presented the debate over voting rights, for establishing lobbying groups in each of the twenty-seven districts represented by members of the House Judiciary Committee, and for using the intensely committed, grassroots networks of several member organizations to generate an avalanche of mail to members of Congress. One Congressman who had been opposed to preclearance reported that he received 4,000 letters urging that the practice be continued and none urging that it end. Another observed, "There are few members, whatever their philosophy, who can look at mail running a thousand to one on an issue and not give serious consideration to voting for the side with the thousand."[36]

The Leadership Conference also presented several witnesses who told the House committee that violations of voting rights continued to be of such magnitude as to justify preclearance. Summarizing the testimony, the *Washington Post* stated editorially that "witness after witness" described "various schemes...to discourage minority voters from going to the polls." Coretta Scott King said "a succession of witnesses" had shown why preclearance was "desperately needed."[37]

It came as no surprise when congressional allies of the civil rights activists cited this testimony as evidence of the need to continue preclearance. Colorado Congresswoman Patricia Schroeder declared, "[T]he states down there, even under the Voting Rights Act, have found clever little ways to tap-dance around [the law]." Congressman Don Edwards characterized the alleged violations as "outrageous." For Schroeder and Edwards, the hearings proved that the South had not mended its ways since 1965 and should spend still more time in the penalty box.[38]

Surprisingly, Henry Hyde eventually agreed with Schroeder and Edwards. After listening to several days of testimony, Hyde said he had "not heard anything that would make me want to advance my own legislation." Hyde said he had received mail "from legislators and officials in the South who really feel that they're being unfairly treated." But few southern officials came forward at the hearings. On the contrary, Hyde said, "all I have heard is the need to continue [preclearance]." Hyde was so appalled by what he heard that he withdrew his proposal. "There are some jurisdictions which deserve to remain covered," he concluded. "You're being dishonest if you don't change your mind after hearing the facts. I was wrong and now I want to be right."[39]

Hyde's about-face captured the attention of the media as well as that of his colleagues in the House of Representatives. But what was the evidence that caused Hyde to cease his opposition to preclearance? None of the 156 witnesses cited an instance of any individual being denied the right to register or vote. Ralph Abernathy mentioned incidents he had observed in 1948, but the testimony before the House committee did not include claims of specific people being denied the right to vote after passage of the Voting Rights Act of 1965. Senator Strom Thurmond later put the question directly to Drew S. Days, a black former assistant attorney general for civil rights: "Do you know of anyone in these covered jurisdictions who has attempted to register or vote and was refused?" Days could not identify any such person.[40]

What, then, caused Hyde to change his mind? Part of the answer, Hyde said, was that many districts had taken "no constructive steps" to make amends for the discrimination of the past. The South no longer used the poll tax, the property tax, literacy tests, or intimidation at the ballot box. Dixie had desisted from negative discrimination against blacks. But it had not made an affirmative effort to facilitate ready access to voting.[41]

Many localities had not made it convenient for blacks to register and vote. They did not allow voters to register at supermarkets, churches, and other often-frequented places. Instead, they required that registration forms be filled out at court houses and city halls. Officials at some polling places allegedly refused to assist handicapped and illiterate voters. In some counties, registration had to be done during normal working hours, and in others registration for federal elections would be held in one place while registration for local elections would be conducted elsewhere.[42]

Jesse Jackson said these provisions were "tantamount to a poll tax" because they required voters to take off time from work and to pay bus fare to get to registration centers and polling places. Gracie Hillman, a voting rights activist from Mississippi, conceded that "you don't have things like the poll tax anymore.... But you've got these other laws on the books that make it damned difficult to do any serious voter registration." Henry Hyde said it was "outrageous" to limit registration hours "from 9 to 5." He said such limitations were "absolutely designed" to discourage voting by "people who are working and have difficulty travelling." Hyde also characterized the location of voting places as "subtle intimidation" and "also wrong."[43]

After withdrawing his proposal to end preclearance, Hyde moved to a fall-back position. Districts should be allowed to "bail out" from preclearance, Hyde said, if they met certain conditions—if the attorney general had not objected to any substantial changes submitted, and if there was evidence of "constructive efforts to enhance minority participation in the electoral process." Unlike Hyde's first bill, which would have ended preclearance except for districts that had been found guilty of discrimination, the new proposal retained preclearance unless a district proved itself to be beyond reproach. "The first proposal would have made preclearance the exception, even in the South; the second left it the rule."[44]

Some civil rights leaders thought Hyde's second proposal had some merit. Ralph Neas said something might be done "to let those counties which...had conscientiously eliminated their discriminatory practices get out from under preclearance." Neas and some others thought the Leadership Conference would benefit from being perceived as reasonable. Neas also calculated that with Hyde's support the 1982 revision of the Voting Rights Act would be reported out of the House Judiciary Committee "with a 3–1, 4–1, even a 5–1 margin, that would begin to give us the irresistible force that otherwise couldn't be counted on, on the House floor."[45]

Although some voting rights activists considered Hyde's second proposal equitable as well as good politics, hard-line activists complained that it would allow some Southern districts to avoid preclearance; in addition, the hard-liners calculated that they had sufficient votes to extend preclearance without making any compromises. Led by Frank R. Parker, who had experience as a voting rights lawyer in Mississippi, the hard-liners threatened to publicly and openly oppose the bill if Neas and the Leadership Conference cooperated with Hyde on bailout. "My integrity was impugned," Neas recalled. "The hostility was unbelievable." One observer reported that "there was a whole lot of screaming and name-calling," and another recalled, "Everybody was yelling at everybody."[46]

To keep his coalition together, Neas insisted on a different bailout proposal, one that voting rights litigators themselves drafted as "the perfect bailout provision—what we would like in the best of all possible situations."[47]

The proposal extended preclearance permanently, and the terms for bailout were made much tougher than Hyde had proposed. Hyde would have denied bailout to any district that had been found guilty of discrimination; the hard-liners would deny bailout to any district that had accepted a consent decree to resolve litigation over voting rights. Hyde proposed that districts be eligible for bailout if the attorney general had not objected to any substantial change; the hard-liners insisted that eligibility be denied to districts which had not received approval for minor changes like moving a polling place. As a condition for bailing out from preclearance, Hyde would have required districts to make "constructive efforts to enhance minority participation"; the hard-liners insisted on stronger language that appeared to make at-large voting and run-off requirements an absolute bar to bailout.[48]

Henry Hyde had drafted a sensible bailout proposal. But Ralph Neas and the Leadership Conference persuaded a majority of the House Judiciary Committee to vote against Hyde's bill. Some members of the committee did not understand the subtleties of specific provisions. Others discounted their reservations because they did not wish to appear to be opposed to voting rights.

In the end, even Henry Hyde voted for the proposal favored by the Leadership Conference. Eventually it passed the Judiciary Committee, 23–1, and was approved in the House by a vote of 385 to 24. As passed by the House, the Voting Rights Act of 1982 permanently extended preclearance and established stringent criteria for bailout. In 1982 hard-line voting rights advocates said that 200 southern counties—one-fourth of the total—could satisfy the stringent bailout criteria, but, as of 1995, none had done so.[49]

Notes

1. Abigail M. Thernstrom, *Whose Votes Count?*, 17.
2. Public Law 80-110 (1965).
3. Ibid.
4. *Report of the Subcommittee on the Constitution*, Senate Judiciary Committee, 97th Congress, 2nd Session, 1982, 61 (cited hereafter as 1982 Subcommittee Report).
5. House Judiciary Committee Hearings, Extension of Voting Rights Act, 97th Congress, 1st Session, 1981, 436 (cited hereafter as 1981 House Hearings); Adam Fairclough, *Race and Democracy: The Civil Rights Struggle in Louisiana* (Athens: University of Georgia Press), 233. For a good account of voting discrimination in Mississippi, see John Dittmer, *Local People: The Struggle for Civil Rights in Mississippi* (Urbana: University of Illinois Press, 1994).
6. 1981 House Hearings, 24; *Time* (11 May 1981): 24–25.
7. 1981 House Hearings, 419–21.
8. Ronnie Dugger, *On Reagan*, 197–8; James J. Kilpatrick, "Voting Rights Bill 'Piles Wrong on Wrong,'" *Washington Star*, 25 March 1965.
9. William Bradford Reynolds, "Power to the People," *New York Times Magazine* (13 September 1987): 18; Reynolds, "Our Magnificent Constitution," *Vanderbilt Law Review*, 40 (1987): 1343–51.
10. Interview with WBR, 28 February 1992.
11. Abigail M. Thernstrom, *Whose Votes Count?*, 41.
12. Ibid., 35; *1982 Subcommittee Report*, 61. In 1970 Congress extended the ban on literacy tests to the entire nation, and in 1970 and 1975 the Voting Rights Act was amended to give protection to foreign-language minorities. By 1980 preclearance was required in parts of twenty-two states, including New York.
13. Hearings Before the Subcommittee on the Constitution, Senate Judiciary Committee, 97th Congress, 2nd Session, 1982, v. II, 137 (cited hereafter as 1982 Senate Hearings); *Time* (11 May 1984): 24–25.
14. 1981 House Hearings, 1512–13.
15. South Carolina v. Katzenbach, 383 U.S. 301 (1966), 360, 359.
16. Ibid., 308, 334, 312, 316. Chief Justice Warren appeared to concede that the Voting Rights Act was a draconian measure, but one that was justified by the severity of the problem it addressed. The implication of the chief justice's opinion was that a suspension of states' rights would not have been justified if the historical experience had been different.
17. McCain v. Lybrand, 465 U.S. 236 (1984), 243, 245.
18. *1982 Subcommittee Report*, 61.
19. *New Republic* (6 December 1980): 11–12; *Time* (11 May 1981): 24–25; *New York Times*, 13 September 1981, 33:1; *New York Times Magazine* (27 September 1981): 107.

20. Laurence I. Barrett, *Gambling With History* (Garden City: Doubleday, 1983), 426; *Washington Post*, 9 May 1981, A8a; *New York Times*, 11 March 1981, II, 20:1; 4 March 1981, 1:3.
21. *New York Times*, 11 March 1981, II, 20:1; 6 July 1981, 9:5; *Washington Post*, 3 October 1981, A3a; *Time*, 11 May 1981, 24–25.
22. Statement of Eddie N. Williams, *1981 House Hearings*, 1836.
23. Statement of Robert N. Brinson, *1981 House Hearings*, 220; *1982 Senate Hearings*, 1657–58.
24. When Hyde proposed to end preclearance, the administration gave Attorney General William French Smith six months to review the matter. During this interval members of the administration maintained public silence on the question.
25. Abigail M. Thernstrom, *Whose Votes Count?*, 91; 1981 House Hearings, 2–3, 483, 436–40; *Washington Post*, 3 June 1981, A23f; 12 June 1981, A17f.
26. *1981 House Hearings*, 927, 921, 187–88, 14.
27. Ibid., 1441–43.
28. Ibid., 89, 1832–55; *Washington Post*, 17 June 1981, A24e.
29. *1981 House Hearings*, 893; *Washington Post*, 21 May 1981, C1a; 29 March 1981, A9f; 25 June 1981, D2b.
30. *1981 House Hearings*, 2012–13, 2022, 2000–2001.
31. *1982 Subcommittee Report*, 18; *1982 Senate Hearings*, 393–94; *Washington Post*, 29 January 1982, A10a.
32. John Bunzel, "Hardball Voting Rights Hearings," *Wall Street Journal*, 19 March 1982, 26:4; 1981 House Hearings, 440–68, 2098–2109.
33. *Wall Street Journal*, 19 March 1982, 26:4; *1982 Subcommittee Report*, 18.
34. Michael Pertschuk, *Giant Killers* (New York: W. W. Norton, 1986), 148–60; Barton Gellman, "The New Old Movement," *New Republic* (6 September 1982): 10–13.
35. *American Spectator* (July 1982): 4–5; *Wall Street Journal*, 19 March 1982, 26:4.
36. Michael Pertschuk, *Giant Killers*, 148–60; *Black Enterprise* (March 1982): 56; *Human Events* (15 May 1982): 3–4.
37. *Washington Post*, 31 July 1981, A20a; *1981 House Hearings*, 1937–41.
38. *1981 House Hearings*, 175, 176.
39. Ibid., 485, 2063; *Washington Post*, 30 July 1981, A7d; Michael Pertschuk, *Giant Killers*, 159. For a similar statement by Virginia Congressman Thomas J. Bliley, see 1982 Senate Hearings, 486.
40. *1981 House Hearings*, 95; *1982 Senate Hearings*, 1368.
41. *Washington Post*, 30 July 1981, A7d.
42. Henry Hyde, "Why I Changed My Mind on the Voting Rights Act," *Washington Post*, 26 July 1981, D7b.
43. *Washington Post*, 11 June 1983, A1f; 17 May 1983, A2a; 1981 House Hearings, 1584; Michael Pertschuk, *Giant Killers*, 159.
44. 1981 House Hearings, 1816–17; Abigail M. Thernstrom, *Whose Votes Count?*, 91.
45. Michael Pertschuk, *Giant Killers*, 162.
46. Ibid., 169; *New Republic* (6 September 1982): 13.
47. Michael Pertschuk, *Giant Killers*, 173.
48. Abigail M. Thernstrom, *Whose Votes Count?*, 90–103.
49. Ibid., 97, 102–3; *1982 Senate Hearings*, 222.

2

At-Large Elections, Minority Vote Dilution, and The Results Test

Some witnesses at the 1981 House hearings on voting rights complained that southern districts were guilty of more than just refusing to take affirmative steps to facilitate registration and voting. They said "a new generation of discriminatory measures" had "replaced the literacy test and the poll tax." Jesse Jackson explained that many procedures, while not denying blacks the right to register or cast ballots, "diluted" the significance of black votes. In many areas, Jackson noted, whites thwarted blacks by electing officials *at-large* rather than by ward or district. According to Jackson, these areas had "simply moved from blatant tyranny to surreptitious tyranny."[1]

Because of racially polarized voting—the tendency of voters to cast ballots for candidates of their own race—minority candidates rarely won at-large elections (elections that encompassed an entire state or metropolis). But minorities often made up a majority of the population in certain parts of a city or region, and minority candidates were likely to win if representatives were chosen from districts whose boundaries coincided with the areas where minorities were concentrated.

Some whites understood this clearly. When the Voting Rights Act became law in 1965, they knew they could no longer deny blacks the right to vote. Therefore, they shifted their strategy to reducing the influence of the black vote. They did so most effectively by establishing at-large elections.

At-large elections were nothing new. In 1960, 60 percent of U.S. cities with populations of more than 10,000 elected their council members at large, while only 23 percent elected them solely from districts. Most of the at-large systems had been initiated in the early 1900s as part of the progressive crusade against the inefficiency of the ward system of government. Under the ward system, each small district had elected its own representative. But the ward leaders often supported local projects for one another without concern for overall cost or the general needs of the wider municipality. To put an end to this, and to facilitate the election of candidates who had broader perspectives, progressives wanted city council members to stand for election in citywide, at-large elections.[2]

When some Southern jurisdictions turned to at-large elections after 1965, however, it was to dilute the political power of blacks. Many whites thought black officials would be incompetent, venal, and corrupt. They thought the election of large numbers of blacks would lead to a deterioration in the quality of government, just as they believed the integration of large numbers of black students had led to problems with discipline, social events, and academic standards at many desegregated public schools.[3]

Opponents of school desegregation had stated their rationale openly but later learned that candor could be used against them in court. Therefore, the opponents of black political empowerment were more circumspect. Without saying why they were doing so, many jurisdictions switched from district to at-large elections for city and county governing boards and for members of the state legislature. Some jurisdictions also eliminated elections for some offices, and others gerrymandered district boundaries to ensure white majorities.

During the late 1960s and 1970s, voting rights lawyers successfully challenged many of these not-so-subtle efforts to cancel the black vote. The court battles against discriminatory structural changes were difficult and many years in duration, but by 1980 so many courts had ruled against efforts to dilute black political power that some observers thought the discriminatory structures had all but disappeared.

But voting rights activists insisted that still more should be done. By 1980 they were saying that the Voting Rights Act should require a different sort of racial gerrymandering—the sort that would maximize the number of elections actually won by black candidates. They insisted that if blacks were not elected in proportion to their percentage of the population, elections should be held by district rather than at large—even if there was no proof that the at-large system had been instituted or maintained for discriminatory purposes. Diane Pinderhughes, then a professor at Dartmouth College, observed that the civil rights movement had entered "a second phase," with blacks striving for "a share of political government" in addition to "citizenship rights." Richard L. Engstrom, a professor at the University of New Orleans, noted that the focus in voting rights was shifting from "the previous emphasis on denial of the vote to a new emphasis on dilution of the votes." The South was facing what Engstrom called "a second generation of electoral discrimination issues."[4]

By 1982 voting rights activists wanted preclearance to be used in ways not anticipated in 1965 but well understood by the time of Ronald Reagan's presidency. They wanted preclearance to be denied if the boundaries of electoral districts did not coincide, wherever possible, with the boundaries of predominantly black neighborhoods. According to journalist Robin D. Roberts, "what many proponents of [voting rights] really want is something far beyond the original purpose of the act. They want the act to be interpreted to require the election of black officials to represent black voters." Political scientist Edward J. Erler made the same point:

> Emphasis has shifted from the issue of equal access to the ballot for racial minorities to the issue of equal results. The issue is no longer typically conceived of in terms of the right to vote but in terms of the right to an effective vote; no longer in terms of disfranchisement but in terms of dilution. The old assumption that equal access to the ballot would ineluctably lead to political power for minorities has given way to the proposition that the political process must produce something more than equal access. The new demand is that the political process, regardless of equal access, must be made to yield equal results.[5]

The Voting Rights Act of 1965 had been intended to enfranchise Southern blacks. "The problem that the bill was aimed at was the problem of registration," explained Burke Marshall, the assistant attorney general for civil rights in the administration of President Lyndon B. Johnson. "If there is a problem of another sort, I would like to see it corrected, but that is not what we were trying to deal with in the bill." Johnson's attorney general, Nicholas deB. Katzenbach, concurred. "The whole bill is really aimed at getting people registered," he said. "Our concern...is to increase the number of citizens who can vote."[6]

In 1969, however, in *Allen v. State Board of Elections*, the Supreme Court reinterpreted the meaning of the act. Despite spirited dissents from Justices Hugo Black and John Marshall Harlan, the Court changed the meaning of disfranchisement. It did so by distinguishing between "meaningful" and "meaningless" votes and by holding that the Voting Rights Act protected blacks from the "dilution" of their political power. One of the points at issue in *Allen* concerned a Mississippi Code of 1966 which allowed counties to change from district to at-large voting for county supervisors. Writing for the Court's majority, Chief Justice Earl Warren held that changes such as this must be precleared by the attorney general in Washington. Warren explained that "the right to vote can be affected by a dilution of voting power as well as by an absolute prohibition on casting a ballot." He said, "The Voting Rights Act was aimed at the subtle as well as the obvious" methods of discrimination. As interpreted by the Warren Court, the Voting Rights Act required Southern states to submit for federal approval not only new laws that might deny blacks the right to register or vote, but also all laws that might have an adverse effect on the political strength of blacks.[7]

The framers of the 1965 law had known that at-large arrangements diminished the prospects of black candidates for public office. Nevertheless, they aimed the Voting Rights Act at disfranchisement; they had not mentioned minority vote dilution. When renewing the legislation in 1970 and 1975, however, Congress, acquiesced in the Supreme Court's redefinition of disfranchisement. In 1978, after conceding that the Voting Rights Act had been interpreted broadly in *Allen*, the Supreme Court itself noted that such construction apparently enjoyed the approval of Congress: "Had Congress disagreed with this broad construction," the Court declared, "it presumably would have clarified its intent when re-enacting the statute in 1970 and 1975."[8]

Congress did more than acquiesce. In 1970 and 1975, when it extended coverage of the Voting Rights Act to Chicanos, Puerto Ricans, and other language minorities, Congress embraced the new approach to minority vote dilution. The law of 1965 had applied only to states that had intentionally practiced racial discrimination. After 1970 the Voting Rights Act also protected language minorities that had not been subjected to traditional forms of disfranchisement, although like blacks their power was fragmented by at-large voting.

One could not plausibly argue that the language minorities needed the protection of preclearance to prevent local authorities from resurrecting ingenious discriminatory subterfuges. One could argue only that affirmative districting was desirable as a method of augmenting Hispanic political power. By extending the protection of the Voting Rights Act to language minorities, Congress tacitly acknowledged that it no longer conceived of voting rights in terms of access to the polls. For Congress, as earlier for the Supreme Court, the emphasis had shifted to one of protecting minority candidates by the advantageous drawing of single-member districts.[9]

Yet Congress had no sooner embraced the Court's evolving approach to disfranchisement than the Court appeared to change its mind. The *Allen* opinion of 1969 and subsequent opinions of the 1970s had required local authorities to restructure electoral processes. But in 1980, in the case of *Mobile v. Bolden*, the high court placed a limitation on affirmative districting.

The case involved the city government in Mobile, Alabama, where the three members of the city commission had been elected at large since 1911. Because the at-large system had been in place before 1964, it enjoyed the same legal status as voting procedures in non-Southern states. Discrimination was forbidden, but preclearance was not required. The local government did not have to demonstrate that this at-large system was not discriminatory. Instead, the plaintiffs had to bear the burden of proof.

The black plaintiffs in *Mobile* noted that blacks made up 35 percent of the local population, but no black had ever been elected to the city commission. They said that a combination of racially polarized voting and at-large elections added up to a case of illegal voting discrimination.[10]

In response, city officials insisted that the at-large system had been adopted to promote good government, not to discriminate against blacks. They said that because "essentially all blacks" had already been disfranchised by a poll tax and literacy test that had been enacted in 1901, the purpose of the at-large system which was enacted ten years later could not have been to disfranchise blacks.[11]

The city officials said at-large voting had been designed to eliminate ward heeling. Prior to 1911 each district had elected its own commissioner. But in those bygone days, elected officials had focused excessively on neighborhood projects and had neglected programs with wider scope. Roads and other projects were built in the neighborhoods, but insufficient attention had been given to promoting the economic development and other larger interests of the metropolitan region. By establishing at-large elections and by providing that each commissioner would administer a separate department with citywide functions, the officials of 1911 had designed a system that was less susceptible to ward parochialism. Mobile's civic leaders said the arrangements of 1911 had been adopted "within the context of the progressive reform movement," and also that "Mobilians, like citizens of other cities swept by the reform movement, sought a city government both more efficient and business-like."[12]

By 1976, when the *Mobile* case was argued, the poll tax and literacy test had long since been abolished. By then blacks were well organized politically and were participating actively in local elections. Knowledgeable observers said that blacks controlled the balance of power in Mobile, and candidates for office actively sought the endorsement of the largest black political organization, the Non-Partisan Voters League. The city maintained that "Mobile's electoral system is entirely open to participation by black citizens, who do in fact participate actively and exercise significant voting power."[13]

The judge of the local district court, Virgil Pittman, admitted that since the Voting Rights Act of 1965, blacks had registered and voted "without hindrance." Nevertheless, Judge Pittman said that this did not satisfy the demands of the Voting Rights Act. Because of the combination of racially polarized voting and at-large elections, it was "highly unlikely that anytime in the foreseeable future" a black would be elected to the city commission. Pittman also found that the all white city commission had not been responsive to the needs of the black community. He mentioned that only 26 percent of the city's employees were black; that there was inadequate drainage in some black neighborhoods; that the streets in black neighborhoods were not as well maintained as streets elsewhere in Mobile; that there were no sidewalks in the vicinity of one predominantly black school; and that there had been instances of police brutality against blacks.[14]

Judge Pittman conceded that because blacks had already been disfranchised before 1911, the at-large system could not have been adopted for the purpose of disfranchising blacks. But Pittman held that the Supreme Court had not required that a discriminatory purpose must be proven in voting cases. Pittman also said that Mobilians of 1911 should have foreseen that the natural consequence of at-large elections would be to dilute black power if the formal disfranchisement of the poll tax and literacy text ceased to exist. There had been no intent to discriminate racially in 1911, Pittman held, but since then the at-large system had become "an effective barrier to blacks seeking public life." At-large elections "result[ed] in an unconstitutional dilution of black voting strength."[15]

To remedy the situation, Judge Pittman ordered that the citywide-elected municipal commission be disbanded. In its place Pittman ordered that Mobile be governed by a mayor and nine council members. Under this "mayor-councilman plan," Pittman explained, the mayor would be elected at large and would have a "city-wide perspective." The nine council members would be elected from single-member districts and supposedly would be more responsive to the needs of their particular constituencies. Pittman also noted that if Mobile was divided into contiguous zones of equal population, about one-third of the districts would have predominantly black electorates. "Segregated housing patterns have resulted in concentration of black voting power."[16]

When the *Mobile* case went to the Supreme Court, several justices were miffed with Judge Pittman. A plurality opinion by Justice Potter Stewart concluded that Pittman had disregarded the Supreme Court's insistence that "a plaintiff must prove that a disputed plan was 'conceived or operated as [a] purposeful devic[e] to further racial discrimination.'" Pittman had paid no attention to the Supreme Court's holding that "it is not enough to show that the group allegedly discriminated against has not elected representatives in proportion to its numbers." A plurality of the Supreme Court believed that Judge Pittman should be rebuked. His decision in *Bolden v. Mobile* was reversed.[17]

In a separate concurrence, Justice Harry Blackmun added another reprimand. Even if there had been purposeful discrimination, Blackmun wrote, Pittman's order to convert Mobile's city government to a mayor-council system "was not commensurate with the sound exercise of judicial discretion."[18]

In reversing Judge Pittman, the Supreme Court declared that the Voting Rights Act had been enacted to make sure blacks could vote, not to guarantee that they would be elected to offices. The opinion of the Court reiterated an important distinction between results and intent. It was not enough to demonstrate that black candidates had not been successful in at-large elections; the Supreme Court held that it was necessary to show that the discriminatory result had actually been intended by those who designed or maintained the at-large system.

The position of the Supreme Court was confusing, however. In addition to the plurality opinion of Justice Stewart, there were two concurring opinions and three dissents. Two justices—Thurgood Marshall and William J. Brennan—believed that plaintiffs in voting cases need show only that at-large elections led to a disproportionately small number of blacks being elected to office. Two other justices—Harry Blackmun and Byron White—accepted the premise that discriminatory purpose must be shown, but thought the facts in *Mobile* supported an inference of purposeful discrimination.

Justice White knew the Supreme Court had established that there must be a discriminatory purpose for there to be a constitutional violation. White himself had written two of the leading opinions that had established this principle. But White also said that under the principles already set down by the Supreme Court, discriminatory purpose could be inferred from the totality of facts in a case. White dissented from the plurality opinion because he thought Judge Pittman had correctly inferred discrimination, even if he had flouted principles that the Supreme Court had established.[19]

When the case was sent back to his courtroom, Judge Pittman admitted that he had been mistaken when he held that it was "not necessary to show a discriminatory purpose." In his first opinion, Pittman acknowledged, he had applied "the wrong legal standard." In re-hearing the case, Pittman complied with the legal rationale that had been set down by the Supreme Court. "A showing of discriminatory purpose (intent) is required to prevail," he wrote. "Effect alone is insufficient." But this time Judge Pittman did as Justice White had suggested. He held that Mobile's at-large system was unconstitutional because a discriminatory purpose could be inferred from the totality of evidence.[20]

Some of this evidence was provided by scholars and paralegal aides who were paid a total of $120,000 to comb the historical record for evidence of discriminatory intent. They discovered two nuggets that Judge Pittman mentioned in his opinion. One was a 1908 Mobile newspaper editorial that said good government could not be achieved unless blacks were disfranchised. Another was a 1909 letter by a prominent Mobilian, Frederick Bromberg, who expressed concern over the possibility that poll taxes and literacy tests might be rescinded at some time in the future. Neither document pertained specifically to the establishment of at-large voting in 1911, although each was written during the time when the movement toward at-large elections was gaining in popular support.[21]

Opinions will differ as to whether this evidence, when added to the evidence Judge Pittman had mentioned in his first opinion—the failure of blacks to win elections and the poor drainage, bad streets, and police brutality—

truly "proved" that the at-large system of 1911 had been instituted or maintained for the purpose of discriminating against blacks. Some members of the white majority apparently wanted to make it more difficult for blacks to win elections. But judges, historians, and other observers would differ as to whether an otherwise legitimate political choice should be invalidated simply because an invidious purpose played some part in the decision-making process. These differences of opinion hardly mattered, however. The decision was to be made by Judge Virgil Pittman, and no one doubted what he would decide. He decided that it was unconstitutional to have at-large voting in Mobile. And this time, because he applied the correct legal standard, the intent standard, Pittman's decision was final.

During the interval between the Supreme Court's *Mobile* opinion and Judge Pittman's final resolution of the case—from April 1980 to April 1982—voting rights activists waged a campaign to amend the Voting Rights Act. NAACP lawyer Julius Chambers said that it was almost impossible to satisfy the intent standard. Earlier in the twentieth century, some officials had not bothered to hide or deny racist motivations; thus,the plaintiffs in *Mobile* were able to discover the incriminating letter and editorial. But that evidence had not come easily. Moreover, Chambers said that in recent years officials had become "too sophisticated to admit their real motivation openly." It was no longer possible to "penetrate the mask of indifference, the smiles that hide the intent to do mischief."[22]

Some of the most influential media rallied in support of the effort to make it easier to prove violations of the Voting Rights Act. An editorial in the *New York Times* said it was unfair to require plaintiffs in voting rights cases to produce evidence that could be found only after arduous research in "historical crannies." The *Washington Post* said it was "virtually impossible" for plaintiffs to satisfy the "unnecessarily tougher standard" the Supreme Court had established in *Mobile*.[23]

Voting rights activists used several metaphors in their effort to illustrate the difficulties created by the *Mobile* standard. Laura Murphy of the American Civil Liberties Union (ACLU) said the intent standard would require that "people come out of their graves and confess that they had a racist motivation." Massachusetts congressman Barney Frank said that because of the Supreme Court's opinion in *Mobile*, "a 'smoking gun' must be shown to successfully prove voting discrimination." Voting rights lawyer Frank R. Parker complained that the Supreme Court was requiring plaintiffs in voting suits to resort to psychoanalysis.[24]

However, an almost contemporaneous case arising from Burke County, Georgia, indicated that the assessment of the voting activists was mistaken, if not insincere. Blacks made up 53 percent of the population in Burke, but only

38 percent of the registered voters, and no black had ever won an at-large election for the county commission. The local district judge, Anthony A. Alaimo, found no direct evidence that at-large elections were intentionally being used to discriminate, but he inferred a discriminatory purpose from the totality of circumstantial evidence in the case. Unlike Judge Pittman in *Mobile*, who initially said discriminatory intent need not be shown but later found that there had been such intent, Judge Alaimo never waffled. He thought Burke's at-large system had been "racially neutral" when it had been adopted in the years before the Voting Rights Act. But he also found the system unconstitutional because it was "being maintained for invidious purposes."[25]

By a vote of 6–3, the Supreme Court, in July 1982, affirmed Judge Alaimo's decision. A dissenting opinion by Justice Lewis Powell noted that Alaimo's finding of unconstitutional discrimination was based "on the same factors held insufficient in *Mobile*." But the majority of the Supreme Court affirmed Alaimo's decision because this district judge purported to be applying the legal standards that the Supreme Court itself had fashioned.[26]

In retrospect it seems that the Supreme Court justices never intended to fashion a tougher standard. In *Mobile,* the Court's plurality had emphasized the importance of distinguishing between discriminatory results and discriminatory intent—but this was a point the Court had made previously. For a majority of the justices, *Mobile* had been an occasion for upholding the prerogatives of the high court by reversing a district judge who was either mistaken or defiant.

Mobile is of historical importance primarily because it gave voting rights activists a plausible reason for urging Congress to change the Voting Rights Act. It would turn out to be a momentous change—one that would forbid at-large elections and require affirmative gerrymandering to increase dramatically the number of blacks who were elected to office.

After reading the Supreme Court's opinion in *Mobile*, Benjamin Hooks and other black leaders "went to a number of Senators and Representatives...and talked about the fact that we were concerned about...the interpretation of the Court." In time they persuaded Congressman Peter W. Rodino of New Jersey as well as Senators Edward M. Kennedy of Massachusetts and Charles McC. Mathias of Maryland to propose an amendment to Section 2 of the Voting Rights Act of 1965. The 1965 law had forbidden all practices that would "deny or abridge the right of any citizen...to vote on account of race or color." After consulting with Hooks and other civil rights activists, these three legislators—Rodino, Kennedy, and Mathias—proposed to forbid any practice "which results in a denial or abridgement" of the right to vote.[27]

This *results* test had a clear purpose. Rodino, Kennedy, and Mathias proposed to do away with practices that resulted in the dilution of black electoral power—practices such as at-large elections—even if there was no proof that the practices were intended to discriminate.

The proposed revision of Section 2 touched on some of the most important civil rights questions of the 1980s. What is racial discrimination? How is it proven? What are the rights of minorities in the political arena? Do they have a right to their own representatives? Is it a sophisticated form of invidious discrimination to maintain neutral policies that have racially disproportionate results?

Despite its significance, the results test received remarkably little attention. In the House hearings, several witnesses mentioned the issue in passing, but only three of the 156 witnesses, all appearing on the afternoon of 24 June 1981, addressed the issue in detail. The proposed amendment to Section 2 received as little attention on the floor of the House as it did in the Judiciary Committee.[28]

For the most part, the mainstream press either disregarded the results test or published false reports about the situation. *Washington Post* columnist William Raspberry wrote that "the civil rights establishment" simply wanted to extend "the present law intact," while *New York Times* reporter Robert Pear said that the House bill "called for a straight extension of the Act." *Times* reporters Adam Clymer and John Herbers, as well as columnist Tom Wicker, also gave readers the mistaken impression that the debate was over extending the Voting Rights Act of 1965 unchanged.[29]

The voting rights scholar Abigail M. Thernstrom later concluded that the major media functioned as part of the civil rights lobby: "Overall, readers of *Newsweek*, *Time*, the *New York Times*, and the *Washington Post* must have thought time had stood still in the South. David Broder [of the *Washington Post*] declared that the gap between black and white registration in the South was just as great in 1981 as it was in 1965—a preposterous assertion." In fact, despite a sizeable increase in the number of white Christian evangelicals who registered to vote in the late 1970s, the proportion of blacks who were registered to vote in the eleven states of the former Confederacy increased from less than one-half the white proportion in 1960 to about four-fifths of the white proportion in 1980. By 1980 a larger proportion of blacks was registered to vote in every Southern state than in the city where Broder worked, Washington, D. C.[30]

Many reporters apparently considered preclearance, bailout, and the standard for proving discrimination to be mere technicalities. "I have not seen much responsible reporting on the legal points at issue," Senator Orrin G. Hatch of Utah stated. According to Hatch, the major newspapers "here in the East...seem to say that this legislation is a wonderful idea; let's just pass it."[31]

Critics also noted that because the House Judiciary Committee gave so little attention to the matter, many members did not understand the difference between the intent standard and the results test. M. Caldwell Butler, a congressman from Virginia, was one member who declared that many of his colleagues did not understand specific provisions of the bill but supported it as "a knee-jerk response." They understood only that they would be characterized as racists if they opposed the proposal.[32]

Some observers also faulted Henry Hyde for distracting attention from the new results test. Because Hyde had proposed to end preclearance, voting rights activists had raised the specter of renewed disfranchisement. The media then depicted the activists as beleaguered defenders of the most successful civil rights measure ever enacted. The fact that the voting rights activists themselves wanted to change the Voting Rights Act was obscured.

Matters were further obscured when Hyde withdrew his opposition to preclearance and announced his support for the Voting Rights Act of 1982. The about-face captured the attention of the media, and the publicity turned out to be a gift to the voting rights activists. Because of Hyde, attention had focused on the question of preclearance rather than on the effort to change the act by substituting "results" for "intent." Henry Hyde turned out to be an unlikely ally for those who wished to expand, not restrict, the reach of the Voting Rights Act.

Notes

1. 1981 House Hearings, 182, 171, 170–81; *Washington Post*, 22 May 1981, A21a. Jackson also took exception to requirements that prohibited single-shot voting or required run-off elections. Single-shot voting is a method a minority can use to increase its influence in an at-large election. In a three-vote context, for example, members of a cohesive minority group could improve their chances by voting only for a single candidate. A majority run-off requirement eliminates the possibility that a minority candidate will win office by getting a plurality of votes in an election when the white vote splits among candidates. If no candidate receives a majority, there must be a second run-off election between the two leading candidates.
2. Edward C. Banfield and James Q. Wilson, *City Politics* (Cambridge: Harvard University Press, 1964), 88. Some historians maintain that business and upper-class professional groups initiated at-large elections to further their own interests. In the early years of the twentieth century, astute observers recognized that the power of ethnic politicians was based on ward voting, and some people calculated that most ethnic politicians would not have the resources to conduct more expensive, citywide campaigns. J. Morgan Kousser has written that "at-large elections had as one of their prime purposes the strengthening of upper-class influence and the corresponding weakening of lower-class influence in politics." Samuel P. Hays reached a similar conclusion: that at-large elections were part of an effort "by upper-class, advanced professional, and large-business groups to take formal political power from the previously dominant lower- and middle-class elements so that they might advance their own conceptions of desirable public policy." See Kousser, "The Undermining of the First Recon-

struction," in Chandler Davidson, ed., *Minority Vote Dilution* (Washington: Howard University Press, 1984), 37; Hays, "The Politics of Reform in Municipal Government in the Progressive Era," *Pacific Northwest Quarterly*, 55 (1964): 157–69. Also see James Weinstein, "Organized Business and the Commission and Manager Movements," *Journal of Southern History*, 28 (1962):, 166–82; and Bradley Robert Rice, *Progressive Cities: The Commission Government Movement in America, 1901–1920* (Austin: University of Texas Press, 1977).

3. Frank R. Parker, *Black Votes Count*, 202, 36, 39 and passim.
4. *Washington Post*, 5 March 1984, C1a; *1981 House Hearings*, 451.
5. *Lancaster News* (South Carolina), 2 October 1981; *1982 Subcommittee Report*, 17; *1982 Senate Hearings*, 489.
6. *Hearings before Subcommittee 5 of the House Judiciary Committee*, 89th Congress, 1st Session, 18 March 1965, 74, 21, 17.
7. Allen v. State Board of Elections, 393 U.S. 544 (1969), 565, 569. *Allen* involved electoral changes from Mississippi that apparently were designed to minimize the political influence of black voters. But the case also decided that Virginia had to seek preclearance for an administrative change that was not motivated by racial animus. It was because of this second point that *Allen* expanded the original understanding of the Voting Rights Act. See James McClellan, "Fiddling With the Constitution," *Louisiana Law Review*, 42 (1981): 22 and passim.
8. Dougherty County Board of Education v. White, 439 U.S. 32 (1978), 38. In *Black Votes Count*, voting rights lawyer Frank R. Parker denied that *Allen* changed the original understanding of the Voting Rights Act. Writing in the *Journal of Law and Politics*, in 1988, Pamela S. Karlan and Peyton McCrary also took exception to the contention that the Congress of 1965 did not intend for the Voting Rights Act to deal with the question of minority vote dilution. Karlan and McCrary have worked for black plaintiffs on various voting rights cases. I have not been persuaded by their arguments.
9. Abigail M. Thernstrom, *Whose Votes Count?*, 31–62.
10. Defendant's Motion to Affirm, reprinted in Philip B. Kurland and Gerhard Casper, *Landmark Briefs and Arguments of the Supreme Court* (Frederick, MD: University Publications of America, 1981), v. 119, 36–59; Brief for Appellees, ibid., 112–31; Brief for the United States as Amicus Curiae, ibid., 250–348.
11. Bolden v. City of Mobile, 423 F.Supp. 384 (1976), 386. For a different view of the origins of at-large voting in Mobile, see Peyton McCrary, "History in the Courts: The Significance of *The City of Mobile v. Bolden*," in Chandler Davidson, ed., *Minority Vote Dilution*, 47–63. McCrary acknowledged that when at-large elections were initiated in 1911, "Obviously there was little immediate threat of blacks themselves being elected to office," but, according to McCrary, "political leaders were aware that the disfranchising mechanisms of 1901 might be open to legal challenge in the federal courts at any time." Therefore, they instituted at-large elections as insurance in case the poll tax and literacy test were invalidated.
12. Jurisdictional Statement, in Philip B. Kurland and Gerhard Casper, *Landmark Briefs*, v. 119, 9–10; Brief for Appellants, ibid., 76–111; Reply Brief for Appellants, ibid., 225–39. Approximately 500 cities established at-large systems in the early years of the twentieth century.
13. Ibid., 17.
14. Bolden v. City of Mobile, 423 F.Supp 384 (1976), 387, 388, 389–92.
15. Ibid., 397–98, 396–97, 389, 402.
16. Ibid., 403–4, 386.

17. Mobile v. Bolden, 446 U.S. 55 (1980), 66.
18. Ibid., 80.
19. Ibid., 94–103.
20. Bolden v. City of Mobile, 542 F.Supp 1050(1982), 1053, 1071.
21. Ibid., 1065–66.
22. *1982 Senate Hearings*, 1252.
23. *New York Times*, 27 April 1982, 22:1; *Washington Post*, 26 June 1982, A19a.
24. *Washington Post*, 7 November 1981, A1a; *New York Times*, 5 February 1982, 31:1.
25. Quoted in Rogers v. Lodge, 458 U.S. 613 (1982), 616.
26. Ibid., 628.
27. *1982 Senate Hearings*, 259, 7, 48.
28. "The Evolution of Section 2 of the Voting Rights Act," typescript in WBR Papers, 8–9.
29. *Washington Post*, 12 June 1981, A17f; *New York Times*, 1 November 1981, 1:3, 35:1; 9 July 1981, 21:1; 10 November 1981, 23:1; 24 January 1982, 1:1. *Times* reporter Stuart Taylor, Jr., did a better job of reporting on the legal points at issue.
30. Abigail M. Thernstrom, *Whose Votes Count?*, 118–19; *Statistical Abstract of the United States*, 103d edition (Washington, 1982), 488.
31. *1982 Senate Hearings*, 550.
32. Ibid., 521.

3

The Debate Over the Revised Section 2

It was not until October 1981, after the new voting rights bill had passed the House of Representatives by a large, momentum-enhancing majority, that the Reagan administration finally announced its position on the legislation.

In the past Ronald Reagan had criticized the selective application of preclearance, and he continued to call for a new federalism that many blacks regarded with suspicion. But Reagan had a keen sense of what was possible politically and knew the Voting Rights Act could not be rescinded. "It was always the administration's view to favor extension of the Voting Rights Act," William Bradford Reynolds recalled. "I never heard from anybody in the administration—first hand, second hand, or other hand—that there was resistance by Reagan or anyone else to extending the Voting Rights Act."[1]

Nevertheless, Reagan had to proceed cautiously because Senate Judiciary Committee chairman Strom Thurmond was strongly opposed to preclearance. To placate Thurmond, Reagan went slow on voting rights. In June 1981, shortly after the House began hearings on the new voting rights legislation, Reagan asked Attorney General William French Smith to report on the subject by 1 October. "We knew we would come out at a different place from Strom Thurmond," Reynolds recalled, but the report would enable Reagan to tell Thurmond that after considering the question carefully, the administration had decided that federal supervision was still needed in the South.[2]

There was also a second reason for giving Smith several months to study the question. Reagan hoped the attorney general would find some formula for maintaining the support of white Southerners without alienating liberals and blacks. Smith tried to do this by combining a continuation of preclearance with a bailout provision that gave districts that had complied with the Voting Rights Act a "realistic possibility" to "win exemption" from preclearance. In a twenty-one page report to Reagan, Smith and Reynolds said the proposed new Voting Rights Act had established bailout standards that were "exceedingly difficult to meet." In addition, they advised Reagan to oppose the "results" standard and to insist on retention of the original wording of Section 2 of the 1965 law.[3]

Smith and Reynolds's proposals touched off a debate within the White House. Some of Reagan's top advisers, including Counselor Edwin Meese, Chief of Staff James Baker, and Deputy Chief of Staff Michael Deaver, recommended that Reagan support the bill that had passed the House by an overwhelming majority and whose passage by the Senate seemed likely. They conceded that it was unfair to continue stigmatizing the South, but they also noted that after seventeen years Southern politicians, and virtually all Republican state party chairmen, had accepted the Voting Rights Act. Meese, Baker, and Deaver also agreed with Mel Bradley, a black member of the White House staff, who argued that support for the House version of the new voting rights legislation would give Reagan an opportunity to show his sensitivity to minority concerns. After conferring with Meese, Baker, and Deaver, Reagan told aides to inform reporters that he would not oppose the House bill.[4]

A press conference was then arranged, with reporters and photographers summoned to the White House on 7 November 1981. But when a member of the White House staff told Reynolds what was in the offing, Reynolds immediately got in touch with Smith. "If Reagan endorses the bill the way it is written, it will mean proportional representation," Reynolds said. "This president cannot do that. If Ronald Reagan endorses this bill, it will be contrary to everything he said he believed in during the campaign. The president's integrity is on the line."[5]

Smith agreed, picked up the telephone, and told the White House, "I want to see the president. I'm coming over. Clear the decks." In the car on the way across town, Smith and Reynolds rehearsed what the attorney general would eventually say to Reagan: "You were the candidate who said he didn't believe in discrimination. You campaigned against quotas. But this bill will mean that lines must be drawn to promote proportional representation by race. You simply cannot do that and face the electorate again with any credibility."[6]

Making use of the friendship he had developed as Reagan's personal lawyer, Smith persuaded the president to reject the advice of those who thought it expedient to go along with the House bill. Instead, Smith convinced Reagan to refuse to endorse the House bill and to hold out for necessary amendments. "This has never happened before," one White House staffer said. "It's the first time I've seen the president change his mind like this after having made a decision."[7]

The White House canceled the press conference that had been scheduled. Later, in March 1982, when Reagan finally addressed the question in public, he insisted on the need for amendments. "To protect all our citizens," Reagan said, preclearance should be continued. "The right to vote is the crown jewel of American liberties, and we will not see its luster diminished." But, Reagan said, it was "a matter of fairness" to provide a better bailout provision that would give jurisdictions that had complied with the Voting Rights Act a realistic opportunity to escape from federal supervision of local elections. In addition, Reagan said that the Voting Rights Act "should retain the 'intent' test under existing law, rather than changing it to a new and untested 'effects' standard." For his part, Smith said "The administration fully supports extension of the Voting Rights Act...in its tried and true form—neither contracted nor expanded."[8]

In testimony before the Senate Judiciary Committee, Smith and Reynolds explained why the administration opposed the effects or results test of the revised Section 2. Reynolds said that since 1965, voting laws had distinguished between districts where racial discrimination was known to be prevalent and the rest of the country. Under Section 5 of the Voting Rights Act, districts with a history of discrimination were already required to prove that any proposed electoral change did "not have the purpose and will not have the effect of denying or abridging the right to vote on account of race or color." When dealing with changes proposed by covered jurisdictions, the Department of Justice did not inquire into intent; it would not preclear changes unless there was proof that the changes had no discriminatory result.[9]

When it came to other regions, however, Section 2 of the Voting Rights Act stated only that citizens should not be denied the right to vote "on account of race or color." As interpreted by the Supreme Court, this provision meant that challenges outside Dixie, or challenges to policies that had been in place in the covered jurisdictions prior to 1964, could not be sustained unless there was proof of discriminatory intent. To understand this important distinction, Smith said, "it really does not require much more than a reading of the statute itself."

> When Congress passed this act in 1965, it very clearly expressed an intents test in Section 2 and it very clearly expressed an effects test in Section 5. If Congress at that time had intended to put an effects test in Section 2, it could just as clearly have done so there as it did in Section 5, but it chose not to do so.[10]

Yet the voting rights bill that the House passed in 1982 substituted an effects or results test for the existing intent standard in Section 2. It prohibited any voting procedure "which results in a denial or abridgment of the right of any citizen...to vote on account of race or color." According to Smith, this substitution imposed upon the entire country a legal test that since 1965, Congress had seen fit to apply only to certain jurisdictions that had been "demonstrably derelict in their failure to protect minority voting rights."[11]

There was no need for this change, Smith believed. Differing from voting rights activists who said the Supreme Court, in its *Mobile* opinion, had set a new and unnecessarily tougher standard for proving discrimination, Smith maintained that *Mobile* signaled no change. Under *Mobile* intent to discriminate had to be proved, but, as before, this could be done by inference from the totality of evidence. Smith insisted that *Mobile* had not established a new legal standard. The Voting Rights Act was still "one of the most effective statutes ever passed by Congress." Smith said there was "much common sense" in the admonition "If it is not broken, don't fix it."[12]

Smith and Reynolds also questioned the constitutionality of the revised Section 2. They referred to the fact that in 1966 the Supreme Court had upheld the constitutionality of preclearance and the effects test of Section 5 only because massive evidence indicated the need for strong federal medicine to combat persistent and egregious violations of the Fifteenth Amendment in the South. But, Smith said, in 1981 and 1982 no evidence had been presented "that there have been voting rights violations throughout the country so as to justify nationwide application of an effects test." Smith speculated that the proposed change in Section 2 might be unconstitutional unless there was "some kind of a record, some kind of evidence, or testimony, that there is an evil out there that needs [correction]." He insisted that "you do not come up with remedies to nonexistent problems!" Smith held that there should be no invasion of the reserved rights of the states without a showing of need.[13]

Smith and Reynolds had an even more fundamental objection to the new voting rights bill. They said that because the revised Section 2 conceived of voting as a group right, rather than an individual right, the new legislation would undermine the basic principle that rights inhere in individuals. They pointed to the dangers of classifying citizens by color and of promoting racial separation. They challenged the assumption that U.S. society was so deeply divided racially that only blacks could represent blacks. They warned that the House bill "would virtually require proportional representation of blacks and other minority groups." By prohibiting any electoral procedure that "results...in a denial or abridgment of the right...to vote," Reynolds said, the new Section 2 substituted "the right to have certain election results" in place of "the right to cast your vote free of racial discrimination."[14]

Reynolds predicted that when it came to interpreting the results test, courts would look for precedents in one of two areas. One was the administrative practice that had grown up around preclearance. The other was the body of law that the Fifth Circuit Court of Appeals had developed in cases involving Title VII of the 1964 Civil Rights Act (the provision that prohibited discrimination in employment). These precedents established the principle that "if you do not have in the elected body [or work force] the same proportion of minorities as you have in the community at large, then you will have a problem."[15]

Smith and Reynolds found an ally in Senator Strom Thurmond, who differed from the administration's position on preclearance. The senator wanted to end that practice or, if that proved impossible, to extend it nationwide. The Reagan administration, in contrast, wanted to continue the system of requiring preclearance only of those jurisdictions that had a history of voting discrimination. But Thurmond joined the administration in opposing the revised Section 2. Thurmond said the revision moved the United States "along a path which measures success by comparing the representation of a group in elective bodies with the proportion of that group in the general population." According to Thurmond, the revision disregarded the individual as the basis of political representation and instead established groups "as the primary units of our political system." The revision was designed "to facilitate proportional representation on the basis of race." It "would have us define discrimination...in terms of the results of elections,...as something other than inhibitions on registering and voting."[16]

Thurmond's view was seconded by Senator Orrin G. Hatch of Utah. Hatch noted that the issue was not "whether or not pure proportional representation will be achieved overnight. It is whether or not future courts and future Justice Departments will look [to] proportional representation as the standard against which all electoral and voting practices are assessed." By focusing primarily on numbers, Hatch said, Section 2 redefined "the very concepts of discrimination and civil rights." It raised "fundamental issues involving the nature of American representative democracy."[17]

Hatch used his position as chairman of the Senate Judiciary Subcommittee on the Constitution to invite testimony concerning the ramifications of the revised Section 2. The results test was "not a very glamorous issue," Hatch conceded, but he thought it had been unconscionable for the House Judiciary Committee to have devoted "only one day [of testimony] to this matter, out of nineteen days." He said it was even worse that the few witnesses who had criticized the House bill had been "accused of racism." Hatch was convinced that many members of the House had not understood the revised Section 2 when it was before them. He was determined to prevent a repetition of this in the Senate, stating "We have to have the guts to stand up and debate these issues."[18]

No organization (other than the Reagan administration) came forward with criticism of the revised Section 2. But a number of professors and academic analysts spoke out in opposition to the revision. Barry R. Gross of the City University of New York (CUNY) said the 1965 Voting Rights Act had been designed to give blacks "uninhibited access to the ballot in an integrated election process," and contrasted this purpose with that of the new Section 2: "minority political power—seats in proportion to minority population." Henry Abraham of the University of Virginia agreed with Gross in the position that proponents of the results test were changing the basic premise of the Voting Rights Act, saying, "Only those who live in a dream world" could fail to perceive that the results test was "tantamount to...proportional representation."[19]

James Blumstein of Vanderbilt University warned that the House bill "pervert[ed] the very meaning of the right to vote." Michael Levin of CUNY said it changed "what we mean by the term 'discrimination.'" By focusing on numbers and statistics rather than on evidence of wrongful purpose, the congressional proponents of the new legislation had joined ranks with civil rights activists who equated discrimination with statistical underrepresentation.[20]

Donald Horowitz of the University of California, Los Angeles (UCLA) similarly insisted that "this playing with words is not harmless." By equating "disparate results" with wrongful discrimination, the proponents of the revised Section 2 were destroying the consensus that had made possible the success of the civil rights movement. The proponents were calling "something discrimination which is not discrimination at all."[21]

Senator Hatch agreed. He challenged "anyone who suggests that the consensus in civil rights in this country was built on this theory.... I do not believe that you can find one person in one hundred in Boston, Baltimore, or Cleveland, black or white, who would define discrimination in this manner."[22]

Senator John East of North Carolina concurred. He accused voting rights advocates of introducing "a wholly new concept." Instead of working for "the right of individuals to register and vote, irrespective of race," they were trying "to guarantee...proportional representation."[23]

The critics conceded that the redefinition of terms served the short-term interests of voting rights lawyers. Indeed, Professor Blumstein thought the reasons behind the proposed revision were essentially "pragmatic." It would be easier for lawyers to show statistical underrepresentation than to prove discriminatory intent. Jerris Leonard, a former assistant attorney general for civil rights, explained that black politicians were using the rhetoric of voting rights as a "smoke screen...for personal political gain." They had become "very sophisticated," Leonard said, and had devised the new Section 2 as a way to improve their prospects. They would do so by making sure that electoral boundaries took account of racial clustering.[24]

Critics distinguished between the interests of the black community as a whole and the interests of black politicians and their lawyers. Susan MacManus, a professor at the University of Houston, conceded that more blacks would be elected if officials were chosen from compact, single-member districts, but she said at-large arrangements would give blacks more "programmatic representation."[25]

To illustrate her point, MacManus mentioned a county that was 20 percent black and had five members on the elected county commission. Under the results test, electoral boundaries would be drawn so as to concentrate black voters in a single district that probably would elect a black commissioner. But with blacks *packed* in a single district, the remaining commissioners would not have to respond to the needs of the black community. Under at-large arrangements, on the other hand, black candidates would rarely be elected to the county commission; but no commissioner could be elected without courting black voters.[26]

MacManus insisted that this example was not just hypothetical. In Houston, she noted, blacks were "tremendously divided on whether a larger minority precinct, defined in terms of blacks, should be created or whether blacks would have more influence if their votes were divided among several precincts." Some prominent blacks "argued for spreading influence among three commissioners rather than having a single black 'figurehead' commissioner."[27]

Similarly, in Dallas, black leaders were divided over the desirability of packing blacks into a single district. The Republican Governor of Texas, William Clements, wanted to create a predominantly black Congressional district, perhaps because he calculated that Republicans would benefit overall if black voters were *drained* from predominantly white areas. But to protect the reelection chances of two liberal white Democrats, many blacks recommended that the black community be divided "to create two or more high-influence districts, rather than one in which [blacks] would be a substantial majority."[28]

Professor Horowitz of UCLA also predicted that proportionality would exalt representation at the expense of influence and power. He thought the revised Section 2 was "wonderful...for the prospective black elected officeholders." But it was "very bad...for their constituents," who would have more influence over public policy if they were not concentrated in districts that were safe for black politicians. Senator Hatch concurred. He predicted that "minority political ghettoization" would leave blacks with "less overall influence and ability to influence the political systems in this country."[29]

Walter Berns of the American Enterprise Institute went beyond those who said blacks would not benefit from the results test. Berns maintained that the revised Section 2 was at odds with the design of the Constitution. According to Berns, proportional representation had been one of the major points at issue in the 1780s between the founding Federalists and the Anti-Federalist opposition. The Anti-Federalists had wanted officials to be elected by small, homogeneous electorates, but the Federalists wanted larger districts that encompassed greater variety. The Federalists did so, Berns said, because they knew that officials chosen in at-large elections would have to appeal to a coalition of diverse interests. Officials chosen in at-large elections would be more inclined to fashion necessary compromises than those elected from smaller, homogeneous districts.[30]

Another critic, political scientist Edward J. Erler, viewed Section 2 in an international perspective. Elsewhere in the world, Erler said, governments based on proportional representation were "highly fragmented and unstable."

Officials elected from small, homogeneous districts often had not been able to find "a common ground that transcends factionalized interests." He warned that Section 2 might lead to a repetition of the same pattern in the United States. Predominantly black districts might elect officials who had no use for whites; white districts might choose representatives who disliked blacks. Instead of institutionalizing parochialism, Erler said, it would be better to continue with a system where candidates could not be elected unless they won support from members of each major group.[31]

In response to those who favored at-large elections, the Leadership Conference on Civil Rights presented several witnesses who spoke in favor of the revised Section 2. Their first contention was that, as Ralph Neas stated, the revision "reflect[ed] the original understanding of Congress in 1965." The purpose of the revision, said Frank R. Parker, was "to restate the original legislative intent of Congress."[32]

The strongest evidence in support of this contention—almost the only evidence—was a statement Attorney General Katzenbach made in 1965. In response to a question from Senator Hiram Fong of Hawaii, Katzenbach had said Section 2 was designed to prohibit "any kind of practice...if its purpose *or effect* was to deny or abridge the right to vote on account of race or color." But this statement was uncharacteristic and was contradicted by Katzenbach himself and other proponents of the Voting Rights Act of 1965. Congress specifically included a results test in Section 5 (applicable only to jurisdictions with a history of voting discrimination). It just as specifically chose not to put the same standard in Section 2 (which applied nationally). Most senators understood this. The 1982 report of a Senate judiciary subcommittee noted that "a single chance remark by an individual does not constitute a conclusive legislative history." The subcommittee correctly characterized Katzenbach's comment as "a wholly isolated remark in the midst of thousands of pages of hearings and floor debates."[33]

Fortunately for voting rights activists, there was another, more plausible, argument for revising Section 2. The Senate hearings were held in January, February, and March 1982—a time when there was confusion concerning the meaning of the Supreme Court's opinion in *Mobile v. Bolden*. At that time voting rights lawyers could plausibly maintain that *Mobile* was "a radical departure by the Supreme Court from prior voting rights cases." A prominent professor of law, Archibald Cox of Harvard University, could say the revised Section 2 was needed to correct the "misrepresentation" of *Mobile v. Bolden*. A former assistant attorney general for civil rights, Drew S. Days, could maintain that a new Section 2 was needed to provide "much needed clarification with respect to standards of proof."[34]

This argument influenced at least one senator. On 27 January 1982 Charles Mathias said laws against voting discrimination "had been thrown into question by the Supreme Court decision in *City of Mobile v. Bolden*." The new legislation was needed to "remove the uncertainty caused by the failure of the Supreme Court to articulate a clear standard in *Bolden*."[35]

Yet this argument was serviceable for only a short time. The remand of the *Mobile* case was decided on 15 April 1982, and the Supreme Court's decision in the *Burke County* case was handed down on 1 July. After those decisions it was clear that the allegedly radical *Mobile* opinion did not represent an extreme change. Intent to discriminate could still be inferred from the totality of evidence.

In addition to contending that the revised Section 2 reflected the original understanding of 1965 and that the revision was needed to restore the legal standard that courts had used before the Supreme Court handed down its opinion in *Mobile*, proponents of the revision presented a third argument. They insisted that the revised Section 2 would not require proportional representation. J. Stanley Pottinger, another former assistant attorney general for civil rights, said he had "heard no one in the civil rights community, literally no one, suggest...there had to be proportional representation." Armand Derfner, an experienced voting rights lawyer, offered similar reassurance. He said the revised Section 2 would apply only to "that small category of places" where at-large elections had resulted in total exclusion of blacks from elected offices. "The cases we are talking about...are cases where Blacks or Hispanics have been simply shut out," Derfner said. The historian J. Morgan Kousser also maintained that the revised Section 2 "only seeks to end a situation in which substantial minorities have no power whatsoever."[36]

Benjamin Hooks of the NAACP assured Congress that there was "no sinister motive, no hidden agenda" lurking behind the revised Section 2. But other voting rights advocates repeatedly stressed how far the United States was from proportional representation. Frank R. Parker conceded that Mississippi had more elected black officials than any state (387 in 1981). But these blacks made up only 7.3 percent of the 5,271 elected officials in a state whose population was 35 percent black. Henry Marsh, the black mayor of Richmond, emphasized that because of at-large elections, blacks were greatly underrepresented in Virginia. Willie Gibson, the president of the South Carolina NAACP, candidly acknowledged that blacks wanted "a redistricting plan in South Carolina that has the possibility of blacks being elected in proportion to their population." Jesse Jackson said that because blacks made up one-third of the population of South Carolina, they "deserve one-third of its representation."[37]

One witness before the House Judiciary Committee put the numbers into a larger context. Geraldine Thompson noted that in the entire South, a region that was more than 20 percent black, blacks made up only 2 percent of the representatives in Congress, 3 percent of the mayors, 3 percent of the state senators, 5 percent of the county supervisors, and 8 percent of the state representatives. The number of elected black officials had admittedly increased dramatically, from fewer than 100 in 1965 to 4,912 in 1980. But Thompson said there was still a long way to go, that for all the gains blacks were still far from the summit of their potential political power.[38]

Drew Days gave some of the most perceptive testimony on this point. Days acknowledged that voting rights activists wanted more political representation for blacks—a great deal more. But he explained that exact or precise proportional representation was not in the offing. Under the revised Section 2, Days said, electoral boundaries would have to coincide with areas where minorities clustered residentially. But this would not cause proportional representation because some blacks—those who lived in predominantly white areas—could not conceivably be packed into predominantly black districts.[39]

One of the best arguments for the revised Section 2 came from Supreme Court Justice Thurgood Marshall. In a dissenting opinion in *Mobile v. Bolden*, Marshall noted that it had been the practice of the Supreme Court to apply different standards when adjudicating discrimination and voting cases. In dealing with discrimination, the Court had held that plaintiffs had to show discriminatory intent; but in dealing with the right to vote, the Court had focused solely on discriminatory effects. In the reapportionment cases of the 1960s, for example, the Court had not required plaintiffs to prove that officials had intended that the votes of citizens in larger districts would not carry as much weight as votes cast by citizens in smaller districts. It was sufficient to show that variation in the size of electoral districts had the result of diluting the votes of those who lived in the larger districts. "Proof of discriminatory purpose [was]...not required to support a claim of vote dilution."[40]

So it should be, Marshall said, with respect to at-large elections. To invalidate these arrangements, plaintiffs should not be required to show discriminatory purpose—not even through inference. It should suffice to show that at-large elections had the result of making it more difficult for minority candidates to win.

Because of reapportionment, politicians had become accustomed to judging electoral arrangements on the basis of results. When it came to school enrollments, university admissions, and employment, many members of Congress believed that disparate impact, by itself, did not suffice to prove the existence of unconstitutional racial discrimination. However, most thought that voting was an exception to this general rule.

But not all. The Reagan administration opposed the revised Section 2, and so did three of the five members of the Senate Judiciary Subcommittee on the Constitution. But this opposition had developed too late to be effective. Neither the administration nor Senator Hatch had taken up the issue until after the revised Section 2 had passed the House. By then the Leadership Conference had persuaded sixty-one senators to sponsor the proposal. If President Reagan had taken his position six months earlier he might have influenced the course of the debate, but delay had rendered him powerless to control the shape of the new voting rights bill.

Nevertheless, Reynolds and others in the Department of Justice belatedly tried to turn things around. They began by emphasizing that the Reagan administration favored a ten-year extension of what they called "the most successful civil rights law ever enacted." The administration insisted that the effectiveness of the Voting Rights Act had not been compromised by the Supreme Court in *Mobile*. They reminded senators that on remand the *Mobile* case was decided in favor of the black plaintiffs who had challenged the at-large system. This, the administration said, proved that "'intent' can be proved without undue difficulty." It demonstrated the falsity of allegations that it was "virtually impossible" to satisfy the standard the Supreme Court had announced in *Mobile v. Bolden*.[41]

In conferences with senators, Reynolds insisted that the administration's opposition to the revised Section 2 "reflected no insensitivity to ensuring civil rights in the voting sphere." Rather, it grew out of "well-reasoned opposition to a proportional representation scheme." Reynolds regarded electoral quotas as "inconsistent with the democratic traditions of our pluralist society." He said the revised Section 2 would "foster the abhorrent notion that blacks can only be represented by blacks."[42]

Reynolds enjoyed some success with these arguments. After a breakfast meeting, Senator Alphonse D'Amato of New York expressed reservations about the revised Section 2. "The fact of the matter is that the Voting Rights Act has been a success," D'Amato said. "I don't think it went too far. But is there a need to go further? Do we want proportional representation? We may be asking for a little more than we want."[43]

Despite the lobbying, only a few senators changed their minds. Close observers reported that only seven of the eighteen members of the full Senate Judiciary Committee opposed the revised Section 2. Two others, Robert Dole of Kansas and Howell Heflin of Alabama, were thought to be undecided. The nine remaining members of the committee were regarded as favoring the change.[44]

Reynolds recognized that the revised Section 2 could not be derailed unless the administration somehow turned things around in the Senate Judiciary Committee. At staff meetings in the Department of Justice, there was candid recognition that to succeed the administration would need the support of the two waverers on the committee. If Dole and Heflin supported the administration, it was said, Senator Dennis DeConcini of Arizona was likely to come on board. The revision could then be defeated in committee, 10–8.[45]

But Heflin and Dole would not budge. Heflin understood that the revised Section 2 was fraught with mischief but also recognized that the major black organizations in his home state favored the revision. As for Dole, he was the leader of his party in the Senate. Whatever personal reservations he might have harbored about the proposed revision, he knew that twenty-six Republican senators had signed on as co-sponsors; he also thought it unlikely that the Reagan administration could turn around enough senators to defeat the proposal. Besides, Dole had presidential ambitions and sensed that the controversy over Section 2 gave him an opportunity to fashion a compromise that would enhance his reputation and save his party from internal wrangling.[46]

Yet, because Dole's staff did not get along well with Reagan's Department of Justice, the compromise did not emerge easily. "His staff was not interested in finding a compromise that we could accept," Reynolds later stated. "It was only interested in pleasing the civil rights groups." Nevertheless, Dole and other Senate leaders wanted to avoid a confrontation that would culminate in a veto, and eventually a compromise was fashioned.[47]

The compromise was developed at a Saturday morning meeting at the White House. Along with Dole and Reynolds, presidential Counselor Edwin Meese, White House Counsel Fred Fielding, and black attorney William T. Coleman were in attendance. After considerable discussion, the impasse was finally broken when the discussants agreed to disavow any commitment to proportional representation while simultaneously agreeing to keep the results test.[48]

Dole then presented the proposal to Congress as a reasonable compromise. Asserting that "intentional discrimination is too difficult to prove to make enforcement of the [voting rights] law effective," Dole proposed to keep the results test. He said, "A voting practice or procedure which is discriminatory in result should not be allowed to stand, regardless of whether there exists a discriminatory purpose or intent." At the same time, Dole proposed additional language clarifying that the revised Section 2 was "not a mandate for proportional representation." The compromise provided that the extent to which minority candidates had been elected was one fact to be considered by judges in voting rights cases. But judges were specifically instructed to consider the "totality of circumstances" and to recognize that "nothing in this section (2) establishes a right to proportional representation."[49]

The revised Section 2, with the Dole amendment, was approved by the Senate Judiciary Committee, 14–4. It then passed the Senate, 85–8, was accepted by the House conference committee, and became Public Law 97–205 when Ronald Reagan signed the bill on 29 June 1982.[50]

Reagan made only a brief allusion to the controversy over Section 2. "This act insures equal access to the political process for all our citizens. It securely protects the right to vote while strengthening the safeguards against representation by forced quota." Writing in the *New York Times*, Howell Raines contrasted the signing of the Voting Rights Act of 1982 "with the jubilant and richly symbolic ceremony in which President Johnson signed the original bill.... Mr. Johnson used fifty pens and handed them out as souvenirs. Mr. Reagan used one pen in a four minute ceremony that ended when he rose from his desk and said, 'It's done.'"[51]

Reagan had little reason to be pleased. The compromise that Dole and Reynolds had fashioned enabled Reagan to avoid a confrontation with Congress and the possible embarrassment of having a veto overridden. It also enabled Reagan to avoid a rift with some fellow Republicans. But these were, at best, prudential considerations.

Reagan said the compromise had his "heartfelt support." But his body language—the four-minute ceremony, the single pen—indicated otherwise. Reagan suspected that despite the disclaimer, the results test would require something akin to proportional representation. He feared that the Voting Rights Act had been changed from a prohibition against discrimination in voting to a prescription for affirmative discrimination in politics.[52]

Nevertheless, in public the administration decided, in the words of one internal memorandum, to "declare victory...and gloss over the losses." Thus, Reynolds no longer described the results test as a scheme to achieve proportional representation. Thanks to Dole's compromise amendment, Reynolds wrote in one letter, the final draft of the bill had removed "the highly offensive concept of proportional representation based on race." "Of equal importance," Reynolds wrote, the compromise shifted "the essential focus of Section 2 away from an emphasis on election results (as in the 'liberal' [Rodino-Kennedy-Mathias] version') and back to a proper concern for individual rights: i.e., protecting for each citizen the opportunity of equal access to the electoral process, free from racial discrimination." Reynolds's comments pointed toward the position the Reagan administration would take later in court, when litigation was required to determine the precise meaning of the Voting Rights Act of 1982.[53]

Although the press generally praised the Dole-Reynolds compromise, some criticism persisted. Writing in *Fortune*, Daniel Seligman characterized "the great bipartisan compromise" as essentially a quota system for electoral politics—a "mindless scheme for converting equal opportunity into equal outcomes." "What's going on here," said Seligman, "is an argument that runs on parallel tracks to the one about affirmative action. There, too, laws designed to create equal opportunity have long since been translated into a push for equal outcomes." Syndicated columnist James J. Kilpatrick was even more blunt. "The Dole 'compromise' is no compromise at all." It was "folly," Kilpatrick insisted, and was based on the "racist assumption...that black voters are not individual voters [but]...group voters...whose bloc power must not be 'diluted.'"[54]

Orrin Hatch—the senator who had most persistently maintained that the revised Section 2 was unwise—confessed that he was tempted to embrace the language of Dole's amendment and "claim compromise if not victory." But Hatch said Dole's amendment was "little more than cosmetics." The Dole amendment disavowed the goal of proportional representation, but by keeping the results test, Hatch claimed Dole had ensured that electoral arrangements that had a disparate impact could not survive a legal challenge. Despite euphemistic platitudes, the Voting Rights Act of 1982 would "inject racial considerations into more and more electoral and political decisions." It would "effect an incalculable transformation in the purpose and objectives of the Voting Rights Act." It would "alter the traditional focus of the act...from equal access to registration and the ballot to equal results and equal outcomes in the electoral process."[55]

For once, voting rights advocates agreed with Hatch. Senator Charles Mathias, one of the original sponsors of the Voting Rights Act of 1982, summed up the attitude of most civil rights activists. Referring to the Dole amendment, Mathias said, "We paid no price at all." Veteran civil rights lawyer Joseph Rauh similarly exulted: "It was no compromise at all. We got everything we wanted."[56]

In assessing the debate over the 1982 Voting Rights Act, the *New York Times* expressed the conventional wisdom of liberals. The *Times* roasted the Reagan administration for "raising a specter of 'proportional representation' and racial quotas—an unworthy argument [that] unnecessarily inflame[d] the debate over voting rights." The *Times* belatedly conceded that the administration wanted "to continue the original [voting rights] act 'as is,'" but said that in the context of 1982 this amounted to "foot-dragging" obstructionism that was at odds with "better race relations and...the right to vote." When the Voting Rights Act of 1982 finally became law, the *Times* offered "a Fourth-of-July salute...to Senator Robert Dole" and "even louder cannon" for the primary sponsors of the new law—Peter Rodino and Don Edwards in the House of Representatives as well as Edward Kennedy and Charles Mathias in the Senate.[57]

Although the *Times* suggested that the legal arguments against the results test had been sophisticated camouflage for bigotry, less partisan observers recognized that the debate over the Voting Rights Act had raised issues of fundamental importance. Senator Dole's amendment had speeded final passage of the legislation (and relieved the Republican Party of a political problem of considerable magnitude). But, as the *National Review* observed, "Such an amicable resolution of such a bitter dispute can mean only one thing: that the language in the bill has been artfully fudged so as to leave it open to conflicting interpretation." In the end the Supreme Court would have to address the points at issue.[58]

Notes

1. Interview with WBR, 11 January 1991.
2. Ibid.
3. *Washington Post*, 16 June 1981, A1d; *Report to the President from the Attorney General Concerning Amending the Voting Rights Act*, 2 October 1981, WBR Papers; *New York Times*, 1 November 1981, 1:3.
4. *Los Angeles Times*, 8 November 1981, 1:3.
5. Interview with WBR, 11 January 1991.
6. Ibid.
7. *Los Angeles Times*, 8 November 1981, 1:3; *New York Times*, 7 November 1981, 1:3.
8. *Washington Post*, 7 November 1981, A1a; *New York Times*, 7 November 1981, 1:2; 27 March 1982, 23:2.
9. *1982 Senate Hearings*, 1657, 1660.
10. Ibid., 74; *New York Times*, 27 March 1982, 23:2; *Washington Post*, 29 March 1982, A11a.
11. *1982 Senate Hearings*, 71.
12. Ibid., 76, 71.
13. Ibid., 68–69, 71, 85–86.
14. Ibid., 1662, 1664; *New York Times*, 2 March 1982, 1:3.
15. *1982 Senate Hearings*, 1665–66, 1660–61.
16. Ibid., 61, 60.
17. Ibid., 644, 3, 2.
18. Ibid., 1405–6, 432, 962.
19. Ibid., 423, 1246; *1982 Subcommittee Report*, 35.
20. *1982 Senate Hearings*, 717, 1344.
21. Ibid., 1310.
22. Ibid., 5.
23. Ibid., 409–10.
24. Ibid., 1349, 1361; *New York Times*, 3 May 1982, II,11:2.
25. *1982 Senate Hearings*, 545, 544.
26. Ibid.
27. Ibid., 545; *New York Times*, 28 February 1982, 28:1.
28. *New York Times*, 28 February 1982, 28:1; Chandler Davidson, ed., *Minority Vote Dilution*, 107.
29. *1982 Senate Hearings*, 1309, 979.
30. Ibid., 228–43.
31. Ibid., 509–10.
32. Ibid., 283, 705.
33. *1982 Subcommittee Report*, 22–23 (emphasis added). For a different interpretation of the legislative history of 1965, see the *Report of the Senate Judiciary Committee*, No. 417, 97th Congress, 2nd Session, 1982, 17.
34. *1982 Senate Hearings*, 711 (statement of Frank R. Parker and Barbara Y. Phillips), 1419, 1367.
35. Ibid., 209, 199.

36. Ibid., 1828, 820; *Los Angeles Times*, 7 February 1982, IV, 15:3. In response to a question from TV journalist Charlayne Hunter-Gault, Derfner said that voting rights activists were concerned "only [with] those egregious situations where the system absolutely locked out minority voters.... All we want is an opportunity of some kind of access to the political system. We're not looking for anything more." Transcript of The McNeil/Lehrer Report, 3 February 1982.
37. *1982 Senate Hearings*, 258, 472, 4, 255; *1981 House Hearings*, 499.
38. *1981 House Hearings*, 1942; Joint Committee on Political and Economic Studies, *Black Elected Officials* (Washington: JCPES Press, 1994), xxii.
39. *1982 Senate Hearings*, 1387–88.
40. Mobile v. Bolden, 114, 115–21. Marshall's comments were rarely mentioned because they were sandwiched between an introduction and conclusion that were so intemperate as to be embarrassingly injudicious. At the outset of his dissent, Marshall said at-large elections rendered blacks "politically powerless with nothing more than the right to cast meaningless ballots." He concluded by warning that if judges continued to tolerate the sort of "sophisticated" discrimination that at-large elections entailed, the judges should "not expect the victims of discrimination to respect political channels in seeking redress." Ibid., 104, 141.
41. Department of Justice Statement on Voting Rights, 30 April 1982, WBR Papers; "Why Section 2 of the Voting Rights Act Should Be Retained Unchanged," undated typescript, ibid.; Kenneth W. Starr, Draft of Op-Ed Piece on Voting Rights Act, 5 February 1982, ibid.; WBR to Benjamin C. Bradlee, 2 February 1982, ibid.; WBR to Nicholas Calio, 6 April 1982, ibid.; Robert A. McConnell to Howard H. Baker, 25 February 1982, ibid.; McConnell to Dennis DeConcini, 16 April 1982, ibid.; 1982 Senate Hearings, 71.
42. WBR, "Response to Testimony Opposing Confirmation," 40, 39, typescript in WBR Papers.
43. *New York Times*, 16 February 1982, II, 2:1.
44. Ibid., 28 April 1982, 25:1; 1982 Senate Hearings, II, 57.
45. Minutes of Meeting on Voting Rights Act, 26 April 1982, WBR Papers.
46. *Human Events* (12 May 1982): 3–4.
47. Interview with WBR, 11 January 1991.
48. Ibid.
49. 1982 Senate Hearings, II, 59–60; *New York Times*, 1 May 1982, 12:5; 4 May 1982, 1:1; 30 June 1982, 16:1; *Washington Post*, 3 May 1982, A14a.
50. Ibid.; *New York Times*, 30 June 1982, 16:1; 42 U.S.C. #1973.
51. *New York Times*, 30 June 1982, 16:1.
52. *Washington Post*, 4 May 1982, A1a.
53. J. V. Wilson to WBR, 29 April 1982, WBR Papers; "The Evolution of Section Two of the Voting Rights Act," ibid., 33–35.
54. *Fortune* (31 May 1982): 78; *Washington Post* 26 May 1982, A23d.
55. *1982 Senate Hearings*, 70, 73, 74; *Washington Post*, 5 May 1982, A3a. Nevertheless, Hatch finally voted for the amended version of the Voting Rights Act of 1982. There were few black voters in Hatch's home state, Utah, but Hatch did not wish to be depicted as an enemy of civil rights as there was the possibility that he would run for national office or be nominated for a seat on the Supreme Court.
56. *Washington Post*, 19 June 1982, A1c; 9 May 1982, D1d.
57. *New York Times*, 29 January 1982, 26:1; 19 March 1982, 30:1; 13 April 1982, 26:1; 4 July 1982, IV, 14:1.
58. *National Review* (11 June 1982): 673.

4

Six Cases: Mississippi, New York City, Selma, Burke County, Montgomery, Greene County

William Bradford Reynolds charted the course for the Reagan administration on voting rights. In most ways that course was congruent with the approach that the major civil rights organizations favored. Nevertheless, because Reynolds parted company with the organizations on a few key cases, the organizations subjected Reynolds to spirited criticism. In 1985, when Reynolds was nominated for a promotion to associate attorney general, the civil rights groups used the confirmation hearings to express their opposition to the civil rights policies of the Reagan administration. They spent more time complaining about the administration's record on voting rights than on anything else.

I

After the 1980 census, when electoral districts were adjusted throughout the country, Reynolds and the Voting Section of the Civil Rights Division took special pains to make sure that the political power of blacks was not diluted by discrimination in the drawing of new electoral boundary lines. Reynolds recognized that, as he put it, "the potential existed for the hard-won gains of black voters to be undermined, not by outright denials of access to the ballot box, as occurred in the past, but by racially motivated vote dilution—that is, by drawing district lines so as to fragment concentrations of black voters and submerge sizable minority voting blocs in districts controlled by white majorities." He said that registration drives would "mean little if, for racial reasons, the reapportionment process unfairly divides black voting strength into several districts while consolidating the strength of white voters."[1]

There are several examples of Reynolds's work to combat minority vote dilution. One occurred in Mississippi, another in New York City, and yet others in several state legislatures that were reapportioned after the 1980 census.

From 1882 to 1966, the boundaries of Mississippi's congressional districts had been drawn from north to south, thereby creating a heavily black district in the Delta area near the Mississippi River. Although most of the people who lived in the Delta were black, the district sent white congressmen to Washington because most blacks had been disfranchised by Mississippi's poll tax and literacy text.

With the passage of the Voting Rights Act in 1965, white Mississippians recognized that large numbers of blacks would soon be voting. When that happened, it seemed likely that a black candidate would be elected in the predominantly black Delta congressional district. To avoid that possibility, the Mississippi legislature, in 1966, set up new congressional districts that ran from east to west. It did so because whites made up the majority of the population in the central and eastern portions of the state. Thus, if the district boundaries ran from east to west, instead of from north to south, whites would be a majority in each congressional district, and Mississippi would continue to send an all-white congressional delegation to Washington.

In 1966 a federal court accepted the configuration that fragmented the predominantly black Delta. A few years later, following modifications made after the census of 1970, the Department of Justice endorsed a similar configuration. But after the 1980 census, when the arrangement was adjusted again, Reynolds refused to preclear the plan. Subsequent negotiation and litigation resulted in an alternative plan that created a predominantly black Delta district that gave black candidates a realistic opportunity to win election to Congress. Finally, in 1986 the voters of the mostly black Second Congressional District elected Mike Espy, who became the first black congressman from Mississippi in the twentieth century.[2]

Mississippi was not the only jurisdiction that used discriminatory techniques that were more subtle than outright denial of the ballot. Another culprit was New York City. The Voting Rights Act was initially targeted at the South, not the South Bronx. But, because of low registration among foreign-language minorities, the Voting Rights Act, as revised in 1970 and 1975, applied to New York City. Gotham, like Dixie, was required to have the attorney general's approval for electoral changes.

After the census of 1980, Reynolds withheld approval when the New York City Council provided substantial black and Hispanic majorities in only eight of forty-five councilmanic districts. According to Reynolds, this represented a "retrogression" from the previous situation where blacks and Hispanics had been able to elect eight of forty-three council members—a retrogression that had occurred despite the fact that the blacks and Hispanics had increased from 24 percent to 44 percent of New York's population in the years since the Census of 1970. Reynolds thought the city had minimized the political influence of its black and Hispanic citizens by drawing boundaries that fragmented their voting strength.[3]

Council members complained about what they called the "intrusion" of the federal government. The *New York Times* said the electoral boundaries had been designed to protect incumbents, nonwhite as well as white—not to promote racial discrimination. But Reynolds explained that under Section 5 of the Voting Rights Act, the city bore the burden "of proving the absence of both discriminatory purpose and effect." This meant that the city "must demonstrate, at a minimum, that the proposed councilmanic redistricting plan would not lead to a retrogression in the position of racial minorities with respect to the effective exercise of their electoral franchise." Because the minority populations were not "so widely dispersed as to preclude the creation of additional minority districts," Reynolds said he was "unable to conclude, as I must under the Voting Rights Act, that the presently proposed councilmanic district lines...were drawn without any discriminatory racial purpose or effect." Reynolds then insisted that the council boundaries be redrawn to facilitate the election of more minority candidates.[4]

Reynolds received a good deal of publicity for his refusal to approve the boundaries for Mississippi's congressional districts and New York's councilmanic districts. But these were only two of 165 voting arrangements Reynolds refused to approve during his first two years as assistant attorney general for civil rights. Reynolds and the Civil Rights Division also objected to policies that made it difficult to register voters during nonworking hours; they objected to laws that limited the ability of illiterate voters to receive assistance in voting; they objected to discriminatory procedures for purging voting lists of voters who had moved away or died; they objected to at-large systems that allegedly reduced the minorities' ability to elect candidates of their choice; they participated in the ultimately successful challenge to at-large voting in Mobile, Alabama.[5]

In six of the Southern states originally covered by the Voting Rights Act, and in three other states as well, Reynolds and the Civil Rights Division interposed objections to the way at least one house of the state legislature had been districted. In addition, Reynolds and the Division set aside proposed congressional redistricting plans from Georgia, New York, Mississippi, and Texas. Subsequently, as Reynolds noted with satisfaction, additional minority candidates were elected to Congress in each of these states.[6]

After the 1980 census, Reynolds and the Civil Rights Division also took on a prodigious task that far outstripped the activity of any previous administration—a careful review of more than 50,000 adjustments that localities had made. In conducting this review, Reynolds had one principal aim: to ensure that the "districting in all covered jurisdictions...was most advantageous to the minority populations." By 1985 Reynolds had rejected 110 redistricting plans (compared to 26 rejections during the four years of the Carter administration).[7]

During the years of Ronald Reagan's presidency, the number of elected black officials increased from 5,038 in 1981 to 7,226 in 1989. This was no accident. The growth in black office holding occurred because Reynolds and the Civil Rights Division, after the 1980 census, fought against efforts to dilute minority voting strength. They "forced states and localities throughout the South, and in some northern states, to redistrict (sometimes several times) or make other voting changes."[8]

Jesse Jackson may deserve some of the credit for Reynolds's record on voting rights. In 1983, when Reynolds toured through Mississippi with Jackson, the *Washington Post* reported that Jackson "lectured [Reynolds] non-stop, regaling him with civil rights horror stories." Jackson pointed out how whites in Belzoni had kept control by refusing to annex a black neighborhood near the center of the town. He explained how whites in Jackson had annexed white suburbs to reduce the influence of a growing black electorate. He introduced Reynolds to blacks who gave voice to a number of complaints: about counties that required double registration—in the voter's home town and also in the county seat; about counties that would not allow registration outside the county courthouse; about wages lost if voters took time off from work to register; about the money it cost for gas to drive to the polls.[9]

Some white Mississippians thought the complaints were exaggerated. One man said the federal government "could have...saved the taxpayers a lot of money" if Reynolds and his entourage had stayed in Washington and used the travel funds to "hire taxis for the people who wanted to come register."[10]

Reynolds conceded that there were "two sides to every story" and that he had heard only one side on his trip to Mississippi. But Reynolds insisted that the visit had made "the whole process of analyzing redistricting come alive to me." After returning to Washington, Reynolds concluded that "the ability to register was not as open and accessible as it might be." Then he sent additional federal registrars to several counties, reiterated that he would not approve any voting districts that diluted minority voting strength, and refused to preclear a record number of Mississippi county redistricting plans. As a result, "by 1988 there were sixty-eight black county supervisors, more than two-and-a-half times the number of black county supervisors elected after the 1979 statewide elections."[11]

In Washington some critics dismissed the trip and the subsequent actions as publicity stunts. Others, who saw films of Reynolds and Jackson arm-in-arm singing "We Shall Overcome," suggested that Reynolds had fallen under Jackson's spell. Writing in the *Washington Post,* Art Harris reported that in

Mississippi Reynolds had been "a sight to behold. He was fired up. He had caught the spirit of Jesse Jackson." By the time Reynolds stepped to the pulpit of a little black church in Canton, "he had a gleam in his eye and a lilt to his speech. Some even suggested that he was getting a touch of soul."[12]

For his part, Reynolds insisted that he had an "absolute intolerance for racial discrimination" all along. "I did not come back from this trip with any different attitude than I went down with," Reynolds said. "My job is to enforce the law in the best way we can. It is not a new direction in our policy."[13]

II

In a 1983 speech to the NAACP, Reynolds acknowledged that "we may reach a different outcome...in some individual cases." But he insisted, "[O]ur overall approaches are quite similar." In some ways it is unfair to focus attention on the instances in which Reynolds and the NAACP differed. They were only a few of more than 50,000 voting decisions that Reynolds made during the period from 1981 to 1985. Some required a difficult choice in a situation where there was sincere disagreement among the attorneys and paralegal staff analysts who were employed by the Voting Section of the Civil Rights Division. No matter which way Reynolds decided, the losing side was sure to criticize the decision. Nevertheless, a consideration of these cases illuminates the points at issue between Reynolds and the critics of the Reagan administration.[14]

One case involved Selma, Alabama, the scene of the major voting rights demonstrations of 1965. During the 1985 hearings on Reynolds's proposed promotion to associate attorney general, Senators Edward M. Kennedy and Howard M. Metzenbaum complained that Reynolds allowed authorities in Selma to move a polling place from a community center in a black neighborhood to a courthouse annex three-quarters of a mile away in a downtown, mostly white area.[15]

Reynolds said he reviewed the situation "very carefully" and "talked to a lot of people" before concluding that the change was "free of discriminatory purpose and effect." Local officials in Selma reported the situation at the community center was confusing because so many activities, including the distribution of food stamps, occurred there. The local officials also said more parking was available at the courthouse annex.[16]

However, Reynolds's decision differed from the recommendation of the staff attorney who had worked on the case. The attorney noted that although the change had been made in 1980, authorities in Selma had waited until 1984 before seeking approval from the attorney general. This was hardly *pre*clearance. In the meantime, the proportion of votes cast by blacks at this polling place declined from 59 percent to 36 percent. Nevertheless, Reynolds approved the change. He said that "voter turnout figures are things that are very hard to ascribe too much significance to, because there are any number of reasons why people may or may not turn out for a particular vote on a particular day." He also noted that he had sent federal observers to "insure that those individuals who want to vote will be able to go there and vote freely."[17]

Reynolds's decision impressed many observers as a close call on a tough question over which reasonable people might differ. But Senators Kennedy and Metzenbaum did not see it that way. Kennedy complained about the extra five dollars it reportedly cost black voters to take a cab to the new polling place (an amount that Reynolds disputed). After stating that he had marched in Selma with Martin Luther King in 1965, Metzenbaum disregarded Reynolds's assertion that "Selma today is much different than the Selma you describe of some twenty years ago." Instead, Metzenbaum characterized Reynolds's decision as "shameful" and "obscene."[18]

Yet another instance of Reynolds's alleged insensitivity to voting rights occurred in Burke County, Georgia. Black plaintiffs in Burke County, like the plaintiffs in *Mobile v. Bolden*, complained that at-large elections illegally diluted black political power. They conceded that blacks made up 58 percent of the county's population and were allowed to register and vote freely. But they also noted that blacks accounted for only 38 percent of the registered voters, and no black had ever been elected to the five-member county commission.

After a lengthy trial, the district court concluded that the at-large system was being maintained for illegal, discriminatory purposes and ordered that the county be divided into five districts with each district electing one county commissioner. Under the order of the district court, the black proportion of the five districts was to be 78 percent, 75 percent, 53 percent, 52 percent, and 43 percent, respectively. Because a larger proportion of blacks were children under the age of eighteen, whites would continue to be a majority of the voting age population in three of the five districts.[19]

In ruling against Burke's at-large system, the district court pointed to evidence of racially polarized voting. The court also held that the all-white county commission had been "unresponsive" to the needs of the black community. The court found that the streets in white neighborhoods were better than those in areas inhabited by blacks and that a disproportionately small number of blacks had been hired for county jobs or appointed to the county's numerous boards and committees. It found that the socioeconomic status of Burke's blacks was depressed, with 73 percent of black households lacking plumbing facilities compared with 16 percent of white households. The court also faulted some county commissioners for helping to organize a white private academy and noted that faded paint over restroom doors at the county courthouse did not entirely conceal the words "colored" and "white."[20]

The Fifth Circuit Court of Appeals and the U. S. Supreme Court later affirmed the district court's decision in the *Burke County* case. The Civil Rights Division had filed briefs in support of the black plaintiffs when the case was before the district and circuit courts. When the case was on appeal to the Supreme Court, however, the division did not intervene.[21]

In 1982 Senator Arlen Specter of Pennsylvania asked Reynolds to explain "the reason that the Justice Department did not file a brief in the Supreme Court of the United States." Senator Patrick J. Leahy of Vermont also inquired about the matter. Reynolds said that "with the resources we have," it was not possible for the department to intervene "in every civil rights case." Reynolds mentioned, though, that "it was not just a workload issue." He said that after considering the case, the decision was made that *Burke County* was "not [a case] that we felt we should become involved in."[22]

Specter then asked Reynolds for his personal opinion on intervention, but Reynolds declined to answer. Reynolds insisted that it would not be appropriate to reveal discussions that had been held within the Department of Justice, "especially when the case is pending." "With the case pending in the Court," he said, "I am not at liberty...to discuss the case or give a legal judgment."[23]

In 1985 Specter and Leahy obtained a copy of a 1982 memorandum Reynolds had written to Solicitor General Rex Lee. In that memorandum, Reynolds stated that personally he thought the appropriate remedy for blacks in Burke County, where blacks made up a majority of the population, was to organize politically rather than to abolish at-large voting. If the Department of Justice had to intervene in the case, Reynolds wrote, "the preferred position" would be to intervene in favor of the county and its system of at-large elections; but because there was not enough time to rewrite the legal briefs the Department had submitted to the lower courts, Reynolds recommended "with considerable disappointment" that the United States not participate in the case.[24]

Specter felt, or feigned, outrage over this decision. He said he had "read many, many cases" and did "not know of one" where the discrimination against blacks was more "egregious." He considered it morally reprehensible for Reynolds to favor at-large voting in a county that was only 58 percent black. In doing so, Specter accepted the argument that a district should not be considered as majority black unless it was at least 65 percent black.[25]

But Reynolds was taking a second look at an argument that impressed many people as dubious. Even the *Washington Post*, on one occasion, conceded, "It makes much more sense to use language literally and say that any district more than half of whose adult residents are black is black majority." As Reynolds saw it, blacks in Burke County made up "well in excess of 50 percent of the voting-age population." If they did not register and vote as frequently as whites, the sensible solution was to organize politically, not to have a court prohibit the system of at-large voting.[26]

Nevertheless, Senators Specter and Leahy were miffed. They accused Reynolds of misrepresenting the position he had taken on the *Burke County* case. Reynolds, apologizing for any false impression, said that he had however made it clear, back in 1982, that he would not discuss his personal opinion of the case but would explain in general terms why the Reagan administration did not file a brief with the Supreme Court.[27]

A furious Leahy characterized Reynolds's explanation as "nitpicking," while Specter said it was "deceptive." Several major newspapers agreed. The *New York Times* accused Reynolds of being "less than candid"; the *Los Angeles Times* said Reynolds played "tricks with the truth"; and the *Washington Post* cited Reynolds's remarks on the *Burke County* case as evidence that Reynolds had "misled senators in describing his own position."[28]

The *Wall Street Journal* assessed the situation differently. In two editorials and an op-ed essay, the *Journal* presented the fullest media account of the credibility question and the *Burke County* case. After reprinting the full text of what Reynolds said to Senator Specter in 1982, the *Journal* concluded that nothing in the testimony had been deceptive. Reynolds had told Specter that he had "a personal view" on the *Burke County* case, but that it would have been inappropriate with the case pending for him to make a statement as to what his personal judgment was on the facts of that case. "If Senator Specter came away misled into believing that he and Mr. Reynolds were in complete agreement," the *Journal* observed, "the voters of Pennsylvania should give [Specter] a hearing test."[29]

More was at issue than a dispute over the *Burke County* case. As the *Journal* noted, in the past liberals and civil rights activists had developed three principal methods for attacking conservative officials. But none could be used effectively against Reynolds. He could not be dismissed as "an unqualified know-nothing," given his previous record as a partner in a prominent Washington law firm, as an assistant to the solicitor general, and as the editor-in-chief of the *Vanderbilt Law Review*. In addition, since Reynolds already had a fortune of his own, it was hard to accuse him of being on the take from one interest or another. Another old standby, "to thunder that a conservative appointee's policies are not only wrong but beyond the pale of decent American behavior," would not fly either, "since Mr. Reynolds's opponents kn[e]w which side most Americans would support if a civil-rights policy poll were taken."[30]

Consequently, according to the *Journal*, Reynolds's opponents took the "credibility" route. Instead of engaging Reynolds head-on with respect to busing, quotas, and affirmative districting, Reynolds's critics turned their policy disagreements "into attacks on his character, using flimsy evidence to boot."[31]

The chief architect of this strategy was neither Arlen Specter nor Patrick Leahy. It was Joseph R. Biden, the Democratic Senator from Delaware. Biden said he found Reynolds's approach to civil rights generally "repugnant," but he differed from "some of the civil rights groups" who wanted Congress to take on the Reagan administration over its opposition to "busing and quotas." That, Biden said, would be "a very stupid strategy."[32]

As the ranking Democrat on the Senate Judiciary Committee, Biden was in a position to shape the strategy of his party. Instead of confronting the Reagan administration on busing and quotas, he instructed his staff to look for questionable voting cases. When Biden's turn came to question Reynolds, he focused on the details of a Louisiana redistricting plan that will be discussed in the next chapter. Leahy and Specter followed Biden's lead with their questions on *Burke County*.[33]

Equally important, prior to Reynolds's appearance before the Senate Judiciary Committee, Biden persuaded committee chairman Strom Thurmond to delay the start of the hearings for several weeks. Biden used the time to have his staff, in cooperation with civil rights leader Ralph Neas and with some disaffected career lawyers in the Civil Rights Division, pore over thousands of pages of documents during long sessions that stretched into the early morning hours. Biden's plan was to allow Reynolds to speak expansively during the first days of the hearings and then trap him by bringing up any inconsistencies between the documents and Reynolds's statements before the committee.[34]

Some observers praised Biden for developing a clever approach. Howard Kurtz of the *Washington Post* credited Biden for claiming "the moral high ground of voting rights" and for raising "questions about Reynolds's credibility." Mary Frances Berry praised Biden for doing "a good job in formulating a strategy."[35]

Others demurred. Griffin Bell described the criticism of Reynolds as "disingenuous" and "unfair." The truth of the matter, Bell said, was that Reynolds was "under attack because of his enforcement of the Justice Department's policies on quotas and discrimination—nothing more, nothing less." Senator Mitch McConnell of Kentucky said it was unfair for senators to "search for some conflict in Mr. Reynolds's testimony, however minor or understandable." After pointing to Senator Biden's staff members at the back of the hearing room ("the bleary-eyed ones" who had pored over transcripts looking for inconsistencies), Senator Alan Simpson of Wyoming declared that Reynolds had been "pecked to death by bug-eyed zealots."[36]

Burke County was not the only case where critics found fault with Reynolds. Controversy also arose in Alabama, where the white mayor of Montgomery, Emory Folmar, developed a plan that reduced the proportion of blacks who lived in the district of a black political enemy, councilman Joe Reed. The case received a good deal of attention because Reed, who had organized the Alabama Democratic Conference, the strongest black political organization in the state, was widely regarded as one of the state's preeminent black leaders. And Folmar was a friend of Ronald Reagan.

Under Folmar's plan, the black majority in Reed's district would have been reduced from 84 percent to 68 percent. Folmar knew the plan could not go into effect unless Reynolds ruled that there was no racial discrimination. Folmar insisted that his districting plan had "nothing to do with race. It is strictly politics." He characterized Reed as "a political enemy of mine from the day we sat down on the council." He said "a 65 percent or above black district can 'safely' select a black representative," and he insisted that he did not care "which black gets elected...as long as it ain't [Reed]."[37]

Folmar hoped that Reed would have problems in the new district. It was 68 percent black, but one-tenth of the prospective black voters were students who lived in the dormitories at a predominantly black university. In the past many students had not voted on election day. The black faculty and professional staff almost always voted, but Folmar calculated that these black professionals might support a moderate black candidate whose policies and rhetoric were less polarizing than Reed's. If they joined with the sizeable white minority that Folmar had folded into the district, one that also would be disposed to favor a black moderate, Reed might be voted out of office. "That was our thought," one of Folmar's associates said. But he conceded that it would take some doing to develop "a credible black rival to Reed in the district."[38]

Folmar knew that districting could not be used to exclude racial groups from the political process or to minimize their political influence. But Folmar and his lawyers noted that the Supreme Court had given wide latitude to political gerrymandering. The Court acknowledged that "district lines are rarely neutral phenomena" and that "political considerations are inseparable from districting and apportionment." While stopping short of saying that no political gerrymander could ever be found unconstitutional, the Court made the burden of proof so difficult that no plaintiff has ever won a claim against a political gerrymander. The Court has said it will not attempt "the impossible task of extirpating politics from what are the essentially political processes of the sovereign States."[39]

Folmar also maintained that, far from diluting black power, his plan would increase the political influence of blacks. He said that no attempt had been made to fragment black voters. In fact, the city's 39 percent black minority had already elected four of the city's nine commissioners. But Folmar explained that fragmentation was not the only way to dilute black power. Dilution could also be accomplished by packing an excessive number of blacks into certain districts. Folmar said that under his plan black candidates would continue to be elected in four districts—where the black proportion of the population would range upward from 62 percent to 89 percent. But because all blacks had not been packed into these four districts, a black minority would be large enough to become a swing vote that could elect sympathetic white candidates in some of the predominantly white districts.[40]

In 1985 voting rights activists and some senators cited Reynolds's approval of Folmar's plan as evidence of the Reagan administration's insensitivity toward blacks. Senator Charles Mathias noted that after Reynolds approved Folmar's plan, black allies of Joe Reed "convinced the Federal Court that [Folmar's plan was] in fact discriminatory." Ralph Neas said that in this instance "the racial discrimination was unbelievably flagrant, to the point where voters were able to go to court afterwards, and win...—something which had never happened before Reynolds's time."[41]

Neas and Mathias did not mention that the judge in the case, Myron H. Thompson, was a liberal Democrat who, before being appointed to the bench by President Jimmy Carter, had been a political enemy of Emory Folmar and an ally of Joe Reed. Judge Thompson conceded that political gerrymanders were not illegal. "To the extent that Folmar's goal was political, and to the extent that he acted out of a desire to reduce the possibility of [Joe Reed's] being re-elected, the Court recognizes and appreciates that such a political goal may not be a violation." But Thompson ruled against Folmar's plan because, according to Thompson, it was "purposefully designed and executed to decrease the voting strength of the black electorate." Thompson held that "Folmar went afoul...when he sought to achieve his goal by purposefully diluting the strength of the black electorate." The judge said it was "solely the voting rights of the black electorate...which are now this court's concern."[42]

III

Another federal judge also overturned a decision Reynolds made in a case that concerned the commissioners who regulated greyhound racing in Greene County, Alabama.

Greene County was 78 percent black, and after 1969 all members of its county commission had been blacks. But Greene's total population was only 11,000, and when it came to electing state representatives the county had been joined with predominantly white areas that sent white representatives to the state legislature in Montgomery. After the 1980 census, Reynolds insisted that Greene should be joined with other predominantly black regions; and in 1983 a new legislative reapportionment act made Greene part of predominantly black areas that elected two blacks, Hank Sanders and Lucius Black, to the state Senate and House of Representatives.

This alarmed the owners of the biggest business in Greene County, the Greenetrack Greyhound Racing Stadium. In 1975 the Alabama legislature had provided that the Greene County Racing Commission should consist of three members appointed by the legislative delegation that represented Greene County in the House and Senate of Alabama. But the owners of the racetrack, led by Paul Bear Bryant, Jr., the principal stockholder and the son of the famous football coach, said that commissioners named by Sanders and Black would appoint excessive numbers of incompetent political cronies to positions at the track. In 1983, when Sanders and Black were about to be elected to represent Greene in the state legislature, the owners of the Greenetrack persuaded the legislature to change the law and to provide that the racing commission should consist of three persons appointed by the governor of Alabama.[43]

At first Reynolds refused to preclear this change, explaining that the reallocation of governmental powers was "retrogressive with respect to minority voting strength." Then he changed his mind and decided that the new policy did not require preclearance. He explained that there was no reduction in the number of elected legislative delegates. The change did not remove the vote from residents of Greene county and did not involve a wholesale transfer of government power from the elected representatives. It was, rather, a modification of duties, similar to changing the responsibility for appointing a fire chief or sanitation commission. A change as to who appointed the racing commissioners was nothing more than a routine modification of duties. Altering the appointing authority for such positions was not, Reynolds decided, a voting practice or procedure that had to be precleared.[44]

Black voters appealed, and a three-judge district court ruled that the change was subject to preclearance. The court did not consider the change ordinary or routine because taxes from the Greenetrack made up almost two-thirds of the total budget of Greene County. The court also noted that the Supreme Court had said the Voting Rights Act was aimed at subtle as well as obvious voting discrimination and should be given "the broadest possible scope."[45]

Unlike Judge Thompson, who had manipulated the law in the Montgomery case to punish a political enemy and to protect an ally, the judges in the Greene County case applied the law without having any ax to grind. In this instance, this writer believes, it was Reynolds who made the mistake; he should have objected to the changed method for appointing racetrack commissioners.[46]

Perhaps one mistake should not be discussed at length, but more was at issue in Greene County than a judgment over approving a reallocation of governmental power. Reynolds carefully considered the information that had been submitted by both the proponents and opponents of the change. Much of this information was technical and legalistic, but other information pointed to a broader picture of poverty, incompetence, and voting fraud.

Predominantly rural Greene was one of the poorest counties in the nation with more than 20 percent of the workers unemployed in 1980 and a median family income that was about one-quarter of the national average. Although the county did not have many of the educated, motivated workers required by high-tech, service, and information-oriented companies, some knowledgeable people, black and white, thought industry could be attracted to the county. They noted that wages and taxes were comparatively low, that Greene had an abundance of cheap land, and that the county was not isolated. The Tennessee-Tombigbee Waterway offered the inexpensive water transportation that many heavy industries needed, and an interstate highway ran through the middle of the county.[47]

The advocates of industrial development found fault with the county's black activists and with the established black political leaders. They noted that when Scott Paper was persuaded to locate in Greene, activists pestered the company with demands that it give preferences to minority loggers and that it deposit a large amount of money in a bank owned by blacks. Put off by what they regarded as aggressive posturing, officials of the Rob Roy textile plant and the McGregor printing company responded to similar demands by closing down their operations. And the Utah Inns, a corporation that wished to build a large motel in the county in the early 1980s, decided to build elsewhere after activists presented the company with demands for affirmative action.[48]

The loss of the Utah Inn was especially important because it nudged a local black businessman, John Kennard, toward organizing biracial opposition to the local black establishment. As one of the owners of the largest black business in the county, a restaurant located across the highway from the dog-racing stadium and next to the land the Utah Inns had planned to develop, Kennard thought the black activists had done more than repel a prospective employer; they had damaged him personally by depriving his restaurant of patronage it would have received from bettors who were lodging at the motel next door.

Beyond this, Kennard, who was also the tax assessor in Greene County, thought many of the local black politicians and office holders were incompetent. The chairman of the county commission owed nearly $12,000 in undocumented travel expenses, and another commissioner owed $1,660. Kennard said the commissioners could not balance a check book, much less oversee a multi-million dollar county budget. On one occasion, in an open meeting, Kennard offered to resign his position as tax assessor if one illiterate county commissioner could read aloud a headline in the newspaper. Kennard predicted that, despite an annual infusion of more than $1 million from Greenetrack taxes, the new commissioners would soon turn what had been an annual surplus of about $500,000 into a substantial deficit.[49]

Kennard also emphasized a point that many whites had been making for some time: that the budget should be balanced by appointing fewer, more efficient government workers, not by raising taxes. He said higher taxes would make it more difficult to attract industry to the county. Like many whites, Kennard said the incompetence of Greene's black officials and the demands of some black activists contributed to poverty by causing white businesses to stay away.[50]

Kennard did more than speak out. He joined with two white lawyers, Walter Griess and Patta Steele, and with a white minister, Marquis Wingard, to organize a biracial coalition to support moderate blacks who were more favorably disposed toward white business. They began in May 1984, when they invited whites to come to the National Guard Armory, a traditional meeting place for whites, to hear speeches by the black candidates. They also issued the following bulletin that explained that battle lines were being drawn for a political confrontation:

> A coalition has been formed. Responsible Whites and Blacks are working in a unified effort to elect qualified, independent candidates. A mixed slate would be ideal, but we must be realistic. As has happened in previous elections, once a White is in the run-off, the [black] radicals have been successful in marketing racism, thereby getting their man into office. The key for the 1984 county election is to support good, responsible Blacks and to keep Whites out of the race.[51]

It was no easy matter to put together a biracial coalition in the black belt of rural Alabama. "In the beginning," Patta Steele recalled, "it was like a junior high school dance, with the girls on one side of the room and the boys on the other. Except this time it was whites and blacks." But the common dissatisfaction with the local black establishment eventually overwhelmed the racial uneasiness, and in 1984 blacks backed by the coalition took six of seven countywide offices from black incumbents that were supported by the civil rights establishment.[52]

Since whites made up only one-quarter of the registered voters in Greene County, the coalition could not have succeeded without support from at least one-third of the black voters. The coalition apparently received some votes from black farmers who were put off by the incumbents' reputation for political chicanery. Some younger blacks with aspirations in politics also gravitated toward the coalition because they had been shut out of the incumbents' inner circle.[53]

But the greatest portion of black support for the biracial coalition apparently came from educated, middle-class blacks—especially those who were middle-aged or older. In the 1960s many of these middle-class blacks had hesitated to participate openly in the civil rights movement because they feared retribution from white employers or clients. Although they supported the movement in private and made financial contributions, their reluctance to take a public stand annoyed those who had marched in the vanguard of the movement. When the young civil rights activists of the 1960s graduated to become the political leaders of Greene County in the 1970s and 1980s, they did not forgive the middle-class "Uncle Toms." Instead, they denied them a role in government. The middle-class blacks dared not protest openly for fear of losing valuable county contracts and jobs. But, when offered the chance, they cast their ballots against the black establishment and for the black candidates associated with the biracial coalition.[54]

The established blacks did not succumb without a struggle. In addition to spending tax money, the county commission influenced the selection of the 132 workers employed by the county. There was more patronage at the Greenetrack, the county's largest employer, and there were contracts for supplying the track and the county government with a variety of supplies and services.

With so much at stake, the establishment rallied around the county's most celebrated civil rights activist, Spiver Gordon. Active in the civil rights movement for more than twenty-five years, Gordon was Alabama vice-president of the organization Martin Luther King, Jr. had founded, the Southern Christian Leadership Conference. He also headed the Greene County Civic League and was a member of the city council in Eutaw, the county seat.

In appearance and style, Gordon personified the civil rights movement. He sported a thick beard and a high, grey-streaked, Afro hairstyle that added several inches—and an intimidating touch—to his sturdy, short-medium frame. The walls of his office were adorned with photographs of rallies and marches with Gordon at the podium or at the head of a picket line, accompanied by leaders such as Martin Luther King, Jr. and Jesse Jackson. By way of contrast, the taller and younger John Kennard was one of the first blacks to graduate from the predominantly white University of Alabama. His restaurant specialized in chicken, ribs, and other varieties of soul food, but it was not decorated with photographs of the civil rights movement. Instead, it featured photographs of John Wayne and other Western movie stars. It was the sort of place where both blacks and whites could feel comfortable. In business, as in politics, Kennard's appeal was biracial.[55]

According to Spiver Gordon, the biracial coalition was a facade erected to obscure the machinations of rich whites who were using black candidates to clear the way for their own eventual return to power. Gordon said white plantation owners and "a few sell-out Tom puppets" were scheming to deprive blacks of their "authentic" leaders.[56]

Wendell Paris, a supporter of Gordon, expanded on this point. He said that after whites had succeeded in electing black moderates, they would move on to elect whites "because they hope to have us split." He said the whites were attempting the reverse of what blacks had done in the late 1960s. "When we first got started we couldn't beat the entrenched white politicians. So what we did as black people was vote for a milder white man to move out the giant. And came back with a black to beat the rookie white. They're reversing that on us."[57]

Some black radicals added a touch of conspiracy to this explanation. Steve Wilson, the editor of the *Greene County Democrat*, said it was the white planters, not the black government, that had an interest in repelling business and thwarting economic development. Wilson explained that if industry brought jobs to the county, the competition for labor would cause wages to rise. When squeezed by higher labor costs, the already struggling white planters would be forced to sell land in small parcels to blacks. According to Wilson, the battle in Greene County was part of a larger third-world struggle between landowners and aspiring peasants.[58]

In addition to presenting these arguments, Spiver Gordon stigmatized his opponents. He characterized John Kennard as a "white folks' nigger," as "a Negro with a little 'n.'" He distributed handbills with Kennard's picture and the legend: "Warning—Beware of this Snake—John 'Tom' Kennard." One of Gordon's prominent supporters, attorney J. L. Chestnut, disparaged Kennard as a "bootlicking...turncoat" who had not taken part in the civil rights demonstrations of the 1960s.[59]

Moving beyond invective, Gordon also resorted to voting fraud. This, at least, was the contention of John Kennard, who formally requested an investigation of the 1984 elections. After the FBI looked into the situation, and acting on the recommendation of U.S. Attorney Frank Donaldson, a grand jury indicted Gordon and four allies, with the case revolving around the propriety of their handling of absentee ballots.[60]

The evidence against "the Greene County Five" was overwhelming. In 1984 more absentee ballots were cast in Greene County than in Jefferson County (the site of Birmingham), which is sixty times more populous than Greene. Sixteen percent of the votes cast in Greene's 1984 Democratic primary were absentee ballots. According to Marty Connors, the director of the Alabama Republican Party, "Anytime more than 2 or 3 percent of the vote is absentee, then you probably have some underworld activity going on." Federal prosecutors said the underworld activity in Greene County had been coordinated by Spiver Gordon.[61]

A lengthy indictment specified that Gordon had used his position as a director of the Greene County Nursing Home to find out which patients were sufficiently aged or infirm so that he could apply for, receive, and cast absentee ballots in their names. Gordon also allegedly convinced people to forge ballots for uninformed relatives and friends who no longer lived in Greene County and then he had his allies sign as witnesses for the ballots. More specifically, Gordon was charged with fraudulently witnessing false signatures on the verification oaths for the ballots of Nebraska and Frankland Underwood.[62]

Two of Gordon's allies, Bobbie Nell Simpson and Frederick Douglass Daniels, were acquitted, but two others accepted plea bargains and admitted to misdemeanor charges. Bessie J. Underwood pleaded guilty to acting as a legal witness to false ballots, and James Colvin, the mayor of the town of Union, admitted to improperly and illegally soliciting and causing the execution of absentee ballots. (In a subsequent case, Colvin was sentenced to seven years in prison and required to make restitution of $150,000 of public money that he had diverted to support an expensive use of illegal drugs.)[63]

But Spiver Gordon was the big man among the Greene County Five. He was the defendant prosecutors most wanted to convict—and convict him they did. After nine days of testimony, the jury found Gordon guilty on four felony counts. Judge E. B. Haltom sentenced Gordon to pay a $1,000 fine, work five hundred hours of community service, and spend three years in a correctional facility. All but six months of the jail term was suspended.[64]

In 1987 the Eleventh Circuit Court of Appeals stated that "there was sufficient evidence to support Spiver Whitney Gordon's convictions for mail fraud arising from the mailing of fraudulently marked absentee ballots." But in 1988 Gordon's conviction was reversed because the Supreme Court, in another case, changed the law of federal mail fraud. In that case the high court ruled that Congress intended the federal mail fraud law to apply only to schemes that involved the deprivation of money or property; it did not intend for the statute to proscribe schemes to defraud citizens of intangible rights, such as the right to honest voting. The circuit court then reversed Gordon's conviction because the government "in prosecuting Gordon...neither alleged or attempted to prove that any person suffered a loss of money or property..., but rather relied exclusively on a deprivation of intangible rights."[65]

During the trial and while the case was on appeal, Gordon's lawyers put forward additional arguments that they hoped might serve as grounds for reversing the conviction. They said the heavily black pool of jurors in Greene

County had been diluted because the district court in Birmingham, where the case was tried, chose its jurors from throughout predominantly white northern Alabama. They also faulted the trial judge for allowing each side, prosecution and defense, six peremptory challenges in choosing the jury. As a result, after the defense struck six whites and the prosecution vetoed six blacks, the jury turned out to be all white.[66]

Gordon and his lawyers also tried to redirect the trial away from the specific evidence and toward a larger issue. They said the federal government had an ulterior motive in prosecuting the case, that the Reagan administration was trying to intimidate rural blacks whose votes otherwise might defeat Alabama's incumbent Republican senator, Jeremiah Denton. If the black vote were "chilled," Gordon and his lawyers said, the Republicans' chances of reelecting Denton and keeping control of the Senate would be enhanced.[67]

Several of Gordon's supporters focused on this alleged conspiracy. Clarence Mitchell, the chairman of the National Black Caucus of State Legislators, said, "The Justice Department is being used as a political tool for Senator Jeremiah Denton." Julian Bond of Georgia said there was "a vicious conspiracy directed from the White House...whose goal is the destruction of a budding political movement in the black belt." In Alabama, state senator Hank Sanders said the voting-fraud trial had "nothing to do with a criminal act"; it was "a purely political trial" that had been instigated by "the very highest levels of our national government."[68]

Gordon and his supporters, veterans of decades in the civil rights movement, recognized that if they alleged racism, the media and some members of Congress would come running. Thus Congressman John Conyers described biracial coalition politics as a desperate ploy of whites that had learned they could no longer outvote blacks in predominantly black areas, saying "So they have decided to go out and select...a black candidate...who will be able to go into office" by combining a minority of the black vote with most of the white votes. Conyers said the same approach had been attempted in many other places, from Detroit to South Africa, where antiblack whites disguised their "political racism and oppression" by giving their support to "black collaborators." Congressman Don Edwards shared this perspective. He regarded voting fraud as a matter of little importance and faulted the Department of Justice for siding with a faction of "Uncle Toms who have sold out to whites."[69]

The most influential newspapers and magazines did not wholly endorse these allegations, but neither did they reject them. The *New York Times* dutifully reported that the trial originally sprang from complaints lodged by black voters but emphasized the accusations against the Reagan administration. *Newsweek* deemed the trial a "mis-fired vote fraud case," and a skeptical article in the *New Republic* asked, "Is clean government the point of these trials?"[70]

The fullest attention in the national media came in misleading articles that Allen Tullos wrote for the *Nation* and *Southern Changes*. One of the articles began with what could have been a press release from Gordon's defense team—an assertion that the voting-fraud prosecution was "an apparent attempt to intimidate black voters in the rural South and push back electoral gains made since the passage of the 1965 Voting Rights Act." Tullos wrote that the case in Greene County and a similar case in nearby Perry County were part of a plot to thwart the emergence of black political power. "That's what this is about," he quoted one local black as saying. "This isn't really about a few absentee ballots.... The local white powers and the feds have said that the Black Belt has gotten too politically strong." Tullos suggested that Senator Denton, who had won election in 1980 by only 36,000 votes and who was sure to face a strong Democratic challenge in 1986, had probably instigated the prosecution.[71]

Tullos also asserted that the Reagan administration had ignored charges of fraud that implicated whites. When earlier put forward by Gordon's attorneys, the trial judge had dismissed this allegation of selective prosection as too frivolous to warrant consideration. But others, including Emory University history professor Dan Carter, repeated the allegation. Carter wrote that "outside observers concluded that white as well as black political figures were involved in voting irregularities," but that "the Reagan administration's justice department targeted black political activists in southern black majority counties—particularly Greene County, Alabama—for voter fraud investigations." It "refused to investigate the actions of conservative white office holders and politicians."[72]

Carter's accusations were false. No white, conservative or otherwise, had held countywide office in Greene since the 1960s, and the Justice Department had received no complaints alleging that whites had committed voting fraud in Greene County. Elsewhere, however, between 1982 and 1984, the federal government secured convictions of 135 vote "thieves," most of whom were white.[73]

It is understandable that the media would focus attention on allegations of selective prosecution and of a government conspiracy to suppress black political power. These charges made for eye-catching headlines. But the real story in Greene County was something else. Everyone there knew that blacks would continue to rule. The question was, which blacks? To the people of Greene County, the candidates of the civil rights establishment stood for certain policies, while the candidates supported by the biracial coalition advocated others. In the election of 1984, at least one-third of the black voters broke ranks. That was the real story—the black vote was not monolithic. Blacks could become tired of traditional leaders and desire a change, just as whites could. And blacks could base their political decisions on something besides race.

William Bradford Reynolds had nothing to do with the voting-fraud prosecutions, which were handled by local U.S. attorneys and by the Election Fraud Branch of the Department of Justice. But as head of the Civil Rights Division, Reynolds was familiar with the situation in Greene County. He knew that many people thought Hank Sanders and Lucius Black, the newly elected black state representatives from the county, would appoint political cronies to the Greene County Racing Commission, and that these cronies would dispense patronage to support a political machine that was stealing votes and stigmatizing its opponents. There is some evidence that this actually came to pass. Between 1983 and 1989, operating expenses at the track increased from 14 percent to 22 percent of the money collected, and the major stockholders complained that the racing commissioners were using jobs at the track "as rewards for loyalty from select people who support certain policies advocated by the racing commissioners and their supporters."[74]

In the end Spiver Gordon's conviction was overturned because the Supreme Court changed the law of federal mail fraud. Since Gordon had contributed much to the civil rights movement, it may be a good thing that he was able to retain his seat on the Eutaw city council and to continue to play an important role in Greene County. But it would be a mistake to accept Gordon's explanation of what had occurred in Greene County. That explanation was concocted by lawyers who put forward an argument that offered possibilities for fund raising and for appealing a conviction, and it was then reiterated and endorsed by journalists and scholars who missed the important story of factionalism among blacks.

The media emphasized that the defendants in the voting-fraud trial were black, that they had the support of the civil rights establishment, and that they made charges of racism. But the media did not assess the strong evidence that the defendants had stolen votes that black citizens had cast for rival black candidates. The media did not emphasize that the voting-fraud trial grew out of a political contest in which two slates of black candidates vied for county offices.

In Greene County the members of the white minority acted as black voters often do. They voted as a bloc. Meanwhile, the black majority behaved as whites often do. They split into factions. The political situation in Greene County was a reverse image of what occurs in U.S. politics. There a substantial number of whites often joins with the overwhelming majority of blacks to support liberal white candidates. In Greene, a substantial number of blacks joined the overwhelming majority of whites to elect black moderates. The black moderates cried foul when they learned that fraudulent ballots were being used against them, and the defendants in the voting fraud trial cried "racist," "turncoat," and "Uncle Tom" when they were caught with their hands in the ballot box.

The factionalism did not end with the voting fraud trial. In July 1984, three white supporters of Spiver Gordon went to court and demanded single-member districts in Greene County. The three could not have found support from many other whites, but they nevertheless filed their suits as a class action "on behalf of all white citizens." Because of racial polarization and at-large voting, they said, no member of the white minority had been elected to the county commission since 1969. Nor was a white likely to be elected unless at least one district was gerrymandered so that its boundaries would coincide with the white residential areas in the town of Eutaw. The plaintiffs said whites lost interest in politics when white candidates were shut out of office. They said businesses were more likely to locate in the county if the elected leaders were not all black.[75]

Advocates of single-member districting conceded that they also had a political purpose. The 1984 elections had boosted the fortunes of black candidates who allegedly had made some kind of deal with whites. But established leaders like J. L. Chestnut were determined to deal "publicly and effectively" with this sort of "Uncle Tomism." Albert Turner, one of the most prominent civil rights activists in Alabama, candidly explained that single-member districts would be configured to remove "the black collaborators" from their white supporters. Garry Spencer, the only incumbent black commissioner reelected in 1984, told Patta Steele that districting would deal a body blow to her biracial coalition. Wendell Paris gloated that with single-member districts, whites and black moderates would "get their one [county commissioner] and we will get our four." John Kennard summarized the matter when he said single-member districts had been put forward as "part of a plan to ensure the election of some blacks and to keep other blacks out of office."[76]

Since the civil rights establishment had lost control of the county commission in Greene, it did not have enough local influence to implement single-member districting. However, after Congress added the results test to the Voting Rights Act in 1982, Senator Hank Sanders steered a new districting plan through the state legislature.[77]

The new state districting law destroyed the biracial coalition in Greene County. "I just want to put it all behind me now," said a disillusioned Patta Steele. "Despite the rhetoric about 'Uncle Toms' and 'selling out' and all the statements that 'real blacks' would not vote for candidates who courted white support, I know that what we were doing was right. Maybe people just aren't ready to accept that blacks and whites can cooperate in politics."[78]

Unfortunately for the county, economic conditions continued to languish, with unemployment increasing to 29 percent by 1989. Many businesses apparently made a point of staying away from predominantly black regions, especially if the local leaders were perceived as inefficient or radical and if the work force was not well educated. Businesses were especially likely to steer clear of Greene because of the persistent political and racial wrangling.[79]

By 1989 the county was so desperate that Spiver Gordon's faction had developed an extraordinary plan. After learning of the problems several cities had disposing of trash and garbage, the local black establishment proposed to build one of the nation's largest landfills on the banks of the Tennessee-Tombigbee Waterway. They calculated that the venture would employ about one hundred workers who would be paid five-to-six-dollars an hour to sort recyclable garbage.[80]

Meanwhile, members of the erstwhile biracial coalition adopted a position not unlike the one the black establishment had taken with respect to Scott Paper and the Utah Inns. They became naysayers and obstructionists. While they conceded that it was difficult to oppose any new business when so many people were struggling to put bread on the table, they noted that the next largest landfill in Alabama employed only eighteen people. They insisted that the civil rights leaders had overestimated the number of new jobs that would be created at the landfill and had underestimated the damage the dump would do to the "ecological balance and health of the people in this area." They predicted that the new jobs would go only to Spiver Gordon's allies, and they said other businesses would not move to Greene County if "the garbage can of Alabama" was established "along the lovely chalk bluffs of the...Tenn-Tom waterway."[81]

Notes

1. WBR, remarks to the National Urban League, 2 August 1983, WBR Papers.
2. Connor v Johnson, 279 F.Supp. 619 (1966); 386 U.S. 483(1967); Jordan v. Winter, 541 F.Supp 1135 (1982); 604 F.Supp. 807 (1984); Frank R. Parker, "The Mississippi Congressional Redistricting Case: A Case Study in Minority Vote Dilution," *Howard Law Journal*, 28 (1965): 397–415.
3. *New York Times*, 28 October 1981, II, 5:1; 18 August 1981, 20:1; 16 February 1982, 19:1; 19 February 1982, II, 3:1.
4. Ibid., 12 September 1981, 1:6 and 22:1; 28 October 1981, II, 5:1.
5. WBR, remarks to Southern Christian Leadership Conference, 11 August 1982 and 26 August 1983, WBR Papers; Civil Rights Division Pamphlet, *Enforcing the Law, 20 January 1981–31 January 1987.*
6. Ibid.; WBR, remarks to National Urban League, 2 August 1983, WBR Papers.
7. *1985 Senate Hearings*, 21, 54, 185.
8. *New York Times*, 31 May 1983, 6:1; WBR, Statement to Senate Judiciary Committee, Hearing on Authorization for Department of Justice, 10 March 1987, WBR Papers; Joint Center for Political and Economic Studies, *Black Elected Officials: A National Roster,* xxii.
9. *Washington Post*, 16 June 1983, A1b; 18 June 1983, A2a; 20 June 1983, A11a; *New York Times*, 20 June 1983, 10:1.
10. *Washington Post*, 18 June 1983, A2a.
11. Ibid., 11 July 1983, A9a; *New York Times*, 16 June 1983, 23:1; 20 June 1983, 10:1; Frank R. Parker, *Black Votes Count*, 157.
12. *Washington Post*, 16 June 1983, A1b.

13. *New York Times*, 17 June 1983, 19:1; *Washington Post*, 19 June 1983, B7c. The trip to Mississippi also led Reynolds to question some arguments put forward by voting rights activists. One was the contention that many blacks had been prevented from registering to vote. Reynolds observed that although large numbers of blacks gathered to hear Jesse Jackson at every stop, few came forward when Jackson urged those who were not registered to come up to registration tables that were set up near Jackson's podium. This led Reynolds to believe that the vast majority of blacks were registered already. "It seemed to me that if there were people out there who were not registered, they would have come forward." Reynolds also came to doubt the contention that, because blacks had been denied the right to vote at courthouses before 1965, it was a subtle form of racial intimidation if polling continued at court houses. He understood that there might be a larger turnout if the balloting was done at community centers where many blacks were accustomed to congregate for social events. But he also observed that in Mississippi blacks "seemed to congregate around the court house every day. Not just affluent blacks, but poor blacks, too." Reynolds concluded, "By and large, the polling places in the Delta were fairly situated." Interview with WBR, 11 January 1991.
14. WBR, remarks to the NAACP, 20 May 1983, WBR Papers.
15. *1985 Senate Hearings*, 36–40, 48–57.
16. Ibid.
17. Ibid.
18. Ibid.
19. Lodge v. Buxton, 639 F2d 1358 (1981).
20. Ibid., 1361–62, 1375–80.
21. Ibid.; Rogers v. Lodge, 458 U.S. 613 (1982).
22. *1982 Senate Hearings*, 1677–78, 1683–86.
23. Ibid.
24. *1985 Senate Hearings*, 86, 888.
25. Ibid., 891.
26. *Washington Post*, 23 April 1982, A28a; *1985 Senate Hearings*, 891.
27. Ibid., 85–91, 886–891.
28. Ibid, 87, 888; *New York Times*, 19 June 1985, 22:1; *Los Angeles Times*, 21 June 1985, II, 4:1; *Washington Post*, 20 June 1985, A20a.
29. *Wall Street Journal*, 26 June 1985, 26:4.
30. Ibid., 14 June 1985, 24:1.
31. Ibid.
32. *Wilmington News Journal*, 25 June 1985; 28 June 1985; *Washington Post*, 24 June 1985, A4a..
33. Ibid.
34. Ibid.
35. *Washington Post*, 24 June 1985, A4a; 28 June 1985, A28e; *Wilmington News Journal*, 28 June 1985; 19 June 1985; *1985 Senate Hearings*, 888, 844–45.
36. *Washington Post*, 26 June 1985, A23f; 27 June 1985, A6a; 28 June 1985, A1b; *New York Times* 29 June 1985, 1:1; *1985 Senate Hearings*, 888–89, 902.
37. Buskey v. Oliver, 565 F.Supp. 1473 (1983), 1479, 1484.
38. Ibid., 1480; interview with G. Dennis Nabors, 29 May 1990.
39. Gaffney v. Cummings, 412 U.S. 735 (1973), 753, 754. Davis v. Bandemer, 106 S.Ct. 1797 (1986).
40. *1981 House Hearings*, 1512–25.

41. *1985 Senate Hearings*, 123, 586.
42. Buskey v. Oliver, 565 F.Supp. 1473 (1983), 1483.
43. Hardy v. Wallace, 603 F. Supp.174 (1985); *Greene County Independent*, 23 March 1989; *Greene County Democrat*, 15 March 1989; 29 March 1989; 17 May 1989.
44. Hardy v. Wallace, 603 F.Supp. 174 (1985), 179–80, 181–82.
45. Ibid., 177, 178.
46. My opinion finds support in the judgment of the District Court that decided the case of the Greene County Racetrack, Hardy v. Wallace, 603 F.Supp. 174 (1985). However, this case was not appealed to the Supreme Court, and when the High Court did consider a similar case, it endorsed the argument that Reynolds had made in the Greene County case: that a change in the authority of an elected official does not have to be precleared because it was not a change "with respect to voting" within the meaning of Section 5 of the Voting Rights Act. Presley v. Etowah County Commission, USLW, 28 January 1992, 4135.
47. Jeff Wolters, "Civil Rights or Government Wrongs? A Study of Black Politics, Voting Fraud, and Allegations of a Federal Conspiracy in the Black Belt" (unpublished senior honors thesis, University of Delaware, 1988), 4–42.
48. Interview with John Kennard, 6 May 1986; *Greene County Democrat*, 21 August 1985; *Greene County Independent*, 8 December 1988.
49. Interview with John Kennard, 6 May 1986; Kennard, interview with Jeff Wolters, 10 August 1987; *Tuscaloosa News*, 21 June 1984.
50. Ibid.
51. Bulletin of People's Action Committee, May 1984, provided by Patta Steele.
52. Patta Steele, interview with Jeff Wolters, 6 August 1987.
53. Interview with Nathan Watkins, 6 May 1986.
54. Jeff Wolters, "Civil Rights or Government Wrongs?" 27–29; Robert L. Brown, interview with Jeff Wolters, 10 August 1987.
55. Author's personal observations.
56. Spiver Gordon, interview with Jeff Wolters, 7 August 1987.
57. *Southern Changes* (May/June 1985): 11.
58. Interview with Steve Wilson, 7 May 1986.
59. Spiver Gordon, interview with Jeff Wolters, 7 August 1987; Jeff Wolters, interview with John Kennard, 10 August 1987; undated handbill, Black People's Action Committee, provided by John Kennard; *Greene County Democrat*, 25 September 1985.

    In his autobiography, a more restrained J. L. Chestnut offered this explanation: "Once the white courthouse crowd could no longer elect whites, they began to promote for office black people who thought the way they did or whom they could control. Instead of white candidates running against black candidates for county commission, school board, and other county offices, you now had white-sponsored black candidates against black candidates." J. L. Chestnut, Jr. and Julia Cass, *Black in Selma* (New York: Farrar, Straus and Giroux: 1991), 375–76, 374–88.
60. Interview with John Kennard, 6 May 1986.
61. *Birmingham Post-Herald*, 28 October 1985. Of 4,236 ballots cast in the Greene County Democratic primary of 1984, 680 were absentee ballots.
62. Grand Jury Indictment, U. S. District Court for the Northern District of Alabama/Western Division, June 1985. No 85-PT-200-W; U.S. v. Gordon, 817 F.2d 1538 (1987), 1542.
63. Jeff Wolters, "Civil Rights or Government Wrongs?" 29–34; *Greene County Independent*, 15 December 1988; 15 February 1989; 16 February 1989.

64. U.S. v. Underwood, 617 F.Supp. 713 (1985); U.S. v. Gordon, 817 F.2d 1538 (1987); 836 F.2d 1312 (1988).
65. U.S. v. Gordon, 836 F.2d 1312 (1988), 1313.
66. U.S. v. Underwood, 617 F.Supp. 713 (1985); U.S. v. Gordon, 817 F.2d 1538 (1987). If Gordon's conviction had not been reversed because of the redefinition of mail fraud, the use of peremptory challenges to strike black jurors might have led to a reversal. After Gordon's conviction, the Supreme Court, in Batson v. Kentucky, 106 S.Ct. 1712 (1986) ruled that prosecutors could no longer challenge jurors because of race.
67. Interview with Albert Turner, 8 May 1986; Spiver Gordon, interview with Jeff Wolters, 7 August 1987.
68. *Tuscaloosa News*, 25 June 1985; Bond, quoted in undated clipping from *Montgomery Advertiser*; *Greene County Democrat*, 30 January 1987.
69. Civil Rights Implications of Federal Voting Fraud Prosecutions, *Hearing before the Subcommittee on Civil and Constitutional Rights of the Committee on the Judiciary*, House of Representatives, 99th Congress, 1st Session, 1985, 121–22.
70. *New York Times*, 17 June 1985, 12:2; *Newsweek* (25 November 1985): 90; *New Republic* (15 July 1985): 22.
71. *Southern Changes* (March/April 1985): 1; (May/June 1985): 5; *Nation* (3–10 August 1985): 78–80.
72. U.S. v. Gordon, 817 F.2d 1538 (1987) ; *Journal of Southern History* (November 1985): 138.
73. Civil Rights Implications of Federal Voting Fraud Prosecutions, 94–105, 160; interview with Frank Donaldson, 10 May 1989. In *U.S. v. Gordon*, 817 F.2d 1538 (1987), 1540, three judges of the fifth circuit court stated, in passing and without specifics, that "some affidavits referenced the illegal voting of absentee whites." But U.S. Attorney Donaldson told me there were no such affidavits. The judges also mentioned "the rival white political organization in Greene County—but, as noted, this organization was a biracial alliance and all of its candidates were blacks. Most of those who voted for the candidates of the alliance were also blacks.
74. *Greene County Independent*, 23 March 1989.
75. Simpson, Elmore, and Zippert v. Greene County, Civil Action filed in U.S. District Court, Northern District of Alabama, 11 July 1984.
76. *Greene County Democrat*, 25 September 1985; interview with Albert Turner, 8 May 1986; Patta Steele, interview with Jeff Wolters, 6 August 1987; *Southern Changes* (May/June 1985): 11; interview with John Kennard, 6 May 1986.
77. *Code of Alabama 1975, 1995 Cumulative Supplement* (Charlottesville: The Michie Company, 1995), Section 11-3-1.
78. Patta Steele, interview with Jeff Wolters, 6 August 1987; interview with Carole and Louis Smith, 7 May 1986.
79. The *New York Times* reported, "Industrial development specialists have disclosed that it was not uncommon for businesses to eliminate southern communities from consideration for new manufacturing plants and other facilities...if they had large black populations. The rationale for such practices, the specialists said, was the belief that black workers were less reliable and skilled than white workers and easier to unionize. The companies also wanted to avoid the race issue in community relations and affirmative action programs."

    The *Greene County Independent* commented, "Business and industry hesitate to locate here in spite of Greene's wealth of natural resources and beauty.

Who wold willingly place himself in a position of being forced to choose political allies even before the first brick is set? How can a company lure employees here only to be met with problems associated with racial divisions in almost every area." See *New York Times*, 15 February 1983, 14:1; *Greene County Independent*, 26 January 1989.

80. *Greene County Independent*, 12 January 1989.
81. Ibid., 12 January 1989; 19 January 1989; 9 February 1989.

5

Congressional Districting in New Orleans

In 1985, when Ronald Reagan nominated William Bradford Reynolds for promotion to associate attorney general, the major civil rights groups used the confirmation hearings to voice their criticism of the administration's voting rights policies. The voting case that received the greatest attention during these hearings concerned New Orleans.

Since 1912 New Orleans had sent two representatives to Congress. The Mississippi River, which wound through the city, and an old commercial canal, which had been used to barge in clam shells from Lake Ponchatrain, were the boundary between the uptown and downtown congressional districts. Jack Wardlaw, a local political writer, reported that many residents considered this boundary "as comfortable as an old shoe." But, after the 1980 census, the Democratic leaders of suburban Jefferson Parish made it clear that they were not satisfied with the traditional arrangement.[1]

Because of shifts in population, the boundaries of congressional districts have to be redrawn after each census to comply with the Supreme Court's mandate that all districts must have almost precisely the same population. In New Orleans more than minor modifications were required because the city, which at one time had been 75 percent larger than the size of an ideal congressional district, had declined by 1980 to the point where it was only 6 percent larger than an ideal district. Meanwhile, the predominantly white suburbs in Jefferson Parish had grown to 87 percent of an ideal district.[2]

In 1981 Lawrence E. Chehardy, John Mamoulides, and other leaders of the Democratic party in Jefferson Parish contended that the population of that parish was such that residents there deserved a majority vote in one congressional district. This could be done, they said, by creating a crescent-shaped district that would wrap around New Orleans and shift the base of Louisiana's First Congressional District from the city to the suburbs of Jefferson Parish. As such a district would fall a bit short of the ideal size of 525,497, they proposed that the difference could be made up by joining suburban Jefferson with smaller white suburbs in St. Bernard and Placquemines parishes and also with the wealthy, predominantly white Algiers section of New Orleans. State Senator Samuel B. Nunez drafted a plan along these lines and took the lead in persuading the state legislature to approve the proposal.[3]

Blacks played no part in originating or developing the Nunez plan. Nevertheless, they rallied in support because the plan had the side effect of creating a 54 percent black Second Congressional District based in downtown New Orleans. Blacks regarded the Nunez plan as an improvement over the previous arrangement, which divided blacks and made them a 36.5 percent minority in the First District and a 40.7 percent minority in the Second District. Senator Joseph R. Biden of Delaware later noted that "it was not so much a case of the legislators getting together in the Nunez plan and saying, 'Now here is how we can create a black district.' It was more, 'How can we protect the suburban white district.' And the byproduct of that was the creation of a black district." Richard Turnley, the chairman of the black caucus in the state legislature, said blacks "really had no role in the development of the Nunez plan.... While the Legislative Black Caucus warmly endorsed the Nunez plan, spoke out in favor of it, and unanimously voted for it, the caucus simply did not participate in its development and the efforts to get it passed."[4]

Eventually, blacks became staunch supporters of the Nunez plan. They noted that blacks made up 29 percent of the population in Louisiana, and they said they would be denied "the right to effective participation in the electoral process" if the boundaries of the state's eight congressional districts were not drawn so as to create at least one district with a black majority. Henry Braden, a black state senator, said that any plan that divided the black vote among different congressional districts made it "impossible for a black candidate to hope to get elected." Richard Turnley said it would be "patently unconstitutional" not to create a single district that included the great majority of blacks in New Orleans.[5]

White and black legislators candidly acknowledged that the Nunez plan would serve another purpose. They said that by providing separate districts for largely black New Orleans and overwhelmingly white Jefferson Parish, the plan "took into account the divergent, frequently antithetical, concerns of city and suburban dwellers." "This plan is good for everybody," said Mary Landrieu, a liberal state representative. "It's good for blacks. It's good for liberals. It's good for Jefferson Parish. It'll keep them on their side of the line and out of our hair." Lawrence E. Chehardy concurred. "No one can adequately represent both New Orleans and Jefferson," he declared, "because they are opposing views." The local newspaper, the *Times-Picayune*, reported that the state's black legislators insisted that blacks "would be best served by... structuring" a New Orleans-based district that "maintained the cohesiveness of the metropolitan black community."[6]

Louisiana's Republican Governor, David C. Treen, saw things differently. He said it was "repugnant" to assert that the interests of blacks and whites were antithetical. "We tend to polarize races when we talk in those terms," he said. Although Treen was "not necessarily opposed" to the idea of a black district, he insisted that there was "no constitutional imperative that that be done." Nor did Treen consider it wise policy. He said that both the whites of Jefferson Parish and the blacks of New Orleans would have more political power if boundaries were drawn so they could influence more than one member of Congress.[7]

Governor Treen's public statements were high-minded. But journalists in Louisiana reported that the governor's opposition to the Nunez plan was based primarily on political considerations. Charles M. Hardgroder observed that "the interest Treen showed in how new districts would be drawn stems obviously from a political view of what would be best for the two Republicans now in Louisiana congressional seats and how new districts would be advantageous to Republican challengers."[8]

Treen was especially concerned about the way the Nunez plan would affect the political future of his political ally, Representative Robert L. Livingston, the Republican incumbent in Louisiana's First District. Livingston's district had been based in New Orleans and had been 36.5 percent black. Under the Nunez plan, however, most blacks would be removed from the district and its base—72 percent of the electorate—would be firmly planted in the suburbs of Jefferson Parish.

Superficially, a mostly Jefferson district appeared hospitable to Republican Livingston. But the Nunez plan would deprive Livingston of traditional supporters along the New Orleans lakefront. By forcing Livingston to stand for election before voters who were not familiar with his previous work, the Nunez plan also denied the congressman one of the advantages of incumbency. Political insiders also noted that the Democrats had a powerful political machine in Jefferson Parish—one that was expected to work for State Senator Nunez if he should challenge Livingston for the congressional seat. Political reporter Jack Wardlaw observed that "Jefferson Parish may look Republican, but it is a political minefield strewn with the bodies of those who failed to align themselves with" the boss of the suburban Democratic party, Lawrence E. Chehardy.[9]

When questioned about his opposition to the Nunez plan, Governor Treen said he did not oppose the idea of creating either a mostly suburban district or a mostly black district, but he opposed the Nunez plan because of the way it affected the state's other congressional districts. "I don't like what it does to the First District," Treen said. "It isn't fair." Asked if he meant unfair to the district or to the incumbent Livingston, Treen answered, "To Representative Livingston."[10]

As the leader of Louisiana's Republican party, Treen naturally was concerned with the political ramifications of redistricting. This concern was especially keen because in the 1960s Treen had personally experienced the effects of a previous gerrymander. In a 1962 challenge to Hale Boggs, the Democratic congressman from New Orleans' Second District, Treen received only 32 percent of the vote. However, in a 1964 rematch Treen received 45 percent of the vote, and in 1968 he received 49 percent in an election that was marred by allegations that Boggs's partisans had committed voting fraud. Then the Democratic state legislature gerrymandered the district by removing suburban Metairie (where Treen lived and was strong) and by including more of downtown New Orleans. Treen's biographer caught the significance of the configuration when he observed that the legislature gave Hale Boggs "a present—a district without Dave Treen in it."[11]

The Second District had been made so secure for Boggs that even when he died in 1972, the congressional seat remained in the family. For the next eighteen years, it would be occupied by Boggs's widow, Lindy.[12]

The earlier gerrymander did not end Treen's political career. Instead, it put him on the course to a 1972 victory in Louisiana's Third Congressional District, which beginning in Metairie and proceeding for 100 miles through the French Cajun country along the Gulf of Mexico, stretched halfway to Texas. From there Treen went on in 1980 to become the first Republican governor of Louisiana in more than a century.[13]

In 1981, when congressional districts were again being modified, Treen and other political observers recognized that the Nunez plan involved more than simply creating separate districts for the whites of suburban Jefferson Parish and the blacks of downtown New Orleans. As political reporter Emile Lafourcade observed, "Political insiders" were saying that the real reason for the new configuration was "much the same as it was the last time the butcher's knife was trotted out—preservation of a Boggs. The last time around it was done for the preservation of the late Congressman Hale Boggs, who was worried Dave Treen was getting too close to unseating him."[14]

In 1981 the insiders said a principal purpose of the Nunez plan was to keep Boggs's widow and successor, Lindy, in office, by carving away as much of the conservative vote in Jefferson as possible. If the traditional boundaries were maintained between Bob Livingston's First District and Lindy Boggs's Second, Boggs would have to be given a large number of suburban voters to achieve the ideal district size; in fact, given the decline in New Orleans's population since 1970 and the increase in the size of the ideal district from 435,000 to 525,000, about 56 percent of Boggs's constituents would be in the suburbs. Some Republicans calculated that by defeating Boggs in the suburbs while Livingston was re-elected in the city, the GOP could then gain a seat in

Congress. Under the Nunez plan, on the other hand, predominantly Democratic blacks from Livingston's First District would be moved into Boggs's Second District. That district would then be safely Democratic.[15]

Nunez's plan called for blacks to be a 54 percent majority in Boggs's district. But because of loyalties based on Lindy Boggs's record as a supporter of civil rights, affirmative action, and social programs, insiders expected blacks to continue to send Lindy Boggs to Congress. They feared the congresswoman would not fare so well if she were compelled to run in a district where white suburbanites made up a majority of the electorate.

Governor Treen then opposed the Nunez plan for several reasons. "Any bill in that form is unacceptable," he announced, "and without question will be vetoed." This was no idle threat, for in Louisiana no governor's veto had ever been overridden. And Treen, taking no chances, made a determined lobbying effort that changed enough minds in the legislature to ensure defeat of the Nunez plan.[16]

Thus the stage was set for compromise. Senator Nunez and Democratic boss Chehardy would have preferred to keep their plan, but they could not override Treen's threatened veto and said it "would be a disaster for the legislature" to wind up "with no plan at all." Nunez consequently invited several congressmen and leaders of the State Senate to a marathon meeting in the capitol basement. After twelve hours of negotiation, they came up with a reapportionment plan that was acceptable to Treen and won a grudging endorsement from Nunez, who conceded that "this is better than no plan at all."[17]

The compromise was popular with the incumbent congressmen, all of whom wound up with districts that were only slightly modified and not likely to give them any problems when they sought reelection. Representative Livingston was especially pleased because he had been saved from the prospect of being thrust into a district in which more than 70 percent of his constituents would have been new to him. The compromise plan was only a minor disappointment to the politicians of Jefferson Parish, who wound up with a large enough share of the First Congressional District to have an good chance of electing one of their own when the incumbent Lindy Boggs retired from Congress.

But the compromise was a disappointment to blacks who wanted a mostly black district in New Orleans. The compromise did increase the black proportion of Lindy Boggs's constituency from 40 percent to 44 percent. However, that was not enough to give blacks much hope of electing a member of Congress, and in the process the black influence was reduced in Bob Livingston's First District. Black legislators complained that none of them had been invited to the basement meeting at which the compromise was hammered out. "The only thing this compromise compromises is the black citizens," said Johnny Jackson, Jr., a black state representative from New Orleans. Lawrence E. Chehardy candidly explained that the black caucus, which consisted of only two state senators and ten representatives, "didn't have enough votes." For that reason blacks were "the one group...that was not going to come out of the session satisfied."[18]

The black politicians had lost in the state legislature. But they still had other cards to play, and they vowed to continue the battle before the attorney general and, if necessary, in court. Lawyers for the black caucus predicted that the Department of Justice would deny preclearance to any reapportionment plan that did not create a mostly black district. State Senator Henry Braden said that "a freshman law student could have [the compromise plan] thrown out by the courts." Governor Treen disagreed. He said he was confident that the plan would satisfy the attorney general and the federal courts.[19]

As noted above, the preclearance provisions of Section 5 of the Voting Rights Act placed the burden of proof on the covered jurisdictions. Local authorities had the burden of demonstrating that any election changes were not motivated by discriminatory purpose and would not have an adverse impact on minority voters. The Department of Justice's regulations for administration stated that if there was doubt as to whether the submitting jurisdiction had satisfied the burden of proof, the attorney general should refuse to preclear the change.[20]

Prior to the 1982 revision of the Voting Rights Act, the "no discriminatory effect" standard of Section 5 was understood to mean that there could be no retrogression from the previous level of black electoral power, the Supreme Court having stated this position in *Beer v. United States*: "The purpose of Section 5 has always been to insure that no voting procedure or changes would be made that would lead to a retrogression in the position of racial minorities with respect to their effective exercise of the electoral franchise."[21]

Louisiana's compromise plan satisfied the effects test because it was not retrogressive. Robert N. Kwan, the attorney who investigated the situation for the Civil Rights Division, noted that the plan actually increased the proportion of blacks in Lindy Boggs' Second District, which had previously had the highest black-population percentage, from 40.7 percent to 44.5 percent. The proportion of blacks in the Eighth District near Baton Rouge had also been increased from 33.2 percent to 38.3 percent. The racial percentages in the other districts remained much the same, except in the First District where Bob Livingston's black electorate decreased by 7 percentage points to 29.5 percent (as compared with a drop of 19 points under Senator Nunez's proposed plan). Kwan concluded that under the compromise plan, "the minority percentage gains and losses seem to even out." He also noted that the Nunez plan, with its proposed black-majority district in New Orleans, could not be considered the standard for measuring retrogression because it was never enacted under state law. Consequently, Kwan concluded that the compromise plan that Louisiana had submitted did "not have a racially retrogressive effect within the meaning of *Beer v. United States*."[22]

When it came to discriminatory purpose, however, Kwan thought the black complainants had a strong case. The complaint was not with the state legislature, which had passed the Nunez plan that would have created a 54 percent black district in New Orleans; it was with Governor Treen, who had threatened to veto that plan. Treen said his motives were political, but Kwan suspected that the governor harbored a racially invidious purpose. Kwan professed to be "somewhat reluctant to probe the racial views of a particular individual," but because of the key role Treen had played in the reapportionment of Louisiana's congressional districts, Kwan thought it necessary to probe the governor's motives.

> The sequence of events in the reapportionment process indicate that the role of Governor Treen in the process, particularly in his public threat of a gubernatorial veto, was central in the reversal of the legislature in its adoption of a plan which would incorporate a majority black Congressional district. Thus, it becomes crucial to examine Governor Treen's motivation.[23]

Kwan conceded that Treen had a number of nonracial reasons for threatening to veto the Nunez plan. Treen wanted to preserve traditional boundaries, advance the interests of the Republican Party, protect Bob Livingston, and make it harder for Lindy Boggs to be reelected. But, after reviewing the record, Kwan concluded that "an inference of racial motivation" could also be drawn "from Governor Treen's background."[24]

In Kwan's mind the key evidence of Treen's invidious racial purpose was Treen's membership, in 1959 and 1960, in the States Rights Party of Louisiana. Treen said his membership grew out of a concern that Congress was undermining local and state governments by concentrating more and more power in the federal government. According to Treen, it made "sense to solve as many of our problems as possible on the local or state level." He said, "This was Thomas Jefferson's thinking. It has always been mine."[25]

Kwan conceded that Treen and the States Rights Party had raised "legitimate questions about the relationship between the federal government and the states." He acknowledged that many of these concerns were still "the subject of contemporary debate." But Kwan thought that "in the context of the history of the state," which in 1959 and 1960 was experiencing Louisiana's version of massive resistance to school integration, Treen's membership in the States Rights Party was evidence of hostility to blacks.[26]

Kwan also mentioned that after winning election to Congress, Treen "almost always voted against positions supported by the Congressional Black Caucus." Treen admittedly was not a bigot. He never engaged in race baiting.

He always defended his votes in terms of sound economics or an abiding commitment to principles of federalism and states' rights. Nevertheless, after considering the totality of Treen's personal history, Kwan concluded that racial considerations had contributed significantly to the Governor's opposition to the Nunez plan. Kwan concluded that Louisiana "had not met its burden of proving the lack of a racial purpose." He recommended "the interposition of a Section 5 objection."[27]

Kwan's recommendation was endorsed by Gerald W. Jones, the chief of the Voting Section of the Civil Rights Division. However, the final decision in this case, as in all preclearance reviews, rested with the assistant attorney general for civil rights, and in this instance William Bradford Reynolds did not approve the recommendation of his staff.

Instead, Reynolds investigated the Louisiana reapportionment plan. He did so because he routinely looked into cases in which his staff did not preclear an electoral change. Even if that had not been his standard operating procedure, Reynolds said, he could not have avoided personal involvement in the case. "I didn't understand how Kwan could make a judgment on Treen's character and motives without ever talking with him. Kwan's charge was as serious a charge as one person could level at another. It was unthinkable that such a charge would be made without giving Treen a chance to answer. Once I received Kwan's report, I insisted on a face-to-face meeting with Treen."[28]

Reynolds had two meetings with Treen and pored over a forty-pound box of documents that Treen provided. He also held "numerous meetings" with his staff, who had interviewed people from all the factions in Louisiana. Then Reynolds reviewed the compromise plan "in minute detail, and went over it carefully over and over again." Finally, on 18 June 1982, after a two-and-one-half-hour meeting with his staff, Reynolds approved the compromise plan.[29]

Reynolds's decision surprised many observers, who noted that while he was considering the Louisiana case, Reynolds had rejected three other districting plans. In one, which seemed to have implications for Louisiana, Reynolds rejected the Georgia legislature's congressional reapportionment plan because it split Atlanta's black community between two districts. The black population in one of the districts had been increased from 50 percent to 57 percent, but Reynolds told the Georgians that they had not provided enough evidence to show that they had not drawn the line though the black community in order to dilute black voting strength. It was possible, Reynolds wrote, "that a legislative reapportionment could be a substantial improvement over its predecessor...and nonetheless continue to discriminate because of race."[30]

In a second case Reynolds concluded that Alabama's plans for redistricting both houses of its state legislature "clearly would lead to a retrogression in the position of black voters" and were "not...necessary to any legitimate governmental interest." Reynolds refused to preclear the plans, as he also refused to preclear redistricting plans submitted by Texas, Virginia, North Carolina, South Carolina, Georgia, and Arizona.[31]

In the third case, which involved Louisiana itself, Reynolds rejected the legislature's plan for reapportioning the state's House of Representatives. Seventeen of the 105 districts had previously contained a black majority, and the black caucus had sought to increase that number to 20. Instead, the legislature reduced the number of black-majority districts to 12. Reynolds acknowledged that the population of New Orleans, where blacks were concentrated, had declined since 1970, but he insisted that the new plan resulted in "an unnecessary dilution of minority voting strength." He demanded more black-majority districts in New Orleans, Baton Rouge, and Rapides.[32]

This case seemed particularly significant. In reaching his decision, Reynolds rejected Governor Treen's pleas that the legislative redistricting be approved. Richard Turnley of the legislative black caucus, recalled that in the Civil Rights Division, attorney Robert Kwan played a major role in persuading Reynolds to reject Louisiana's plan for legislative reapportionment. "Kwan did a fantastic job. He turned the thing around for us."[33]

When it came to the congressional redistricting, however, Reynolds rejected Kwan's advice and sided with Governor Treen. Reynolds precleared the plan because he thought it was "a political redistricting and that politics was what was involved." What Treen did was "courageous and correct," Reynolds said. He believed the Nunez plan had originated as "a power grab" by Democratic politicians in Jefferson Parish, who were "trying to protect Lindy Boggs and do a number on Bob Livingston." Then, "when Governor Treen tried to stop this political business, they accused him of racism." In an appearance before a senate committee in 1985, Reynolds used more measured language:

> My conclusion was that the line-drawing was one that was very much motivated by political considerations, and had not been done in a manner or with a purpose of denying or minimizing minority voting strength, but indeed, had been driven very much by a lot of political considerations.[34]

In reaching this conclusion, Reynolds accepted one of the premises of his staff: "that there was not racial animus we could ascribe to the legislature." The legislature, after all, had passed the Nunez plan, which called for a black-majority congressional district in New Orleans. For Reynolds, as for his staff, preclearance "depended on Governor Treen's attitudes.... In order to preclear,...we had to make it clear that the Governor did not have a racial motive." If a "racial motive or racial animus" could be ascribed to Treen, "then we could not preclear it."[35]

Unlike staff attorney Robert Kwan, Reynolds did not equate Treen's states' rights philosophy with racism. Instead, like Treen, Reynolds thought the separation of powers and the division of sovereignty did more to protect individuals and minorities than concentrating power in the federal government.[36]

Reynolds acknowledged that the Voting Rights Act placed the burden of proof on the submitting jurisdiction. He agreed that "in layman's terms," it was "fair to say that the benefit of the doubt is given to those opposing preclearance rather than to those who are seeking preclearance." He said he was "prepared to object" if there was "a racial motive on the part of the Governor." But after meeting with Treen, after quizzing him carefully, and after reviewing the case "in very great detail," Reynolds precleared the congressional reapportionment plan because he was "able to conclude" that Treen was "[not] animated by racial animus or by racial purpose." Reynolds said, "There's not a biased bone in Dave Treen's body.... Even the blacks in Louisiana understood that Treen threatened to veto the Nunez plan for political reasons."[37]

Louisiana's black leaders had not challenged Treen's motives, but they were determined to exhaust every avenue of appeal. Thus they proceeded to the United States District Court. "We feel three impartial judges who are not Republican appointees will see the matter quite differently," attorney William L. Quigley declared.[38]

The judges did see things differently, but they did so because by the time they reached a decision in September 1983, the Voting Rights Act had been changed. The Supreme Court had not yet rendered an authoritative interpretation of the 1982 amendment to Section 2 of the Voting Rights Act. However, the new statute clearly went beyond the nonretrogression standard that the Court had established in *Beer v. United States* in that the results test of the amended Section 2 measured discrimination by comparing the representation of blacks in electoral bodies with their proportion of the general population. It said that if blacks were underrepresented in public office, local officials must make affirmative efforts to promote the election of more blacks.

Because Section 2 had been revised, Judges Henry A. Politz, Fred J. Cassibry, and Robert F. Collins had no difficulty deciding the New Orleans case. They explained that the 1982 amendment had "dispense[d] with the requirement that a plaintiff demonstrate intentional discrimination in the imposition or maintenance of the disputed electoral structure." Applying the new results test to the case before them, the judges ordered Louisiana to "enact a valid new plan for the election of members of the United States House of Representatives"—one that would maximize the likelihood that at least one black person would be elected to Congress from Louisiana.[39]

The decision of the court came as no surprise and was not appealed. Reynolds conceded that he "probably would have ruled the same way" if the revised Section 2 had been in place when he made his decision. "I would not have been able to preclear the plan, and would have objected to it." The court did not find discriminatory intent, as Reynolds had been required to do. Instead, it found discriminatory effect—but only because the nonretrogression standard of *Beer* had been superseded by a more stringent results test.[40]

The court's decision did not end the New Orleans case for Reynolds. Two years later Senator Biden cited the case as the centerpiece of his criticism of the civil rights policies of the Reagan administration and as the major reason for his opposition to confirming Reynolds as associate attorney general.

Biden's opposition was something of a surprise. He and Reynolds were born in the same year, 1942, and both were reared in Wilmington, Delaware. Delaware's other senator, Republican William V. Roth, had praised Reynolds's high standards of "integrity [and] professionalism" and had introduced Reynolds to the Senate Judiciary Committee as "a man of high principles [and] impeccable moral character, who has the courage to stand on conviction." Biden acknowledged to Reynolds that several of their mutual friends, "people that I know and you know from home, people I respect a great deal, tell me how good you are." Biden also said Reynolds was "one of the best lawyers" he had met during his years in the Senate, "and you are clearly not a racist. You are not out there, saying, 'Man, I want to get those blacks.'"[41]

Biden also said he agreed with Reynolds on two controversial civil rights questions. "I happen to agree with you on your view of quotas," Biden said. "I happen to agree with you on busing." Biden said busing was a counterproductive policy that had failed educationally and alienated "the great middle class" from the civil rights movement. Biden had even sponsored legislation that restricted the use of federal money to defray the cost of court-ordered busing.[42]

Biden insisted, "As far as I am concerned, this [confirmation] hearing is not about quotas, not about busing." What, then, was it about? A reporter for the *Washington Post* quoted Biden as saying Reynolds's approach to civil rights was "repugnant." But at the hearings, Biden said only that Reynolds was "an insensitive guy" who did not put "the rights of minorities on the front burner." Biden proposed to illustrate this by focusing on Reynolds's record on voting rights.[43]

Before the hearings began, Biden and his aides collected documents and got in touch with hostile witnesses. Then Biden shifted his focus away from busing and affirmative action to voting rights. "Some of the civil rights groups wanted to make this an issue of busing and quotas," Biden recalled. "I thought this would be a very stupid strategy." To illustrate Reynolds's "insensitivity," Biden focused on a single case, the case of congressional districting in New Orleans. Each time Biden's turn came to question

Reynolds—eight times in all—he inquired about the situation in New Orleans. He asked about nothing else.[44]

Some observers credited Biden with a strategic masterstroke, but others were not so generous. Dennis W. Shedd, the Chief Counsel and Staff Director of the Senate Judiciary Committee, insisted that Biden did not determine the strategy, saying, "It all comes from the civil rights groups." Shedd asserted that NAACP lawyer Lani Guinier and Ralph Neas of the Leadership Conference on Civil Rights "wrote all the questions and gave them to Biden and other senators."[45]

For his part, Reynolds regarded Biden as "a political animal with no scruples or principles," a man "driven by the desire to promote his own career." Even in 1985, Reynolds said, Biden was contemplating his abortive 1988 campaign for the presidency. Because Biden had tangled with the established black leaders over busing, he needed to regain the confidence of this crucial component of the Democratic coalition. In addition, Reynolds said Biden was "preoccupied with the fear that Teddy Kennedy would upstage him. He was afraid Kennedy would take the lead in defeating my nomination." Since Biden had frequently criticized busing and quotas, he could hardly find fault with Reynolds or the Reagan administration on these grounds. But, Reynolds said, "Biden could not campaign effectively for the presidency unless he came out in opposition to the policies of the Reagan administration." The New Orleans case gave Biden that opportunity. "It was politics. Just politics. Biden wanted to let the civil rights establishment know he disapproved of the policies of the Reagan administration."[46]

Opinions differ concerning the importance of the New Orleans case. Reynolds did not think the case was crucial in fostering the suspicion that he was biased against blacks. He conceded, though, that Biden's cross-examination may have reinforced the suspicion that Reynolds was not being entirely candid with the Senate Judiciary Committee. In response to one of Biden's questions, Reynolds said he had met with people who opposed the New Orleans plan. Reynolds's records did not mention any such meetings, however, and he later confessed that he probably was confused. He said he had attended many meetings involving similar cases and had read about one hundred letters from critics of the New Orleans plan.[47]

Yet, unlike Senators Arlen Specter and Patrick Leahy, and the editors of the *New York Times* and *Washington Post*, who made much of alleged discrepancies in Reynolds's statements about the *Burke County* case, Biden did not make anything of Reynolds's faulty recollection about meeting with opponents of the New Orleans plan. "As far as I am concerned," Biden said, "this hearing is...not about integrity."[48]

Biden's caution may have been due to the fact that civil rights activists had earlier misled him with respect to Reynolds's integrity. They said Reynolds had deviously backdated a memorandum that explained his decision to approve the New Orleans plan. The memorandum was actually written in mid-July 1982, they said, but had been dated to 18 June. They led Biden to believe that Reynolds had committed "a very nefarious act, which was to try to avoid applying" the stricter results test of the Revised Section 2, which became law on 29 June. Upon investigation, Biden discovered that Reynolds's decision had been announced on 18 June. Letters had been sent to Louisiana on that date, and the newspapers had reported the story then. In mid-June Reynolds wrote the memorandum in question "for the files." It was written in longhand, typed into a computer diskette that contained other documents, and finally printed in July. Then it was dated 18 June because it had been drafted to record the reasons for the decision of that day. Biden also noted that the Voting Rights Act required the attorney general to render a decision within sixty days after receiving a submission for preclearance. Since the New Orleans plan had been submitted on 19 April 1982, Reynolds had to make his decision by 18 June.[49]

Instead of challenging Reynolds's integrity, Biden raised the specter of "insensitivity." He said that only someone with Reynolds's "lack of sensitivity" would conclude that Governor Treen's decision "had nothing to do with, was not in any way based on race."[50]

Biden repeatedly insisted that Reynolds was deficient in sensitivity. To illustrate this point, Biden, on several occasions, asserted that one member of the Louisiana legislature, Representative Charles Emile Bruneau of New Orleans, had opposed the Nunez plan for racial reasons. After noting that the city already had a black mayor, Ernest Morial, Bruneau allegedly told Lawrence E. Chehardy, "We already have a nigger mayor. We don't need another nigger bigshot."[51]

Reynolds and his staff attached little significance to Bruneau's comment. In passing the Nunez plan, Reynolds said, the legislature had disregarded whatever Bruneau may have said. For his part, Bruneau denied making the statement.[52]

Reynolds's assessment of the matter was sound. Leaving aside the accuracy of the hearsay allegation, Reynolds said it would not make sense to deny preclearance "just because there is within the legislative body one or two people who are advancing a position for racial reasons." This was especially true when the legislature had voted for the Nunez plan and against Bruneau.[53]

Nevertheless, Biden used Bruneau's alleged statement to foster the suspicion that Reynolds was not protecting black voting rights. On five separate occasions, Biden questioned Reynolds about the "nigger bigshot" comment. By the end of the hearing, other senators were also using the phrase. So was the press.[54]

By focusing on Bruneau's comment, Biden created the perception that Reynolds was insensitive to the right to vote. In so doing, Biden contributed to the defeat of Reynolds's nomination for associate attorney general. The focus on voting rights in general, and the New Orleans case in particular, also enabled Biden to mend fences with black leaders that had been miffed by Biden's opposition to forced busing for racial integration. This was something that had to be accomplished before Biden could make his bid for the Democratic presidential nomination in 1988.

But Biden's posturing did not have much effect on politicians in Louisiana. In 1983 the state legislature, complying with the order of the federal court, dutifully engaged in affirmative districting to promote the election of at least one black congressman. Going beyond the Nunez plan, the legislature created a new Second Congressional District that was 58 percent black.

State Representative Johnny Jackson, Jr. hoped that Lindy Boggs would say, *Look, after all these years of support by the black community, now is the time for me to step down.* But other blacks encouraged Boggs to seek reelection because they liked her voting record and valued her seniority. In 1984, after winning about 37 percent of the votes cast by blacks, Boggs defeated Israel M. Augustine, a black state-court judge who had been her long time supporter. Mrs. Boggs was reelected in 1986 and 1988, and in 1990 became only the second great-grandmother ever to sit in Congress. When Mrs. Boggs retired in 1991, the congressional seat finally passed to an African-American, William Jefferson.[55]

New Orleans' erstwhile Republican congressman, Bob Livingston, grumbled about the redistricting. For a while he toyed with the idea of abandoning the new First Congressional District to run against Senator J. Bennett Johnston, who was up for reelection in 1984. But Livingston soon discovered that the suburbanites of Jefferson Parish appreciated his conservative brand of politics. He was reelected handily, winning 86 percent of the vote in 1984. He won again in 1986, 1988, 1990, 1992, and 1994, and in 1987 came close to being elected governor of Louisiana. Livingston became so popular in his new district that the leader of the local Democrats acknowledged, "The only way Bob Livingston will not be reelected in this district is if he decides not to run."[56]

Governor Treen did not fare so well. He failed in his bid for reelection in 1984, and in 1987 and 1988 the Senate Judiciary Committee stymied Ronald Reagan's efforts to appoint Treen to the Fifth Circuit Court of Appeals. Some observers noted that the NAACP and other civil rights groups lobbied against the nomination because Treen had opposed the "deliberate, conscious drawing of congressional district lines for the purpose of achieving a majority black district." In response to pressure from civil rights groups, the observers said, the Senate Judiciary Committee refused to conduct a hearing on Treen's nomination.[57]

Treen said the story was more complex. The failure to schedule a confirmation hearing was not caused simply by liberal Democrats who were responding to pressure from civil rights groups. It resulted also from the machinations of Louisiana's Democratic Senator Johnston, who wanted to postpone Treen's confirmation hearing until the Reagan administration offered a judicial appointment to one of Johnston's supporters.[58]

Because of Johnston's maneuvering and the opposition of the civil rights groups, for nine months the Senate Judiciary Committee refused to consider the nomination that President Reagan submitted in July 1987. Finally, in April 1988, Treen grew weary and asked that the nomination be withdrawn. He explained that he had suffered a financial loss over the nine months because during that time he could not become involved in legal business that might come before the Fifth Circuit Court. He also noted that there were others who shared Reagan's general judicial philosophy "and whose public profiles would hardly provide an excuse for delaying consideration of their nominations."[59]

Congressman Livingston insisted that "Brad Reynolds wasn't the only person whose career advancement was thwarted" because of the dispute over congressional districting in New Orleans. "Dave Treen also lost out." But Treen expressed no regrets. Actually, he said, the nine month hiatus gave him an opportunity to reflect and to learn more about himself. He discovered that he really enjoyed the active life of legal work and politics, and he came to doubt that he was temperamentally suited for a "cloistered" life on the federal bench. In the end, Treen said, he withdrew because he decided he did not want to be a judge.[60]

In some ways the Republican party emerged as the biggest winner. When the dispute over congressional districting began in 1981, two of Louisiana's eight members of Congress were Republicans. When the dust settled after the battle, Republicans occupied four of the eight seats.

This came as no surprise to many politicians. Treen recalled that when he was governor, some Republicans had urged him to cooperate with blacks. "They said we should pack traditionally Democratic black voters into one or two districts. Write off those districts. Then Republicans would have a better chance to win the remaining districts."[61]

Treen rejected this argument. He thought any such arrangement would be morally wrong. He said racial gerrymanders would be "a divisive force in the community" and that the government had "no business designing districts along racial or religious lines."[62]

Treen insisted that blacks would have fared well under the plan he had proposed and also under the modification of that plan that the Fifth Circuit Court rejected. Under these plans, blacks would have had substantial influence (about 35 percent) in Bob Livingston's First District and even more clout (about 44 percent) in Lindy Boggs's Second District. Treen also noted, at the time and subsequently, that because of demographic trends, blacks would become a majority of the population in Boggs's Second District by 1986. If the court had not stepped in, Treen said, the blacks of New Orleans would have elected a black member of Congress as soon as Boggs retired and would have continued to have influence in Livingston's district.[63]

But the court did step in. It insisted that the great majority of blacks should be packed into a single congressional district. As a result, a black candidate eventually was elected to office—but not until after Boggs retired. In the meantime, the influence of blacks in other districts actually declined, while Republicans increased their representation.

"The irony of the thing," Treen observed, "is that losing this case helped the Republican party." Another irony, he said, was that blacks actually lost influence. Treen told blacks that if they applied their New Orleans and Louisiana plans all over the country, they would have "ten percent of Congress, and that's all." He predicted that they would have "more black congressmen, but no influence on the rest of Congress."[64]

There is much to be said for Treen's analysis, but a case can also be made for Treen's black critics. One of them, State Senator Henry Braden, explained that if voters are racially polarized, as was the case in New Orleans, a racial minority does not have much influence, even if it is a sizable minority. If the electorate is polarized over issues such as welfare spending or affirmative action, the member of Congress will have to cater to the interests of the majority, which meant that blacks could expect little from Congressman Livingston, even if they did make up 35 percent of his constituency.[65]

Nor could they expect much from Congresswoman Boggs, as long as the majority of voters in Boggs's district were white. Braden and another black state senator, Richard Turnley, conceded that blacks had no quarrel with Boggs's voting record *after* her district became predominantly black, but it had not always been this way, they said. When whites had made up the majority of her constituents, even Lindy Boggs had been reluctant to go all out for black causes. It took a black district, Braden and Turnley said, to insure that the opinions of blacks would be represented in Congress.[66]

Notes

1. *New Orleans Times Picayune*, 25 October 1981.
2. Major v. Treen, 574 F.Supp. 325 (1983), 329.
3. Ibid., 332; *New Orleans Times Picayune*, 17 October 1981; 4 May 1981; 1 October 1981; 2 October 1981; 8 October 1981; 11 October 1981; 20 October 1981; 24 October 1981; 30 October 1981; 4 November 1981; 5 November 1981; 7 November 1981.

4. *1985 Senate Hearings*, 1001–2; Robert N. Kwan, "Section 5 Submission Analysis: Reapportionment of Congressional Districts in the State of Louisiana," ibid., 425.
5. Major v. Treen, 574 F.Supp. 325 (1983), 327; *New Orleans Times Picayune*, 30 October 1981; 2 February 1982.
6. Major v. Treen, 574 F.Supp 325 (1983), 332, 330; *New Orleans Times Picayune*, 7 November 1981; 5 November 1981; 13 November 1981.
7. *New Orleans Times Picayune*, 27 October 1981; 10 November 1981.
8. Ibid., 7 November 1981.
9. Ibid., 11 October 1981.
10. Ibid., 7 October 1981; 10 November 1981.
11. Grover Rees III, *Dave Treen of Louisiana* (Baton Rouge: Moran Publishing Corp., 1979), 49–65, 59.
12. Lindy Boggs, *Washington Through a Purple Veil: Memoirs of a Southern Woman* (New York: Harcourt Brace & Co., 1994).
13. Grover Rees III, *Dave Treen of Louisiana*, passim.
14. *New Orleans Times Picayune*, 17 October 1981.
15. Ibid.
16. Ibid., 7 November 1981; 10 November 1981.
17. Ibid., 11 November 1981; 12 November 1981.
18. Ibid., 12 November 1981; Major v. Treen, 574 F.Supp. 325 (1983), 334.
19. *New Orleans Times Picayune*, 10 November 1981; 30 October 1981; 15 November 1981; 13 November 1981; 11 November 1981.
20. McDaniel v. Sanchez, 452 U.S. (1981); 28 CFR section 51.39(e), quoted in *1985 Senate Hearings*, 1000.
21. Beer v. U.S., 425 U.S. 130 (1976), 141.
22. *1985 Senate Hearings*, 419–20, 437.
23. Ibid., 420, 429, 421.
24. Ibid., 439, 430.
25. Grover Rees III, *Dave Treen of Louisiana*, 44.
26. *1985 Senate Hearings*, 428.
27. Ibid., 430, 439.
28. Interviews with WBR, 14 April 1989 and 28 February 1992.
29. *1985 Senate Hearings*, 398–409, 76–77, 1018; *New Orleans Times Picayune*, 18 April 1982.
30. *New Orleans Times Picayune*, 17 February 1982.
31. Ibid., 7 May 1982; *1985 Senate Hearings*, 686.
32. *New Orleans Times Picayune*, 8 November 1981; 15 November 1981; 2 February 1982; 3 June 1982.
33. Interview with Richard Turnley, 26 October 1990.
34. Interview with WBR, 14 April 1989; *1985 Senate Hearings*, 1004, 30.
35. *1985 Senate Hearings*, 68.
36. *New York Times Magazine*, 13 September 1987, 18 ff; *Vanderbilt Law Review*, 40 (1987): 1343–51.
37. *1985 Senate Hearings*, 1001, 68, 1004, 116; interview with WBR, 14 April 1989.
38. *New Orleans Times Picayune*, 19 June 1982.
39. Major v. Treen, 574 F.Supp. 325 (1983), 342, 354, 355.
40. *1985 Senate Hearings*, 119, 95.
41. Ibid., 3, 1015, 121.

42. Ibid., 27; Raymond Wolters, *The Burden of Brown: Thirty Years of School Desegregation* (Knoxville: University of Tennessee Press, 1984), 234.
43. *1985 Senate Hearings*, 999, 491; *Washington Post*, 24 June 1985, A4a.
44. *Washington Post*, 24 June 1985, A4a.
45. *Washington Post*, 24 June 1985, A4a; Dennis Shedd, interview with Stephen Auch, 17 April 1989.
46. Interview with WBR, 14 April 1989.
47. Ibid.; *1985 Senate Hearings*, 30, 67.
48. *1985 Senate Hearings*, 998–99; *Washington Post*, 21 June 1985, A5a; 28 June 1985, A25f.
49. *1985 Senate Hearings*, 606–7, 491, 493–94, 391–93, 410.
50. Ibid., 491.
51. Ibid., 31, 68, 120, 440, 999, 1003.
52. Ibid., 68, 440, 1001.
53. Ibid., 1001.
54. Ibid., 31, 68, 99, 120, 999, 1003; *Washington Post*, 5 June 1985, A6e.
55. *New Orleans Times Picayune*, 15 December 1983; 16 December 1983.
56. Interview with Lawrence E. Chehardy, 26 October 1990.
57. Interview with Robert Livingston, 20 September 1990; Attachment A, Statement of David C. Treen, June 1982, Treen Papers.
58. Interview with David C. Treen, 27 October 1990.
59. David C. Treen to Ronald Reagan, 22 April 1988, Treen Papers; Statement of David C. Treen, 26 April 1988, ibid.
60. Interview with Robert Livingston, 20 September 1990; interview with David C. Treen, 27 October 1990.
61. Interview with David C. Treen, 27 October 1990.
62. Statement of David C. Treen, June 1982 (quoting William O. Douglas), Treen Papers.
63. Interview with David C. Treen, 27 October 1990.
64. Ibid.
65. Interview with Henry Braden, 27 October 1990.
66. Ibid.; interview with Richard Turnley, 26 October 1990.

6

Legislative Districting in North Carolina

Thornburg v. Gingles was the most important voting rights case of the 1980s. *Gingles* (which is pronounced "jingles," as in "Jingle Bells") posed a familiar question—whether at-large elections were a surreptitious form of illicit racial discrimination. But this North Carolina case was appealed all the way to the Supreme Court and became the first major test of the 1982 revision of Section 2 of the Voting Rights Act.[1]

During the early stages of the case, the Reagan administration sided with the voting rights activists. North Carolina differed from other Southern states in that 60 of the state's 100 counties were not subject to preclearance. The Voting Rights Act did not apply to these 60 counties because although they had required prospective voters to pass a literacy test, more than 50 percent of their eligible voters had voted in the 1964 presidential election. The remaining 40 counties were subject to preclearance because they also gave literacy tests *and* less than half of their adults had voted in 1964. These 40 counties could not make any changes in voting policies without the approval of the attorney general, and in 1981 and 1982 William Bradford Reynolds twice rejected districting plans submitted by the state's General Assembly. He insisted that North Carolina must create single-member districts that were mostly black, if that could be done without extreme gerrymandering.[2]

Since colonial times it had been the practice in North Carolina not to divide counties in the formation of districts for the State House and State Senate. In 1968 this practice had been codified as part of the state's constitution, and during the administrations of Presidents Johnson, Nixon, Ford, and Carter, the Department of Justice had not objected.[3]

During the Reagan years, however, Reynolds did object. He ruled that the practice of not dividing counties "necessarily submerge[d] cognizable minority population concentrations into larger white electorates." By placing substantial concentrations of blacks in countywide districts that had even more substantial white voting majorities, Reynolds said, the state had diluted black political power.[4]

In response, the General Assembly abandoned 300 years of tradition and submitted a revised districting plan that divided several counties into single-member districts. Reynolds acknowledged that the revised plan represented some progress but found the improvement insufficient to permit preclearance. He approved the plan only after the General Assembly convened a second time and made still more changes. Leslie Winner, a voting rights lawyer in North Carolina, conceded that at this stage Reynolds and the Reagan administration "did just what we wanted them to do."[5]

Because the Reagan administration refused to countenance the no-division-of-counties policies, the number of blacks elected to the General Assembly more than doubled. Between 1971 and 1982 there had been, at any given time, only two to four blacks in the 120-member State House of Representatives; from 1975 to 1983 there were either one or two blacks in the 50-member State Senate. In 1982, after the districts were redrawn to satisfy Reynolds, eleven blacks were elected to the State House and two to the Senate.[6]

Nevertheless, Reynolds did not require enough affirmative gerrymandering to satisfy many voting rights activists. The activists complained in particular about Reynolds's approval of a single-member, multicounty senatorial district in northeastern North Carolina that was only 55.1 percent black when one with a 60.7 percent black configuration could have been developed. Voting activists said that because a disproportionately large number of blacks were younger than age eighteen and because voter registration for blacks lagged behind whites, blacks would not have an effective voting majority if a district was only 55 percent black.

Voting activists also noted that Reynolds's opposition to the no-division-of-counties policy applied only to the forty North Carolina counties that were subject to preclearance. It did not, and could not, apply to the state's other sixty counties.

After Section 2 of the Voting Rights Act was revised in 1982, the sixty noncovered counties, like jurisdictions throughout the country, were forbidden from using any voting practice "which results in a denial or abridgement of the right of any citizen...to vote on account of race." Voting activists said this meant that wherever there was a sufficiently large concentration of minority voters—and in North Carolina this was the case in seven additional state legislative districts—electoral boundaries had to be fashioned so that black candidates were likely to win elections.[7]

Voting activists emphasized that despite black successes in the districts that Reynolds had fashioned for the 1982 elections, the number of elected black officials remained quite low in comparison with the total black population. In a state that was 22.4 percent black, the thirteen blacks in the General Assembly amounted to only 7.6 percent of the total number of state legislators. Also blacks held only 9 percent of the city council seats, 7.3 percent of county commission seats, and 4 percent of the sheriffs' offices.[8]

The black plaintiffs in *Gingles* mentioned more than the failure to win a proportional share of elective offices. They emphasized that North Carolina had a long history of segregation and disfranchisement. Pointing to statistics on income, unemployment and health conditions, they also noted that blacks as a group generally had a lower socioeconomic status than whites.[9]

In addition, the black plaintiffs argued that North Carolina's elections were characterized by racist appeals that led to racially polarized voting. As an example, they noted that one white candidate had recently distributed photographs of his white opponent in the company of Jesse Jackson, and that another white candidate had sent out fliers warning that his black opponent would bus the "bloc" vote to the polls. The plaintiffs said subtle racial messages were being "telegraphed" by white candidates who urged voters to cast their ballots for "*continued* progress" and for candidates who would "serve *all* the people."[10]

Some observers said the analysis of these fliers as arguably racial appeals was simply not credible. Others took exception to the black plaintiffs' definition of racially polarized voting. Building on the testimony of Professor Bernard Grofman, the plaintiffs said an election was racially polarized if most blacks voted differently from most whites. If this view were to be accepted, this meant that an election would be characterized as *racially polarized* if only 49 percent of whites cast their ballots for a candidate who received 51 percent of the black vote.[11]

A three-judge district court (James Dickson Phillips, Earl Britt, and Franklin Dupree) endorsed Professor Grofman's definition of racially polarized voting—the definition that made even a minor degree of polarization legally significant. The judges held that racial polarization was "substantively significant" if "the results of the individual election would have been different depending upon whether it had been held among only the white voters or only the black voters."[12]

The judges further held that the fact that blacks had not achieved proportional representation did not, by itself, constitute a violation of the Voting Rights Act. After all, the revised Section 2 contained the so-called Dole Compromise—which said that "members of a protected class" did not have "a right to [be] elected in numbers equal to their proportion in the population." But the amended section also said that in evaluating a case "the extent to which members of a protected class have been elected to office...is one circumstance which may be considered." Taking everything into account—the depressed socioeconomic status of blacks, the existence of racially polarized voting, and the lack of proportional representation—Judges Phillips, Britt, and Dupree ordered North Carolina to create the maximum feasible number of single-member districts with sizeable black majorities.[13]

North Carolina promptly complied with the order of the court. The state disassembled the seven at-large districts and created thirty-one smaller districts with one legislator elected from each.[14]

While complying with the court order, North Carolina also filed an appeal that gave the Supreme Court the opportunity to explain how the lower federal courts should interpret the 1982 revision of Section 2. The Supreme Court invited the Department of Justice to participate in the case, and as things turned out, the participation of the Reagan administration was anything but routine. In legal briefs that infuriated civil rights lawyers—briefs that marked the first time the United States ever sided with a Southern state in a lawsuit that involved black voting rights—the administration argued that the district court's interpretation of the Voting Rights Act was "fundamentally flawed." The principal architect of this argument was William Bradford Reynolds.[15]

In his legal briefs for *Gingles*, Reynolds conceded that because of the revision of Section 2, the plaintiffs were warranted in challenging the configuration of two of the seven disputed at-large districts. "As to these districts," he wrote, "the [Supreme] Court should summarily affirm the judgment of the district court."[16]

But Reynolds insisted that the district court had presented a mistaken rationale and had made the wrong decision, with respect to the other five districts. According to Reynolds, the district court had committed two major errors. It misjudged the significance of electoral victories that blacks had won in the five districts that remained in dispute. And it used a simplistic definition of racially polarized voting.

Reynolds noted that in four of the districts that held at-large elections for the State House in 1982, blacks had won five of the twenty-two available seats. Since blacks made up 23.4 percent of the electorate in these districts, this rate of success (22.7 percent) was close to the black proportion of the registered voters. In 1982 blacks had not done as well in the one disputed Senate district. Although 16.8 percent of the registered voters there were black, white candidates had won all of the four at-large seats. Reynolds noted, however, that this district had chosen a black man to represent it in the State Senate from 1975 to 1980.[17]

According to Reynolds the success of black candidates proved there was no minority vote dilution in the disputed at-large districts. Reynolds conceded that it would have been possible to create single-member districts with safe black voting majorities, but he insisted that blacks had "no right to the creation of safe electoral districts merely because they could feasibly be drawn."[18]

Reynolds thought the three district judges had erred because they had assumed, contrary to the intent of Congress, that the revised Section 2 guaranteed electoral success in proportion to the black percentage of the population. That, he wrote, was "the only explanation" for the judges' decision. Since blacks had achieved nearly proportional success in the at-large districts, it was apparent that they already enjoyed "an equal opportunity to participate in the electoral process." Thus the claim that more should be done to facilitate the election of blacks was implicitly based on a commitment to proportional representation.[19]

Reynolds may have reacted strongly because the district court had rejected a districting plan that Reynolds had imposed by his refusing on two occasions to preclear the state's alternative plans. The Reynolds plan helped blacks to increase their numbers in the state legislature from six to thirteen in 1982 (and to sixteen by the time Reynolds sent his brief to the Supreme Court in 1985). The district judges ruled the black electoral successes were "too recent" in relation to the long history of discrimination to establish that blacks now enjoyed an equal opportunity to participate in politics, while Reynolds' position was that to disregard the results of the 1982 elections amounted to disregarding "the only election[s] ever conducted under the challenged plan."[20]

Reynolds also questioned the assumption that it was in the interests of minority voters to provide black politicians with safe, predominantly black districts. If the maximum number of 65 percent black districts were set up, the number of blacks elected from the disputed districts would probably increase from five to six. But Reynolds said that this sort of packing would reduce overall black influence; that by draining blacks out of the remaining, predominantly white districts, it would deny blacks the ability to influence the white representatives; and thus, "judged simply on the basis of 'results,'" the at-large plans in the disputed districts had "enhanced—not diluted—minority voting strength."[21]

Reynolds recognized one other point. Although the *Gingles* lawsuit had been brought as a class action on behalf of all blacks, several black North Carolinians gave court testimony in favor of the disputed at-large systems. They said single-member districts would enhance the careers of some black politicians—the ones who appealed primarily to black voters but not to whites—but single-member districts would also damage the prospect of black politicians who were trying to establish biracial coalitions. The established civil rights groups talked about the need to end minority vote dilution and to increase black political power, but Reynolds thought that single-member districts would aid some black candidates at the expense of other black candidates.[22]

Reynolds also took exception to the district court's definition of racially polarized voting. As noted, the court held that the failure of blacks to win a proportional number of positions was not, by itself, enough to justify a judicial prohibition of at-large elections. However, the court held that there could be no at-large elections if blacks were underrepresented *and* most whites did not vote for candidates favored by the majority of blacks.[23]

Reynolds and his staff objected that this definition went beyond what proponents of the revised Section 2 had demanded. In testimony before Congress, they had said that the results test would "apply only in those places where there is already an extraordinary amount of [racial] division," and that the goal of the results test was "to create an opportunity—nothing more than an opportunity—to participate in the political system." They proposed to invalidate at-large elections in places where black candidates had been completely "shut out" of office and whites had been able to elect all representatives.[24]

Reynolds had joined in legal efforts to end at-large elections of this sort. He had participated in the effort to overturn the at-large system in Mobile, Alabama. But Reynolds thought the North Carolina court was mistaken to hold that even a small variation in voting patterns, combined with even a slight underrepresentation of blacks, was sufficient to condemn at-large elections.

Reynolds said the district court's approach to polarized voting was simplistic. Following the lead of Professor Grofman, the expert witness for the plaintiffs, the court had accepted a bivariate statistical analysis that demonstrated a correlation between race and the level of voter support for candidates. Reynolds, however, said the court should have recognized that variations in racial voting patterns could have been caused by a number of factors. He felt the court should have allowed North Carolina to introduce a multivariate study that compared the voting preferences of blacks and whites after controlling for income, education, age, and religion. Other district courts had recognized that "race or national origin may mask a host of other explanatory variables." But the North Carolina judges did not consider nonracial factors. Instead, they simplistically held that racial polarization existed if most white voters did not support the candidate preferred by the majority of blacks.[25]

Because the North Carolina case presented an important issue—the proper construction of the 1982 revision of Section 2 of the Voting Rights Act—and because the Reagan administration thought the district court's opinion was badly flawed, Reynolds urged the Supreme Court to review the case "at more than a perfunctory level." He said the district court had ignored one key aspect of the new law—a point that had been crucial to a "compromise" that had been "enacted after intensive legislative struggle."[26]

Reynolds emphasized that Congress had passed the revised Section 2 only after Senator Robert Dole had added language that assured that blacks and other protected minorities did not have "a right to [be] elected in numbers equal to their proportion of the population." Focusing on this disavowal of proportional representation, Reynolds said, "Congress could not have expressed more clearly its intention not to invalidate [at-large elections] where minority candidates have had an equal opportunity to be elected—even if they did not necessarily win a proportional share of the seats."[27]

When the Supreme Court heard the *Gingles* case, however, the justices received an extraordinary, thirty-page legal brief. In it Senator Dole and nine other members of Congress said that Reynolds and the Reagan administration had misinterpreted the Voting Rights Act. The brief maintained that the victories of several blacks in North Carolina's at-large elections did not prove there had been no violation of the Voting Rights Act.[28]

Dole and the others said their "primary concern" in this case was to ensure that Section 2 was "interpreted and applied in a manner consistent with Congress' intent." They said that "electoral success by blacks in the challenged districts" was not dispositive because Congress did not intend for "definitive weight" to be given to any "single factor." The "literal language" and the legislative history of Section 2 indicated that Congress wanted the courts to consider the "totality of circumstances." Dole rejected Reynolds's argument that Congress, when it said the revised Section 2 did not assure proportional representation, precluded a claim in districts where blacks had already come close to proportional representation. He said that this argument would mistakenly "require the Court to ignore the totality of circumstances...in favor of focusing on only the most recent electoral returns." Dole then asked the Supreme Court to affirm the decision of the three-judge district court which, he said, "appeared to undertake just the sort of 'totality of circumstances' analysis as is required by Section 2."[29]

The Supreme Court did as Dole asked. In *Gingles*, the Court upheld the decision of the three-judge district court. But when it came to legal reasoning, the Court was fractured, with the justices writing six different opinions.

In the lead opinion for five members of the Court, Justice Brennan held that minorities who challenged at-large arrangements had to satisfy three necessary preconditions. Minorities could, as in the past, present evidence relating to socioeconomic conditions, the history of discrimination, and the responsiveness of elected officials to the particular needs of the minority group. To challenge an at-large system successfully, however, three points were crucial: minorities had to prove that the electorate was racially polarized, that minorities won a disproportionately small number of elections, and that they were sufficiently large and compact to become a majority in putative single-member districts. Because the majority opinion attached such importance to these points, they came to be known as the Gingles standard.[30]

Most voting rights lawyers were pleased with the Supreme Court's decision in *Gingles*. Their side had won the case and, equally important, the

Court had established a new standard that made it easier to challenge at-large systems throughout the nation. The totality-of-circumstances approach had required minority plaintiffs to do work that was arduous, expensive, and time-consuming: they were required to do research on the history of local race relations; they had to determine whether government policies and services were responsive to the needs of minority groups; they had to scrutinize campaign speeches for evidence of coded racism; and, to do this, they had to employ sympathetic historians and social scientists.

Voting rights lawyers understood that it would be easier, and less expensive, to work with the *Gingles* standard. After *Gingles*, at-large elections would be ended if voting rights lawyers demonstrated that the electorate was racially polarized and that an underrepresented minority group was sufficiently compact and cohesive to become a majority in a single-member district.

In explaining the Supreme Court's decision, Justice Brennan also rejected the multivariate approach that Reynolds had recommended. Brennan said this approach, because it focused on what caused different races to vote differently, "would frustrate the goals Congress sought to achieve." Brennan worried that multivariate studies would discredit the very linchpin of vote-dilution lawsuits—the concept of racially polarized voting. He felt that after controlling for income, it might turn out that middle-income blacks and whites voted pretty much the same way, and that low-income members of both races did likewise. In that case, there then would be no racially polarized voting even if most whites, the majority of whom were in the middle-income brackets, opposed candidates supported by most blacks, the majority of whom were in lower-income brackets. Brennan said this approach to racially polarized voting was "pernicious" and would "thwart the goals Congress sought to achieve when it amended [Section] 2."[31]

Justice O'Connor, on the other hand, declared that Justice Brennan's rationale struck "a different balance" than Congress had intended because it implied that minority groups had "a right to a form of proportional representation" if they were large enough to be a majority in a single-member district.[32]

Writing for four members of the Court, O'Connor recognized that there was an inherent tension between the language of the revised Section 2 and its real purpose. The language called for equal opportunity to participate in political processes and disavowed proportional representation. But the prevailing understanding was that Congress wanted affirmative districting to increase the likelihood that black leaders would be chosen to represent compact and cohesive black communities.[33]

O'Connor must have been tempted to say the law meant what it said—that nothing in this law established a right to have members of a protected class elected in numbers equal to their proportion in the population—but she knew that statement was at odds with another part of the revised Section 2, namely, the results test. Consequently, O'Connor endorsed the judgment of the district court while asserting that Justice Brennan's opinion came "closer to an absolute requirement of proportional representation than Congress intended."[34]

O'Connor feared that lower courts would fuse Brennan's *Gingles* standard with the idea that racial polarization existed if most blacks voted differently from most whites. If that was done, O'Connor warned, the courts would foster a rigid, mechanical understanding of what constitutes equal political opportunity.

O'Connor would soon be proven right. Armed with *Gingles*, voting rights lawyers moved from county to county, forcing new election arrangements for school boards, city councils, county commissions, and state legislatures. Judges threw out at-large voting systems all across the country and replaced them with small single-member districts. Many of the single-member districts had black majorities, and as expected, these *majority-minority* districts almost always elected black representatives. The number of black elected officials, which had stood at 5,038 in 1981, at the outset of the Reagan administration, and had increased to 6,424 when the *Gingles* decision was handed down in 1986, reached 7,370 by 1990.[35]

These figures indicate that *Gingles* was not the only factor responsible for the increase in black officeholding. Voting rights lawyers had previously won most of their cases, and before *Gingles* Reynolds and his predecessors at the Civil Rights Division had been using the preclearance provisions of Section 5 to prevent minority vote dilution. If a local districting plan was not fairly drawn, and especially if it involved retrogression from the previous system, Reynolds would not preclear the plan. As noted above, during their first four years in office Reynolds and the Reagan Justice Department rejected 110 redistricting plans (compared to 26 rejections during the four years of the Carter administration).

There were occasional instances, like the one in North Carolina, when Reynolds did not agree with the demands of voting rights activists. But overall, Reynolds and the Reagan administration worked hard to change the political map. This approach helped increase the number of blacks in the North Carolina legislature from four in 1981 to sixteen in 1986. Then, because of *Gingles*, the number increased again, to seventeen in 1990.

With something approaching the maximum feasible representation already accomplished in the North Carolina state legislature, voting activists turned their attention to other offices. Faced with a new lawsuit based on *Gingles*, the North Carolina legislature redrew judicial districts in such fashion that eight new black judges were elected in 1988, bringing the total number of black judges in the state to eleven out of seventy-three. There were also substantial increases in the number of new black school board members, city council members, and county commissioners. Voting rights lawyer Leslie Winner, who used the *Gingles* standard to force new election procedures in 19 of North Carolina's 100 counties, explained that "as a result of *Gingles*, blacks are getting elected in record numbers."[36]

There were similar developments throughout the country. As lower courts applied the *Gingles* formula to the cases before them, plaintiffs found it so easy to win that many local governments ceased their efforts to defend at-large elections. In 1990 the Justice Department reported that more than 1,300 jurisdictions had changed their methods of electing officials in response to Section 2 litigation or the threat of litigation. Michael Crowell, a lawyer who had represented local governments in voting cases, explained that if a concentrated black minority was underrepresented, and if most whites did not vote for candidates preferred by most blacks, the local government would lose. It would also "end up paying not only its own attorneys but the attorneys' fees for the plaintiffs.... In one county in North Carolina that sum reached several hundred thousand dollars." As a result, because of the potential costs involved, many cities and towns agreed to plans that voting rights activists put forward.[37]

These plans almost always called for single-member districts that practically ensured that black leaders would represent predominantly black districts. But this did nothing to increase the political influence of suburban and rural blacks who were so dispersed that they could not feasibly be packed into districts with black majorities. Consequently, voting activists began to consider plans that would increase the influence of dispersed minorities.

In doing so, they ran into a road block the Supreme Court had erected in *Gingles*. By requiring that the minority group in a voting-dilution case "must be able to demonstrate that it is sufficiently large and geographically compact to constitute a majority in a single-member district," Justice Brennan's opinion seemed to have placed the protection of Section 2 beyond the reach of dispersed minorities.[38]

Dispersed minorities were more likely to have political power in an at-large district that allowed cumulative voting. This, at least, was the opinion of Richard L. Engstrom, a political scientist who worked on several voting rights cases. Engstrom explained that in the usual at-large system, each voter was allowed to mark as many ballots as there were positions to be filled. If five people were to be elected, each voter would be allowed to choose as many as five different candidates. Under cumulative voting, however, voters were not restricted to casting a single vote for any particular candidate. Instead, they would be allowed to cumulate or aggregate their votes behind one or more candidates. In the five-vote context, a voter could vote in the traditional fashion, casting a vote for each of five different candidates; or the voter could cast two ballots for one candidate and three for another or even cast all five votes for a single candidate, a practice called *plumping*.[39]

Engstrom said cumulative voting was more democratic than the one-vote-per-candidate format because it allowed voters to cast ballots that reflected the intensity of their preferences for different candidates. Equally important, cumulative voting afforded better protection against minority vote dilution. Unlike packing, which protected only those blacks who were concentrated residentially, cumulative voting would protect the dispersed members of a politically cohesive minority.

Engstrom wrote that the Supreme Court's opinion in *Gingles* was "extremely unfortunate" because it afforded no protection for dispersed minorities. More than that, by focusing on the minority's ability to elect members of the group, rather than viewing minority political power as the ability to influence and interact with others, *Gingles* undermined the black political power it purported to promote. Engstrom suggested that a well-informed construction of the results test would provide for packing in some districts but would make provision elsewhere for cumulative voting in at-large elections.[40]

Cumulative voting is frequently used in elections for corporate boards of directors, and so far it has been used in more than thirty instances to augment the power of dispersed black minorities. In Worcester County, Maryland, a federal judge replaced at-large elections for the Board of Commissioners with a cumulative voting plan. And in Alabama, three municipalities, a county commission, and a county school board have settled lawsuits by voluntarily accepting cumulative voting plans. Voting rights lawyer and scholar Pamela S. Karlan has written that in these instances it was not possible "to draw a single-member district plan that would provide black voters with an equal opportunity to elect their preferred candidates."[41]

In other cases black plaintiffs have asked federal judges to impose limited voting—a similar method for boosting the political power of minorities. In this approach, voters in at-large elections are permitted to vote for only a portion of the seats that are up for election. They might, for example, be limited to casting three votes in an election for seven members of a county commission. As of June 1993 limited voting had been instituted in about thirty-two jurisdictions.[42]

There are still other possibilities. Edward Still, an Alabama lawyer who represented blacks in several voting lawsuits, presented a blizzard of graphs, equations, and calculations in support of his pet plan, the *Single Transferable Vote*. Under this system, nearly complete proportionality can be achieved by allocating seats to parties on the basis of the percentage of votes received. For this to work, however, voting must be extremely polarized racially, and blacks would have to organize their own political party—a move that Edward Still acknowledges "would have the effect of segregating blacks and probably hindering further amelioration of racial tensions."[43]

The methods are diverse—cumulative voting, limited voting, the single transferable vote—but the purpose is not. Voting rights activists want to increase black political power (or, as they might prefer to phrase it, to make sure that blacks have the opportunity to influence policy by electing candidates of their choice). Before 1965 white Southerners ingeniously used poll taxes, literacy tests, and white primaries to deny blacks the right to vote. By the 1980s, voting activists said that it was "time for federal courts to be equally creative" in developing remedies for perceived minority vote dilution.[44]

Voting activists generally assumed that blacks were better off if the system ensured the election of some blacks than if it gave them influence over a larger number of candidates. For this reason, they preferred single-member districts to at-large arrangements, but some sympathetic observers questioned this assumption of the activists. Thus Matthew Cooper, a liberal journalist, noted that the election of black candidates, by itself, did not ensure that any public policies would be changed. On the contrary, redistricting could lead to a situation where state houses, county commissions, and even Congress were "dominated by two factions—blacks who are unaccountable to whites, and whites who are unaccountable to blacks." Another journalist, David DeBuisson, observed that "'safe districts' could easily isolate [blacks] from the political mainstream." DeBuisson reported that by 1985 some people in North Carolina were already referring to the *Gingles* districts as "black homelands."[45]

James Wallace, Jr., an attorney who represented North Carolina during the *Gingles* litigation, did not use inflammatory language, but he strongly believed single-member districts reduced the influence blacks exercised over white representatives, "abolish[ing] coalition politics among the races."

> The way I view it, and I appreciate that many blacks don't see it this way, is that blacks said, "Well, we may not be able to win votes in the General Assembly, and maybe we can't have any real strong influence there. But at least for the first time our children can have role models. That's what is most important to us now." The overriding thought seems to be," Let us have some important positions, and then later we will deal with how to be more effective."[46]

Kathryn Abrams, a law professor specializing in voting rights, also wondered if *Gingles* had not "created more problems than it resolved." She conceded that the election of black officials had been "a crucial first step" that provided role models and boosted "political self-esteem," but she argued that more should be done.[47]

As Abrams saw it, the problem with *Gingles* was that it focused on the election of black officials, not on augmenting the political influence of minority groups. She felt the courts seemed to forget that in a democracy a minority cannot exercise real power unless it makes advantageous alliances with a substantial portion of the majority. If the judges had construed Section 2 more perceptively, she believed, so as to maximize the influence of blacks, they would have redrawn district lines "to create groups of minority voters with such potential influence" that they could "break the cycle of avoidance that has characterized polarized politics."[48]

Abrams acknowledged that social scientists had not determined how large a minority population had to be to get the attention of white officials, but she felt that the 65 percent black districts that were optimal for electing black leaders were not conducive to biracial politics. Abrams conceded that some black-majority districts were needed to ensure the election of black role models. She thought, however, that wherever possible the majority-minority districts should be reduced to barely more than 50 percent. In those cases, more blacks would then be available for gerrymandering as substantial, influential minorities in what Abrams called "strong plurality" districts. Abrams conceded that this approach might lead to the election of fewer blacks, but she thought any loss would be compensated by an increased ability to enact programs that most blacks favored.[49]

Abrams wanted the courts to rule that the revised Section 2 required the sort of districting that would be conducive to biracial coalitions. This, she maintained, was the best way to maximize black political power; this is what the *Gingles* court would have required if the justices had dealt more intelligently with the problem of minority vote dilution.

Abrams may have underestimated the benefits blacks derived from electing black representatives. At a theoretical level, however, there is something to be said for her analysis. Packing blacks into districts that are 65 percent black does militate against intergroup cooperation and biracial politics.

But that was exactly what the major civil rights groups wanted. When *Gingles* was argued before the Supreme Court, Justice Stevens elicited an extraordinary concession from Julius Chambers, the NAACP lawyer. Chambers agreed that the abolition of at-large elections and the creation of single-member districts would not ensure that more blacks would be elected to office. His position was that while it could mean that the same number of blacks would be elected, those elected would be "different ones." Chambers believed single-member districts were better because blacks that were chosen from districts with solid black majorities, unlike the blacks that were elected at-large, would be authentic representatives of the black community.[50]

In making this argument, Chambers was reiterating a point that veteran civil rights activists Spiver Gordon and Albert Turner had made in Alabama. Gordon characterized the black candidates of a biracial coalition in Greene County as "white folks' niggers" and "sell-out Tom puppets," whereas Turner candidly acknowledged that single-member districts in Perry County would be arranged to remove "black collaborators" from their "white supporters."[51]

Others made similar statements. In Virginia, Curtis House, a black minister and civil rights leader, complained that blacks could not win at-large elections unless they made "some kind of deal" with whites. In an opinion explaining its reasons for creating a 65 percent black district in Atlanta, three judges of the Fifth Circuit Court of Appeals gratuitously repeated charges that an elderly black legislator who opposed the new plan was an "Aunt Jane." In an amicus brief prepared for the *Gingles* case, the Lawyers' Committee for Civil Rights Under Law explained that "entrenched political forces" could manipulate at-large elections by supporting "hand-picked minority candidates." In another amicus brief for *Gingles*, Legal Services of North Carolina asserted that "black leaders who have been outspoken about issues of concern to the black community cannot get white support, and thus cannot win at-large elections."[52]

Voting rights lawyer Lani Guinier would later pay a price for expressing similar views. In 1993 President Bill Clinton nominated Guinier to fill Reynolds's former position as assistant attorney general for civil rights, but Clinton withdrew the nomination after he learned that Guinier had suggested, among other things, that black officials who were elected by largely white electorates were not *authentic* blacks.[53]

Actually, Guinier's statements about authenticity were only one of several problematical sets of comments. Although Guinier had worked tirelessly during the early 1980s as an advocate of race-based, single-member districts, by late in the decade she had second thoughts about the approach to which she once was committed. In dense, almost incomprehensible articles written for law reviews, she set forth a voting rights paradigm: She explained that the first generation of voting activists had sought to end discrimination against black voters; the second generation of activists then worked to facilitate the actual election of blacks by establishing single-member districts; but a third approach, which had gained support after *Gingles*, looked toward structuring the legislative process to enhance the power of black officeholders.[54]

According to Guinier, most blacks who were elected from single-member districts—the authentic blacks—favored "a redistributive agenda." They wanted policies that would take money and prerogatives away from people who were well-to-do and give them to those who were not. But when they pushed for such policies, they discovered that they lacked *clout*. Within the legislative bodies, they had been "marginalize[d]" and "isolat[ed]" by a majority that wielded its "disproportionate power" to defeat redistributive proposals.[55]

To improve the prospects for redistributive policies to benefit "the dispossessed," Guinier proposed several new approaches to voting. She said that blacks should demand that single-member districts be supplemented, where appropriate, with cumulative voting in at-large elections, and that they should also demand a series of antimajoritarian measures that would require white legislators to bargain with their black counterparts. Specifically, Guinier mentioned the need for a "minority veto" or a "concurrent majority"; if either of these procedures were in place, a law could pass only if it was supported by a majority of both black and white legislators. Guinier explained that such provisions would make it necessary for white legislators to accommodate blacks in order to get any legislation enacted.[56]

Guinier equivocated when it came to how these "supermajority arrangements" should be brought about. Writing in the *Michigan Law Review*, she suggested that her proposals were not required by either the Constitution or the Voting Rights Act. However, in a later article for the *Virginia Law Review*, Guinier indicated otherwise. Since the Voting Rights Act prohibited minority vote dilution, she wrote, it followed that the act should protect the power of blacks after they entered the halls of government. Thus, if courts imposed her recommendations and required a concurrent majority, Guinier reasoned that they would not be making new law but instead would give meaning to a law that was already on the books. "Far from actually making law, the federal courts [would] merely apply a law made," she wrote. Stuart Taylor, Jr., a journalist for the weekly *Legal Times*, described Guinier's approach as a "mandate for the courts to change the rules so as to insure not only that black voters have substantially proportionate representation, but also that black representatives—or rather those who are authentic—can win a 'fair number of contested policy decisions.'"[57]

After Guinier's proposals received wide publicity, President Clinton withdrew the nomination—and said that he could not defend some of Guinier's views. In the larger context, *l'affaire Guinier* indicated that by the early 1990s voting activists had belatedly recognized a point that Reynolds had recognized in the 1980s—that judged simply on the basis of results, blacks did not gain much from creating the maximum number of districts that were safe for black politicians.

The consequences of *Gingles* were problematical in terms of augmenting black political influence, but the case turned out to be an unmitigated boon to the Republican party. As blacks were packed into the maximum feasible number of districts that were about 65 percent black, the remaining districts became whiter and less Democratic—and therefore, fertile soil for Republican candidates. The big losers were white liberals. In North Carolina, after the at-large system was replaced with race-conscious, single-member districts, the number of Republicans in the General Assembly increased from twenty-four in 1982 to fifty in 1984.[58]

In state after state, the story was similar—white Democrats lost when they were separated from black constituencies. Thus, in South Carolina in 1984, after the state created two black state-legislative districts, conservative Republicans defeated liberal Democratic incumbents in the surrounding four districts from which black voters had been siphoned. In Alabama, Republican strength almost doubled after legislative districts were redrawn in 1983. Again, many of the gains came in districts where the number of black voters had been depleted. In 1994, after some forty years as the minority party on Capitol Hill, the Republicans finally won a majority of the seats in the U.S. House of Representatives. Analysts attributed about fifteen of the Republican victories in 1994 to the fact that predominantly Democratic blacks had been siphoned out of some districts to create black-majority districts elsewhere.[59]

Some Republicans were content to say that when it came to districting, their interests happily coincided with those of blacks. Others did not pass up the opportunity to comment on the irony of the situation. One observed, "You know, the federal government goes through the South, and says you have been very bad to your blacks. You have to desegregate your restaurants, your schools, and your hotels. And, yes, you have to segregate your districts." That was just "fine" with Tom Bethell, a conservative columnist who was one of the first to recognize that the revised Section 2 would come back to haunt liberal reformers. If blacks were placed in districts that were about 65 percent black, Bethell noted, "the remaining districts will tend to be more Republican (since blacks are overwhelmingly Democratic)" and white liberal Democrats were "likely to be the losers." Another conservative journalist, Pat Buchanan, predicted that "by the law of unintended consequences, the victims of this form of racial politics will be the same white liberals most enthusiastically endorsing it. Militant blacks, searching for an all-black district that can guarantee them permanent public office, will collaborate with white Republicans anxious to be rid of Democratic-voting black constituents. Together, they will re-segregate America."[60]

Some liberal white North Carolinians agreed. They said that single-member districts left blacks politically isolated and guaranteed that fewer white liberals, and more conservatives, would be elected to office. One such liberal was Margaret R. Tennile, who was identified in the local press as "the last of a political breed in Forsyth County—a white Democratic member of the House of Representatives." With a mixture of Old South charm and political savvy,

Mrs. Tennile had been elected to the House five times. But in 1984, after district lines had been redrawn, Tennile and two other liberal white Democratic incumbents from Forsyth were defeated. They lost because of what University of North Carolina professor Thad Beyle called "the suburban effect." With blacks clustered together in black-majority districts, the liberal Democrats lost an important part of their political base and had to stand for reelection in districts that were more suburban and conservative.[61]

Single-member districts led to a form of politics that was better focused and less costly; but Tennile complained that as a result of this, black legislative candidates rarely campaigned in white neighborhoods and fewer white legislators counted blacks as an important part of their constituencies. "The thing that has distressed me more than anything else," she said, "is what it has done to our community. I think it has helped polarize this community to a greater extent."[62]

This point of view was echoed by Louise Brennan, another liberal white Democrat who failed to be reelected. Brennan recalled that before redistricting she and other liberal Democrats had been able to win "because we had black support." But after *Gingles* they could no longer prevail because they had been placed in districts that were not just predominantly white. The new suburban districts seemed to be more racially polarized than ever, with a growing number of whites regarding the Democrats as "a black party."[63]

Some voting activists tried to shift the blame for the demise of the Democrats. Leslie Winner noted that the Republican gains in North Carolina occurred when the Republican tide was rising—at a time when Ronald Reagan won the state's presidential electors, James G. Martin was elected governor, and Jesse Helms was reelected to the U. S. Senate.[64]

Yet even Winner conceded that redistricting had done more to help local Republicans than the coattails of the president, the governor, or the senator. If the work against at-large elections and for single-member districts had damaged Democrats, she believed it was a price that had to be paid. "In the end, she said, "my answer is that white Democrats are not entitled to save their own necks at the expense of black representation, even if that is the net effect."[65]

The effect was no surprise to Republican insiders. When *Gingles* was before the courts, three Republican groups supported the black plaintiffs. Asserting that at-large elections harmed Southern Republicans as well as blacks, Governor Martin filed a brief that urged the Supreme Court to decide in favor of single-member districts. The Republican National Committee took a similar position and, as noted above, so did Senator Dole.[66]

The Reagan administration, on the other hand, opposed racial redistricting in the *Gingles* case. Reynolds said there was no need to create safe districts for minorities in areas where blacks were already winning a nearly proportional share of the at-large elections. North Carolina had moved so far beyond tokenism that it was no longer necessary to guarantee the election of some black officials. In these circumstances, Reynolds said, packing would not lead to the election of many more blacks; it would lead, rather, to a racial polarization in politics and to a loss of black influence over white officials.[67]

Notes

1. Thornburg v. Gingles, 478 U.S. 30 (1986).
2. "Extreme gerrymandering" is hard to define, but for an example see the discussion in Shaw v. Reno, 61 USLW 4818 (1993).
3. The previous administrations had not objected because North Carolina had not submitted the practice for preclearance—apparently because the practice was informal and antedated the time (1964) after which preclearance was required.
4. Gingles v. Edmisten, 590 F.Supp. 345 (1984), 350.
5. Ibid., 351; *Charlotte Observer*, 2 December 1981.
6. Thornburg v. Gingles, 478 U.S. 30 (1986), 40; Gingles v. Edmisten, 590 F.Supp. 345 (1984), 365; *Charlotte Observer*, 29 January 1982.
7. 42 U.S.C. #1973.
8. Gingles v. Edmisten, 590 F.Supp. 345 (1984), 365.
9. Ibid., 359–63.
10. Ibid., 364.
11. Bernard Grofman, "Criteria for Districting: A Social Science Perspective, 33 *UCLA Law Review* (1985): 77–184.
12. Gingles v. Edmisten, 590 F.Supp. 345 (1984), 355, 368. In point of fact, the judges noted, in the disputed at-large districts "81.7 percent of white voters did not vote for any black [candidates]."
13. Ibid., 365, 355, 352–57; 42 U.S.C. #1973.
14. Gingles v. Edmisten, 376–84; *New York Times*, 30 April 1985, 17:1; *Washington Post*, 30 June 1985, A8a.
15. *New York Times*, 30 April 1985, 17:1; Rex E. Lee, William Bradford Reynolds et al., Brief for the United States as Amicus Curiae, October 1984, Thornburg v. Gingles, Supreme Court Library (cited hereafter as Lee-Reynolds Brief); Charles Fried, William Bradford Reynolds, et al., Brief for the United States as Amicus Curiae Supporting Appellants, October 1985, ibid., (cited hereafter as Fried-Reynolds Brief).
16. Lee-Reynolds Brief, 6.
17. Lee-Reynolds Brief, 6; Fried-Reynolds Brief, 5–6.
18. Lee-Reynolds Brief, 20.
19. Lee-Reynolds Brief, 12; Fried-Reynolds Brief, 27.
20. Gingles v. Edmisten, 590 F.Supp. 345 (1984), 367; Lee-Reynolds Brief, 17.
21. Lee-Reynolds Brief, 16.
22. Interview with WBR, 14 April 1989.
23. Gingles v. Edmisten, 590 F.Supp. 345 (1984).
24. *1982 Senate Hearings*, 821, 803 (testimony and statement of Armand Derfner), 1182–87, 1204–14 (testimony and statement of Frank R. Parker); Rogers v. Lodge, 458 U.S. 613 (1982), 616; Lee-Reynolds Brief, 13, 19.
25. Fried-Reynolds Brief, 29–30; Thornburg v. Gingles, 478 U.S. 30 (1986), 61–67.

26. Lee-Reynolds Brief, 11; Fried-Reynolds Brief, 6.
27. 42 U.S.C. #1973; Lee-Reynolds Brief, 9, 18; Fried-Reynolds Brief, 6–8, 10–12, 15–16, 27
28. Robert J. Dole et al., Amicus Curiae Brief on Behalf of Appellees, Thornburg v. Gingles, Supreme Court Library.
29. Ibid., 2, 5, 3, 29.
30. Thornburg v. Gingles, 478 U.S. 30 (1986).
31. Ibid., 71, 73, 62, 66, 70, 64–65.
32. Ibid., 95, 85, 105.
33. Ibid., 84.
34. 42 U.S.C. #1973; Thornburg v. Gingles, 478 U.S. 30 (1986), 94. In his concurring opinion in Holder v. Hall, 62 LW 4728 (1994), Justice Clarence Thomas discussed the "tension" between the language and the real meaning of the 1982 amendment.
35. Joint Center for Political and Economic Studies, *Black Elected Officials: A National Roster*, xxii.
36. *St. Louis Post Dispatch*, 26 March 1989.
37. Frank R. Parker, *Black Votes Count*, 179, 167; Michael Crowell, "North Carolina Local Government After *Gingles*," *Popular Government*, 54 (Summer 1988): 18.
38. Thornburg v. Gingles, 478 U.S. 30 (1986),50. Pamela S. Karlan has noted that several lower courts have understood *Gingles* to mean that geographic compactness is an essential precondition for a showing of minority vote dilution, as expressed in the following: "[U]nless blacks are sufficiently numerous to constitute the majority of the electorate in a single-member district, their votes have not been diluted." "Maps and Misreadings: The Role of Geographic Compactness in Racial Vote Dilution Litigation," *Harvard Civil Rights-Civil Liberties Law Review*, 24 (1989): 206, 210, 173–248.
39. Richard L. Engstrom et al., "Cumulative Voting as a Remedy for Minority Vote Dilution," *Journal of Law and Politics*, 5 (1989): 476–80.
40. Ibid., 472 and passim.
41. Paul Craig Roberts and Lawrence M. Stratton, *The New Color Line* (Washington, D.C.: Regnery Publishing, Inc., 1995), 123, 146; *Harvard Civil Rights-Civil Liberties Law Review* 24 (1989): 234.
42. Ibid., 223–31; *Popular Government*, 54 (Summer 1988): 19; *Newsweek* (14 June 1993): 28.
43. Edward Still, "Alternatives to Single Member Districts," in Chandler Davidson, ed., *Minority Vote Dilution*, 258, 249–67.
44. Statement of Pamela S. Karlan, *Harvard Civil Rights-Civil Liberties Law Review*, 24 (1989): 248.
45. Washington Monthly, (September 1987): 11; *Greensboro News & Record*, 19 December 1985.
46. *Charlotte Observer*, 2 August 1983; James Wallace, interview with Sheila O'Connor, 8 August 1989.
47. Kathryn Abrams, "'Raising Politics Up': Minority Political Participation and Section 2 of the Voting Rights Act," *New York University Law Review*, 63 (June 1988): 464, 519–20.
48. Ibid., 461.
49. Ibid., 524 and passim.
50. *Washington Post*, 5 December 1985, A4a; *New York Times*, 5 December 1985, II, 25:1.

51. Spiver Gordon, interview with Jeff Wolters, 7 August 1987; Handbill of Black People's Action Committee; interview with Albert Turner, 8 May 1986.
52. *1982 House Hearings*, 405–15; *Washington Monthly* (September 1987): 14; Frank R. Parker et al., Brief for the Lawyers' Committee for Civil Rights Under Law, 17, Thornburg v. Gingles, Supreme Court Library; David H. Harris et al., Brief for Legal Services of North Carolina, 17, ibid.
53. Lani Guinier, "The Triumph of Tokenism," *Michigan Law Review*, 89 (March 1991): 1103 and passim; *New York Times*, 23 May 1993, IV, 14:1.
54. Lani Guinier, "No Two Seats: The Elusive Quest for Political Equality," *Virginia Law Review*, 77 (November 1991): 1415 and passim.
55. *Michigan Law Review*, 89 (March 1991): 1086 and passim; *Virginia Law Review*, 77 (November 1991): 1436, 1441, 1446 and passim.
56. *Michigan Law Review*, 89 (March 1991): 1135, 1140, 1140 n. 302 and n.303, 1149 and passim.
57. Ibid., 1154; *Virginia Law Review*, 77 (November 1991): 1510, 1509; *New York Times*, 4 June 1993, 16:1.
58. *Washington Post*, 30 June 1985, A8a; Monitor Leadership Directories, *State Yellow Book* (New York and Washington, 1994): 605, 608.
59. *New Republic* (2 September 1985): 23; *Washington Monthly* (September 1987): 12; Daniel B. Polsby and Robert D. Popper Jr., "Racial Lines," *National Review* 20 February 1995): 53.
60. *Washington Monthly* (September 1987): 12; *American Spectator* (July 1982): 4–5; *Human Events* (22 May 1982): 17.
61. *Raleigh News and Observer*, 16 April 1989.
62. Ibid.
63. Louise Brennan, interview with Sheila O'Connor, 8 August 1989.
64. *Raleigh News and Observer*, 16 April 1989.
65. Ibid.
66. James G. Martin, Amicus Curiae Brief, Thornburg v. Gingles, Supreme Court Library; Republican National Committee, Amicus Curiae Brief, ibid.; Robert Dole et al., Amicus Curiae Brief on Behalf of Appellees, ibid.
67. *Washington Post*, 5 December 1985, A4a.

7

Conclusion to Part I

How should one assess the voting rights record of the Reagan administration and of William Bradford Reynolds? The answer of the established civil rights groups, an answer generally reiterated in the major media, was that Reagan and Reynolds "set a new record for non-enforcement, retreats, and defaults in voting rights."[1]

Voting rights activists acknowledged that Reynolds objected to more discriminatory voting changes than any previous assistant attorney general for civil rights. But they found fault with Reynolds for opposing a proposal to put a results test into Section 2 of the Voting Rights Act and for advancing, in *Thornburg v. Gingles*, an interpretation that would have made it more difficult to achieve the maximum number of single-member districts that had a black majority. Voting rights activists also criticized Reynolds for questioning the principle that districts must be at least 65 percent black if African-Americans were to have an equal chance to participate in politics and to elect representatives of their choice. The activists also focused on a few instances in which Reynolds overruled staff recommendations and precleared changes that subsequently were struck down by federal courts. Partly because of this criticism, in 1985 the Senate Judiciary Committee refused to confirm Reynolds as associate attorney general.

Most of these criticisms do not withstand scrutiny. Because he recognized that the revised Section 2, if unamended, would lead to something akin to proportional representation, Reynolds expressed legitimate reservations that touched on the fundamental nature of U.S. government. He was correct in holding that a mechanical application of the 65 percent rule could actually reduce black influence in some instances; and the overruling of staff recommendations usually turned out to involve minor matters like changing a polling place or the filing, or timing, of an appeal.

Voting rights activists made much of four instances in which courts later disagreed with Reynolds's decisions. But these cases, when examined carefully, do not support their indictment. In the New Orleans congressional districting case, *Major v. Treen*, Reynolds had good reason to conclude that

Governor David Treen acted for political, not racial reasons; and the court, in setting aside Reynolds's decision, applied a new test (the results standard) that had not been available when Reynolds acted on the case. In the Montgomery city-council case, *Buskey v. Oliver*, Reynolds's decision was set aside by a judge who had been a political ally of the victorious party.[2]

One of the other cases, *Thornburg v. Gingles*, concerned reapportionment in North Carolina; and the fourth, *Hardy v. Wallace*, involved the appointment of dog-racing commissioners in Greene County, Alabama. The issues in these cases were complex, and as will be noted below, the Supreme Court later embraced Reynolds's arguments.[3]

Another criticism is also wide of the mark. It is that Reynolds generally favored affirmative districting for partisan reasons—because the policy redounded to the benefit of the Republican party. When blacks were packed into majority-minority districts, the remaining jurisdictions were whiter and more hospitable to the GOP.

As a example of this criticism journalist Matthew Cooper, after noting that Reynolds was "remarkably vigilant, albeit not as aggressive as the civil rights groups want" in pushing for the creation of predominantly black, single-member electoral districts, warned liberals and Democrats to "beware of Republicans bearing voting rights suits." He wrote that while Reynolds "talked about his color-blind vision," he was working to boost the fortunes of the GOP.[4]

Abigail M. Thernstrom, a leading scholar of voting rights, also expressed this criticism. After the Senate Judiciary Committee rejected Reynolds's nomination for associate attorney general, Thernstrom wrote that Reynolds was "hanged for the wrong crime," adding, "not that he was innocent." According to Thernstrom, the crime was not that Reynolds parted company with voting rights activists on a few cases, but that he was bending the law for partisan reasons.[5]

Thernstrom noted that Reynolds's overall record on voting "differ[ed] little from the one that the civil rights groups themselves would create." Because he recognized that "what is good for black candidates is good for Republicans," Reynolds used "the number of blacks in office" to measure compliance with the Voting Rights Act. To advance the interests of his political party, she said Reynolds sanctioned "routes around the law."[6]

It may be that single-member districts benefitted the GOP, but it seems to this writer that Cooper and Thernstrom, when they vilified Reynolds, ignored the fact that by 1980 a well-developed body of voting rights law prescribed single-member districts as the antidote to minority vote dilution. By the time the Reagan administration came into office, the original Voting Rights Act of 1965 had experienced a metamorphosis, if not an outright transformation. The federal courts had reinterpreted a law that originally protected only the right to register and vote, and had turned it into a guarantee against minority vote dilution. Then, after the Voting Rights Act was revised in1982, voting rights activists insisted that the law required that district lines must be drawn to enable blacks to win something approaching the maximum feasible number of offices.

The resistance of Southern whites was partly responsible for the reinterpretation. By 1969 it was clear that equal access to the polls would not suffice to eradicate racially discriminatory voting practices. In some cases, at-large elections and other structural arrangements were being manipulated to prevent the election of blacks. Consequently, the Supreme Court, in *Allen v. State Board of Elections*, recognized that "the right to vote can be affected by a dilution of voting power as well as by an absolute prohibition on casting a ballot."[7]

Allen was a departure from the original understanding of the Voting Rights Act, but Congress acquiesced in the reinterpretation when it renewed the legislation in 1970 and 1975. In 1982, when Congress renewed the law a third time, it further expanded the concept that the Voting Rights Act prohibited minority vote dilution as well as outright disfranchisement.

As noted in the introduction to this book, Reynolds thought government policies should be color-blind and nondiscriminatory. Nevertheless, although this was Reynolds's personal preference for public policy, he was preeminently a lawyer who recognized that when it came to electoral districting, both Congress and the Supreme Court had rejected the argument that race-conscious districting was per se unconstitutional. On the contrary, Congress and the Supreme Court had held that the conscious use of race in districting was required to facilitate the election of members of underrepresented racial groups.

Yet this was not an instance in which Reynolds was enforcing a policy he regarded as mistaken. On the contrary, Reynolds understood the need for a broad interpretation of the Voting Rights Act. He understood that after this law was enacted in 1965, some jurisdictions had used an arsenal of weapons to resist black political empowerment: sometimes boundary lines were changed; sometimes elected offices were abolished and the appointive process was substituted; and sometimes elections were switched to an at-large basis. Because of the resistance to black political power, Reynolds believed there was a need for affirmative action in voting rights, although because of the Dole amendment to the Voting Rights Act of 1982, Reynolds insisted that the affirmative measures should not involve proportional representation.

In opposing proportional representation, Reynolds foresaw some of the problems that would concern voting rights activists in the 1990s. He recognized that an emphasis on single-member districts, while useful for ensuring that blacks would be elected to office, might lead to a situation where black officials would be marginalized and isolated within the legislative body. Long before the idea seems to have occurred to voting rights lawyer Lani Guinier, Reynolds recognized that the election of black officials, by itself, would not ensure that public policies would change.

Unlike Guinier and most other voting rights activists of the 1980s, Reynolds thought blacks could participate effectively in politics even if a district were less than 65 percent black. He understood that in some situations it might be necessary to have predominantly black districts, but he did not see the need for race-conscious, single-member districting in areas where more than a token number of African-Americans had already been elected to office.

"If we are really going to move to a point that will help blacks and avoid racial polarization," Reynolds said, "we should be much more sensitive to the need for districts where blacks can be influential in forming political coalitions." In many instances where blacks made up only a minority of the electorate, he observed, they would have real power because "officials will have to take account of the interests of blacks, or the officials will not remain in office very long." In some cases, Reynolds insisted, African-Americans would be better off if there were a smaller number of blacks in office, but more officials who depended on the votes of black constituents.[8]

For eight years Reynolds was the nation's ranking voting rights enforcer. As such, his job was to strike the balance that Congress intended when it enacted and amended the Voting Rights Act. He won the vast majority of voting cases he was involved in, and after he left office, the Supreme Court belatedly endorsed arguments that Reynolds had put forth in his two biggest voting rights losses.

In *Hardy v. Wallace*, Reynolds decided that a change in the authority of elected officials did not come within the meaning of the Voting Rights Act. He held that the federal government need not preclear a decision to shift the responsibility for governing the Greenetrack Greyhound Racing Stadium away from elected officials just because the reallocation of duties occurred simultaneously with the first election of blacks. In 1985 a district court overruled Reynolds. Because revenues from the track provided a large portion of the public funds in Greene County, Alabama, the court held that a reallocation that diminished the decision-making authority of black officials came within the scope of the Voting Rights Act.[9]

In 1992, however, in a case from Etowah County, Alabama, the Supreme Court endorsed the legal argument that Reynolds had made in the Greene County case. Once again, the authority of newly elected black officials was diminished (with the reallocation of authority in Etowah pertaining to the maintenance of roads). Voting rights activists again argued that reallocations of decision-making authority were just as unacceptable as gerrymandering boundaries to the disadvantage of blacks or switching elections from a single-member district to an at-large basis. But six justices of the Supreme Court held that the framers of the Voting Rights Act did not intend for preclearance to apply to reallocations of authority.[10]

Then, in 1993, the Supreme Court endorsed some of the arguments that Reynolds had fashioned for *Thornburg v. Gingles*. There Reynolds had argued that North Carolina need not abolish at-large elections in areas where blacks had won numerous elections, even if the blacks' proportion of victories fell short of their proportion of the overall population. The state, Reynolds argued, need not take affirmative steps to facilitate the election of the maximum feasible number of black candidates.[11]

Reynolds lost *Gingles* in 1986, but in three decisions of the 1990s, the Supreme Court emphatically and repeatedly placed limits on affirmative racial districting. In so doing, the Court endorsed a rationale that was similar to the argument that Reynolds had made in *Gingles*: the Court held that government officials, when they drew district boundaries, could consider the racial balance in order to prevent minority vote dilution; but they could not make race the predominant consideration in order to ensure proportional representation or to maximize the number of blacks who were elected to office.[12]

The first decision of the 1990s arose from another North Carolina voting case. After the census of 1990, North Carolina had tried to give blacks approximately proportional representation in the House of Representatives by fashioning black majorities for two of its twelve congressional districts. To accomplish this, one of the black districts was given an extraordinary shape. It was "approximately 160 miles long and, for much of its length, no wider than the I-85 corridor. It winds in snake-like fashion through tobacco country, financial centers, and manufacturing areas 'until it gobbles in enough enclaves of black neighborhoods.'"[13]

In *Shaw v. Reno*, the Supreme Court decided that this went too far. North Carolina had gone beyond *Gingles*, which had required that a putative majority-minority district must be "geographically compact." It had fashioned a district of such dramatically irregular shape that the configuration could not be understood as anything other than "an effort to segregate the races for purposes of voting." In so doing, the Court held, North Carolina "reinforce[d] the perception that members of the same racial group—regardless of their age, education, economic status, or the community in which they live—think alike, share the same political interests, and will prefer the same candidates at the polls." The Court said the North Carolina plan bore "an uncomfortable resemblance to political apartheid."[14]

One year later, in 1994, the Supreme Court moved closer to the position that Reynolds had staked out in *Gingles*. In *Johnson v. De Grandy*, a case that arose from Florida, where electoral districts had already been drawn to ensure that the proportion of minority representatives in the state legislature would approximate the percentage of minorities in the electorate, the Court held that the Voting Rights Act did not require that additional efforts be made to facilitate the election of the maximum feasible number of minority candidates. "[T]he Voting Rights Act does not require maximization," Justice O'Connor emphasized in a concurring opinion.[15]

Then, in a 1995 decision, *Miller v. Johnson*, the Supreme Court reiterated that government officials should not take account of race in order to maximize the number of black officeholders. In Georgia, lines had already been drawn so that blacks could (and did) win two of the state's eleven seats in the U.S. House of Representatives. In a state where blacks made up 27 percent of the population, however, this amount of representation (18 percent) fell short of proportionality. Therefore, after the census of 1990, the Department of Justice (of the Republican Bush administration) refused to preclear Georgia's congressional districting boundaries until the state maximized black representation by creating a third predominantly black district.[16]

Georgia finally received approval from the federal authorities in Washington, after the state created a third black district. It did so by modifying an arrangement that the ACLU had initially designed (and that the ACLU had called its "max-black plan"). It combined four compact, densely populated, predominantly black urban areas with geographically extensive rural counties that were sparsely populated and largely black.[17]

Race was the predominant consideration in crafting this district. It was unusual for a congressional district to unite, as this one did, portions of Atlanta, Augusta, and Savannah with one another and with rural areas that were as much as 260 miles away. Other than race, the populations of these areas had little in common. Nevertheless, as congressional districts went, the shape of the new Georgia district was not particularly bizarre. In fact, a map of the district resembled a large quadrilateral with the cities neatly positioned at three of the corners.[18]

When *Miller v. Johnson* went before the Supreme Court, the Clinton administration argued that regardless of Georgia's intention, those who opposed the plan had failed to satisfy the test that the Supreme Court had established in *Shaw v. Reno*. They had not demonstrated that the district's shape was so bizarre that it could not be explained other than on the basis of race.[19]

By a vote of 5–4, however, the Supreme Court ruled that President Clinton's lawyers had "misapprehend[ed]...our holding in *Shaw*." The ruling in *Shaw* "was not meant to suggest that a district must be bizarre on its face before there is a constitutional violation." The Court insisted on a crucial distinction. Government officials could consider race to combat minority vote dilution, but they could not use race to *maximize* the number of black office holders.[20]

The Court admitted that this distinction could be "difficult to make," but the Court's holding was remarkably similar to the argument that Reynolds had unsuccessfully made in the *Gingles* case of 1986. By the 1990s the Supreme Court had belatedly recognized the need to place limits on racial gerrymanders. Justice Scalia explained that

> Racial classifications of any sort pose the risk of lasting harm to our society. They reinforce the belief, held by too many for too much of our history, that individuals should be judged by the color of their skin. Racial classifications with respect to voting carry particular dangers. Racial gerry-mandering, even for remedial purposes, may balkanize us into competing racial factions; it threatens to carry us further from the goal of a political system in which race no longer matters—a goal that the Fourteenth and Fifteenth Amendments embody, and to which the Nation continues to aspire.[21]

Notes

1. William H. Freivogel, "Reagan Administration Fought Rear-Guard Action on Enforcement," *St. Louis Post-Dispatch*, 26 March 1989.
2. Major v. Treen, 574 F.Supp. 325 (1983); Buskey v. Oliver, 565 F.Supp. 1473 (1983).
3. Thornburg v. Gingles, 478 U.S. 30 (1960); Hardy v. Wallace, 603 F.Supp. 174 (1985).
4. *Washington Monthly* (September 1987): 14, 11.
5. *New Republic* (2 September 1985): 21.
6. Ibid., 22, 23, 21; Thernstrom, *Whose Votes Count?*, 170. Thernstrom maintained that before 1982, and arguably until *Gingles* was decided in 1986, the "no retrogression" standard of *Beer v. U.S.* was the proper test for judging minority vote dilution. She complained that Reynolds nevertheless judged electoral districts on the basis of whether they were "fairly drawn"—that is, whether they conduced toward the election of a fair number of blacks. This argument impresses me as dubious for the period before 1982 and wrong for the period after 1982. In any case, I believe it is a weak foundation for challenging Reynolds's character and integrity.
7. Allen v. State Board of Elections, 393 U.S. 544 (1969), 569.
8. Interview with WBR, 28 February 1992.
9. Hardy v. Wallace, 603 F.Supp. 174 (1985).
10. Presley v. Etowah County Commission, 60 USLW 4135 (1992).
11. Thornburg v. Gingles, 478 U.S. 30 (1986).
12. Shaw v. Reno, 61 USLW 4818 (1993).
13. Ibid., 4822, 4820.
14. Thornburg v. Gingles, 478 U.S. 30 (1986), 50–51; Shaw v. Reno, 61 USLW 4818 (1993), 4822, 4823.
15. Johnson v. De Grandy, 62 USLW 4755 (1994), 4763.
16. Miller v. Johnson, 63 USLW 4726 (1995).
17. Ibid., 4728.
18. Ibid.
19. Ibid.

20. Ibid., 4729.
21. Ibid., 4730; Johnson v. De Grandy, 62 USLW 4755 (1994), 4764. Justices Thomas and Scalia also questioned the direction the Court had been taking ever since it sanctioned the concept of minority vote dilution in the *Allen* case of 1969, and Justice Kennedy said that race-based, majority-minority electoral districts were "entrench[ing] the very practice and stereotypes the Equal Protection Clause is set against." Holder v. Hall, 62 USLW, 4728 (1994), 4733 ff; Shaw v. Reno, 61 USLW 4818 (1993), 4826.

Part II

Affirmative Action

Introduction to Part II

Title VII of the 1964 Civil Rights Act declared that individuals should not be subjected to racial discrimination when they applied for a job or were considered for a promotion or a contract. Over the course of the next two decades, however, Title VII was reinterpreted to permit, and sometimes to require, affirmative racial preferences if nondiscrimination led to a significant, statistical underrepresentation of blacks and some other minority groups. The focus of those who enforced Title VII changed—as it also changed for those responsible for enforcing the laws on voting rights and school desegregation—from an emphasis on the rights of individuals to a preoccupation with the representation of groups.

Thanks to the Civil Rights Act, much of the old-fashioned discrimination against black workers came to an end. But civil rights activists were also concerned about policies that did not seem discriminatory at first glance but often had the effect of making it difficult for blacks to get ahead. They noted that some employers used intelligence and ability tests, while others required their employees to be literate or to have graduated from high school or college. The activists said that emphasis on testing and credentials was a subtle form of racial discrimination. They said that employers were using the new criteria as screening devices to keep blacks out of the workplace.

Many Americans undoubtedly distrusted inflated claims about the value of tests and credentials, but most did not regard *paper* requirements as a subtle form of racial discrimination. Therefore, when it came to enacting legislation to correct bias in employment, Congress did not prohibit testing. Bureaucrats in the Equal Employment Opportunity Commission eventually fashioned new standards that militated against testing and required affirmative race-conscious measures to introduce larger numbers of blacks into the work force; and the Supreme Court gave a qualified endorsement to this emphasis on numerical balance in an important case of 1971, *Griggs v. Duke Power Company*. Congress then seemed to accept this approach when it amended the Civil Rights Act in 1972 without criticizing *Griggs*.

But Congress never ruled against color-blind policies that affected blacks disproportionately. When it came to employment, Congress did not redefine goals the way it did with voting; in employment policy, there was nothing comparable to the 1982 revision of the Voting Rights Act of 1965.

Because the Civil Rights Act of 1964 was not altered fundamentally, and because the rule of law required that statues be applied as written and intended by the legislature, Ronald Reagan and William Bradford Reynolds held they had no choice but to oppose racial preferences and quotas. Because Congress had prohibited racial discrimination when it enacted the Civil Rights Act of 1964, Reagan and Reynolds said that employers must be color-blind and nondiscriminatory.

Beyond this, Reagan and Reynolds said that the use of racial discrimination in allocating limited opportunities inevitably infringed on the legitimate interests of people who were not members of the preferred race. While such discrimination might seem *benign* to those who benefited from the preferences, they held that it was not fair to others who were denied opportunities because of their race.

8

The Civil Rights Act, 1964

Students of the Reagan administration encounter a striking paradox. Those who favored strong affirmative employment policies accused the administration of disrespect for the law. Defenders of the administration said the same thing about the critics. Who was right? This question is fundamental to assessing the record of Ronald Reagan and William Bradford Reynolds.

I

Opinions differed because by the 1980s there was no consensus about the meaning of the Civil Rights Act of 1964. Title VII declared it an unlawful employment practice for labor organizations or businesses to discriminate against any individual because of race, color, religion, sex, or national origin. But what did that mean?[1]

According to some observers, the Civil Rights Act had no precise meaning; thus, the legal philosopher Ronald Dworkin argued that it was impossible for courts to discover, years after the event, the collective understanding that Congress had in mind when it prohibited discrimination. Discrimination could mean that an employer made distinctions or treated people differently because of race, or it could mean that the employer did not have a racially balanced work force. It was inevitable, Dworkin wrote, that "different judges, who disagree about morality, will therefore disagree about the [civil rights] statute."[2]

Some people complained that judges were undemocratically substituting their own political judgment for the judgment of the elected representatives of the people; but Dworkin said such criticism was wrong because it mistakenly assumed that Congress, in passing the law, had manifested an "institutionalized intention," a "collective understanding," that could be divined.[3]

Dworkin was not alone in denying the possibility of understanding the civil rights law. A number of legal scholars and epistemologists set themselves to the task of pointing out ambiguities, complexities, and inconsistencies. They read the text in such a way as to deny what most people had thought the law meant when it was enacted. They argued that it was not possible to know whether Congress, when it prohibited discrimination, established a policy that pointed toward equality of opportunity for all individuals or toward equality of results for different groups. Yale law professor Paul Gewirtz said the wording of the 1964 Civil Rights Act was "utterly vague."[4]

Others, however, insisted that the Civil Rights Act must have a settled meaning. They also thought that, under the U.S. system of separation of powers, it was the responsibility of elected legislators to enact laws, and that of bureaucrats and judges to give effect to the intent of the lawmakers. Even a liberal writer like Walter Goodman of the *New York Times* chastised "distinguished philosophers of the law like Ronald Dworkin" for advancing "ingenious arguments for their notions of equality, and never mind...what legislators thought they were legislating." Goodman complained that professors and judges had made themselves into "a priesthood, with the gift of extracting astounding meanings from the entrails of laws that seemed so plain to the unanointed mortals who voted them into existence."[5]

Civil rights activists and sympathizers recognized that many Americans did not subscribe to Dworkin's theory. It smacked too much of rejecting the possibility of distinguishing between truth and error, and it seemed to make the Civil Rights Act of 1964 mean what it would have said had it been written by left-liberal egalitarians.

Consequently, some of those who favored equality of results took a different tack. They conceded that the foundation for correct legal interpretation was to go to the language of the law and to the intention of the legislators who enacted it. But they argued that the purpose of the Civil Rights Act was to improve conditions for blacks. Therefore, they said, it was inconsistent with the basic policy of the act to construe it to forbid benign discrimination that was intended to help blacks.

Writing in the *Washington Post*, columnist Dorothy Gilliam pointed in this direction. She noted that when the Civil Rights Act was debated in 1964, many blacks had "a two-part objective." They wanted, first, to end racial discrimination against blacks; but, "recognizing that grievous imbalances had accrued during the long history of segregation and oppression," they also sought "to correct the system by balancing the scales in an affirmative way."[6]

Some scholars also made this point. David Garrow insisted that the civil rights movement sought more than "the elimination of racial discrimination [and]...a 'colorblind' approach to American society." Mike Davis said that "the ultimate goals" of the civil rights movement were "the mass incorporation of black labour into the high-wage economy [and] surmounting the barriers of de facto segregation in Northern schools and suburbs."[7]

Other scholars emphasized that the civil rights movement was divided over its goals. William H. Chafe noted that during the 1960s some civil rights activists began "to alter radically their understanding of the issues, rejecting the individualist and integrationist approach associated with the early movement and opting instead for a collectivist strategy." According to Chafe, most civil rights activists initially wanted "to forget about race, to have color-blind admissions to jobs and schools, to have black Americans treated as individuals with the color of their skin forgotten." But all along "there were others in the movement who sustained a vision of larger, more collective, more structural change." Eventually many of the leaders, including Martin Luther King, Jr., came to "a new understanding of what was necessary in American society to achieve racial justice." They rejected "the individualist and integrationist approach associated with the early movement and opt[ed] instead for a collectivist strategy" that pointed toward a "redistribution of wealth and power."[8]

In the Reagan Justice Department, Reynolds recognized that some leaders of the civil rights movement had favored racial preferences to benefit blacks, but he thought the advocates of affirmative discrimination were a minority element in the civil rights coalition of 1964. Reynolds believed that the great majority of the Congress that passed the Civil Rights Act subscribed to the core notion that no person should gain any advantage or suffer any hardship because of racial discrimination.[9]

In the Congress of 1964, Reynolds said, there had been a collective understanding that Title VII of the Civil Rights Act would prohibit the use of race-conscious criteria for hiring or promoting employees. Reynolds noted that the foremost proponent of the legislation, Senator Hubert Humphrey, unequivocally rejected the suggestion that Title VII was intended to countenance race-conscious preferences. According to Humphrey, Title VII "provide[d] that race shall not be a basis for making personnel decisions." It did "not provide that any preferential treatment...[should] be given to Negroes or to any other persons or groups. It [did] not provide that any quota systems may be established to maintain racial balance in employment. In fact, [it] would prohibit preferential treatment."[10]

Humphrey was not alone in expressing these views. Senator Edmund Muskie of Maine, another key supporter of the 1964 Act, expressed a similar understanding: "Every American citizen has the right to equal treatment—not favored treatment...just equal treatment." Senator Harrison Williams of New Jersey, another supporter of the act, assured skeptics that the new law could not possibly sanction preferences for blacks. "[How] can the language of equality "favor one race or one religion over another?" he asked. "Equality can have only one meaning," he said, "and that meaning is self-evident to reasonable men. Those who say that equality means favoritism do violence to common sense."[11]

Senator Joseph Clark, a Democrat from Pennsylvania, and Senator Clifford Case, a Republican from New Jersey, were designated the bipartisan "captains" for the bill. In a special interpretive memorandum, they specifically rejected the suggestion "that the concept of discrimination is vague." In fact, they said, "[I]t is clear and simple and has no hidden meanings": it meant that no individual person could be favored or penalized because of race; further, it did not mean that racial groups were entitled to any particular statistical representation.

> There is no requirement in Title VII that an employer maintain a racial balance in his work force. On the contrary, any deliberate attempt to maintain a racial balance...would involve a violation of Title VII because maintaining such a balance would require an employer to hire or to refuse to hire on the basis of race... He would not be obliged—or indeed permitted—to fire whites in order to hire Negroes, or to prefer Negroes for future vacancies, or, once Negroes are hired, to give them special seniority rights at the expense of the white workers hired earlier.[12]

To make this point as clearly as possible, the interpretive memorandum stated, "There is no requirement in Title VII that employers abandon bona fide qualification tests where, because of differences in background and education, members of some groups are able to perform better on these tests than members of other groups. An employer may set his qualifications as high as he likes, he may test to determine which applicants have these qualifications, and he may hire, assign, and promote on the basis of test performance."[13]

The *New York Times* expressed the prevailing contemporary understanding of the 1964 Civil Rights Act when it assured its readers that the new legislation "would not...require anyone to establish racial quotas." To underscore this point, the *Times* insisted, "To the contrary, such quotas would be forbidden as a racial test. The Bill does not require employers or unions to drop any standard for hiring or promotion or membership—except the discriminatory standard of race or religion."[14]

II

Ronald Reagan and William Bradford Reynolds understood the Civil Rights Act the way most people had in 1964. These views were also consistent with the conclusions of the two best scholarly histories of the Civil Rights Act of 1964: *Equality Transformed*, by Herman Belz; and *The Civil Rights Era*, by Hugh Davis Graham.

According to Belz, "at the time the Civil Rights Act was passed, equality of opportunity was a concept that, as much as possible in political life, had an agreed-upon if not self-evident meaning... [T]he Civil Rights Act of 1964 was intended to establish color-blind employment opportunity."[15]

It was not that the concept of benign discrimination was unknown in 1964. Belz noted that as early as 1962 the Congress of Racial Equality (CORE) had "made compensatory preference for blacks the object of protests against job bias." To compensate for the negative discrimination of the past, Roy Wilkins of the NAACP also urged that blacks "should be placed in the positions from which they [had been] excluded until racial imbalance was corrected."[16]

By 1963, Belz noted, preferential treatment had become a controversial question. The supporters of civil rights in Congress understood that some black leaders favored race-conscious benign discrimination, but the congressional sponsors knew that civil rights legislation would not pass unless it renounced all forms of racial preference. Accordingly, assurances were given, and an amendment added, to the effect that there could be no finding of racial discrimination without proof of a hostile intent to injure members of a racial group. Other amendments provided that plaintiffs would have the burden of proof and that racial imbalance could not be considered proof of discrimination.[17]

According to Belz, "Title VII was intended to settle the controversy over quotas and preferential treatment that existed in the early 1960s." It did so by avowing "the nondiscrimination principle that was at the heart of the bill." The sponsors of the Civil Rights Act gave repeated assurances that it was not "in any way intended or capable of being interpreted to promote race-conscious preferential practices."[18]

The research of Hugh Davis Graham led to similar conclusions. Graham noted that by 1963 even moderate black leaders like Whitney M. Young of the National Urban League were saying that "the 'simple act of granting "equal opportunity" to Negro citizens' and the mere disappearance of old barriers could not compensate for 300 years of discrimination." Young insisted that "equal opportunity is not sufficient," that employers should "give preference" to blacks, and that the national government should engage in compensatory, preferential spending for social programs. Young demanded "realistic compensation (not necessarily in money alone) and realistic reparation for past injuries."[19]

Other black leaders made similar demands. James Farmer of CORE favored compensatory preferences. So did Herbert Hill of the NAACP. Farmer and Hill no longer regarded employment discrimination as an invidious and injurious act. Rather, they defined discrimination statistically as a differential; it was the gap between black- and white-employment rates. They said that equal treatment was desirable if it produced equal results, but if equal treatment did not lead to equal results, the gap should be closed by taking affirmative action to achieve a better racial balance.[20]

Yet there was a problem with this approach. As Graham noted, "[I]t violated the American creed that rights inhered in individuals rather than in groups, and that immutable factors like race and ethnicity should be irrelevant as employment criteria." He noted further that even "such pillars of the liberal establishment as the *New York Times*...and Senator Hubert Humphrey rejected...the notion of racial preference." Graham pointed out that they did so in Title VII itself, which made it clear that discrimination could not be properly inferred from statistical patterns in employment, and they did so by repeatedly asserting that the legislation would not permit employers to give racial preferences of any sort.[21]

They did so as well, Graham wrote, by adding amendments to Title VII. Thus the word "intentionally" was added to Section 703(g) of Title VII to make it clear that discrimination could not properly be inferred from statistical differences. Another amendment (Section 703[h]) protected differences in compensation or conditions of employment that resulted from seniority systems. Another provision in Section 703(h) authorized employers to use ability and aptitude tests, provided they were developed by professional psychologists and were not in-house tests that could be manipulated to serve discriminatory purposes.[22]

Thus, the historical research of Belz and Graham supports Reagan and Reynolds's contention that the Civil Rights Act of 1964 resulted from a collective understanding in Congress. The purpose of Title VII was to improve economic conditions for blacks by establishing the principle of nondiscrimination and by guaranteeing equal employment opportunity. Congress wanted to help blacks by prohibiting the use of race-conscious criteria in the work place. Reynolds was right when he said that both the legislative history and the language of Title VII mandated "color blindness in employment decisions." He was right when he said Congress had "rejected special interest legislation in the area of civil rights." He was right when he said Congress had made it "clear that the rights protected...are universal in their application to *all* persons."[23]

But Reynolds was wrong about one thing. A recurring theme in Reynolds's speeches was that the original dream of the civil rights movement—the dream of equal opportunity and color-blind nondiscrimination—"began to fade in the 1970s." It was "in the 1970s," Reynolds said, that "the colorblind ideal that had been the civil rights rallying cry for more than a decade began to give ground to a new demand. Instead of race neutrality, 'racial balance,' and 'racial preference' were increasingly advanced as necessary means of overcoming racial discrimination." It was "during the 1970s," that "the quest for equality of opportunity gradually evolved into an insistence upon equality of results."[24]

The research of Herman Belz and Hugh Davis Graham has demonstrated something else—that the effort to alter the original understanding of the Civil Rights Act began even before the ink on the legislation was dry. Belz and Graham have shown that civil rights activists who were committed to equality of results joined the bureaucratic agencies that were established or augmented to enforce the Civil Rights Act. From the outset, these agencies implemented the new law in a way that was at odds with the spirit and the letter of the Civil Rights Act. Belz and Graham have been particularly severe in their criticism of the Equal Employment Opportunity Commission (EEOC), which Graham characterized as a "subversive bureaucracy." But much the same could have been said of the U. S. Commission on Civil Rights; the Office of Federal Contract Compliance; the Office of Civil Rights in the Department of Health, Education and Welfare; and the Civil Rights Division in the Department of Justice.[25]

The research of Belz and Graham makes it clear that Reynolds was too generous when he assessed the conduct of civil rights activists. Reynolds said the activists had embraced racial preferences only after they became "impatient" with the pace of the progress that resulted from fighting against racial discrimination and working for equality of opportunity. Belz and Graham have shown that from the outset the activists were not concerned with discrimination but with ensuring that minorities were distributed in numbers equal to their proportion of the population. Belz and Graham have further shown that the activists knew that their efforts ran contrary to "a normal, traditional, and literal interpretation of Title VII."[26]

Reynolds said the activists "were motivated by the best of intentions" (but warned about "men of zeal, well meaning but without understanding").[27]

Belz and Graham were more severe in their judgments. Graham noted that the transformation of civil rights was related to a larger problem of "clientele capture." Just as some of the bureaucracies that were set up to regulate business and economic activity were *captured* by the interests they were supposed to regulate, so the civil rights bureaucracy was captured by activists who did not subscribe to the ideas that underlay the Civil Rights Act. According to Graham, the civil rights bureaucrats had a "fundamental disagreement" with the law they were supposed to enforce, but they were careful, however, to avoid a candid public discussion of their ideas about what discrimination meant and what equality required.[28]

Belz was especially harsh. Since "the purpose of Title VII [was] to improve the economic status of blacks by guaranteeing equal employment opportunity based on the nondiscrimination principle," Belz considered it a grievous breach of faith for bureaucrats who were sworn to enforce the law to impose racial preferences in the name of law enforcement. The bureaucrats thought (and sometimes said) that it was not enough to cease discrimination. They wanted compensatory preferences to remedy what they regarded as the effects of past discrimination—though, as Belz insisted, "[t]he rule of law" requires that laws be enforced as they are written and understood.[29]

In accounting for this misfeasance, Paul Craig Roberts and Lawrence M. Stratton have emphasized the role of Alfred W. Blumrosen, a Rutgers law professor who was the EEOC's first compliance chief. "Blumrosen disdained the Civil Rights Act's definition of discrimination," Roberts and Stratton concluded, "preferr[ing] a definition that Congress had rejected." He redefined discrimination as "anything that yielded statistical disparities."[30]

Blumrosen was able to do this because Franklin Delano Roosevelt, Jr., the EEOC's first chairman, spent much of his time yachting. "Staffers jokingly changed the lyrics of the song 'Anchors Aweigh' and sang 'Franklin's Away' during his frequent absences. Roosevelt resigned before the year was out, and his successors stayed little longer. The EEOC had four chairmen in its first five years, which enhanced Blumrosen's power."[31]

Blumrosen knew he was treading on thin legal ice. He recognized that the Civil Rights Act forbade invidious racial discrimination, not the use of defensible tests and standards that a disproportionately large number of blacks failed to pass or satisfy. Nevertheless, Blumrosen "bet" that his *creative* interpretation of the Civil Rights Act would be upheld by the courts. History would prove him right.[32]

III

By themselves, Blumrosen and other like-minded civil rights bureaucrats could not have transformed the Civil Rights Act. They succeeded because they eventually persuaded federal courts that the act required an end to practices and policies that resulted in what was called the underutilization of blacks. According to this theory, which is called the *disparate impact* theory, the failure of blacks to be proportionally distributed in various occupations was presumed to be due to forms of institutional discrimination that are in violation of the Civil Rights Act.[33]

One of the early judicial cases that moved toward disparate impact (and away from the *harmful intent* theory of discrimination) involved the Crown Zellerbach Corporation. Before 1963 many of the company's jobs in production and maintenance were officially restricted for whites. After desegregation, all applicants for the jobs were required to attain certain minimum scores on professionally developed examinations. Since Crown Zellerbach had not required such tests in the days when jobs were segregated, there was the suspicion that the company was using the tests as a covert system of discrimination. But, as noted, Congress had sanctioned the use of professionally developed tests when it enacted Section 703(h).

After it turned out that whites generally scored better than blacks on both the verbal and the nonverbal portions of the tests, a black man by the name of Robert Hicks challenged the company's use of the tests. Although Hicks presented no evidence to prove that Crown Zellerbach had used the tests for the purpose of discriminating against blacks, the district court concluded that in the circumstances of the case, an inference of discrimination was warranted. The court further stated that "a practice need not be adopted with the purpose or intent of discriminating to be invalidated under Title VII." The court embraced an argument that the EEOC put forward: that "a practice which significantly prefers whites over Negroes...must fall before Title VII unless the employer can show business necessity for it."[34]

The *Crown Zellerbach* court did not define *business necessity*, although the phrase suggests the notion of a practice that is indispensable for the company. This impression was reinforced when, in a case from Mississippi, the Fifth Circuit Court indicated that it would not be enough for employers to show that practices with a disparate impact led only to increased efficiency.

The Mississippi case concerned the highway patrol, where only six of the ninety-one patrolmen who were added to the force in the early 1970s were black. These black patrolmen made up only 6.6 percent of the recent hires in a state where blacks constituted 37 percent of the general population. The disparity was so great that the Fifth Circuit Court declared that "these figures alone negate the State's argument that its practices are nondiscriminatory."[35]

The Fifth Circuit Court found special fault with Mississippi for requiring that patrolmen must possess a high-school diploma and must make a score of at least 110 on the Army General Classification Test. The court acknowledged that many whites also failed to make the grade—"that in the search for high quality patrol officers, both whites and blacks have been rejected in substantial numbers." But the court ruled that because of disparate impact, Mississippi must develop different hiring criteria.[36]

Not all judges of the Fifth Circuit Court were comfortable with the decision. While agreeing that "no properly qualified person should be denied appointment...on account of race," Judge J. P. Coleman was troubled by the court's "open hints that minimum requirements for eligibility may be reduced, that the requirement of a high school diploma or its equivalent may be dispensed with, and that the State may not really satisfy itself of the intelligence of [members of the highway patrol]." Coleman declared that neither the Fourteenth Amendment nor the Civil Rights Act meant that citizens "must be subjected to arrest, imprisonment, and even more deadly dangers at the hands of incompetent officers of whatever race."[37]

But Coleman was a lone dissenter. In the opinion he drafted for the court, Judge Walter Pettus Gewin explained that "to eliminate the effects of past discrimination," it was necessary to require "clear and convincing evidence [of] the necessity of any...objective requirements which black applicants have difficulty in satisfying." Lest there be any uncertainty about the court's meaning, Chief Judge John R. Brown and Judge John Minor Wisdom, in a separate concurrence, wrote that "until all traces of discrimination against blacks were removed, blacks would be accorded the same treatment as that accorded whites in the era of discrimination."[38]

Elsewhere in the South, district and circuit courts proffered a different interpretation of the Civil Rights Act. In a case involving the Duke Power Company of North Carolina, both district and appellate courts allowed the company to require that potential employees must have graduated from high school, even though such a requirement affected blacks adversely.[39]

Prior to 1965, Duke Power had openly discriminated on the basis of race. It had refused to hire blacks for skilled and semiskilled work at the Dan River Steam Station, a power-generating facility. It employed blacks only in the labor department, where the highest-paying jobs paid less than the lowest-paying jobs in other departments. In 1955 the company also instituted a policy of requiring a high-school education for initial assignment to any department except that of labor. The company also required prospective workers to make satisfactory scores (that is, scores equivalent to those achieved by an average high-school graduate) on two professionally developed intelligence tests.

In 1970 Willie Griggs and twelve other black laborers at the steam station claimed that Duke's use of the high school and testing requirements violated the Civil Rights Act. Griggs acknowledged that the company no longer barred blacks from work in any department at the steam station. Griggs also acknowledged that discrimination on the basis of education was not intrinsically illegal. But he argued that Duke's requirements should not be allowed to stand in North Carolina, where in 1960 only 12 percent of blacks (as compared with 34 percent of whites) had graduated from high school, where only 6 percent of blacks passed the tests (as compared with 58 percent of whites), and where schools that were predominantly black were generally inferior to those that were predominantly white.[40]

In these circumstances, Griggs said, nondiscrimination in the present was not enough to remedy the effects of past discrimination. The educational requirements, which appeared racially neutral on their face, actually worked to continue the effects of the state's inferior black schools.

While acknowledging the disparate impact, the district court ruled in favor of the company. It did so because the Civil Rights Act had prohibited only "intentional" discrimination, because Section 703(h) authorized testing, and because Section 703(j) rejected the possibility of preferential treatment to compensate for racial imbalance. The district court also emphasized that there was a business justification for the requirements because the company's policy had been to promote from within. Consequently, the company wanted employees to have more than the minimum skills needed to perform an entry-level job. It wanted entry-level employees who possessed enough education and intelligence to merit promotion to supervisory positions at some time in the future. It also wanted employees who could read and understand manuals relating to boilers, turbines, and other complicated mechanical and electrical equipment that was used at the Dan River Steam Station.[41]

On appeal, the Fourth Circuit Court affirmed most of the district court's holdings. Like the district court, the circuit court thought it significant that the company used "an intracompany promotion system to train its own employees for supervisory positions." Because of this, the circuit court said, the company's educational requirements were valid under Section 703(h)—which authorized the use of professionally developed tests. The tests were "job related" and served "a legitimate business purpose" because they gave the company "some reasonable assurance that its [entry-level]employees could advance into supervisory positions."[42]

Significantly, both the district court and the circuit court explicitly rejected the EEOC's interpretation of the Civil Rights Act. In Willie Griggs's case, and in many similar cases, EEOC argued that educational requirements and tests that had disparate impact should be prohibited unless social scientists convincingly demonstrated that the requirements accurately predicted a person's ability to perform a particular job. Since there was no convincing evidence that high school graduates were better than dropouts when it came to shoveling coal or performing other entry-level labor at the Dan River Station, EEOC maintained that the company had illegally seized upon educational requirements as a means of camouflaging racial discrimination.

The circuit court conceded that "great weight" should be given to an interpretation that had been developed "by an agency which was established to administer the statute," but the circuit court nevertheless concluded that the EEOC's disparate impact doctrine should not be read into the act. According to the Fourth Circuit Court, the disparate impact theory was "clearly contrary to compelling legislative history" and, with respect to intelligence tests, was also at odds with the history and language of Section 703(h).[43]

Thus, by 1971 the Civil Rights Act had come to mean different things in different parts of the United States. In the Fourth Circuit (which included several Southern states along the Atlantic seaboard), employers were allowed to give intelligence tests to prospective workers and to establish educational requirements. They were allowed to do so even if there was an adverse effect on blacks—as long as there was a credible argument that the tests and requirements served a useful business purpose and as long as there was no proof that they were being used to discriminate because of race. By way of contrast, in the Fifth Circuit (which included several states on the Gulf of Mexico), the Civil Rights Act was interpreted to prohibit tests and requirements that had a disparate impact—unless employers could prove that the tests and requirements were necessary to obtain satisfactory performance of particular jobs.

In 1971 the Supreme Court settled the conflict between the two circuits. In *Griggs v. Duke Power Company*, the high court sided with the Fifth Circuit. It ruled that the Civil Rights Act forbade employers from requiring a high-school education or a passing score on an intelligence test as a condition of employment, because neither standard was shown to be precisely related to successful performance of specific entry-level jobs and because the tests and requirements operated to disqualify a greater proportion of black applicants than white.[44]

In the opinion he wrote for the Court, Chief Justice Burger said that the Civil Rights Act proscribed "not only overt discrimination but also practices that are fair in form, but discriminatory in operation." Burger said "[T]he touchstone is business necessity." He said that neither the high-school completion requirement nor the general intelligence tests had been shown to bear "a demonstrable relationship" to the performance of the entry-level jobs in question.[45]

The chief justice conceded that the company had no discriminatory purpose. The requirements had been instituted because the company thought they "generally would improve the overall quality of the work force." But Burger said that this was not enough: "Good intent or absence of discriminatory intent does not redeem employment procedures or testing mechanisms...[that affect blacks adversely] and are unrelated to measuring job capability."[46]

Burger included some statements to soften the tone of the Court's opinion. He admitted that "Congress did not intend by Title VII...to guarantee a job to every person regardless of qualifications." He wrote that "the Act does not command that any person be hired simply because he was formerly the subject of discrimination, or because he is a member of a minority group," and also stated, "Discriminatory preference for any group, minority or majority, is precisely and only what Congress has proscribed." He did not argue that Congress, when it prohibited discrimination, intended to prohibit whatever civil rights activists considered undesirable.[47]

Instead, Burger maintained that when it came to comprehending the collective understanding that Congress had in mind when it passed the Civil

Rights Act, deference should be given to the guidelines the EEOC had developed. EEOC said that Congress had recognized that a test that was useful for one purpose was not necessarily valid for another. An intelligence test that might be adequate to determine fitness for a supervisory job might be grossly unfair if used in hiring a machine operator. According to EEOC, Congress intended to permit only the use of tests that were related to specific jobs.[48]

Thus the Court embraced the theoretical idea that the Civil Rights Act should be understood to mean what its framers thought it meant when they passed the legislation. But while the Court conceded this point, it sided with the civil rights activists on the practical points at issue. It did so by concluding that Alfred Blumrosen and the EEOC's construction of the Civil Rights Act was well supported by the legislative history. If an employment practice affected minorities adversely, the *Griggs* Court said, employers had to bear the burden of proving that the practice was job-related and necessary for the success of the business.

What can be said by way of assessing *Griggs*? Professor Graham concluded that the Court had misconstrued history. Its "interpretations in 1971 of the legislative intent of Congress in the Civil Rights Act would have been greeted with disbelief in 1964."[49]

Professor Belz was equally blunt. He conceded that *Griggs* gave the civil rights activists a stunning victory by adopting the disparate impact theory. But, like Graham, Belz concluded that the Supreme Court had redefined the meaning of equality in the work place and had adopted a theory of discrimination that was at odds with the requirements and the intent of the Civil Rights Act.[50]

While Graham and Belz questioned the accuracy of the Court's legal history, others challenged the social science that was implicit in *Griggs*. *Griggs* assumed that there was only a weak correlation between scores on intelligence tests and job performance. But the records in hundreds of personnel departments have established that performance on broadly based intelligence tests correlated with job performance in dozens of areas and that these tests also appear to predict job performance equally well for blacks and whites.[51]

How, then, can one account for *Griggs*? Professor Belz pointed to the race riots of the late 1960s. He said discrimination was redefined in terms of disparate impact because leaders of the dominant institutions came to regard such definition as "the price society had to pay to prevent further violence in the black community." Belz wrote, "Considered in the abstract, few Americans then or now accept the notions of group rights and equality of results." But such notions were implemented in the name of the Civil Rights Act because by the late 1960s, elite opinion considered this approach to be "a politically expedient response to the race riots."[52]

There was more. *Griggs* came down at a time when most Americans were confident that the national economy could easily absorb the cost of affirmative action. The opinion of the Supreme Court was written in 1971, at the end of the post-World War II era of steadily rising prosperity and at a time when some prominent economists were writing books about the problems of affluence. Others were telling congressional committees that Americans would soon enjoy a twenty-two hour work week. In 1972 actuaries in the Social Security system said that for the foreseeable future, real wages in the United States would rise at the rate of 56 percent every two decades.[53]

With these assumptions in vogue, almost anything seemed affordable. Most people did not worry about the cost of using affirmative preferences to remedy adverse impact. Even if Congress had not been thinking in terms of remedies for disparate impact when it passed the Civil Rights Act, it seemed in the early 1970s that no one would really suffer if blacks were given special breaks and were not required to measure up to conventional standards.

There was, in addition, an historical argument for *Griggs*. Some proponents of racial preferences said that Congress approved the disparate impact theory and ratified *Griggs* when it amended Title VII in 1972. Katherine J. Thompson, a proponent of this view, conceded that *Griggs* was at odds with the principle of color-blind nondiscrimination that underlay the Civil Rights Act of 1964, but she maintained that the Congress of 1972 was so pleased with *Griggs* that it added amendments that amounted to a ratification of disparate impact.[54]

One of the 1972 amendments to Title VII increased the authority of the EEOC, the government agency that had pioneered and developed the concept of disparate impact. In 1964 members of Congress were concerned that the EEOC would become such a strong advocate for blacks that it could not serve as an impartial forum for discrimination cases. Accordingly, the legislation of 1964 authorized EEOC to investigate allegations of discrimination and to attempt to conciliate differences, but under the 1964 legislation, EEOC was denied authority to issue cease and desist orders against discriminatory employers. It could not even take alleged violators to court. Only the Department of Justice (in addition to individual plaintiffs) was authorized to initiate lawsuits. In 1972, however, EEOC was authorized to issue cease and desist orders and to bring civil suits for violation of the Civil Rights Act.[55]

Another amendment of 1972 increased the remedial authority of the federal courts. In 1964 federal judges had been authorized to order "such affirmative action as may be appropriate" in order "to make persons whole for injuries suffered on account of unlawful employment discrimination." In 1972 the power of the judges was augmented by new language that authorized a court to order, in addition to affirmative action, "any other equitable relief [that] the court deems appropriate."[56]

In explaining the reasons for the 1972 amendments, several members of Congress said they belatedly had come to recognize that employment discrimination went beyond ill will and intentional wrongs. The Senate Report that accompanied the 1972 amendments summed up this view, stating that "employment discrimination as viewed today is a...complex and pervasive phenomenon. Experts familiar with the subject now generally describe the problem in terms of 'systems' and 'effects' rather than simply intentional wrongs." These experts, the report noted, said it was "institutional racism" if a company used merit standards of hiring or promoting and if those standards failed to produce a proportional outcome for blacks.[57]

Along with statements about institutional racism, some members of Congress referred to the Supreme Court's decision in *Griggs*. The Congress that enacted the amendments of 1972 recognized that under *Griggs* there could be violations of Title VII even if employers did not intend to discriminate. The Congress of 1972 also seemed to have *Griggs* in mind when it increased the authority of the EEOC and when it specifically authorized judges to give "any other equitable relief the court deems appropriate."[58]

The Congress of 1972 also rejected an antipreference amendment introduced by Senator Sam Ervin of North Carolina. This ammendment stipulated that no court or government agency should require an employer "to practice discrimination in reverse by employing persons of a particular race...in either fixed or variable numbers, proportions, percentages, quotas, goals, or ranges." This proposal lost, 22 to 44.[59]

Thus, it can be argued that the Congress of 1972 altered the antidiscriminatory core of the Civil Rights Act of 1964. The Congress of 1972 rejected Senator Ervin's proposal to ban racial preferences and, instead, increased the authority of the EEOC and the discretion of federal judges. At the same time, some members of Congress praised *Griggs* and indicated satisfaction with the prospect that *Griggs* would continue to govern the interpretation of Title VII. Katherine J. Thompson has concluded that "[a]n examination of the legislative history of the 1972 amendments to the Civil Rights Act of 1964 reveals that the disparate impact theory of discrimination was ratified in the 1972 amendments."[60]

Other scholars are not convinced. Michael Evan Gold has rejected the argument that the Congress of 1972 shifted the basic premise of the 1964 Civil Rights Act. The argument would be convincing, Gold conceded, if Congress had amended in any relevant way the section of the 1964 law (Section 703) that contained the basic definitions of discrimination. But Congress did not do so. The argument would have some force if Congress had deleted a reference in Section 706(g) that required proof that an employer had intentionally engaged in discrimination before a court could order relief; but although the Senate proposed such a deletion, the House of Representatives insisted on preserving the intent requirement. Nor did Congress amend the provision with which *Griggs* was most concerned, the provision that authorized testing (Section 703(h)); instead, it rejected a proposal that would have required that tests must be job-related.[61]

Herman Belz, in agreeing with Gold, wrote, "Congress did not revise the substantive requirements of Title VII." Belz noted, in addition, that the Senate's rejection of Senator Ervin's proposals "cannot properly be regarded...as constituting statutory approval of preferential treatment." Hugh Davis Graham concurred. "Historically," he wrote, "the Supreme Court has resisted inferences of congressional intent from *nonaction*."[62]

Graham further explained that passage of the 1972 amendments was influenced by political calculations that had little to do with a consideration of the legal merits of *Griggs*. In 1972 President Richard M. Nixon, a Republican, favored preferences as a tactic to split apart two traditionally Democratic voting blocs—blacks and organized labor. By reserving for blacks a proportion of jobs on government projects, Nixon calculated, the Republicans might win support from established civil rights groups; and by forcing contractors to disregard the prerogatives of the predominantly white, union hiring halls, Nixon could also retaliate against unions that were a major source of funds for the Democratic party.[63]

The *Philadelphia Plan* proved to be the instrument for implementing Nixon's strategy. First developed in 1965 as a means for combating discrimination in the construction trades, the Philadelphia Plan postponed the award of federal construction funds to successful low bidders until the winning contractors promised to hire a certain number of blacks in all job categories. This required contractors to disregard the portion of union contracts that required them to employ only workers sent from union halls.

A good case could be made for the Philadelphia Plan in the 1960s, when a government official reported that there were only 25 to 30 blacks among the 8,500 members of seven of the twenty-two building trades in Philadelphia. Although the seven discriminatory unions made up only 4 percent of the union members in Philadelphia, and other unions had much better records, it made sense to the Department of Labor that they insist that an acceptable number of blacks should be employed on projects that were funded by the government.[64]

By the late 1960s the discriminatory unions had better records, and the Philadelphia Plan fell into disuse. In Philadelphia, the 5,000-member Local 542 of the operating engineers, which had been all white in 1960, included 800 to 900 minority workers and 150 minority apprentices by 1967.[65]

Under the guidance of Nixon's Department of Labor, however, the Philadelphia Plan was revived, revised, and expanded. In 1969 an assistant secretary announced that a new Philadelphia-style plan would be put into effect "in all the major cities across the Nation." He explained that specific "standards for percentages of minority employees" were necessary and said that "visible, measurable goals to correct obvious imbalances are essential." Moreover, the original Philadelphia Plan, which had been tailored to correct local pockets of discrimination in construction, would be applied to all federal contractors. According to Nixon's director of the Office of Federal Contract Compliance (OFCC), "The rate of minority applicants recruited should approximate or equal the ratio of minorities to the applicant population in each location."[66]

At the heart of Nixon's revised Philadelphia Plan was a model of proportional representation. The OFCC would hold up government contracts if the number of blacks employed did not fall within a specific target range. The target range generally represented a splitting of the difference between the proportion of blacks in the community and the proportion in the relevant labor pool. Thus, for plumbers and pipe fitters in Philadelphia, the target range in 1973 was 22 percent to 26 percent—because blacks made up 30 percent of the metropolitan population and 12 percent of the skilled construction workers.[67]

The Nixon administration tried to finesse the Civil Rights Act's ban on quotas and preferences. It said the numerical figures were merely "targets" or "goals." It said the new policies were "not intended and will not be used to discriminate against any qualified applicant or employee." But the administration's rhetoric could not obscure the reality. The targets and ranges were thinly disguised minority quotas. Nixon's plan was at odds with Senator Humphrey's assurance that the Civil Rights Act would prohibit government officials from requiring the "hiring, firing, or promotion of employees in order to meet a racial 'quota' or to achieve a certain racial balance."[68]

By a vote of 52 to 37, the Senate passed a rider that denounced Nixon's plan as violative of the 1964 Civil Rights Act, but the administration rallied its forces in the House of Representatives to defeat the Senate rider, 208–156. "The contest confounded normal alignments," Hugh Davis Graham observed, "as labor joined the Southern Democrats in opposition [to Nixon], and the Nixon administration joined the civil rights liberals." Thus, Nixon "even[ed] the score against labor," which had opposed him in several past elections.[69]

There were long-range consequences that Nixon did not anticipate. Senator Ervin would get his revenge when he chaired the Senate committee that investigated the Watergate scandal. In addition, opposition to the Philadelphia Plan and racial quotas eventually emerged in the Republican party. In the 1980s, under the leadership of Reagan and Reynolds, Republicans would repudiate Nixon's legacy in affirmative action.

In the short term, however, Nixon's gambit worked well. In the presidential campaign of 1972, Nixon offered the revised and expanded Philadelphia

Plan as a way to improve the economic conditions of blacks. He confounded Democrats by driving a wedge between two of their core constituencies—organized labor and civil rights groups. There was a congressional majority for the amendments of 1972, but that majority resulted from the exigencies of politics rather than from a calculated rejection of the principle of nondiscrimination.

IV

When they accused one another of disregarding the law, critics and partisans of Reagan and Reynolds pointed to different historical records. When Reagan said that liberal judges and bureaucrats had "turned our civil rights laws on their head," he meant they had taken a law that forbade discrimination—the Civil Rights Act of 1964—and had twisted it into a statute that was being used to "enforce discrimination in favor of some groups." When New York attorney Thomas Barr accused the Reagan administration of "a disregard for the rule of law," he meant that Reagan and Reynolds rejected the preferential policies that judges and bureaucrats (and the Nixon administration) had been using to promote the interests of blacks.[70]

Reagan and Reynolds had a straightforward understanding of the Civil Rights Act. For them, the act was a nondiscrimination law. It meant that no individual should benefit or suffer because of that person's race.

The argument of the administration's critics was multifaceted. Some legal theorists said the government should feel free to enforce any racial policy because it was impossible to know the intention of the Congress of 1964. Others said the Civil Rights Act of 1964 allowed for benign discrimination; and that any doubt on this score was resolved in 1972 when Congress rejected Senator Ervin's proposal, increased the authority of the EEOC, and authorized federal judges to give victims of discrimination "appropriate" equitable relief.

Critics of the Reagan administration said the concept of disparate impact inevitably pointed toward proportional representation. Therefore, they said, when members of the Congress of 1972 referred approvingly to the *Griggs* decision, they implicitly endorsed the idea that a policy was discriminatory if it did not lead to proportional employment of the races. A spokesman for the EEOC said that the 1972 amendments meant that "Congress said the EEOC view [of the Civil Rights Act] was correct and gave us the power to *force* employers and unions to adopt *our* view."[71]

Reynolds answered every point. He noted that the amended law of 1972 still defined discrimination in terms of individual rights in that it prohibited discrimination against "any individual...because of such individual's race."

It required that courts, before awarding relief, must find that employers or unions had purposely engaged in discrimination. It also said that equitable relief should not be given to anyone who suffered "for any reason other than discrimination on account of race."[72]

Reynolds especially took issue with critics who inferred congressional intent from nonaction. The critics' argument was that because Congress did not enact Senator Ervin's proposal to ban preferences and because Congress did not repudiate *Griggs*, it tacitly assented to disparate impact and to preferences for proportionality.

In response, Reynolds said it was not possible to infer intent from nonaction. There were too many alternative explanations: one was that in 1972 President Nixon was more adroit politically than Senator Ervin; another was that affirmative action was so controversial that Congress generally gave it wide berth and had acquiesced in whatever was done by a succession of presidents, courts, and bureaucrats; and a third was that the Senate voted against Ervin because the senator was trying to prolong a filibuster by proposing "a barrage of amendments." In voting against Ervin's proposed ban on preferences, Reynolds wrote, "[I]t is entirely possible that Senators seeking to end the filibuster (and who voted against all proposed amendments) were voting not on the merits of each amendment, but on the judgment that the filibuster could be ended only by voting down each of the filibusterer's amendments."[73]

Reynolds also noted that it was not clear, in 1972, that disparate impact would require preferences to achieve proportionality. In *Griggs*, Chief Justice Burger wrote that "discriminatory preference, for any group, minority or majority, is precisely and only what Congress has proscribed." In another post-*Griggs* case, the Supreme Court declared that it was "clear beyond cavil that the obligation imposed by Title VII is to provide an equal opportunity for *each* applicant regardless of race, without regard to whether members of the applicant's race are already proportionately represented in the work force."[74]

Reynolds also rejected one of the critics' basic premises. The critics said that before departing from the affirmative preferences that the Nixon administration had implemented and that had continued during the administrations of Presidents Ford and Carter, the Reagan administration should seek authorization from Congress. In making such demands, Reynolds said, the critics were saying that more had to be done in the 1980s to repeal preferences than the initiators of the policy had done in the 1970s. The critics said, in effect, that policies that had been created by unelected judges and bureaucrats could be ended only by surmounting the checks and balances of the legislative process. To Reynolds, this was unfair, because the civil rights organizations that were not strong enough to persuade Congress to endorse proportionality in 1964 and 1972 still did have enough influence at that time to prevent Congress from disestablishing the preferential policies that EEOC bureaucrats and federal judges had put into place.[75]

Beyond this, there was the matter of decision making in a democracy. Reynolds knew that the debate over the true meaning of equality would continue—but in the presidential election campaigns of 1980 and 1984, Ronald Reagan said the civil rights laws required equality of opportunity, not equality of results. In those election campaigns, Reagan promised to move the nation back to the principle of the 1964 Civil Rights Act—color-blind nondiscrimination. As Reynolds saw it, his job was to develop a legal strategy to implement Reagan's promise.[76]

Notes

1. Public Law No. 88–352 (1964), codified as amended at 42 U.S.C. #2000 (1982).
2. *New York Review of Books* (20 December 1979): 41.
3. Ibid., 39 and passim.
4. *New Republic* (12 August 1991): 19.
5. *Harper's* (March 1985): 73.
6. *Washington Post*, 11 November 1985, B3d.
7. *Nation* (4 May 1985): 535, 537; *New Left Review*, 143 (January-February, 1984): 18.
8. "The End of One Struggle, the Beginning of Another," in Charles W. Eagles, ed., *The Civil Rights Movement in America* (Jackson: University Press of Mississippi, 1986), 134, 131, 137, 135–36.
9. WBR, speech to Fourth Annual Conference on Equal Employment Opportunity, 20 October 1981, WBR Papers; interview with WBR, 28 February 1992.
10. 110 *Congressional Record* (1964), 6553, 11848; Ronald Dworkin, "How to Read the Civil Rights Act," *New York Review of Books* (20 December 1979): 40; WBR, speech to American Bar Association, 9 August 1982, WBR Papers; Clint Bolick, "Legal and Policy Aspects of Testing," *Journal of Vocational Behavior*, 33 (December 1988): 320.
11. 110 *Congressional Record* (1964), 12614, 8921; William Bradford Reynolds, "Tending the Civil Rights Garden," *Wake Forest Law Review*, 25 (1990): 202, 201.
12. 110 *Congressional Record* (1964), 7212–15.
13. Ibid., 7213.
14. *New York Times*, 8 May 1964, 32:2.
15. Herman Belz, *Equality Transformed* (New Brunswick: Transaction Publishers, 1991), 8, 17.
16. Ibid., 20, 21. For a thorough discussion of the civil rights leaders' support for affirmative preferences, see Paul D. Moreno, "Fair Employment: Law and Policy, 1933–1972" (Ph.D. diss., University of Maryland, 1994).
17. Then Justice Rehnquist made the same point: "It may be that one or more of the principal sponsors of Title VII would have preferred to see a provision allowing preferential treatment of minorities written into the bill. Such a provision, however, would have to have been expressly or impliedly excepted from Title VII's explicit prohibition of all racial discrimination in employment. There is no such exception in the Act. And a reading of the legislative debates concerning Title

VII, in which proponents and opponents alike uniformly denounced discrimination in favor of, as well as discrimination against Negroes, demonstrates clearly that any legislator harboring an unspoken desire for such a provision could not possibly have succeeded in enacting it into law." United Steelworkers v. Weber, 443 U.S. 193 (1979), 222.

18. Herman Belz, *Equality Transformed*, 24. Everett M. Dirkson, the Republican minority leader in the Senate, played an important role in adding amendments to the civil rights bill. Since Southern Democrats were filibustering the bill, and a two-thirds vote was required to end the filibuster, Dirkson was in a key position. "The bill can't pass unless [we] get Ev Dirkson," President Johnson declared. Dirkson demanded the amendments as his price for breaking the filibuster and supporting the civil rights bill. See Paul Craig Roberts and Lawrence M. Stratton, *The New Color Line*, 79–81.
19. Hugh Davis Graham, *The Civil Rights Era: Origins and Development of National Policy, 1960–1972* (New York: Oxford University Press, 1990), 111–13.
20. Ibid., 117–20.
21. Ibid., 120.
22. Ibid., 147, 149–50.
23. Herman Belz, *Equality Transformed*, 26; WBR, remarks at Equal Opportunity Conference, 20 October 1981; WBR, remarks to National Urban League, 2 August 1983, WBR Papers.
24. WBR, remarks at Amherst College, 29 April 1983; at American Bar Association, 9 August 1982; at Washington Center, 4 January 1984, WBR Papers.
25. Hugh Davis Graham, *The Civil Rights Era*, 152, 190.
26. WBR, remarks at Equal Employment Opportunity Conference, 20 October 1981, WBR Papers; Hugh Davis Graham, *The Civil Rights Era*, 248.
27. WBR remarks at Equal Employment Opportunity Conference, 20 October 1981, WBR Papers.
28. Hugh Davis Graham, *The Civil Rights Era*, 469, 248.
29. Herman Belz, *Equality Transformed*, 26.
30. Paul Craig Roberts and Lawrence M. Stratton, Jr., "Color Code," *National Review* (20 March 1995): 40.
31. Ibid.
32. Ibid., 45. Also see Paul D. Moreno, "Fair Employment," chapter 9, and several articles by Alfred W. Blumrosen: "Administrative Creativity: The First Year of the EEOC," *George Washington Law Review*, 38 (1970): 695–703; "Strangers in Paradise,: *Griggs v. Duke Power Co.* and the Concept of Employment Discrimination," *Michigan Law Review*, 71 (1972): 59–110; "The Duty of Fair Recruitment Under the Civil Rights Act of 1964," *Rutgers Law Review*, 22 (1968): 465–536; "The Group Interest Concept, Employment Discrimination, and Legislative Intent," *Harvard Journal on Legislation*, 20 (1983): 99–135; and "The Law Transmission System and the Southern Jurisprudence of Employment Discrimination," *Industrial Relations Law Journal*, 6 (1984): 1043–92.
33. To avoid cases where blacks were only slightly "underutilized," EEOC developed an 80 percent rule. "A selection rate for any race, sex, or ethnic group which is less than four-fifths (4/5) (or eighty percent) of the rate for the group with the highest rate will generally be regarded by the Federal enforcement agencies as evidence of adverse impact, while a greater than four-fifths rate will generally not be regarded by Federal enforcement agencies as evidence of ad-

verse impact." Uniform Guidelines on Employee Selection Procedures (1978), 29 C.F.R. #1607.4D (1989).

34. Hicks v. Crown Zellerbach, 319 F.Supp. 314 (1970), 318.
35. Morrow v. Crisler, 491 F.2d 1053 (1974), 1055.
36. Ibid., 1056, 1063.
37. Ibid., 1061–62.
38. Ibid., 1055, 1056, 1057.
39. Griggs v. Duke Power Company, 292 F.Supp. 243 (1968); 420 F.2d 1225 (1970).
40. Ibid.; Griggs v. Duke Power Company, 91 S.Ct. 849 (1971), 853.
41. Griggs v. Duke Power Company, 292 F.Supp. 243 (1968), 248. The District Court said that, as a practical matter, it was impossible to eradicate "all the consequences of past discrimination." Even a proscription of fair policies that affected minorities adversely would not eradicate all the continuing effects of past discrimination. Besides, by stating that the Civil Rights Act should "receive only prospective application," Congress indicated that it had not contemplated an assault on disparate impact.
42. Griggs v. Duke Power Company, 420 F.2d 1225 (1970), 1230, 1231, 1234.
43. Ibid., 1234.
44. Griggs v. Duke Power Company, 91 S.Ct. 849 (1971).
45. Ibid., 853.
46. Ibid., 853, 854.
47. Ibid., 853.
48. Ibid., 854–55.
49. Hugh Davis Graham, *The Civil Rights Era*, 387.
50. Herman Belz, *Equality Transformed*, chapter 2 and passim.
51. See below, Chapter Nine. Also see Richard J. Herrnstein and Charles Murray, *The Bell Curve*, chapters 3 and 20.
52. Herman Belz, *Equality Transformed*, 65.
53. Thomas Byrne Edsall and Mary D. Edsall, *Chain Reaction*, 251; Neil Howe and Philip Longman, "The Next New Deal," *Atlantic*, 269 (April 1992): 95.
54. *Industrial Relations Law Journal*, 8 (1986): 105–16.
55. Herman Belz, *Equality Transformed*, 23–24, 76.
56. Ibid., 76; 42 U.S.C. #2000; *Equal Employment Opportunity Act of 1972*, 86 Stat. 103, amending 42 U.S.C. #2000; Franks v. Bowman Transportation Company, 424 U.S. 747 (1976), 762–64.
57. *Senate Report* No. 92–415 (1971), 5.
58. 118 *Congressional Record* (1972), 590, 697, 1161–62, 3978.
59. Hugh Davis Graham, *Civil Rights and the Presidency* (New York: Oxford University Press, 1992), 212–13.
60. *Industrial Relations Law Journal*, 8 (1976): 116–17.
61. Ibid., 117–19.
62. Herman Belz, *Equality Transformed*, 76–77; Hugh Davis Graham, *Civil Rights and the Presidency*, 214.
63. Hugh Davis Graham, *Civil Rights and the Presidency*, 160.
64. Ibid., 156–57.
65. Ibid., 157.
66. Ibid., 160, 166–67.
67. Ibid., 161, 168.
68. Ibid., 161–62, 164.

69. Ibid., 166.
70. *New York Times*, 16 June 1985, 25:1; *Los Angeles Times*, 16 June 1985, 5:2; *Report of the Lawyers' Committee for Civil Rights Under Law, 1985 Senate Hearings*, 239.
71. Herman Belz, *Equality Transformed*, 84.
72. 42 U.S.C. #2000e, Sections 703(e) and 706(g).
73. WBR, Brief for the United States, Williams v. City of New Orleans, January 1983, (Fifth Circuit Court of Appeals, Case 82-3435), 38, 35.
74. Interview with WBR, 28 February 1992; Griggs v. Duke Power Company, 401 U.S. 424 (1971), 431; Furnco Construction Corporation v. Waters, 438 U.S. 567 (1978), 579.
75. Interview with WBR, 28 February 1992.
76. WBR, remarks at American Bar Association Conference, 9 August 1982; remarks to the Florida Bar, 8 February 1985, WBR Papers.

9

The Social Science Critique of Affirmative Action

While civil rights activists criticized the policies of the Reagan administration, several economists and psychologists published studies that questioned whether affirmative action did any good. William Bradford Reynolds was influenced by the social science evidence on affirmative action, but his approach was shaped primarily by his understanding of the meaning of the Civil Rights Act.

I

Many liberals had embraced disparate impact and benign preferences during a time of prosperity, a time when per capita income was increasing annually. When *Griggs* was decided in 1971, few Americans were concerned about the cost of affirmative action. During the decade after *Griggs,* however, the national economy received a series of jolting blows. There was an Arab oil boycott, double-digit inflation, and the intensification of international competition in a global economy. Within the United States, the economy shifted away from manufacturing and toward services and computer technology. These trends combined to increase the value of general intelligence, formal education, and advanced skills.

The interaction worked to the detriment of blacks who, on the average, trailed behind whites and Asians when it came to educational achievement and job skills. As James P. Smith and Finis R. Welch have noted, "It is easy to forget how little schooling the average black male worker had, even as late as 1960, and how large black-white education differences were in that year." At that time, 80 percent of the black male work force had not finished high school, and only 3 percent had college degrees. In 1960 white men on average had attended school for 2.7 years more than blacks.[1]

As the differential in schooling narrowed, to 1.5 years in 1980, blacks did better on some standard tests. School desegregation and expensive compensatory programs may also have helped. Nevertheless, a substantial gap remained. In 1982, when the College Board first reported on how different groups performed on the Scholastic Aptitude Test (SAT), the difference between the median scores of blacks and whites was more than 200 points. After comparing blacks and whites with family incomes of more than $50,000, there remained a difference of 150 points.[2]

Many egalitarians said the tests were invalid or culturally biased. Some psychologists, on the other hand, regarded criticism of the tests as akin to "'breaking a thermometer because it registers a body temperature of 101' or 'like the ancient practice of killing the messenger who brought bad news to the emperor.'" Despite criticism, most people considered the tests as an index to the sort of intellectual ability needed for higher-level jobs.[3]

With prosperity no longer taken for granted, the quality of the work force in the United States came under scrutiny. A number of books and press reports indicated that academic standards had declined since the 1950s and that many schools had failed to prepare pupils to enter the labor market. There were unflattering comparisons to the productivity of foreign workers.[4]

Against this background, the public began to pay heed to those who said the nation should take steps to become more competitive. Some reports pointed to the need to provide more incentives for investment. Others mentioned bloated administrative costs and the need for better leadership in the executive suites. There was also increased interest in finding better ways to select and use workers. Consequently, during the 1980s there was a surge in the use of drug tests and health projections to screen out bad risks. Along with this went a resurgence of interests in using personnel and intelligence tests to identify better prospects.[5]

In the 1950s and 1960s, personnel tests were widely used to match prospective employees with suitable jobs. Even before *Griggs*, however, the tests came in for criticism because minorities generally scored lower on them. According to one survey, the percentage of employers that used any sort of objective tests dropped from 90 percent in 1963 to 42 percent ten years later, and after *Griggs*, there was further decline in the use of tests. Instead of bearing the legal and other expenses that were required to prove the business necessity of tests that affected blacks adversely, most employers scrapped the tests.[6]

Some industrial psychologists said this trend aggravated the economic problems. James L. Sharf of George Washington University boldly asserted that "the trashing of objective employment standards in the pursuit of equal employment results...contributed to this nation's productivity decline." Another industrial psychologist, John E. Hunter of Michigan State University, estimated that a rigorous and systematic use of testing could increase productivity by the staggering amount of about $80 billion (in 1980, when total corporate tax revenue at all levels was $59 billion). Frank L. Schmidt of the University of Iowa calculated that the dollar cost to firms whose personnel offices no longer used a standard battery of intelligence tests was about $8,500 per year for an entry-level computer programmer in 1978—more for budget analysts, less for other jobs.[7]

Measuring the overall cost of affirmative action was difficult. Nevertheless, some analysts made estimates. After summarizing the relevant economic-impact studies, journalists Peter Brimelow and Leslie Spencer calculated the cost of preferences and quotas in 1992 at about 4 percent of annual gross national product—"about as much as we spend on the entire public school system." They derived this figure after adding the cost of compliance to the cost incurred from hiring less-efficient workers.[8]

Some egalitarians said there was an important dividing line between the qualified and the unqualified. They said that all that was important was that employees be *qualified*—that they be above some minimum qualification level. At the University of Delaware, an affirmative action officer said that in areas where minorities were underutilized, "a less qualified minority or woman" should be hired in preference to "a more qualified white male." The director of the Office of Women's Affairs then said, "It's federal law. If [two candidates] are both qualified to do the job, then affirmative action says that if there is under utilization, you'll hire the one from the protected class." Another administrator said the university was "not lowering its standards...because unqualified people are not being hired."[9]

Personnel psychologists like Frank Schmidt conceded that preferences usually did not lead to the employment of unqualified workers; they led, rather, to the hiring of lesser-qualified employees over those who were better qualified. But Schmidt insisted that any decline in standards was "very costly in terms of lost productivity." To illustrate his point, Schmidt mentioned the situation at U. S. Steel. Before *Griggs*, the company had selected applicants into its skilled-trade apprentice programs from the top down, with rankings based on the applicants' scores on a battery of tests. Afterwards, the company lowered standards and required only minimum scores equal to about seventh-grade work. The lower standards enabled the company to avoid adverse impact, but at the expense of productive efficiency. In fact, Schmidt reported, the cost to the company was 80 percent to 90 percent as great as it would have been if testing had been completely abandoned.[10]

Most of the loss attributed to minimum competency selection systems came from white workers. Schmidt explained that because standards were reduced for all workers, and because most jobs still went to whites, "the cumulative productivity loss from hiring less productive members of the majority group is much greater than the loss due to less productive minority workers."[11]

The key point was not whether the productivity loss was associated with the employment of whites or blacks. It was that the abandonment of valid job-aptitude tests led to declining productivity. "When the less competent employees reach a critical mass," Schmidt said, other employees abandoned their former rules of conduct and the "lower performance standards bec[a]me the standards of the organization." Schmidt was convinced that the abandonment of testing had led to "substantial economic losses."[12]

The United States was in a bind. Because of group differences in education and job skills, fairness in terms of equal employment results for blacks required a lowering of standards. Efficiency and profits (and also fairness to individuals who were members of high-scoring groups) had to be traded away to achieve equality of results.

To reduce their losses, some companies resorted to a practice known as "within-group scoring" or *race norming*. They did so with the support of officials who worked for the Reagan administration in the Department of Labor and in the United States Employment Service. These officials urged employers to make expanded use of the General Aptitude Test Battery, a standard test the government had developed to match prospective employees with appropriate jobs. To avoid the legal expenses and the general hassle associated with using a test that had a disparate impact, however, the Employment Service kept separate rosters for blacks and for whites and then recommended the highest scorers from each group. That way blacks would receive a proportion of the jobs that was commensurate with their proportion of the labor pool.

By not telling employers that the black and white candidates had normed scores and came from different lists, the Employment Service effectively eliminated adverse impact. Even if employers learned about the race norming, many continued to rely on the Employment Service for referrals because the loss in productivity from using race-normed scores was less than the loss that would occur if the tests were scrapped or if minimum competency standards were established. Race norming was a compromise that enabled employers to comply with *Griggs* while maintaining a degree of efficiency in their personnel systems.

It was paradoxical that career bureaucrats supported double standards even during the Reagan years, and Reynolds challenged the practice when he learned of it in 1986. Until Reynolds stepped in, however, the U. S. Employment Service promoted the use of these "efficient" racial preferences.[13]

Although Reynolds squelched the federal government's practice in 1986, race norming did not receive much public attention until 1990, when Robert G. Holland published articles on the subject in the *Richmond Times Dispatch*. Holland explained that the U. S. Employment Service and several state employment agencies had been grading tests "within group." Instead of being measured against all the other applicants for a job, a candidate would be measured against a group composed only of members of his or her own racial group. Instead of being told the actual score they made on the test, applicants would be told their percentile ratings within their group—but they would not be told their score was a percentile ranking. Instead, they were led to believe that their score reflected their standing in comparison with a group representative of all those who took the test. Holland explained how this worked:

> Say four men—one black, one Hispanic, one white, one Asian—came into a Virginia Employment Service office in search of a job. If the prospective employers wanted tested applicants, the four would all take the same Validity Generalization version of the General Aptitude Test Battery (VG-GATB), a test with both paper-and-pencil and manual dexterity sections. Assume that each made a composite score of 300 and that all four were interested in an accountant's position.
>
> None of them would ever see that 300 score. Instead, the numbers would be fed into a computer, and what would emerge would be the applicants' percentile ranking, with the owner of the highest ranking presumed to be the best qualified worker. But, you may say, with identical scores they would all be in the same percentile.
>
> If you say that, you are reckoning without the ingenuity of the bureaucrats in charge of racial balance. For in fact, the black would be ranked in the 87th percentile; the Hispanic in the 74th percentile; and the Asian and the white way down in the 47th.[14]

Holland's story captured wide public attention. His original essay was reprinted in the *Washington Times*. Another piece appeared in the *National Review*, where Holland focused on individual people as well as the general issue. "As always," he wrote, "the real victims are the individuals behind the abstractions. A white job-seeker who is given a low score will not be recommended for a job for which he may be fully qualified; furthermore, he will get an additional blow to an ego already bruised by being unemployed. One veteran factory worker, Larry P. Holman, who had been laid off and was trying to start over..., told me, 'I thought on top of everything else, I'm stupid.'"[15]

Holland also published part of the GATB percentile conversion table that was being used in Virginia and in forty other states.

Percentile Conversion Tables

> Jobs are grouped into...broad families: Family I includes, for example, machinists, cabinet makers, and tool makers; Family II includes helpers in many types of agriculture, manufacturing, and so on; Family III includes professional jobs such as accountant, chemical engineer, nurse, editor;

Family IV includes exterminators, butchers, file clerks. A raw score of 300 would convert to the following percentile rankings:

	I	II	III	IV
Black	79	59	87	83
Hispanic	62	41	74	67
Other	39	42	47	45

Contemporaneously with the concern about productive efficiency and with the controversy over race norming, Linda S. Gottfredson published important studies on personnel placements. On the basis of statistical analyses, Gottfredson concluded that an IQ of 105 was generally required for getting good grades in a college-preparatory curriculum; and an IQ of about 115 was generally a prerequisite for graduating from college with the grades and test scores that would qualify one for admission to a professional or graduate school. Gottfredson also pointed to research that indicated that the average IQ of high-level executives and of physicians was about 125, and that few people in these professions were found below IQ 115. Gottfredson further estimated that the minimum IQ for high-school teachers was around 108; for police officers and fire fighters, 91; and for truck drivers and meat cutters, 86.[16]

Gottfredson then explained adverse impact by pointing to the relatively small pool of blacks who had the scores that seemed to be necessary for high-level jobs. Since 21 percent of blacks and 22 percent of whites have IQs between 91 and 100, she noted, one would expect an approximately proportional distribution of blacks and whites in jobs that drew workers primarily from this range (for example, butchers and truck drivers); and since only about 2 percent of blacks have IQs between 111 and 120 (as compared with about 17 percent of whites), one would expect that whites would be disproportionately represented in more-advanced jobs. As one proceeded up the IQ scale, the distribution of scores was even more skewed—with whites twenty-five times more likely than blacks to have scores in excess of 120. When it came to a score of 650 on the Graduate Record Quantitative Exam, a score that Gottfredson considered "a rough threshold for success in a first-rate graduate program in the physical or social sciences," the ratio of blacks to whites was 1 to 192.[17]

The work of sociologists like Gottfredson and of industrial psychologists like Sharf, Schmidt, and Hunter challenged the basic premises of egalitarianism. A major tenet of that ideology was that there were no important racial differences in intelligence or other capabilities. Consequently, any differences in test scores had to be due to bias in the tests, to cultural variations, or to societal discrimination against blacks.

Egalitarian psychologists and sociologists developed a number of theories to challenge cognitive tests. One theory, the theory of test invalidity, held that the test-score differences between individuals or groups were irrelevant because the tests did not really predict job performance. Another theory, the theory of low utility, argued that even valid tests were irrelevant because the differences in job performance did not have any significant economic impact. Other theories held that the tests predicted performance for whites but not for blacks (the theory of single group validity), or that they were predictive for all groups but to a different degree, with the tests having higher validity for whites than for blacks (the theory of differential validity).

In response, testing experts pointed to a large body of research. They said the test differences were real and not a result of bias. They said the tests predicted performance on the job, and that differences in measured intelligence had economic impact. Rejecting "the popularly held belief that general ability tests are racially biased—that is, that they underpredict the job performance of blacks," Gottfredson insisted that "lower test scores among blacks and Hispanics are accompanied by lower job performance, just as in the case of whites."[18]

Some egalitarians questioned the correlations between the workers' test scores and the performance ratings they later received. The ratings were suspect, the egalitarians said, because most of the supervisors who gave the ratings were whites whose assessments may have been influenced by personal attitudes and racial prejudice. In reply, industrial psychologists cited studies that indicated that low scorers generally received slightly higher ratings from supervisors than they would have received if the ratings had been based on more objective measures of job performance (such as accidents, customer complaints, stock shortages, etc.).[19]

Other egalitarians proposed what is sometimes called "the convergence theory." They conceded that workers who made high scores on intelligence tests would do better than low scorers during the early months on the job, but they predicted that as the low scorers gained experience with the actual work, the initial advantage of the high scorers would be eroded over time. They said that the cost of scrapping tests would exist only in the early phases on the job and that in time any differences in job performance would tend to disappear. But Frank Schmidt spoke for many industrial psychologists when he said that if tasks were not so repetitive as to become a matter of habitual routine—that is, when the tasks were complex enough to require continued processing of information—"mental ability continues to correlate with performance indefinitely over time."[20]

Another egalitarian theory, the theory of marginal utility, held that the correlation between test scores and performance on the job was too low to justify the adverse impact. A debate over statistics ensued, with some egalitarians placing the correlation coefficient around 0.3 while those who were more favorably disposed toward testing placed it at 0.5 or higher. Egalitarians said that if the industrial psychologists were weather forecasters, they would not know enough to say with certainty whether one should take an umbrella to work. The psychologists answered that there was good reason to pay attention to weather reports, even if some predictions were mistaken. They said objective tests were the best single predictor of employee performance—better than personal references or interviews, better than academic grades or credentials.[21]

With testing embroiled in controversy, and with the Department of Justice challenging the practice of race norming, in 1986 the Department of Labor sought guidance from the National Academy of Sciences. Working through the National Research Council, the National Academy then convened a committee of experts: fourteen scholars agreed to serve on the Committee on the General Aptitude Test Battery; another twenty-nine scholars served as members of a liaison group; John A. Hartigan, a statistician from Yale University, was chosen as the chairman of the panel. The Labor Department asked the scholars to assess whether the GATB test was valid as a predictor of job performance, whether the validity was strong enough to enhance worker productivity, and whether there was scientific justification for race norming. In response, the NAS panel published a 354-page book that included graphs, charts, and an extensive survey of the relevant scholarly literature. There is a risk of oversimplification in summarizing the findings of a complex book, but, essentially, the answer to all the questions was yes.[22]

Because the NAS panel endorsed race norming, many people initially thought it had sided with the egalitarians. This impression was reinforced when several anti-egalitarian scholars criticized the panel for favoring the adjustment of the scores of black and Hispanic test takers. James Sharf accused the committee of putting "a scientific fig leaf on a naked political argument." Constance Holden challenged the justification that the committee gave for race norming. Jan H. Blits and Linda Gottfredson insisted that "whether the nation should adopt race norming should be decided by public officials and ultimately by the citizens: to pretend that science can supply an answer is only to pervert science by politicizing it."[23]

Blits and Gottfredson were right on both counts. The scientific case for norming was dubious, and once the public learned about the practice, there were demands for Congress to end it. Accordingly, Senator Alan Simpson of Wyoming introduced an amendment to the Civil Rights Act of 1991. While there was much about that legislation that was ambiguous and confusing, one thing about the new law was clear—it prohibited employers and government agencies from adjusting the results of tests on the basis of race.[24]

Thus the conservative side eventually prevailed in the battle over race norming. The industrial psychologists also prevailed on the other questions that had been put to the NAS panel: that panel concluded that the GATB was valid for predicting the job performance of both blacks and whites, and also concluded that the validity was strong enough to improve the productivity of the work force. "We probably cannot afford not to use [the GATB]," said the panel chairman John A. Hartigan.[25]

In supporting the GATB, the NAS panel also endorsed a concept known as "validity generalization." Developed by Frank Schmidt and John Hunter in the late 1970s, validity generalization was the industrial psychologists' answer to *Griggs*, which had said that if an employment policy or practice had a disparate impact, employers could rebut the presumption of discrimination by demonstrating the business necessity of the procedure in question. *Griggs* also said that if an employment test affected blacks adversely, employers must make separate validity studies for each job.

Such demonstrations were costly and difficult to provide. If blacks did worse than whites on any test, and if the employer still wanted to use the test, the employer was required to bear the expense of demonstrating that the relationship between the test and performance on the job was not different for minorities from what it was for others. Nathan Glazer reported that in 1975 the cost of validation ranged upward from a minimum of $40,000 to $50,000 per test for each job. Nor was it sufficient for a company to provide a single validation for a test. If the Du Pont Company validated a test for machinists at a plant in Virginia, it would still have to validate the test for use at a second factory in Tennessee because courts held that the conditions at the two sites might be different.[26]

Validity generalization provided a way around the need for expensive, separately validated tests. It did so by demonstrating that the results of one test of cognitive ability could be generalized from one place to another and from one job to many more. Validity generalization meant that a general measure of mental ability that is valid for some jobs is valid for most jobs. Essentially, the advocates of validity generalization argued that general mental ability—as measured on tests that examined the ability to reason, to think abstractly, and to solve problems—predicted the performance of workers better than other measures. They acknowledged that as the complexity of jobs decreased, so did the validity of mental ability in predicting job performance. For some of the simpler occupations that involved an automatic, habitual repetition of tasks, tests of psychomotor ability generally had a higher correlation with success on the job. But, according to John Hunter, "the more complex the job, the better cognitive ability predicts performance ratings." Advocates of validity generalization said that in general and for the great majority of jobs, mental ability was more important than either specific aptitude or special training. They stressed that in a changing modern economy, with its emphasis on services and computer technology, the ability to learn, unlearn, and relearn was especially important.[27]

Validity generalization was based on hundreds of studies of the correlation between general intelligence and job performance. According to industrial psychologists, some 515 studies conducted by the U.S. Employment Service went far toward proving that "cognitive ability tests are valid predictors of performance on the job and in training for all jobs...in all settings." Another 500 studies by the U.S. Armed Forces yielded similar results. In military drills, for example, tank crews with higher average IQ scores made more *kills* than crews with lower average scores. Even when it came to kitchen patrol, there was a positive correlation between the scores servicemen made on the Army General Classification Test and the supervisors' assessments of their work.[28]

Since validity-generalization studies showed that performance on most jobs was related to performance on general mental tests, personnel experts argued that employers should be allowed to use validity generalization to defend tests in disparate-impact cases. *Griggs* required employers to demonstrate the business necessity of hiring procedures that had adverse impact; but if validity generalization was correct—if performance on general mental tests substantially predicted performance on the job—there would be no more need for employers to provide studies of particular jobs in particular situations. Instead, they could comply with *Griggs* by citing the work of the scholars whose research had been reviewed and assessed by the NAS panel.[29]

Civil rights lawyers were aghast at this prospect. If validity generalization won acceptance in court, one lawyer acknowledged, "validity would always be presumed, and it would necessarily follow that no employer could *ever* lose a testing case."[30]

Civil rights lawyers did not have the expertise to carry on a debate in the social science journals. But they were skeptical about the scholars' claims that testing could lead to marked increases in productivity, and they were prepared to fight in court. Throughout the Reagan years, they would insist that the industrial psychologists had not presented enough evidence to justify the use of tests that seemed to consign blacks disproportionately to jobs in the lower ranks of the occupational hierarchy. They said there was a difference between "the appearance of science and its reality." They said the levels of correlation were not sufficient to warrant adverse impact. They said that the prospective gains in productive efficiency were not enough to justify "any substantial degree of harm to minorities or to women."[31]

II

During the Reagan years civil rights lawyers and some liberal economists argued that affirmative action was responsible for some of the job advancement of members of minority groups. This argument reassured activists that their work had not been in vain. It also was in accord with the common-sense intuition that efforts intended to assist African-Americans were actually helping them.

There was some empirical support for this proposition. Those who believed that affirmative action was a success, when judged by its results in terms of benefits for blacks, could point to increases in the number of black fire fighters and police officers hired after affirmative action programs were implemented. They noted similar increases in the numbers of blacks who were admitted to competitive colleges and professional schools and issued a 184-page report that concluded that affirmative action had promoted minority hiring. They pointed to a Labor Department study that showed that more blacks were employed by contractors that did business with the government (and therefore had to satisfy affirmative action guidelines) and to a study by the Potomac Institute, which credited affirmative action for much of the progress blacks had made in getting better jobs.[32]

Some of these studies were partisan and tendentious, but social scientists who were not members of the civil rights lobby also reported that affirmative action "worked." Some noted that "since the early 1960s blacks have been overrepresented in white collar and professional occupations relative to the number of candidates in the IQ range from which these jobs are usually filled." Others reported that there had been an overall narrowing of the wage gap, with the income of black workers increasing from about 43 percent of white wages in 1940 to 73 percent in 1980. There was also marked improvement in the relative occupational position of blacks, with the proportion of blacks employed in white-collar, managerial, and professional jobs increasing from less than one-half the white proportion before 1950 to more than three-quarters by the late 1970s.[33]

Nevertheless, some economists questioned whether civil rights laws were responsible for the progress. Thomas Sowell of the Hoover Institution at Stanford University acknowledged that "the notion that the Civil Rights Act and 'affirmative action' have had a dramatic impact on the economic progress of minorities has become part of the folklore of the land." But Sowell thought this view was "established primarily through repetition and vehemence, rather than evidence." The number of blacks in higher-level occupations had increased, but Sowell said this was part of an historical trend that began before the Civil Rights Act was passed. According to Sowell, "the advance of blacks was even greater during the 1940s—when there was little or no civil rights policy—than during the 1950s when the civil rights revolution was in its heyday."[34]

James P. Smith of the Rand Corporation and Finis R. Welch of UCLA also noted that the greatest improvement in narrowing the racial wage gap had occurred during the 1940s. The advances slowed during the 1950s but picked up during the 1960s and early 1970s. Overall, Smith and Welch concluded, there was as much progress in the twenty years prior to 1960—before civil rights activism and before affirmative action—as during the twenty years afterward.[35]

A number of factors contributed to narrowing the racial wage gap. The U.S. economy grew rapidly during the forty years after 1940, shifting from an emphasis on agriculture and manufacturing to an economy that was oriented toward technology and services. Sharecropping in cotton, the primary activity of Southern blacks before World War II, was almost eliminated. Large numbers of black farmers and agricultural workers migrated to the cities of the South and the North, transforming the black population from predominantly rural to largely urban. Many of these blacks initially found good-paying jobs in industry, but in time the U.S. economy—especially the manufacturing sector—had to face the challenge of increased international competition. This competition dealt especially severe blows to the industrial sector where black workers had made advances in manufacturing jobs. The overall pattern, according to economists James J. Heckman and J. Hoult Verkerke, was well known:

> Beginning in 1965, the rate of improvement in black relative wages and occupational status accelerated. However, since 1975, relative black economic status has not advanced and may have deteriorated slightly.[36]

With so many factors interacting, it is difficult to calculate the importance of any particular component. After making a number of complicated, statistical regression analyses, Smith and Welch concluded that two elements were especially influential. One was the black migration away from the low wages of the rural South, to which Smith and Welch ascribed much of the reduction in black poverty; the other was a reduction in the differential between blacks and whites in average years of schooling, from 3.68 years in 1940 to 1.51 in 1981. Compared with the benefits that resulted from moving to cities and the higher income associated with spending more years in school, Smith and Welch said that the benefits from civil rights laws in general and affirmative action in particular seemed "at best" to have altered the wage gap only "marginally."[37]

Other economists, while conceding that trends in migration and education were important for explaining the closing of the wage gap, did not discount the effects of the civil rights laws. In 1968 William M. Landes, an economist at the University of Chicago, calculated that the relative wages of blacks were about 5 percent higher in states that had fair employment laws. In an influential study published in 1981, Richard B. Freeman, an economist at Harvard University, maintained that the ratio of black to white income increased after passage of the Civil Rights Act at a faster rate than in the period before 1964. These and other studies indicated that antidiscrimination laws did improve the relative economic conditions of blacks. James P. Heckman and J. Hoult Verkerke concluded that "the coincidence of increased federal antidiscrimination pressure in the mid-1960s with the acceleration in the rate of black progress beginning in 1965 makes it plausible that federal pressure caused the improvement in black status."[38]

Standard principles of economics can account for the improvement. By criminalizing job discrimination, the Civil Rights Act counteracted racial prejudices and protected companies that wanted to compete in open markets. The antidiscrimination laws were a boon to employers who wanted to maximize profits by hiring workers who had the greatest marginal utility.[39]

Prior to 1964 many firms would not hire black workers, even if the blacks would work for less and would produce more than white employees. The employers would not do so for fear of suffering the reprisals that could follow violations of racist customs and mores. But after passage of the Civil Rights Act, with the government prohibiting discrimination, there were countervailing pressures. Employers who wanted to hire blacks felt free to do so. Blacks benefited because many employers welcomed the larger supply of workers.

In this respect, the Civil Rights Act worked exactly as its principal sponsor had anticipated. In 1964 Senator Humphrey had identified discrimination against blacks as the cause of their lower wages, their relatively high unemployment, and their confinement to low-skilled jobs. Humphrey said the purpose of Title VII was "to open employment opportunity for Negroes in occupations which have been traditionally closed to them." But this could not be done without "requir[ing]...an end to the discrimination which now prevails." Humphrey predicted that the income disparities between blacks and whites would diminish as greater opportunities became available for black workers.[40]

Yet even economists who pointed to increased progress after 1964, economists such as James Heckman and J. Hoult Verkerke, acknowledged that after 1975 the relative economic status of blacks either did not advance or declined slightly. According to Heckman and Verkerke, the stagnation or deterioration was "most likely due to the collapse of the U.S. manufacturing industry and the attendant loss of many relatively high-paying, low-skill jobs."[41]

Other economists blamed some of the stagnation and deterioration on the civil rights movement in general and on *Griggs* in particular. Liberals had argued that the civil rights laws had complemented the trends in migration and education to produce economic progress after 1964. During the 1980s, some conservatives similarly maintained that *Griggs* had unintended consequences that combined with increased foreign competition to aggravate the economic conditions of blacks.

Chief Justice Burger's opinion in *Griggs* was problematically vague. At one point, Burger said the "touchstone" for determining the validity of an employment test was "business necessity." But elsewhere he suggested a standard that would be easier to satisfy; he said tests could pass muster if they were "related to job performance" or if they "fulfill[ed] a genuine business need."[42]

Given the ambiguity of the *Griggs* opinion, it was hard for employers to know what they must do. Some understandably concluded that *Griggs* gave license to the imagination, ingenuity, and political predilections of the lawyers and judges who would argue and decide adverse impact lawsuits.

Whether *Griggs* required employers to show that their tests were genuinely necessary or only job-related, the demonstrations were expensive and arguably inconclusive. The only thing that was certain was that *Griggs* imposed costs and legal risks on employers who did not hire blacks in statistically proportionate numbers. In the short term, many employers responded by hiring more blacks. But they feared that the employment of workers with low marginal utility would cause their companies to go the way of firms that do not maximize profits—out of business.

To avoid this fate, some employers moved to regions where blacks made up smaller proportion of the relevant labor pool. They moved to distant counties, states, and countries. They moved away from inner cities and toward predominantly white suburbs where long daily commutes and bad systems of public transportation were sufficient to put the jobs beyond the reach of most black workers.

The employers of the 1970s and 1980s professed to be eager to hire blacks who were well qualified for jobs. They employed some blacks. They recognized that generalizations about the inefficiency of black workers were not universally true. But since the Supreme Court had made it difficult to use tests to predict which workers were likely to have higher-than-average productivity, many employers used knowledge of race (and of residence in undesirable neighborhoods) as shorthand.

Some observers defended the companies. Because of the intensity of international economic competition, they said that companies could not afford to discriminate against well-qualified workers. Moreover, because of the research of industrial psychologists, companies had reason to believe they could improve efficiency if they insisted that employees must graduate from high school (or college, or graduate school) and must make good scores on professionally developed personnel tests like the GATB.

There is evidence that some firms took *Griggs* into account when they decided to relocate away from concentrations of black population. In a court case involving a subsidiary of the Standard Oil Company, evidence was presented that the company wanted to "build its plant in a city with a minority population no greater than 35% of the total population, allegedly because it had previously experienced difficulty meeting affirmative action goals with proportionately larger minority populations." The *New York Times* reported that it was common knowledge among economists that many firms would not build plants or offices in predominantly black areas.[43]

There was also the problematical example of the automobile industry. After black rioters devastated Detroit in 1967, the big three automobile companies tried to appease blacks by putting into effect "a complete reversal of traditional industrial hiring practices." As the labor economist Herbert R. Northrup wrote, "Instead of hiring the fittest and best personnel obtainable in the labor market, the companies were literally searching for the most marginal that can possibly be utilized." Chrysler and General Motors dropped previous policies against hiring people who had police records, and Ford sent recruiters into black neighborhoods to hire people on the spot. All three companies increased efforts to hire blacks who had previously been considered "unemployable."[44]

Leaders of the companies were candid in explaining their objectives. At General Motors the chairman of the board, James M. Roche, said that more had to be done than "to wait for the qualified applicant to present himself at our employment office." At Ford, Henry Ford II invited the interest of "people who would not normally come to us—not to screen *out* doubtful candidates but to screen *in* if possible."[45]

As a result of these efforts, by 1968 the proportion of blacks in the work force of this high-wage industry had increased to 14.5 percent of all employees and to 18.6 percent of blue-collar workers. However, even Herbert Northrup, who applauded this instance of affirmative action, acknowledged that there were problems. He wrote that "the introduction of large numbers of Negroes into huge automobile plants has brought with it the mores of the slums—violence, gambling, lawlessness." He noted that management personnel said "the turnover of Negroes was much higher than whites." Some supervisors said that "the Monday absentees, and the sickness and accident claims were dominated by Negroes."[46]

Many knowledgeable observers chose not to discuss these problems. David Halberstam never mentioned the matter in his generally perceptive 752-page book on the decline of the U.S. auto industry. But others suggested that Japanese companies, while observing the taboo on candid discussion, decided to locate their plants in areas with minimal black populations. Andrew Hacker, a white professor of indisputably liberal sentiments, accusingly noted that Toyota located one of its U.S. assembly plants in Harlan County, Kentucky, where the population was 95 percent white, while Honda chose a rural area near Marysville, Ohio, where 97 percent of the residents were white. Isuzu located its major U.S. plant in Lafayette, Indiana, which is 1.7 percent black.[47]

The Japanese auto makers said they were not running away from blacks. Instead, they mentioned the advantages of both cheap land and avoiding organized labor in small towns and rural areas. But after they chose their new locations, the Japanese companies established policies that effectively screened out most blacks. Honda required workers to live within twenty miles of the plant, and every potential employee had to go through three interviews that were aimed at discovering attitudes toward work and, arguably, at screening out applicants who would welcome union organizers. Toyota gave its prospective workers fourteen hours of tests that measured interpersonal skills and corporate loyalty as well as literacy, mathematics, and technical knowledge. As a result, in areas where much of the adult population had not finished high school, almost all of Honda and Toyota's employees had high-school diplomas, and some had college degrees. Unlike U.S. auto makers, who traditionally reserved interviews and tests for white-collar workers who were being considered for management posts, the Japanese companies paid careful attention to anyone who would work on the shop floor. Civil rights activists railed about the practice, but in 1990 the Honda Accord was the best selling automobile made in United States.[48]

Generalizing from evidence of this sort, Judge Richard A. Posner, sitting on the Seventh Circuit Court of Appeals, concluded that companies were taking account of disparate impact. "When deciding where to locate a new plant or where to expand an existing one," Posner wrote, "a firm will be attracted (other things being equal) to areas that have only small percentages of blacks in their labor pools." The black economist Thomas Sowell observed that affirmative action "has meant mutually canceling incentives to hire and not to hire."[49]

The tendency to abandon or avoid both the inner cities and the rural black belt was established before *Griggs*, and it is difficult to disentangle the effects of the war against testing and credentials from all the other considerations that were involved. But because *Griggs* made it more costly for firms to operate in areas where the labor pool contained a high percentage of blacks, its effect was similar to that of legally mandated, higher minimum wages. Just as some employers found it cost-effective to mechanize rather than pay higher wages to marginally productive workers, others took the cost of affirmative action into account when they made decisions about building, expanding, or moving their plants.

Contemporaneous with civil rights laws that prohibited discrimination and with interpretations that both required busing for racial balance in the schools and forbade disparate impact in the work force, there was an extraordinary decline in blue-collar employment in the urban areas where the black population was disproportionately concentrated. Over a period of twenty-five years, the central cities of the thirty-three most populous metropolitan areas lost 880,000 manufacturing jobs, while manufacturing employment in their suburbs grew by 2.5 million. Meanwhile, black men, who historically had been more likely than whites to be employed, began to experience rising levels of unemployment. During the 1970s, the labor-force participation of black men fell below that of white men in all age groups, with the decline particularly steep for younger men. Among teenaged blacks, whose rate of unemployment had been almost identical to that of whites in the early 1950s, unemployment increased to more than twice the white rate by 1980.[50]

In the cities the decline in manufacturing jobs was partly offset by the expansion of professional, managerial, and office work; but because of the racial differential in educational achievement and because educational standards were still used as prerequisites for employment in most white-collar jobs, the expansion of office work did not compensate low skilled blacks for the loss of blue-collar jobs. The result in most cities was a serious mismatch between the training and abilities of inner-city blacks and the jobs available to them. One influential study reported that after *Griggs* almost all of the national growth in entry-level and other low-skilled jobs occurred "in the suburbs, exurbs, and non-metropolitan areas far removed from growing concentrations of poorly educated urban minorities."[51]

Prominent students of what has been called the urban "underclass" have offered different interpretations of the statistics and trends. William Julius Wilson, a black sociologist and a man of the left, has criticized civil rights leaders for not anticipating that the restructuring of the economy would eliminate jobs that were disproportionately held by inner-city blacks. He has called upon the government to develop a national economic plan—especially a jobs plan—to deal with de-industrialization and the mismatch between jobs and skills. Wilson has acknowledged, however, that many unemployed workers with low skills refused to take the low-wage jobs that are available in the cities—in hospitals, hotels, warehouses, building maintenance and the like. In recent years, "[A]ttitudes concerning low-status work have changed," Wilson wrote. "[Black] workers today are less willing to accept the kinds of low-paying and menial jobs that their grandfathers and fathers readily accepted."[52]

Charles Murray, a white social-policy analyst, has offered an explanation for the changing attitude toward work. Instead of emphasizing the mismatch between jobs and skills, Murray criticized the government for establishing social and welfare programs that undermined the work ethic by subsidizing indolence and by removing the "spur" of poverty. He noted that government welfare and social programs were greatly expanded after 1965, and that by the early 1970s, unwed mothers who did not work received about as much (or more) from welfare as unskilled men could earn at minimum-wage jobs—a situation that seemed to reduce the incentive for unskilled men to take jobs. Rather than marry their girlfriends, the men adapted by sponging off the mothers of their children and by engaging in a variety of part-time jobs and hustles. Meanwhile, there was a dramatic plunge in the proportion of black men who were steadily employed, and an increase in the proportion of black babies born out of wedlock (from about 17 percent in 1950 to 48 percent in 1980 to more than 60 percent in the 1990s).[53]

Instead of calling for a jobs program, Murray had censured the existing government programs. In addition to eroding the work ethic, he said that these programs undermined family stability by freeing mothers from financial dependence on the fathers of their children and by relieving the fathers of responsibility for supporting the children. Murray conceded that the welfare programs were initiated out of a sense of compassion and concern. But he maintained that the programs, because they reduced the incentives to work and to get married, backfired and made things worse.[54]

Whatever the cause of the rising unemployment and increasing family instability among blacks, economists recognized that it offset much of the progress that was made during the civil rights era. Blacks had made progress in closing the wage gap and also moved forward in terms of occupational status. But because of rising unemployment and the increase in families headed by single women, there was no progress for blacks in terms of overall income.

Indeed, the decline in labor-force participation was so great that it cast doubt on the whole idea of progress. The statistical evidence of progress was based on comparisons of blacks and whites who were employed. It did not take account of those who no longer had jobs. Thus, some of the alleged improvement was spurious because unemployment was much higher among low-skilled blacks than among similar whites. James Heckman and J. Hoult Verkerke explained that "the relatively greater proportion of black labor market dropouts has manufactured some fraction of black relative wage growth as a statistical artifact."[55]

Did affirmative action have unintended negative consequences? Charles Murray thought it did. William Julius Wilson was reluctant to concede the point, although he acknowledged that "affirmative action programs were not designed to deal with the problem of the disproportionate concentration of blacks in the low-wage labor market."[56]

Wilson recognized that an increasing stratification of the black community was accompanying the enforcement and interpretations of the laws that prohibited discrimination and adverse impact. So did Martin R. Kilson, a black political scientist at Harvard, who noted that many middle-class blacks were taking advantage of new opportunities and were "pulling away from the black lower strata." But the job-market experience of lower-class black men was just the opposite. It was so bad that many left their jobs (and their wives and children, who could survive on welfare). As a consequence of "the extraordinary rise in female black households," Kilson reported, there was considerable slippage in aggregate black family income relative to white family income—from 62 percent in 1975 to 57 percent in 1981.[57]

Thomas Sowell reiterated these points. He reported that during the 1970s, when affirmative action was receiving more emphasis than ever before, the most disadvantaged black families—those headed by women, with no husband present—suffered a decline in real income. "During the affirmative action era," Sowell wrote, "blacks with less education and less job experience—the truly disadvantaged—have been falling farther and farther behind their white counterparts...[while] blacks with more education and more job experience have been advancing economically, both absolutely and relative to their white counterparts."[58]

The overall trend was clear: well-educated blacks had benefited under affirmative action while the disadvantaged fell behind. By 1980 college-educated black couples with husband and wife working had achieved incomes higher than white couples of the same description. The top fifth of blacks was receiving a growing proportion of all income received by blacks, while each of the bottom three-fifths was receiving a declining share. In within-race comparisons, income inequality among black families was growing markedly, and growing more rapidly than income differentials among white families.[59]

Stephen L. Carter, a black professor at Yale Law School, also noted this trend. He observed that "one need not argue that affirmative action is the cause of increasing income inequality...to understand that it is not a solution."[60]

William Raspberry, a usually liberal, black columnist for the *Washington Post*, assessed the situation in stronger language. In 1984 he wrote that "America today really does treat blacks as individuals. It looks at education, test scores, economics, and other evidences of individual merit." As a consequence, "meritorious blacks" were moving ahead.[61]

These upwardly mobile blacks, according to Raspberry, recognized that affirmative action would do little for "the unskilled, uneducated, unambitious, economically crippled 'underclass.'" But blacks of the upper and middle classes recognized that *they* could benefit from preferences. They cited statistics "to prove that blacks in the aggregate are under-represented in college, graduate school or top management," although they knew full well that poor blacks would not be candidates for admission to Ivy League colleges or to corporate board rooms.[62]

Affirmative action was being used as part of what Raspberry called a "bait-and-switch game." Statistics about poor blacks were put forward as a rationalization to get a larger number of top positions set aside for blacks as a group, but the real purpose was to insulate well-to-do blacks from competition. If the leading universities accepted the theory of *no adverse impact*, the children of blacks who were well-off would no longer have to compete with their white or Asian counterparts. Instead, Raspberry explained, they would compete with black children from the slums—"a competition they are likely to win." Similarly, "black executives who hold good jobs get promoted to better ones; blacks who already sit on important corporate boards get other directorships. The people who provide the statistical base get nothing."[63]

III

In questioning the motives of those who favored affirmative racial preferences, Raspberry lapsed obliquely into psychology. When it came to the effects of affirmative action on the mental state of blacks, however, the most perceptive criticism of the civil rights establishment came from three black scholars: Shelby Steele of San Jose State, Thomas Sowell of the Hoover Institution, and Stephen L. Carter of Yale.[64]

While the architects of the *Griggs* standard worried about the adverse impact of tests and credentials, Steele warned about the adverse psychological effects of affirmative preferences. He said the basic assumption of affirmative action was that blacks could not measure up to the intellectual standards of whites and Asians; therefore, there was a need for preferences to "do for us what we cannot do for ourselves." In the process, affirmative action reinforced suspicions of black inferiority and called into question the legitimate achievements of well-qualified blacks who got ahead on the basis of merit.[65]

Steele recognized that these costs should be balanced against the success of blacks who managed to move ahead only because of the opportunities provided by affirmative action. He acknowledged that his own children would have a better chance of being admitted to a prestigious university "if they will only designate themselves as black on their college applications." But Steele thought that one of the worst effects of preferential treatment—"the lowering of normal standards to increase black representation"—was that it reinforced a "debilitating doubt" that already existed in the minds of many blacks.[66]

One of the hindrances to black progress, Steele said, was a kind of psychological demoralization, "an enlargement of self-doubt," an anxiety that was related to suspicions of racial inferiority. Blacks knew they belonged to "the most despised race in the human community of races." In the past it had been common for whites to ascribe the relatively low test scores of blacks (and the high rates for crime, illegitimacy, and substance abuse) to racial inheritance.[67]

Standards of etiquette eventually changed, and after about 1960 it was no longer polite to voice such views publicly. Nevertheless, some prominent psychologists continued to insist that genetic variation played a significant role in group differences in IQ scores. The elite media sometimes gave the impression that only a few maverick experts subscribed to this view and that the great majority believed that group differences were purely the result of environmental factors. But when Mark Snyderman and Stanley Rothman surveyed more than 600 experts in the field of psychological measurement in 1988, they discovered that most of the experts believed that IQ tests measured the ability to solve problems and to reason abstractly; most experts believed that heredity accounted for much of the variation within racial groups; and most believed that the IQ gap between blacks and whites was due in part to genetic inheritance.[68]

It is possible to argue about the representativeness of the sample used for Snyderman and Rothman's survey. Clearly, there were many psychologists who rejected the suggestion of genetic differences. But regardless of the distribution of opinion among psychologists, the message of the race/IQ controversy seemed to be: "We have scientific evidence that blacks, because of genetic inadequacies, cannot be expected to do well at tasks that require great intelligence."[69]

If few blacks could succeed in open competition (except in nonintellectual fields like athletics and entertainment), then proportional representation could not be achieved without preferences, which then, in turn, reinforced white suspicions of black inferiority. Even worse, according to Shelby Steele, the preferences imputed "a certain helplessness to blacks that diminishes our self-esteem" and caused blacks to internalize the message of inferiority that they received from the larger society.[70]

Some blacks doubtless accepted the view that their race was inferior. But Steele observed that others simply took solace in "the comforts and rationalizations [that] their racial 'inferiority' affords them," using preferences as an excuse to avoid hard work and diligent study. Affirmative action did not "teach skills, or educate, or instill motivation," Steele wrote. It simply guaranteed that blacks and some other minorities would compete only with one another for whatever positions had been set aside. Instead of "developing a formerly oppressed people to the point where they can achieve proportionate representation on their own (given equal opportunity)," preferences went "straight for the proportionate representation." They encouraged blacks to rely on a form of reparations. In the process, they sapped the initiative and self-reliance of the alleged beneficiaries.[71]

The dependency and racial anxiety induced by preferences were so great, Steele wrote, that by the 1980s blacks were "more oppressed by doubt than by racism." Because of prevailing suspicions, opportunity had come to seem "more like a chance to fail than a chance to succeed." Because of "opportunity aversion," many black students did not take their studies seriously; and those who attended predominantly white colleges enforced "a kind of neo-separatism that includes black 'theme' dorms, black student unions, [and] Afro-houses." Some blacks snidely disparaged fellow blacks who worked hard at their studies; they accused them of acting "white." Similar criticism was directed at those who worked hard at their jobs. Much of this criticism stemmed from self-doubt—a lack of confidence that, according to Steele, also caused the most obvious entrepreneurial opportunities in black communities to be "routinely ignored."[72]

Steele thought blacks had the potential to do as well as other groups if they worked hard. Instead, he wrote, too many complained "that institutional racism is automatically present in the work place; that political conservatism is by definition anti-black; that blacks were not 'given' enough chances to advance; that blacks are exploited economically and otherwise." Further, because blacks had internalized the "message of inferiority," they "demanded concessions from government, industry, and society at large while demanding very little from blacks by way of living up to the opportunities that have already been won."[73]

Unlike William Raspberry, Shelby Steele did not question the motives of those who established preferences. He thought they were trying to "balance the scales of history" by awarding a form of compensation for the centuries of discrimination against blacks. But good intentions were not enough. "After twenty years of implementation," Steele concluded, "affirmative action has shown itself to be more bad than good."[74]

Thomas Sowell shared Steele's concern about what affirmative action was doing to "the minds and hearts of human beings." Like Steele, Sowell concluded that racial preferences undermined black confidence and conveyed the message that blacks were "losers who will never have anything unless someone gives it to them."[75]

Sowell was also concerned as to how preferential policies would affect the psychology of whites. He warned that "a multi-ethnic society like the United States can ill-afford continually to build up stores of inter-group resentments." Sowell noted that slave rebellions, race riots, and lynchings had claimed a few thousand lives throughout the course of U.S. history. By way of contrast, hundreds of thousands of people had lost their lives in truly massive racial riots and pogroms in Indonesia, Sri Lanka, Uganda, and elsewhere. Sowell warned that Americans should "never think that the disintegration and disaster that has hit other multi-ethnic societies 'can't happen here'.... We have not escaped this fate by nobility but by circumstance." Sowell wrote that Americans were not made of different flesh and blood from other people; if they went down the road to polarization, they would find interracial violence at the end of it. Sowell warned of "what people are capable of, when the stage has been set for tragedy," and cautioned that those who sanctioned affirmative preferences were sowing the seeds for a possible disaster in the future.[76]

If it were necessary to take such risks to lift up blacks, Sowell felt, then perhaps a case could be made for racial preferences, but he had confidence in the ability and potential of his fellow blacks. If they would turn a deaf ear to white racists and civil rights activists, who told them "by word and deed that skills are not the real issue," the masses of blacks could prevail in the "arduous process of acquiring [the] skills and discipline" that "have worked for all sorts of groups in all sorts of countries, down through history."[77]

Beyond that, Sowell reiterated one of the standard points of the economists who criticized affirmative action: that "most of the things that polarize Americans—busing and quotas, for example—have no...record of advancing the disadvantaged." Under affirmative action, Sowell wrote, "those with little education or job experience, or from broken families—have fallen even further behind [while] the benefits of preferential programs go disproportionately to those more fortunate." Affirmative preferences may have helped "a black professor get an endowed chair" but were of no benefit to "the black teenager trying to get a job." In summation Sowell wrote, "What the masses of blacks get from affirmative action is mainly the resentment of the rest of society."[78]

Unlike Thomas Sowell, Stephen L. Carter was not concerned as to how preferences might affect whites. At one point in his book, *Reflections of an Affirmative Action Baby*, Carter confessed that he hardly knew what to make of the argument that preferential programs were unfair to whites.[79]

Carter joined Steele and Sowell, however, in decrying the "terrible psychological pressures that racial preferences often put on their beneficiaries." Like Steele and Sowell, Carter thought that affirmative action was based on the assumption "that black people cannot compete intellectually with white people." Consequently, affirmative programs reinforced the suspicion that successful blacks had moved ahead as a result of preferences rather than because of merit. In this way, the affirmative programs tarnished "the legitimate achievements of highly qualified black professionals." In addition, Carter noted that affirmative programs did little for the black people who were most in need. Taking everything into account, he felt affirmative action was "unfair, denigrating, counterproductive, or unnecessary."[80]

Others, such as Derek Bok, the president of Harvard University, warned that the abandonment of racial preferences would lead to a dramatic reduction in the number of blacks at selective colleges and professional schools. Bok said this reduction would then have "a devastating effect on the morale and aspirations of blacks" (and would also strengthen "racial stereotypes on the part of many whites").[81]

Carter disagreed. He had "far too much faith in [the] competitive capacity [of blacks] to anticipate some apocalypse" if affirmative preferences were cut back. Carter insisted that blacks did not need special treatment in order to succeed in the professions; they did not need to be considered "the best blacks, competing only with one another for the black slots." The blacks' goal, he believed, should be "to prove that we can compete with anybody, to demonstrate that the so-called pool problem, the alleged dearth of qualified entry-level candidates who are not white, is at least partly a myth."[82]

Unlike Thomas Sowell, who was one of the nation's preeminent conservative economists, Stephen Carter was a man of the left. He favored more government spending for medical care, more government spending for preschool programs, and more government spending to improve the infrastructure of inner-city areas. He mentioned Lyndon B. Johnson's Great Society and War on Poverty as examples "of the kind of societal commitment that is required even now."[83]

Unfortunately, according to Carter, major spending programs were not possible because affirmative action had become a substitute that provided racial justice on the cheap. The costs were paid by the working- and middle-class whites who lost out in competition for jobs and contracts. Blacks who were already well off received some benefits; and well-to-do whites also benefited, because affirmative action became a substitute for the higher progressive taxes that were needed to finance major domestic-spending programs.[84]

Carter endorsed several of the points that William Julius Wilson emphasized in his book of 1987, *The Truly Disadvantaged.* Like Carter, Wilson recognized that racial preferences, although beneficial to more-advantaged blacks, did little for those who were most in need. He believed that the so-called underclass needed a combination of public employment and government-subsidized on-the-job training and apprenticeships, but that such programs were no longer possible because affirmative racial preferences had destroyed much of what was left of the New Deal coalition of working-class whites and blacks.[85]

In the past this coalition had enacted higher taxes to finance government spending programs. By the 1980s, however, the coalition was rent asunder.

The fissure was due in large part to a white backlash against affirmative action. When the national leaders of the Democratic party embraced affirmative preferences and moved away from the idea that race should not be a source of advantage or disadvantage for anyone, many working- and middle-class whites bolted the Democrats. They thought that Democratic talk about "fairness" and "affirmative action" was essentially a cover for "favoritism" for minorities and "reverse discrimination" against whites.

Ronald Reagan's victories in the presidential elections of 1980 and 1984 created a difficult situation for those who believed that government-spending programs could alleviate the problems of poor blacks. William Julius Wilson and Stephen L. Carter had second thoughts about affirmative action because they thought that white resentment over preferences and quotas had destroyed the coalition of working- and middle-class blacks and whites. They criticized affirmative action because they wanted to reestablish a coalition that could enact the sort of spending programs that they thought would help people who were truly disadvantaged.[86]

IV

Even before he became president, Ronald Reagan sensed that many traditionally Democratic, working-class whites regarded affirmative preferences as a serious obstacle to their own advancement on the job and also opposed busing for integration because they thought an influx of blacks would damage the quality of education at the public schools their children attended. Reagan recognized that racial policy could be used as a powerful wedge to break up what had been the liberal coalition of the poor, minorities, and working- and middle-class whites.[87]

Reagan thought the Democrats were vulnerable because the tenets of liberalism had changed from the pre-1964 emphasis on equality of opportunity to a post-1964 emphasis on racial preferences to achieve equal outcomes. He recognized that by 1980 many whites favored the principle that the civil rights movement had pronounced in years past—opposition to every form of state-sanctioned racial discrimination. He recognized that by campaigning for conservative egalitarianism—equality of opportunity rather than equality of results—he could win the support of many low- and middle-income whites who previously voted Democratic.[88]

After winning the presidency, Reagan was careful to maintain the support of the crossover Reagan Democrats. As Thomas and Mary Edsall have noted, the Reagan administration "maintained a steady public drumbeat of opposition to government benefits targeted to blacks, to affirmative action, and to all race-based special preferences," and portrayed "opposition to the use of race and sex preferences...as deriving from a principled concern for fairness: as a form of populist opposition to the granting of special privilege." Further, the Reagan administration defined "'reverse discrimination' as the symbol of liberalism run amok," and offered assurance to whites of ordinary means "that under Republican direction the federal government was no longer tilted in favor of minority competitors for jobs, schools...or college entrance."[89]

To many, William Bradford Reynolds initially seemed an unlikely candidate to appease the Reagan Democrats. Journalist Tom Bethell wondered whether Reynolds, or anyone else of his elite background, would have the courage to confront a liberal establishment that had switched the definition of equal rights. William D. D'Onofrio, an antibusing activist, later recalled that when he first met Reynolds in 1981, "I left unconvinced that Reynolds was the right man" to be assistant attorney general for civil rights.[90]

D'Onofrio and South Carolina senator Strom Thurmond initially thought University of Texas law professor Lino A. Graglia would be a better choice to head the Civil Rights Division. Graglia had several strengths. He was the author of *Disaster By Decree*—a brilliant critique of the court rulings that led to forced busing. He was a gifted public speaker and a trenchant writer who had few peers when it came to analyzing the Constitution and the civil rights movement. A graduate of the City College of New York, Graglia also had the advantage of not bearing a trace of either the southern mint julep or the northern Brahmin.[91]

Reynolds's background—as an Ivy League graduate, as a member of one of the nation's premier families of industrialists, and as a direct descendant of the most famous of the voyagers on the *Mayflower*—led many conservatives to wonder whether Reynolds would sympathize with the working- and middle-class people who were the victims of affirmative discrimination. As many conservatives saw it, the system of affirmative preferences had been designed by people who were well-off and already had achieved most of their career objectives. Most were white. Some were tenured professors who, many conservatives thought, were bent on inveigling blacks into supporting liberal social policies in return for dependency-inducing benefits and preferences. Others, these same conservatives believed, were wealthy people who, ensconced behind the porticoes and columns of their spacious homes, wanted to make sure that crime and sporadic racial riots did not escalate into convulsive domestic violence. To control people "whom society is not able to successfully train to live by the rules of society," one psychiatrist explained, it was necessary to make some concessions. But, according to many conservatives, it turned out that most of the sacrifices were to be made by young working- and middle-class whites, especially ethnic-Americans, who did not subscribe to the ethos of the privileged liberals and who had not yet achieved their career objectives.[92]

In addition to coming in for suspicion because of his wealth and lineage, one of Reynolds's statements in 1981 alarmed many conservatives. During the confirmation hearing for assistant attorney general, Reynolds gave voice to a standard maxim of the Reagan Justice Department: that whenever anyone "suffered injury as a result of another's unlawful discriminatory practices," that individual "should be awarded a full measure of relief, including affirmative action relief." When questioned further, however, Reynolds extemporaneously said, "In addition to that, I think those people who *potentially* were the subjects of that discriminatory conduct should also be put back into the position that they would have been in had there not been that discrimination."[93]

This answer pleased Senator Arlen Specter. By saying that those who "potentially" suffered from discrimination were entitled to affirmative relief, Specter said, Reynolds had indicated that he would continue to support policies that aided groups that were "in a less-favored position than they would have otherwise been." "That is correct," Reynolds said, "where there has been a determination of discrimination and a showing of injury, or potential injury."[94]

But Reynolds's comment alarmed Senators Jeremiah Denton, John East, and Orrin Hatch. Like Specter, they understood Reynolds's use of "potentially" to mean that he would not limit affirmative relief to actual victims of discrimination but would continue to support policies that gave special preferences on the basis of membership in a group.[95]

Reynolds regained the support of Denton, East, and Hatch by explaining that when he mentioned people who "potentially" suffered from discrimination, he was referring to instances where there was proof that members of a minority group had not applied for jobs because the employer's discriminatory conduct was so well known that it was understood that a member of a minority group would have "no opportunity...to obtain the job." In a letter to Senator Hatch, Reynolds rephrased what he had said extemporaneously in testimony and, in so doing, summarized the policy that he would adhere to consistently during his eight years as assistant attorney general for civil rights:

> Any litigant who can demonstrate that he or she has suffered injury as a result of another's unlawful discriminatory practices should be awarded a full measure of relief, including affirmative action relief if necessary, in order to insure that the injured person is placed in the position he or she would have attained had there been no discrimination. Beyond this, I believe that the government should not seek race-conscious remedies which afford preferential treatment to "protected groups."
>
> The overriding objective must be to ensure that those in the work force obtain employment on the basis of individual worth and merit, without regard to race, color, religion, sex or national origin.... Affirmative action programs which fail to adhere to this fundamental principle...will be considered unacceptable.[96]

The next four chapters will show that Reynolds adhered to this approach tenaciously during the eight years of the Reagan administration. Why he did so is a matter for conjecture. As an attorney who had specialized in commercial litigation, Reynolds by training and background was predisposed to agree with the economic arguments against affirmative preferences. Those preferences, after all, handed out jobs according to membership in groups that had attained political power. To Reynolds, it seemed obvious that this approach distorted the market, fostered inefficiency, and imposed costly burdens on the economy. He thought civil rights activists, using the pretext of equity rather than the socialist argument for efficiency, had put politics (and lawyers) in charge of the workplace.[97]

But Reynolds did not emphasize the economic arguments against affirmative action. This contrasts with other members of the Reagan administration, such as Charles Fried, the solicitor general with whom Reynolds coauthored several of the Reagan administration's legal briefs against affirmative racial preferences. Fried repeatedly warned against the politicization of the economy. He lamented that "when the government...tells private businesses and institutions that they must hire more blacks..., we are taking a large step in the direction of a command economy, an economy where the bureaucracy replaces market forces." Fried warned that many "affirmative action extremists" harbored a grudge against free enterprise and that they wanted to give government bureaucrats "control over the most intimate and crucial part of the economy: the employment relation." Fried was alarmed that they would impose "a collectivist conception of equality" that would give government "a hold on parts of private institutions that had previously eluded its grasp."[98]

Reynolds agreed with Fried. He recognized that the post-1964 reinterpretation of discrimination had converted the Civil Rights Act into a measure of social engineering that jeopardized the market economy. He recognized that civil rights activists were using arguments for equity to increase the power of politics over the economy. He agreed with an observation of the journalist Peter Brimelow: "While conservatives have been congratulating themselves about [the demise of communism and the decline of socialism] overseas, the U.S. has been silently and steadily transformed by a race- and gender-based socialism."[99]

But Reynolds did not emphasize this line of thought. In the scores of speeches and articles he prepared on affirmative action, there were only occasional references to economics. Reynolds said that well educated, middle-class blacks who would have done all right in any case were the only beneficiaries of affirmative preferences. He said that "the disadvantaged who were said to benefit from the programs actually received nothing." He said, in addition, that the focus on preferences led the country to ignore "potentially more effective solutions to the problems we seek to solve," and that it diverted attention away from the need to improve educational standards and to create more jobs in urban centers of the United States. But these were fleeting comments.[100]

Reynolds had more to say about the psychological arguments against affirmative preferences. He mentioned that the "better educated and more affluent blacks" paid a price for the "modest gains" they received from affirmative preferences in that they did not receive the recognition that would accompany advancement that was merited and awarded after free and open competition. Instead, "they carried with them into the work force the general recognition that they were 'affirmative action' employees, and thus all-too-frequently were visited with the stigma that they could never have secured their position on merit alone."[101]

Reynolds also warned of the harmful effects that racial preferences had had on the attitudes of whites. In addition to reinforcing the impression of black inferiority, Reynolds said, preferential policies increased group polarization. They created "resentment between fellow workers, divided the country, and engendered new tensions." Preferences pointed the United States "down the road leading to a society ordered along racial lines where a person's standing in the eyes of the government turned on the pigmentation of one's skin." Preferences encouraged Americans "to look upon people as possessors of racial characteristics, not as the unique individuals they are."[102]

Reynolds accepted the essence of *Griggs*—that any test or standard that had an adverse racial impact must have a legitimate business purpose. Reynolds said that if a requirement used for hiring or promotion affected minorities adversely, "the burden shifts to the employer to demonstrate that the hiring or promotion practice is job related."[103]

But Reynolds also thought that civil rights lawyers had concocted dishonest arguments to show that reasonable tests of ability and achievement were somehow unfair and prejudiced. He thought the adverse impact theory was being misapplied to promote equality of results, and that sometimes "under representation" was mistakenly equated with "discrimination." He said, "It is simply not the case that applicants for any given job come proportionally qualified by race, gender and ethnic origin." Because different groups had differences in interest, industry, and ability, a selection process that was entirely free of invidious discrimination would not produce proportional representation.[104]

When it came to race norming, Reynolds expressed strenuous objections. He said employers should be allowed to use tests that were job related and that the tests should be scored honestly.

All things considered, however, Reynolds made only sparing use of the arguments of psychologists and of market-oriented economists. He knew these arguments combined to make a powerful case against affirmative action—but Reynolds's emphasis was elsewhere.

For Reynolds there were a few key points. One was that the civil rights laws—the laws he was sworn to enforce—called for color-blind nondiscrimination. He said this was clear "not only in the language of the Civil Rights Act of 1964, but also in the legislative debate preceding its passage." The civil rights groups had lobbied for affirmative preferences; but time and again Congress rejected special-interest legislation in the area of civil rights. Reynolds held that "[i]n every major enactment since 1964, Congress has made clear that the rights protected by our federal civil rights statutes are universal in their application to *all* persons."[105]

Reynolds also thought affirmative preferences were fundamentally at odds with the nation's constitutional and philosophical traditions. According to Reynolds, the rights of citizens derived "from the uniquely American belief in the primacy of the individual." He believed "[t]he right to be free from racial discrimination inheres in all individuals, not just those who can claim membership in some 'preferred' group."[106]

Beyond this lay a matter of simple justice. Reynolds said it was wrong—"morally wrong"—for the government to discriminate on the basis of race. A painting on one of his office walls recalled an event that the artist Norman Rockwell had memorialized. It was a scene of federal marshals protecting a well-dressed young black girl who was being taunted as she made her way toward a desegregated school. As Reynolds saw it, this girl was being judged by the color of her skin rather than by the content of her character. Reynolds thought racial discrimination was wrong in the 1950s and still wrong in the 1980s.[107]

Notes

1. *Journal of Economic Literature*, 27 (June 1989): 531–32.
2. Ibid.; Richard J. Herrnstein and Charles Murray, *The Bell Curve*, 291–92; College Entrance Examination Board, Profiles, *College Bound Seniors, 1981* (New York: College Entrance Examination Board, 1982), 32, 41, 51, 60, 70; Thomas Sowell, "Playing the Numbers Game with Civil Rights," *Wall Street Journal*, 20 January 1983, 24:3; David J. Armor, "Why is Black Educational Achievement Rising?" *The Public Interest* (Summer 1992): 65–80.
3. Barbara Lerner, "Washington v. Davis: Quantity, Quality, and Equality in Employment Testing," *Supreme Court Review*, (1976): 293.
4. For the most influential example of this literature, see National Commission on Excellence in Education, *A Nation at Risk: The Imperative for Educational Reform* (Washington: National Commission on Excellence in Education, 1983).
5. John A. Hartigan and Alexandra K. Wigdor, eds., *Fairness in Employment Testing* (Washington: National Academy Press, 1989), 17 and passim.
6. I. A. Ryanen, "Commentary of a Minor Bureaucrat," *Journal of Vocational Behavior*, 33 (1988): 381.
7. *Journal of Vocational Behavior*, 33 (December 1988): 239, 279–80; John A. Hartigan and Alexandra K. Wigdor, *Fairness in Employment Testing*, 19.

8. *Forbes*, (15 February 1993): 80.
9. *The Review* (University of Delaware), 8 November 1989. Stephen L. Carter has also written about this. "I am reminded of a conversation I had some years ago with a veteran civil rights litigator who, concerned at charges that affirmative action sometimes results in hiring unqualified candidates, drew a sharp distinction between *unqualified* and *less qualified*. An employer, he mused, does not have to hire the *best* person for the job, as long as everyone hired is *good enough* to do the job. Consequently, he reasoned, it is perfectly fine to require employers to hire black applicants who are less qualified than some applicants, as long as the black candidates are capable of doing the job." *Reflections of an Affirmative Action Baby* (New York: Basic Books, 1991), 51.
10. *Journal of Vocational Behavior*, 33 (December 1988): 279–80.
11. Ibid., 288.
12. *Forbes* (15 February 1993): 99.
13. John A. Hartigan and Alexandra K. Wigdor, *Fairness in Employment Testing*, 21, 34, 48–49; Richard A. Epstein, *Forbidden Grounds* (Cambridge: Harvard University Press, 1992), 237–38.
14. *National Review* (3 September 1990): 35–36.
15. Ibid.
16. *Journal of Vocational Behavior*, 33 (December 1988): 303.
17. Ibid., 302.
18. *The Public Interest* (Winter 1990): 19.
19. *Journal of Vocational Behavior*, 33 (December 1988): 287,
20. Ibid., 286.
21. Ibid., 334 and passim.
22. John A. Hartigan and Alexandra K. Wigdor, *Fairness in Employment Testing*.
23. *Science*, 244 (2 June 1989): 1036–37; *The Public Interest* (Winter 1990): 18–25.
24. Linda Gottfredson, "The Science and Politics of Race Norming," *American Psychologist* (November 1994): 955 ff.
25. John A. Hartigan and Alexandra K. Wigdor, *Fairness in Employment Testing*, 1–14 and passim.
26. Nathan Glazer, *Affirmative Discrimination* (New York: Basic Books, 1975), 57.
27. *Journal of Vocational Behavior*, 29 (December 1986): 343.
28. Ibid.; *American Psychologist* (October 1981): 1128; Richard Herrnstein and Charles Murray, *The Bell Curve*, 71–79; Robert Gordon, paper delivered at the University of Delaware, 12 March 1992.
29. Two of the major studies on validity generalization are John E. Hunter, Frank L. Schmidt, and Gregg B. Jackson, *Meta-Analysis: Cumulating Research Findings Across Studies* (Beverly Hills, Sage, 1982); and Hunter, *Test Validation for 12,000 Jobs* (Washington: Department of Labor, 1983).
30. *Journal of Vocational Behavior*, 33 (December 1988): 350.
31. Ibid., 350, 334.
32. Andrew Hacker, *Two Nations: Black and White, Separate, Hostile, Unequal* (New York: Charles Scribner's Sons, 1992), 113, 121; Derek Bok, "Admitting Success: The Case for Racial Preferences," *New Republic* (14 February 1985): 14–16; *Washington Post*, 2 July 1984, A3f; *New York Times*, 19 June 1983, 16:1; 12 December 1983, 26:1; *Commonweal* (21 June 1985): 356–57; *New Orleans Times Picayune*, 19 June 1983, 25:1; Herbert A. Hammerman, *A Decade of New Opportunity: Affirmative Action in the 1970s* (Washington: The Potomac Institute, 1984).

33. Richard Herrnstein and Charles Murray, *The Bell Curve*, 479; Reynolds Farley and Walter R. Allen, *The Color Line and the Quality of Life in America* (New York: Oxford University Press, 1989); James P. Smith and Finis R. Welch, "Black Economic Progress After Myrdal," *Journal of Economic Literature*, 27 (June 1989): 521–28; Richard B. Freeman, "Black Economic Progress after 1964: Who Has Gained and Why?" in Sherwin Rosen, ed., *Studies in Labor Markets* (Chicago: University of Chicago Press, 1981), 248–55.
34. Thomas Sowell, *Civil Rights: Rhetoric or Reality?* (New York: William Morrow and Company, 1984), 50, 49.
35. *Journal of Economic Literature*, 27 (June 1989): 519–64.
36. *Yale Law and Policy Review*, 8 (1990): 276.
37. *Journal of Economic Literature*, 27 (June 1989): 539–47, 546, 531, 555.
38. *Journal of Political Economy*, 76 (July/August 1968): 544; Sherwin Rosen, ed., *Studies in Labor Markets*, 247 ff; *Yale Law and Policy Review*, 8 (1990): 277–78.
39. See Milton Friedman, *Capitalism and Freedom* (Chicago: University of Chicago Press, 1962), 108–15.
40. 110 *Congressional Record* (1964), 6548; Alfred W. Blumrosen, "Society in Transition," *Yale Law and Policy Review*, 8 (1990): 260.
41. *Yale Law and Policy Review*, 8 (1990): 276, 285.
42. Griggs v. Duke Power company, 91 S.Ct. 849 (1971), 853, 854.
43. Terry Properties, Inc. v. Standard Oil Company, 799 F.2d (1986), 1527; *New York Times*, 15 February 1983, 14:1.
44. Herbert R. Northrup, *The Negro in the Automobile Industry* (Philadelphia: Wharton School of Finance and Commerce, 1970), 109–12.
45. Ibid., 110–11.
46. Ibid., 80, 106–9.
47. David Halberstam, *The Reckoning* (New York: William Morrow and Company, 1986); Andrew Hacker, *Two Nations*, 133; *Wall Street Journal*, 12 April 1988, 1:1. Toyota's main facility is in Georgetown, Kentucky, in Scott County.
48. *Wall Street Journal*, 12 April 1988, 1:1; 1 December 1987, 1:1.
49. *University of Pennsylvania Law Review*, 136 (1987): 519; Thomas Sowell, "Are Quotas Good For Blacks?" *Commonweal* (June 1978): 40.
50. William Julius Wilson, *The Truly Disadvantaged* (Chicago: University of Chicago Press, 1987), 100–102; Charles Murray, *Losing Ground* (New York: Basic Books, 1984), 72, 74.
51. William Julius Wilson, *The Truly Disadvantaged*, 42.
52. William Julius Wilson, *The Declining Significance of Race* (Chicago: University of Chicago Press, 1978), 96, 107–8.
53. Charles Murray, *Losing Ground*, 75–81, 125–29.
54. Ibid., passim.
55. *Yale Law and Policy Review*, 8 (1990): 278n.
56. William Julius Wilson, *The Declining Significance of Race*, 110.
57. *The Public Interest* (Summer 1981): 68, 61.
58. Thomas Sowell, *Civil Rights: Rhetoric or Reality?*, 51–52.
59. Ibid.; *The Public Interest* (Summer 1981): 63.
60. Stephen Carter, *Reflections of an Affirmative Action Baby*, 71–72.
61. *Washington Post*, 28 November 1984, A21a.
62. Ibid; *Wilmington News Journal*, 30 August 1990.
63. Ibid.

64. Some readers will be surprised by the omission of the economist Glenn Loury from my list of black critics of affirmative action. Loury criticized black leaders for placing excessive emphasis on affirmative action and for failing to do more to uplift the moral values and social norms of their communities. But it would not be correct to characterize Loury as a critic of affirmative action. He noted that racial preferences were problematical; however, his major point was not that affirmative action was wrong but that it had received excessive emphasis at the expense of the need for black self-improvement. In one essay for the May 1981 issue of the *American Economic Review*, Loury even defended affirmative action. Also see, "Beyond Civil Rights: The Better Path to Black Progress," *New Republic* (7 October 1985): 22–25; "The Moral Quandary of the Black Community," *The Public Interest,* (Spring 1985): 9–22; and *One By One From the Inside Out: Essays and Reviews on Race and Responsibility in America* (New York: The Free Press, 1995).

    Clarence Pendleton, Clarence Thomas, Walter Williams, and Robert Woodson were additional, influential black critics of affirmative action.
65. Shelby Steele, *The Content of Our Character* (New York: St. Martin's Press, 1990), 119.
66. Ibid., 111, 117.
67. Ibid., 116, 44.
68. Mark Snyderman and Stanley Rothman, *The IQ Controversy* (New Brunswick: Transaction Publishers, 1988). Also see Richard N. Herrnstein and Charles Murray, *The Bell Curve.*
69. Jeff Howard and Ray Hammond, "Rumors of Inferiority," *New Republic* (9 September 1985): 20.
70. Shelby Steele, *The Content of Our Character*, 90.
71. Ibid., 28, 121, 115.
72. Ibid., 54, 50, 52.
73. Ibid., 72, 27, 68.
74. Ibid., 112–13.
75. Thomas Sowell, quoted by Russell Nieli, ed., *Racial Preference and Racial Justice* (Washington: Ethics and Public Policy Center, 1991), 416.
76. *Commentary* (June 1978): 43. Also see Thomas Sowell, *Preferential Policies: An International Perspective* (New York: William Morrow, 1990).
77. *Washington Post*, 12 August 19984, B1e.
78. Ibid.
79. Stephen L. Carter, *Reflections of an Affirmative Action Baby*, 17.
80. Ibid., 14, 47, 59, 102.
81. *New Republic* (4 February 1985): 15.
82. Stephen L. Carter, *Reflections of an Affirmative Action Baby*, 11, 17, 66–67.
83. Ibid., 82–83.
84. Ibid., Chapter 4.
85. William Julius Wilson, *The Truly Disadvantaged*, 110 and passim.
86. For more on this point, see Michael Lind, *The Next American Nation* (New York: The Free Press, 1995).
87. The Democratic pollster Stanley Greenberg provided support for Reagan's view. When Greenberg conducted in-depth, two-hour interviews in Macomb County, Michigan, he discovered that many working- and middle-class whites opposed busing intensely and regarded affirmative preferences as "a serious obstacle to

their personal advancement in the work place." Their opposition to busing and preferences was so intense that it shaded toward being a profound aversion toward blacks. By the 1980s, reverse discrimination against whites had become "a well-assimilated and ready explanation for [the] status, vulnerability and failures" of many whites. They emphasized that blacks were responsible for a disproportionate number of crimes. "Blacks constitute the explanation for [the] vulnerability [of whites] and for almost everything that has gone wrong with their lives; not being black is what constitutes being middle class; not living with blacks is what makes a neighborhood a decent place to live." For a summary and discussion of Greenberg's polls, see Thomas D. Edsall and Mary D. Edsall, *Chain Reaction*, 182 and passim; and Peter Brown, *Minority Party*, (Washington, D.C.: Regnery Gateway, 1991): 78–79 and passim.

88. For a good example of Reagan's thought on this point, see his 1977 speech to the American Conservative Union, reprinted in Ronald Reagan, *A Time for Choosing*, 181–201.
89. Thomas D. Edsall and Mary D. Edsall, *Chain Reaction*, 202, 144, 173, 192.
90. *American Spectator* (March 1986): 9–11; Conservative Caucus of Delaware, Newsletter, 7 March 1989.
91. In an interview on 11 January 1991, Reynolds said that Attorney General William French Smith knew that Graglia had a keen mind and was well versed on civil rights law. But, because Graglia had written about the Constitution and civil rights, he was a known quantity. The major civil rights groups would have organized a vigorous opposition to Graglia, and Smith did not wish to begin the administration with that sort of controversy.
92. Walter Menninger, quoted in *Topeka State Journal*, 23 April 1970; Martin Shapiro, "Fathers and Sons: The Court, the Commentators, and the Search for Values," in Vincent Blasi, ed., *The Burger Court* (New Haven: Yale University Press, 1983), 234; *National Review* (18 March 1991): 58, 60.

Upon first learning that Reynolds was being considered for the civil rights post, several conservative members of Congress requested an audience that turned into an interrogation. In the spring of 1981 Senator Thurmond invited Reynolds to come to his office for a talk; but when Reynolds arrived for what he thought would be an informal, cordial discussion, he found thirty-five chairs arranged in a semicircle. The chairs were occupied by prominent Republican members of Congress, who were accompanied by staff attorneys from both the Senate and House Judiciary Committees.

The assembled Republicans made it clear that they expected the next assistant attorney general for civil rights to move away from hiring preferences and forced busing. It was time, they said, to seek other, better ways to combat job discrimination and school segregation. They reminded Reynolds that Ronald Reagan had called for a policy of nondiscrimination, and that William French Smith had criticized several courts and the administration of Jimmy Carter for "compromis[ing] the principle of color blindness through over reliance on mandatory busing to desegregate our schools" and for coming "perilously close...to fostering discrimination by establishing racial quotas in other areas."

For an hour Thurmond and the others quizzed Reynolds on legal points. Reynolds recalled the experience as "the toughest inquisition I had ever faced." He left the meeting with the impression that he had not passed muster. But when he went to Smith's office the attorney general was speaking on the telephone with Thurmond, and the senator from South Carolina was saying that "Brad" was a good candidate for the position.

Interviews with WBR, 11 January 1991 and 13 November 1992; *New York Times*, 23 May 1981, 9:5.

93. Nomination of William Bradford Reynolds to be Assistant Attorney General, Civil Rights Division, Senate Judiciary Committee, *Hearings*, 97th Congress, 1st Session, June 24 and July 17, 1981, 81–82, 90.
94. Ibid., 90, 130.
95. Ibid., 130.
96. Ibid., 99–103.
97. See *American Spectator* (November 1992): 741; *Forbes* (15 February 1993): 80.
98. *Washington Post*, 27 January 1983, A23a; Charles Fried, *Order and Law*, 100, 20.
99. *American Spectator* (November 1992): 741.
100. WBR, remarks to American Trucking Association, 29 October 1984; remarks to Council of Jewish Organizations, 23 October 1983; remarks to Delaware Bar Association, 22 February 1982, WBR Papers.
101. WBR, remarks to American Trucking Association, 29 October 1984, WBR Papers.
102. WBR, remarks to Chamber of Commerce, 26 September 1984; remarks to Labor Policy Association, 13 March 1982; remarks to Bureau of National Affairs, 14 June 1984; remarks to Washington Center Legal Symposium, 4 January 1984, WBR Papers.
103. WBR, remarks to Bureau of National Affairs, 2 June 1983, WBR Papers.
104. WBR, remarks to Affirmative Action Association, 20 September 1984; remarks to University of Maryland Center for Philosophy and Public Policy, 19 October 1984; remarks to Bureau of National Affairs, 8 February 1982, WBR Papers.
105. WBR, remarks at Equal Employment Opportunity Conference, 20 October 1981; remarks to National Urban League, 2 August 1983, WBR Papers.
106. WBR, remarks to Washington Center Legal Symposium, 4 January 1984, WBR Papers.
107. WBR, remarks at Amherst College, 29 April 1983, WBR Papers; personal observation of author. The name of Rockwell's painting is *The Problem We All Live With*.

10

Charting a New Course: The Case of the New Orleans Police Department

In the presidential campaign of 1980, Ronald Reagan promised the sort of color-blind nondiscrimination that Congress had in mind when it enacted the Civil Rights Act of 1964, and as the head of the Civil Rights Division, William Bradford Reynolds developed a policy to implement Reagan's campaign promises. Reynolds did not break with the recent past in every regard. Under Reynolds, 97 percent of the Civil Rights Division's employment-discrimination cases were on behalf of either racial, ethnic, and religious minorities or women. In some ways, Reynolds was more active than his predecessors. Under Reynolds's direction, the division filed more employment-discrimination cases per year than it had during the four years of the Carter administration, and it increased the annual amount of back pay awarded to victims of discrimination by almost 50 percent.[1]

Under Reynolds, the division also pressed a number of disparate impact cases. The most important of these involved twenty-nine municipalities in the suburbs of Chicago and Detroit. These predominantly white communities required municipal workers to live in the municipalities. This requirement was racially neutral on its face, but Reynolds challenged it as a subtle form of illegal discrimination. After the division won its case against Cicero, Illinois, the other municipalities agreed to eliminate the residency requirement and to recruit black applicants.[2]

But Reynolds's opposition to broad racial preferences and quotas put him on a collision course with the civil rights establishment. It also put him at odds with many officials in the Equal Employment Opportunity Commission (EEOC) and with others at the U.S. Commission on Civil Rights.

In addition, Reynolds's opposition to broad racial preferences was inconsistent with two Supreme Court decisions. In the *Weber* case of 1979 the Supreme Court gave its approval to a collective-bargaining agreement in which the United Steelworkers and Kaiser Aluminum reserved half of the openings in some training programs for blacks. Then, in the *Fullilove* case of 1980, the Court gave its blessing to the Public Works Employment Act of 1977, in which Congress required that at least 10 percent of federal grants for local projects must be set aside for minority groups.[3]

The Supreme Court was divided over the 10 percent set-aside, with the justices writing five separate opinions—none of which commanded the support of a majority of the Court. And although only two justices dissented from the Court's approval of the 50 percent quota in the *Weber* case, the Court's majority emphasized that "the only question" before the Court was the narrow issue of whether the civil rights law forbade employers and unions from voluntarily agreeing to give racial preferences to blacks. Phrased this way, *Weber* was as much a victory for entrepreneurial liberty as for racial quotas. In *Weber*, the Court also refused to "define in detail the line of demarcation between permissible and impermissible affirmative action plans."[4]

Despite the qualifications, Reynolds thought *Weber* could not be reconciled with Reagan's campaign rhetoric. Reynolds supported back pay, constructive seniority, and other kinds of relief if they were narrowly tailored to restore victims of discrimination to the place they would have enjoyed absent the discrimination. But he did not support preferences in a case like *Weber*, where there had been no finding that Kaiser Aluminum had discriminated against blacks. Without a finding of discrimination, the preference was not a remedy for a proven wrong.

For Reynolds, *Weber* represented a judicial foray into social engineering. The justices had not approved a settlement between adverse parties. They had, rather, placed their imprimatur on a plan that aimed to remedy the purported wrongs of society by creating a new, racially balanced social order. In Reynolds's view, it was a racial preference plan that helped blacks who were not the victims of discrimination, and, furthermore, it was a plan that, because of race, denied opportunities to innocent white workers.

Feeling as he did about *Weber*, Reynolds was alarmed by comments that President Reagan made at a press conference in December 1981. A reporter asked Reagan if he agreed with Reynolds that *Weber* should be overturned. When Reagan said he could not remember the case, the reporter said it involved "a voluntary agreement to conduct affirmative action programs for training minorities." With the case thus shorn of its quota quotient, Reagan said he favored voluntary agreements for training. Shortly thereafter, the *New York Times* published an editorial praising Reagan for parting company with Reynolds.[5]

Recognizing that Reagan's answer was problematical, Reynolds and Attorney General William French Smith briefed Reagan about the *Weber* case. Reagan then told journalists that he had not known the details of the Supreme

Court's ruling at the time of the press conference, and that after being apprised, he thought the high court had decided the case wrongly and should take another look at the legality of preferences and quotas for hiring and promotion.[6]

I

At the outset of the administration, there were several cases that seemed to offer the possibility for overturning *Weber*. One case involved schoolteachers in Boston, where District Judge W. Arthur Garrity had found local authorities guilty of operating a segregated school system. To correct the wrong of discriminating against blacks, Judge Garrity ordered a controversial plan of busing for racial balance. He also ordered Boston to hire one black teacher for every new white teacher until the overall proportion of black teachers reached 20 percent—the percentage of blacks in Boston. This was necessary, he said, to provide role models and to bring black students and their parents "fully into the school community and decision making process and to counteract their past isolation."[7]

In 1981 the number of teachers had to be reduced because of a tax reduction initiative commonly known as Proposition 2½. The school board then discovered that it could not maintain a 20 percent black teaching corps if it honored the contract it had signed with the teachers' union. That contract contained a standard seniority provision for layoffs ("last hired, first fired"), which, if honored, would have reduced the proportion of black teachers in Boston from 19 percent to 8 percent. The court therefore gave the school board permission to ignore the seniority clause, with the result that white teachers—some with more than ten years of service—were laid off, while new black teachers were still being hired.[8]

The American Federation of Teachers protested on behalf of the white teachers, who, the union said, were not responsible for any discrimination and should not have to bear the burden. The president of the union said that "colorblind, race-neutral seniority systems are perhaps the most important safeguard won by the American labor movement in its 100 years of struggle for job equality for all Americans." Reynolds was tempted to intervene in the case but backed off because of legal complications that arose from the fact that the litigation grew out of a school-segregation case.[9]

Initially, the situation with respect to Boston's police and fire fighters seemed to offer the Reagan administration a better opportunity. Here, the district court had not entered a finding of purposeful discrimination. It found only that the proportion of Hispanics and blacks employed in Boston's police and fire departments in 1970 (3.6 percent and 0.9 percent, respectively) was less than the city's 16 percent minority population. The court also said that the department used culturally biased entrance examinations that were not job related. Thus the case initially grew out of an application of the *Griggs* adverse impact doctrine. The district court ordered that one minority officer be hired for each nonminority officer until the percentage of minorities in the departments was commensurate with the percentage of minorities in the community.[10]

As was the case with the Boston schoolteachers, in 1981 the police and fire departments had to lay off workers because of the financial limitations that resulted from the voter-initiated tax cut. Finding that layoffs according to seniority would reduce the percentage of minorities (from 11.7 to 6.2 in the police department and from 14.7 to 9.1 in the fire department), the court declared the seniority provision inoperative and ordered that layoffs be made so as to preserve the proportion of minority fire fighters and police officers. As a result, some white officers with eleven years of service were laid off while minority officers with only two years of service were retained.[11]

The case of the Boston fire fighters and police officers was ideal for the Reagan administration. It was an employment discrimination case that was not complicated by association with school segregation. It was attractive because the trial court had not found intentional discrimination in addition to adverse impact. It especially appealed to the administration because Section 703(h) of the Civil Rights Act of 1964 specifically immunized seniority systems from challenge.[12]

Because the case looked like a winner for the administration, Reynolds and Solicitor General Rex E. Lee prepared a legal brief in support of the white fire fighters and police officers. By the time the case got to the Supreme Court in 1983, however, the financial situation in Boston had improved, and the laid-off workers had been reinstated. In light of this, the Supreme Court vacated the judgment of the lower court and declared the case moot. The workers had their jobs back, but the Reagan administration's hopes for a strong ruling against reverse discrimination were dashed.[13]

It was not unusual for the Supreme Court to dispose of a case on narrow grounds and thus avoid making a decision on a controversial question that has broad application. But by declining to resolve the matter, the high court did more than deny the Reagan administration a victory. It left the lower courts free to do as they pleased at a time when, as the *Washington Post* observed, "[A]ll over the country employers are 1) grappling with the need to implement affirmative action plans and 2) threatened by reverse discrimination suits."[14]

II

Reynolds tried to end the uncertainty by pressing ahead with lawsuits that challenged preferential policies in the police departments of Detroit and New

Orleans. Usually the Department of Justice waits until a court accepts a case before filing a brief. Because of "a pressing public need for whatever clarification can be achieved," however, the Reagan administration urged the Supreme Court and the Fifth Circuit Court of Appeals to intervene in cases they had not yet agreed to consider. Specifically, the administration urged the Supreme Court to set aside a court-approved plan that stipulated that in Detroit one black sergeant had to be promoted to lieutenant for each white sergeant promoted until 50 percent of all lieutenants were black. The administration also asked the full Fifth Circuit Court to reject a similar promotion quota that a divided three-judge court had approved for New Orleans.

When the Supreme Court, once again, sidestepped the question by refusing to review the Detroit case, lawyers speculated about the reason. It may have been that the Court was so fragmented on affirmative preferences that the justices did not wish to cause greater confusion by rendering a splintered opinion. In any event, a disappointed but determined Reynolds said that ultimately the Supreme Court would "have to resolve this issue.... We have to have from the Court the ultimate decision on whether we are going to proceed along the lines of assigning everyone to a group—a racial or sex group—or whether we are going to proceed on the basis of individual initiative or merit and allow every individual an equal opportunity to compete for the job."[15]

The administration was more successful in the Fifth Circuit Court. Here the judges agreed that the issues raised by affirmative action in the New Orleans Police Department should be considered by all the judges of the circuit.

In 1981 the city of New Orleans had entered into a lengthy and comprehensive agreement with a group of disgruntled black police officers. As in Detroit, the most controversial aspect of the New Orleans plan was a requirement that one black police officer must be promoted for every white officer until blacks made up 50 percent of the officers of every rank. But this was only one of the provisions that were spelled out in a thirty-three-page affirmative action plan.

The plan also called for a revision of the standards used for recruitment and hiring. Although blacks made up 55 percent of the population in New Orleans and 67 percent of those who applied for positions on the police force, only 48 percent of the black applicants passed the entry exam. Therefore, the city agreed to make "intensified" efforts to recruit more blacks. Black officers were to be sent on recruiting missions to local high schools, and black recruits were to be given a senior "buddy" to counsel them during the training period. To prevent disparate impact in hiring or promotion, any written tests were to be revised by the civil service commission in consultation with testing experts.[16]

The testing experts were instructed to perform an "item analysis" and to eliminate any question that produced "a statistically significant adverse impact against blacks." If there still were differential rates of passing after the tests had been revised, the city agreed to calculate "a separate frequency distribution" to ensure that tests did not have an adverse impact. The city said it would do whatever was necessary "to ensure that blacks will advance through the ranks at the same pace as nonblacks."[17]

The city essentially promised to engage in race norming—although the promise was phrased in such thick jargon that many people did not understand this at the time. In a general way, though, there was no confusion about what the experts were supposed to do. White police officers said the tests were being rigged. District Judge Morey Sear offered a more sedate comment. He said the goal was to "adopt procedures to assure that the proportion of blacks that graduate from the police academy at least meets the proportion of blacks who pass the written hiring examination."[18]

In 1981, nearly three-quarters of the officers in the New Orleans Police Department signed protests, and groups of white, Hispanic, and female officers went to court to challenge the New Orleans plan. They said the city had deprived them of equal protection of the laws by rigging tests and reserving half the promotions for blacks. They said they had "the right to compete for the benefits of public employment on the basis of individual worth and accomplishment, fairly ascertained, without the influence of irrelevant factors such as race." According to Sidney Bach, one of their lawyers, the issue was this: "At what point does reverse discrimination become unconstitutionally impermissible?"[19]

Judge Sear allowed the white, Hispanic, and female officers to intervene in the case, but he ruled against them on every point except one. He approved all of the New Orleans plan except the provision calling for promotion of one black policeman for every white until blacks made up one-half of all upper ranks in the department. He said that quota would jeopardize the careers of nonblack police officers and was not necessary to remedy past discrimination.[20]

On appeal to the Fifth Circuit Court, a divided panel of three judges endorsed every aspect of the New Orleans plan, including the quota for promotions. Criticizing Judge Sear's finding that the quota would greatly reduce the promotion chances of nonblack officers, Judges Albert Tate and John Minor Wisdom stated the following: "This reasoning overlooks that the present great disparity between the numbers of blacks and non-blacks is due to past discriminatory practices, and that 'temporary' affirmative action quotas are an acceptable and approved remedy to redress long-term past discriminatory practices."[21]

Tate and Wisdom did not identify the discriminatory practices but pointed to statistics. As of 28 August 1981 blacks made up 23 percent of the 1,007 nonranked police officers in New Orleans, but the number of blacks in the upper ranks was disappointingly small. Among 187 sergeants, there were only five blacks; among sixty-seven lieutenants, only 2; and among twenty-nine captains and majors, zero.[22]

Tate and Wisdom then inferred discrimination because, they wrote, "it is ordinarily to be expected that nondiscriminatory hiring practices will in time result in a work force more or less representative of the racial and ethnic composition of the population in the communities from which employees are hired."[23]

Since Tate and Wisdom regarded adverse impact as evidence of discrimination, it followed that the promotion quota was "appropriate [and] necessary to afford complete relief to the...black officers." Because blacks had been victims of discrimination in the past, Tate and Wisdom wrote, they were entitled to "preferential treatment...even though some of the burden of remedying past discrimination is borne by other employees themselves innocent of the wrongdoing."[24]

It was at this point that Reynolds asked the full Fifth Circuit Court to review the New Orleans case. Reynolds said the district court had been right to reject "the race-conscious promotion quota at issue in this case." He said that the divided panel, in approving the quota, disregarded Title VII of the Civil Rights Act and ignored "fundamental principles of equity and the equal protection guarantees of the U.S. Constitution."[25]

Reynolds's argument in the New Orleans case was a shot across the bow of the civil rights establishment. "We came from out of nowhere and did the unheard-of," he later recalled. He explained that since President Carter's Department of Justice had not participated in this case when it was before the district court, it was unusual for the full circuit court to grant Reynolds's request for a review and to allow the Department of Justice to intervene belatedly in the litigation. It was especially unusual because the EEOC had previously participated in the case on the other side. Thus Reynolds was entering the case at the eleventh hour with a request that the full circuit court should set aside a consent decree that another agency of the U.S. Government had previously requested. Under the circumstances, Reynolds regarded it as "a major accomplishment" to be permitted to intervene in these circumstances.[26]

Reynolds's legal brief, which was coauthored with Charles J. Cooper, threw down the gauntlet on constitutional grounds and on the basis of traditional principles of equity, as well as on the narrower question of what was permissible under Title VII. Reynolds and Cooper broke no new ground in saying that employers must cease and desist from racial discrimination, must open up their recruitment efforts to minorities, and must give affirmative relief to blacks who had been victims of discrimination; but they also said that affirmative relief should be restricted to individuals who had been the victims of discrimination and not given to others who belonged to the same race but had not themselves suffered discrimination. In saying that affirmative relief should be restricted to actual victims of discrimination, Reynolds and Cooper departed from the group-oriented policy that EEOC had always favored, that President Nixon had adopted in the early 1970s, and that subsequent administrations had followed.[27]

At the time the Supreme Court had not established the "line of demarcation between permissible and impermissible affirmative action plans." It had also not settled the question of whether affirmative relief should be given only to individuals who had suffered from discrimination. But spokesmen for the established civil rights groups noted that Reynolds's argument ran counter to the approach of the EEOC and of some circuit courts of appeal. "The significance of this case is extraordinary and so is the administration's position," said Barry L. Goldstein of the NAACP-associated Legal Defense Fund. "What they're doing is arguing for a fundamental change in the way the civil rights laws have been interpreted."[28]

Reynolds began his argument in *New Orleans* by pointing to what he called an "ancient requirement" of equity law, "that the right and remedy must be congruent." To explain the essence of fairness, he quoted from a nineteenth-century work by Professor John Norton Pomeroy:

> [A person] whose primary right has been violated immediately acquires a secondary right to obtain an appropriate remedy from the wrongdoer, while the wrongdoer himself becomes subjected to the secondary duty of giving or suffering such remedy. It is the function of courts, both of law and of equity, directly to enforce these remedial rights and duties.[29]

In referring to other Supreme Court decisions, Reynolds maintained that the Court had "never wavered" in insisting that a remedy must correspond to a wrong. In one school-desegregation case, the Court asserted that "all remedies" must be designed "to restore the victims of discriminatory conduct to the position they would have occupied in the absence of such conduct." In another desegregation case, the Court said that remedies must be "tailor[ed]" so as to be "commensurate" with "specific violations." In these cases, and in others, the Supreme Court had made it clear that court orders to remedy discrimination "can extend no farther than the violation itself."[30]

Reynolds's critics accepted this. However, they maintained that discrimination involved more than giving benefits or penalties to an individual because of his or her race; it involved institutional arrangements that discriminated against blacks as blacks and favored whites as whites. Gertrude Ezorsky wrote that "institutional racism" was responsible for the statistical overrepresentation of blacks at the bottom of the occupational ladder. She said that the "ultimate goal" of affirmative action was to counteract this "by moving the black work force toward approximate statistical parity."[31]

Some judges endorsed this point of view. Thus John Minor Wisdom said discrimination was so deeply rooted in the nation's system that "an effective remedy must be color conscious." He wrote that "[i]n light of the pervasive past discriminatory practices and the present effects of these practices," it was necessary to give special preferences to individuals who had not been victimized personally but who belonged to a race that had suffered discrimination in the past. Also, to overcome the hidden structures of white domination and the continuing effects of past discrimination, it was necessary to take account of race; that is, to treat blacks equally, they must be given special preferences.[32]

Reynolds rejected this defense of "benign" discrimination. He said it ignored "the fact that occupation selection in a free society is determined by a host of factors, principally individual interest, industry and ability." Because of differences in cultural styles and historical experiences, he said, "the career interests of individuals do not break down proportionally." Because different groups have distinctive constellations of values, "it simply is not the case that applicants for any given job come proportionally qualified by race."[33]

Reynolds regarded discussions of group differences as interesting speculation. In the end, he thought, no one knew for certain whether the differentiation was the result of discrimination or of deeply rooted cultural values. It was clear to Reynolds, however, that the Congress that enacted the Civil Rights Act had not favored benign discrimination and had not equated underrepresentation with discrimination. Whatever the merits of the proquota argument, it was not what the legislators had in mind in 1964.[34]

A large portion of Reynolds's sixty-page brief in *New Orleans* was devoted to showing that Congress, when it enacted Title VII of the Civil Rights Act, specifically prohibited judges from using racial quotas to remedy systemic discrimination. Reynolds quoted a dozen supporters who insisted that Title VII would not require or permit racial quotas. Senator Humphrey had sounded this refrain when he said that "contrary to the allegations of some opponents," there was nothing in the act that would give "any power...to any court to require hiring, firing, or promotion of employees in order to meet a racial 'quota' or to achieve a certain racial balance." Humphrey said, "That bugaboo has been brought up a dozen times, but it is nonexistent."[35]

In addition to noting the statements of the congressional sponsors, Reynolds pointed to the language of the act. The act made it unlawful for an employer or labor union to discriminate against "any individual... because of such individual's race." It said that if a court found such discrimination it could order "such affirmative action as may be appropriate." But the act also said that no court order should benefit anyone "if such individual...[had lost out] for any reason other than discrimination on account of race."[36]

Advocates of benign discrimination could not cite statements from the legislative debates that supported preferences or quotas. In terms of legislative history their best argument was that Congress, in 1972, voted down Senator Ervin's proposals to ban preferences. The post-*Griggs* Congress of 1972 also amended Section 706(g) to authorize judges to give "any other equitable relief as the court deems appropriate." Those who favored preferences noted that by this time some lower courts had ordered or upheld numerical quotas to benefit blacks. They said the Congress of 1972 "assumed that the present case law...would continue to govern the...construction of Title VII."[37]

Reynolds considered this argument untenable. He said the Congress of 1972 did not fundamentally revise the Civil Rights Act. The law continued to establish that workers had an individual right not to be discriminated against because of race. "Section 703 was left unchanged." He pointed out that it used the word "individual" twenty-four times in saying that it was unlawful for an employer "to discriminate against any individual...because of such individual's race"; and that Section 706 still said that no court order should require an employer to hire or promote anyone for any reason other than "discrimination on account of race."[38]

The most that could be said about the Congress of 1972 was that it rejected antiquota amendments introduced by Senator Ervin, and that some members praised *Griggs*. But, as noted above, Reynolds (and professors Herman Belz and Hugh Davis Graham) refused to find a delegation of power in congressional inaction or acquiescence, especially where such delegation was at odds with the language, the structure, and the preponderance of the legislative history of the Civil Rights Act.[39]

Reynolds insisted that the Civil Rights Act authorized courts to enforce principles of equity in the traditional context of personal rights. The law did not require racial balance. It required action to end discrimination and to restore every victim of discrimination to his or her rightful place. Once that was accomplished, the effects—all the effects—of unlawful discrimination would be remedied. For Reynolds, a one-to-one promotion quota such as that contained in the New Orleans plan violated the Civil Rights Act. For him, there was nothing remedial about a plan that required the promotion of people whose personal right to nondiscriminatory treatment had not been violated; and there was nothing equitable about harming the prospects of innocent white, Hispanic, and female police officers in order to benefit blacks who had not proved they were victims of discrimination.

Reynolds agreed with critics who said it would be difficult to identify all the victims of past discrimination. Therefore, victim specific relief probably would not achieve the racial balance that would have occurred in the work force absent discrimination.[40]

However, Reynolds insisted that the failure to afford remedial relief to some victims was "in no way ameliorated (much less remedied), by conferring preferential promotion priority on other, randomly selected members of the discriminatee's race." Reynolds wrote that "a person suffering from appendicitis is not relieved of his pain by an appendectomy performed on the patient in the next room, even if the latter is a member of the same race."[41]

Reynolds thought the real goal of those who favored preferences was not to remedy discrimination but to achieve racial balance. As he saw it, however, the Constitution and laws of the United States did not require any particular balance. The government's interest was to ensure that all citizens received equal protection and that no person suffered discrimination because of his or her race. If racial preferences were not narrowly restricted to benefit specific victims, Reynolds said, they would not prevent discrimination; on the contrary, they would guarantee that there would be discrimination. They would create new groups of victims. Reynolds said that "any preferential treatment accorded to nondiscriminatees—or to discriminatees beyond those measures necessary to make them whole—necessarily deprives innocent incumbent employees of *their* 'rightful places.'"[42]

In *New Orleans*, Reynolds also raised a constitutional issue. Even if the Civil Rights Act had not protected individuals of every ethnic group against racial discrimination, and even if quotas for groups did not exceed traditional principles of equity jurisprudence, Reynolds said that the New Orleans plan violated the equal protection clause of the U.S. Constitution.

Quoting from the opinion of the Supreme Court in *Korematsu v. United States* (1944), Reynolds said that it was well settled that "all legal restrictions which curtail the civil rights of a single racial group are immediately suspect" and that "courts must subject them to the most rigid scrutiny." Reynolds noted that Justice Lewis Powell, in announcing the Court's judgment in *University of California v. Bakke* (1978), had said that "it is the individual who is entitled to judicial protection against classification based upon his race or ethnic background because such distinctions impinge upon personal rights." Justice Powell went on to say that the equal protection clause "cannot mean one thing when applied to one individual and something else when applied to a person of another color. If both are not accorded the same protection, then it is not equal."[43]

Proponents of the New Orleans quota answered that the Supreme Court (in the Japanese curfew and internment cases of World War II) had authorized racial classification and the imposition of burdens if there was a good reason for the policies. The proponents then argued that the "operational needs" of the New Orleans Police Department required the promotion of blacks, saying that the public was more likely to cooperate with a police force whose members reflected the racial balance in the community. "Because of the importance of public assistance to effective law enforcement," they said, "the government has an interest in a police department in which the blacks have a fair share of policing responsibilities."[44]

Reynolds noted that similar arguments had "long been [used] in the service of racial discrimination." Some whites had argued against assigning black teachers to predominantly white public schools, on the basis that the assignments would cause a loss of public confidence in the schools; and some municipalities had assigned only black police officers to patrol predominantly black areas, on the grounds that black officers were "able to communicate with the inhabitants of the Negro area better than white officers and [were] better able to identify Negroes and investigate criminal activities in that zone."[45]

For years, Reynolds noted, courts had consistently and rightly rejected such racial classifications. Reynolds insisted that "a free society is anchored in the concept of equality before the law." Quoting from an NAACP brief in another case, he wrote, "To place police efficiency ahead of equality is to destroy that concept and to destroy the fundamental right of human dignity."[46]

Reynolds's *New Orleans* argument was coherent and spirited. At one time most liberals would have found it persuasive. By the 1980s, however, they recoiled from the argument that affirmative relief should be restricted to individuals who were actual victims of discrimination. Tom Wicker of the *New York Times* complained that Reynolds had "flatly reversed the policy on 'affirmative action' that had been developed by predecessor[s]...under two Republican and two Democratic Presidents."[47]

To appreciate the extent of the change, Reynolds's *New Orleans* brief can be contrasted with the briefs the Carter administration submitted for the *Bakke* and *Weber* cases of 1978 and 1979.

In *Bakke*, the University of California Medical School at Davis reserved 16 percent of the spaces in its entering class for disadvantaged blacks, Chicanos, and Asians (while disadvantaged whites were routed through the regular admission process). Because the university had not discriminated in the past, there was nothing remedial about the set-aside. The chairman of the admissions committee candidly explained that because the average score of the disadvantaged minorities on the Medical College Admission Test (MCAT) was much lower than the average score of whites, a quota was "the only way" to achieve the admission of substantial numbers of blacks. Under the quota plan, he said, all minority students would be "qualified," though their average score on the science portion of the MCAT placed them in only the 35th percentile (as compared with an average of 83d percentile for other students).[48]

Applying the "strict scrutiny" test for racial classifications that "result in detriment to a person because of his race," the Supreme Court of California rejected the quota. It said the quota deprived "persons who were not members of a minority group of benefits which they would otherwise have enjoyed." Further, the California court said, "To uphold the University would call for the sacrifice of principle for the sake of dubious expediency and would represent a retreat in the struggle to assure that each man and woman shall be judged on the basis of individual merit alone."[49]

On appeal to the U.S. Supreme Court, the Carter administration defended the 16 percent quota. Carter's lawyers argued that "race must sometimes be taken into account to achieve the goal of equal opportunity." They said "minority sensitive programs" like that at the California medical school should be used "to overcome the effects of years of discrimination." They said that "as long as prior discrimination has present effects, mere neutrality is insufficient." They recognized that the University of California had not been found guilty of discrimination, but they said that because "societal discrimination" had been "pervasive," the university could take race "into account to prevent racially disadvantageous outcomes, not simply to rectify past discrimination."[50]

In its *Weber* brief, the Carter administration expanded on these points. Here Kaiser Aluminum had established a one-for-one quota for admission to training programs for skilled-craft jobs at its plant in Gramercy, Louisiana. Because Kaiser, like the University of California, had not been found guilty of past discrimination, the district court and the court of appeals rejected the quota. The district court found that the black employees selected for the training program "had never themselves been the subject of any unlawful discrimination." Therefore, the court said, it was not appropriate to use race as a criterion for admission to the program. In the absence of prior discrimination, the court of appeals added that "a racial quota loses its character as an equitable *remedy* and must be banned as an unlawful racial *preference* prohibited by Title VII."[51]

In response, the Carter administration said that blacks had been "subjected to pervasive and systematic employment discrimination." Because blacks had been victimized as a group, Carter's lawyers said, members of the group were entitled to benefit from "a race-conscious selection device."[52]

This was essentially the argument that some civil rights activists had made in 1964 and that Congress had rejected then. But Carter's lawyers said that Congress, in amending the Civil Rights Act in 1972, had authorized the use of race-conscious remedies. It did so because it did not enact Senator Ervin's proposals to ban such remedies and because it "was aware of" (and therefore tacitly endorsed) court orders and bureaucratic regulations that had established numerical relief even "in the absence of proof of previous discrimination."[53]

The lawyers for Carter and Reagan had different conceptions of equality. For the Carter administration, affirmative racial preferences and quotas were all right because they purported to benefit members of groups that had been the victims of widespread discrimination. Carter's lawyers did not demand proof of discrimination by specific employers against specific people. Their goal was racial balance in the work force. In contrast, Reagan's lawyers wanted to restrict race-conscious preferences to instances where they would restore particular victims of discrimination to their rightful places.

In developing the Reagan administration's position on affirmative action, Reynolds did more than depart from the policies of the Carter administration. He also took the lead in squelching the Equal Employment Opportunity Commission and hastened a reorganization of the U. S. Commission on Civil Rights.

When Reynolds challenged the racial quota system in the New Orleans Police Department, the EEOC prepared a separate brief that criticized Reynolds's legal arguments. Disputing Reynolds's version of the legislative history of 1964 and 1972, the EEOC reiterated the standard line of the established civil rights groups: that the framers of the Civil Rights Act favored race-conscious quotas; and that any doubts on this score were put to rest in 1972 when Congress rejected Senator Ervin's proposals to ban quotas, when it acquiesced in *Griggs*, and when it made no effective objection to district- and circuit-court decisions that ordered or upheld numerical affirmative action plans. The EEOC's brief said that there was "nothing in the language...or legislative history...to indicate that Congress intended to preclude courts from approving prospective race-conscious relief simply because the benefits of such relief are not restricted to actual victims of past discrimination."[54]

The views of the EEOC were not a surprise. From its founding in 1964, Alfred W. Blumrosen and other staff members had rejected the idea that the economic conditions of blacks could be improved by nondiscrimination and equal employment opportunity. Instead, they used adverse impact charges to force employers to hire blacks on a numerical basis. Some members of the staff were even opposed to investigating individual complaints, for fear that attention to specific instances would get in the way of the effort to define inequality as a statistical pattern of underutilization. Professor Belz has pointed to a pattern of misfeasance at EEOC, and Professor Graham concluded that "few new agencies...have been as subversive of their founding charter."[55]

The EEOC's legal brief in *New Orleans* was predictable, but for Reynolds it was also an annoying indication of disunity within the Reagan administration. At a White House meeting, Reynolds convinced presidential counselor Ed Meese and Attorney General William French Smith that the administration should speak with only one voice and that the commission should be pressured into silence.[56]

The EEOC acquiesced, but an independent legal foundation submitted the commission's brief to the Fifth Circuit Court anyway. Clarence Thomas, then the chairman of the commission, initially voted to submit the brief and "strongly urge[d] the Department of Justice to reconsider its position in light of the EEOC's objections." It was not until 1984 that Thomas announced his support for the concept that affirmative preferences should be restricted to identifiable victims of discrimination. During Ronald Reagan's second term, the EEOC shifted to an antiquota policy.[57]

Reynolds hastened the transformation, but Thomas played the key role in moving the EEOC toward the Reagan Right. The second-highest-ranking black in the administration, Thomas was a proud man who could quote Malcolm X from memory on the importance of racial pride and self-help. He fought against post-*Griggs* pressures to make employers adjust tests to allow as many blacks as whites to pass, on the grounds that these pressures were based on the assumption "that blacks lack intelligence" and that they "can't perform as well as whites."[58]

Under Thomas's leadership, the EEOC broke away from more than twenty years of defining discrimination as the statistical underutilization of blacks. Instead of regarding civil rights as a matter of corporate struggle and group equity, Thomas, like Reagan and Reynolds, focused on individuals who said they had been victimized by discrimination. Under his leadership the EEOC, in 1986, processed a record number of 66,000 complaints.[59]

While the *New Orleans* case was being argued, the U.S. Commission on Civil Rights weighed in with a letter urging President Reagan to allow the EEOC to send its brief to the Fifth Circuit Court. The letter of the Civil Rights Commission was one of a series of nagging annoyances to Reagan and Reynolds; and since the Civil Rights Commission, like the EEOC, was part of the executive branch of government, Reagan moved to bring the commission into line with the policies of the administration. He did so by replacing pro-quota commissioners with others who opposed quotas but had strong records of support for civil rights.

The process began in November 1981 when Reagan dismissed commission chairman Arthur S. Flemming. At that time no one challenged the president's right to replace one commissioner with another. In fact, Flemming had been appointed to the commission in 1974 to replace the Reverend Theodore Hesburgh, who had been fired after he criticized the Nixon administration for its opposition to court-ordered busing to integrate the public schools. By 1981 it was Flemming, who also supported forced busing and hiring quotas, who had become an irritant to an incumbent administration. In one interview Flemming said that the Thirteenth, Fourteenth, and Fifteenth Amendments, enacted after the Civil War, "introduced proportional representation" along with outlawing slavery and giving citizenship rights to former slaves.[60]

In 1981 Reagan also fired Stephen Horn, the vice-chairman of the commission. To replace Flemming, Reagan picked Clarence Pendleton, a black man who had been an official with the National Urban League in San Diego. To replace Horn, he chose Mary Louise Smith, a white woman who had once been chairman of the Republican National Committee. After joining the commission, Smith surprisingly supported busing and quotas; but Pendleton, in what he called "a drastic departure from the traditional civil rights thinking," opposed these measures as "bankrupt" policies that led to "an emphasis on statistical parity rather than equal opportunity."[61]

Despite Pendleton's appointment, the commission did not concern itself with instances in which people had been treated differently because of their race. It continued to define discrimination as underrepresentation, and its reports pointed to statistics that showed that blacks were not being elected, hired, and promoted in numbers commensurate with their proportion of the population. The commission also said that because of adverse impact, it was a violation of civil rights for the government to reduce spending for social programs. It further irritated Reagan by reporting, falsely, that the administration had reduced spending for the enforcement of civil rights.[62]

By 1983 Reagan had had enough. He proposed to stop the carping by replacing three proquota commissioners with three antiquota Democrats. He also proposed to substitute a Chicana woman for a black man as the director of the commission's professional staff.

In terms of background and long commitment to civil rights, Reagan's nominees were more distinguished than the people they were to replace. Linda Chavez, the new staff director, was a former civil rights activist who had been working as an assistant to the president of the American Federation of Teachers. Robert Destro was a law professor who had had a volunteer civil rights law practice for many years. Political scientist John Bunzel was a former president of San Jose State University who had worked for the admission of more blacks to Princeton as far back as 1948. Morris Abram, a former president of Brandeis University, had played an important role in the voting rights litigation of the 1960s, had defended civil rights workers facing the death penalty in Georgia, and helped persuade John F. Kennedy to use his influence to get Martin Luther King released from jail in 1960.[63]

Despite these qualifications, Reagan's reorganization did not go smoothly because two proquota commissioners, Mary Frances Berry and Blandina Cardenas Ramirez, asked for a court order invalidating their dismissals from the commission, saying that the framers of the legislation that created the commission had intended for the commissioners to have independence and to be free from political interference. Berry and Cardenas said they would not relinquish their posts and would continue to attend meetings and to vote on whatever business was before the commission.[64]

Liberals rallied to the defense of the proquota commissioners. Harvard professor Lawrence Tribe said that Congress intended for the commission to be independent, and therefore the courts should "construe the law to bar the sort of action that President Reagan took." The *New York Times*, which previously had acknowledged that "the President has a right to appoint individuals who share his views," changed course and noted that the president's power to dismiss commissioners "isn't spelled out in law."[65]

In response, lawyers for the administration said that a government official who has the power to appoint also has the power to remove the appointees, unless a statute says otherwise. They presented copies of President Carter's letters appointing Berry and Cardenas to serve "during the pleasure of the President of the United States for the time being." They also asked the rhetorical question, If the president could not fire commissioners, who could? If, as Berry and Cardenas argued, the answer was no one, then the commissioners would serve for life or at their own pleasure.[66]

The courts never rendered a definitive answer on the president's legal authority to replace commissioners because Congress, in November 1983, approved a compromise to restructure the Civil Rights Commission. The compromise provided that the president and Congress would each appoint four members to an eight-member commission.[67]

Reagan then gained control of the commission. He did so by reappointing Clarence Pendleton, Morris Abram, John Bunzel, and by replacing the proquota Republican Mary Louise Smith with an antiquota, female high school science teacher—Esther Gonzalez-Arroyo Buckley. The Democrats in Congress reappointed Mary Frances Berry and Blandina Cardenas Ramirez, but the House Republicans picked the president's erstwhile choice, Robert Destro, to replace Jill Ruckelshaus, a Republican who supported quotas. The Senate Republicans then named Francis Guest, a black man from Tennessee, to replace the proquota Rabbi Murray Saltzman.

The reorganized commission quickly moved in new directions. Staff director Linda Chavez canceled several ongoing studies, including one that focused on how cuts in federal aid harmed black students, and another that was critical of technology for having an adverse impact on women and blacks.[68]

Chavez said she would continue a study of voting rights and redistricting but cautioned that "careful attention should be paid that the [study] does not assume that the concept of fair representation necessarily implies that unless minorities are elected in proportion to their numbers in the electorate [they] have been denied their full rights to be fairly represented." She also recommended a study of affirmative action in higher education—one that would assess the "general decline in academic standards [that] coincided with the advent of affirmative action," and that also would question whether unprepared students who were admitted under preferential plans were damaged because they later had to leave school without obtaining degrees.[69]

In addition to redirecting the staff reports, the new commission switched to the side of the Reagan administration in the debate over affirmative preferences. By a vote of 6–2, the commission condemned quotas as a new form of discrimination that created "a new class of victims." The commission also said that decisions on social policy were outside the purview of civil rights, and it renounced prior studies that attacked budget cuts as harmful to minorities. By way of explanation, commission chairman Clarence Pendleton said that racial discrimination and civil rights lost their special hold on the conscience of the nation when they became identified with social and economic policies, and that discrimination is always wrong, even when its victim was a white male.[70]

Members of the civil rights establishment were outraged. Mary Frances Berry lamented that the commission had become "a lapdog for the administration instead of a watchdog." Walter Mondale called the new commissioners "trained puppets of the White House." William Coleman said that the commission's "traditions of independence and nonpartisan continuity" had been "sacrificed on the altar of political conformity."[71]

The new commissioners resented the aspersions. Clarence Pendleton observed that the issue of the commission's independence was not raised when the commission agreed with the policies of previous administrations. Morris Abram promised to follow "the dictates of my conscience" and said he had "not been asked with respect to this appointment what I may or may not do." John Bunzel predicted that the new commission would be "totally independent—of the White House [and] of the Leadership Conference on Civil Rights."[72]

Of course, the Reagan administration did not have to inquire into the opinions of Abram and Bunzel, as their views were a matter of public record. The civil rights establishment professed to be concerned about the independence of the commission, but the real concern was that the new commissioners would embarrass the civil rights establishment. In addition, there was the possibility that the new commissioners, because of their eminence and eloquence, would undermine liberal support for quotas and preferences. That this was one of Abram and Bunzel's goals was indicated by the testimony they gave to the Democratic National Platform Committee in 1984:

> We come before you as longstanding Democrats who have supported for 40 years the efforts of this party to provide rights and opportunities for all individuals independent of race, color, religion, sex, or national origin. Twenty years ago we joined with other individuals and groups in urging Congress to pass the Civil Rights Act that was designed to bring Americans together, not to separate or di-

vide them. The purpose of that historic act was to take race out of the equation, to cut out the tumor of racial categories that had been poisoning our whole society for too long. The nation's commitment to equality of opportunity had been reaffirmed.

During the last decade or so, however, congressional policy has undergone many changes—but not because there has been a great reversal of public opinion. As verified by every poll, the American people remain committed to the goal of equal opportunity. Yet today in many quarters the principle of equal opportunity is being replaced by another principle, namely, equality of results. We are now told, for example, that racial preferences should be given to certain persons by virtue of their group membership. That is why there is so much talk today about quotas.

In the name of a new equality, the policy of color-blindness, which had long been the moral touchstone and mandate of our Constitution and is a requirement of the 1964 Civil Rights Act, has been severely modified....

We come before you today because we believe the time is at hand for the Democratic Party to state clearly and unambiguously how it feels about this redefinition of equality.... Does the Democratic Party believe that the principle of nondiscrimination should be replaced with the principle of race-based entitlements [?]...Where does the Democratic Party stand?[73]

New Orleans gave Reynolds and his allies the opportunity to advance a position on affirmative action and to enforce unity within the Reagan administration. The case was also important in its own right. In 1984, by a vote of 7–6, the Fifth Circuit Court gave the administration a victory by ruling against the proposed one-to-one black-white promotion quota. Reynolds described the decision of the court as "a breakthrough." It was "the first judicial recognition that there was something wrong with consent decrees that assigned racial preferences."[74]

But Reynolds's victory was qualified because the court also rejected the administration's claims that affirmative relief should be limited to actual victims of past discrimination. While holding that there was no "insurmountable barrier" to the use of general preferences, the court ruled against "the extent of preferential treatment" that was at issue with the one-for-one promotion quota in New Orleans.[75]

Writing for the six dissenters, Judge John Minor Wisdom rejected almost every one of Reynolds's points. He said that the Constitution did not require that "strict scrutiny" be given to racial classifications that purported to benefit blacks. He endorsed the liberal line on the legislative history of 1972. He accepted the argument that the "operational needs" of the police department were "sufficiently compelling" to justify the promotion quota. He "wholly reject[ed] the concept of 'identifiable victims,'" saying that institutional racism against blacks was so "systemic" that the remedy must point toward "restructuring the system" on a "color conscious" basis.[76]

Taking a different tack on behalf of three members of the seven-judge majority, Judge Patrick E. Higgenbotham endorsed the essential points in Reynolds's argument. He agreed that "we are a nation of persons, not groups," and that the legislative history of the Civil Rights Act made it plain that courts did not have the authority to approve quotas to achieve a racial balance.[77]

Judge Higgenbotham said that New Orleans had done nothing wrong in failing to maintain a statistically proportionate work force. "The illegality [was] in discriminating against black persons," and that illegality could be remedied by giving back pay and the proper rank to those who had been denied promotions. "Nothing," he wrote, "justifies the jump from such permissible relief to that of what can fairly be described as an obligation to proportionally employ." Higgenbotham rejected "the notion that 'the black race' is an independent legal entity and that relief for past discrimination against black persons should take the form of special advantages granted in the future to 'the black race.'"[78]

Upon learning that the Fifth Circuit Court had ruled against the New Orleans quota plan, city attorney Salvador Anzelmo promised to go to the Supreme Court if necessary to win approval for the quotas. Cooler heads eventually prevailed, and in 1987 the courts approved a settlement that called in part for creating thirty-one new sergeant, lieutenant, and captain jobs for blacks. This was a far cry from the one-for-one promotion quota plan. Ron Wilson, an attorney for the black officers, acknowledged that the settlement "provided for a very, very limited number of black promotions; it is not an ongoing affirmative action sort of situation." Sidney Bach, who represented the white officers in the litigation, said his clients had their day in court and would not challenge the settlement.[79]

The importance of the *New Orleans* case is not to be found in the final settlement. The case was important because it provided the occasion for the Reagan administration to develop its approach to affirmative action. The *National Review* noted this in 1983 when it praised Reynolds and his deputy Charles Cooper "for finally swinging the weight of the Executive Branch behind the simple, colorblind precept of fairness and justice held by most Americans." The *Wall Street Journal* concurred when it commended "the Reaganites" for bringing a "truly important question into the open: whether racial quotas are fair according to the basic tenets of our political order."[80]

Notes

1. U. S. Department of Justice *Enforcing the Law* (Washington, 1987), IV2, IVc, IVd.
2. Ibid., IV; *St. Louis Post Dispatch*, 26 February 1989.

3. United Steelworkers of America v. Weber, 443 U.S. 193 (1979); Fullilove v. Klutznick, 448 U.S. 448 (1980).
4. United Steelworkers of America v. Weber, 443 U.S. 193 (1979), 200, 208.
5. *New York Times*, 18 December 1981, II, 6:1; 30 December 1981, 14:1; 9 January 1982, 24:6.
6. *Washington Post*, 5 January 1982, A6e.
7. *Washington Post*, 24 June 1982, A7a; Morgan v. Kerrigan, 388 F.Supp. 581 (1975).
8. Ibid.; *Washington Post*, 2 July 1982, A19a.
9. *Washington Post*, 24 June 1982, A7a.
10. Castro v. Beecher, 334 F.Supp. 930 (1971); 459 F.2d 725(1972); 365 F.Supp. 655 (1973); 386 F.Supp. 1281 (1975).
11. Rex E. Lee, William Bradford Reynolds, et al., Brief for the United States as Amicus Curiae, Boston Firefighters v. Boston NAACP, U. S. Supreme Court, 1982, Case 82-185; *Washington Post*, 17 March 1983, A19f.
12. Teamsters v. United States, 431 U.S. 324 (1977); United Air Lines v. Evans, 423 U.S. 553 (1977).
13. Boston Firefighters v. Boston NAACP, 461 U.S. 477 (1983).
14. *Washington Post*, 18 May 1983, A26a.
15. Baker v. City of Detroit, 458 F.Supp. 379 (1978); 483 F.Supp. 930 (1979); 504 F.Supp. 841 (1980); Bratton v. City of Detroit, 704 F.2d 878 (1983); 712 F.2d 222 (1983); 464 U.S. 1040 (1983); 465 U.S. 1074 (1983); *Washington Post*, 11 January 1984, A2c.
16. *New Orleans Times Picayune*, 17 December 1982, 1:2; Williams v. City of New Orleans, 543 F.Supp. 662 (1982); 694 F.2d 197 (1982), 993.
17. Williams v. City of New Orleans, 543 F.Supp. 662 (1982), 682–83, 685.
18. Ibid., 685.
19. Ibid., 681; *New Orleans Times Picayune*, 24 December 1982, 13:3; *Washington Post*, 6 April 1983, A6a.
20. Williams v. City of New Orleans, 543 F.Supp. 662 (1982), 685–86; *New Orleans Times Picayune*, 17 December 1982, 1:2.
21. Williams v. City of New Orleans, 694 F. 2d 987 (1982), 996.
22. Ibid.
23. Ibid., 995, quoting Teamsters v. United States, 431 U.S. 324 (1977), 340 n.20.
24. Ibid., 989, 996.
25. *New York Times*, 8 January 1983 , 11:1.
26. Interview with WBR, 5 August 1993.
27. William Bradford Reynolds and Charles J. Cooper, Brief of the United States as Intervenor, Willilams v. City of New Orleans, Fifth Circuit Court of Appeals, New Orleans (cited hereafter as Reynolds-Cooper Brief).
28. United Steelworkers v. Weber, 443 U.S. 193 (1979), 208; *New York Times*, 7 June 1983, 18:1.
29. Reynolds-Cooper Brief, 9, quoting John Norton Pomeroy, *A Treatise on Equity Jurisprudence, As Administered in the United States of America* (San Francisco: A. L. Bancroft and Company), 1881–83.
30. Ibid., 10, 13, 16, quoting Milliken v. Bradley, 418 U.S. 717 (1974); and Dayton V. Brinkman, 433 U.S. 406 (1977), 417.
31. Gertrude Ezorsky, *Racism and Justice: The Case for Affirmative Action* (Ithaca: Cornell University Press, 1991), 2, 32, 55.
32. Williams v. City of New Orleans, 729 F.2d 1554 (1984), 1573.

33. WBR, remarks to Association of American Law Schools, 6 January 1985, WBR Papers.
34. Interview with WBR, 5 August 1993. Reynolds was skeptical when I mentioned that some psychologists thought there were racial differences in cognitive ability. He thought racial differentiation resulted either from discrimination or from dissimilar cultural values.
35. 110 *Congressional Record* (1964), 6549.
36. 42 U.S.C. 2000e, Section 703(a) and Section 706(g).
37. See Brief of the United States and the Equal Employment Opportunity Commission, United Steelworkers v. Brian F. Weber, in Philip Kurland and Gerhard Caper, eds., *Landmark Briefs and Arguments of the Supreme Court*, vol. 112, 302–6, 336–41.
38. Reynolds-Cooper Brief, 33 and appendix.
39. Ibid.; Herman Belz, *Equality Transformed*, 76–77; Hugh Davis Graham, *Civil Rights and the Presidency*, 214–15.
40. Reynolds-Cooper Brief, 18.
41. Ibid., 18–19.
42. Ibid., 52, 18–20.
43. Ibid., 48–49; Korematsu v. United States, 323 U.S. 214 (1944), 216; University of California v. Bakke, 438 U.S. 265 (1978), 299, 289–90.
44. *Williams v. City of New Orleans*, 729 F. 2d 1554 (1984), 1575.
45. Reynolds-Cooper Brief, 54–55, quoting from *Baker v. City of St. Petersburg*, 400 F.2d 294 (1968).
46. Ibid., quoting from the NAACP's brief for the appellants in Baker v. City of St. Petersburg.
47. *New York Times*, 22 April 1983, 31:1.
48. Brief for the United States as Amicus Curiae, Regents of the University of California v. Allan Bakke, in Philip Kurland and Gerhard Casper, eds, *Landmark Briefs and Arguments of the Supreme Court*, vol. 99, 307, 314; University of California v. Bakke, 438 U.S. 265 (1978), 277 n.7.
49. Philip Kurland and Gerhard Casper, *Landmark Briefs and Arguments of the Supreme Court*, vol. 99, 319, 321.
50. Ibid., 301, 303, 354, 341, 221. For an account of the discussions among Carter's lawyers, see John C. Jeffries, Jr., *Justice Lewis F. Powell, Jr.* (New York: Charles Scribner's Sons, 1994), 461–65. Also see Bernard Schwartz, *Behind Bakke: Affirmative Action and the Supreme Court* (New York: New York University Press, 1988).
51. Philip Kurland and Gerhard Casper, *Landmark Briefs and Arguments of the Supreme Court*, vol. 112, 283285.
52. Ibid., 294, 292.
53. Ibid., 304, 335, 340.
54. Brief of the Equal Employment Opportunity Commission, submitted as an appendix to the brief of the Douglas Foundation, Williams v. City of New Orleans, Fifth Circuit Court of Appeals, 1983,case 82-3435; Williams v. City of New Orleans, 729 F.2d 1554 (1984), 1572 n.5.
55. Herman Belz, *Equality Transformed*, 25–30, 70–81; Hugh Davis Graham, *Civil Rights and the Presidency*, 122.
56. *Washington Post*, 7 April 1983, A1a.
57. *Washington Post*, 28 April 1983, A17a; Herman Belz, *Equality Transformed*, 189.

58. *Atlantic Monthly* (February 1987): 73, 72.
59. Ibid., 72, 73, 78.
60. *New York Times*, 2 March 1982, 22:1; 6 December 1974, 56:4; *Psychology Today* (June 1984): 52.
61. *New York Times*, 3 October 1982, IV, 5:1; 13 October 1982, 18:1.
62. *Wall Street Journal*, 22 March 1983, 32:2.
63. Ibid., 15 July 1983, 26:3.
64. *New York Times*, 27 October 1983, II, 13:1.
65. Ibid., 1 June 1983, 14:2; 2 March 1982, 22:1; 15 September 1983, 26:1.
66. Ibid., 27 October 1983, 13:1; 1 November 1983, 23:1; *Wall Street Journal*, 28 June 1983, 34:3.
67. *New York Times*, 5 November 1983, 26:1; 1 December 1983, 28:1.
68. *Washington Post*, 7 January 1984, A1b.
69. Ibid.
70. Ibid., 18 January 1984, A1b; *Wall Street Journal*, 22 March 1983, 32:3.
71. *Washington Post*, 18 January 1984, A1b; *Wall Street Journal*, 20 July 1984, 16:1; *New York Times*, 5 November 1983, 13:5.
72. *Washington Post*, 18 January 1984, A1b; *New York Times*, 23 May 1983, 15:1; *Wall Street Journal*, 21 December 1983, 24:3.
73. *Wall Street Journal*, 15 June 1984, 30:4.
74. Interview with WBR, 5 August 1993.
75. Williams v. City of New Orleans, 729 F.2d 1554 (1984), 1557, 1564.
76. Ibid., 1574, 1572 n.5, 1575, 1573.
77. Ibid., 1566.
78. Ibid., 1567, 1566, 1569.
79. *New Orleans Times Picayune*,24 April 1984, 1:1;; 13 June 1989, 1:1.
80. *National Review* (4 February 1983): 95–96; *Wall Street Journal*, 8 December 1983, 30:1.

11

False Dawn

If quotas were not the answer, what was? William Bradford Reynolds said publicly that punitive damages should be assessed against employers who were guilty of discrimination. In addition, he stressed the importance of advertising and recruiting programs that would reach "deep into communities previously ignored or barely tapped," and also called for special programs that would train members of minority groups to the point where they could compete with members of other groups. He acknowledged that the training and advertising involved racial preferences (because they would be targeted for blacks and other minorities), but this did not bother him because Congress had this in mind when it passed the Civil Rights Act. Then, moving beyond punitive damages as well as affirmative recruiting and training, Reynolds favored make-whole relief for individuals who were actual victims of discrimination.[1]

Thus, it would not be correct to say that Reynolds opposed affirmative action. He favored what he called "the original and undefiled" sort of affirmative action that was popular in the 1960s, opposing race-conscious quotas, goals, and set-asides that gave nonvictims a preference based on race. Reynolds freely acknowledged that the United States had an "undeniable legacy of discrimination," but he differed from the major civil rights groups when it came to policies that were designed to remedy discrimination and its effects.[2]

Reynolds said the remedies for discrimination should be *color-blind* and *victim specific*. He said a remedy would be color-blind if it was based on victim status rather than race; and since the goal was to punish discriminators and to compensate actual victims, relief should consist of punitive damages and the award of a job or a promotion (together with back pay and seniority) to the individuals who had been victims of discrimination.

Essentially, Reynolds insisted that individuals must show they had been injured before the courts ordered that special measures be taken for their benefit. It might seem like a small point, yet insistence on victim specificity would end quotas and all that Reynolds considered objectionable about the civil rights agenda of the 1970s.

Some members of the Reagan administration had reservations about Reynolds's position. They thought the administration's goal should be to scotch what one of them called "the sinister tendency toward a bureaucratic-collectivist state"; they said the administration should stop the politicization of the economy that was "implicit in government-imposed racial and gender preferences"; and they argued that victim specificity went beyond what was needed to combat excessive government control over the economy.[3]

Of those who expressed reservations about victim specificity, one of the most articulate was Charles Fried, a Harvard law professor who became solicitor general during Ronald Reagan's second term. The problem with victim specificity, Fried felt, was that by the time a lawsuit was over, some of the victims would have scattered and thus would not be compensated. In these cases, discrimination would go unremedied. It was because of this, Fried suggested, that some people who opposed both government management of the economy and equality of results nevertheless favored racial preferences. Fried thought some people (including some members of the Supreme Court) could be peeled away from the coalition that supported egalitarian social engineering if the Reagan administration would allow for "preferential remedies when an employer had been shown to discriminate."[4]

When Fried said that victim specificity was not essential, he "found out how deeply Brad Reynolds...felt about the concept of color-blindness." He recalled that Reynolds "bridled at government-imposed preferences and 'race-conscious relief,' even as a remedy for proven discrimination." Reynolds gave Fried to understand that "victim specificity was the order of the day; it was the President's policy."[5]

Fried was put off by Reynolds's manner, as well as the message. "After a confrontation with [Reynolds]," he wrote, "you needed a stiff drink and a long walk." Years later, he remembered the "cold contempt" Reynolds displayed at some meetings. Even on the occasions when Reynolds refrained from full discussion of an issue, "what he did say dripped scorn and was rich in spoken or implicit accusations of apostasy and unmanly cowardice." For his part, Reynolds took umbrage when Fried said that "victim specificity was an unnecessary and unacceptable addition to a sound antidiscrimination policy."[6]

Michael Horowitz, a White House lawyer, was even more outspoken than Reynolds in making the case against racial preferences. Fried recalled one occasion when "Mike treated me to the kind of tirade—fervent and heartfelt—for which he had become famous":

> [D]eregulatory, economic-liberty concerns were beside the point; this was a moral issue; when Lincoln freed the slaves, questions of efficiency and government interference did not come into it; and where racial justice is the issue, he would not gag at any amount of government control. Racial preferences of any kind were

unjust, I was told. People like me did not understand how struggling white working people were hurt and outraged to see their efforts disregarded in favor of others, who were no more deserving and had not suffered anything more or worse than they had. These were the people who had elected Ronald Reagan, not fancy-pants neocons[ervatives] like me.[7]

On some occasions, Reagan's first solicitor general, Rex E. Lee, was another, but more friendly, adversary of Reynolds. Formerly the dean of the law school at Brigham Young University, Lee was in charge of the office that represented the government in the Supreme Court. It was a difficult position because Reagan believed the Supreme Court was flat out wrong on a number of issues beyond those of racial quotas and forced busing: the president thought the Court had been wrong in deciding that it was unconstitutional for states to restrict a woman's right to have an abortion; the president thought the Court had been wrong in refusing to allow prayer in the public schools; and he also thought the Court had unnecessarily hobbled local law enforcement and had mistakenly extended First Amendment protections to obscenity and pornography.

Lee agreed with Reagan. But as an experienced litigator, Lee recognized that "you just don't win cases...[by] going before the Supreme Court...and telling its members point blank that they were wrong." If he did this, Lee believed, he would be guilty of "bad lawyering." Lee said, "In a close case—as so many of the cases are in the Supreme Court—the lawyer's impertinence might well cost the client the one or two votes needed to win."[8]

In addition, Lee recognized that the positions taken by the solicitor general enjoyed special influence with the Supreme Court. They did so because the solicitor general was regarded as representing not just the political views of the administration but also the broad interests of the country, which is why, Lee noted, the solicitor general's legal briefs are filed in the name of "the United States."[9]

Thus Lee was wary of cases involving the so-called Reagan Agenda—the cases where the administration tried to persuade the Court to interpret the law in ways that matched Reagan's political positions. Lee regarded school prayer as "an albatross around my neck," and he ducked the *Bob Jones* case on the grounds that he had once represented the Mormon Church in a similar lawsuit.[10]

Like most litigators, Lee wanted to win, and during his four years as solicitor general, he won 77 percent of his cases—well above the average of other solicitors (about 67 percent). In one year during Lee's four-year tenure, the United States won a higher percentage of its cases in the Supreme Court than in any year since the Justice Department began keeping statistics, but Lee was convinced that this success was possible only because he exercised restraint when it came to campaigning for the agenda of the administration.[11]

Although he was concerned about the solicitor's need to preserve his standing with the Supreme Court, Lee acknowledged that there were occasions when he should stand forthrightly for principles that the Court was not then prepared to embrace. "There could be long-range objectives to be served by such a filing," he said. But "there are large costs, and it is rarely advisable." Lee said, "You can dip your bucket into the well [of high principle] once or twice a year." Anything more, would compromise the effectiveness of the solicitor.[12]

In 1983, Lee "dipped it" with a legal brief that questioned the reasoning of the Supreme Court's decisions that legalized abortion. He knew the Supreme Court was not likely to agree at that time, but he hoped that some day the Court would rally around a position that he considered legally correct and firmly rooted in basic principles of morality. In the short term, though, Lee thought his office and the Reagan administration had paid heavily for challenging the Court on abortion. "Any time you come into a highly visible case and you lose," he said, "you pay some costs."[13]

Reynolds was more inclined to battle for principle and to ignore the short-term consequences. Regardless of what the Supreme Court decided, Reynolds thought Lee's brief on abortion was well crafted and legally correct. He knew Bob Jones University was not likely to prevail in court, but he took the case because he thought the university was right on the legal issues. Because he thought the Supreme Court had misinterpreted the establishment clause, Reynolds also urged Lee to make an issue of school prayer (although Lee finally persuaded Reynolds to back off on this question).[14]

Charles Fried later complained, with some exaggeration, that Reynolds "proposed a constant stream of suicidally radical...projects." He wrote that "working with Brad Reynolds was the toughest part of my job—as it had been for Rex Lee." Journalist Lincoln Caplan maintained that "constant hounding from the Reagan Right," from people "like Bradford Reynolds," finally caused Lee to resign as solicitor general. Perhaps so, although the only disputes between Reynolds and Lee that ever went public concerned the government's position on school prayer and on publicly sponsored nativity scenes.[15]

Lee shared Reynolds's misgivings about the Court's decisions on religion, but said "[I]t's obvious the Court isn't going to depart from them." Lee said he had "no qualms about taking a position that might not be immediately persuasive, but which might bear fruit down the road." But he said it usually "isn't smart to lecture the Justices about where they went wrong.... If I had done what was urged on me in a lot of cases, I would have lost those cases and the Justices wouldn't have taken me seriously in others."[16]

Because of his more cautious approach to litigation, Lee was initially reluctant to push the argument that the proper remedy for discrimination should not go beyond make-whole relief for specific victims. In *Weber*, after all, the Supreme Court had sanctioned voluntary preferences for the entire class of blacks in a case where the employer had never been found guilty of discrimination; and throughout the nation other employers had avoided lawsuits by agreeing to preferential arrangements (called consent decrees) that were supervised and enforced by local courts.

Reynolds wanted to challenge *Weber*. He publicly said the case had been wrongly decided. He also wanted the U.S. Government to contest the preferential consent decrees. He wanted to establish the proposition that relief, even for proven cases of discrimination, must be victim specific. What one observer called "a furious battle" ensued, with most of the career lawyers in the solicitor general's office opposing Reynolds. So did Rex Lee, for a while.[17]

In 1983, however, Reynolds found a consent decree that caused Lee to shift and to argue for victim specificity. Reynolds liked the case because it involved an employer who had never been found guilty in court and a consent decree that gave a racial preference to blacks who had not been actual victims of discrimination. Lee liked the case because it involved seniority and because the preference had not been devised voluntarily but had been imposed by order of a court. The case was *Memphis Firefighters v. Carl Stotts*.[18]

Legal battles over the composition of the Memphis fire department dated to 1974, when the administration of President Ford sued the city over alleged racial discrimination. An inspection of class photographs at the fire department's training center indicated that no blacks had been employed before 1955, when sixteen were hired. Three more blacks were hired in 1965, and after that a few blacks were hired each year, although it was not until 1972 and 1973 that the number of new jobs given to blacks approximated their proportion (35 percent) of the city's overall population. Blacks were also underrepresented in other departments of the city government.[19]

City officials never admitted to any misconduct, but to avoid the time and expense of a lawsuit, the city and the Department of Justice accepted a consent decree that provided for a "long term goal" of achieving throughout the municipal government "proportions of black and female employees in each job classification approximating their respective proportions in the civilian labor force." The city government also accepted interim goals of filling 50 percent of entry-level vacancies with blacks and of giving blacks and women at least 30 percent of the positions (such as accountant or engineer) that required a professional degree.[20]

Because the city government agreed to a consent decree, there was no judicial hearing and no findings of fact in the case. By accepting the decree, the city did not concede that it had violated the law, and President Ford's Justice Department waived any further relief.[21]

Notwithstanding the 1974 consent decree, Carl Stotts, a black employee of the Memphis fire department, brought a class-action lawsuit in 1977, alleging that he had been denied a promotion because of his race. In 1979 another black fire fighter, Fred Jones, filed a similar suit.

In 1980 the city government again settled, without admitting to any misconduct, by accepting a consent decree that supplemented the decree of 1974. "The decree [of 1980] reaffirmed the City's commitment to achieve the long-term goal of increasing minority representation in each job classification to levels approximating the level of minority representation in the Shelby County labor force." The city provided $60,000 to settle complaints about promotions, and promised that minorities would fill "at least 50 [percent] of the vacancies" in city government and would receive at least 20 percent of any promotions.[22]

Then, in 1981, the city experienced financial problems that required a reduction in personnel throughout the municipal government. To balance the budget the city proposed a number of demotions and layoffs that would be based on the traditional policy of seniority ("last hired, first fired"). In the fire department, the forty employees with the least seniority (fifteen of whom were blacks) were to be laid off.[23]

In response, Carl Stotts and his lawyers asked the local district court, which was supervising the consent decrees of 1974 and 1980, to set aside the city's seniority policy and to forbid the demotion or layoff of any black employees. Stotts said the proposed demotions and layoffs would have "a devastating and retrogressive effect on minority employment," which had increased in the fire department from about 4 percent in 1974 to 12 percent in 1980. He acknowledged that the proposed layoffs would reduce the black proportion of the department by only one percentage point (from 12 percent to 11 percent), but he emphasized that the demotions would affect almost one-half of the fifteen blacks who were drivers and 55 percent of the twenty-nine blacks who were lieutenants.[24]

In 1955 Stotts had been a member of the first class of black fire fighters, and he later became a charter member and a vice-president of the local union. In 1983, however, Stotts said "[T]here was segregation in the past [and] it's payoff time now." He said seniority would have to go, even if, as other union members said, it was "the backbone of any union" and the only way to give working people job security. The union president said morale was "at an all time low," and the local press recounted stories of slashed tires, stolen boots, and fistfights at the firehouses. Stotts acknowledged that the dispute over seniority had caused "a bad, bad, bad morale problem."[25]

Judge Robert M. McRae recognized that the city had never been proved guilty of discrimination, but said, "[I]t would be naive not to realize that...this

City was very discriminatory towards black people for years." For that reason, and because seniority had a disproportionately adverse effect on blacks, McRae suspended seniority and ordered that demotions and layoffs be structured so as not to decrease the percentage of blacks in any rank of the fire department.[26]

A divided Sixth Circuit Court of Appeals affirmed this decision. Writing for the court, Judges Damon J. Keith and Robert M. Duncan acknowledged that in enforcing a consent decree, courts should not depart from the provisions of the decree itself. However, ignoring the fact that the city and the municipal workers' union had signed a memorandum of understanding with respect to seniority, and that the consent decree of 1974 mentioned seniority, Keith and Duncan modified the decree they purported to enforce. They did so by seizing on standard boilerplate language that authorized the supervising court to issue "such further orders as may be necessary or appropriate to effectuate the purposes" of the decree. Since the general purpose of the consent decree was to move toward the proportional employment of blacks, they reasoned, a seniority policy—even one that was mentioned in the decree itself—could not be enforced if it ran counter to the general, long-term purpose of racial balance.[27]

The city of Memphis, the fire department, and the municipal government workers' union then filed separate appeals with the Supreme Court. The Court agreed to hear the case, and William Bradford Reynolds and Rex Lee requested special leave to intervene. *Memphis* (or *Stotts*, as it is usually called) was the case Reynolds had been waiting for.

Reynolds and Lee could have made the narrow argument that dispensing with seniority was not an honest effort to implement the terms of the original decree.[28] Alternatively, they could have followed the bold argument that Reynolds and Charles Cooper developed in *New Orleans*: that relief that went beyond color-blind victim specificity was at odds with traditional principles of equity and was violative of the equal protection clause. But, because *Stotts*, unlike *New Orleans*, involved seniority, Reynolds and Lee's legal brief emphasized that the decisions of the lower courts were opposed to what Congress intended when it explicitly gave special protection to seniority in the Civil Rights Act of 1964. Then, during the oral argument before the Supreme Court, Lee emphasized that the decisions of the lower courts were out of step with what the Supreme Court itself had previously decided. It was an ingratiating argument that, if accepted by the Supreme Court, would make the law, as a practical matter, require color-blind victim specificity.

Reynolds and Lee began by noting that Section 703(h) of the Civil Rights Act protected seniority. They said the lower courts paid no attention to a compromise that was not only essential to getting the act passed but that also reflected the belief that it was wrong, even in the name of racial equality, to take seniority benefits away from white workers. They said the lower courts in *Stotts* had disregarded the fact that Congress intended "to accord special status to seniority systems and the stability that they provide to labor relations." They said the lower courts "completely ignore[d] that seniority is not just another term in a collective bargaining agreement."[29]

Critics of the Civil Rights Act of 1964 had warned that the act would destroy existing seniority systems. In response Senators Joseph Clark and Clifford Case, the bipartisan "captains" for the act, placed an interpretive memorandum in the *Congressional Record* outlining the following position:

> Title VII would have no effect on established seniority rights.... If a business has been discriminating in the past and as a result has an all-white working force...the employer's obligation would be simply to fill future vacancies on a non-discriminatory basis. He would not be obliged, or indeed permitted—to fire whites in order to hire Negroes, or to prefer Negroes for future vacancies, or, once Negroes are hired, to give them special seniority rights at the expense of the white workers hired earlier.[30]

Senator Clark also placed in the *Congressional Record* a Justice Department statement concerning Title VII:

> It has been asserted that Title VII would undermine vested rights in seniority. This is not correct. Title VII would have no effect on seniority rights existing at the time it takes effect. If, for example, a collective bargaining contract provides that in the event of layoffs, those who were hired last must be laid off first, such a provision would not be affected in the least by Title VII. This would be true even in the case where owing to discrimination prior to the effective date of the title, white workers had more seniority than Negroes. Title VII is directed at discrimination based on race, color, religion, sex, or national origin. It is perfectly clear that when a worker is laid off or denied a chance for promotion because under established seniority rules he is "low man on the totem pole" he is not being discriminated against because of his race.[31]

In addition to emphasizing the legislative history, Reynolds and Lee noted that Section 706(g) specified the sort of relief that was to be provided if a court determined than an employer was guilty of racial discrimination. They said courts could enjoin future discrimination, could order the reinstatement or hiring of individuals who were victims of discrimination, and could adjust seniority to allow the victims to be slotted into the places they would have enjoyed absent discrimination. But seniority could not be abrogated for the benefit of individuals who were not themselves the victims of discrimination.[32]

In his oral argument before the Supreme Court, Rex Lee also said that the issue in *Stotts* was "squarely controlled" by the Supreme Court's own holdings in two cases of the 1970s. In *Franks v. Bowman* (1976), the Supreme Court gave seniority to black truck drivers who had proved they were victims of discrimination. The drivers had not asked for the elimination of seniority, the Court noted. They asked only to be "slotted" into the seniority system in the position they would have enjoyed but for the illegal discrimination. Then, in *Teamsters v. United States* (1977), the Court awarded "constructive" seniority to 30 blacks who produced "convincing evidence of discrimination and harm" but not to 300 others "as to whom there was 'no evidence to show that these individuals were either harmed or not harmed individually.'"[33]

In another case, *Connecticut v. Teal* (1982), the Court noted that "the principal focus" of the Civil Rights Act had been on "the protection of the individual." The Court said, "Indeed, the entire statute and its legislative history are replete with references to protection for the individual." This was the reason the Court, in *Teamsters*, would not award seniority to those who had not shown they individually suffered. The most it could do, since the employer had been found guilty of discriminating, was award seniority to individuals who proved they were "actual victims" by at least applying for jobs during the time when the employer practiced discrimination.[34]

The arguments were weighty. But many observers were surprised when six members of the Supreme Court, in *Stotts*, ruled for seniority over affirmative action. They were astonished when they read the opinion of the Court, which was, as the *Washington Post* reported, "broadly worded and potentially far-reaching." According to the *Post*, the opinion "extend[ed] far beyond questions of seniority" and "seemed to embrace the Reagan Administration's central argument on civil rights: that federal anti-discrimination law bars the use of quotas and other such remedies for employment discrimination."[35]

A jubilant Rex Lee, calling Stotts "a slam dunk," said, "If you want to attribute to me the statement that this is one of the greatest victories of all time, I won't dispute you." Because the Court embraced the argument that affirmative relief must be tied to discrimination against specific victims, Lee said, "[T]his is a decision of far-reaching implications." Barry Goldstein of the NAACP Legal Defense Fund admitted that the ruling was a "sharp departure...an unfortunate decision which may substantially undercut the benefits that have been obtained through enforcement of the civil rights acts."[36]

For civil rights activists, it was bad enough that the *Stotts* Court decided that inferior courts could "award competitive seniority only when the beneficiary of the award has actually been a victim of illegal discrimination." It was worse that the opinion of the Court was written by Byron White, a justice who, in *Weber*, had supported an explicit affirmative quota even in the absence of proven discrimination. It was disastrous that large parts of the opinion were cribbed from the arguments of Rex Lee and William Bradford Reynolds.[37]

With citations to Senators Humphrey and Clark and to the language of the Civil Rights Act, Justice White said employers could not be "ordered to hire and promote persons in order to achieve a racially balanced work force even though those persons had not been victims of illegal discrimination." Unlike Justice Potter Stewart, who in 1976 said the legislative history of the 1972 amendments was "susceptible of different readings," Justice White's opinion for the Court rejected the contention that the 1972 amendments authorized affirmative preferences for nonvictims. It said, in addition, that previous opinions of the Supreme Court, especially *Teamsters*, had made it clear that "mere membership in the disadvantaged class" was not enough to warrant an affirmative remedy. "Each individual must prove that the discriminatory practice had an impact on him." The purpose of Title VII was "to provide make-whole relief only to those who have been actual victims of illegal discrimination."[38]

Naturally, Reynolds was elated by the Court's support for victim specificity. As he saw it, the nation had been "at a critical crossroads." Some people and organizations favored group rights, racial quotas, and proportional representation; but the Reagan administration stood for individual rights, nondiscrimination, and equality of opportunity. Now, it seemed, the Supreme Court had "propelled [the nation] down the road we have been urging."[39]

For Reynolds, *Stotts* was "an exhilarating decision"—one that vindicated his views on affirmative action and one that would bring an end to "that stifling process by which government and society view its citizens as possessors of racial characteristics, not as the unique individuals they are." For Reynolds, *Stotts* promised each citizen the opportunity "to compete on merit...to go as far as that person's energy, ability, enthusiasm, imagination, and effort will take him and not be hemmed in by the artificial allotment given to his group in the form of a quota."[40]

Reynolds recognized that some observers viewed *Stotts* narrowly, as applying only to seniority, but he said "the better reasoned view" was that *Stotts* placed limits on affirmative action and prohibited quotas. The Supreme Court had ruled that remedies for discrimination could not go beyond make-whole relief for actual victims of discrimination. As Reynolds said in a 1984 address at the University of Maryland, the Court did not merely hold

> that federal courts are prohibited from ordering racially preferential layoffs to maintain a certain racial percentage.... To be sure, it did so rule; but the Court said much more, and in unmistakably forceful terms.... After *Stotts*, it is abundantly clear that [the Civil Rights Act] does not tolerate remedial action by courts that would grant to nonvictims of discrimination...an employment preference based solely on the fact that they are members of a particular race or gender.[41]

Reynolds's reading of *Stotts* was understandable. There was a natural tendency for members of the Reagan administration to regard *Stotts* as a definitive victory in their war against quotas. This was especially the case because, as Reynolds noted, it had been "a struggle to maintain our position in the face of an awful lot of shrill criticism, much of it political."[42]

Reynolds was not alone in his view of *Stotts*. Speaking at Northwestern University, Justice John Paul Stevens said that *Stotts* was "a far-reaching pronouncement concerning the limits on a court's power to prescribe affirmative action." And Justice Harry Blackmun, one of the three dissenters in *Stotts*, lamented that the Court had effectively "interred" the use of quotas, goals, and other broad racial preferences. Reynolds insisted that these justices "did not overstate the case."[43]

Many court watchers concurred. The liberal columnist Joseph Kraft noted that the *Stotts* opinion "was framed to cover hiring and promotions and any other employment practice as well as layoffs." Fred Barbash, the Supreme Court reporter for the *Washington Post*, provided an especially astute analysis in explaining that the "remedies" section of the Civil Rights Act authorized courts to order an end to discrimination and to provide "such affirmative action as may be appropriate." However, in response to critics who said the act would be used to require employers to achieve a racially balanced work force, Barbash said that Congress had placed an explicit limit on the courts' remedial powers when it held that racial preferences must be limited to remedying instances of racial discrimination.[44]

The conservative columnist George F. Will characterized *Stotts* as a rebuke to obstinate lower courts that had disregarded provisions that had been essential to securing passage of the Civil Rights Act. The lower courts had also ignored the Supreme Court's own rulings in *Teamsters* and *Franks v. Bowman*. The Supreme Court, according to Will, was reasserting control over renegade judges who had allowed themselves to become "instruments of groups who want racial quotas but who know that to get them they must do an end run around democracy—around, that is, the process of establishing policy by legislation rather than judicial fiat." Will characterized *Stotts* as "the most important civil rights ruling of the decade."[45]

Regarding *Stotts* as he did, Reynolds seized the opportunity to challenge other consent decrees. Memphis, after all, was not the only city that had preferential arrangements for racial groups. By the spring of 1985, Reynolds had initiated proceedings that questioned the use of numerical goals and quotas in fifty-six cities. Reynolds said he had done so because, after *Stotts*, the Department of Justice was obliged "to take a hard look at the decrees now in existence and to assess the extent to which those decrees call for relief that seems under this decision to be inappropriate."[46]

Some cities quickly brought their affirmative action plans into line with Reynolds's understanding of *Stotts*. San Diego, which had previously agreed to give Hispanics 33 percent of its jobs as fire fighters, librarians, and meter readers (and 25 percent of the jobs in professional and technical fields), eliminated numerical goals and quotas from its court-approved affirmative action plan. The city said it would speak to the needs of minorities with special sensitivity and affirmative recruiting but without numerical formulas.[47]

Some judges also went along. In New Jersey, Judge H. Lee Sarokin reluctantly reversed his earlier decision that white public employees must be laid off before employees from minority groups. In the District of Columbia, Judge Charles R. Richey struck down a plan that used quotas to foster the promotion of blacks in the fire department.[48]

Elsewhere, however, municipal governments resisted Reynolds. In Los Angeles, Mayor Tom Bradley said Reynolds's challenge to that city's affirmative action plan was "foolish" and would "result in expensive, time consuming litigation and will reopen old wounds that have long been healed." In Norfolk, the city attorney said that "no community that has been through this...is anxious to go back and revisit it." In Detroit, the fire commissioner denied that there were precise quotas, although he acknowledged that the city sought rough proportionality in hiring and promotions. "When we hire," he said, "we just want the department to look like the city."[49]

The Reagan administration tried to resolve differences through discussion, but Indianapolis mayor William Hudnut was so adamant that the Department of Justice finally took the city to court to overturn quotas in the police and fire departments. It was an unlikely locale for a showdown, for at that time Indianapolis was the largest city in the country where the mayor was a Republican. According to *Newsweek*, Hudnut was not a liberal but a "pragmatist" who thought quotas were necessary in order to have effective law enforcement in predominantly black neighborhoods. The *New York Times* quoted a black police major as saying that without quotas the city would "have a 95 percent white Anglo-Saxon Protestant police department going into lower-income neighborhoods. And that would be chaotic."[50]

In explaining the decision to fight the Department of Justice in court, Mayor Hudnut said that *Stotts* applied to layoffs but denied that it extended to hiring and promotions. In making this point, he touched on the basic legal argument of those who equated racial justice with approximate statistical parity.[51]

From the day *Stotts* came down, informed observers recognized that the perception of the decision was almost as important as the decision itself. Thus, while members of the Reagan administration emphasized the broad reach of the rationale and language of the Court's opinion, members of the civil rights lobby stressed that the Court's discussion came in the context of a seniority system. Former EEOC head Eleanor Holmes Norton predicted that the impact of the decision would be confined to disputes involving seniority. Columnist William Raspberry said that hiring and promotion were different from seniority. The *New York Times*, while conceding that *Stotts* prohibited "blanket preference for one racial group at the expense of another," also emphasized that "the extent to which the decision goes beyond seniority...depends on how courts use that language in the future."[52]

In addition to distinguishing between seniority and hiring or promotions, proponents of affirmative discrimination made other legal points. They said *Stotts* was concerned only with the modification of consent decrees and not with fully litigated court orders. They said *Stotts* dealt with government employment, and that private businesses could still engage in affirmative discrimination, even if it involved the abrogation of seniority plans. They said that if the *Stotts* Court had meant to condemn all race-conscious action, the opinion would have been more explicit than it was. They noted that several inferior courts rejected the interpretation of the Reagan administration.[53]

With so much controversy over the meaning of *Stotts*, most businesses and local governments decided to sit tight. By 1985 Reynolds recognized that there were legal miles to go. He thought the civil rights lobby and inferior courts had combined to deny the administration the victory it had won in *Stotts*, and he wanted "to go back to the Supreme Court and get the Justices to say it again." He did, and eventually they did—although the ensuing litigation lasted for years and resulted in some modifications that will be discussed in the next chapters. In the short term, however, Reynolds's broad reading of *Stotts* became an issue in the 1985 Senate hearings on Reynolds's nomination to be associate attorney general.[54]

The Senate hearings to consider Reynolds's promotion took place ten months after *Stotts*. They occurred against the background of resistance to Reynolds's efforts to bring scores of cities into line with his understanding of the Supreme Court's ruling. For these reasons, as Kentucky's Senator Mitch McConnell observed, parts of the confirmation hearing came close to being "a symposium on the meaning of the *Memphis Fire Fighters* decision."[55]

Representatives from the established civil rights groups insisted that, *Stotts* notwithstanding, *Bakke* and *Weber* had established the proposition "that colorblindness is ineffective." They accused Reynolds of "a blatant misconstruction" of *Stotts*, which they said dealt only with whether broad affirmative remedies could override seniority in layoff situations (and then only if government was the employer and if a court had modified a consent decree). They censured Reynolds for injecting "political ideology [in]to the legal process." They said the Civil Rights Division had forsaken its raison d'etre—that it was no longer an "effective champion of the interests of minority groups."[56]

In response, Reynolds made two points: with respect to *Stotts*, he said litigation was already under way to seek further clarification from the Supreme Court; with respect to the more general purpose of the Civil Rights

Division, he said he was not opposed to race-conscious remedies because they supposedly helped blacks. He mentioned what he was for: "that...every single individual in this country is entitled to the full measure of protection under our civil rights laws." And he said what he was against: "what I am against, Senator, is discrimination; and I view discrimination as the giving of a preference to one individual who is not a victim at the expense of another innocent third party, solely by reason of that individual's race or gender."[57]

One cannot know with certainty, but the furor over *Stotts* may have tipped the confirmation scale against Reynolds. Democratic senators like Edward M. Kennedy and Howard M. Metzenbaum would have opposed Reynolds in any case, but Republican Arlen Specter was genuinely troubled by what he regarded as Reynolds's tendency to exalt his own understanding of *Stotts* over contrary views that had already been expressed by some circuit courts of appeal.[58]

Beyond this lay a more fundamental point. Most people did not follow the complex legal arguments over racial preferences and quotas, but because of *Stotts*, Reynolds had received publicity that went far beyond that which is usually accorded an assistant attorney general. Civil rights activists knew that Reynolds opposed quotas. They knew he had persuaded the Supreme Court to move in that direction. They knew he had become a symbol of the Reagan administration's effort to change civil rights policies. If the public opinion polls were correct, most Americans agreed with Reynolds, but the general public, unlike the civil rights organizations, was not organized around the question of racial preferences. In the Senate confirmation hearings, as so often in politics, victory went to interests that were well organized.

Notes

1. WBR, remarks at University of Maryland, 19 October 1984; remarks to American Trucking Association, 29 October 1984, WBR Papers.
2. Ibid.
3. Charles Fried, *Order and Law*, 105.
4. Ibid.
5. Ibid., 105, 106.
6. Ibid., 41, 42.
7. Ibid., 106.
8. Lincoln Caplan, *The Tenth Justice*, 145.
9. *Los Angeles Times*, 25 July 1983, 10:1.
10. Ibid. For more on *Bob Jones*, see the Appendix below.
11. Lincoln Caplan, *The Tenth Justice*, 251, 69; *Los Angeles Times*, 25 July 1983, 10:1.
12. Lincoln Caplan, *The Tenth Justice*, 146; *Los Angeles Times*, 10 July 1983, 10:1.
13. *Los Angeles Times*, 10 July 1983, 10:1.
14. Lincoln Caplan, *The Tenth Justice*, 100.

15. Charles Fried, *Order and Law*, 41; Lincoln Caplan, *The Tenth Justice*, 107. Lee mentioned economic reasons for the resignation. "My wife and I went shopping, and she reached for some English muffins. They were the Thomas's brand, and I said to her, 'We can't afford those.' I don't want to dwell on this, but I can't afford to send three kids to college and support four others on a government salary. That's the immediate reason why I'm leaving."

    For a spirited right-wing critique of Lee's work as Solicitor General, see James McClellan, "A Lawyer Looks at Rex Lee," *Benchmark* (March-April 1984): 1–16.
16. Lincoln Caplan, *The Tenth Justice*, 107.
17. Charles Fried, *Order and Law*, 106, 107.
18. While cooperating on this case, Reynolds and Lee continued to differ in their approaches. Michael Carvin, a Civil Rights Division lawyer who worked with them on the case, recalled that Reynolds had to "get down in the trenches and fight Rex Lee every step of the way. Lee's initial preference was to fuzz over crucial matters like victim specificity." Interview with Michael Carvin, 2 March 1993.
19. Stotts v. Memphis Fire Dept., 679 F.2d 541 (1982), 578–79.
20. Consent Decree, 27 November 1974, U.S. v. City of Memphis, Civil Action No. C-74-286, Supreme Court Library.
21. Firefighters v. Stotts, 467 U.S. 561 (1984), 565.
22. Stotts v. Memphis Fire Dept., 679 F.2d 541 (1982), 548.
23. Firefighters v. Stotts, 467 U.S. 561 (1984), 566, 567.
24. Stotts v. Memphis Fire Dept., 679 F.2d 541 (1982), 549; Preliminary Injunction Hearing, 8 May 1981, Civil Action C-74-286; Supreme Court Library; Oral Ruling of Court, 8 May 1981, ibid.
25. *Memphis Commercial Appeal*, 6 December 1983; *Memphis Press Scimitar*, 7 May 1983.
26. Oral ruling of the Court, 8 May 1981, Civil Action C-74-286.
27. Stotts v Memphis Fire Dept., 679 F.2d 541 (1982), 568, 555–56, 566. More particularly, Judges Keith and Duncan held that Judge McRae had not abused his discretion in setting aside seniority.
28. The Supreme Court later made this point. Firefighters v. Stotts, 467 U.S. 565 (1984), 575.
29. Rex E. Lee, William Bradford Reynolds, Charles J. Cooper et al., Brief for the United States as Amicus Curiae, Firefighters v. Stotts, 14, 13, Supreme Court Library (cited hereafter as Lee-Reynolds Brief).
30. 110 *Congressional Record* (1964), 7213.
31. Ibid., 7207.
32. Lee-Reynolds Brief, 12, 13, 15.
33. Oral Argument before the Supreme Court, Firefighters v. Stotts, 6 December 1983, 20–28, Supreme Court Library; Franks v. Bowman Transportation, 424 U.S. 747 (1976); International Brotherhood of Teamsters v. United States, 431 U.S. 324 (1977), 331, 332.
34. Connecticut v. Teal, 457 U.S. 440 (1982), 453–54; International Brotherhood of Teamsters v. United States, 431 U.S. 324 (1977), 327, 367–71.
35. *Washington Post*, 13 June 1984, A1e.
36. Ibid.
37. Firefighters v. Stotts, 81 L.Ed. 483 (1984), 484.

38. Firefighters v. Stotts, 467 U.S. 561 (1984), 580, 582 n.15, 579; International Brotherhood of Teamsters v. United States, 431 U.S. 324 (1977), 354 n.39.
39. *Washington Post*, 14 June 1984, A1a.
40. Ibid.; WBR, remarks to National Foundation for the Study of Equal Employment Policy, 14 November 1984; remarks to Bureau of National Affairs, 14 June 1984, WBR Papers.
41. WBR, remarks to Association of American Law Schools, 6 January 1985; remarks at University of Maryland, 19 October 1984, WBR Papers.
42. *Washington Post*, 14 June 1984, A1a.
43. *New York Times*, 20 October 1984, 9:5; WBR, remarks to the Association of American Law Schools, 6 January 1985, WBR Papers.
44. *Washington Post*, 17 June 1984, D7a and A3a.
45. Ibid., 17 July 1984, D7a.
46. *New York Times*, 14 April 1985, IV, 4:1; *Los Angeles Times*, 14 June 1984, 1:5.
47. *New York Times*, 9 May 1985, 12:3.
48. Ibid., 22 June 1984, 3:1; 2 April 1985, 10:2.
49. Ibid., 4 May 1985, 1:1; 14 December 1984, 32:2; *Los Angeles Times*, 6 June 1985, 1:5.
50. *Newsweek* (13 May 1985): 39; *New York Times*, 30 April 1985, 1:6; 1 May 1985, II, 28:1.
51. *New York Times*, 5 May 1985, IV, 6:4.
52. *Washington Post*, 13 June 1984, A1e; 15 June 1984, A23d; *New York Times*, 14 June 1984, 17:1.
53. *New York Times*, 10 February 1985, 1:5; 14 April 1985, IV, 4:1; 4 May 1985, 1:1; *Fortune* (23 July 1984): 95–96; EEOC v. Local 638, Sheet Metal Workers, 753 F.2d 1172 (1985); Vanguards v. City of Cleveland, 753 F.2d 479 (1985); Deveraux v. Geary, 765 F.2d 268 (1985).
54. Charles Fried, *Order and Law*, 109.
55. *1985 Senate Hearings*, 26.
56. Ibid., 260, 192, 342, 313.
57. Ibid., 43–44, 91, 33.
58. Ibid., 6, 8, 40ff.

12

The Nadir

The Fourteenth Amendment made it unconstitutional for a state to deny any person "the equal protection of the laws." A principal sponsor explained that the provision guaranteed that states would give blacks and whites exactly the same treatment: "Whatever law punishes a white man for a crime shall punish the black man precisely in the same way and to the same degree. Whatever law protects the white man shall afford 'equal' protection to the black man. Whatever means of redress is afforded to one shall be afforded to all."[1]

Then the Civil Rights Act of 1964 made it illegal for businesses or unions "to discriminate against any individual...because of such individual's race." The principal sponsors of the act said this meant that the law could not be used to make employers "meet a racial 'quota' or...to achieve a certain racial balance," and that under the law, courts "could not order that any preference be given to any particular race."[2]

There is nothing obscure or arcane about this. The Constitution and laws of the United States prohibit racial discrimination. Nevertheless, the Supreme Court, in the *Weber* and *Fullilove* cases of 1979 and 1980, ruled in favor of explicit racial quotas and set-asides. Then, in the *Stotts* case of 1984, the Court ruled against a broad racial preference and said the policy of the Civil Rights Act was to give relief "only to those who have been actual victims of illegal discrimination."[3]

By the time of the *Stotts* decision, however, many people had concluded that racial preferences and quotas were necessary to eradicate the effects of past discrimination against minorities, to achieve a better racial balance, to prevent race riots, or to avoid litigation. Because of the persistence of affirmative discrimination, William Bradford Reynolds asked the Supreme Court to clarify what it had decided in *Stotts*.

But clarification was not to be found—at least not in the short term. In three cases of 1986 the Court made a number of technical legal points and generally compounded the confusion. Then, in 1987, the Court embraced the principles of those who favored racial preferences and quotas. In 1989, however, the Court repudiated these principles and sided with Reynolds. It may be that Reynolds's persistence finally paid off, or perhaps it was the criticism of economists and psychologists that turned around the Court. More certainly, the effect of presidential elections was felt. The antiquota Court of 1989 included two new Reagan appointees, and in the 1990s, after George Bush appointed Clarence Thomas to the Supreme Court, the antiquota majority was ascendant.

I

The first-named plaintiff in one of the three cases of 1986 was a kindergarten teacher who had lost her job in Jackson, Michigan. In the second case the plaintiff was a Cleveland fire fighters' union that objected to a court-approved plan that required race norming. The third case involved a New York sheet metal workers' union that was trying to evade a court order to increase the proportion of its minority membership to 29.23 percent. All the cases were concerned with the scope of permissible relief. The question was whether racial preferences could be given to people who were not actual victims of illegal discrimination. It turned out, though, that the differing factual situations were important to the outcomes of the cases.

Wendy Wygant was the kindergarten teacher who had been laid off because of an affirmative action provision in her union's collective bargaining agreement, a provision that was added to the contract in 1972 because of statistical imbalance. Prior to 1953 no black teachers had been employed in the public schools of Jackson. In 1972 when blacks made up 15.9 percent of the students in the district but only 8.5 percent of the teachers, the board of education and the teachers' union agreed to a goal of increasing the number of black teachers until the proportion of black teachers was commensurate with the proportion of black students. The collective bargaining agreement also said that if it was necessary to reduce the number of teachers, those with the most seniority would be retained, except that the percentage of black teachers laid off could not be larger than the overall percentage of minority teachers at the time of the layoff.

By 1981 the proportion of blacks had increased to 13.5 percent of the teachers and 25 percent of the students, but layoffs were needed because the overall number of students was declining. In accordance with the terms of the collective bargaining agreement, tenured white teachers were dismissed while blacks on probationary status were retained. Wendy Wygant and seventeen other whites then claimed they were laid off because of their race in violation of Title VII of the Civil Rights Act and of the equal protection clause of the Fourteenth Amendment. The Title VII claim was dismissed because the teachers went to court without first filing a complaint with the EEOC. Consequently, the only question in the case concerned the constitutionality of the racial preference.[4]

In the Cleveland case, no white fire fighters were laid off, but several lost out on promotions because of a preferential plan that was implemented in 1983. At that time minorities made up about 47 percent of the population of the city; but only 20 percent of the city's fire fighters were Hispanic or black, and only 4.5 percent of those who held the rank of lieutenant or above belonged to these minority groups. To change the statistical balance, the city and a group of black fire fighters known as the Vanguards of Cleveland agreed that sixty-six promotions to lieutenant would be split evenly between minority and nonminority fire fighters. They further agreed to the goal of having minorities make up between 20 and 25 percent of the officer ranks within four years. Promotional examinations would still be given, but to achieve the goals, the minority and nonminority candidates would be paired. The highest-scoring black or Hispanic would be coupled with the highest-scoring white—although this meant that some whites would not be promoted even though they made higher scores than blacks or Hispanics who were promoted.[5]

The nonminority fire fighters objected to the agreement. In fact, when the proposal was submitted to the union in 1982, it was rejected by 88 percent of the membership. James Andrews, the president of the union, said that if the city wanted to make amends for past discrimination, it should give compensation in the form of money rather than promotions at the expense of whites who had done no wrong. Jim Peters, a white captain in the fire department, explained that because of racial pairing, the cost of affirmative action had been passed on to rank-and-file fire fighters who were paying "a $3,000 a year penalty by not moving up in rank." Peters said, "That's where the injustice comes in." Battalion Chief Tom Stepic agreed. "Who's paying the price?" Stepic asked. "Me and Paul and Jimmy and Ted...and we ain't done anything against minorities."[6]

Notwithstanding the resentment and objections of the fire fighters' union, the district court entered the city's agreement with the black Vanguards as a consent judgment. The union then appealed, and a divided panel of the Sixth Circuit Court affirmed, holding, "The district court did not abuse its discretion in finding that the consent decree was fair, reasonable, and adequate." The union then appealed to the Supreme Court.[7]

The third case of 1986, the most complicated of the three, involved Local 28 of the Sheet Metal Workers' Union. For several years this New York union resisted court efforts to reform its racial policies. When the case finally went to the Supreme Court, Justice Lewis F. Powell wrote that "it would be difficult to find defendants more determined to discriminate against minorities."[8]

In the brief he filed that argued against quota relief even in this case, Reynolds acknowledged that the union was guilty of "pronounced and protracted discrimination." Reynolds parted company with the established civil rights groups "only with respect to the appropriate remedy." Instead of an explicit quota, Reynolds recommended that "sanctions should be directed at those responsible for the union's contumacy." He said, "If you are trying to punish a person for thumbing his nose at court orders," "the way to do it is through criminal contempt, whopping fines and the most rigid kind of recruitment program you can devise." It was wrong, Reynolds said, to penalize innocent people by not allowing more than an agreed-upon number of their group to be admitted to the union.[9]

Among the union practices that the courts faulted, the greatest censure was directed at the entrance examination that was used for admission to the union's four-year apprenticeship program. The exam covered spatial relations, mechanical reasoning, and arithmetic, subjects that were relevant for workers who made and installed ducts for ventilating, air conditioning, and heating. The problem was that blacks and Hispanics did not fare well on the exam and, after *Griggs*, a union could not use a test that had adverse impact unless it proved that the examination was related to actual performance on the job.

In this case the New York sheet metal workers presented what they referred to as "validation" in the form of research and testimony by Professor Judah Gottesman of the Stevens Institute of Technology. Nevertheless, the trial judge, Henry F. Werker, concluded that the union did not prove the entrance test was "significantly job-related" because Gottesman's evidence was "spotty and largely equivocal." Under cross-examination, Gottesman said he could design a better exam than the one the union was using. He also said there was a .25 correlation coefficient between performance on the exam and performance on a demonstration that students had to give at the end of their four-year apprenticeship.[10]

Statisticians regard a correlation of .25 as *significant* but not *strong*—that is, that what is measured on the test is relevant to performance on the job. But although the association is sufficient to satisfy statisticians, it was not enough for Judge Werker, who characterized the "evidence of validity" as "meagre" and insufficient to satisfy the *Griggs* standard. He noted that some of those who scored "in the *bottom* half" on the entrance exam later performed "successfully as apprentices and journeymen"; and he thought the test was a device which, while "neutral on [its] face, operate[d] to exclude non-whites capable of performing effectively."[11]

The use of an inadequate entrance exam was the key point in the case against the sheet metal workers' union, as Judge Werker and the appellate courts devoted more space to describing and condemning the test than to anything else. But there were other practices that also came in for censure. One was the requirement of a high school diploma for admission to the apprenticeship program. Another was a requirement that candidates list all arrests for offenses other than minor traffic violations. Yet another was the failure to organize nonunion sheet metal shops. The court also faulted the union for restricting the size of its membership by not accepting blowpipe workers, most of whom were not white.[12]

All of these practices had an adverse impact on blacks and, in the opinion of Judge Werker, amounted to a sophisticated form of illegal racial discrimination. To remedy this wrong, Werker gave the union six years to increase its nonwhite membership from 3.2 percent to 29.23 percent (the proportion of nonwhites in the labor force of New York City). The judge also ordered that 60 percent of the spaces in the apprenticeship program must be set aside for nonwhites and appointed an administrator with broad powers to supervise the union.[13]

The union appealed. Far from viewing the entrance examination as a form of racial discrimination, union members said the test was a good-faith effort to comply with an earlier directive from the State Commission for Human Rights (which had insisted that objective tests should be substituted for the previous practice of restricting admission to the apprenticeship program to candidates sponsored by union members). The union said it did not include blowpipe workers because they were semiskilled operatives who worked with prefabricated round ducts (and earned only one-half the hourly wage of sheet metal workers who used square or rectangular ducts that often had to be custom made). They explained the failure to organize nonunion shops as part of a policy of maintaining high wage rates. As for the court's 29.23 percent quota, the union said the figure was unrealistic. Since many union members lived outside the city, the union said the proper statistical comparison—if a statistical comparison had to be used to measure discrimination—was not with the proportion of nonwhites in the labor force of New York City but with the proportion in the larger metropolitan area (about 15 percent).[14]

The union lost every appeal. It was also slapped with a contempt citation and a fine of $150,000 plus 2 cents for each hour worked by a union member. It was fined because after six years the percentage of nonwhites in the union had increased from 3.2 to 10.8 (instead of the court-ordered 29.23). The court also found fault with the union for allowing older members to work overtime (thereby "underutilizing the apprenticeship program to the detriment of nonwhites"). The court further criticized the union for establishing cram courses to prepare the sons and nephews of members for the entrance examination (although this did not affect the racial ratio because 60 percent of the places in the apprenticeship program were set aside for nonwhites).[15]

When it came to clarifying the meaning of *Stotts*, the Reagan administration could have wished for more attractive cases. Because it involved no finding of discrimination and the forced layoff of white workers, *Wygant* posed the question of proper remedies in an appealing factual situation. In *Cleveland*, however, the city admitted to discrimination, and the racial preferences pertained only to promotion. In *Sheet Metal Workers* there was a judicial finding of discrimination and a union that had dragged out the litigation for fifteen years. The union was determined to take its appeal to the Supreme Court, even if it did not have the support of the Reagan administration.[16]

Reynolds and Solicitor General Charles Fried eventually filed briefs that argued against racial preferences in each case, and Reynolds made the oral argument before the Supreme Court in *Cleveland*. They said that Sections 703(h) and 706(g) had been placed in the Civil Rights Act to ensure that court-ordered remedies for discrimination did not discriminate against innocent persons. They said that to give meaning to this policy, the Supreme Court, in *Stotts*, had properly held that a court could order affirmative relief to compensate people who were victims of discrimination—while at the same time holding that courts could not bestow benefits on people who were not victims.

"The unambiguous meaning of *Stotts*," according to one of Fried and Reynolds's legal briefs, was that "a court...may not award affirmative equitable relief to non-victims at the expense of innocent third parties." Fried and Reynolds said the lower federal courts were mistaken when they held that *Stotts* applied only when seniority rights were abridged. They said the lower courts, in *Wygant* and *Cleveland*, were wrong to distinguish those cases from *Stotts* on the grounds that they involved voluntary consent decrees (while *Stotts* was concerned with a court's modification of a consent decree).[17]

Fried and Reynolds's brief in *Wygant* was particularly vivid. Because the Michigan teachers had gone to court without first taking their complaint to the EEOC, they had forfeited the right to bring an action under the Civil Rights Act. Thus Fried and Reynolds argued that the teachers had been denied the equal protection that the Fourteenth Amendment guarantees to all persons. Solicitor General Fried saw *Wygant* as an opportunity "to press for a clear statement that the Constitution does indeed force government to be colorblind, thus trumping the doctrinal intricacies of Title VII."[18]

Fried and Reynolds began their *Wygant* brief with a dramatic assertion that they were making "the same argument" that Thurgood Marshall had made in the 1950s when *Brown v. Board of Education* was before the Supreme Court. They even quoted Marshall's statement that "the Fourteenth Amendment prohibits a state from making racial distinctions in the exercise of governmental power." Fried and Reynolds said that there would "always be voices seeking to carve out exceptions" to the "magnificent" principle of "equality before the law"; but because the population of the United States was "the most diverse in the world—indeed, probably in the history of the world"—it was especially important for the Supreme Court to uphold "the equality of all persons before the law regardless of race, religion, or ethnic background."[19]

More legalistically, Fried and Reynolds pointed to previous Supreme Court holdings that government actions that discriminate on the basis of race are "constitutionally suspect" and subject to the "most rigid scrutiny." The case for racial discrimination had to be "compelling," they said; and compensating for past discrimination was the only interest that was compelling enough to justify racial classifications. Race-conscious measures had to be "precisely tailored" to remedy the effects of previous discrimination without abridging the rights of innocent third parties.[20]

Fried and Reynolds's arguments had the virtue of being clear and comprehensible. The same cannot be said for the opinions that the Supreme Court rendered in the cases. The Court ruled for Wendy Wygant (and against racial preferences when it came to layoffs). However, in *Cleveland* it upheld racial preferences for promotions, and in *Sheet Metal Workers* it affirmed the 29.23 percent solution.[21]

The justices could not agree on why they did what they did. They published fourteen separate opinions, which covered 180 printed pages in the *U.S. Reports*. Only one of the fourteen opinions commanded the support of a majority of the Court. Justice Sandra Day O'Connor said that "the diverse formulations and the number of separate writings put forth by various Members of the Court...[did] not necessarily reflect an intractable fragmentation in opinion with respect to certain core principles." But, in truth, the multiple opinions did little except to sow confusion as to the meaning of the Constitution and the Civil Rights Act.[22]

The perception of a Supreme Court opinion is almost as important as the opinion itself. This is especially true if the Court's opinion is muddled. Consequently, members of the civil rights lobby and their sympathizers were quick to put their "spin" on the 1986 cases. Barry Goldstein of the Legal Defense Fund called the decisions "a tremendous victory for affirmative action" and "a clear rejection of the position argued by the Reagan Justice Department." Ralph Neas of the Leadership Conference hailed the rulings as a "tremendous victory for civil rights."[23]

Goldstein and Neas had reason to be elated. In affirming the racial preferences and quotas that were at issue in *Cleveland* and *Sheet Mètal Workers*, the Supreme Court rejected Reynolds's argument that the law required public policy to be color-blind except when correcting the effects of particular discrimination against identified victims. The *Washington Post* reported that the Court had "explicitly repudiat[ed] the central principle of the Reagan administration's civil rights policies." The *New York Times* said the Court's rulings amounted to "a rejection of the policies and arguments that the Reagan Administration has been advancing for six years." *Human Events* lamented that the Court had held "that minorities, under certain conditions, are entitled to...preferential treatment in the workplace, even when they have not been personal victims of discrimination."[24]

Nevertheless, the splintered Court was ambivalent about affirmative action and seemed to say that racial preferences should be used only as a remedy for egregious discrimination. It is difficult to make sense of opinions that split so many legal hairs, but the Court was moving toward an idea that, in Supreme Court talk, went by the name of "narrow tailoring." It said racial preferences were permissible as a remedy for proven discrimination. It also said preferences need not be strictly compensatory—that is, they need not be confined to identifiable victims of discrimination—but the preferences could not be so broad as to trammel the rights of identifiable, innocent third parties.

Thus the Court renounced the preference in *Wygant* because it caused identifiable white teachers to be laid off and because the school district had never been found guilty of discrimination against blacks. The Court upheld the other preferences because the city of Cleveland admitted to discrimination, because the sheet metal workers' union was found guilty after a trial, and because the preferences were at the expense of diffuse groups of white candidates for promotion or employment.

Columnist William Raspberry wrote that the Court had decided "that it sometimes make sense to do a little race-specific tilting when it comes to hiring, but that it is usually a good idea to be race-neutral when it comes to layoffs." Another columnist, Charles Krauthammer, thought that "a rather odd and elegant rule of thumb" was emerging:

> To determine whether reverse discrimination is permitted, the important point is not whether the original (black) victims can be identified—the Administration's position—but whether the current (white) victims can be identified. The idea is diffusion, to produce a truly "societal" remedy for the "societal" injury of racial discrimination, and to cushion blameless individuals for having to pay for the failings of the larger society.[25]

James J. Kilpatrick expressed the opinion of many conservatives when he characterized the Court's position as "untenable." He insisted that "[v]ague ramblings about the 'diffusion' of discrimination 'among society generally' have no place where individual rights are at stake." He expressed the wish that Justice Lewis Powell had stuck to a principle he had asserted in *Bakke*: that "the guarantee of equal protection cannot mean one thing when applied to one individual and something else when applied to a person of another color."[26]

Many liberals, on the other hand, praised the ambiguity of the Court's opinions. Unlike George F. Will, who said the justices were "drowning" in legal technicalities, Robert Pear characterized the Court's opinions in the *Cleveland* and *Sheet Metal Workers*' cases as "135 pages...full of nuance and thoughtful distinctions." Robert J. Samuelson regarded the Court's "web of judicial distinctions" as a way of "accommodating the legitimate claims of rival groups." William Raspberry predicted that "most Americans would approve" of the "middle course" the Court was charting "between quotas and pure colorblindness." An editorial in the *Washington Post* said that it was "healthy...to muddle along in the middle" because most people were not "fully comfortable either embracing affirmative action or rejecting it."[27]

Solicitor General Fried was not greatly disturbed. He bridled at government-imposed racial preferences, but not simply because they deprived innocent whites of their individual rights. In fact, Fried personally thought it made sense to require employers or unions that had been found guilty of discrimination to institute quotas to increase the number of minorities in their work force.[28]

In some ways Fried was an unlikely choice for solicitor general. A Harvard law professor who had never argued before any court until he addressed the Supreme Court on behalf of the Reagan administration in 1985, Fried was a refugee from the state socialism of his native Czechoslovakia. He thought many rank-and-file liberals had a sentimental attachment to quotas as necessary for racial progress, but he also thought some leaders of the proquota lobby harbored ulterior motives. He thought they were closet collectivists who wanted to use racial regulations to achieve government management of the U.S. economy. When he first became a consultant to the Reagan administration in 1982, Fried proposed a plan to divide the socialist ideologists from rank-and-file liberals by allowing preferences in those relatively rare instances where employers or unions had been shown to discriminate, but Fried lost that argument within the administration. [29]

After the Supreme Court in *Stotts* seemed to have endorsed the proposition that race-conscious relief had to be victim specific, Fried argued quite forcefully for victim specificity. He did not argue effectively, however. Quoting Thurgood Marshall's earlier statements of opposition to every form of racial discrimination impressed some observers as bad lawyering. By exposing Marshall's inconsistency, they said, Fried alienated possible swing votes and made it more difficult for the Reagan administration to sell its case against racial preferences. Such theories necessarily involve a degree of speculation, but Justice William J. Brennan, in a portion of the *Sheet Metal Workers*' opinion that was joined by three other justices, directed especially sharp criticism at Fried's "misguided" arguments.[30]

In the end, though, the Supreme Court of 1986 gave Fried what he had favored in 1982. The Court held that employers or unions that had been found guilty of discrimination could be required to give racial preferences that were not victim specific.

Reynolds did not fare so well. Because the Court rejected the argument that relief must be victim specific, Reynolds said the rulings in *Cleveland* and *Sheet Metal Workers* were "disappointing" and "extremely unfortunate." Reynolds's boss at the Department of Justice, Attorney General Ed Meese, acknowledged that "[t]here is no question that the Court did not agree with the position advanced by the Administration. I admit that they ruled against us in both of these cases."[31]

The concessions had hardly been published when a resilient Reynolds found comfort from some aspects of the Court's decisions. Five days after the decisions in *Cleveland* and *Sheet Metal Workers*, Reynolds wrote that there was much more in the Court's opinions than a rebuke to the Reagan administration, saying that the Court, while rejecting the administration's position that broad racial preferences should never be used, had also rejected the argument that such preferences could be a recommended or preferred form of relief. "The Court,...while declining to say 'never' to hiring by race, said 'hardly ever,'" Reynolds said. It placed, he explained, "explicit and stringent restrictions" on preferences that went beyond make-whole relief for actual victims; and it said broad preferences must be limited to correcting "flagrant and egregious" acts of "pervasive" discrimination, and that they must be "carefully tailored" so as not to "unnecessarily trammel" the rights of others.[32]

In addition, Reynolds noted that *Wygant* was decided in favor of the administration (and set the stage for an award of $424,466 to the white teachers). In *Wygant,* the Court said that local governments could not justify broad racial preferences with citations to general "societal discrimination" or to social science theories like the desirability of having more minority teachers as role models. The Court said the Fourteenth Amendment applied equally to all individuals; and before any racial classification would be constitutionally tolerated, there must be the most compelling reason—a proven wrong that could not be remedied by any less intrusive action.[33]

Thus, Reynolds came to regard the affirmative action cases of 1986 less as a defeat than as an invitation to more litigation. He would be back in 1987 to ask if the Court really meant what it seemed to say: that racial preferences must be narrowly tailored to remedy proven discrimination and to do so in the manner that intruded least on the rights of innocent third parties.

II

When Reynolds returned to the Supreme Court in 1987, the principal legal issue concerned the meaning of "narrow tailoring," as it had arisen in the context of lawsuits that challenged preferences in California and Alabama. The California preference was part of a plan to change the social order, but it grew out of a relatively uncomplicated factual situation. In Alabama the preference was limited, but the facts in the case were complex. Together, the two cases provide another window for viewing affirmative action.

The California case pitted a white man against a white woman. Paul Johnson and Diane Joyce worked for the public transportation agency of Santa Clara County, and both wanted to be promoted to the position of road dispatcher. After the agency gave the position to Diane Joyce, Paul Johnson went to court with allegations of illegal sex discrimination. He said that the county had acted in violation of the 1964 Civil Rights Act, which explicitly prohibited sex discrimination as well as race discrimination.

Before joining the agency as a road clerk in 1967, Paul Johnson had worked for seventeen years as a dispatcher and supervisor for a private company. He first applied for a promotion to road dispatcher in 1974, coming in second. To increase his experience and thus improve his prospects for a promotion in the future, Johnson requested and received a demotion to road maintenance worker. Then, when the dispatcher's job came open again in 1979, Johnson applied a second time. With a score of 75 on the qualifying examination and many years of experience as a dispatcher, Johnson thought he would get the job.[34]

Diane Joyce had several years' experience as a bookkeeper and clerical worker before 1972, when she got a job as a senior account clerk at the transportation agency. She also wanted the job as road dispatcher and to improve her chances, Joyce, like Johnson, had worked as a road maintenance worker, "doing everything from flagging traffic to shoveling hot tar." When the road dispatcher's position became available in 1979, Joyce made a score of 73 on the qualifying exam and applied for the job.[35]

Johnson expected to be chosen over Joyce. He had years of experience as a dispatcher as well as a higher score on the qualifying exam, and a committee of three agency supervisors recommended Johnson after an interview. The supervisor of road operations told Johnson that he had been chosen and that the promotion required only routine approval from the director of the transportation agency. For nine months—from September 1979 to June 1980—Johnson was assigned out of class to work full-time in the job.

But Johnson had not reckoned with affirmative action. While the promotion was pending, Diane Joyce telephoned the county's affirmative action officer and explained that she was eligible for appointment as a road dispatcher. "No woman has ever held this position before," she said and asked, "Are you interested?" Other telephone calls and meetings ensued, and eventually the director of the agency, James Graebner, stepped in and gave the promotion to Diane Joyce.[36]

Graebner usually did not involve himself in routine appointments and promotions, but a friend and a close observer have described him as "sort of liberal," a man who "had no problems with affirmative action." He decided for Diane Joyce once he learned that both candidates (in the words of Paul Johnson's counsel, to which Graebner assented) "met the M.Q.s, the minimum. Both were qualified." According to Melvin Urofsky, the author of a scholarly monograph on the case, Graebner "quite openly admitted [that] Joyce's sex had not only been a positive factor; it had been the main factor leading to her selection."[37]

Graebner was so indifferent to the relative merits of the candidates that he did not even bother to look at their files before making the promotion. Perhaps this was because he was not indifferent to his own career prospects, as he knew that supervisors in Santa Clara County, as elsewhere, were being evaluated on the basis of their affirmative action statistics. In 1976, Santa Clara had adopted a plan that sought the "attainment of a County work force whose composition...includes women, disabled persons and ethnic minorities in a ratio in all categories that reflects their distribution in the Santa Clara County area work force." The purpose was not to remedy prior sex discrimination against women, as the district court specifically held that the transportation agency had "not discriminated in the past, and does not discriminate in the present against women in regard to employment opportunities in general and promotions in particular."[38]

Nevertheless, not one woman was employed in any of the Transportation Agency's 238 skilled-craft positions—a situation that the trial judge apparently ascribed not to discrimination but to societal attitudes that made few women eager to work with machine tools. In Santa Clara County, road dispatchers were classified as skilled-craft workers.

The county's affirmative action plan said that supervisors were expected to show "a statistically measurable yearly improvement in the hiring, training and promotion of minorities [and] women." At the trial, Graebner indicated that once he had determined that a woman was on the list of those who were minimally qualified and "capable of performing the work," he decided to give the job to Diane Joyce. In response to questions from the county's attorney, Graebner said he "tried to look at the whole picture" and that Paul Johnson and Diane Joyce were "essentially equal in qualification." But under cross-examination, Graebner also said that he and the affirmative action officers were "less interested in the particular individual [Diane Joyce]" and viewed the case as an opportunity to meet affirmative action goals by appointing a member of "a protected group."[39]

"As it turned out," Melvin Urofsky has written, "Graebner's version of what happened seemed to support every one of Paul Johnson's assertions."

District Judge William A. Ingram found that Diane Joyce's gender was "the determining factor," and he concluded that Paul Johnson was "more qualified for the position of Road Dispatcher than Diane Joyce." The judge wrote that "but for [Johnson]s sex, male, he would have been promoted to the position," and that "but for Diane Joyce's sex, female, she would not have been appointed to the position."[40]

The case from Alabama differed in important respects. For starters, it involved a judicial finding of discrimination in each of two separate lawsuits. One involved racial discrimination against black clerical and professional workers; the other involved discrimination in Alabama's highway patrol.

When it came to the employment of clerical workers, the state followed a "rule of three," under which at least three persons were certified as eligible, and the appointing officer was authorized to reject the highest-scoring individual as long a someone from among the top three was selected. Forty-nine blacks, whose names were affixed to the court records, complained of illegal discrimination when they were passed over in favor of whites who made lower scores on the qualifying examinations. Testimony and other evidence at the trial led District Judge Frank M. Johnson to find, in 1970, that Alabama had systematically discriminated "against qualified Negro applicants for clerical positions." In 1968 the state employed more than 1,000 clerical workers, and only 1 was black.[41]

The evidence with respect to the highway patrol was also overwhelming. From the inception of the patrol in 1935 until the trial date in 1972, there had never been a black trooper, and the principal named plaintiff, Philip Paradise, Jr., was refused an application form when he inquired about the possibility of a position on the force. Judge Johnson found that the highway patrol had "engaged in a blatant and continuous pattern and practice of discrimination in hiring."[42]

To remedy the situation with respect to the clerical workers, Judge Johnson prohibited further discrimination, ordered that the first available clerical positions be offered to the forty-nine named blacks, and required the state to do something it had previously refused to do—to recruit at predominantly black schools and colleges and to advertise with newspapers and radio stations that served mainly black markets. The judge also required that at least 25 percent of the places where civil service examinations were given must be "predominantly Negro schools or other institutions." These orders were tame in comparison with measures that later would be required elsewhere, but they succeeded in increasing the number of black clerical workers to something approaching proportionality.[43]

Judge Johnson thought something stronger in the way of judicial medicine was needed to remedy the discrimination in the highway patrol. Accordingly, in addition to enjoining discrimination and requiring affirmative advertising and recruiting, Johnson ordered the patrol to hire "one Negro trooper for each white trooper hired until approximately 25 percent of the Alabama state trooper force was comprised of Negroes." Alabama appealed to the Fifth Circuit Court, which in 1974 affirmed all aspects of the order (including the one-for-one hiring quota). By then 325 blacks had passed the written and oral qualifying examinations for state trooper. Although the average score of these blacks was lower than the average for whites, enough blacks were on the *qualified* register to enable the state to comply with the quota. Beginning in 1975, the department instituted a one-for-one hiring plan, and by 1983 more than 22 percent of the overall trooper force was black.[44]

Yet this did not end Alabama's legal problems, for in the meantime blacks had gone to court to complain about the dearth of black officers in the highway patrol where, as of November 1978, not one of the 232 state troopers at the rank of corporal or above was a black. The state said this was the inevitable legacy of having been compelled (by the one-for-one hiring quota) to employ black troopers whose average score on the entrance examinations was below the average for their white counterparts; thus, it was not surprising, the state said, that most blacks would make lower scores a few years later when they took promotion exams. Blacks, on the other hand, complained of test bias and noted that the promotion exam had never been validated. The state, for its part, pointed out that it took several years to correlate scores on the entry and promotion examinations with later performance as state troopers or officers.[45]

Alabama's explanations were valid but legally irrelevant because *Griggs* had prohibited the use of tests that were not validated and that affected blacks adversely. To extricate itself from its legal problems, in 1979 the state promised to develop promotion examinations that were valid—that is, correlated with performance on the job—and that would have little or no adverse impact.[46]

The promise (which eventually became a consent decree involving the U.S. Government, the state of Alabama, and the intervening black complainant Philip Paradise) was noble but naive. Because blacks, on average, trail behind whites on tests of reading and writing from first grade onward, and because verbal skills are important for troopers who must file reports and testify in court, it was not possible to develop a test that was both valid and without adverse impact. Alabama had made a promise it could not keep. And when the state did not keep its promise, it incurred the wrath of a federal judge.

In 1981, before the fury descended, Alabama had asked for approval to give a written examination for promotion to the rank of corporal. At first Reynolds refused—because the test had not been validated. But Reynolds changed his mind after Alabama pointed out that it is impossible to validate a test unless it is given, and after the state noted that operational needs required that at least fifteen troopers be promoted to the rank of corporal. The federal and state governments and Philip Paradise then agreed to a second consent decree that provided that the examination would be given and scored and that the promotion register would be reviewed to determine whether the test had an adverse impact on blacks.[47]

It turned out that the racial gap was even greater than most testing experts would have predicted. Of the 262 candidates who took the corporal's examination, 60 were black, and although these 60 blacks made up 23 percent of the test takers, only 5 blacks (less than 2 percent of the test takers) were among those in the top half of the register, with the highest-scoring black ranked eightieth. Therefore, a rank-ordered use of the test would have resulted in no blacks being promoted to corporal had even as many as 79 troopers been promoted.[48]

Because of the adverse impact, Reynolds informed Alabama that it should submit an alternative proposal for making promotions. Reynolds insisted that the alternative should do what the state had promised in its consent decree of 1979; it should provide for promotions without having an adverse impact on blacks. In response, Alabama promoted 4 blacks and 11 whites—thereby avoiding adverse impact by giving blacks a proportion of the promotions (26 percent) that was more than commensurate with the proportion of blacks in the troop and in the pool of candidates for corporal (23 percent). Of the 66 promotions given during the next five years, 15 (23 percent) went to blacks.[49]

Reynolds was willing to accept this, but Philip Paradise, the intervening black plaintiff, rejected the arrangement. Instead, he returned to district court and asked Judge Myron H. Thompson to order that one black trooper must be promoted for each white. Judge Thompson then established a one-for-one promotion plan that was to remain in effect until blacks made up at least 25 per cent of each rank.[50]

As a practical matter, Judge Thompson's order meant that 8 blacks (instead of only 4) would be promoted to corporal in 1984. In some ways it seemed like a negligible difference, but Reynolds and Charles Fried took the case to the Supreme Court anyway. They were convinced that the one-for-one promotion quota was at odds with the narrow tailoring that the Supreme Court had prescribed in *Wygant*, *Cleveland*, and *Sheet Metal Workers*. They thought, in addition, that the one-for-one promotion plan was arbitrary and capricious, as they said that Alabama's behavior did "not smack of recalcitrance or obstructionism." Since 1975 the state had "faithfully complied with the one-for-one hiring quota," and after 1981 it had promoted black troopers at a rate commensurate with their availability. Fried said it was autocratic for Judge Thompson to impose a one-for-one promotion quota against this background; it smacked of "spanking a child when he's good to show that you would spank him when he's bad."[51]

After *Wygant*, *Cleveland*, and *Sheet Metal Workers*, Fried and Reynolds no longer argued that it was illegal to give racial preferences to individuals who had not been identified as actual victims of discrimination. Instead, they said that the sex preference in Santa Clara County and the promotion quota in Alabama went beyond the boundaries the Supreme Court had established.

This seemed obvious in the *Santa Clara* case. In *Wygant* the plurality opinion noted that the Supreme Court had never held that "societal" discrimination alone was sufficient to justify a racial classification; instead, the Court insisted that there must be "some showing of prior discrimination by the governmental unit involved before allowing limited use of racial classifications in order to remedy such discrimination."[52]

In *Santa Clara County*, the transportation agency was not trying to remedy past discrimination against women; the trial judge had found that the agency "ha[d] not discriminated in the past, and does not discriminate in the present." Instead, the agency was giving preference to a sex because it wanted to overcome the effect of societal attitudes that had limited the entry of women into certain jobs. The purpose was not to remedy discrimination but to achieve the sort of society that might have existed if social attitudes had been different in the past.[53]

As Fried and Reynolds saw it, this sort of social engineering was at odds with the limitations the Court had established in *Cleveland* and *Sheet Metal Workers*. While those cases had authorized the use of race-conscious relief for persons who were not identifiable victims of discrimination, six members of the Court had said the affirmative preferences could be used only in narrowly confined circumstances. The Court had chosen a middle course that would permit racial or gender preferences for individuals who had not themselves suffered specific discrimination, but only if there had been discrimination against their group and only if the preferences were narrowly tailored to fit the circumstances of the case and to protect the interests of innocent persons.[54]

Unless the Court of 1987 was prepared to disregard the limitations it had established in 1986, Fried and Reynolds maintained, Diane Joyce should lose her promotion. The facts in the case revealed "not [a] carefully tailored remedial action but a rather extreme example of casual social engineering heedless of individual rights." If the Court decided for Diane Joyce, it would achieve "the perverse result of authorizing an employer that has never engaged in discriminatory practices to now, for the first time, embark on such an invidious course."[55]

The Alabama case was more problematical. Fried and Reynolds thought the state had behaved properly during the 1970s, but because there had been a record of egregious discrimination before then, it could therefore be argued that a quota for promotions was needed to eradicate the continuing effects of the illegal discrimination. Nevertheless, Fried and Reynolds thought the one-for-one promotion quota exceeded the boundaries of narrow tailoring. As Alabama, after all, was already giving about 25 percent of the promotions at issue to lower-scoring blacks, the existing policy already imposed a heavy penalty on a small number of whites who competed for the promotions, but giving one-quarter of the promotions to blacks was at least arguably "tailored" to fit the number of blacks in the relevant labor force. Doubling the number of promotions that were reserved for blacks would only compound the penalty and abandon the pretense of narrow tailoring.

Fried and Reynolds argued that Judge Thompson's 50 percent promotion quota should not stand because it was not tailored to fit the facts of the case. They said Thompson's one-for-one order greatly exceeded the percentage of blacks in the relevant labor market and damaged the career prospects of identifiable whites. In language that suggested just how arbitrary they thought Judge Thompson had been, Fried and Reynolds wrote that "the promotion quota was the wrong gun...aimed at the wrong head," and that Thompson was "holding innocent white state troopers hostage." They said the real purpose of the judge was to advance a "preconceived notion of a desirable 'racial balance,'" and that it was a purpose that was at odds with earlier Supreme Court statements to the effect that the condition that offended the Constitution was racial discrimination (subtle or otherwise), not the lack of racial balance.[56]

In the end the Supreme Court's decision in the Alabama case went against Fried and Reynolds. In some ways the ruling was an important show of support for affirmative action, but it also demonstrated that deep divisions existed within the Supreme Court. The vote was 5–4, and there were five separate opinions, with no more than four justices endorsing any one statement.[57]

The Court had continued a practice of the recent past—that of handling affirmative action on a case-by-case basis and without giving lower courts a clear set of principles to follow. In an opinion for a four-member plurality, Justice Brennan held that the one-for-one promotion quota *was* narrowly tailored to fit the facts of the case. Justice Stevens concurred in the decision (but not the opinion) of the plurality. In a dissent joined by Chief Justice Rehnquist and by Justice Scalia, Justice O'Connor said the one-for-one promotion quota *was not* narrowly tailored and was unduly burdensome to white troopers. Justice White dissented separately.[58]

Reynolds tried to make light of the defeat. "In the face of proven, persistent discrimination," he said that the Supreme Court had carved out a "narrow exception" to the general rule against racial preferences. A more-upbeat Barry Goldstein of the Legal Defense Fund hailed the decision as a victory for affirmative action and as proof that Reynolds and Fried had been wrong when they said the Court's rulings in 1986 had meant that affirmative racial preferences could "hardly ever" be used. The *Washington Post* reported that the decision "underscored the Reagan administration's failure after six years to make significant headway in winning Supreme Court support for its civil rights arguments."[59]

The full dimensions of the administration's defeat became apparent in March 1987, when the Supreme Court handed down its opinion in the *Santa Clara County* case. By a vote of 6–3, the Court held that the Civil Rights Act allowed employers to favor women over better-qualified men and that an employer could give affirmative preferences even if there was no proof that there had been discrimination against women. The Court said that government employers, as well as private companies, could use affirmative preferences for the purpose of bringing a work force into line with the makeup of the local population or labor market. The Court held that employers who were trying to achieve a better balance in their work force should not be held liable for reverse discrimination against men or whites.[60]

There were some qualifications in the opinion that Justice Brennan crafted for five members of the Court. He noted that Santa Clara's plan called for a relatively mild form of affirmative action in which no specific number of positions was set aside for women or blacks; race and sex were simply taken into account as two of several factors in individual employment decisions. Brennan said that the plan was carefully designed to correct the "underrepresentation of women in 'traditionally segregated job categories'," and that "any differences in qualifications" between Paul Johnson and Diane Joyce were "minimal."[61]

A more important qualification was left unstated. In *Santa Clara County*, Justice Brennan's majority was interpreting the Civil Rights Act. Because of the way Paul Johnson had framed his case, Brennan did not and could not use *Santa Clara County* to determine the requirements of the equal protection clause.

As of 1987, however, there could be no mistaking the fact that the Court had broadly extended the authorization for affirmative action. In the *Cleveland* and *Sheet Metal Workers'* cases of 1986, the Court had rejected victim specificity, but it had not rejected the idea that affirmative preferences could be used only as a *remedy* for discrimination. The Court had said the antidiscrimination provisions of the Civil Rights Act could be honored in the breach by giving preferences to individuals who had not suffered personally—but only if it was shown that there had been illegal discrimination against their group. However, in *Santa Clara County*, the Court held that there need be no showing of discrimination; it was enough if the employer wanted to correct the underrepresentation of women or blacks in the work force.

In a separate concurring opinion, Justice Stevens explained that the Court was building upon, and extending, its earlier precedents. Stevens acknowledged that the language of the Civil Rights Act prohibited "discriminatory preferences for any group, minority or majority," and, therefore, it created an obligation not to discriminate against men or Caucasians. Stevens conceded that if the Court had respected the intention of the Congress that passed the law, Paul Johnson "would unquestionably prevail in this case."[62]

However, Stevens explained that, beginning with *Bakke* and *Weber* and continuing with *Cleveland* and *Sheet Metal Workers*, "a majority of the Court interpreted the antidiscriminatory strategy of the statute in a fundamentally different way"; that is, it allowed discrimination that was intended to benefit members of minority groups even if the discrimination trammeled the rights of whites. For Stevens, "the only problem" was whether to adhere to "the actual intent of the authors of the legislation" or to a line of interpretation that the Court had been developing. "Without hesitation," Stevens opted for the latter course. He said he did so because "stability and the orderly development of the law" required fidelity to the Court's recent pattern.[63]

Columnist George F. Will characterized Stevens's concurrence as "a guileless admission" that the Court was "legislating its sense of justice and its preferred social-welfare policies." In a dissenting opinion (joined by Chief Justice Rehnquist and Justice White), Justice Scalia said the Court had "effectively replace[d] the goal of a discrimination-free society with the quite incompatible goal of proportionate representation by race and sex."[64]

Conservative commentators greeted *Santa Clara County* with cries of anguish. James J. Kilpatrick lamented that the Court had stood the Civil Rights Act on its head in that "[i]n the name of 'affirmative action,' [it] went further than it ever has in approving discrimination in reverse." Norman Podhoretz complained that the Court, "far from acting as a guardian of the law, ha[d] become a law unto itself, and therefore a lawless institution." Joseph Sobran said the decision reminded him of Jonathan Swift's description of lawyers—"a body of men among us, brought up from their youth in the art of proving by words multiplied for the purpose, that white is black, and black is white."[65]

The defeat in *Santa Clara County* represented the lowest point in Reynolds's tenure as assistant attorney general for civil rights. In the early years of the Reagan administration, he had argued that the equal protection clause and the Civil Rights Act prohibited racial classifications but allowed action to remedy illegal discrimination against actual victims. In the *Cleveland* and *Sheet Metal Workers*' cases of 1986, however, the Court had rejected victim specificity and had authorized racial preferences in cases where there was a finding that there had been discrimination against blacks. Then, in 1987, the Court said that employers who had never practiced discrimination could discriminate if their purpose was to achieve a better balance in the work force.

There was speculation that both Reynolds and Charles Fried would resign. It was said that the administration's "strident assault on affirmative action" had backfired and made the Court more resolutely proquota than it otherwise would have been. Some critics censured Reynolds for criticizing Justice Brennan in an out-of-court speech at the University of Missouri. One federal appeals judge said that Fried had so antagonized Justice Stevens that the Reagan administration could "cross Justice Stevens's vote off if Fried appeared" to argue a case before the Court.[66]

But the speculation about Reynolds failed to take account of his character. "Just because you lose," one of Reynolds's colleagues noted, "does not mean that your position is wrong." Reynolds still thought his legal reasoning was correct. He also felt a sense of obligation to President Reagan. He recalled that in 1985 Reagan had given a radio speech in support of Reynolds's promotion to associate attorney general, and now, after *Santa Clara County*, Reagan made another public statement, saying that he "disagree[d] with the decision of the Supreme Court."[67]

Reynolds recognized that the administration had little hope of prevailing with a majority of the nine sitting justices, but he also knew that four of the justices who favored affirmative discrimination were quite elderly and could not hold on much longer. A new appointment of two would give the Reagan administration the chance to regain the ground it had lost, and Reynolds expected to have a hand in shaping the appointments.

Moreover, from Reynolds's perspective there were redeeming features even in *Santa Clara County*. One derived from the limited nature of the Court's ruling. Plaintiff Paul Johnson had not claimed that he was denied the equal protection guaranteed by the U. S. Constitution. Johnson wanted a promotion, and he wanted to get it quickly and with a minimum of legal expense. Therefore, instead of basing his complaint on the Constitution, Johnson said the county had acted in violation of the 1964 Civil Rights Act, which forbade discrimination on the basis of both sex and race. Thus, *Santa Clara County* pertained only to the proper construction of the Civil Rights Act. It did not address the meaning of the equal protection clause, and when Reynolds returned to court in 1988, he would ask the justices to use the equal protection clause to trump *Santa Clara County*.

In addition, Justice Scalia's dissent in *Santa Clara County* was an especially powerful statement that had caused other justices to add footnotes to their opinions. It even caused the usually pro-preference editors of the *Wash-*

ington Post to conclude that the *Santa Clara County* court had gone too far in embracing an "extreme" version of affirmative action. For years Chief Justice Rehnquist had expressed views similar to Reynolds's and had been preeminent on the Court in terms of clear expository prose. Now, with Scalia on the Court, conservatives also had the support of the Court's best phrasemaker. In addition, Justices O'Connor and White could also be expected to weigh in with comments that were well considered even if less eloquent. Instead of surrendering, Reynolds decided to hold the fort and provide reinforcements for Rehnquist, Scalia, O'Connor and White.[68]

Notes

1. Statement of Thaddeus Stevens, *Congressional Globe*, 39th Congress, 1st Session (1866), 2459.
2. Statements of Emmanuel Celler and Hubert H. Humphrey, *Congressional Record*, 110 (1964), 1518, 6549.
3. Firefighters v. Stotts, 467 U.S. 561 (1984), 580.
4. Wygant v. Jackson Board of Education, 546 F.Supp. 1195 (1982), 1203 and passim.
5. Vanguards of Cleveland v. City of Cleveland, 753 F.2d 479 (1985); Local 93 v. City of Cleveland, 478 U.S. 501 (1986).
6. Brief for the United States as Amicus Curiae, Local 93 v. City of Cleveland, Supreme Court Library; *New York Times*, 4 July 1986, 7:1; *Washington Post*, 25 February 1986, A7a.
7. Vanguards of Cleveland v. City of Cleveland, 753 F.2d 479 (1985), 485.
8. Local 28 v. EEOC, 478 U.S. 421 (1986), 485.
9. Reply Brief for the EEOC, Local 28 v. EEOC, 1, 6, Supreme Court Library; *Washington Post*, 7 July 1986, A11a.
10. EEOC v. Local 638, 401 F.Supp. 467 (1975), 480, 479.
11. Ibid., 480, 478.
12. Ibid., 481–85.
13. Ibid., 489; EEOC v. Local 638, 532 F.2d 821 (1976), 831 n.5.
14. EEOC v. Local 638, 532 F.2d 821 (1976), 826; 401 F.Supp. 467 (1975), 485; 565 F.2d 31 (1977), 40–41.
15. EEOC v. Local 638, 753 F.2d 1172 (1985), 1176–77; 532 F.2d 821 (1976), 826.
16. Charles Fried, *Order and Law*, 110–11.
17. Brief for the United States as Amicus Curiae, Local 93 v. City of Cleveland, 7 and passim, Supreme Court Library.
18. Charles Fried, *Order and Law*, 111.
19. Brief for the United States as Amicus Curiae, Wygant v. Jackson Board of Education, 4, 7, 6, 8, Supreme Court Library.
20. Ibid.
21. Wygant v. Jackson Board of Education, 476 U.S. 265 (1986); Local 93 v. City of Cleveland, 478 U.S. 501 (1986); Local 28 v. EEOC, 478 U.S. 321 (1986).
22. Wygant v. Jackson Board of Education, 476 U.S. 265 (1986), 287; Local 28 v. EEOC, 478 U.S. 421 (1986), 424. The flavor of the Court's 1986 handiwork on affirmative action is suggested in the preface to the opinion in the *Sheet Metal Workers* case: "BRENNAN, J., announced the judgment of the Court with re-

spect to Parts I, II, III, and VI, in which MARSHALL, BLACKMUN, POWELL, and STEVENS, J.J., joined, and an opinion with respect to Parts IV, V, and VII, in which MARSHALL, BLACKMUN, and STEVENS, J.J., joined. POWELL, J., filed an opinion concurring in part and dissenting in part.... WHITE, J., filed a dissenting opinion.... REHNQUIST, J., filed a dissenting opinion, in which BURGER, C.J., joined."

23. *New York Times*, 3 July 1986, 1:4; *Detroit Free Press*, 3 July 1986.
24. *Washington Post*, 3 July 1986, A1d; *New York Times*, 3 July 1986, 1:4; *Human Events* (19 July 1986).
25. *Washington Post*, 21 May 1986, A25d; 6 June 1986, A19a.
26. *Wilmington News Journal*, 2 June 1986.
27. *Washington Post*, 25 May 1986, C8a; 11 July 1986, D1a; 3 July 1986, A22a; *New York Times*, 3 July 1986, 1:4.
28. Charles Fried, *Order and Law*, 105, 113.
29. Ibid., 23, 96, 101, 105.
30. *New York Times*, 5 July 1986, 32:1; Local 28 v. EEOC, 478 U.S. 421 (1986), 444–81.
31. *New York Times*, 3 July 1986, II, 9:1; *Detroit Free Press*, 3 July 1986.
32. *USA Today*, 7 July 1986.
33. *Washington Post*, 13 June 1986, A9a; *Jackson Citizen Patriot*, 16 October 1986 and undated clipping (probably January 1987); *Grand Rapids Press*, 4 July 1986.
34. Melvin Urofsky, *A Conflict of Rights*, 6 and passim.
35. Ibid., 8.
36. Ibid., 2.
37. Ibid., 244, 11; Johnson v. Transportation Agency, 480 U.S. 618 (1987), 663–64.
38. Johnson v. Transportation Agency, 480 U.S. 616 (1987), 658, 659.
39. Ibid., 661, 625, 655; Brief for the United States, Johnson v. Transportation Agency, 2 Supreme Court Library.
40. Melvin Urofsky, *A Conflict of Rights*, 62; Johnson v. Transportation Agency, 480 U.S. 616 (1987), 663–64.
41. U.S. v. Frazer, 317 F.Supp. 1079 (1970), 1085–87.
42. NAACP v. Allen, 340 F.Supp. 703 (1972), 705.
43. U.S. v. Frazer, 317 F.Supp. 1079 (1970), 1090–97.
44. NAACP v. Allen, 340 F.Supp. 703 (1972), 707–8; 493 F.2d 614 (1974), 621; Second Reply Brief for the United States, U.S. v. Paradise, 4, Supreme Court Library.
45. Paradise v. Shoemaker, 470 F.Supp. 439 (1979), 442; Reply Brief for the United States, U.S. v. Paradise, 10 n. 4, Supreme Court Library; NAACP v. Allen, 340 F.Supp. 703 (1972), 706.
46. Paradise v. Prescott, 585 F.Supp. 72 (1983), 74.
47. Paradise v. Prescott, 580 F.Supp. 171 (1983), 172–73; Brief for the United States, U.S. v. Paradise, 6–8, Supreme Court Library.
48. Paradise v. Prescott, 580 U.S. 171 (1983), 173.
49. Brief for the United States, U.S. v. Paradise, 6–11, Supreme Court Library; *Birmingham News*, 14 November 1986.
50. Paradise v. Prescott, 585 F.Supp. 72 (1983), 74, 75.
51. Reply Brief for the United States, U.S. v. Paradise, 5, 4, Supreme Court Library; *Birmingham News*, 12 November 1986.
52. Wygant v. Jackson Board of Education, 476 U.S. 275 (1986), 274.

53. Johnson v. Transportation Agency, 480 U.S. 616 (1987), 659.
54. Brief for the United States, Johnson v. Transportation Agency, 7 and passim, Supreme Court Library.
55. Ibid., 9, 23.
56. Brief for the United States, U.S. v. Paradise, 26, 16, 34, Supreme Court Library.
57. United States v. Paradise, 480 U.S. 149 (1987).
58. Ibid.; *Wall Street Journal*, 26 February 1987, 5:1.
59. *Washington Post*, 26 February 1987, A1d; *New York Times*, 26 February 1987, 1:6.
60. Johnson v. Transportation Agency, 480 U.S. 616 (1987).
61. Ibid., 622, 631, 641 n.17.
62. Ibid., 642–43.
63. Ibid., 644.
64. *Washington Post,* 2 April 1987, A25a. Scalia explained that the Court's previous interpretations of Title VII, especially the opinion in *Griggs,*subjected employers to a potential lawsuit and the cost of validating for job relatedness if there was an imbalance in the representation of minorities or women in the employer's work force. Then, in *Santa Clara County*, the Court held that "employers were free to discriminate through affirmative action, without fear of 'reverse discrimination' suits by their nonminority or male victims." Thus, Scalia concluded, Title VII was "not merely repealed but actually inverted," and also wrote, "A statute designed to establish a color-blind and gender-blind workplace has...been converted into a powerful engine of racism and sexism, not merely *permitting* intentional race- and sex- based discrimination, but often making it, through the operation of the legal system, practically compelled." Johnson v. Transportation Agency, 480 U.S. 6 16 (1987), 658, 676, 677.
65. *Wilmington News Journal*, 2 April 1987; *Conservative Chronicle*, 15 April 1987.
66. *Washington Post*, 28 March 1987, A4c; *New York Times*, 13 September 1986, 1:6; Melvin Urofsky, *A Conflict of Rights*, 131.
67. *Newsweek* (6 April 1987): 8; *Washington Post*, 7 March 1987, Ad.
68. *Washington Post*, 27 March 1987, A26a.

13

Endgame

I

While awaiting the appointment of new justices, William Bradford Reynolds worked to keep the Reagan administration true to the president's principles. As noted above, in 1983 and 1984 he played a role in persuading the EEOC and a revamped Civil Rights Commission to embrace color-blind victim specificity, but the Office of Federal Contract Compliance (OFCC) continued to march to the beat of a different philosophy.

Established by the Secretary of Labor in 1965, the OFCC was responsible for enforcing the affirmative action obligation in President Lyndon B. Johnson's Executive Order 11246. Initially, the office focused on affirmative advertising and recruiting; it did not press for hiring preferences or quotas, which were then thought to be in violation of the Civil Rights Act of 1964. By the 1970s, however, the OFCC was urging federal contractors to hire more blacks as a condition of doing business with the government.[1]

Order No. 4 was the principal vehicle for the transformation. As revised by the Nixon administration in December 1971, this order required government contractors to develop "goals and timetables" for correcting any "under utilization" of enumerated minorities "at all levels and in all segments of the work force," with *underutilization* defined as "having fewer minorities in a particular job class than would reasonably be expected by their availability." It was to be determined by comparing "the percentage of the minority work force...with the total work force in the immediate labor area." If contractors did not make satisfactory progress toward proportional utilization of minorities, they could lose their government contracts.[2]

Newsweek reported that between 1977 and 1985 only fifteen employers lost their contacts for violations of Executive Order 11246, and OFCC officials said this relatively small number proved that goals and timetables were not being used as a substitute for quotas. They said that when there was a discrepancy between utilization and availability of minorities, they simply asked the employer to make a good-faith effort to ensure that the gap was closed. They canceled contracts only when they encountered obstinate resistance.[3]

Critics of the OFCC, on the other hand, said there was no real distinction between goals and quotas. "What the Office of Contract Compliance frequently tells a company," one critic said, "is, 'You haven't met your goal, so the remedy is: Meet your goal.' And that's a quota. To meet it, the company has to hire people in the preferred group, even if it means turning down better qualified people in other groups."[4]

The civil rights coalition wanted to keep the system as it was. They said the OFCC program, which by the 1980s covered 15,000 companies with 23 million workers, was one of the nation's most effective civil rights programs. The president of the National Association of Manufacturers said that it had led to "dramatic progress...in incorporating talented minorities and women into our work force." Howard Kurtz of the *Washington Post* wrote that critics of OFCC had set up "a straw man—that government is using illegal 'quotas' to enforce the law." An editorial in the *Post* declared, "Quotas are not the issue here; they are not being required or imposed."

> The issues are whether the government should continue to press within the modest confines of this program for greater opportunities to be made available to blacks and members of other minorities...and whether the [OFCC] should continue to compare racial and other employment percentages in particular firms with the same percentages in the work force as a whole. The sensible answer to both questions is yes.[5]

The Reagan Justice Department sided with the critics of OFCC. As Reynolds saw it, the regulations promulgated during the Nixon administration had changed the race neutral approach of the original executive order. The revised Order No. 4 put in place "an elaborate scheme of race and sex quotas (euphemistically camouflaged as 'goals and timetables') that compel federal contractors and sub-contractors to engage in hiring and promotions on the basis of skin color and gender in order to cure 'under representation.'"[6]

Reynolds said the result was predictable. To satisfy the bureaucratic numbers game, federal contractors "denied jobs and promotions to better qualified non-minorities because of race and sex." Equally important, they also "denied jobs and promotions to fully qualified minorities and women once the designated numerical threshold was reached."[7]

Upon becoming assistant attorney general, Reynolds recalled that "the thing that struck me most was that almost every single affirmative action program stopped when they reached the 10 percent ceiling." Years later, he reflected, "Everybody had 10 percent. Nobody had 11 percent even though in the construction business there were a lot of blacks who could swing a hammer, hit a nail, use a saw or work on bricklaying."[8]

Reynolds explained that employers feared that egalitarian bureaucrats and judges would accuse them of discrimination if blacks were concentrated at the bottom of the occupational hierarchy. Therefore, the employers "structured a system where minority executives were put in EEO [equal employment and affirmative action] jobs with high titles." Then, to avoid racial imbalance, "qualified blacks were turned away from unskilled and semi-skilled jobs." The situation was not unlike that in the U.S. Army where a black quota of 10.6 percent was established during World War II. When the quota was removed after the war, the proportion of black enlisted men quickly increased to 25 percent. Reynolds thought rank-and-file black workers of the 1980s would also benefit from "lifting the quota lid."[9]

In the meantime, a sympathizer in the Department of Labor gave Reynolds documents that pertained to fifty-five incidents in which companies were forced to meet racial and gender goals in order to keep their government contracts. Civil rights leaders said fifty-five cases were not many when one considered that Executive Order 11246 applied to some 15,000 companies. Nevertheless, Reynolds's evidence indicated that there were more cases than the civil rights leaders had previously acknowledged. When he released the documents to the press, Reynolds blacked out the names of the companies, except for that of the United Bridge Company of Lenaxa, Kansas, which had complained publicly when it was cited for its failure "to exert adequate good faith effort to achieve the minimum minority utilization goal of 12.7 percent for Truck Drivers and the minimum female utilization goal of 6.9 percent" for each of six job categories.[10]

Because of cases such as this, in 1985 Reynolds and Attorney General Ed Meese drafted an executive order that would have *prohibited* the OFCC from using statistical evidence to determine if contractors were discriminating against women or blacks. Reynolds and Meese said they were trying to "carry out the original intent of the civil rights movement," but the *Washington Post* characterized the proposal as a "giant step backward," the "most regressive step on civil rights in five years."[11]

Within the Reagan administration, Secretary of Labor Bill Brock came to the support of the OFCC. It would be enough, Brock felt, to revise the original Executive Order 11246 with a sentence or two that repeated the language of the 1964 Civil Rights Act—language that called for color-blind nondiscrimination. In response, Reynolds and Meese said that a few sentences would not stop bureaucrats who had made careers out of establishing and overseeing numerical racial measures.[12]

A spirited debate ensued. Some cabinet members sided with Secretary Brock in defense of only a slight revision of the status quo, while others supported Meese and Reynolds. Most conservatives wanted to prohibit the statistical goals. With the stroke of a pen, they believed, President Reagan could deliver a crushing blow against quotas and put an end to the government's policy of forcing firms with federal contracts to practice racial discrimination.[13]

Action of this sort had been considered but postponed in 1981, when the Reagan administration wanted to focus on its program for reviving the economy. It had been deferred again in 1984, for fear of raising a divisive issue during an election year. But by 1985 the economy was performing well and Reagan had been reelected. The time had come, *Human Events* said, for Reagan to "back Meese over Brock on quotas."[14]

There was no doubt about where Reagan stood on the merits of the issue. He had repeatedly insisted that "all persons should be judged on the basis of individual merit and ability, not skin color or gender." He condemned civil rights bureaucrats who, he said, "have turned our civil rights laws on their heads, claiming they mean exactly the opposite of what they say." He said that "goals and timetables" amounted to "a quota system."[15]

But there was a political problem. While members of the administration had been debating the question, leaders of the civil rights lobby organized their forces. By early 1986, 69 members of the U.S. Senate and 180 members of the House of Representatives had signed letters urging Reagan not to sign the new executive order. "This is the largest coalition ever on a civil rights issue," said Ralph Neas of the Leadership Conference. Neas added that if Reagan ignored the sentiment there would be "a political firestorm that [would] hurt Republicans." The economist Thomas Sowell, who favored Meese and Reynolds's proposal, observed that there was "a whole empire of bureaucrats, politicians, media pundits, hustlers, and traditional civil rights organizations, who will cry bloody murder if the President tries to make 'equal opportunity' mean what it says, instead of meaning preferential treatment."[16]

Reagan considered the question at length but, in the end, did nothing. With 69 senators and 180 members of the House on record in opposition, Reagan decided that the political cost of supporting Meese and Reynolds's proposal would outweigh the benefits.

Meese had not pushed the issue. In fact, Meese also came to believe that the political cost of signing would be too high. For his part, Reynolds understood the political situation. Gary McDowell has noted that the incident illustrated an important point about Reagan and Meese (and Reynolds): that they were dedicated to principle but also had "a keen-eyed, unblinking acknowledgment of practical political realities." It also showed how Reagan treated his most trusted aides. Unlike George Bush, who repudiated one of his aides, Michael Williams, when Williams made the politically controversial decision to oppose scholarships that were restricted for blacks, Reagan simply allowed the controversy over the executive order to fade away without announcing a decision. In that way, Reagan avoided portraying Meese and Reynolds as losing parties. Reynolds later recalled, "Reagan didn't do everything I recommended, but he never pulled the rug out from under me."[17]

Some conservatives were angry. The columnists Rowland Evans and Robert Novak lamented that the administration had lost its spark and had grown "too cautious and consensual in its long enjoyment of unprecedented popularity ratings." At the Department of Justice, press officer Terry Eastland criticized White House staffers who did not share the president's convictions on civil rights. The problem with the civil rights policies of the Reagan administration, Eastland claimed in an article in *Commentary*, was that the White House did not provide much leadership but instead left Brad Reynolds and the Department of Justice to march into battle on their own.[18]

II

Reagan's backing away from the proposed revision of 11246 meant that litigation would continue to be the primary vehicle for advancing the administration's civil rights program. Consequently, Reynolds looked for new cases that could be used to challenge affirmative discrimination. In 1988, in cooperation with Solicitor General Charles Fried, he intervened in three lawsuits that were already under way. One questioned the doctrine of adverse impact, another concerned the right to challenge consent decrees that contained racial preferences, and the third took exception to the practice of setting aside a fixed proportion of construction work for minority contractors. In 1989, the Supreme Court decided all three cases in favor of the Reagan administration. With those decisions, the drift toward a quota society was arrested.

In 1977, Congress provided that 10 percent of all federal grants awarded by the Department of Commerce should be given to minority business enterprises. White contractors challenged the law as a denial of equal protection, but the Supreme Court upheld the set asides by a vote of 6–3. The opinion of the Court was confusing, however, for a majority of justices could not agree on the rationale. They wrote five different opinions, none of which was joined by more than three members of the Court.[19]

For some time Reynolds and Fried had been planning to challenge racial set-asides, and in 1987 they found a case, *City of Richmond v. J. A. Croson*, that could be used to that end. Richmond had instituted an unusually high, 30 percent set-aside even though there was no evidence that minority firms had suffered from discrimination. There was evidence of statistical imbalance: between 1978 and 1983 black contractors received less than 1 percent of the municipal contracts that were awarded, even though black people made up 52 percent of the population of the city (and black politicians had become a majority on the city council). But there was no evidence that blacks had been excluded from the bidding pool or passed over when they submitted competitive bids. Fried and Reynolds also noted that the Fourth Circuit Court of Appeals had already rendered a strongly worded opinion against Richmond's set-aside program. In this case, for once, the Reagan administration could take a position in the middle—a stance that Fried thought would make it easier to win support from Justice O'Connor and perhaps from some other members of the Court.[20]

When the city advertised for bids on the installation of some stainless steel fixtures in the city jail, the J. A. Croson Company of Ohio expressed interest in the job and asked five minority firms if they would subcontract 30 percent of the work. When none of the minority firms expressed interest or tendered a quote before the day when bids were due, Croson submitted a low bid of $126,530. A local minority firm then offered to supply fixtures—but for a price that was $6,183 higher than the price Croson had included in its bid. Croson asked that it be allowed either to raise the overall contract price accordingly or that the city waive the set-aside requirement; but the city told Croson that the price could not be increased and that the contract would be rebid if Croson did not use the minority subcontractor. Croson then sued, on the grounds that the Richmond set-aside program was at odds with the equal protection clause of the U.S. Constitution.[21]

The district court upheld the plan in all respects, as did a divided panel of the Fourth Circuit Court. The Supreme Court then remanded the case for further consideration in light of its intervening decision in *Wygant*, and a second divided panel of the court of appeals struck down the Richmond plan as violative of the equal protection clause.[22]

On remand, the court of appeals acknowledged that the boundaries of *Wygant* were subject to dispute because the views of the Court in that case were expressed in a plurality opinion and two concurrences. Nevertheless, the appellate court found that the core of the Supreme Court's holding was that affirmative racial preferences could not pass muster under the equal protection clause unless they were designed to *remedy* past discrimination; that is, there had to be findings of prior discrimination—not just generalizations about societal discrimination but findings of "prior discrimination by the government unit involved." *Wygant* was found to have erected "more than a trivial hurdle for localities that wish to draw racial distinctions." *Wygant* required that racial preferences be limited (narrowly tailored) "to what is necessary to redress a practice of past wrongdoing."[23]

The court of appeals held that Richmond's set-aside plan did not satisfy either prong of the equal protection requirement: there was no finding of prior discrimination by the city or by its contractors, and the 30 percent quota was not narrowly tailored in that it was not tied to a showing that 30 percent of the subcontracting firms in Richmond were owned by minorities. The court said that "the figure simply emerged from the mists." It also said the city's statistical comparisons were "spurious" because only 4.7 percent of all construction companies in the United States were minority owned, and 41 percent of them were located in California, New York, Illinois, Florida, and Hawaii.[24]

The opinion of the Fourth Circuit Court was written in prose that was uncommonly clear and stylish. The author was J. Harvie Wilkinson III, a former University of Virginia law professor who had previously been at one time a law clerk for Justice Lewis Powell and at another the editorial page editor of the *Virginia-Pilot* in Norfolk. Wilkinson was also the author of a memoir and of two well regarded scholarly books, and for one year in the early 1980s he had worked for Reynolds in the Civil Rights Division. Although only thirty-nine-years old when he became a member of the Fourth Circuit Court, Wilkinson quickly became an influential member of that body, and his work on the bench, Reynolds said, was "as good as we anticipated [it] would be."[25]

In ruling against Richmond's set-aside plan, Wilkinson did not insist on the victim specificity he had favored when he worked for Reynolds, but he held that *Wygant* required employers to limit racial preferences to eradicating the effects of *their own* prior discrimination.

This impressed Charles Fried as unduly restrictive. Fried thought racial preferences would be limited sufficiently if they were allowed in instances where there was proof of discrimination. Reynolds, on the other hand, thought it was illogical to talk about narrow tailoring if a racial preference was designed to remedy the discrimination of another party. But by 1988 Reynolds recognized that the Reagan administration would have a better chance of prevailing in the Supreme Court if it did not insist that there must be prior discrimination on the part of the employer involved. Accordingly, the brief that Fried and Reynolds prepared for the Supreme Court in *Croson* called for narrow tailoring and proof of discrimination, but did not insist on either victim specificity or prior discrimination by the city of Richmond.[26]

It proved to be a winning strategy. The Supreme Court rejected Judge Wilkinson's holding that a city must limit racial preferences to eradicating the effects of its own prior discrimination. But, by a vote of 6–3, the Court also rejected Richmond's argument that cities enjoyed sweeping discretion to define and attack the effects of societal discrimination, doing so in language that delivered a major set back to every sort of set-asides.

In her opinion for the Court's majority, Justice O'Connor held that the equal protection clause protected the individual rights of whites as well as blacks. She said that remedying past discrimination was the only legitimate reason for racial preferences, and that any preferences must pass the test of "strict scrutiny." This meant that preferences must be accompanied by findings of prior discrimination and must be tailored to overcome that wrong. O'Connor said that when it came to using a suspect classification, like race, it was not enough to justify a program by saying that it was intended to remedy societal discrimination; and that for the government to favor one race over another was a serious constitutional matter that could be justified only as an effort to remedy identifiable discrimination. Although preferences need not be victim specific, O'Connor said that they must be strictly limited and could be used only when there were no other effective racially neutral measures that would have less untoward impact on innocent third parties.[27]

From a legal point of view, *Croson* was important because Justice O'Connor's majority used the equal protection clause to trump the 1987 opinion that Justice Brennan had cobbled together in *Santa Clara County*. As noted in chapter 12, Paul Johnson, the passed-over candidate for road dispatcher, did not develop a constitutional theory. He wanted a promotion, and he wanted to get it in the fastest and cheapest way. Consequently, he relied solely on the argument that his employer had violated Title VII of the Civil Rights Act. The case finally went to the Supreme Court after public-interest law firms intervened and paid the costs, but when the case went up on appeal, it presented only an issue of statutory law and did not involve a constitutional argument about equal protection. Justice Brennan then held that affirmative racial preferences did not violate Title VII if women or minorities were manifestly underrepresented. In *Croson,* however, Justice O'Connor held that the equal protection clause established a more exacting two-part test: there must be proof of discrimination *and* proof that the wrong could not be remedied with race-neutral measures.

The concurring opinions in *Croson* suggested that other members of the Court were prepared to go beyond Justice O'Connor to protect against reverse racial discrimination. In a concurring opinion, Justice Scalia reiterated a view that Chief Justice Rehnquist and Justice White had previously affirmed: that governments may allocate benefits on the basis of race only to eliminate their own discrimination and only to compensate identified victims of that discrimination. In elegant language, Scalia observed that

> [t]he difficulty of overcoming the effects of past discrimination is as nothing compared with the difficulty of eradicating from our society the source of those effects, which is the tendency—fatal to a Nation such as ours—to classify and judge men and women on the basis of their country of origin or the color of their skin. A solution to the first problem that aggravates the second is no solution at all.[28]

Then, to make matters worse for the civil rights lobby, the newest member of the Court, Justice Kennedy, said that he agreed with Justice Scalia in that he wanted to make it "crystal clear...that legislation must be based on criteria other than race." Nevertheless, Kennedy joined Justice O'Connor's opinion for two reasons: one was that "a rule of automatic invalidity for racial preferences in almost every case would be a significant break with...precedents that require a case-by-case test"; the other was that Kennedy thought the strict scrutiny rule that Justice O'Connor had announced would forbid "the use even of narrowly drawn racial classifications except as a last resort." If that was not the case, Kennedy implied, he too would enlist under the banner of victim specificity.[29]

Most observers recognized that the Supreme Court had dealt a severe blow to hard affirmative action. Charles Krauthammer, who had supported racial preferences in the past, acknowledged that the Court was "drawing a narrower and narrower circle—a noose—around any government action that is race-conscious." George F. Will, a critic of such plans in the past, praised the Court for "roll[ing] back the racial spoils system that exists for certain government-favored minorities."[30]

A bitter, thirty-four-page dissent confirmed the impression that the Court had turned decisively. In an opinion joined by Justices Blackmun and Brennan, Justice Marshall said the Court had sounded "a full-scale retreat from [its] longstanding solicitude to race-conscious remedial efforts." It had "launche[d] a grapeshot attack on race-conscious remedies in general." It had taken "a giant step backward in...affirmative action jurisprudence."[31]

Five months later, in June 1989, the Court released another opinion that tightened the noose around affirmative preferences. Because it involved a procedural question—the standing to sue — *In re Birmingham Reverse Discrimination* did not receive much attention in the press, but when coupled with the strict scrutiny standard of *Croson,* the procedural ruling in *Birmingham* was a major blow against quotas.

The factual situation in *Birmingham* was similar to that in other cases that have already been described in that the Alabama city had discriminated against blacks in municipal employment and in other respects. After a trial in 1976, but before judgment, the city and the NAACP agreed to remedy the discrimination by establishing the goal of employing women and blacks in each city job classification "in percentages which approximate their respective percentages in the civilian labor force of Jefferson County." The city further agreed to hire blacks for one-half of the new jobs as fire fighter and fire lieutenant and for one-quarter of the positions in the engineering department. The district court then entered this agreement as a consent decree.[32]

After entering the consent decree provisionally, the court held a fairness hearing to consider any objections to the plan. The predominantly white Birmingham Firefighters Association appeared and moved to intervene on the ground that the plan would adversely affect the rights of its members. Seven individual whites also asked the court to enjoin the plan. In 1981, however, the court issued an order approving the fairness of the decree and denying both the injunction and the petition to intervene in the lawsuit.[33]

In Birmingham, as elsewhere, it turned out that a hiring quota was not sufficient to guarantee the proportional promotion of blacks. To compensate for the lower average scores that blacks made on promotion examinations, the city and the NAACP then extended the quotas to cover promotions. In 1985, when whites complained that it was illegal to pass over them in favor of lower-scoring blacks, the district court held that whites could not challenge the practice because it was made pursuant to a court-approved consent decree.[34]

In denying whites the right to challenge consent arrangements that employers had worked out with other parties, the district court seemed to contravene a cardinal principle of Anglo-American jurisprudence: that third parties should not be required to submit to bargains in which their interests are either ignored or sacrificed. But the district court was not alone in holding that consent decrees were immunized from charges of discrimination. When it came to consent decrees in employment discrimination cases, the courts of appeal in the second, fifth, sixth, and ninth circuits also ruled that members of the majority could be deprived of legal rights in proceedings to which they were not parties. The courts explained that there was "a strong public policy in favor of voluntary affirmative action plans," reasoning that parties would be discouraged from negotiating such agreements if they could be subjected to attacks from third parties.[35]

This was precisely why *Birmingham* was an important case. Unlike the construction set-asides, where white contractors were allowed to challenge the quotas and had an economic incentive to do so, white workers could not contest consent decrees that supposedly were remedies for discrimination. As long as these consent decrees were invulnerable to attack by third parties, the Supreme Court's insistence on strict scrutiny and narrow tailoring would do little for the so-called Reagan Democrats or for Republicans of ordinary means.

Reynolds recognized this and accordingly urged the Supreme Court to allow third parties to challenge employment related consent decrees. In June 1989, by a vote of 5–4, the Court agreed. Chief Justice Rehnquist explained that a consent decree among certain parties resolved the issues among them but should not restrict "the rights of strangers to those proceedings." To hold otherwise, Rehnquist wrote, would be at odds with the nation's "deep-rooted historic tradition that everyone should have his own day in court."[36]

As stated by the chief justice, the Court's decision seemed unremarkable, even common-sensical. Once again, however, a decision of the Court provided the occasion for jeremiads from the civil rights lobby and its sympathizers. Journalist David Broder accused the Reagan administration of using the *Birmingham* case "to roll back history," and Representative Don Edwards called the Court's decision a "blow to 25 years of progress." An editorial in the *New York Times* lamented that the Supreme Court was "tearing down a legal structure that was fair, workable and working." An editorial in the *Washington Post* suggested that the decision would lead to a "chaos of interminable litigation."[37]

That was the rub. In the past, civil rights activists had used litigation to persuade judges to read the Civil Rights Act every which way but straight, but after the Court's ruling on *Birmingham*, they feared an explosion of legal challenges from those who opposed racial preferences. They had reason for concern, for the *Birmingham* decision meant that the consent decrees that settled many discrimination suits, which had been considered immune from legal attack by outside parties, could now be just an early skirmish in a round of litigation. The Supreme Court had set the stage for challenges, not only to future consent decrees but also to decrees that had already been entered. During the first year after the *Birmingham* decision, white workers filed reverse discrimination suits in Atlanta, Boston, Chicago, Memphis, Oakland, Omaha, and San Francisco.[38]

In the third important civil rights case of 1989, the Supreme Court changed the ground rules that had governed adverse impact cases for eighteen years. Beginning with the *Griggs* case of 1971, the Court held that the Civil Rights Act called into question any employment practice that affected blacks adversely. After *Griggs*, Title VII was held to mean that whenever a practice had a disparate impact the employer must prove there was a strong business justification for the practice.

Reynolds was not opposed to using statistics to draw inferences of discrimination. In 1983, Reynolds wrote that in instances where minorities were seriously underutilized, it was fair and legally correct for the employer to shoulder "the heavy burden of demonstrating that its hiring practices have...been nondiscriminatory." During Reynolds's tenure as assistant attorney general, the Civil Rights Division filed several disparate impact lawsuits.[39]

But Reynolds also knew there were problems with the implementation of *Griggs*. One concerned the sort of proof that employers were required to present. In *Griggs*, the Court had waffled. At one point the Court said employers must prove that any standard or test that affected blacks adversely was a "business necessity"; at another point, the Court said it would be sufficient if the standard had a "manifest relationship to the employment."[40]

Lower courts then augmented the confusion with more varying formulations: one panel of judges from the Seventh Circuit Court of Appeals held that employers had to prove only that a practice with adverse impact was "reasonable" and contributed to "efficient" business operations; another panel in the Fifth Circuit wrote that "indispensability is not the touchstone," that a practice with adverse impact need only "promote the proficient operation of business"; yet another panel, from the Tenth Circuit, held that a practice with adverse impact "must be essential, the purpose compelling."[41]

Because the courts were not clear in articulating what it took to satisfy *Griggs*, some employers protected themselves against adverse impact lawsuits by removing imbalances. One way was by moving away from areas where minorities were concentrated. Another was by setting aside a designated share of jobs for minorities—a practice that ran counter to the framers' insistence that the Civil Rights Act was not intended or capable of being interpreted to promote race-conscious preferences to eliminate an underrepresentation of minorities.

Reynolds thought *Griggs* could be useful in ferreting out instances where an employer's standards and practices served only to keep out minorities. He thought it right and proper that employers should have to make a reasonable defense of any practice that affected minorities adversely, but Reynolds also thought some civil rights lawyers and judges were using *Griggs* to challenge reasonable employment practices simply because the employer did not hire the *right* percentage of minorities or women. He thought some employers were handing out jobs in racial proportions to avoid the cost of intimidating lawsuits and the possibility of ultimate liability. He was on the lookout for a case that could be used to constrain *Griggs*.

That case was *Wards Cove Packing Company v. Frank Atonio*. At first appearance, the facts in the case looked terrible to Reynolds. Wards Cove was operating salmon-canning factories in remote regions of Alaska but had a racially segmented work force that resembled that of a plantation economy. Most of the unskilled cannery workers were either Filipinos or natives (Inuits or Aleuts), while most of the skilled machinists, carpenters, and office workers were white. The skilled and unskilled workers were housed in separate dormitories and ate in separate dining halls. The accommodations were labelled racially with terms like "Filipino Mess" and "Native Bunkhouse." Even the salmon-butchering machine had a name with racial overtones, the "Iron Chink."[42]

When looked at closely, however, *Wards Cove* was a good case for the Reagan administration. There were reasonable explanations for the segmentation of the work force—and in ruling against the packing company, the Ninth Circuit Court of Appeals had developed an extreme interpretation of *Griggs*.

Most of the skilled workers were taken to Alaska in May or June, a few weeks before the salmon runs of the summer months. Their job was to repair the facilities from winter damage as well as assemble and prepare the canning equipment. Boat crews arrived next, and then, finally, the cannery workers, who made up the bulk of the summer work force. Since salmon are extremely perishable and must be processed within a short time of being caught, the cannery workers put in long hours during the duration of the fish runs, which lasted usually about six to eight weeks. After the fishing season, the cannery workers departed, but most of the skilled workers remained for a few weeks to winterize equipment and to take care of paper work.

The work crews were housed by time of arrival, with the skilled crews assigned to bunkhouses that were better insulated. The company said this was a sensible adaptation to weather conditions in the colder spring and fall and not an indication of a sinister desire to operate a segregated company town. When it came to the separate dining halls, the company noted that the predominantly Filipino Seattle Local 37 (of the International Longshoremen's Union) had demanded Filipino cooks and cuisine in the collective bargaining agreement it had negotiated with the company. The company further explained that its use of Local 37 was largely responsible for the skewed distribution of its labor force. When hiring skilled workers, the company relied on applications received at the mainland home offices in Seattle and Astoria, Oregon. However, for cannery workers, it relied on crews dispatched by Local 37, which for peculiar historical reasons was run by and dispatched primarily Filipinos. The company said it used Local 37 because it was the exclusive bargaining representative for cannery jobs, not because of the racial composition of the crews it dispatched.

Upon examination, the underrepresentation of minorities in skilled jobs—the crux of the allegation of disparate impact—was a statistical artifact that resulted from the use of Local 37. The minority plaintiffs said there was disparate impact because nonwhites made up a larger portion of the cannery workers (52 percent) than of the skilled work force (24 percent). But after hearing testimony from labor economists, the trial judge, Justin L. Quackenbush, found that minorities made up only 10 percent of the workers in the relevant labor market (Alaska and the Pacific Northwest). If members of Local 37 were excluded from statistical comparisons, 90.2 percent of the unskilled jobs and 91.6 percent of the skilled jobs were held by whites.

Judge Quackenbush thought the plaintiffs' use of statistics made no sense. From their comparison, it could just as easily be deduced that native Alaskans and Filipinos were "significantly over represented in the cannery worker jobs." It could even be argued that minorities were overrepresented in the most-skilled jobs, where they made up 17 percent of those hired for medical jobs in the 1970s and 15 percent of those hired for office work. Because the statistics used to establish adverse impact had "little probative value," Judge Quackenbush entered a judgment for the company.[43]

On appeal, the Ninth Circuit Court reversed Judge Quackenbush and found for the minority plaintiffs. The court held that the statistics showing a higher percentage of nonwhite workers in the cannery jobs were enough to establish a prima facie case of disparate impact. It held that once disparate impact was established, the burden of proof shifted to the company to prove the "business necessity" of any challenged practice. The company had offered reasonable explanations of why its cannery workers were disproportionately Filipino and why it used separate hiring channels, dormitories, and mess halls, but it had not proved that these practices were necessary for the successful operation of its business.[44]

Reynolds and Fried regarded the opinion of the Ninth Circuit Court as perverse. *Griggs* called for the removal of "artificial, arbitrary, and unnecessary barriers to employment," but the judges of the Ninth Circuit Court had interpreted this as carte blanche to achieve what they considered rough justice. In the brief they prepared for the Supreme Court, Fried and Reynolds said it was inappropriate to compare the proportion of nonwhites in cannery jobs with the proportion that were machinists, electricians, accountants, or boat captains. The proper comparison would have been between the racial composition of the skilled jobs and the racial composition of the qualified labor pool. They said the statistical disparity the plaintiffs pointed to (and that the Ninth Circuit Court had endorsed) did not suffice to make out a prima facie case of disparate impact as there was no disparate impact simply because most jobs on the cannery line were held by nonwhites while most non-line positions were held by whites. Fried and Reynolds said the charges against the company should have been dismissed.[45]

Fried and Reynolds noted that the company could have eliminated the alleged disparate impact without making any change in its hiring practices for skilled jobs: by ceasing to rely on Local 37 as a hiring channel for cannery jobs, the statistical imbalance in the work force would have disappeared or dwindled to insignificance. If that were to have happened, the Ninth Circuit Court would be satisfied, but many Filipinos would have lost their jobs. Surely, Fried and Reynolds maintained, Title VII should not be understood to require such an ironic result.[46]

But Fried and Reynolds wanted to do more than teach judges and civil rights activists a lesson about the proper use of statistics. They also wanted to reduce the burden employers faced after there had been a correct statistical demonstration of disparate impact (that is, after there had been a showing that the proportion of jobs or promotions that went to minorities was significantly less than their proportion of the qualified labor force). They stated that it was "virtually impossible" for employers to prove that a practice was essential to the survival of their businesses, and that if the standard were set that high, employers would avoid disparate impact liability "by adopting quotas or otherwise turning their attention away from job qualifications and toward numerical balance." And when that happened, Fried and Reynolds held, economic efficiency would be sacrificed, the spirit of the equal protection clause would be ignored, and the letter of the Civil Rights Act disregarded.[47]

Therefore, Fried and Reynolds said that companies should be allowed to defend against disparate impact by offering a reasonable business justification. They said it should not be enough to proffer "a negligible contribution to a business purpose," but it should suffice to demonstrate that there were "legitimate business reasons."[48]

In addition, once disparate impact had been established, Fried and Reynolds argued that the burden that shifted to the employer should be one of production rather than of persuasion. This meant that an employer could be required to produce evidence that the practice in question served a reasonable business purpose. Once the employer produced evidence of business justification, the plaintiff could introduce contrary evidence. But Fried and Reynolds said the burden of proving that the imbalance in hiring or promotion was because of race rather than for a sound business reason should always remain with the plaintiff.[49]

When the decision of the Supreme Court came down, a five-member majority agreed with Fried and Reynolds on every point. Justice White's opinion said that the Ninth Circuit Court's use of statistics was "fundamentally misconceived" and even "nonsensical." It said that the cannery work force in no way reflected the pool of qualified applicants for skilled jobs, and that the "proper comparison" would be "between the racial composition" of the [skilled] jobs and the racial composition of the qualified...population in the relevant labor market."[50]

The Court could have decided the case on the statistics, but Justice White went on to endorse Fried and Reynolds's second point. He said that if the plaintiffs proved that an employment practice caused a pattern of disparate impact, it would be enough for the company to present evidence that the practice served a legitimate business purpose. In a passage that paraphrased a portion of Fried and Reynolds's brief, Justice White instructed the lower courts to make "a reasoned review of the employer's justification." White said that "a mere insubstantial justification" should not suffice, "because such a low standard of review would permit discrimination to be practiced through the use of spurious, seemingly neutral employment practices." But White also wrote that there was "no requirement that the challenged practice be 'essential' or 'indispensable' to the employer's business."[51]

Justice White then proceeded to endorse Fried and Reynolds's third point: that the burden of proving that a disputed practice did not serve a legitimate business purpose remained with the disparate impact plaintiffs "at all times." White explained that this was in accord with "the usual method" that required that those who allege a violation have the burden of proving that the violation occurred. White acknowledged that some of the Supreme Court's previous opinions had been understood to say that disparate impact cases were an exception to the general rule—that employers had to assume the burden of persuasion once a statistical case of disparate impact had been made out. But White said those earlier opinions "should have been understood to mean an employer's production—but not persuasion—burden."[52]

In *Wards Cove*, the Court also made another point that Reynolds had frequently asserted during his tenure as assistant attorney general. The Court said that placing the burden of proof on employers, when combined with loose statistics and a high standard of business necessity, left employers with only one way to avoid the expensive and time-consuming task of defending the indispensability of the methods used to select or promote workers. This was "to adopt racial quotas, insuring that no portion of [the] work force deviates in racial composition from the other portions thereof." The Court noted that this was "a result that Congress expressly rejected in drafting Title VII."[53]

In 1989 the Supreme Court changed the direction of affirmative action jurisprudence. In *Croson*, the Court said the equal protection clause of the Constitution required that racial classifications, even classifications that supposedly were "benign," must be subjected to "strict scrutiny." It said that racial classifications could survive only if they were intended to advance a compelling interest, and that redressing prior discrimination was the only interest that was sufficiently compelling to justify a racial classification. Government agencies (and others whose actions were intertwined with the activities of government) would be permitted to remedy the present effects of past discrimination, but discrimination for social engineering, for the purpose of creating a more diverse work place or society, would be out-of-bounds. In addition, the Court said that even if prior discrimination had been proved, a race-conscious remedy must be narrowly tailored so as not to trammel the rights of innocent third parties.

Then, in *Wards Cove*, the Court said that plaintiffs who alleged discrimination must bear the burden of proving discrimination, and that they must satisfy a higher standard than they had previously been required to meet. And in *Birmingham*, the Court said that the third parties, if they thought they were the victims of reverse racial discrimination, were entitled to their day in court.

Most conservatives were elated. "Thanks in large part to Ronald Reagan's skill in making good judicial appointments," *Human Events* declared, "businesses will no longer feel pressured as many have up till now, to meet racial and sexual quotas at enormous cost to their efficiency and output, just to avoid arbitrary legal harassment." Without endorsing the pro-Reagan value judgments, Linda Greenhouse of the *New York Times* concurred. In the recent past, she wrote, employers had sought to avoid the cost of disparate impact litigation by "redress[ing] striking imbalances in their work forces." Because of *Croson* and *Wards Cove*, there was less incentive to hire by the numbers. Because of *Birmingham*, there was reason to fear reverse discrimination suits.[54]

Of course, Reynolds was pleased. "As a practical matter," he said at the time, "that's the whole ball game." The timing of the Supreme Court's decisions was especially gratifying. *Croson* was released on 23 January 1989, three days after the Reagan administration left office, and *Birmingham* and *Wards Cove* came down six months later. They served as vindication for Reynolds after eight years during which he had been denied promotion by the Senate and reviled by most civil rights leaders and by many in the media. The decisions of 1989 left no doubt that Reynolds finally succeeded in a goal that appeared to elude him during his eight years in office: he had shifted the direction of the Supreme Court on affirmative action.[55]

While characterizing the Supreme Court's opinions of 1989 as wrongheaded, civil rights activists agreed about the importance of the cases. Benjamin Hooks said the Court had become "more dangerous" than racist sheriffs like Bull Connor. Ralph Neas explained that Connor, "as horrible as he was, affected a relatively small number of people but this Court has weakened the protections of our civil rights laws, thus exposing millions of Americans to new discrimination."[56]

Several major newspapers also reacted with dismay. The *Washington Post* lamented that the Court had "vitiated and basically abandoned" *Griggs* as "an 18-year misunderstanding." The *Los Angeles Times* complained that the Court had "demolished a perfectly sound structure of civil rights case law." The *New York Times* declared that the Court had shown an "alarming disrespect for law and its own precedents." An article in the *New York Times Magazine* later explained that "[t]he Establishment's reasoning, never openly stated, would have gone something like this: Sure, affirmative action generates white victims of reverse discrimination, but there aren't very many of them and they don't suffer too greatly. They go to Colgate instead of Cornell. Big deal. The most clearly outstanding whites...don't suffer at all. In return, we are able to take some of the edge off of what has been the most explosive issue in our history, the one that set off our bloodiest war and our worst civil disturbances."[57]

In retrospect, the statements of the civil rights leaders and their sympathizers seem wide of the mark. "Notwithstanding the gnashing and wailing of the 'civil-rights' community over the Supreme Court's recent decisions," the *National Review* declared, "the most striking thing about these decisions is their utter mundaneness." In *Croson*, the Court said racial set-asides must be narrowly tailored to remedy proven discrimination. In *Birmingham*, it said white workers were entitled to their day in Court. In *Wards Cove*, it said the burden of proof in employment discrimination suits rested with the employee or would-be employee rather than with the employer. That three such unremarkable propositions could occasion "doomsday rhetoric" from the civil-rights community indicted how far the country had "drifted in the direction of a racial spoils system." Competition for preferences was setting one ethnic group against another. For the *National Review*, as for Reynolds and others in the Reagan Justice Department, the only hope of avoiding an even worse situation was to drop the entire notion of group entitlements.[58]

Notes

1. There is a widespread, mistaken impression that President Johnson's Executive Order 11246 established the policy of pressuring government contractors to give racial preferences to black workers. In fact, the policy of encouraging preferences for blacks (and later for women and members of other stipulated groups) was the product of bureaucratic and judicial rulings of the 1970s.
   Russell Nieli set the record straight:

   > The relevant section of Executive Order No. 11246...reads: "The contractor will not discriminate against *any* employee or applicant for employment because of race, creed, color, or national origin. The contractor will take *affirmative action* to ensure that applicants are employed, and that employees are treated during employment, *without* regard to their race, creed, color or national origin...." The term "affirmative action,"...refers to positive steps to be taken by an employer to guarantee that race, ethnicity, and religion shall *not* be used as criteria in the making of employment decisions. "Affirmative action" in the sense LBJ used the term thus meant "active non-discrimination." *Policy Review* (Summer 1989): 90–91,

   Nicholas Lemann noted that

   > [t]he original, executive-order definition of affirmative action is that it requires employers only to search aggressively for qualified minority applicants—through advertising, for instance, or special recruitment efforts. Once found, these new minority applicants would go into the same pool with everybody else and the final selection would be made on a color-blind basis." *New York Times Magazine* (11 June 1995): 42.

   As noted above in chapter 11, Reynolds and the Reagan administration adhered to the original approach to affirmative action.
2. 41 C.F.R. (1971), Section 60-2.10; Herman Belz, *Equality Transformed*, 91–93; Hugh Davis Graham, *The Civil Rights Era*, 342–43; Graham, *Civil Rights and the Presidency*, 168.
3. *Newsweek* (30 December 1985): 66–68; *New York Times*, 27 November 1985, 22:3.
4. *Human Events* (25 January 1986).
5. *Los Angeles Times*, 18 December 1985, II, 4:1; *Washington Post*, 27 July 1986, D1a; 19 February 1986, A20a.
6. *New York Times*, 9 December 1985, 22:3.
7. Ibid.

8. WBR, remarks to Washington Center Legal Symposium, 4 January 1984, WBR Papers; interview with WBR, 28 February 1992.
9. Interview with WBR, 28 February 1992; Richard M. Dalfiume, *Desegregation of the U.S. Armed Forces* (Columbia: University of Missouri Press, 1969), 59, 202 and passim.
10. *Washington Post*, 29 March 1986, A5a; *New York Times*, 29 March 1986, 1:5; *Los Angeles Times*, 29 March 1986, 4:1; *Human Events* (12 April 1986).
11. *New York Times*, 15 August 1985, 1:6; *Washington Post*, 16 January 1986, A11a; 16 August 1985, A22a.
12. *National Review* (13 December 1985): 14; *Newsweek* (30 December 1985): 66–68; *Human Events* (2 November 1985).
13. Cabinet members James Baker, Elizabeth Dole, Margaret Heckler, Samuel Pierce, and George Schultz supported Brock. Three other members of the cabinet (William Bennett, John Herrington, and James Miller) sided with Reynolds and Meese, as did EEOC chairman Clarence Thomas and Civil Rights Commission chairman Clarence Pendleton. Donald Regan, the President's chief-of-staff, did not want the issue to go to Ronald Regan with a divided cabinet vote.
14. *Human Events* (25 January 1986).
15. Ibid., 2 November 1985; Ronald Reagan, *A Time for Choosing*, 163.
16. *Washington Post*, 11 January 1986, A3a; *Wilmington News Journal*, 8 December 1985.
17. Gary L. McDowell, "Affirmative Inaction," *Policy Review* (Spring 1989): 32–37; interview with WBR, 28 February 1992.
18. *Washington Post*, 14 July 1986, A11d; *Commentary* (January 1989): 37.
19. Fullilove v. Klutznick, 448 U.S. 448 (1980).
20. Charles Fried, *Order and Law*, 119–20, 127; Croson v. Richmond, 822 F.2d 1355 (1985), 1359; Richmond v. Croson, 488 U.S. 469 (1989), 479–80.
21. Richmond v. Croson, 488 U.S. 469 (1989), 482–83.
22. Ibid., 483–85; Croson v. Richmond, 779 F.2d 181 (1985); 822 F.2d 1355 (1987).
23. Croson v. Richmond, 822 F.2d 1355 (1985), 1358 (quoting Wygant v. Jackson, 476 U.S. 267 [1984], 274), 1362.
24. Ibid., 1360, 1359; Richmond v. Croson, 488 U.S. 469 (1989), 481.
25. *Wall Street Journal*, 18 February 1988, 48:1.
26. Charles Fried, *Order and Law*, 105, 127; Brief for the United States, Richmond v. Croson, Supreme Court Library; *Commentary* (January 1989): 6.
27. Richmond v. Croson. 488 U.S. 469 (1989), 493 and passim.
28. Ibid., 520–21.
29. Ibid., 518–19.
30. *Washington Post*, 3 February 1989, A25e; 29 January 1989, D7f.
31. Richmond v. Croson, 488 U.S. 469 (1989), 561, 529.
32. In re Birmingham Reverse Discrimination Employment Litigation, 833 F.2d 1492 (1987), 1494 n.5.
33. Martin v. Wilks, 490 U.S. 755 (1989), 759–60; In re Birmingham, 833 F.2d 1492 (1987), 1495.
34. Martin v. Wilks, 490 U.S. 755 (1989), 760; In re Birmingham, 833 F.2d 1492 (1987), 1495–96.
35. Martin v. Wilks, 490 U.S. 755 (1989), 761; In re Birmingham, 833 F.2d 1492 (1987), 1498, summarizing Thaggard v. City of Jackson, 687 F.2d 66 (1982); Dennison v. City of Los Angeles, 658 F.2d 694 (1981); EEOC v. McCall Printing Corp., 633 F.2d 1232 (1980).

36. Brief for the United States, Martin v. Wilks, Supreme Court Library; Martin v. Wilks, 490 U.S. 755 (1989), 762.
37. *Wilmington News Journal*, 20 January 1986; *New York Times*, 13 June 1989, 1:6; 14 June 1989, 26:1; *Washington Post*, 14 June 1989, A22a.
38. Jared Taylor, *Paved With Good Intentions* (New York: Carrol and Graf Publishers, 1993), 144.
39. *Washington Post*, 20 August 1983, A13b.
40. Griggs v. Duke Power Company, 401 U.S. 424 (1971), 431, 432.
41. Aguilera v. Cook County Police, 760 F.2d 844 (1985), 847; Chrisner v. Compete Auto Transit, 645 F.2d 1251) (1981), 1262; Williams v. Colorado Springs School District, 641 F.2d 835 (1981), 842.
42. Wards Cove v. Atonio, 109 S.Ct. 2115 (1989), 2119–21; Respondent's Brief, Wards Cove v. Atonio, 1–2, Supreme Court Library; Petitioner's Brief, 4–9, ibid.
43. Atonio v. Wards Cove, 768 F.2d 1120 (1985), 1128. The trial lasted for twelve days and involved the testimony of more than 100 witnesses and the submission of more than 900 exhibits and 1,000 statistical tables. Judge Quackenbush's seventy-three-page opinion is reported at 34 E.P.D. 437.
44. Atonio v. Wards Cove, 810 F.2d 1477 (1987).
45. Griggs v. Duke Power Company, 401 U.S. 424 (1971), 431; Brief for the United States, Wards Cove v. Atonio, 16–21, Supreme Court Library.
46. Brief for the United States, Wards Cove v. Atonio, 20–21, Supreme Court Library.
47. Ibid.
48. Ibid., 24–27.
49. Ibid., 25–27.
50. Wards Cove v. Atonio, 109 S.Ct. 2115 (1989), 2122, 2121.
51. Ibid., 2126.
52. Ibid.
53. Ibid., 2122.
54. *Human Events* (17 June 1989); *New York Times*, 7 June 1989, 16:3.
55. *Wall Street Journal*, 16 June 1989, 6:3. As Charles Fried saw it, the Supreme Court had called a halt to aggressive plaintiffs' lawyers and some judges who were using a "sensible rule [*Griggs*] to threaten employers with crushing liability if they used entirely reasonable employment qualifications." In addition to *Wards Cove*, Fried mentioned a case where a federal judge, on the basis of disparate impact, invalidated a requirement that prospective blood tank technicians must have a high school diploma. Others mentioned other judges—one who told a police department that when hiring new officers it could not take into account the applicants' felony conviction records; another who ruled that prospective mass transit workers could not be required to pass a drug test. (See *Washington Post*, 16 June 1989, A27a; *Policy Review* [Summer 1991]: 48; New York Transit Authority v. Beazer, 440 U.S. 568 [1979].) These cases lend credence to Robert H. Bork's judgment—that the *Wards Cove* Court had "made some moderate and overdue adjustments" to a rule that had produced results contrary to the intention of the Civil Rights Act. (See *Wall Street Journal*, 30 June 1989, 12:4.)
56. *New York Times*, 10 July 1989, 14:1; *USA Today*, March 1990, 18; *Washington Post*, 6 June 1989, A1a; 16 June 1989, A27a.
57. *Washington Post*, 9 June 1989, A26a; *Los Angeles Times*, 8 June 1989, II, 5:1; *New York Times*, 12 June 1989, 18:1; Nicholas Lemann, "Taking Affirmative Action Apart," *New York Times Sunday Magazine* (11 June 1995): 54.
58. *National Review* (14 July 1989): 15–16.

14

Conclusion to Part II

Critics of the Reagan administration often said that it was naive to assume that an end to negative discrimination was all that blacks needed to succeed in the United States. They insisted that it was not enough simply to establish the right to compete on a free and open basis. Some of these critics would have been surprised to know that Ronald Reagan and William Bradford Reynolds agreed with them in that they also wanted to do more that just end discrimination. Reagan developed a broad economic program, while Reynolds urged the courts to return to the sort of affirmative action that most Americans favored and that Congress had in mind when it passed the Civil Rights Act of 1964.

Reagan said that "the well-being of blacks—like the well-being of every other American—is linked directly to the health of the economy," and to stimulate economic growth, Reagan pressed for a program that was called "supply-side economics." If Congress would eliminate unnecessary government regulations and reduce income taxes across-the-board by 30 percent, Reagan said, there would be so much economic growth that the government would actually collect more taxes at the lower rate than it had collected previously. In addition, Reagan proposed to get serious about inflation (which had increased from 6.5 percent in 1977—the first Carter year—to 7.6 percent the following year, to 11.3 percent in 1979, and ultimately to 13.5 percent in 1980). To reverse this trend, Reagan proposed to restrain the increase in the money supply and to limit budget deficits by holding the line on social and welfare spending.[1]

Reagan regarded his economic policy as a success. There were problems as the nation went through a difficult period of adjustment and restructuring, and the budget deficit also increased. But the rate of inflation declined to 10.3 percent in 1981, 3.2 percent in 1983, 3.6 percent in 1985, and 3.6 percent in 1987. In the meantime, economic expansion led to the creation of about 17 million new jobs—more than in all of Europe during the same period.[2]

Most civil rights leaders, on the other hand, pointed to other statistics. Partly because so many black families were becoming headed only by women, the overall income of black families declined by about 3.7 percent during the Reagan years. The evidence with respect to unemployment was also disturbing. After seeing statistics that indicated that black joblessness increased in 1984 while white unemployment declined, the journalist Carl Rowan concluded that it was a "cruel cliché" to say that everyone would benefit from a rising economy. John Jacob of the National Urban League lamented that "[w]hile White Americans celebrate a long overdue economic recovery and a falling unemployment rate, Black America is buried in a depression of crushing proportions."[3]

Nevertheless—in addition to calling for deregulation, tax cuts, and a lower rate of inflation—Reagan wanted to end many welfare programs. Addressing the annual convention of the NAACP in 1981, Reagan discarded his usual crowd-pleasing anecdotes and spoke in terms that were somber and stern: "I did not come here today bearing the promise of Government handouts which others have brought." He said that it was time to recognize that government spending for welfare programs had created "a new kind of bondage." Blacks had been freed from slavery in the 1860s, and, according to Reagan, the time had arrived for liberation from dependence on initiative-sapping welfare programs and from overreliance on jobs in the public sector.[4]

The NAACP delegates gave Reagan what was probably the coolest reception of his presidency. There was no heckling, but Reagan was taken aback by the stony silence. Other blacks were not so circumspect. Jesse Jackson said there was "an element of racism in the budget cuts." Carl Rowan declared that more blacks had been hurt by the economic policies of the Reagan administration "than ever were wounded by the Ku Klux Klan."[5]

Most black leaders recognized that no one was likely to starve because of Reagan's proposed budget cuts, but they said that every dollar saved by cutting welfare benefits would reduce the standard of living of people whose standard was already low. They noted that blacks, who made up only 12 percent of the total population, made up one-half of those who received Aid to Families with Dependent children (AFDC), one-third of those who received medicaid and food stamps, and one-third of those who lived in public housing.[6]

Reagan never gave another speech to the NAACP, but in 1982 he candidly told a group of black Republicans that the economic condition of most blacks would have been better if the social and welfare programs associated with Lyndon B. Johnson's Great Society had never been implemented. Reagan said that the economic expansion and low inflation of the 1950s and early 1960s were destroyed (and the character of many welfare recipients damaged) because the federal government "began eating away at the underpinnings of the private enterprise system." As a consequence, Reagan said, by 1980 more people were living in poverty than in 1969. After two decades of earnest legislation, of wars on poverty and riots in the streets, the gap in income between blacks and whites was as large as it had been in 1969, and the percentage of households that depended on welfare had increased by 20 percent.[7]

Reagan said this was because the Great Society programs had a number of unintended, negative consequences. Because of the increased availability of welfare from the government, many women could get by without a working husband. Consequently, there was an "increasing breakdown of families" and a steady growth in the number of children born out of wedlock. Because of "misguided welfare programs instituted in the name of compassion," a "national problem" had been turned into a "national tragedy." Reagan said, "Let us have the courage to speak the truth.... Policies that increase dependence and break up families are not progressive—even though they are invariably promised, passed, and carried out in the name of fairness, generosity, and compassion." As Reagan saw it, the key ways to combat poverty were marriage and work, but these were precisely the activities that welfare discouraged.[8]

In the early 1980s, many liberals found it difficult to understand what Reagan was getting at. The Catholic journal *America* said that when Reagan "blamed the current economic distress of many black families on the antipoverty programs," he was using a "logic" that was "too obscure to follow." The *New York Times* similarly could not understand what Reagan meant when he called for a second emancipation from "a new kind of bondage," "Emancipation from what?" the *Times* asked. According to the *Times*, "[A]ssistance programs like welfare and food stamps can only ease the pressures of life at the margins." For many people, "government social welfare programs" were the "only hope."[9]

Many Reagan Republicans also criticized liberals for fostering a number of pernicious attitudes and opinions. They said that liberals, when they criticized traditional sexual mores, touted the merits of recreational drugs, and hobbled law enforcement, unleashed scourges that had a disproportionately adverse impact on black communities. They also criticized liberals for popularizing the notion that discrimination, rather than a lack of education and marketable skills, was the main obstacle to black economic progress.[10]

In addition to rejecting what they regarded as failed liberal ideas and policies, some Reagan Republicans also developed an affirmative program for improving the condition of blacks. It called for tax breaks for those who operated businesses in economically depressed areas (the so-called urban enterprise zones). It proposed an end to complex licensing regulations that made it difficult for blacks to get a start in some occupations. It recommended tenant management or ownership of public housing. It favored a system of educational vouchers to enable poor families to choose the best school for their children. It proposed tough anticrime measures to deal with those who had ravaged many black neighborhoods.[11]

These programs might have benefited poor blacks. But with Democrats in control of at least one house of Congress throughout the 1980s, the Reagan administration was not able to override the liberal lobbies that were aligned in opposition.

As a Reagan Republican, William Bradford Reynolds agreed with the president's assessment of welfare and supported the conservative proposals to assist poor people. As chief of the Civil Rights Division, Reynolds also insisted that punitive damages should be assessed against employers that practiced racial discrimination, and he stressed the importance of advertising and recruiting in black and other minority communities. He also called for special programs to train members of minority groups so that they would have the skills to compete with members of other groups. In addition, Reynolds favored make-whole relief—the award of a job or a promotion, together with back pay and seniority—for people who were actual victims of discrimination.

Reynolds insisted that this was the sort of affirmative action that most Americans favored and the sort that Congress intended when it passed the Civil Rights Act of 1964, but he opposed race-conscious quotas, goals, and set-asides. He said broad racial preferences would lead to questions about the qualifications of minorities. He feared that preferences would give rise to seething anger among workers who lost out because of the preferences, and he warned the preferences would put U.S. corporations at a competitive disadvantage in the global economy. Most of all, Reynolds argued that racial preferences were at odds with the principle of color-blind nondiscrimination that underlay the Civil Rights Act of 1964 and the equal protection clause of the United States Constitution.

In 1984, Reynolds won a major victory in the Supreme Court. In *Stotts v. Memphis Firefighters*, the Court placed its imprimatur on Reynolds's arguments for victim specificity as the best way to reconcile affirmative action with the principles of nondiscrimination and equal protection. The Court said that the policy of the Civil Rights Act was to give affirmative relief "only to those who have been actual victims of illegal discrimination."[12]

The Supreme Court backed away from victim specificity in 1986 and 1987, but it sounded only a limited retreat. In *Richmond v. Croson*, in 1989, the Court held that the Constitution required "strict scrutiny" of all race-based action by state and local governments. Racial preferences and set-asides could be used, but only if they were "narrowly tailored to remedy the effects of prior discrimination" and only if there was proof that there was no alternative racially neutral remedy that would have a less untoward impact on innocent third parties.[13]

Then, in *Wards Cove v. Atonio*, another case of 1989, the Court shifted the burden of proof in two important ways: it ruled that under Title VII of the Civil Rights Act a company could justify practices that had a disparate impact by presenting evidence that the practices served a legitimate business purpose; and it held that the burden of proving that the disputed business practices did not serve a legitimate purpose fell on those who brought the allegations of illegal discrimination.

Reeling from their defeats in court, civil rights leaders turned to Congress and demanded legislation to overturn the Supreme Court's interpretation of the Civil Rights Act. "We can't rely on the Court any more," declared Ralph Neas. "But we have a strong bipartisan consensus in Congress.... We are confident that remedial legislation will be enacted." The major press agreed. The *Washington Post* urged Congress to "rewrite the law." The *Los Angeles Times* chimed in with an editorial entitled, "It's Up to Congress Now."[14]

A two-year battle ensued, with a compromise measure enacted in 1991 after Congress was unable to override President George Bush's veto of what was called the Civil Rights Act of 1990. A thorough discussion of the legislative history would be out of place here (as the Reagan administration ended in January 1989), but the matter deserves mention.

Taking aim at the interpretation of Title VII that the Supreme Court had proffered in *Wards Cove*, the civil rights lobby wanted employers to bear the burden of proving that any disparate impact was caused by practices that were essential to effective performance of specific jobs. Taking aim at yet another case of 1989, *In re Birmingham Reverse Discrimination*, the lobby wanted to restrict the right of third parties to challenge consent decrees in employment discrimination cases. In the summer of 1989, Senator Edward M. Kennedy and Representative Augustus Hawkins sponsored legislation incorporating these two intents.

The proposed legislation passed both the Senate (65–34) and the House of Representatives (272–154), but supporters could not muster enough votes to override a veto by President Bush. Bush recognized that the *Birmingham* provisions allowed for the notification of third parties and their right to intervene when consent agreements were initially made; but this seemed inadequate because many people would not realize they had been hurt until after the consent decree was implemented, by which time, under the Kennedy-Hawkins bill, they would have no redress. More troubling to Bush were the *Wards Cove* provisions, which the president said would force businesses to use racial and gender quotas to avoid expensive lawsuits.

Bush said the inevitable effect of the Kennedy-Hawkins bill would be to require employers to hire by the numbers. Employers would have to do so because the legislation amounted to something like a "double whammy." It said that employers with an unbalanced work force had to both bear the burden of proof and show that the employment practices that contributed to the imbalance were "essential to effective job performance." Bush said that since this burden of proof was set so high, employers would resort to quotas in order to avoid costly lawsuits they could not win.[15]

Senator Kennedy said that Bush, when he mentioned quotas, was raising a "false cry" and using a "disreputable tactic." The *New York Times* agreed. Characterizing Bush's veto as "a temporary setback," the Leadership Conference on Civil Rights promised to return to Congress with similar legislation. "The Civil Rights Act will be law in the spring of 1991," Ralph Neas predicted; "It isn't a question of 'if,' it is a question of 'when' we pass it."[16]

Some conservatives feared that Bush would abandon the fight against racial preferences. *Human Events* warned that a "sell out" was in the offing, and J. A. Latham, Jr., a former staff director at the U.S. Commission on Civil Rights, insinuated that the Bush administration would cave in because it "does not want to appear opposed to 'civil rights,' and it has no principled civil rights policy of its own." With a reference to history, Latham explained why it was difficult to oppose anything with "civil rights" in its title:

> What has happened is a modern version of "waving the bloody shirt." After the Civil War, as the Republican Party grew increasingly corrupt and lost the noble ideals that had inspired its earlier days, it would fend off political attacks by "waving the bloody shirt." That is, the party would tout its historic role in saving the Union and freeing the slaves in the Civil War, rather than face up to its later corruption. Similarly, today's civil rights groups which have degenerated into advocating an unseemly spoils system, wave the bloody shirt of the civil rights movement whenever anyone dares to bring its current leadership and ambitions into question.[17]

Bush did give some ground. At a Rose Garden ceremony in the spring of 1990, he had set two conditions for acceptance of a civil rights bill: it could not require or encourage racial quotas, and it could not reverse the principle that a person or company is innocent until proven guilty. But Bush could not prevail on the second point because Kennedy had the support of a handful of Republican senators on the due process question, and they would insist that corporations and other institutions must do more than offer a reasonable explanation for any practice that affected minorities adversely. They would insist that the companies must justify any such practices. Two-thirds of the Senate was poised to override a presidential veto on this question.

At this point, Bush hit upon the sound strategy of giving ground on the burden of proof but drawing the line at quotas. Liberal Democrats did not relish the prospect of openly having to defend so controversial a position as racial quotas. "Quotas, schmotas," said Senator Kennedy, reassuring his supporters that the allegations of the administration were baseless. The quota argument was "phony," the *New York Times* agreed. "The Republicans' marketing of the quota issue has been brilliant," wrote Michael Kinsley in the *New Republic*, but it was "the cynical concoction of a divisive issue...for narrow electoral advantage."[18]

Notwithstanding the lamentations, Bush was not exploiting an unjustified fear of racial preferences for political gain. Even some supporters of the Kennedy-Hawkins bill admitted that proponents of the legislation were not being candid. Yale law professor Paul Gewirtz chided those who said the bill would not encourage discrimination in reverse. He wrote that "honest observers, as well as common sense, will tell you that to some extent a disparate impact test does encourage racial preferences."[19]

Far from being a "phony" issue, the debate over the implicit quotas and preferences of the Kennedy-Hawkins bill touched on issues of major importance. "What's at stake," Professor Gewirtz wrote, "are different ideas of what discrimination means and what equality requires, different views about affirmative action preferences (not simply 'quotas'), and different stances toward meritocratic criteria. A great deal turns on the path our society takes."[20]

Gewirtz favored affirmative preferences. He thought they were "a justifiable means of overcoming the continuing effects of our country's long history of discrimination." Others said preferences were needed to counteract ongoing discrimination, to promote diversity, to overcome the inadequacies of existing standards, to avert racial riots, or to buy racial peace.[21]

Despite these arguments, the Bush administration opted for individual rights and equality of opportunity. It did so partly for political reasons. It recognized that "the Bush majority, every bit as much as the Reagan majority, [was] built in part upon deep dissatisfaction with the violence done traditional American ideals by racial preferential treatment." It recognized that many grassroots Republican voters feared that the well-to-do, Yale-educated president would abandon his working-class supporters to gain plaudits from liberals in academia and in the media.[22]

On the surface, most of the opposition to the Kennedy-Hawkins bill was legalistic. Opponents said Kennedy and Hawkins "want[ed] to make employers' situations so threatening that they would engage in reverse discrimination as insurance against ruinous litigation." They said that if racial disproportion was regarded as discrimination, the natural inclination of employers would be to spare risk and expense by hiring people according to a quota.[23]

In addition to this legal argument, there was a subtheme that many opponents of the Kennedy-Hawkins bill were hesitant to discuss publicly: it was that the statistical underrepresentation of blacks was not testimony to the impropriety of the tests and credentials that were used for hiring or promotion; rather, the underrepresentation was an indication of the need to improve the qualifications and behavior of blacks.[24]

Here we come to what some observers discreetly called "the pool problem." The orthodox view—assiduously cultivated by most civil rights leaders—was that discrimination was responsible for the underrepresentation of blacks in the nation's better jobs. If so, the discriminatory practices needed to be changed. But some people said the underrepresentation of blacks pointed to the need to change the group, as the problem was that the available pool of qualified blacks was too small to generate the *correct* statistics.

In some ways this argument resembled historic racism. Yet most critics of the Kennedy-Hawkins bill were careful to distinguish their argument from the racism of yesteryear. They did not say that as a result of evolution in geographically distinct regions, blacks differed from whites in some relevant hereditary characteristics. Instead, they said that a series of disadvantageous experiences had caused a disproportionately large number of blacks to develop attitudes that were dysfunctional in the modern world and that a tangle of pathology was responsible for the underrepresentation of blacks in good jobs. They said that proportional representation could not be achieved (without a disastrous sacrifice of efficiency) unless more blacks developed an ethic of personal responsibility. They said that affirmative action sent the wrong message—that blacks could get ahead through set-asides rather than by conforming to traditional standards.[25]

While observers analyzed the situation, members of the Bush administration went to work on the Kennedy-Hawkins bill. Believing that they could not prevail against the civil rights lobby on the burden of proof, the administration agreed that employers should have the burden of justifying employment disparities. At the same time, the administration pressed for language that would make it easier for employers to justify their practices. The Kennedy-Hawkins bill would have required employers to show that a challenged employment practice was "essential" to the performance of a specific job, but in the end Bush got a bill that required employers to demonstrate that the challenged practice was "job related for the position in question and consistent with business necessity."[26]

The administration also succeeded in introducing ambiguities into other portions of the Kennedy-Hawkins bill. An early version had stated that the purpose of the bill was "to overrule the proof burdens and meaning of business necessity in *Wards Cove*." The final law declared that the purpose was "to codify the concepts of 'business necessity' and 'job related' enunciated by the Supreme Court in *Griggs*...and in the other Supreme Court decisions prior to *Wards Cove*." The administration pushed hard for this change because one of these decisions, *Watson v. Fort Worth Bank*, said, "The ultimate burden of proving that discrimination...has been caused by a specific employment practice remains with the plaintiff *at all times*."[27]

When President Bush signed the Civil Rights Act of 1991, most liberals concluded that Congress had defeated the Court. Some conservatives also accused the administration of "caving in," an allegation that Pat Buchanan emphasized when he challenged Bush in the Republican presidential primaries of 1992. After Bush was defeated for reelection, it became a refrain of conservative postmortems to blame the defeat in part on Bush's approach to "the so-called Civil Rights Act of 1991."[28]

Defenders of President Bush, on the other hand, noted that the meaning of the new law would have to be determined by litigation and praised the administration for putting enough ambiguity into the law to persuade the courts that "the great civil rights lobby push to overturn *Wards Cove* was a bust." Richard Vigilante summed up this view in an article for the *New Republic*:

> Bush vetoed Kennedy-Hawkins and was upheld, but that was only the first act: there were more than enough votes to override a veto for a compromise bill perceived as moderate. Both sides set out on long struggle to control the compromise, fighting for language that a majority of Congress would accept but would go their way in court.... [In the end] the Bushites...won [the] critical battle in the details.[29]

It is hard to know who won the battle of 1990–91. The Bush administration put some "fudgewords" into the statute, and the Supreme Court (which by 1991 included two Bush appointees in places previously occupied by the proquota justices, William J. Brennan and Thurgood Marshall) may in time resolve the ambiguities against the civil rights lobby. Reynolds thought that would be the likely outcome.[30]

Equally important, the civil rights lobby did not persuade Congress to modify the Supreme Court's holding in *Richmond v. Croson*. It could not do so because *Croson* involved an interpretation of the equal protection clause, not of Title VII, and amending the Constitution is harder than changing a statute. Even the most sanguine members of the civil rights lobby recognized that an amendment was beyond their reach.

Because of *Croson*, the effects of the Civil Rights Act of 1991 will be limited. White people who think they are victims of reverse racial discrimination will ignore Title VII and instead appeal to the Constitution, arguing that the equal protection clause requires that racial preferences must be narrowly tailored to remedy instances of proven discrimination. Few preferences seem likely to survive this sort of scrutiny.

This is not to say that the Civil Rights Act of 1991 was inconsequential. Once again, the civil rights lobby indicated that it could command the support of blocs of voters and demonstrated that it could use its connections with the major media to shape the public perception of an issue. The lobby showed it had power. It reaffirmed a point it had made on several prior occasions: in 1982, when it persuaded Congress to revise the Voting Rights Act to overturn the Supreme Court's ruling in *Mobile v. Bolden*; in 1985, when it pressured the Senate Judiciary Committee to reject the nomination of William Bradford Reynolds for associate attorney general; in 1987, when it kept Robert H. Bork off the Supreme Court; in 1989, when it defeated the nomination of a black Republican, William Lucas, to succeed Reynolds as head of the Civil Rights Division; in 1991, when it pulled out all stops trying to prevent the appointment of Clarence Thomas to the Supreme Court.

After *Croson,* many institutions that had never been found guilty of prior discrimination continued with special preferences and quotas for minorities. Corporations persevered with double standards for employment and promotions, and colleges did likewise with respect to admission and financial aid. In an article entitled "Permafirm Action," Abigail Thernstrom observed that affirmative action efforts had become "so institutionalized that court decisions will have the most marginal effect.... [I]t almost doesn't matter what the Supreme Court does."[31]

In the short term, Thernstrom was right. Both the Republican administration of George Bush and the Democratic administration of Bill Clinton ignored *Croson*. Neither challenged the practices of government agencies and government-supported companies or institutions that disregarded the standards the Supreme Court had established.[32]

In the longer run, however, *Croson* is likely to matter. This is especially true because the Supreme Court, despite its vagaries in the 1970s and 1980s, had belatedly sided with those who oppose racial favoritism. In doing so, the Court endorsed the widely popular principle that citizens should not be disadvantaged because of their race or ancestry.

Of course, it may turn out that *Croson* will do no more to end set-asides, racial preferences, and double standards than the *Bakke* decision did to end quotas in university admissions. But history does not inevitably repeat itself. Thanks in part to the work of Reynolds and other lawyers for the Reagan Justice Department, the prevailing opinion of the 1990s was turning against affirmative action. Many elite leaders and institutions still favored "benign" preference, either as a means of achieving racial justice or as a way to buy racial peace, but as journalist Nicholas Lemann noted, in the country at large there was "an enormous well of pent-up hostility to affirmative action." Democratic pollster Stanley Greenberg reached a similar conclusion after conducting in-depth, two-hour interviews with groups of white voters in Macomb County, Michigan. The discussions would begin

> with one person raising the subject [affirmative action] almost apologetically. Then it just opened up. People would start telling stories of how opportunities in their lives had been blocked by special privileges given blacks—promotions they didn't get, small business loans they didn't qualify for. And once they started, you could hardly stop them. If they had their way, they would spend the whole two hours talking about nothing else.[33]

These sentiments came to the fore in the Congressional elections of 1994. Almost overnight, it seemed, affirmative action was transformed from a conservative issue to a mainstream concern. As this book goes to press, all the leading contenders for the 1996 Republican presidential nomination have made statements opposing racial preferences, and even President Clinton asked for an internal review that would enable him to back away from at least some of the programs that were causing so much anger among rank-and-file white voters.

Given the increasing unpopularity of affirmative action, civil rights leaders did not ask Congress for help in 1995 when the Supreme Court reaffirmed the principles of *Croson* and applied them to the federal government as well. The civil rights leaders recognized that by the mid-1990s Congress (dominated by Republicans for the first time in forty years) had become at least as skeptical of "benign" racial preferences as the Supreme Court.[34]

The facts of economic life also reinforced the movement against affirmative racial preferences. When the preferences began in the late 1960s and early 1970s, the United States was enjoying a quarter-century of steady economic growth. When the Supreme Court handed down its *Griggs* opinion in 1971, it seemed that the national economy could easily afford the cost of affirmative preferences. Then, as other nations recovered from the ravages of World War II, the situation changed rapidly, and the United States found itself struggling for its economic life in a new global economy.

In the 1970s, civil rights activists and bureaucrats said the industrial and manufacturing economy of the post-World War II United States required "workers with little formal education and few specific skills," and that those who worked in mining, paper, steel, and heavy manufacturing "could quickly acquire the necessary skills on the job." They said "most Blacks were qualified for these jobs," and any standards that had a disproportionate impact "supported an inference that employers had discriminated unlawfully." They said employers could not justify "such exclusionary practices as a business necessity."[35]

The bureaucrats and civil rights activists were wrong about the importance of skills on the assembly line. However, in *Griggs* they persuaded the Supreme Court to adopt their view, and the Court then pressed the view on the rest of the country. In doing so, the civil rights lobby and the Supreme

Court contributed to the erosion of standards and probably to the decline of the manufacturing sector of the U.S. economy as well.

Liberal activists, judges, and bureaucrats may question this assessment, but by the 1990s even many of them recognized that the United States had come to the end of the *Griggs* economy. The office tower had replaced the smokestack as the symbol of U.S. enterprise. There was some brave talk about "overcom[ing] the complexity" and "mak[ing] disparate impact theory work in the new economy," but most civil rights activists acknowledged that an increasing proportion of good jobs required literacy, numeracy, cognitive skills, or the ability to work with the public. Despite passage of the Civil Rights Act of 1991, the future of disparate impact was bleak. There was a growing recognition, in the country and in Congress, that if the United States was to succeed in the new global economy, the setting of reasonable standards must no longer be regarded as synonymous with racial discrimination.[36]

Notes

1. *Washington Post*, 30 June 1981, A1b; *New York Times*, 3 July 1981, 10:1; "Consumer Price Index," *Statistical Abstract of the U.S., 1990* (Washington: Department of Commerce, 1990), table 757; William A. Niskanen, *Reaganomics: An Insider's Account of the Policies and the People* (New York: Oxford University Press, 1988).
2. "Consumer Price Index," *Statistical Abstract of the U.S., 1990*, table 757. The economist Milton Friedman and the economics reporter Warren T. Brooks calculated that as a percentage of gross national product, the total national debt amounted to 107 percent of annual GNP in 1945, 46 percent in 1960, 18 percent in 1974 (the low point), 22 percent in 1980, and 37 percent in 1987. *Human Events* (16 January 1988); (27 August 1988).
3. Lou Cannon, *President Reagan: The Role of a Lifetime* (New York: Simon & Schuster, 1991), 516; Marilyn Moon and Isabel V. Sawhill, "Family Income: Gainers and Losers," in John L. Palmer and Isabel V. Sawhill, eds., *The Reagan Record* (Cambridge: Ballinger Publishing Company, 1984), 336; *Washington Post*, 27 January 1985, C8a; 23 January 1985, A23b; *Jet* (6 February 1984): 4.
4. *New York Times*, 30 June 1981, 1:2.
5. *New York Times*, 2 June 1981, 1:3; *Washington Post*, 19 May 1982, A23d.
6. *New York Times*, 2 June 1981, 1:3.
7. *Washington Post*, 30 June 1981, A1b; 16 September 1982, A1b; *New York Times*, 16 September 1982, 1:1; 21 September 1982, 26:1.
8. *New York Times*, 2 August 1983, 14:1;; *Washington Post*, 19 February 1986, A21f; *National Review* (19 August 1983): 1037; (5 August 1983): 916–17.
9. *America* (20 November 1982): 303; *New York Times*, 1 July 1981, 26:1.
10. See Ed Meese, "GOP Must Reach Out for the Black Vote," *Human Events* (14 January 1989); Clint Bolick, *Changing Course: Civil Rights at the Crossroads* (New Brunswick: Transaction Books, 1988); Bolick, *Unfinished Business: A Civil Rights Strategy for America's Third Century* (San Francisco: Pacific Research Institute for Public Policy, 1990); Bolick, "G.O.P. Can Capture the Civil Rights

Issue," *Wall Street Journal*, 18 March 1991; Bolick, "The Emerging Republican Majority: Blacks and the G.O.P.," *National Review* (6 August 1990): 33–35.
11. Ibid.
12. Firefighters v. Stotts, 467 U.S. 561 (1984), 580.
13. Richmond v. Croson, 488 U.S. 469 (1989), 508.
14. *Los Angeles Times*, 18 June 1989, I4a; 16 June 1989, II6a; *Washington Post*, 9 June 1989, A26a.
15. *Wall Street Journal*, 17 May 1990, 18:3; *Human Events* (26 May 1990).
16. *Washington Post*, 8 June 1990, A1d; 20 July 1990, B3d; *Wall Street Journal*, 19 July 1989, 12:5; 20 October 1990, 20:1; 25 October 1990, 5:1; *New York Times*, 24 April 1991, 24:1.
17. *Human Events* (26 May 1990); (14 July 1990); *Barron's*, 26 March 1990, 9.
18. *Wall Street Journal*, 19 July 1989, 12:5; *New York Times*, 24 April 1991, 24:1; *New Republic* (24 June 1991): 4.
19. *New Republic* (12 August 1991): 20.
20. Ibid., 18.
21. Ibid., 20; Gertrude Ezorsky, *Racism and Justice: The Case for Affirmative Action*; Nicholas Lemann, "Taking Affirmative Action Apart," *New York Times Magazine* (11 June 1995): 36ff.
22. *National Review* (14 July 1989): 15–16.
23. For examples, see columns by George F. Will (*Wilmington News Journal*, 20 May 1989), Charles Krauthammer (*Washington Post*, 18 May 1990, A19e), and Susan Mandel (*National Review* [28 May 1990]: 32–33).
24. For an example, see Glenn C. Loury, *One By One From the Inside Out*, passim.
25. Ibid., passim. Also see the works of Thomas Sowell and Shelby Steel, cited above in Chapter 9.
26. Paul Gewirtz, "Fine Print," *New Republic* (18 November 1991): 10–13.
27. Ibid.; Watson v. Fort Worth Bank, 108 S.Ct. 2777 (1988), 2790.
28. For an expression of the liberal view, see William T. Coleman, Jr. and Vernon E. Jordan, Jr., "How the Civil Rights Bill was *Really* Passed," *Washington Post*, 18 November 1991, A21a. For examples of conservative criticism, see the columns by Mona Charen, Don Feder, and Jeffrey Hart in the *Conservative Chronicle*, 8 November 1992, and by Kate Walsh O'Beirne in the *National Review* (30 November 1992): 32–33.
29. *New Republic* (31 August 1992): 20.
30. Interview with WBR, 28 February 1991.
31. *New Republic* (31 July 1989): 19, 17.
32. For more on the massive resistance to *Croson*, see Michael Greve, "Segregation, 90s Style," *Weekly Standard*, 25 December 1995, 31–35.
33. *New York Times Magazine* (11 June 1995): 39; *Human Events* (25 January 1986).
34. Adarand Constructors v. Pena, 63 USLW 4523 (1995).
35. Eleanor Holmes Norton, "The End of the *Griggs* Economy," *Yale Law and Policy Review*, 8 (1990): 199.
36. Ibid., 204.

Part III

School Desegregation

Introduction to Part III

Charles Evans Hughes, a former chief justice of the Supreme Court, once noted, "We are under a Constitution, but the Constitution is what the judges say it is." Nothing illustrates this better than the course of the law on school desegregation. Before 1954 the Supreme Court interpreted the equal protection clause to allow public schools to practice racial discrimination to separate the races, as long as the separate facilities were (theoretically) equal. Between 1954 and 1968, the Court reinterpreted the clause to prohibit racial discrimination in assigning children to public schools. Then, after 1968, the Court required many school districts to take race into account in order to increase racial mixing. The justices said that busing for racial balance would undo the effects of discrimination and thereby give meaning to equal protection, but skeptics suspected that the Court's real purpose was to uplift black youths by ensuring that they were socialized in racially balanced, predominantly white schools.[1]

But this was constitutional law, not statutory law. When it came to school desegregation, there was nothing comparable to the Voting Rights Act of 1982, in which Congress changed the law on voting rights, and there was nothing like the congressional acquiescence in the "no disparate impact" approach to affirmative action. In the field of public education, Congress never departed from the policy it established in the Civil Rights Act of 1964, when "desegregation" was defined as "the assignment of students to public schools...without regard to their race," but "not...the assignment of students to public schools in order to overcome racial imbalance."[2]

When courts ordered that children must be taken out of their neighborhoods to increase racial mixing in the public schools, many parents took actions in response. Some moved to different neighborhoods; some enrolled their children in private schools; and others participated in protests and demonstrations. Some observers said that parochialism and racism were responsible for the opposition to busing, but Ronald Reagan did not agree. He thought court-ordered busing was bad for education, and he recognized, in addition, that busing was an issue that Republicans could use to win support at the polls.

Thus Reagan's Republican platform of 1980 "condemn[ed] the forced busing of school children to achieve arbitrary racial quotas." It said busing had "failed to improve the quality of education, while diverting funds from programs that could make the difference between success and failure for the poor, the disabled, and minority children." One of William Bradford Reynolds's jobs was to develop a legal strategy that would translate these campaign promises into public policy.[3]

Notes

1. Speech, 3 May 1907, quoted in William Lockhart, Yale Kamisar, and Jesse Choper, *Constitutional Law*, 3d ed.. (St. Paul: West Publishing Co., 1970), 7.
2. Public Law 88-352 (1964), 246.
3. *National Party Conventions, 1831-1980* (Washington: Congressional Quarterly, Inc., 1983), 135.

15

From *Brown* to Busing

Scholars have described the evolving law on school desegregation as "inscrutable," "incoherent," and "a patchwork of unintelligibility." At the very least, the jurisprudence of school desegregation was complex.[1]

When the Supreme Court, in *Brown v. Board of Education of Topeka* (1954), ruled that it was unconstitutional for government authorities to separate the children of different races by assigning them to segregated public schools, the opinion of the Court was originally understood to mean that the government could not constitutionally discriminate on the basis of race. On the Sunday after *Brown* was handed down, the *New York Times* expressed this common understanding.

> It is forty-three years since John Marshall Harlan passed from this earth. Now the words he used in his lonely dissent in...*Plessy v. Ferguson* in 1896 have become...the law of the land. Justice Harlan said: "Our Constitution is color-blind and neither knows nor tolerates classes among citizens." [*Brown*] dealt solely with segregation in the schools, but there was not one word in Chief Justice Warren's opinion that was inconsistent with the earlier views of Justice Harlan. This is an instance in which the voice crying in the wilderness finally becomes the expression of a people's will and in which justice overtakes and thrusts aside a timorous expediency[2]

The black plaintiffs in *Brown* agreed with the *New York Times*. They acknowledged that the Constitution allowed for some discrimination against groups (as with the all-male military draft), but they said the equal protection clause required not only that discrimination must be justified but also that especially weighty evidence was necessary to justify racial discrimination. They said no such evidence had been presented in *Brown* and that, in fact, discrimination against people with dark skins was just as arbitrary and capricious as discrimination against people who had blue eyes or blond hair. According to Thurgood Marshall, who argued *Brown* for the NAACP, racial segregation fell within a group of unreasonable classifications that were prohibited by the equal protection clause.[3]

The black plaintiffs made these points repeatedly and unequivocally. They said that classifications "based solely on race or color" were "arbitrary and unreasonable" and "the very kind the equal protection clause was designed to prohibit." They said it was their "dedicated belief" that the Constitution was "color-blind." They said that the Fourteenth Amendment had "stripped the state of power to make race and color the basis for governmental action."[4]

The plaintiffs also renounced discrimination as a remedy for previous discrimination. They said they were

> not asking for affirmative relief.... The only thing that we ask for is that the state-imposed racial segregation be taken off, and to leave the county school board...to assign children on any reasonable basis they want to assign them on....
>
> What we want from this Court is the striking down of race....
>
> Do not deny any child the right to go to the school of his choice on the grounds of race or color...[Do] not assign them on the basis of race.... If you have some other basis...any other basis, we have no objection. But just do not put in race or color as a factor.[5]

The idea that official racial discrimination was prohibited also seemed to be implied in *Bolling v. Sharpe* (decided the same day as *Brown*), in which the Supreme Court ruled against segregation in the public schools of the District of Columbia. In so ruling, the Court reiterated that "the Constitution of the United States, in its present form, forbids...discrimination by the General Government, or by the States, against any citizen because of his race."[6]

That *Brown* prohibited racial discrimination also seemed to be the message later in 1954 when the Court invalidated laws requiring segregation of municipal parks, buses, tennis courts, and the like. The Court did not explain its rationale, but it reversed and remanded the segregation "for consideration in light" of *Brown*. Civil rights activists and sympathizers understood this to mean that the Court had declared that all classification by race was unconstitutional per se.[7]

In 1955 this impression was reinforced by the implementation decision in *Brown*, which was worded so as to condemn "discrimination" rather than "segregation" in education. Three years later, in a case that arose in Little Rock, Arkansas, the Court held that *Brown* had established that children have "the constitutional right...not to be discriminated against in school admission on grounds of race or color."[8]

In response to the decisions of the Supreme Court, lower federal courts affirmed that racial discrimination was prohibited and that the Constitution required the government to treat each person as an individual without regard to race. Stated most fluently, perhaps, by Circuit Judge John J. Parker in

Briggs v. Elliott (1955), this point of view was frequently called the *Briggs* dictum, and for more than a decade it was the authoritative construction of *Brown*: "It is important that we point out exactly what the Supreme Court has decided and what it has not decided.... The Constitution...does not require integration. It merely forbids discrimination."[9]

Few principles are more appealing than that citizens should not be disadvantaged by their government because of their race or ancestry. Thus, despite some opposition, *Brown* quickly won general acceptance. Public opinion polls indicated that by 1956 most Americans were opposed to official racial discrimination.[10]

Responding to this sentiment, Congress in 1964 enacted a Civil Rights Act that placed the legislature's stamp of approval on the emerging consensus. Section 407 authorized the attorney general to initiate school desegregation actions, and Section 401 defined what that meant: "'Desegregation' means the assignment of students to public schools and within such schools without regard to their race, color, religion, or national origin, but 'desegregation' shall not mean the assignment of students to public schools in order to overcome racial imbalance."[11]

This double definition—defining what desegregation did not mean as well as what it did—was the result of an extraordinary debate in Congress. Critics of the civil rights bill warned that disingenuous federal bureaucrats and judges would use "desegregation" to impose racial balance on public schools. In response, supporters of the bill, such as California Senator Thomas Kuchel, asserted that one point should be "thoroughly understood." To answer what Kuchel called "scare charges," the sponsors of the legislation "specifically provided in section 401(b) of the bill that 'desegregation' shall not mean the assignment of students to public schools in order to overcome racial imbalance."[12]

The principal sponsor of the Civil Rights Act in the Senate, Senator Humphrey, gave similar assurances. Humphrey said that explicit definitions had been included, to soothe fears that the legislation might be used to empower the federal government to order the busing of children around a city in order to achieve a certain racial balance or mix in the schools. The purpose of the civil rights bill was to prohibit racial discrimination, not to seek any sort of racial balance. "I do not believe in duplicity," Humphrey declared. "The bill does not attempt to integrate the schools, but it does attempt to eliminate segregation in the school system."[13]

In addition, Humphrey introduced into the *Congressional Record* a recent court decision, *Bell v. City of Gary*, in which the Seventh Circuit Court held that the Constitution, as interpreted by the Supreme Court, "does not mean that there must be an intermingling of the races in all school districts. It means only that [students] may not be prevented from intermingling or going to school together because of race or color." Humphrey assured the Senate that this was only the most recent decision holding that the Constitution did not require compensatory discrimination. Other decisions could have been cited to the same effect. The federal courts had ruled that black students could not be separated from others solely because of their race; but it was no concern of the Constitution if the races were separated because of geographic or transportation considerations or other similar criteria.[14]

Senator Robert Byrd of West Virginia, an opponent of the civil rights bill, said he still was "not convinced" that federal bureaucrats might not try to impose racial balance by threatening to cut off federal funds. In response, Senator Humphrey said he wanted "to put the troubled mind of the distinguished Senator at rest." Humphrey mentioned that he was "manager of the bill," and, consequently, his assurance that such balance could not be required would be of "some importance" in any interpretation or application of the legislation.[15]

Humphrey then explained that federal courts would not permit policies that required racial balance. Over the course of a decade, an unbroken line of cases—extending from *Brown* to *Briggs* to *Gary*—had established that while the Constitution did not require integration, it most assuredly did prohibit discrimination. According to Humphrey, this meant that busing for integration would be unconstitutional. He said, "The busing of children to achieve racial balance would be...a violation [of the Constitution], because it would be handling the matter on the basis of race and we would be transporting children because of race."[16]

Despite this legislative history, officials in the federal Office of Education soon changed the meaning of "desegregation" from a prohibition of racial discrimination to a requirement that racial discrimination must be used if greater "integration" would result. "Every assurance written into the [Civil Rights] Act and reiterated by its sponsors and supporters that it could not be made the basis of a requirement of integration proved to be worthless."[17]

How did this reinterpretation come about? The usual answer is that school districts brought forced integration upon themselves. Because of massive, persistent resistance to *Brown*, it is said, a forbearant federal government finally ran out of patience and recognized that there was no alternative but to force integration upon recalcitrant districts.[18]

But this explanation will not withstand scrutiny. "Massive resistance" to school desegregation was a phenomenon of the 1950s, not of the 1960s, and occurred primarily in small towns and rural areas in the Deep South. Even in the 1950s, there was compliance with *Brown* in the border states and in several Southern cities, and after passage of the Civil Rights Act in 1964, the pace of school desegregation quickened throughout the South.

> At the end of the 1963–1964 school year, only half the Negro children in the border states and barely one percent of the 2.84 million in the [Deep South] were attending white schools. But by September 1965, goaded by fear of losing urgently needed federal funds, all but 170 of the 5,045 school districts in the South had begun to integrate classes. Probably more southern Negroes entered white schools in 1965 than in the entire 11-year period since the desegregation decision of 1954."[19]

The acceleration in the rate of desegregation occurred because Congress reinforced *Brown* by passing the Civil Rights Act. It was also a result of prodding from the Office of Education, which insisted that the Civil Rights Act of 1964 required school districts to cease racial discrimination as a prerequisite for receiving federal aid.

But the end of discrimination did not lead to anything like proportional integration. Because of differing patterns of racial concentration in different residential areas, proportionally balanced integration usually was not achieved when students were assigned to neighborhood schools. Nor was balanced mixing achieved if students were allowed to choose schools, since only a minority of blacks and almost no whites volunteered to attend schools where their race was in the minority. Even in schools where the overall enrollment was racially balanced, considerable so-called resegregation occurred within individual classrooms after students were grouped according to academic achievement.

Consequently, the Office of Education developed new guidelines for administering the Civil Rights Act. Beginning in 1966—just as desegregation was spreading through the South—the office disregarded the congressional declaration that "'desegregation' shall not mean the assignment of students to public schools in order to overcome racial imbalance." Instead, the office changed the meaning of desegregation from a prohibition of racial discrimination for the purpose of separating the races to a requirement of racial discrimination to mix them.[20]

It did so because bureaucrats in the office were not content when desegregation did not produce balanced racial mixing. Like their counterparts at the EEOC—who, from the outset, wanted to define job discrimination in terms of equality of results rather than equality of opportunity—key people in the Office of Education favored integration and had no use for mere desegregation.

In the past the Office of Education had been a cautious agency, but in the 1960s it employed a group of bureaucrats who had participated in the civil rights movement and who favored nothing less than a second Reconstruction to abolish racial imbalance in the public schools. One especially influential integrationist was Harold Howe II, the Commissioner of Education. A grandson of Samuel Chapman Armstrong, a Union army general who established the Hampton Institute to educate former slaves in 1868, Howe—the son of the college's president, the Reverend Arthur Howe—was reared in Hampton. Although himself educated at the private Taft School and at Yale University, Harold Howe, by the 1960s, had developed the conviction that integrating the public schools was the key to solving the nation's racial problems. As Commissioner of Education, he threw his support behind the efforts of the civil rights activists-turned-bureaucrats who were redefining desegregation to require integration.[21]

In Congress, the office's guidelines for interpreting the Civil Rights Act came in for criticism, but there was no explicit repudiation of the new policy. Some members recognized that the office had changed the meaning of desegregation, but others were not aware of what was happening or seemed to believe, with the *New York Times*, that it was "not Federal arrogance but hardened local prejudice" that was responsible for the turnabout.[22]

The initial results were mixed when the 1966 guidelines were challenged in court. In the Fourth Circuit, the court of appeals rejected the guidelines. In an opinion written by the chief judge, Clement F. Haynesworth, the court held that the mandate of *Brown* was satisfied if students were assigned to school on a racially nondiscriminatory basis. In the case before the court, all students had been allowed to attend the school of their choice and there was no evidence of any sort of intimidation. In these circumstances, the court rejected the bureaucrats' argument that school authorities were required to assign students to achieve "a greater intermixture of the races." The court held that "if each pupil, each year, attends the school of his choice, the Constitution does not require that he be deprived of his choice."[23]

However, in the Fifth Circuit, the court of appeals rejected freedom of choice and declared that the 1966 guidelines were "required by the Constitution and...within the scope of the Civil Rights Act of 1964."[24]

The opinion for the Fifth Circuit Court was written by John Minor Wisdom, a judge who at one time seemed an unlikely candidate to change the meaning of school desegregation. Appointed to the federal bench by President Dwight D. Eisenhower, Wisdom had written in 1958 that *Brown* established that the government could not discriminate on the basis of race: "In the School Segregation cases...the Supreme Court held that classification based on race is inherently discriminatory and violative of the Equal Protection Clause of the Fourteenth Amendment."[25]

By 1966, however, Wisdom had "grown" to understand that *Brown* imposed an "affirmative duty...to furnish a fully integrated education to Negroes as a class." Lest there be any uncertainty about his meaning, Wisdom italicized his holding that "*the only adequate redress for a previously overt system-wide policy of segregation directed against Negroes as a collective entity is a system-wide policy of integration*." When properly understood,

Brown required more than the disestablishment of segregation; it also imposed "an absolute duty to integrate."[26]

It would be hard to overstate the importance of the opinion that Judge Wisdom wrote and that a panel of judges of the Fifth Circuit Court later affirmed, 8–4. Wisdom held that there could be no middle course—that is, one with no discrimination and no compulsion either to separate or to integrate. Earlier decisions that distinguished between desegregation and integration were overruled. J. Harvie Wilkinson has written that "Wisdom transformed the face of school desegregation law." Lino A. Graglia concluded that Wisdom changed "the constitutional mandate...from a prohibition of racial discrimination to separate the races to a requirement of racial discrimination to mix them."[27]

Since the Constitution has come to mean whatever the judges say it means, Judge Wisdom's interpretation of equal protection was legally plausible. However, an additional effort by Wisdom to reconcile the mandatory integration of the 1966 guidelines with the Civil Rights Act of 1964 could be termed sophistry. Swept up in the strong currents of opinion that existed when the civil rights movement was in its heyday, Wisdom wrote, "No army is stronger than an idea whose time has come," and for the judges of the Fifth Circuit Court, as previously for the bureaucrats at the Office of Education, the time had come for compulsory integration. Wisdom said this was "commanded by *Brown,* the Constitution, the Past, the Present, and the wavy fore-image of the Future."[28]

The judges of the Fifth Circuit said they approached their decision "with humility" and with the recognition that "as far as possible federal courts must carry out congressional policy," but then they proceeded to defeat the very purpose of the Civil Rights Act. In 1964, Congress called for desegregation. The essence of the new law was the principle that racial discrimination was wrong. That was the "idea whose time had some," but in 1966 and 1967 the Fifth Circuit Court held that the Civil Rights Act and the Constitution required color-conscious affirmative discrimination to undo the effects of past discrimination.[29]

In 1968 the Supreme Court settled the conflict between the Fourth Circuit (where "no racial discrimination" was still the official policy) and the Fifth Circuit (where racial assignments were required to promote integration). In *Green v. County School Board of New Kent County*, the high court sided with the Fifth Circuit.

In *Green*, the Supreme Court held that students must be assigned so as to achieve substantial integration. With this decision the era of desegregation came to an end. Purporting to do no more than apply the holding of *Brown* to the case at hand, the Supreme Court changed the constitutional mandate from a prohibition of segregation to a requirement that affirmative steps must be taken to achieve a substantial amount of racial interaction.

Situated about halfway between Richmond and Williamsburg in Virginia, New Kent was a rural county with only two schools and 1,300 students, 740 of whom were black. Each of the schools was a combined elementary and high school, and prior to *Brown* the schools were racially segregated, with blacks assigned to the George W. Watkins School in the western portion of the county and whites to the New Kent School on the east side. Until 1965, Watkins continued to have an all-black student body, faculty, and staff, and New Kent remained all-white. Then, to qualify for federal money after passage of the 1964 Civil Rights Act, school authorities adopted a plan that gave students free transportation to whichever school they wished to attend. There were 35 black students who chose New Kent in 1965, 111 in 1966, and 115 in 1967, but no white student ever chose to attend Watkins. In 1967, one white teacher was employed at Watkins and one black at New Kent. Thus the Watkins School remained almost all-black, while New Kent School was 83 percent white.[30]

Jack Greenberg, the NAACP's chief legal counsel, personally took charge of the New Kent lawsuit. He saw to it that the legal briefs and oral arguments focused on a crucial question; namely, Did a school district satisfy its obligations under *Brown* "simply by ceasing its illegal practices," or should it be required to take "affirmative steps to thoroughly dismantle the dual segregated system"? To clarify the issue, the black plaintiffs admitted that in New Kent, "each child was given the unrestricted right to attend any school in the system." Elsewhere there might be pressures to restrict freedom of choice, but in New Kent the choice was conceded to be completely free and unencumbered. Defense attorney Frederick T. Gray told the Supreme Court that "115 children of the colored race have elected to go to the white school,...and there is not a shred of evidence that anyone has been, in any way, abused; that any parent has lost his job; that any pressure has been exerted."[31]

Nevertheless, lawyers for the NAACP argued that freedom of choice was illusory. They said blacks could not choose freely because of the way they had been reared. Most had decided to remain at the previously all-black school because they knew that was what most whites wanted them to do. Neither the blacks nor the whites of New Kent County could "unshackle themselves from the psychological effects of [the] imposed racial discriminations of the past."[32]

Several justices agreed. During the oral argument, Chief Justice Warren said the system in New Kent was "booby trapped" by "social and cultural influences and the prejudices that have existed for centuries there." Justice Marshall had to be reminded that the black plaintiffs had conceded that their choice was free and unrestricted. Justice Brennan, by putting "freedom of choice" in quotation marks in the opinion he drafted for the Court, implied that blacks could not choose freely.[33]

In *Green* the Supreme Court held that New Kent had not complied with the 1955 *Brown* order "to effectuate a transition to a racially nondiscriminatory school system." The racially imbalanced pattern of enrollment—with one school almost all-black and the other mostly white—was said to indicate that different schools were intended for students of different races. The schools were not racially segregated as they once had been, but they were still racially imbalanced. "It was such dual school systems," the Court said, "that...*Brown I* held to be unconstitutional and...*Brown II* held must be abolished." The Supreme Court accordingly ordered New Kent to provide for more racial mixing.[34]

In some ways Justice Brennan's opinion was more subtle than Judge Wisdom's path-breaking opinion for the Fifth Circuit Court. *Green* did not speak of integration. As Professor Graglia has noted, "[A] Constitutional requirement of racial discrimination to increase integration...would have been most difficult to justify as such. Instead of attempting such justification, the Court imposed the requirement—by what it actually did—while insisting that it was requiring only that all racial discrimination be eliminated. It was thus able to maintain the enormous advantage of seeming to combat racism, as in *Brown*, while in fact imposing a racist requirement."[35]

The rationale that integration was not constitutionally required for its own sake but was simply a remedy for the formal segregation of the past also seemed to mean that the requirement would be applied only to the South. This served to minimize national attention and to make the decision seem but another step taken by a patient Court to counteract still another attempt by the recalcitrant South to evade the requirement of *Brown*.

The essential question in *Green* concerned the point at which a school board had fulfilled its duty to provide equal protection of the laws. New Kent said it had satisfied its obligations by ceasing racial discrimination and by offering free choice. It said that "desegregation" was different from "integration," that school districts were not required to achieve racially balanced enrollments, and that the availability of free choice was sufficient quite apart from the amount of mixing that resulted. The Supreme Court decided to the contrary, ruling that the school board must reorganize its program so that no school would be racially identifiable. New Kent was "charged with the affirmative duty to take whatever steps might be necessary to convert to a unitary system in which racial discrimination would be eliminated root and branch."[36]

Chief Justice Warren observed that the New Kent case changed "the traffic light...from *Brown* to *Green*." In response, several lower courts demanded substantial mixing in the public schools of the South. One district judge in

North Carolina explained that "the actions of School Boards and district courts must now be judged under *Green v. New Kent County* rather than under the milder leash of *Brown v. Board of Education.*" Other courts concurred. One panel of judges from the Fifth Circuit held that the fundamental question was not whether schools were operated without racial discrimination but rather: "The ultimate inquiry is whether the [school] board is fulfilling its duty to take *affirmative* steps...to find realistic measures that will transform its formerly *de jure* dual segregated school system into a 'unitary, nonracial system of public education.'" One panel of judges declared that a point had been reached in the process of school desegregation "where it is not the spirit, but the bodies that count." Another said: "Good faith is not, and cannot be, the standard.... [I]t comes down to figures.... If the result is satisfactory it is because of the numbers, not the effort or subjective motivation. If the result is unsatisfactory it is because of the numbers." In 1969 the Fourth Circuit Court declared: "The famous *Briggs v Elliott* dictum—adhered to by this court for many years—that the Constitution forbids segregation but does not require integration...is now dead."[37]

Three years after *Green*, the Supreme Court clarified its meaning. In a North Carolina case, *Swann v. Charlotte-Mecklenburg Board of Education* (1971), the Court indicated that substantial integration was required, and districtwide busing could be used to achieve it.[38]

The facts in *Swann* were very different from those in *Green*. The Charlotte-Mecklenburg School District ranged over an area of 550 square miles and served 84,000 students in 1968. Black students made up 29 percent of the total student body and were heavily concentrated in one portion of the city of Charlotte. Token desegregation had begun shortly after *Brown*, and after 1966 students were assigned, irrespective of race, to neighborhood schools. Black students who lived in predominantly black areas were allowed to transfer to schools elsewhere, but most decided to attend schools that were close to home. Because of the confluence of residence and choice, about two-thirds of the black students attended schools that were all-black or almost all-black.[39]

After *Green*, integrationists challenged the Charlotte system. They said it was one thing to require, as *Brown* had, that children must be assigned to public schools on a nondiscriminatory basis; it was something else to require, as *Green* had, that school boards must take affirmative action to achieve substantial integration. Agreeing with this argument, District Judge James B. McMillan held that "the rules of the game have changed, and the methods and philosophies which in good faith the Board [of Education] has followed are no longer adequate to complete the job which the courts now say must be done."[40]

Judge McMillan therefore imposed a busing program, the goal of which was to achieve an equal dispersion of blacks and whites. He started "with the thought...that efforts should be made to reach a 71–29 ratio in the various schools so that there will be no basis for contending that one school is racially different from others." He allowed that "variations from that norm may be unavoidable" but insisted that "pupils of all grades [should] be assigned in such a way that as nearly as practicable the various schools at various grade levels have about the same proportion of black and white students."[41]

On appeal, the Supreme Court affirmed, but not before considering the points at issue. Justice Black wanted to overrule Judge McMillan's order because Black thought busing for racial balance was at odds with *Brown*'s command, "that there was to be no legal discrimination on account of race." Black also maintained that the legislative history of the 1964 Civil Rights Act established that "the purpose of Congress was to deny the courts exactly what the [plaintiffs] in this case are urging, namely, that pupils be transported to achieve a racial balance."[42]

Chief Justice Burger also wanted to reverse Judge McMillan but discovered that he and Justice Black were alone in thinking there should not be a constitutional command to prohibit racially neutral policies (like assigning children to schools in their neighborhood) that did not lead to substantially proportional racial mixing. Five justices (Brennan, Douglas, Harlan, Marshall, and Stewart) favored busing for integration. For them there was no middle ground. These five seemed to believe that because government authorities in North Carolina had once operated segregated schools, they should now make amends by taking affirmative action to compel integration. Further complicating the situation for Burger and Black, the two remaining justices (Blackmun and White) seemed willing to go along with the integrationists.[43]

Justices Brennan, Douglas, and Marshall reflexively favored busing for integration. However, the moderate Justices Stewart and Harlan also favored the policy. In one memorandum, Stewart told Burger it was "fallacious" to argue "that the basic meaning of *Brown*...was a requirement of 'colorblindness' in the administration of public school systems." If a school board had sanctioned racial discrimination in the past, Stewart wrote, it could not discharge "its affirmative duty by establishing a system which does not 'take race into account.'" Harlan agreed. Although he revered his grandfather (who had asserted in 1896 that "[o]ur Constitution is color-blind"), Harlan thought *Brown* had created a "duty to mix the races," and, writing to Burger, stated that "mixing is permissible, if indeed not a required *remedial* tool for the disestablishment of state-enforced dual school systems."[44]

Recognizing that there were not enough votes on the Court to obtain a decision against busing, Burger voted with the majority so that he could assign himself the job of writing the Court's opinion. He hoped to include enough caveats to limit the damage.

The integrationists on the Court allowed Burger to say that the Court "has not ruled, and does not rule that 'racial balance' is required under the Constitution"; that "the basic constitutional requirement" was "that the State not discriminate between public school children on the basis of race"; and that desegregation plans should be "feasible," "workable," "effective," and "realistic."[45]

Equally important, the majority allowed Burger to stress that the objective of desegregation was to remedy the formal segregation of yesteryear. The goal was to remove the "vestiges of state-imposed segregation," Burger wrote. To this end, affirmative assignments could be required "in a system with a history of segregation," but if there were no such history, "it might well be desirable to assign pupils to schools nearest their homes."[46]

The majority also allowed Burger to write that after school authorities had complied with the Court's orders, their systems would be "unitary," and it would not be necessary "to make year-by-year adjustments of the racial composition of student bodies once the affirmative duty to desegregate has been accomplished." (As will be noted in chapter 20 below, the Rehnquist Court of the 1990s would make much of these caveats.)[47]

But the Court of 1971 made Burger write six drafts of the *Swann* opinion. They made him say that district judges and local authorities were required to make "every effort to achieve the greatest possible degree of actual desegregation." They made him approve busing as one way to implement the mandate of *Green*. They made him call for pro-integration techniques that could be "administratively awkward, inconvenient and even bizarre in some situations"—techniques such as the "gerrymandering of school districts and attendance zones" and the "'pairing,' 'clustering,' or 'grouping' of schools with attendance assignments made deliberately to accomplish the transfer of Negro students out of formerly segregated Negro schools and the transfer of white students to formerly all-Negro schools." They made Burger assert that if authorities had kept the races apart in the past, they must now take affirmative steps to eradicate the vestiges of segregation.[48]

The *Swann* opinion that finally came down in Burger's name was far from the opinion that the chief justice had tried to write. After reading *Swann*, Griffin Bell, then a judge of the Fifth Circuit Court, told a reporter, "There is a lot of conflicting language here." The *New Republic* characterized the opinion as "a negotiated document looking in more than a single direction." Nevertheless, as Bernard Schwartz has written, the ambiguities of the opinion could not "obscure the fact that the *Swann* decision was a categorical affirmance of Judge McMillan's far-reaching desegregation order." Burger's fellow justices had forced him to further the process he wanted to limit—the process of compulsory integration.[49]

By holding that integration was not required for its own sake but only to disestablish a pattern of officially compelled racial separation, the remedy theory of *Green* and *Swann* implied that affirmative assignments could not be required of school districts that had never previously assigned students on the basis of race. But in 1973 the Supreme Court adjusted the legal rationale so that busing could be required outside the South. It did so in *Keyes v. School District No. One*, a case that arose in Denver, Colorado.[50]

In 1969 more than 96,000 students were enrolled in Denver's 119 public schools, with whites making up 65 percent of the total; Hispanics, 20 percent; and blacks, 14 percent. The schools had never been segregated on the basis of race, a practice that was explicitly prohibited by the constitution of Colorado, but Hispanic and black students were disproportionately concentrated in downtown schools that served the areas where most Hispanics and blacks lived. In 1969 attorneys for the NAACP went to court and argued that the racial imbalance that resulted from using neighborhood assignments amounted to illegal segregation.[51]

After a lengthy lawsuit, the Supreme Court gave the NAACP a victory. The Court held that, despite appearances to the contrary, Denver had been practicing official segregation. The Court so held because the school board, instead of taking advantage of an opportunity to increase racial mixing in the well-to-do, predominantly white Park Hill section in northeast Denver, had opened a 450-student elementary school (the Barrett School) that was situated so as to serve a nearby, mostly black enclave.

Although the school board had built 100 schools in the twenty years before *Keyes*, construction of the Barrett School was the only instance that Justice Brennan specifically mentioned in the opinion he wrote for five members of the Court. Nevertheless, Brennan generalized about "a practice of concentrating Negroes in certain schools by structuring attendance zones"; and he also rejected the appraisal of the district judge, who concluded that the assignment of a few-hundred black students to the Barrett School had only a minimal effect on the pattern of racial imbalance that prevailed elsewhere in Denver. Instead, Brennan developed what would be called "the *Keyes* presumption"—the presumption that if an attendance zone between two individual schools was gerrymandered to limit racial interaction, then the racial imbalance that prevailed elsewhere in a large metropolitan district was not adventitious.[52]

In some ways *Keyes* was not an especially expansive opinion. The *Keyes* Court did not hold that racial separation, concentration, or imbalance amounted to illegal segregation. The Court continued to say that affirmative integration was not required per se but only as a remedy for the negative discrimination of the past.

But, by indirection, the *Keyes* presumption paved the way for busing for racial balance in the North and West. It did so because civil rights lawyers could always find some instance of school location or attendance boundaries that contributed to racial imbalance. Once a school board was found to have committed a "segregative act," district judges were to presume that racial imbalance elsewhere in the school system was the result of other segregative actions. Then, to correct such segregation, the judges were authorized to require affirmative polices such as busing for racial balance throughout the district.

The justices themselves appeared to recognize that the *Keyes* presumption was problematical. Breaking from the pattern of unanimity that had characterized all previous Court decisions on school desegregation, the newest member of the Court, then Justice Rehnquist, wrote a dissent that rejected the *Keyes* presumption and questioned the idea that compulsory integration followed from *Brown*. Justice Douglas wrote a concurring opinion, and Chief Justice Burger concurred only in the result. Justice White took no part in the decision, and Justice Powell filed an opinion concurring in part and dissenting in part. The Court had boarded the bus, but with misgivings.

Justice Powell's remarks were especially thoughtful. As a result of *Green*, Powell wrote, *Brown* had been "transformed into the present constitutional doctrine" of "affirmative duty." When it came to large metropolitan districts, however, Powell thought it mistaken to consider affirmative action a remedy. In point of fact, the large districts were being asked to correct patterns of racial imbalance that were not caused by official action but by economic and residential conditions and by patterns of migration that were "largely unrelated to whether a particular State had or did not have segregative school laws." Powell therefore advised the Court to abandon the pretense that affirmative action was a remedy for official segregation. He thought the Court should "hold, quite simply" that local authorities must achieve approximate racial balance in the school districts of the North as well as in the South.[53]

Nevertheless, Powell recorded his "profound misgivings" about the "large-scale or long distance transportation of students" that would be required to achieve racial balance. He feared that the time and distance of travel would "significantly impinge on the educational process." He said neighborhood schools possessed "several valuable aspects"—such as saving money that would otherwise be used for long-distance busing, minimizing the safety hazards for children who were traveling to school, and allowing youths more time for study or for extra-curricular activities. Powell acknowledged as well the widespread belief, long recognized in constitutional law, that the child was "not the mere creature of the State" but the ward of parents or guardians who had the right and obligation to nurture, support, and educate their children.[54]

Powell anticipated opposition from people who would say the government should not shuffle children around without regard to the preferences of their families. He knew many parents purchased homes in particular areas because the neighborhood schools would have children from like-minded families and would reinforce the values the parents wished to instill in their offspring. He recognized that many parents understood the influence of the peer group and wanted to sequester their children from lower-class children in general and especially from what would later be called the "underclass." Despite the reassurances of liberal sociologists, he knew that many parents were convinced that their children would not benefit from integration.

Powell had to tread gingerly. He was touching on issues that cause so much bitterness that their discussion has become almost taboo. He said he "pass[ed] no judgment" on the views of such parents; he was merely acknowledging that they would regard busing for integration as an interference with "the concept of community" and with their "liberty to direct the upbringing and education of children under their control."[55]

This was not fright fantasy. It was an accurate prediction of what actually happened when judges, armed with the *Keyes* presumption, required busing for integration not just in southern cities like Charlotte, but in northern cities like Denver, San Francisco, and Boston. The compulsory transportation of school children out of their neighborhoods to increase school racial mixing touched off widespread, bitter resentment because busing affected the lives of average people significantly and directly. Busing gave rise to demonstrations, dissent, and middle-class flight. Eventually, it also contributed to a decline in the quality of public education and to a realignment in politics.

The Supreme Court has said that the enforcement of constitutional principles cannot be compromised because of public opinion; but the justices were aware of the wide public dissatisfaction with busing and knew that in some ways the national mood in the 1970s was "reminiscent of that in southern state legislatures in the late 1950s." In 1970 President Nixon issued an extraordinary eight-thousand-word statement that said that in requiring busing for integration, judges had moved beyond desegregation and were trying to overcome the effects of residential racial concentration. In 1974 the House of Representatives voted, 293–117, to prohibit busing students past the nearest public school. Polls indicated that less than 20 percent of the population supported busing for racial balance, and that a majority favored a constitutional amendment to ban school assignments that were based on race, creed, or color.[56]

When the justices encountered opposition after the *Brown* decision of 1954, they allowed the nation time to adjust to new principles, saying that desegregation should be implemented "with all deliberate speed" and at "the earliest practicable date." When the busing cases of the early 1970s gave rise to complaints about judicial "usurpation" and "tyranny," the Court again drew back. It did so in *Milliken v. Bradley*, a case that concerned busing for racial balance in the metropolitan region near Detroit.[57]

In Detroit the district judge, Stephen Roth, acknowledged that the city had never separated students on racial grounds and had made some efforts to promote integration. He found, for example, that the school board had "followed a most advanced and exemplary course in adopting and carrying out what is called the 'balanced staff concept'—which seeks to balance faculties in each school with respect to race, sex, and experience, with primary emphasis on race." By 1970 Detroit employed "black teachers in a greater percentage than the percentage of adult black persons in the City of Detroit," and the city had a "higher proportion of black administrators than any city in the country." In one instance the school board held open 240 positions in schools that were at least three-quarters white, "rejecting white applicants for these positions until qualified black applicants could be found and assigned."[58]

The efforts of the school board had not been uniformly pro-integration, however, for Judge Roth also found that the board had built some schools in the center of racially concentrated areas, thereby minimizing integration. The board also allowed students in neighborhoods that were undergoing racial transition to transfer to schools elsewhere in Detroit, thereby enabling white students to "escape" from schools that were becoming "identifiably Negro." Since the board was an agent of the state of Michigan, Judge Roth also found the state culpable.[59]

Judge Roth recognized that the racial composition of Detroit's schools, which by 1973 had become 70 percent black, resulted primarily from a pattern of migration that saw large numbers of blacks move into the city while even larger numbers of whites departed for the suburbs. But the judge held that the school board's actions were additional "causal factors in the segregated condition of the public schools of the city of Detroit." Because the school board was guilty of segregative acts, and because the Supreme Court had established the *Keyes* presumption, Judge Roth ordered that affirmative action be taken to integrate the schools.[60]

Roth knew that an order for racial balance throughout the city would stimulate white flight. Instead of achieving integration, a busing plan that was limited to the city of Detroit would probably lead to a resegregated school district that would be at least 90 percent black. Therefore, Roth decided to look beyond Detroit. To get a 75 percent-white majority in the schools, he ordered that whites and blacks should be dispersed through three counties and fifty-four school districts with a total enrollment of 780,000 students. Roth said he would try to limit the students' busing time to eighty minutes a day but acknowledged that some youngsters would have to spend as much as three hours each day in transit to and from school.[61]

On appeal, a divided Sixth Circuit Court voted 6–3 to affirm most of Judge Roth's order. The majority said that "any less comprehensive a solution than a metropolitan area plan would result in an all black school system immediately surrounded by practically all white suburban school systems."[62]

In an opinion by Chief Justice Burger, the Supreme Court reversed and censured the lower courts for requiring a metropolitan plan simply because a plan that was limited to Detroit "would not produce a racial balance which they perceive as desirable." Racial balance was not required as such, the Supreme Court insisted, but only as a remedy for unconstitutional actions. Burger wrote that the logic of desegregation—the undoing of segregation—required that affirmative action to achieve integration must be limited to culpable school districts.[63]

Because the suburban districts near Detroit had never been found guilty of segregative actions, the Supreme Court insisted that they must be left out of any remedial plan. There was nothing in the Constitution, the Supreme Court held, that required that independent school districts must be consolidated to make all schools predominantly white. "The mere fact of different racial composition in contiguous districts does not itself imply or constitute a violation of the Equal Protection Clause."[64]

The Court's decision in *Detroit* hit integrationists like a slap in the face. The *Green* Court had sanctioned "whatever steps might be necessary" to achieve the "root and branch" eradication of the last vestiges of segregation. The *Swann* Court told federal judges to "make every effort to achieve the greatest possible degree of actual desegregation." But those decisions were handed down in 1968 and 1971. By 1974, when *Detroit* was decided, the Warren Court had passed into history. Four of President Nixon's appointees were on the bench, and they ruled that there was no warrant for an interdistrict plan to achieve integration unless there had been interdistrict actions to promote segregation.[65]

The Court's decision against metropolitan busing was by the narrowest of margins, 5–4, but the *Detroit* opinion was a significant turning point. *Brown* had been the watershed of school desegregation; *Green, Swann,* and *Keyes* represented the high tide for integration; *Detroit* marked the water's edge.

The dissenting justices understood that *Detroit* was a turning point. Justice Marshall said that a busing plan that was limited to the city would be "a hollow remedy" that would leave the schools "segregated in fact." He warned that because of *Detroit*, black and white children would grow up as strangers to one another, with most blacks in the central cities and most whites in the suburbs. Marshall conceded that this might seem "the easier course," but he predicted that it would be a choice "our people will ultimately regret." Marshall said the Court's decision was less a product of sincere doubts about the rationale for integration than a reflection of the public mood that the courts were going too far.[66]

In *Detroit*, each of President Nixon's four appointees to the Court agreed with the president's basic position on busing. Nixon had said, in effect, *Brown* was right, but *Green* was wrong—that the decision to end segregation was correct but the decision to require integration was a mistake. It was ironic that *Detroit* came down on 25 July 1974, only two weeks before Nixon was forced out of office, but *Detroit* was a victory for the soon-to-be-deposed president.

This made the decision all the more difficult for many people to accept. The battle over forced busing had been one of the major points at issue between liberals and conservatives during the early 1970s, and now, thanks to Nixon's justices, the Court had set up a roadblock that put most suburbs beyond the reach of liberal social engineering. Tom Wicker of the *New York Times* gave voice to the views of many integrationists when, after conceding that there was "no doubt whatever that public opinion has turned massively against the kind of cross-busing that would have been required to unify Detroit schools with 53 surrounding suburban school systems," he lamented that the Supreme Court had retreated from "a noble goal."[67]

The Supreme Court took another step away from busing in a 1977 case that involved the public schools of Dayton, Ohio. Here the racial enrollments in the city's sixty-six public schools were not balanced because students were assigned to schools close to home and blacks were not evenly dispersed throughout the neighborhoods of the city. The district court found that the school board was guilty of some segregative actions—such as allowing students to transfer outside the normal attendance zones and assigning 72 percent of the black teachers to schools in black neighborhoods. Nevertheless, the court said these actions were "isolated" and were only minimally responsible for the racial imbalance in the schools; therefore, the court limited its remedy to eliminating the transfer option and assigning faculty to achieve a racial balance at each school.[68]

The Sixth Circuit Court of Appeals reversed and ordered a districtwide busing plan. It did so on the grounds that *Keyes* had established that once a school district was found to have engaged in segregative behavior, it must take affirmative action to achieve the maximum amount of actual integration.[69]

The Supreme Court, in an opinion by then Justice Rehnquist, vacated the judgment of the Sixth Circuit Court and ordered the district court to "tailor 'the scope of the remedy' to fit 'the nature and extent of the constitutional violation.'" Even if intentional infractions were found, the Supreme Court said, lower courts should not impose a remedy which was out of proportion to the constitutional violation. A basic principle of equity was to restore victims to the position they would have enjoyed in the absence of illegal action. In school-segregation cases this meant that the district court should

> determine how much incremental segregative effect these violations had on the racial distribution of the...school population as presently constituted, when that distribution is compared to what it would have been in the absence of such constitutional violations. The remedy must be designed to redress that difference, and only if there has been a systemwide impact may there be a systemwide remedy.[70]

"*Dayton* was a godsend to northern school districts," one observer noted. "It meant that school boards might indulge in marginal behavior—minor indiscretions—without being subjected to city-wide busing as a result." Departing from the *Keyes* presumption, *Dayton* said federal courts should not use isolated instances of segregation as justification for imposing districtwide busing for racial balance. In the North and West, it seemed, busing would be limited. Thanks to *Detroit*, it would not cross district lines into the suburbs. Thanks to *Dayton*, most cities in the region would be spared cross-town busing.[71]

However, unlike Chief Justice Burger (who kept a majority of the Court in support of the principles of *Detroit*), Justice Rehnquist could not keep his majority for limiting the *Keyes* presumption. When *Dayton* was remanded for further proceedings, the district judge, after a supplemental evidentiary hearing, concluded that the occasional lapses of the school board had occurred more than twenty years previously and, therefore, had no effect on the current pattern of racial imbalance. But the Sixth Circuit Court reversed the district judge, resurrected the *Keyes* presumption, and ordered busing to achieve racial balance in all sixty-six schools in the city.[72]

Nor was this all. In similar litigation arising from Columbus, Ohio, another district judge decided that similar infractions—allowing transfers and assigning most black teachers to schools in black neighborhoods—had a persisting, systemwide effect that could be remedied only by citywide busing for racial balance. The Sixth Circuit Court then affirmed.[73]

When the litigation from Columbus reached the Supreme Court in 1979, and when the Dayton case returned there at about the same time, the high court approved citywide busing in each instance. Writing for five members of the Court, Justice White held, first, that the lower courts' findings of facts were "not...clearly erroneous," and, in addition, held that the pro-busing orders were not based on a "misapprehension of the controlling law." He mentioned that *Green* and *Swann* had "imposed an affirmative duty to desegregate." *Dayton* had admittedly "reiterated the accepted rule that the remedy...should be commensurate with the violation," but the district court in *Columbus* and the Sixth Circuit Court in *Dayton* had found the sort of discrimination that, under *Keyes*, warranted "an inferential finding of systemwide discriminatory intent."[74]

In a dissent joined by Justice Powell, Justice Rehnquist took strong exception to the decisions of 1979. In effect, Rehnquist observed, the lower courts had held that if a school board committed an infraction (such as allowing optional transfers or siting a school in the midst of a racially homogeneous area), or even if the board failed to take advantage of opportunities to promote integration, a court could order the diffusion of black and white students throughout the school district. On appeal, the Supreme Court then held that the actions of lower courts should be set aside only if they were "clearly erroneous." This holding, according to Rehnquist, created "the disturbing prospect of very different remedies being imposed on similar school systems because of the predilections of individual judges."[75]

Searching history for metaphors, Rehnquist said that "like Pilate," the Supreme Court had "washed its hands of disparate results in cases throughout the country." By deferring to the lower courts (except in extreme cases where the courts' rulings were clearly erroneous), the Supreme Court had authorized district judges to act as "Platonic Guardians" and to run local school systems. In giving such latitude, the Supreme Court had established a procedure that would lead to violations of Cicero's maxim not to "lay down one rule in Athens and another rule in Rome."[76]

In a separate concurring opinion, Justice Powell also took exception to the Court's decisions in *Columbus* and *Dayton II.* By "stringing together a chain of 'presumptions,' not one of which is close enough to reality to be reasonable," Powell wrote, the Sixth Circuit Court in *Columbus* and *Dayton* arrived at "the remarkable conclusion—[one that was] not supported by evidence in either case, and as a general rule seems incredible—that the absence of integration found to exist in a high percentage of the 241 schools in Columbus and Dayton was caused entirely by intentional violations of the Fourteenth Amendment by the school boards of these two cities." In point of fact, Powell believed, any actions taken by the school boards were slight indeed compared to more general socioeconomic reasons for the nonintegration of blacks.[77]

Powell also warned that compulsory integration would "provoke responses that will defeat the [courts'] integrative purpose," predicting that "resentment against judicial coercion" would stimulate "resegregation." Powell said that unlike school officials, parents were not bound by court orders and were free to send their children to private schools or to move to suburban school districts. Either option could be expensive, but Powell noted that "experience demonstrates that many parents view these alternatives as preferable to submitting their children to court-run school systems." This turned out to be true in Columbus and Dayton, where white enrollment in the public schools declined precipitously (from 71,000 to 35,000 in Columbus and from 31,000 to 15,000 in Dayton).[78]

Many observers ascribed *white flight* to racism, but Powell said that it was "at least as likely that the exodus is in substantial part a natural reaction to the displacement of professional and local control that occurs when courts go into the business of restructuring and operating school systems." He thought Americans "instinctively resent coercion, and perhaps most of all when it affects their children and the opportunities that only education affords them."[79]

Powell acknowledged that "proved discrimination by state or local authorities should never be tolerated." He said it was "a first responsibility of the judiciary to put an end to it where it has been proved." But in *Columbus* and *Dayton* (and in some other cities, too, Powell implied) courts had relied on "fictions and presumptions" to justify "wide-ranging decrees and [judicial] supervision over school systems." Because of white flight, and because of the dubious legal rationale for court-ordered busing, Powell thought the time had come "for a thoughtful re-examination of the role of courts in confronting the intractable problems of public education."[80]

Instead of reconsideration, however, the Supreme Court withdrew to the sidelines. It was not until twelve years later, in 1991, that the Court handed down another important opinion on busing for racial balance. In the meantime it allowed the inferior federal courts to set different rules for different communities (e.g., in the state of Georgia, Athens was required to have busing for racial balance, but Rome was not).[81]

By the time Ronald Reagan became president, a pattern had emerged. The Supreme Court's opinion in *Detroit* had established that there should be no busing to achieve racial balance across district lines unless (as in Louisville, Kentucky) a suburban district was found to have taken action to promote segregation. If a single school district had committed segregative acts, however, that district was required to make amends, with the extent of the atonement depending on whether the lower federal courts relied on the *Keyes* presumption or the test the Supreme Court had announced in the first *Dayton* case. If the lower court used *Keyes*, it would require affirmative steps to achieve an even racial balance in all the schools of the district. If the lower court used *Dayton*, the remedy would redress only the incremental segregative effects caused by the school board but not the general demographic imbalance that resulted from larger social and economic forces. As Justice Rehnquist had predicted, there was room for individual judges to exercise their "predilections."[82]

One instance of this occurred in Delaware in 1975 when a divided three-judge district court—without finding that suburban districts had committed any segregative acts—breached the suburban line and consolidated ten mostly white districts with a 90 percent-black district in the city of Wilmington. In this instance the district court held that the state government was responsible for racial imbalance because it had built highways that facilitated residential separation, because it had not dispersed public housing, and because it had encouraged the consolidation of small, rural districts that had too few students to operate a high school while not taking affirmative steps to consolidate the larger but racially imbalanced schools near Wilmington. The fact that even the black members of the state legislature had voted for these policies made no difference to the judges. They ruled that "to a significant extent," the state government was responsible for "the net outmigration of white population and [the] increase of city black population in the last two decades."[83]

To remedy this wrong, the judges ordered a plan that Justice Rehnquist described as "more Draconian than any ever approved by this [Supreme] Court." Eleven independent, locally elected school boards were dissolved, with their places taken by a single court-appointed school board.

> [w]ithin this judicial school district, which comprise[d] in excess of 60 percent of all the public school students in the State of Delaware, every single student [was] reassigned away from his or her local school for a period of no less than three years [for most whites] and for as long as nine years [for most blacks]. The plan was designed to accomplish a racial balance in each and every school, in every grade, in all of the former eleven districts, mirroring the racial balance of the total area involved.[84]

Other judges considering similar evidence had concluded that the huge tide of black immigration into the nation's cities, and the white flight to the suburbs, was due to a myriad of social, economic, and personal factors. But the district court in Delaware held that the state was responsible and imposed the maximum amount of actual racial mixing. Lawyers for Delaware complained that the district court was evading the mandate of *Detroit*, but the Delaware court knew that *Detroit* had been rendered by a vote of 5–4, and apparently hoped that the majority opinion of *Detroit* would become a minority view by the time the Delaware case went up on appeal.[85]

As things turned out, when Delaware's appeal got to Washington in 1980, the Supreme Court decided not to consider the case. The Court's newest member, Justice Stevens, recused himself, because he had once practiced law with Delaware's chief lawyer, Philip B. Kurland. With only eight justices available, the case might well have ended in a 4-to-4 deadlock, and Chief Justice Burger said it was "a total waste of time" to have a full-scale review in these circumstances.[86]

The Delaware case was an exception, however. Despite the leeway allowed to inferior federal courts, there were only a few cases of forced busing across district lines and a few instances of voluntary busing to distant magnet schools. Forced busing rarely reached into the suburbs.[87]

Within the cities, however, there was a good deal of busing. Yet when city-only plans were imposed, many whites (and also middle-class blacks) moved to the suburbs. In city after city, the whites who remained in the central cities were disproportionately single people, young couples without children, or older people whose children were already grown. This was nothing new. As early as 1967, the journalist Joseph Alsop, after noting that the 500,000 blacks of Washington, D.C., produced ten times as many school-age children as the 250,000 whites, observed that this meant "that just about every white couple [in the city] has moved to the suburbs, at least as soon as it came time to send the children to school." What had been peculiar to Washington and some other cities in the 1960s became commonplace by the 1980s.[88]

As the Reagan administration took office in 1981, this is how things stood: the Supreme Court had moved beyond *Brown*. Within school districts in the South, racial balance was generally required and busing could be used to achieve the necessary amount of mixing; elsewhere, depending on the predilections of the judges, busing could also be required either for racial balance or to eliminate the incremental effects of isolated segregative actions, but the buses did not cross district lines—except in rare instances where outlying districts were guilty of segregative acts, or in cases where district judges were willing to engage in a sort of brinkmanship with the Supreme Court. After establishing this pattern, the Court then stepped back to see how things would work out. For more than a decade after 1979, the Court declined to hear cases that involved busing for racial balance.

Unlike the Supreme Court, the Reagan administration did not have the luxury of time. As a candidate for president, Ronald Reagan said the government should not assign students to school "on account of race." His platform in 1980 "condemn[ed] the forced busing of children to achieve arbitrary racial quotas," and Reagan promised that he would work to give parents the ability to choose the schools their children would attend. One of William Bradford Reynolds's jobs was to translate these campaign promises into public policy.[89]

Notes

1. James S. Liebman, "Implementing *Brown* in the Nineties," *Virginia Law Review*, 76 (April 1990): 352–53.
2. *New York Times*, 23 May 1954, 10:1.
3. Leon Friedman, ed., *Argument: The Oral Argument Before the Supreme Court in Brown v. Board of Education of Topeka, 1952–1955* (New York: Chelsea, 1969), 38, 45.
4. Andrew Kull, *The Color-Blind Constitution* (Cambridge: Harvard University Press, 1992), 157; G. W. Foster, Jr., "The North and West Have Problems, Too," *Saturday Review* (20 April 1963): 72.
5. Leon Friedman, *Argument*, 47, 375, 402.
6. Bolling v. Sharpe, 347 U.S. 497 (1954), 499.
7. Florida ex rel Hawkins et al., 347 U.S. 971 (1954); Andrew Kull, *The Color-Blind Constitution*, 162.

8. Brown v. Board of Education, 349 U.S. 294 (1955); Cooper v. Aaron, 358 U.S. 1 (1958), 17.
9. Briggs v. Elliott, 132 F.Supp. 776 (1955), 777.
10. Herbert H. Hyman and Paul B. Sheatsley, "Attitudes Toward Desegregation," *Scientific American* 195 (December 1956): 35–39.
11. Public Law 88-352 (1964), 246
12. 110 *Congressional Record* (1964), 6560.
13. Ibid., 12715, 12717.
14. Bell v. City of Gary, 324 F.2d 209 (1963).
15. 110 *Congressional Record* (1964), 12716.
16. Ibid., 12717; Lino A. Graglia, *Disaster By Decree: The Supreme Court Decisions on Race and the Schools* (Ithaca: Cornell University Press, 1976), 51.
17. Lino A. Graglia, *Disaster By Decree*, 51.
18. For an example of this point of view, see the editorial in the *New York Times*, 7 December 1966, 46:1.
19. John A. Garraty, *The American Nation* (New York: Harper & Row, 1966), 831. For annual and regional tabulations of the percentage of black children attending school with whites, 1954–1972, see Gerald N. Rosenberg, *The Hollow Hope* (Chicago: University of Chicago Press, 1991), 50.
20. U.S. Office of Education, Revised Statement of Policies for School Desegregation Plans (1966); Raymond Wolters, *The Burden of Brown*, 152–53; James R. Dunn, "Title VI, the Guidelines and School Desegregation in the South," *University of Virginia Law Review*, 53 (1967): 42–88; "The Courts, HEW, and School Desegregation," *Yale Law Journal* 77 (1967): 321–65.
21. Raymond Wolters, *The Burden of Brown*, 153; Gary Orfield, *The Reconstruction of Southern Education* (New York: Wiley, 1969), xi and passim; *Current Biography* (1967): 185–88; Stephen C. Halpern, *On the Limits of the Law* (Baltimore: John Hopkins Press, 1995), 52–57 and passim.
22. *New York Times*, 7 December 1966, 46:1.
23. Bowman v. County School Board, 382 F.2d 326 (1967), 327, 329.
24. United States v. Jefferson County Board of Education, 372 F.2d 836 (1966), 848.
25. Dorsey v. State Athletic Commission, 168 F.Supp. 149 (1958), 151.
26. United States v. Jefferson County Board of Education, 372 F.2d 836 (1966), 869, 846 n.5.
27. United States v. Jefferson County Board of Education, 380 F.2d 385 (1967), 389; J. Harvie Wilkinson, *From Brown to Bakke: The Supreme Court and School Integration* (New York: Oxford University Press, 1979), 111; Lino A. Graglia, *Disaster By Decree*, 59.
28. United States v. Jefferson County Board of Education, 372 F.2d 836 (1966), 849, 878.
29. Ibid., 848, 883.
30. Green v. County School Board, 391 U.S. 430 (1968); Philip Kurland and Gerhard Casper, eds., *Landmark Briefs and Arguments of the Supreme Court,* vol. 66, 1–298.
31. Philip Kurland and Gerhard Casper, eds., *Landmark Briefs and Arguments of the Supreme Court*, vol. 66, 31, 225, 231–32, 259, 262; Green v. County School Board, 382 F.2d 338 (1967), 32.
32. Philip Kurland and Gerhard Casper, eds., *Landmark Briefs and Arguments of the Supreme Court*, vol. 66, 25, 38.

33. Ibid., 223–25; Green v. County School Board, 391 U.S. 430 (1968), 441.
34. Green v. County School Board, 391 U.S. 430 (1968), 435, 439.
35. Lino A. Graglia, *Disaster By Decree*, 73, 83. Also see Bernard Schwartz, *Super Chief: Earl Warren and His Supreme Court* (New York: New York University Press, 1983), 703–6.
36. Green v. County School Board, 391 U.S. 430 (1968), 437–38.
37. Bernard Schwartz, *Super Chief*, 706; Swann v. Charlotte-Mecklenburg, 300 F.Supp. 1358 (1969), 1372; Henry v. Clarksdale Municipal Separate School District, 409 F.2d 682 (1969), 687; Indianola Municipal Separate School District, 410 F.2d 626 (1969), 631; Montgomery County Board of Education v. Carr, 402 F.2d 782 (1968), 786; Walker v. Brunswick County School Board, 413 F.2d 53 (1969), 54, n.2.
38. Swann v. Charlotte-Mecklenburg Board of Education, 402 U.S. 1 (1971); Bernard Schwartz, *Swann's Way* (New York: Oxford University Press, 1986).
39. Swann v. Charlotte-Mecklenburg, 300 F.Supp. 1358 (1969), 1360, 1372; 402 U.S. 1 (1971), 6–7. For a thorough and especially well-written account of the history of school desegregation in Charlotte, see Davison M. Douglas, *Reading, Writing, and Race* (Chapel Hill: University of North Carolina Press, 1995), 50, 123–24, and passim.
40. Brown v. Board of Education, 349 U.S. 294 (1955), 300; Swann v. Charlotte-Mecklenburg, 300 F.Supp. 1358 (1969), 1372.
41. Swann v. Charlotte-Mecklenburg, 306 F.Supp. 1299 (1969), 1312, 1313–14. Under the plan that Judge McMillan imposed, black enrollment at individual schools would range from 9 percent to 38 percent.
42. Bernard Schwartz, *Swann's Way*, 101, 177–78.
43. Ibid., 88–129 and passim.
44. Ibid., 125, 39, 144.
45. Swann v. Board of Education, 402 U.S. 1 (1971), 31.
46. Ibid., 15, 26, 28.
47. Ibid., 23–24, 5–6, 31–32.
48. Bernard Schwartz, *Swann's Way*, 114 and passim; Swann v. Board of Education, 402 U.S. 1 (1971), 26, 27.
49. *Newsweek* (3 May 1971): 27; *New Republic* (1 May 1971): 12; Bernard Schwartz, *Swann's Way*, 186.
50. Keyes v. School District No. 1, 413 U.S. 189 (1973).
51. Ibid., 196.
52. Ibid., 201, 208–9. More precisely, the "*Keyes* presumption" was that "a finding of intentionally segregative school board actions in a meaningful portion of a school system...creates a presumption that other segregated schooling within the system is not adventitious. It establishes...a prima facie case of unlawful segregative design on the part of school authorities, and shifts to those authorities the burden of proving that other segregated schools within the system are not also the result of intentionally segregative actions."
53. Ibid., 220, 223, 224; John C. Jeffries, *Lewis F. Powell*, 290–305.
54. Keyes v. School District No. 1, 413 U.S. 189 (1973), 238, 239, 245, 247.
55. Ibid., 246, 247.
56. Cooper v. Aaron, 358 U.S. 1 (1958), 16, 22; Gary Orfield, *Must We Bus?* (Washington: The Brookings Institution, 1978), 248; Lino A. Graglia, "When Honesty is 'Simply Impractical'," *Michigan Law Review*, 85 (April-May 1987): 1172;

U.S. News and World Report (11 March 1974): 76; *Integrated Education* (November-December 1976): 24.

In 1974 Ben J. Wattenberg summed up the findings of the Gallup organization: "In 1970, Gallup began polling on school busing: the question dealt with 'busing of Negro and white school children from one school district to another.' The response was 86–11% against. In 1971, the same question yielded a 76–18% 'against,' with blacks also in opposition 47–45%. In the years since, those ratios have remained roughly constant; massive white opposition, a split black view." *The Real America* (Garden City: Doubleday and Co., Inc., 1974), 252. Also see William G. Mayer, *The Changing American Mind* (Ann Arbor: University of Michigan Press, 1982), 24–25.

57. Brown v. Board of Education, 349 U.S. 294 (1955), 301, 300; Milliken v. Bradley, 418 U.S. 717 (1974).
58. Bradley v. Milliken, 338 F.Supp. (1971), 589–91.
59. Ibid., 587–89.
60. Ibid., 592; Lino A. Graglia, *Disaster By Decree*, 207–15.
61. Bradley v. Milliken, 345 F.Supp. 914 (1972).
62. Bradley v. Milliken, 484 F.2d 215 (1973), 245.
63. Milliken v. Bradley, 418 U.S. 717 (1974), 740.
64. Ibid., 744–47, 756 (concurring opinion of Justice Stewart).
65. Green v. County School Board, 391 U.S. 430 (1968), 437–38; Swann v. Charlotte-Mecklenburg, 402 U.S. 1 (1971), 26.
66. Milliken v. Bradley, 418 U.S. 717 (1974), 808, 815.
67. *New York Times*, 28 July 1974, IV, 7:1.
68. Dayton v. Brinkman, 433 U.S. 406 (1977), 412 and passim; 443 U.S. 52 (1979), 525 n.11.
69. Brinkman v. Gilligan, 503 F.2d 684 (1974); 518 F.2d 853 (1975); 539 F.2d 1084 (1976).
70. Dayton v. Brinkman, 433 U.S. 406 (1977), 420.
71. J. Harvie Wilkinson, *From Brown to Bakke*, 246.
72. Dayton v. Brinkman, 433 U.S. 406 (1977), 421; Brinkman v. Gilligan, 446 F.Supp. 1232 (1977), 1237; 583 F.2d 243 (1978).
73. Penick v. Columbus Board of Education, 429 F.Supp 229 (1977).
74. Columbus Board of Education v. Penick, 443 U.S. 449 (1979), 454, 463, 464, 459, 465, 467; Dayton v. Brinkman, 443 U.S. 525 (1979), 525–27.
75. Columbus v. Penick, 443 U.S. 449 (1979), 491.
76. Ibid., 525, 492.
77. Ibid., 481, 480, 482.
78. Ibid., 484, 483; National Association for Neighborhood Schools, *Bulletins*, 39 (April-May 1985); 52 (December 1988); and 53 (February-March 1989).
79. Columbus v. Penick, 443 U.S. 449 (1979), 485, 489.
80. Ibid., 487, 481.
81. Telephone interviews with officials in Athens and Rome (Lucian Harris and Jimmie Morris), 5 January 1993.
82. Newburg Area Council v. Jefferson County Board of Education, 510 F.2d 1358 (1974); Columbus v. Penick, 443 U.S. 449 (1979), 491.
83. Evans v. Buchanan, 393 F.Supp. 428 (1975), 434, 436n, 438; Raymond Wolters, *The Burden of Brown*, 204–28.
84. Delaware State Board of Education v. Evans, 446 U.S. 923 (1980), 923.

85. Evans v. Buchanan, 393 F.Supp. 428 (1975), 448, 449; statement of Philip B. Kurland, 15 January 1975, docket 300, Civil Action 1816, U.S. District Court, Wilmington; Raymond Wolters, *The Burden of Brown*, 204–28.
86. Raymond Wolters, *The Burden of Brown*, 223–24; *Wilmington Morning News*, 29 April 1980.
87. School desegregation expert Christine H. Rossell stated that she knew of "no mandatory reassignment plan implemented in the North since 1981 and of only two implemented in the South since 1981." *The Carrot Or the Stick* (Philadelphia: Temple University Press, 1990), p. xiii. James S. Liebman has mentioned seven instances of court-ordered integration in the 1980s. "Desegregating Politics," Columbia Law Review, 90 (October 1990), 1468–69.
88. *New Republic* (22 July 1967): 19.
89. Ronald Reagan, *A Time for Choosing*, 171; *National Party Conventions, 1831–1980* (Washington: Congressional Quarterly, Inc., 1983), 135.

16

Coercion or Choice: The Forked Road to School Desegregation

Upon taking office as assistant attorney general for civil rights, William Bradford Reynolds faced a difficult problem. He had to reconcile Ronald Reagan's opposition to court-ordered busing with the Supreme Court's insistence that "every effort" must be made "to achieve the greatest possible degree of actual desegregation."[1]

I

On one occasion Reynolds recalled a story about a conversation that Lord Balfour supposedly had with Colonel Edward House in 1917. According to the story, Balfour inquired about what should be done to acquire a good knowledge of public opinion in the United States, and House advised Balfour first to spend a few days with wealthy people on Long Island, New York. "Then you will know what the great mass of American men and women think, for they will think just the opposite of your Long Island friends."[2]

Similarly, Reynolds's opinions on school desegregation can be characterized by first describing their antithesis. Reynolds's views differed from those ideas that prevailed in the legal and constitutional culture of the Ivy League, ideas propounded by scholars such as Paul Gewirtz of Yale, James S. Liebman of Columbia, and Jennifer L. Hochschild of Princeton. Reynolds said that in this respect, as with Lord Balfour's wealthy friends of 1917, the elite wisdom was "out of touch with the mass of Americans."[3]

By 1980 many Americans had come to question the sincerity of the judicial rationale for mandatory integration. In theory the courts required only that students be assigned to public schools on a nondiscriminatory basis. Judges said that it was no concern of the Constitution if racial imbalance was the result of economic or geographic factors or of personal choice; they said that court-ordered integration was remedial—that is, it was designed to restore the victims of discrimination to the places they would have occupied if government officials had not committed segregative acts. Then they proceeded to require racial balance in every grade throughout entire school districts.

Some observers questioned the integrity of the judges. They said that when judges imposed racial balance, they were requiring "something that no one honestly believed would have occurred in the absence of the alleged constitutional violations." They said that the effects of any official segregation were slight indeed compared to the personal, social, and economic factors that were primarily responsible for racial imbalance. They accused judges of being "disingenuous" when they said their goal was only to rectify the segregation that had been caused by state actions. In fact, the judges wanted to eliminate all racial clustering, "whether it resulted from individual actions of families or from state action." They said judges were shifting the goal, without candidly admitting what they were doing, "from eliminating state-imposed segregation to instituting state-imposed integration."[4]

Professor Paul Gewirtz, of the Yale Law School, conceded that this criticism was superficially plausible. In *Green v. New Kent County*, for example, it seemed that the county had done all that *Brown* said it must do. By allowing all students to attend the school of their choice, the county had desegregated its schools and was assigning children on a nondiscriminatory basis.[5]

When the Supreme Court nevertheless held that the New Kent plan was unacceptable, the Court seemed to require more than it said it was requiring. So also in other cases, when the Court ruled against assigning students to the nearest neighborhood schools. The Court said it "ha[d] not ruled, and does not rule that 'racial balance' is required." It said it was necessary only to assign students on "a non-racial basis"—but then the Court ordered that students must be assigned so as to maximize racial integration.[6]

Gewirtz developed a clever psychological argument that explained why the Court's remedial rationale actually required mandatory integration. He said that when it came to race relations, most people could not choose freely because their socialization had been shaped by racist influences that were deeply rooted in U.S. history. One of the influences, inextricably intertwined with others, was the segregative action of government officials.

Because socialization had been influenced by "discriminatory conditions over the years," Gewirtz said, the views of whites and blacks were "tainted" and "distorted." That was why most students of both races, in New Kent County and throughout the United States, did not choose to attend schools in which their race would be the minority. Most people did not understand that it was in their own best interest to have racially balanced public schools. When offered the opportunity to choose integration, they declined the choice because they had subconsciously "adapted to the regime of discrimination."[7]

By always putting the phrase *freedom of choice* in quotation marks, Gewirtz suggested, the *Green* Court implied that there was no true freedom, that the justices did not allow the New Kent plan because they thought the choices there were still influenced by the official segregation of the past. Because they recognized that the psychological effects of segregation would persist for many years, the justices went beyond prohibiting official discrimination and required affirmative steps to eliminate the vestiges of discrimination—specifically, the Court required the mixing of black and white students because the Court recognized that the "effects of past violations persist even after the violations stop."[8]

Gewirtz also said that the Supreme Court, in *Green* and its progeny, implied that compulsory integration should continue "almost indefinitely." Anything less would fail to change the "perceptions and understandings" that had been shaped during "decades or centuries of discrimination." Freedom of choice and neighborhood schools would not suffice, the Court held, until the psychological vestiges of government-sponsored segregation had been eradicated—that is, until the great majority of both blacks and whites recognized that balanced mixing was good for everyone.[9]

Gewirtz left no doubt that he personally favored coerced integration, but he said his primary goal was to explain the rationale of the Supreme Court. The Court, he said, had not established racially balanced integration as the end goal. It opted instead for a remedial policy to correct the persistent effects of past discrimination.

Gewirtz's assessment of the Court's rationale was inventive, but was it correct? The Court itself never did more than hint at this underlying psychology, but had it done more than that, there would have been criticism, as Gewirtz's interpretation smacked of elitism and authoritarianism. It was, in addition, too convoluted to gain wide support. Consequently, other integrationists, like James S. Liebman of the Columbia University School of Law, said the civil rights movement should abandon the remedial approach and start over with a forthright argument for integration.[10]

Liebman shared Gewirtz's censorious view of U.S. history. Believing that government-sponsored discrimination had "saturated" the experience of the United States and "tainted" it with "corruption," Liebman had no quarrel with the argument that governments should now make amends by forcing students to mix in racially balanced proportions.[11]

Many Americans, however, did not think that official discrimination was the cause of racial imbalance. They thought nonintegration resulted primarily from personal choice and socioeconomic factors. Thus, the remedial theory impressed many people as a bad-faith rationalization.

Therefore, Liebman advised integrationists to proceed openly. They should simply say that racial justice required the United States to have integrated schools. Because students were young and impressionable, and because public education was a principal activity of local and state governments, Liebman thought that the schools were the ideal place to promote integration and to redeem a contaminated society. Integrated education was the best way to reform "the malignant hearts and minds of racist white citizens."[12]

Jennifer Hochschild of Princeton University also considered racially balanced integration a moral imperative, but she thought racism was so deeply entrenched that integration could not be achieved unless the country abandoned democratic processes. Believing that ordinary citizens were too benighted to realize that everyone would benefit from integration, she wrote, "The populace (or at least a majority of voters) does not want mandatory desegregation." Therefore, if integration were to be achieved, she said that it would have to be imposed by "authoritative, committed leadership," and that "Democracy" should "give way to liberalism." Quoting John Dewey, Hochschild said that "what the best and wisest parent wants for his child, that must the community want for all its children." If Americans would not voluntarily choose to have racially balanced schools, she said that "they must permit elites to make that choice for them."[13]

One reviewer described Hochschild's book, *The New American Dilemma*, as a "startling" but "straightforward" argument for coercion. For "complete desegregation" to be achieved, Hochschild explained, metropolitan busing from city to suburb would have to become commonplace, a situation that could be achieved only if the Supreme Court overturned its *Detroit* ruling and broke down the barriers between city and suburban school districts. In addition, teachers would have to surrender seniority rights, counties and towns would have to give up financial control over local schools, and parents would have to relinquish the right to send their children to private schools.[14]

Above all else, integrationists emphasized the desirability of metropolitan busing. They said that that was the only way to make sure that blacks and whites would not grow up as strangers to one another. Even Ronald P. Formisano, an historian who focused on the failure of busing in Boston, thought it would have been a good idea to impose a metropolitan plan that included affluent whites as well as blacks and urban ethnics. The biggest problem with busing in Boston, according to Formisano, was that this city-only plan applied only to the relatively poor blacks and whites of Boston itself and did not extend to outlying suburbs.[15]

Some integrationists believed that racial balance should be pursued by any means necessary. Thus, in addition to promoting metropolitan busing, they would close off the possibility of escape to private schools. While Hochschild "question[ed]" the "parents' rights to send their children to private schools," Formisano mentioned "the *presumed* right of private schools to exist." To protect the "autonomy" of children from the "tyranny" of their parents,

Liebman recommended that children be required to attend "schools that are not entirely controlled by parents." He said the state should make sure that children were exposed to "a broader range of...value options than their parents could hope to provide." "[F]amily life," Liebman explained, was too often "marked by exclusiveness, suspicion, and jealousy as to those without."[16]

According to Liebman, one goal of desegregation was to withdraw control from white parents and to give white children "a wider range of choices about the persons with whom they might associate and the values they might adopt as they approach adulthood." A principal purpose was to deny parents the right to send their children to schools that would reinforce "the 'personal features' and values those parents have chosen as their own."[17]

II

The academic integrationists were in earnest. They did not equivocate. They openly expressed views that others were too circumspect to declare. But to Reynolds, these arguments for integration rang false. The celebration of coercion reminded him of what the historian Crane Brinton wrote about Robespierre: "If Frenchmen would not be free and virtuous voluntarily, then he would force them to be free and cram virtue down their throats."[18]

Surely, Reynolds thought, there must be a better approach than applying more coercion and curbing the freedom of families. Eventually, Reynolds developed a two-part plan that emphasized (1) the right of students to transfer to schools outside their neighborhood, and (2) the need to upgrade the quality or distinctiveness of neighborhood schools. Instead of restricting parental rights, Reynolds hoped to expand choice in a way that would increase integration voluntarily.

Shortly after taking office, Reynolds reread *Brown* and concluded that "the 'civil rights establishment' [was] all wrong." To Reynolds, the prevailing contemporary understanding of *Brown* made better sense than the interpretations of integrationists. Like the *New York Times* of 1954, Reynolds understood *Brown* to mean that government could not discriminate on the basis of race. *Desegregation* meant that students must be assigned to public schools on a nondiscriminatory basis.[19]

Reynolds recognized that *Brown* could be read differently. He knew that when the case was argued, the NAACP had maintained, as a secondary theme, that black children were psychologically injured if they attended segregated schools. On the basis of evidence from the social sciences, the NAACP said that segregated blacks developed a sense of inferiority that adversely affected their motivation and impaired their education, and that under segregation it was difficult for blacks to learn the social skills needed for easy interaction with whites. The NAACP also said segregation made it difficult for black and white children to develop mutually respectful racial attitudes.[20]

At one point in his opinion for the Supreme Court, Chief Justice Warren mentioned this theme, saying that segregated schools gave black children "a feeling of inferiority as to their status in the community that may affect their hearts and minds in a way unlikely ever to be undone."[21]

The full ramifications of Warren's sociological theorizing would not be apparent immediately, but scholars have subsequently noted that the rationale for *Brown* was muddled. *Brown* said that racial discrimination amounted to a violation of the equal protection clause, while the companion *Bolling* opinion emphasized that discrimination was too arbitrary to satisfy the requirements of the due process clause. But *Brown* also said that racial segregation damaged the personality of human beings. On one hand, *Brown* suggested the per se illegality of racial distinctions, and on the other, it suggested that discrimination would be all right if it was used to break down racial isolation and to achieve substantial racial interaction.[22]

Reynolds recognized that *Brown* rested partially on what he called "imperfect sociological underpinnings." But he said integrationists were "misguided" when they said *Brown* required substantial racial mixing. In fact, Chief Justice Warren had alluded to the social science evidence only briefly—perhaps as a gracious way of acknowledging the efforts of scholars who had worked for the victorious NAACP. Then, Reynolds said, the Court plumped for the color-blind ideal that had been the dominant goal of the civil rights movement for several decades: it said racial classifications were too arbitrary and irrational to satisfy the equal protection clause; it "flatly and unequivocally condemned race-consciousness as a tool for assigning school children"; it ordered public schools to adopt "nondiscriminatory" admission policies; it endorsed "the colorblind ideal that had been the civil rights rallying cry." *Brown* was a victory for the NAACP, which for decades previously and for several years thereafter maintained that "the state has a duty...to be 'colorblind' and not to act so as to encourage racial discrimination."[23]

The meaning of desegregation changed in 1968, when the Supreme Court handed down its decision in *Green v. New Kent County*. Upon rereading *Green*, however, Reynolds recognized that the Court had imposed a requirement of racial balance while insisting that it was requiring only that all racial discrimination be eliminated. Justice Brennan's opinion never used the words *racial balance* or *integration*, and he did not explicitly reject the idea that while the Constitution forbids discrimination, it does not require integration.

It was disingenuous for the *Green* Court to say the goal was still desegregation rather than racially balanced integration, but Reynolds took the words of the Court at face value. He emphasized that *Green* "did not alter the fundamental premise established in [*Brown*]." *Green* did not require "race-consciousness as a tool for assigning school children." "No mention was made of...'racial balance.'" The *Green* Court "held simply that the Constitution requires racially nondiscriminatory student assignments and the eradication of the segregative effects of past intentional racial discrimination."[24]

The North Carolina busing case, *Swann v. Charlotte-Mecklenburg Board of Education*, was more problematical. Here, Reynolds admitted, the Court "embarked on a new course," as it "ordered into effect race-conscious student assignment schemes, employing for the first time the techniques of mandatory busing, alteration of attendance zones, and 'racial-balance' assignments of school children."[25]

Nevertheless, upon rereading the opinion that Chief Justice Burger wrote for the Supreme Court, Reynolds discovered that even *Swann* was not as bad as he feared. He saw that the Court "for the first time" said that school districts might be required to go beyond "strict race neutrality" and to make affirmative efforts to achieve "the greatest possible degree of actual desegregation." But the Court also said that it had "not ruled...that 'racial balance' is required under the constitution." The Court said that it was "[not] deviat[ing] from [*Brown*] in the slightest degree." The objective was still "to eliminate from the public schools all vestiges of state-imposed segregation." At one point, the Court said the remedy for segregation might be "administratively awkward, inconvenient, and even bizarre in some situations," but it also said court orders should not only be "effective" and "feasible," but in addition they should promise "realistically to work."[26]

Reynolds knew that many federal judges understood *Swann* to mean that they should require hard affirmative action—policies that were "awkward, inconvenient, and even bizarre"—to achieve "the greatest possible degree of actual desegregation." Reynolds said that, consequently, "racial balance—rather than racial neutrality—became the overriding concern in school desegregation decrees." By the end of the 1970s, "forced busing" was "the predominant desegregation tool, with little attention being paid to the practical consequences of such judicial reordering of our public education system."[27]

Reynolds thought this view of *Swann* was mistaken. He said that the Supreme Court had not given the lower federal courts unconditional authority to use race-conscious measures to achieve racial balance. *Swann* "did not contemplate indiscriminate use of busing without regard to other important, and often conflicting, considerations." The *Swann* Court "spoke in measured terms, expressing reserved acceptance of busing as but one of a number of remedial devices available for use when...it was 'practicable,' 'reasonable,' 'feasible,' 'workable,' and 'realistic.'"[28]

When Reynolds became assistant attorney general a decade after *Swann*, he said ten years of experience had proved that busing was a failure. He noted that instead of achieving balanced integration, busing stimulated a middle-class flight that left many schools more segregated than ever; and that instead of improving the quality of education, busing led to a loss of parental and community support and in the process "robbed many public school systems of a critical component of a good educational program."[29]

Therefore, Reynolds said, busing for racial balance had not turned out to be "feasible," "workable," "effective," and "realistic"; it did not achieve either "racial balance" (which *Swann* said was not required) or "the greatest possible degree of actual desegregation" (which was). To make matters worse, Reynolds believed, many courts of the 1970s had been so concerned with the issue of racial proportionality that they forgot other important matters: they allowed "the social objective of racial balance" to displace *Brown*'s explicit mandate for "racial neutrality in student assignments"; and they lost sight of the improved educational quality that was the implicit purpose of desegregation.[30]

Reynolds said the time had come to move away from the "misguided preoccupation with forced busing" and to develop a different approach to achieve the goals of *Brown*, *Green*, and *Swann*. He said the Supreme Court would sanction such a move because the Court recognized that the law must take account of experience.[31]

Reynolds acknowledged that it was imperative to eliminate all unconstitutional racial separation. He said the Reagan administration was "firm in its resolve to ferret out any and all instances of unlawful segregation and to bring such practices to a halt," but Reynolds also called for careful investigations to determine whether racial imbalance in the public schools was really the result of segregative actions by government officials. In addition, he called for voluntary programs to promote racial mixing—programs such as magnet schools and modest adjustments of attendance zones. By improving the quality of urban schools, he said, it would be possible to "buil[d] in incentives to promote desegregation."[32]

The next four chapters will describe and assess Reynolds's approach, but one point should be mentioned here. From the outset of his tenure as assistant attorney general, Reynolds said the Civil Rights Division would curtail its use of the *Keyes* presumption. When investigating racial patterns, the Division would not assume that isolated segregative acts in one part of a school district were responsible for racial imbalance elsewhere in the district. It would, rather, "define the violation precisely" and limit the remedy "only to those schools in which the racial imbalance was the product of the intentionally segregative acts of state officials."[33]

III

Like Reynolds, Ronald Reagan thought it was a mistake to force children to leave their neighborhoods to attend distant, racially balanced schools. And Reagan also recognized that opposition to busing was popular with most voters. He knew that the yellow school bus had become a symbol of intrusive social engineering and sensed that, for many people, the buses might as well have been emblazoned with words like *liberals* or *Democrats*."[34]

Reagan proposed to take political advantage of the situation. He told the American Conservative Union in 1977 that he wanted to "combine the two major segments of contemporary American conservatism into one politically effective whole." He wanted to make Republicans of people who were interested in social issues like forced busing. By combining them with economic conservatives, Reagan sought to create "a new, lasting majority."[35]

The election returns in 1980 and 1984 confirmed Reagan's analysis. By opposing busing (and by taking conservative stands on other social issues), Reagan won the support of many former Democrats. One of these Reagan Democrats summed up a prevailing view when she said, "[Busing] taught me a little about the liberal philosophy. They thought they knew what was best for my son.... They think they know better than we do." Rather than submit to busing for racial balance, many people moved to other areas or withdrew their children from the public schools.[36]

Much of the documentation of middle-class flight came from research by the prominent sociologist James S. Coleman. This was ironic, for in the late 1960s and early 1970s, Coleman had filed depositions and given interviews in which he touted the benefits that black children would receive if they were dispersed and educated in predominantly white classrooms. Eventually Coleman became known as "The Scholar Who Inspired Busing."[37]

Coleman's integrationist sociology emphasized the role of peer-group culture in affecting attitudes toward schoolwork. It held that the quality of a school depended on its "class climate," and that middle-class schools were better. Since most whites were "middle class," and most blacks were not, the purpose of integration was to create schools with "enough middle-class students to establish the class character of the school and...a substantial number of lower-class children to benefit from it."[38]

Coleman said the best situation for effective integration was one in which blacks made up between 20 percent and 30 percent of the total number of students. In such an environment, blacks could escape the effects of being socialized in a lower-class culture without suffering at the same time from psychological isolation. As explained by Coleman, the theory was that "children who themselves may be undisciplined, coming into classrooms that are highly disciplined, would take on the characteristics of their classmates and be governed by the norms of the classrooms, so that the middle-class values would come to govern the integrated classroom. In that situation both white and black children would learn."[39]

In 1975, however, Coleman shocked integrationists when he reported that the peer culture of the black minority often overwhelmed that of the majority. Thus, "characteristics of the lower-class black classroom, namely a high degree of disorder, came to take over and constitute the values and characteristics of the classroom in the integrated school."[40]

Integrationists were further dismayed when Coleman reported that middle-class parents, blacks as well as whites, responded by fleeing to the refuge of private schools or to public schools in predominantly white suburbs. They had done so, Coleman said, because many integrated schools "failed to control lower-class black children" and had to spend "90 percent of the time...not on instruction but on discipline."[41]

Integrationists subjected Coleman's new findings to bitter criticism. They said middle-class flight was a temporary and minimal phenomenon. They said similar changes were occurring in almost all cities that had large black populations, including some that never experienced massive integration. In 1975 one of Coleman's critics, Christine H. Rossell, concluded that school desegregation caused "little or no significant white flight, even when it is court ordered and implemented in large cities."[42]

By 1980, however, most experts—regardless of their policy preferences—acknowledged the problem of middle-class flight. By then, most of the nation's large cities had lost more than 40 percent of their white students. By then, even Professor Rossell conceded that Coleman had been right.[43]

The magnitude of the flight was especially great if the proportion of blacks in the central city was large and if court-ordered busing did not involve suburban school districts. In that case, parents could keep their city jobs and still "escape" from busing by moving to the suburbs. Thus, between 1968 and 1976, 78 percent of the white students left the public schools of Atlanta, while white enrollment in Detroit and San Francisco declined by 61 percent, and Boston "lost" 46 percent of its white students.[44]

It was more difficult to flee if there was only one school district for an entire county, but in a premier case of interdistrict consolidation (New Castle County, Delaware), the number of white students declined by 50 percent after ten years while the number enrolled in private schools increased by one-quarter. Meanwhile, in racially balanced countywide districts with sizeable black populations, the proportion of whites attending private schools generally ranged between 25 and 50 percent (as compared with a national average of about 10 percent).[45]

Experience thus indicated that court-ordered racial balance would not materialize. Often, after judges assigned students to racially balanced schools, parents who thought their children would not benefit from the mixing would evade the court order by sending their children to private schools or by moving to new neighborhoods. In addition, many families with children avoided areas that were under court orders when they moved into metropolitan regions. For one reason or another, it was difficult to sustain racial balance.[46]

The Reagan Justice Department pointed to middle-class flight as one of the reasons why busing was unworkable. "In many communities where courts have implemented busing plans," Attorney General William French Smith declared, "resegregation has occurred." Reynolds said it did not make sense "to put in place something that has been such a failure."[47]

Ronald Reagan emphasized these points during a 1984 campaign speech in Charlotte, North Carolina. In choosing to make his remarks in Charlotte, Reagan picked a city that integrationists frequently mentioned as a prime example of a place where busing worked well. They said Charlotte had experienced a minimum of white flight because its busing plan was countywide and there were no independent suburbs to escape to. Charlotte was also said to be a place where, as journalist Frye Gaillard put it, "test scores were good, and generally getting better, and [where] nobody doubted the intangible advances—those changes in mood and racial climate which...'made Charlotte-Mecklenburg synonymous with trying to do what's right.'" Charlotte was a place where, thanks to busing, whites had learned "that they could live peacefully in the presence of blacks," and a city that "had finally come to terms with the old problems of race."[48]

Reagan thought otherwise. During his visit to Charlotte, he departed from his standard text and criticized Democrats for their support of "busing that takes innocent children out of the neighborhood school and makes them pawns in a social experiment that nobody wants." He reiterated that busing had "failed."[49]

Liberals fumed. The *Charlotte Observer* published an indignant editorial under the headline, "You Were Wrong, Mr. President." Tom Wicker of the *New York Times* and William Taylor of the Center for National Policy Research said Charlotte was only one of several cities where balanced integration was working reasonably well.[50]

But it turned out that Reagan was not off the mark. In 1978, after eight years of busing, 80 percent of Charlotte's black high school juniors, twice the number of whites, failed the minimum competency examinations that were required for high school graduation. An analysis of test-score statistics indicated that "in virtually every category the differential in black and white scores [was] greater" than it had been before busing. In 1991 *Newsweek* reported that crime among black youths had increased to the point where Charlotte was on the verge of becoming a "fortress city." By then, more than thirty new private academies had been established for students who were leaving the public schools.[51]

In 1992 the *New York Times* reported that busing was being "abandoned even in Charlotte." White enrollment had declined from 71 percent of the total to 57 percent. Enrollment in private schools had almost tripled, and "test scores of blacks continue to lag." The public schools were still under a court order to integrate, but 63 percent of the parents thought the busing program should not continue. "We may be number one in integration," one community leader said, "but we have low teacher morale,...and students aren't performing."[52]

IV

According to Ronald Reagan, there was a second major problem with forced busing. It was not just unpopular; it also failed to give blacks a better education.

It was known at the time of *Brown* that blacks, on average, trailed whites in academic achievement, but most educators said this was because most blacks were then taught in grossly inferior schools. It was assumed that blacks would do better after schools were desegregated.

The most substantial support for this assumption came from a report by a team of researchers headed by James S. Coleman. Commissioned by the U.S. Government and published in 1966 under the title, *Equality of Educational Opportunity*, the report presented information on the facilities available at some 4,000 schools and on academic knowledge as measured by tests given to 570,000 students and 60,000 teachers.[53]

The report indicated that many buildings had been upgraded and that by 1966 the equipment and other measurable resources at schools where most students were black were substantially equal to those at mostly white schools. Surprisingly, however, the racial gap in test scores had not narrowed and there was very little difference in the average scores made by blacks, whether they attended schools that were mostly black, mostly white, or mixed in various proportions.

Yet the full impact of these findings was muted because the summary of the study emphasized that black children in predominantly white schools scored slightly higher than other blacks. From this, Coleman concluded that integration was the key to improving the academic performance of disadvantaged blacks. In courtroom testimony and depositions, he touted the benefits that black children would receive from integrated education.[54]

Coleman's research and comments led several judges to conclude that racial balance was constitutionally required to give blacks an equal educational opportunity. In Washington, D.C., Judge J. Skelly Wright wrote that "Negro students' educational achievement improves when they transfer into white or integrated educational institutions." In Charlotte, Judge James M. McMillan mentioned the "alarming contrast in performance" between black and white students, which he said "cannot be explained solely in terms of cultural, racial or family background" and could be reduced by "transferring underprivileged black children from black schools into schools with 70% or more white students." In Denver, Judge William E. Doyle said that racial imbalance was "a major factor producing inferior schools and unequal educational opportunity."[55]

These statements reflected the conventional wisdom of integrationists of the 1960s and early 1970s. By 1975, however, Coleman had concluded that it was a mistake to assume that integration would improve the schoolwork of black children. The blacks who first integrated Southern schools and who provided the basis for Coleman's earlier conclusions were well-motivated volunteers who enrolled under freedom of choice plans and were superior students from families who cared about education. It was simply "wishful thinking," Coleman admitted, to believe that similar academic improvement would result from the massive integration of blacks under court orders.[56]

Sociologist David Armor, an integrationist and once a leader of campus radicals at Berkeley, reached a similar conclusion. After reviewing the best case studies of busing, Armor reported that most of the integrationists' major premises were wrong. Integrationists predicted that achievement would improve as black students moved to integrated schools, but it turned out that there were no significant gains in test scores. Integrationists predicted that busing would enhance interracial harmony, but instead of reducing racial hostility, the mixing of groups with different mores and achievement levels aggravated negative feelings. They predicted that integration would bolster the confidence and aspirations of blacks, but Amor found that the higher academic standards and stiff competition in predominantly white schools had the opposite effect. The one positive finding was that black students who attended predominantly white schools were more likely to attend college and to enroll in what are generally considered higher-quality institutions. But even this was a mixed blessing, because so many of these blacks dropped out of college that they did not graduate at a higher rate than the blacks who had attended predominantly black schools.[57]

In 1975 Nancy St. John, another committed integrationist, also renounced her earlier belief that educational benefits would flow to black children in integrated classrooms. After reviewing 120 studies of the relation between school racial composition and race relations, St. John reported that for every instance in which mixing led to increased interracial friendship, there was another case of both heightened racial tensions and race chauvinism. As for academic achievement, the most that could be said for large-scale integration was that test scores usually did not decline.[58]

Sometimes, however, academic scores did decline. After reading some careful studies, even James S. Coleman thought this was the case. He concluded that what once appeared to be fact—that integration would help blacks without harming whites—turned out to be fiction.[59]

Coleman's recantation stunned integrationists. Scavenging the research literature, they focused attention on studies that depicted integration as a success, minimized the incidence of white flight, and said integration did not damage the academic achievement of whites and "without doubt...improves black academic achievement." Some said that integrated students were "less likely to express negative views about members of the other race and are significantly more comfortable in integrated work and social settings than are black and white graduates of segregated schools," while others said that black and white adults who attended racially balanced schools were more likely to live in integrated neighborhoods and to have personal relationships across the color line.[60]

Although most of these studies were, at best, briefs that brought together the evidence on one side of a controversial question, the major media generally adopted the integrationist line. *Newsweek* told its readers that "educationally, integration has been shown to be at worst harmless and often beneficial. Repeated studies have nearly always reached the same conclusion: black children profit from integration efforts, while white children do not suffer." The *New Republic* mistakenly reported that "research overwhelmingly indicates that blacks in a desegregated environment learn more than their segregated peers, and that white students do not suffer at all."[61]

Even some integrationists, however, acknowledged that there were problems when integration was not "fully and carefully carried out." Research indicated that competition with nonblack students caused integrated blacks to lose self-confidence, but for integrationists, this only underscored the need for careful planning to minimize competition. They said teachers should encourage "cooperative learning" instead of "individualistic or competitive relations among students." Integrationists wanted students to be organized as part of heterogeneous teams, with each pupil given responsibility for part of a group project and with the same grade given to all members of the group. In this way individual grades would be eliminated and children would "spend less time worrying about class rank."[62]

Several problems stemmed from the fact that blacks trailed behind whites in average academic achievement. On standard achievement tests, the average black first-grade student was about one year behind the average white. At age thirteen the average black was almost three years behind the average white, and by age eighteen the differential had increased to more than three years.[63]

This would have caused no educational problems if individual students were grouped with others of similar achievement, or as Thurgood Marshall recommended at the time of *Brown*: "Put the dumb colored children in with the dumb white children, and put the smart colored children with the smart white children." However, by the time of Ronald Reagan's presidency, few integrationists subscribed to this logic. They said that it did not make good sense to have racially imbalanced classes after having gone to all the trouble or busing for integration.[64]

What, then, should be done? Integrationists wanted to place the full range of a given-age cohort in the same class—a practice known as heterogeneous grouping (or *mainstreaming* if it included disabled or retarded youths). In this setting, advanced students could spend part of the day tutoring the slower learners, who would "be inspired to emulate, to understand, and to cherish the bright, [while] the bright...will understand, cherish and learn from them." Some parents feared that heterogeneous classrooms would leave the brighter students bored and the slower children uncomprehending, but integrationists said there would be benefits because teachers would be forced to move toward "individualized" instruction. As a consequence, all students would be liberated from boring lectures by authoritative teachers, and slow learners would feel better because differences in academic performance would not be so obvious when students interacted privately with the teacher rather than publicly.[65]

Integrationists also observed that fast learners inevitably moved ahead of slower students if all received the same amount of time and instruction. Therefore, they recommended an alternative approach known as *mastery learning*—a method that held back fast learners while students who missed items on quizzes were given extra teaching and learning time until they mastered a subject. Some called this the "Robin Hood" approach, taking teaching time from the academically rich and giving it to the academically poor. It appealed to egalitarians because it offered the promise of equality of educational outcomes. To head off criticism, fast learners sometimes received cultural "enrichment"—art, music, field trips—while waiting for slower students to master basic academic subjects.[66]

Of course it was customary to make more capable students wait until slower learners caught up. Even conventional teachers paced their classes so that they would not have to shift to new topics until most students were ready to move on. Mastery theorists, however, proposed to make the process more explicit and to extend the delays to accommodate the bottom 10 percent of the class. When combined with cooperative learning, peer tutoring, and heterogeneous grouping, mastery learning changed the pace of instruction.[67]

As a result, there was less distance between high and low scores on some standardized examinations. Students from the bottom quartile showed slow but steady improvement on the Scholastic Aptitude Test (SAT), with the average score of black students increasing by 49 points during the 1980s alone; but at the same time, top students suffered a dramatic setback. Thanks to an influx of high-scoring Asian American students, the proportion of SAT test takers who scored over 600 in mathematics was the same in 1991 as it had been in 1972 (17.9 percent), but on the verbal portion of the exam the percentage of students scoring over 600 declined from more than 11 percent to less than 7 percent. The actual number of students scoring above 600 or above 700 on the verbal SAT was lower in the early 1990s than it had been twenty years earlier.[68]

Nevertheless, the average SAT score of blacks still lagged more than 150 points behind that of whites, and some integrationists devised more recommendations to cope with the continuing inequality. They said teachers should avoid excessive emphasis on academic subjects and should be judged in terms of their ability to foster "equal status contact between groups." To facilitate good race relations, they recommended that students be seated around large tables rather than at individual desks and urged teachers to plan assignments so that students with different abilities could work together on projects. They said academic honor rolls should be abolished and more emphasis should be placed on extracurricular activities.[69]

There were still more recommendations. In the 1970s the black psychologist Kenneth B. Clark emphasized the importance of the teachers' expectations. He insisted that black students would do better if only their teachers believed they could do well in school (instead of emphasizing that poor black youths had so many cards stacked against them). In the 1980s, after Clark's so-called Pygmalion effect failed to materialize, others promoted multiculturalism and Afrocentrism as methods for improving the self-image and confidence of black students. If the results of integration were disappointing, integrationists said, it was because "real" integration had rarely been tried. They criticized teachers and schools for lagging in the implementation of reforms.[70]

V

Because of resistance from many teachers and schools, the pace of change differed from one place to another, yet in general the new methods that accompanied integration changed the course of educational history in the United States. In the late 1950s and early 1960s, U.S. schools had emphasized academic courses that challenged the brightest students. Then, as the civil rights movement turned from desegregation to integration, identifying the gifted and stimulating high achievement seemed less important than eliminating educational policies that had disparate impact. Black leaders brought their demands to the schools and, as historian Diane Ravitch has noted, "before long the pursuit of excellence was overshadowed by concern about the needs of the disadvantaged." Progressive education enjoyed a renaissance in the 1970s when, as the *Wall Street Journal* observed, "the liberal educational reformers had a running field as open as it ever gets in the public policy game."[71]

Yet by 1980 there was a growing recognition that public education had suffered. Instead of solving complex problems that went beyond the schools, reformers, it seemed, had undermined the quality of academic instruction. This impression was fostered by historical comparisons showing a decline in top- and overall-SAT scores and was reinforced by international comparisons that showed U.S. students lagging behind students of other nations in science and mathematics.

Ronald Reagan thought there was a link between education and productivity, and he feared the economic consequences of a redistribution of trained capability to other nations. His Secretary of Education, Terrel H. Bell, shared the belief that the U.S. economy would decline "if we don't turn around education and make it one of our top national priorities." To "call attention to an alarmingly persistent decline in quality education," Bell decided "to stage an event that would jar the people into action on behalf of their educational system." He set up a National Commission on Excellence in Education, which was given eighteen months to prepare a hard-hitting report that would sound a credible alarm. In a speech made when the commissioners were appointed, Bell indicated that the focus should be on academic standards. "We've been focusing so much on the minimum," he said, "so much on bringing the bottom up...[that] we're not challenging the outer limits of abilities and talents."[72]

The report of the commission, *A Nation at Risk*, did not mince words. It said the United States had "lost sight of the basic principles of schooling, and of the high expectations and disciplined effort needed to attain them." It said the nation's schools had been overloaded with a "multitude of often conflicting demands"; they had been required "to provide solutions to personal, social, and political problems that the home and other institutions either will not or cannot resolve." "[T]hese demands" had exacted "an educational cost as well as a financial one." In memorable language, *A Nation at Risk* declared, "[T]he educational foundations of our society are presently being eroded by a rising tide of mediocrity that threatens our very future as a Nation and a people.... If an unfriendly foreign power had attempted to impose on America the mediocre educational performance that exists today, we might well have viewed it as an act of war. As it stands, we have allowed this to happen to ourselves."[73]

Initially, *A Nation at Risk* enjoyed great influence. Within two years there were a dozen major national reports and almost 150 state-level reports that called, as the dean of one college of education observed, for "the same set of educational reforms: more time devoted to the study of basic core disciplines and more rigorous assessment of the academic achievements of students and their teachers." The nation seemed to be on the road back to basics.[74]

Many of Ronald Reagan's supporters were pleased. They said attempts to group students heterogeneously—"to put potential A's, C's, and failure in the same class...—would result in severe detriment to the educational development of normal and gifted students, and...would drive the normal and gifted into private schools." They said public schools did not push their brightest students "primarily because we fear it will increase inequality and hurt the self-esteem of other children." As a result, they said, "the most talented" were "shortchanged."[75]

The National Commission did not forthrightly discuss the tension between equality and excellence in education. But some observers insisted that students who disrupted the education of others, or those who threatened or assaulted fellow students, had no place in normal schools and should be reassigned to alternative reform schools. While acknowledging that disciplinary policies would punish a disproportionate number of black youths, psychologist Byron M. Roth insisted that children of all races were entitled to orderly schools: "Whenever new and fruitful ideas are brought forward by educational research, none of them can possibly have any impact until they can be implemented in safe and orderly schools."[76]

Still others, such as the editors of the *Chicago Tribune*, insisted that there could be no excellence "without more tracking and ability grouping, without paying more attention to our gifted children, and without accepting the fact that equality of opportunity does not necessarily mean equality of results." The *Tribune* noted that "challenging standards" and "fast track learning opportunities" would be of special benefit to bright black students whose families could not afford to send their children to private schools.[77]

Instead of developing programs for the best and the brightest, the *Tribune* observed, the public schools had taken on "responsibilities for children's nutrition, health, sex education and driver training" as well as for "racial integration and social equality." As a result, the schools' "ability to teach reading, writing, math, science and history" had been "diluted." The *Tribune* said, "If we really want schools that turn out students of high achievement, we should make it clear that teaching academics is their clear priority and make other institutions responsible for pushing all the other social goals."[78]

Many egalitarians, on the other hand, regarded talk about overloading the schools with social responsibilities as code language for racism. Saying that the report of the National Commission was "mediocre," they wrote additional books about the crisis in the classroom.

One tactic of these new writings was to shift away from basic academic subjects and to focus on other matters that *A Nation at Risk* had also mentioned. One example of this was an influential book by Ernest L. Boyer of the Carnegie Foundation that emphasized getting better teachers as the key to improving education. To this end, Boyer recommended that teachers be treated as true professionals, with higher salaries and an end to daily frustrations and petty humiliations.[79]

Other influential reports accused *A Nation at Risk* of exaggerating the extent of the academic decline. Gerald W. Bracey, a researcher for the National Education Association, brushed over the declining performance of top students on the SAT and said that overall, after taking account of the backgrounds of the larger number of students who were taking standard tests, the average performance had not declined. Another researcher who accentuated the positive was Michael W. Kirst of Stanford, who said that, despite deficiencies in elementary and high school, U.S. colleges and graduate schools were as good as any in the world. Kirst asked rhetorically, "Is there a better technical university in Japan or Germany than MIT, Cal Tech, or Stanford?" To Kirst, educational competition did not end at age seventeen, and when postsecondary systems were compared, it seemed that the United States was "like football teams that are behind at half time but catch up with the competition late in the fourth quarter."[80]

Other influential reports by Theodore Sizer and John Goodlad, former deans of education at Harvard and UCLA, also took exception to *A Nation at Risk* and rejected the back-to-basics approach. Still others said *A Nation at Risk* was "elitist," "a xenophobic screed" that addressed only the needs of the bright and academically talented while neglecting students who were disadvantaged, handicapped, or members of racial minorities. Harold Howe II, of Harvard—the former Commissioner of Education who had played an important role in reinterpreting the 1964 Civil Rights Act—lamented that *A Nation at Risk* did not explicitly mention school desegregation. Fred Hechinger, the principal education writer for the *New York Times*, weighed in with additional criticism.[81]

With prominent education writers and researchers either advising different tactics or calling attention to its inadequacies and omissions, *A Nation at Risk* lost its force, and the public schools continued with their emphasis on uplifting the disadvantaged. In time, egalitarians even co-opted the language of *A Nation at Risk* by developing expensive new programs for what were called *at-risk students*—students who were likely to drop out because they were poor, abused, handicapped, addicted to drugs, or suffering from psychological problems. By the 1980s, *equality* had become a dominant cultural value—a value that paradoxically was especially ensconced at elite institutions like the Carnegie Foundation, Harvard University, and the *New York Times*.

During the debate over *A Nation at Risk*, however, some experts broke ranks and said the schools should focus more attention on the academic preparation of college-bound students. They said too many teachers were being judged "by how well they can reach the least-able student in the system, the slowest one in the class." They complained, "Instead of trying to spur children on to set high standards," teachers were "invest[ing] their energies in making sure that slow learners do not come to think of themselves as failures." If schools did not emphasize academic subjects above all, they said, the schools would fail to achieve their own purpose and everything else as well.[82]

By the 1980s such comments had become a mainstay of the rhetoric of the Reagan Right. At one time, however, some civil rights leaders had also emphasized that schools should stress academic subjects. In an article published in 1935, W. E. B. Du Bois had insisted, "[T]he Negro needs neither segregated schools nor mixed schools. What he needs is Education." In an address to the National Education Association, Du Bois expanded on the point.

> Whenever a teacher's convention gets together and tries to find out how it can cure the ills of society there is simply one answer: the school has but one way to cure the ills of society and that is by making men intelligent. To make men intelligent, the school has again but one way, and that is, first and last, to teach them to read, write and count. And if the school fails to do that, and tries beyond that to do something for which a school is not adapted, it not only fails its own function, but it fails in all other attempted functions. Because no school as such can organize industry or settle the matter of wage and income, can found homes or furnish parents, can establish justice or make a civilized world.[83]

By the 1980s, the leaders of the national civil rights organizations had rejected Du Bois's emphasis. They pressed for racially balanced integration (and its attendant educational "reforms"). At the local level, however, many blacks demurred. Disillusioned and frustrated by the failure of integration to improve the quality of education for black children, many parents placed renewed emphasis on neighborhood schools. They said there was an important difference between schools that were black because the neighborhood was black and the institutions created by the forced segregation that existed before *Brown*. Byron Rushing, a black state representative in Massachusetts, gave voice to this opinion when he said, "There's nothing wrong with [black schools] if it's simply a matter of geography." In Atlanta, Gary, Indianapolis, Wilmington, and other cities, local black leaders balked at integration because it caused blacks to lose control over urban school boards they had only recently come to dominate. Polls indicated that about 50 percent of blacks (and more than 80 percent of whites) were opposed to busing for racial balance.[84]

Many blacks resented the notion that sitting in a classroom with whites would improve the education of blacks. They said that whatever benefits some children might obtain from attending more orderly schools would be offset by reinforcing racist stereotypes and by deflecting the attention of blacks away from the importance of hard work and self-reliance. By placing so much emphasis on integration, *Washington Post* columnist William Raspberry observed, black leaders were giving the false impression that learning was "a passive enterprise...something that happens to children." He said that they were using racial imbalance as an excuse, when they should have stressed that black youths could learn, even in mostly black schools, if they had good teachers and worked conscientiously.[85]

Some blacks also complained that their children inevitably bore the brunt of the inconvenience associated with busing. The "optimal mix" called for whites to make up about 75 percent of a school's enrollment, but that meant that blacks would have to be bused into white areas for about nine of the twelve years of public schooling, while whites would be sent into black areas for only three years.

One of the most surprising voices in the chorus of black critics was that of Derrick Bell. A radical law professor who at one time was in charge of dozens of school integration lawsuits for the NAACP, Bell changed his mind in the 1980s. He complained that the rationale for racial balance perpetuated "the demeaning and unproven assumption that blacks must have a majority-white presence in order either to teach or to learn effectively."[86]

Bell also speculated about "the most distressing aspect of school desegregation"—the fact that "few...desegregated districts show black scholastic achievement scores equal to those of whites." Part of the explanation, he felt, was that many integrated blacks felt isolated and rejected in predominantly white schools; but also, Bell thought, because of the threat of white flight, some desegregated schools gave priority to the needs and concerns of whites—things like advanced-placement courses and grouping students by ability—and neglected "the often specialized interests and educational needs of black children."[87]

Bell was vague when it came to defining the "educational needs," but other blacks were specific. One educational psychologist, Spencer Holland, said that black boys from female-headed households would do better if they were taught by black men in all male classes. Another psychologist, Janice Hale-Benson, said blacks had a different learning style—one that preferred inductive to deductive reasoning—and implied that black children were doing poorly in school because they were forced to respond to a white pedagogy. Others pointed to the need for black studies and even an Afrocentric curriculum. Still others said that black English was a distinctive language and that black students were doing poorly because most instruction took place in standard English, a language the students did not fully understand.[88]

Critics observed that many black students avoided intellectual engagement and disparaged academic work as "acting white." Some said this was a response to the rumors of black intellectual inferiority that existed in the larger culture, while others thought it was a defense mechanism for blacks who were forced to compete with better-prepared whites and Asians. One black writer for the *Washington Post* confessed that she had second thoughts about integration after noting the contrast between her own graduation from a predominantly black high school, where blacks received all the honors, and the commencement ceremony at an integrated school in the suburbs, where hardly any awards went to blacks.[89]

William Bradford Reynolds was familiar with the educational questions that were the subjects of discussion and debate in the 1980s and knew that many blacks were against busing. He said, in addition, that middle-class flight had damaged public education by making it more difficult for parents to become involved in school activities and to cooperate with their children's teachers. He also noted that there were instances where white flight was so widespread that integration had led to "racial isolation on a broader scale."[90]

When it came to the effect of desegregation on academic achievement, Reynolds recognized that there was no consensus among experts. He noted, though, that in 1984 the National Institute of Education convened a panel of seven social scientists to review the research on school desegregation and black achievement, and he was well aware of its results. The panel included two scholars whose own research had indicated that integration had positive effects on black achievement; two who had found negative effects; two who discovered no significant effects; and a seventh member who served as a moderator. After reviewing 157 separate studies, only one member of the panel (Robert Crain of Johns Hopkins University) concluded that blacks benefited substantially from integration. Reynolds himself personally believed that the test scores of blacks improved only minimally, if at all, under race-conscious student assignment plans.[91]

Reynolds's expertise was in legal analysis. For him, the social science research was important because the Supreme Court, in its *Swann* decision of 1971, had said that experience should be taken into account in fashioning remedies for discrimination. The *Swann* Court had sanctioned busing as a desegregation technique when particular circumstances warranted its use, but it also said that remedies should be "effective," "reasonable," "feasible," "workable," and "realistic."[92]

As Reynolds saw it, the Supreme Court had written on a blank slate when it first addressed the busing question in 1971. After ten years of experience and the results of hundreds of busing decrees, Reynolds said that it was time to move beyond busing and develop a new, noncoercive approach to school desegregation. He said busing had been "misused, overused, and all-too-often injudiciously used to the considerable detriment of the overall objective of desegregation and the quality of public education." Because busing had "failed so dramatically to live up to the expectations of the social engineers that forced it upon us," he said that it was time "to look elsewhere for a more appropriate and effective response."[93]

Reynolds insisted that the U.S. Government should take action against unlawful discrimination, but because of political realities as well as his own personal views, Reynolds would not pursue either of the approaches that integrationists favored. Reynolds was not about to challenge the legal barricades that the Supreme Court had placed in the way of cross-district, metropolitan busing for racial integration. Nor would he press for closing private schools. Integrationists would not get their hearts' desire during the 1980s.

Integrationists said that Reynolds, when he refused to press for court-ordered busing for racial integration, was "dismantl[ing] the remedies that previous administrations, both Democratic and Republican, have sought and obtained." They accused him of disobeying "the indisputable law of the land." Writing for the Lawyers Committee for Civil Rights, attorney Thomas D. Barr said that the Supreme Court had made it clear that "mandatory measures" were "normal and accepted" remedies. The Court, according to Barr, had said "that voluntary plans were inadequate to fulfill the promise of educational opportunity," and the Court had indicated that forced busing was "absolutely essential to the fulfillment of [the school boards'] constitutional obligation" to desegregate.[94]

John Shattuck of the ACLU agreed. He wrote, "There is no room for debate about what the law requires." To Shattuck, *Green* and its progeny had made two points clear: that freedom of choice plans were inadequate, and that the government had an affirmative obligation to make sure that public schools were integrated. "This is not a dispute over busing," Shattuck wrote. "It is a dispute over the role of government in eliminating discrimination."[95]

Shattuck and Barr did not assess the evidence that forced busing had been generally ineffective and in some ways counterproductive. Nor did they deal with Reynolds's argument that the Supreme Court had merely approved of busing as a permissible tool of school desegregation when it was found to be "practicable," "reasonable," and "feasible." Instead, they said that by rejecting forced busing, Reynolds had shown contempt for the Supreme Court and disrespect for the law.

This was strong criticism, but Reynolds stood his ground. Instead of pressing for forced busing and compulsory attendance at public schools, Reynolds proposed to use incentives to encourage voluntary mixing. Integrationists complained that voluntarism would never lead to enough mixing, but Reynolds insisted that any successful plan would have to take account of the fact that most Americans regarded freedom as a fundamental value. A successful approach would also take cognizance of the social science research on education. Considering everything, Reynolds regarded choice as the key element for any plan that hoped to produce the maximum feasible amount of "actual desegregation."[96]

Notes

1. Swann v. Charlotte-Mecklenburg, 402 U.S. 1 (1971), 26, 27,
2. William Bradford Reynolds, "Renewing the American Constitutional Heritage," *Harvard Journal of Law and Public Policy,* 8 (Spring 1985): 233–34.
3. Ibid., 234.
4. Raymond Wolters, *The Burden of Brown*, 227, 289; James S. Coleman, *Equality and Achievement in Education* (Boulder: Westview Press, 1990), 211, 226.
5. Paul Gewirtz, "Choice in the Transition," *Columbia Law Review*, 86 (May 1986): 736.
6. Swann v. Charlotte-Mecklenburg Board of Education, 402 U.S. 1 (1971), 25 n.9, 26; Green v. County School Board, 391 U.S. 430 (1968), 432.
7. Paul Gewirtz, *Columbia Law Review* 86 (May 1986): 745, 749, 746.
8. Ibid., 751.
9. Ibid., 796, 753.
10. James S. Liebman, "Desegregating Politics: 'All-Out' School Desegregation Explained," *Columbia Law Review*, 90 (October 1990).
11. Ibid., 1597, 1595 and passim.
12. Ibid., 1496, 1617.
13. Jennifer L. Hochschild, *The New American Dilemma: Liberal Democracy and School Desegregation* (New Haven: Yale University Press, 1984), 129, 124, 145, vii, 203.
14. *New Republic* (11 March 1985): 36; Jennifer L. Hochschild, *The New American Dilemma*, 155–56.
15. Ronald P. Formisano, *Boston Against Busing* (Chapel Hill: University of North Carolina Press, 1991), chapter 10 and passim.
16. Jennifer L. Hochschild, *The New American Dilemma*, 156; Ronald P. Formisano, *Boston Against Busing*, 239 (emphasis added); *Columbia Law Review*, 90 (1990): 1639, 1650, 1650 n.801 (quoting John Dewey).
17. James S. Liebman, "Implementing *Brown* in the Nineties," *Virginia Law Review*, 76 (April 1990): 365.
18. Crane Brinton, *A History of Civilization* (New York: Prentice Hall, 1955), vol. 2, 115.
19. William Bradford Reynolds, "The 'Civil Rights Establishment' Is All Wrong," *Human Rights* (Spring 1984): 34; WBR, remarks at the Lincoln Institute, 28 September 1983; remarks at the University of Virginia, 5 October 1983, WBR Papers.

20. See Leon Friedman, ed., *Argument*, passim.
21. Brown v. Board of Education, 347 U.S. (1954) 495, 494.
22. See Charles Black, "The Lawfulness of the Segregation Decision," *Yale Law Journal* 69 (1960): 421; Edmund Cahn, "Jurisprudence," *New York University Law Review*, 30 (1955): 150; Herbert Wechsler, "Toward Neutral Principles of Constitutional Law," *Harvard Law Review*, 73 (1959): 1; Andrew Kull, *The Color-Blind Constitution*, 113–26, 154–55, and passim; Dinesh D'Souza, *The End of Racism*, 192–96.
23. WBR, remarks at the Chautaqua Conference, 30 June 1987; remarks for the National Association for Neighborhood Schools, 10 August 1984; remarks at the University of Virginia, 5 October 1983; remarks at the Lincoln Institute, 28 September 1983 (quoting from a jurisdictional statement that Jack Greenberg prepared for the NAACP in *Anderson v. Martin*, 375 U.S. 399 (1964), WBR Papers.
24. WBR, remarks at Metropolitan Center for Educational Research, 13 September 1984; statement to Subcommittee on Civil and Constitutional Rights, House of Representatives, 19 November 1981, WBR Papers.
25. WBR, remarks at Metropolitan Center for Educational Research, 13 September 1984, WBR Papers.
26. WBR, statement to Subcommittee on Separation of Powers, House of Representatives, 16 October 1981, WBR Papers; Swann v. Charlotte-Mecklenburg, 402 U.S. 1 (1971), 26, 25n, 11, 15, 28, 31.
27. WBR, remarks at Amherst College, 29 April 1983; remarks at Metropolitan Center for Educational Research, 13 September 1984, WBR Papers.
28. WBR, testimony before the Subcommittee on Separation of Powers, Senate Judiciary Committee, 16 October 1981; statement before Subcommittee on Civil and Constitutional Rights, House Judiciary Committee, 19 November 1981, WBR Papers.
29. Ibid.
30. WBR, remarks at the Metropolitan Center for Educational Research, 13 September 1984, WBR Papers.
31. Ibid.; WBR, testimony before the Subcommittee on Separation of Powers, Senate Judiciary Committee, 16 October 1981, WBR Papers.
32. WBR, testimony before the Subcommittee on Separation of Powers, Senate Judiciary Committee, 16 October 1981, WBR Papers; *Human Rights* (Spring 1984): 40.
33. WBR, statement to the Subcommittee on Civil and Constitutional Rights, House Judiciary Committee, 19 November 1981, WBR Papers.
34. Peter Brown, *Minority Party*, 3.
35. Ronald Reagan, *A Time for Choosing*, 185.
36. Peter Brown, *Minority Party*, 11; Thomas Byrne Edsall and Mary D. Edsall, *Chain Reaction*, 164.
37. *National Observer*, 7 June 1975.
38. Ibid.; Brunson v. School Board No. 1, 429 F.2d 820 (1970), 824.
39. *National Observer*, 7 June 1975.
40. Ibid.
41. Ibid.
42. Christine H. Rossell, "School Desegregation and White Flight," *Political Science Quarterly*, 90 (Winter 1975): 688.
43. Christine H. Rossell, *The Carrot or the Stick* (Philadelphia: Temple University Press, 1990), xii, xiv; Diane Ravitch, "The 'White Flight' Controversy," *The Public Interest* (Spring 1978): 146–47; James S. Coleman, *Equality and Achievement in Education*, 168–97.

44. Diane Ravitch, "The 'White Flight' Controversy," *The Public Interest* (Spring 1978): 146–47.
45. Raymond Wolters, *The Burden of Brown*, 246–47. For a description of the situation in two rural areas with countywide school districts, see ibid., 65–127, 129–74.
46. James S. Coleman, *Equality and Achievement in Education*, 213.
47. William French Smith, quoted by WBR, testimony before the Subcommittee on Separation of Powers, Senate Judiciary Committee, 16 October 1981, WBR Papers; *Washington Post*, 5 December 1983, A1b.
48. Frye Gaillard, *The Dream Long Deferred* (Chapel Hill: University of North Carolina Press, 1988), 172–73, 158, 156.
49. Ibid., xv.
50. *Washington Post*, 10 October 1984 A15c (for a reprint of the editorial); *New York Times*, 7 June 1985, 27:2.
51. *New York Times*, 7 June 1985, 27:2; *Wall Street Journal*, 21 January 1985, 22:3; *Newsweek* (10 June 1991): 17.
52. *New York Times*, 15 April 1992, II, 11:1.
53. James S. Coleman, et al., *Equality of Educational Opportunity* (Washington: U.S. Department of Health, Education, and Welfare, 1966); Frederick Mosteller and Daniel P. Moynihan, *On Equality of Educational Opportunity* (New York: Vintage Books, 1972), 5.
54. James S. Coleman, *Equality of Educational Opportunity*, 21; Deposition, 23 July 1966, Civil Action 82-66, U.S. Court of Appeals, Washington, D.C.; Testimony, 5 August 1966, ibid.
55. Hobson v. Hansen, 169 F.Supp. 401 (1967), 420; Swann v. Charlotte-Mecklenburg, 306 F.Supp. 1291 (1969), 1297; Keyes v. School District No. 1, 313 F.Supp. 61 (1970), 81.
56. *National Observer*, 7 June 1975.
57. David Armor, "The Evidence on Busing," *The Public Interest* (Summer 1972): 90–126.
58. Nancy St. John, *School Desegregation: Outcomes for Children* (New York: Wiley, 1975).
59. *National Observer*, 7 June 1975; James S. Coleman, "School Desegregation and City-Suburban Relations," 1978 paper reprinted in *Court-Ordered School Busing: Hearings before the Subcommittee on Separation of Powers, Senate Judiciary Committee*, 97th Congress, 1st Session (1981), 454–59.
60. James S. Liebman, "Desegregating Politics: 'All-Out' School Desegregation Explained," *Columbia Law Review*, 90 (1990): 1624, 1627.
61. *Newsweek* (15 September 1980): 101–2; *New Republic* (24 February 1982): 5–7.
62. Jennifer L. Hochschild, *The New American Dilemma*, 163, 177, 83 and passim; *Newsweek* (10 May 1993): 73.
63. James S. Coleman, *Equality of Educational Opportunity*, 21; Frederick Mosteller and Daniel P. Moynihan, *On Equality of Educational Opportunity*, 14–15; Christopher Jencks, *Inequality* (New York: Basic Books, 1972), 81; Abigail Thernstrom, "The Drive for Racially Inclusive Schools," *Annals of the American Academy of Political and Social Science* (September 1992): 133.
64. Leon Friedman, ed., *Argument*, 402.
65. Carl Hansen, "No Retreat in the Drive for Excellence," typescript in files of the Board of Education, Washington, D.C.; Janet Ward Schofield and H. Andrew

Sagar, "The Social Context of Learning in an Interracial School," in Ray C. Rist, ed., *Desegregated Schools* (New York: Academic Press, 1979), 189.

66. Marshall Arlin, "Time, Equality, and Mastery Learning," *Review of Educational Research* (Spring 1984): 65–86.
67. Ibid.
68. Daniel J. Singal, "The Other Crisis in American Education," *Atlantic Monthly* (November 1991): 60–61 and passim; Frank B. Murray, "The Paradoxes of a University at Risk," in Jan Blits, ed., *The American University* (New York: Prometheus Books, 1985), 108.

    The president of the College Board reported that between 1976 and 1994 the average SAT score of African-Americans increased by 54 points. Donald M. Stewart to *New York Times*, 5 November 1994, 22:4. Also see, David J. Armor, "Why Is Black Educational Achievement Rising?" *The Public Interest* (Summer 1992): 65–80. Richard J. Herrnstein and Charles Murray reported that the number of students who scored 700 or higher on the SAT-Verbal declined by 41 percent, from 17,560 in 1972 to 10,407 in 1993 (despite a larger raw number of students taking the test in 1993 compared to 1972). *The Bell Curve*, p. 428,
69. Jacqueline Scherer and Edward J. Slawski, "Color, Class, and Social Control in an Urban Desegregated School," in Ray C. Rist, ed., *Desegregated Schools*, 117–54; Janet Ward Schofield and H. Andrew Sagar, "The Social Context of Learning in an Interracial School," ibid., 155–99; Jennifer L. Hochschild, *The New American Dilemma*, passim.
70. Raymond Wolters, *The Burden of Brown*, 49–52. There is a large literature on multiculturalism and Afrocentrism; see Molefi Asante and Diane Ravitch, "Multiculturalism: An Exchange," *American Scholar* (Spring 1991): 267–76.
71. Diane Ravitch, *The Troubled Crusade: American Education, 1945–1980* (New York: Basic Books, 1983), 233–34; *Wall Street Journal*, 28 April 1983, 30:1. Also see Robert L. Hampel, *The Last Little Citadel* (Boston: Houghton Miflin Company, 1986), 105, 137, 140 and passim.
72. *U.S. News and World Report*, 18 July 1983, 52; *New York Times*, 25 August 1981, III, 5:1; Terrel H. Bell, *The Thirteenth Man* (New York: The Free Press, 1988), 115.
73. National Commission on Excellence in Education, *A Nation at Risk: The Imperative for Educational Reform* (Washington: The Commission, 1983), 5–6.
74. Frank B. Murray, in Jan Blits, ed., *The American University*, 101–2.
75. *New York Times*, 19 April 1981, IV, 15:3; *Chicago Tribune*, 5 September 1983, 8:1.
76. 76. Byron Roth, *Prescription for Failure*, 337,292. Also see Stewart Purkey and Marshall Smith, Effective Schools: A Review," *Elementary School Journal*, 83 (1993): 427–52.
77. *Chicago Tribune*, 5 September 1983, 8:1.
78. Ibid.
79. Ernest L. Boyer, *High School* (New York: Harper and Row, 1983).
80. *Phi Delta Kappan* (October 1991): 104–17, 118–20; (April 1993): 613–18.
81. Theodore R. Sizer, *Horace's Compromise* (Boston: Houghton Miflin, 1984); John I. Goodlad, *A Place Called School* (New York: McGraw-Hill, 1984); Terrel H. Bell, *The Thirteenth Man*, 134; Harold Howe II, "Education Moves to Center Stage: An Overview of Recent Studies," *Phi Delta Kappan* (November 1983): 167–72; *New York Times*, 2 August 1983, III, 7:1.

82. Daniel Singal, "The Other Crisis in American Education," *Atlantic Monthly*, (November 1991): 67.
83. W. E. B. Du Bois, "Does the Negro Need Separate Schools?" *Journal of Negro Education* (July 1935): 355; Du Bois, quoted by Diane Ravitch, "A Bifurcated Vision of Urban Education," in Jane Newitt, ed. *Future Trends in Educational Policy* (Lexington: Lexington Books, 1979), 80.
84. *Time* (17 December 1990): 102; Raymond Wolters, *The Burden of Brown*, 206, 211; *Georgetown Law Review* (June 1988): 1881; *New York Times*, 2 March 1981, II, 4:1.; Ben J. Wattenberg, *The Real America*, 252; William G. Mayer, *The Changing American Mind*, 24–25.
85. *Washington Post*, 16 September 1985, A17b.
86. Derrick A. Bell, Jr., "A Reassessment of Racial Balance Remedies," *Phi Delta Kappan* (November 1980): 177.
87. Ibid.; Derrick A. Bell, "Learning from Our Losses," *Phi Delta Kappan* (April 1983): 575.
88. *Washington Post*, 2 March 1987, A11d; 18 November 1987, A25b; Abigail Thernstrom, "The Drive for Racially Inclusive Schools," *Annals of the American Academy of Political and Social Science* (September 1992): 135; Joseph Adelson, "What Happened to the Schools?" *Commentary* (March 1981): 37–38.
89. *Washington Post*, 23 September 1985, A16a; 14 March 1987, A1a; 25 March 1987, A23a; 20 April 19986, C1b.
90. WBR, remarks to Metropolitan Center for Educational Research, 13 September 1984, WBR Papers.
91. National Institute of Education, *School Desegregation and Black Achievement* (Washington, 1984); Max Green, "Thinking Realistically About Integration," *New Perspectives* (Fall 1984): 35–36; Sarah Glazer, "Magnet Schools," *Editorial Research Reports* (15 May 1987): 232; WBR, remarks to National Association of Neighborhood Schools, 10 August 1984, WBR Papers.
92. Swann v. Charlotte-Mecklenburg, 402 U.S. 1 (1971), 31.
93. William Bradford Reynolds, "The Reagan Administration and Civil Rights, *University of Illinois Law Review* (1986): 1003.
94. *1985 Senate Hearings*, 240, 244, 245–46, 248.
95. John Shattuck, "Malign Neglect: Reagan vs. Black America," *New Republic* (11 October 1982): 16–19.
96. Ibid; WBR, remarks to Education Commission of the States, 27 September 1981, WBR Papers; Swann v. Charlotte-Mecklenburg, 402 U.S. 1 (1971), 31.

17

Breaking Away

Opposition to forced busing was only one of the educational policies that William Bradford Reynolds implemented for the Reagan administration. It was just the starting point in developing a new plan. In addition, Reynolds fostered *magnet schools* that offered attractive innovations or that focused on special fields like science, foreign languages, or the performing arts. The idea was to appeal to parents who otherwise would be reluctant to send their children to integrated schools. By taking race into account when admitting students to magnet schools, Reynolds hoped to achieve more racial interaction than was possible through forced busing. He regarded magnets as "a reasonable and meaningful alternative" to forced busing ("a policy which we believe has proved ill-advised and ineffective"). By the end of the Reagan years there were 5,000 magnet schools, four times as many as there had been in 1980. Although most school districts were still a long way from achieving balanced integration in every school, the magnets generally were regarded as a worthy innovation.[1]

I
Seattle

In 1981 and 1982, Reynolds modified the position that the Carter administration had already staked out in school-desegregation cases that arose in Seattle, East Baton Rouge, and Chicago. Reynolds's approach to these cases pointed toward the policy he would develop more fully when the Reagan administration initiated and litigated its own school-desegregation cases.

In Seattle, there never had been official discrimination against blacks, but the different ethnic and racial groups were disproportionately concentrated in different neighborhoods. By the mid-1970s, about 63 percent of Seattle's 54,000 public school students were white, with blacks, Asians, Hispanics and native Americans making up the remaining 37 percent. Although students were allowed to transfer from their neighborhood schools if the transfers reduced racial imbalance, the proportion of students at several schools differed from the districtwide average by more than 20 percent. In 1978, to combat racial imbalance, the school board adopted a policy that reassigned entire neighborhoods to achieve ethnic and racial balance. Similar student-assignment policies were also adopted in two other Washington cities, Tacoma and Pasco.

As soon as the race-conscious policy was announced, it ran into opposition from a citizens' group known as CiVIC (Citizens for Voluntary Integration Committee). CiVIC professed to be *for* integration but said a stable racial balance was more likely to be achieved by providing magnet schools that would voluntarily attract students who were interested in a particular specialty or emphasis. There were about 4,000 "voluntary racial transfers" when Seattle established such a program in 1977, and CiVIC urged the school board to allow more time for voluntarism to work. However, the school board proceeded with busing after it calculated that an additional 8,000 transfers would be needed to achieve racial balance throughout the city.[2]

CiVIC then drafted and submitted to the voters at the 1978 general election an initiative that provided that students who did not volunteer to transfer should be assigned to neighborhood schools (unless there was overcrowding, health or safety hazards, or a court order to remedy illegal segregation). The initiative became a state law after it was approved by 66 percent of the voters statewide and by 61 percent of the voters in Seattle.

The Seattle school board, supported by the Carter administration, then challenged the constitutionality of the initiative, and the district court and a divided Ninth Circuit Court held that the new law was unconstitutional. Essentially, the initiative was set aside because the judges thought the voters of Washington were motivated by a malign, discriminatory purpose. Legalistically, the judges said it was illegal to forbid out-of-the-neighborhood assignments for racial reasons while allowing such assignments to deal with nonracial problems such as overcrowding or safety hazards.[3]

Reynolds then asked the Supreme Court to reverse the decision of the lower courts. In doing so, the Reagan administration parted company with the Carter administration—a departure that Reynolds knew would elicit criticism from civil rights stalwarts who considered it anathema for a state to rebuke local school boards that were trying to promote integration. Reynolds recognized, in addition, that his chances on appeal were uncertain, for some of the justices of the Supreme Court were reflexively pro-integration. Nevertheless, Reynolds decided not to duck the case.

Reynolds thought the sponsors of the initiative had a convincing legal argument in that they had significantly allowed for court-ordered busing to non-neighborhood schools if there was a judicial finding of illegal discrimination. This was important because no decision of the Supreme Court had ever required a school district to adopt a mandatory busing policy simply for the sake of racial integration. In the absence of a judicial finding that there had been official racial discrimination that must be remedied by a race-conscious policy—and there had been no such finding in Seattle—Reynolds believed there was nothing unconstitutional about a state policy that assigned children to the nearest neighborhood school.[4]

In addition, Reynolds considered CiVIC an especially congenial group. He liked their name, Citizens *for* Voluntary Integration, and he liked their style, which the district judge praised when he said CiVIC had acted "legally and responsibly...[and] has not directed its appeal to the racial biases of the voters." Reynolds also agreed with several of the arguments that CiVIC put forward: that parents would have more influence if their children attended neighborhood schools; that racial balance by itself would not improve the quality of education; that tax money for education would be better spent on education than on transportation; that forced busing would eventually increase racial imbalance by inducing middle-class flight; and that voluntary magnet schools were the best way to maintain stable, long-term integration.[5]

Nevertheless, in 1982 the Supreme Court ruled against Reynolds and CiVIC. Like the judges of the lower federal courts, a majority of the justices of the Supreme Court divined an unspoken but malign discriminatory purpose in CiVIC. More technically, the Court held that by prohibiting local school boards from assigning students on a race-conscious basis, while leaving local authorities free to develop most other policies without state intervention, the new state law partook of unconstitutional racial discrimination. Critics of the Reagan administration gloated that the Supreme court had "rejected [Reynolds's] position" and hoped the rebuff would dissuade Reynolds from changing other positions that the Carter administration had staked out. But the vote in the Supreme Court was 5–4, and Reynolds continued to believe that, in time, the Supreme Court would recognize the value of voluntary magnet schools.[6]

II
East Baton Rouge

In East Baton Rouge, Louisiana, the controversy over school desegregation went back to the 1950s, when the public schools had been formally segregated. During the 1960s the schools were reorganized, and all students were assigned, without regard to race, to neighborhood schools. By 1970 there was also a majority-to-minority transfer provision that allowed students to transfer from a school in which their race was in the majority to one in which their race was in the minority, but, still, the racial balance varied from school to school because blacks and whites tended to live in different areas.[7]

In 1975, when there were about 70,000 students enrolled in 110 schools, 20 schools were all-black and 2 were all-white. Of the other schools, 40 were 90 percent or more of one race, and another 20 were within 20 percentage points of the districtwide racial mix (65 percent white and 35 percent black).[8]

Despite the racial imbalance, most citizens of East Baton Rouge thought their schools were desegregated. Desegregation did not depend on the number or percentage of black and white children enrolled in particular schools, they said, but on whether there was any policy or concerted effort to use race as a means of preventing children from attending schools in the district of their residence. The city said it had complied with the order of the Fifth Circuit Court, which in 1961 had told East Baton Rouge that "the race or color of the pupil can not be a factor entering into [school] assignment." The city noted also that in 1963 and 1975 the district court had held that the schools of East Baton Rouge were "a unitary, desegregated school system...that is being operated in compliance with the Constitution."[9]

The prevailing sentiment in East Baton Rouge was heartfelt and plausible, but it failed to take account of the evolution and inversion of school-desegregation law. Anticipating the Supreme Court's holdings in *Green* and *Swann,* the Fifth Circuit Court declared in 1966 that local school boards had an "affirmative duty...to furnish a fully integrated education to Negroes as a class." It held that "the duty to desegregate" required more than treating students "on a non-racial basis." It said that "the law imposes...an absolute duty to integrate," that "racial mixing of students is a high priority," and that "a disproportionate concentration of Negroes in certain schools cannot be ignored."[10]

The Fifth Circuit Court also said the law did "not require a maximum of racial mixing." Every school did not have to achieve "a racial balance accurately reflecting the racial composition of the community."[11]

Thus there was considerable ambiguity about what was required. For example, in 1967 one judge (and the future attorney general), Griffin Bell, said that the law of school desegregation was couched in so much "vagueness" that it was impossible to understand. However, in 1978, in the East Baton Rouge litigation, a panel of three judges from the Fifth Circuit Court overturned the district court's decision that the schools were "desegregated...[and] in compliance with the Constitution." Instead, the circuit court ordered the local authorities to achieve more racial integration in the schools.[12]

To achieve more integration, the Carter administration proposed a plan that District Judge John V. Parker characterized as "a classic pair 'em, cluster 'em, and bus 'em plan." The essence of the plan was to match predominantly white and black schools and then bus the children so that all the instruction at a particular grade level would occur in only one school. If all first graders attended one school and all second graders another, the government planners explained, racial balance would be achieved. Under the Carter plan, students who stayed in the system from first grade through high school would attend as many as eight different schools.[13]

Judge Parker rejected the Carter plan, saying it was not advisable for children to be "constantly changing schools throughout their educational process." Parker also noted that the Carter plan required busing "for long distances over...some of the most dangerous traffic arteries in the State of Louisiana." He said there was nothing in the evolving jurisprudence of school desegregation that required children to be treated "as so many sticks of black and white dots to be shifted around and around in order to satisfy some mostly illusory racial numbers game." A three-judge panel from the Fifth Circuit Court then affirmed Judge Parker's decision.[14]

The school board was willing to take some affirmative steps. It offered to pair a few schools, cluster a few more, adjust some attendance boundaries, and establish a number of magnet schools to foster integration without coercion. But the school board feared that extensive mandatory reassignments would cause an exodus of white students. One attorney expressed the prevailing apprehension when he predicted that forced busing would lead to a resegregated situation where there would be "two school systems—a private school system and a public school system."[15]

Judge Parker eventually decided that the school board's proposal was as unacceptable as that put forward by the Carter administration. There was no assurance, Parker said, that "a neighborhood school-voluntary magnet plan" would achieve what the Supreme Court had in mind when it said that segregation must be eliminated "root and branch." Therefore, Parker fashioned his own plan to achieve a proper racial balance for East Baton Rouge. In May, 1981, he closed fifteen elementary schools, paired six schools, and lumped thirty-five others into ten clusters.[16]

Like most compromises, Parker's plan came in for criticism. Outraged white parents staged protest marches through Baton Rouge, while black parents complained about the closing of schools in black neighborhoods. Many whites transferred to private schools, while the NAACP complained that even Judge Parker (who confessed that he was concerned about white flight) had left eleven elementary schools with enrollments that were predominantly of one race.[17]

Reynolds was also unhappy with the court order in Baton Rouge. He had approved when Judge Parker rejected the Carter plan, but he thought Parker was mistaken to disallow the school board's magnet plan, and he was especially disturbed when 7,000 white students (about 21 percent of the white total) withdrew from the public schools during the year after Parker's plan was handed down. Reynolds recognized that the fear of white flight was no justification for shirking the constitutional duty to desegregate public schools, but he also recalled that the Supreme Court, while requiring "every effort to achieve the greatest possible degree of actual desegregation," also counseled that court orders should be "reasonable," "feasible," and "workable."[18]

As Reynolds saw it, the problem with Judge Parker's order was not that it countenanced race consciousness, for the Supreme Court had mistakenly established the legality of such an approach. The problem was that Parker had imposed a plan that was so widely perceived as unfair that thousands of whites were leaving the public schools of East Baton Rouge, thereby making it impossible to achieve the professed goal of a better racial balance. Reynolds thought this was unnecessary as well as nonsensical, since stable integration could be achieved by skillfully establishing voluntary magnet schools.

Consequently, Reynolds took the unprecedented step of asking the Fifth Circuit Court not to review the East Baton Rouge case until after the Civil Rights Division had an opportunity to confer with Judge Parker. Reynolds wanted to show the judge how "voluntary incentives, attractive to parents" could desegregate the schools "more effectively than the measures presently in effect." To assist in this task, Reynolds hired Professor Christine H. Rossell to draft an ingenious plan to achieve desegregation by luring liberal and higher-social-class whites into black neighborhoods (where Montessori-type schools would be featured) and by inducing working-class black parents to send their children to white neighborhoods (where fundamental, back-to-basics schools would be set up).[19]

Reynolds had trouble selling the plan in the Civil Rights Division, where some career lawyers were still seething because Reynolds had refused to support the Carter plan—the "pair 'em, cluster 'em, and bus 'em" plan—when it was before the trial court. Two attorneys were reassigned after they said they would be embarrassed to present Professor Rossell's plan, but Reynolds found other lawyers who took on the case. For his part, Judge Parker was eager to consider the new approach.[20]

However, Reynolds dropped the Rossell plan early in 1983. The problem was not with the NAACP, which predictably said the plan was "unconstitutional"; Reynolds backed away from the plan because the school board of East Baton Rouge asked for more time to consider the proposal. "We just couldn't convince those people that the courts would insist on some form of race-conscious affirmative action," said Mike Carvin, one of Reynolds's deputies. "They continued to say that 'racial neutrality' was enough and that *Brown* had decreed that students should be assigned on a 'racially nondiscriminatory' basis."[21]

Faced with stalling by the local school board, Reynolds withdrew the proposal. "We continue to believe that the constitutional requirement of desegregating schools can be better achieved without the disruptive and counterproductive use of forced transportation," Reynolds said, but he thought that "for us to have any chance to get [Judge Parker] to accept this approach," there had to be "a firm commitment from the school board." Since that was not forthcoming, Reynolds saw no point in proceeding, saying, "We have insisted from the outset that a school board's commitment is the vital ingredient in implementing an educational incentive plan, and...that we would decline to proceed in court without such a commitment."[22]

It was embarrassing for Reynolds to withdraw the plan. But the East Baton Rouge case was not a complete loss, for it gave the Reagan administration the opportunity to signal its opposition to forced busing and to develop voluntary alternatives.

For public education in East Baton Rouge, the result was equivocal. Under Judge Parker's plan, the white proportion of the student body declined from the 65 percent it had been in 1975, when the lawsuit began, to 47 percent in 1993. By then, academic standards at many schools had declined and, according to Ken Sills, an attorney for the school board, the parish had developed "a new and different form of segregation"—with private schools for those who were white and affluent and public schools for others.[23]

III
Chicago

Chicago's public schools were not formally segregated prior to *Brown,* but after 1960 the situation there was similar to that in Baton Rouge. Because blacks and whites tended to live in different parts of the city, because the well-to-do kept their distance from the impoverished, and because children were assigned to neighborhood schools, the public schools were desegregated but the enrollments were not balanced in terms of race or class.

The Board of Education of Chicago thought there was nothing illegal about this. *Brown* said that it was unconstitutional "to separate [blacks] from others...solely because of their race," thereby implying that it was no concern of the Constitution if students did not mix because of economic or other nonracial considerations that produced a disparate pattern of residential settlement.[24]

Newspaper coverage in Chicago reported that there were sound educational reasons for assigning children to neighborhood schools. About 15 percent of the public money for education in rural and suburban areas was spent on transportation, but in urban areas with neighborhood schools, that money could be used for programs that were directly related to education. Parents also found it easier to make their influence felt in neighborhood schools, which often were cultural centers that reinforced the prevailing values of the community.

In the late 1950s and early 1960s, when whites still made up a majority of the students in Chicago, the school superintendent, Benjamin Willis, built scores of schools smack in the middle of racially concentrated neighborhoods. Had Willis considered integration more important than community, he would have chosen sites on the boundaries of diverse neighborhoods, but Willis strongly believed in neighborhood schools. Instead of adjusting boundaries or transferring students when neighborhood schools could not keep up with the growth of population in their vicinity, Willis set up trailer-like mobile units (which critics derisively dubbed "Willis wagons") in the school yards.[25]

U.S. education commissioner Harold Howe II barred federal education funds from Chicago in 1965, on the grounds that Willis's policies were a spurious form of racial discrimination. However, President Lyndon B. Johnson, after conferring with Chicago's Mayor Richard J. Daley, restored the money. It was not until 1979 that Howe's interpretation finally prevailed. As a condition for continued federal aid, the Carter administration insisted that Chicago must take affirmative steps to achieve more racial mixing. When Chicago balked at busing, the matter was referred to the Department of Justice. A lawsuit was scheduled for trial in September 1980.[26]

By 1980, however, thousand of blacks had moved into Chicago while an even larger number of whites left the city. This caused public school enrollments to shift to the point where the black proportion of the overall student enrollment increased to 61 percent while the white proportion declined to 18 percent. In view of the racial percentages, some people thought the emphasis on racial balance was, as the *Chicago Tribune* declared, "more than a little ridiculous." Mayor Jane Byrne was adamantly opposed to forced busing, as were ethnic aldermen like Roman Pucinski of the 41st Ward in Northwest Chicago. Nor was opposition confined to the city. Attorney General William French Smith seemed to have Chicago in mind when he said that desegregation plans should be "tailor[ed]...to the facts of each case" and should emphasize programs "that actually improve the quality of education."[27]

The Carter administration had recognized that there were limits to the amount of integration that could be achieved when only 18 percent of the students were white. Although the administration formally demanded the mandatory reassignment of one-fourth of Chicago's 450,000 public school students, it was willing to settle for less. The local authorities also favored compromise. Consequently, on 24 September 1980, just as the Carter administration's case against Chicago was set to go to trial, the administration and the local school board negotiated a consent decree. The administration dropped its lawsuit, and the school board agreed to develop and implement "a system-wide plan to remedy the effects of past segregation of black and Hispanic students in Chicago."[28]

Most members of the school board were of two minds. On the one hand, they wanted to resist the Carter administration. They disputed the practice of calling a school with a racially mixed enrollment "segregated" if its mixture departed from the systemwide racial ratio by more than 15 or 20 percentage points. They continued to believe that a segregated school was one from which some pupils were excluded because of their race. They thought desegregation law had gone badly wrong when it turned from state-imposed separation to mandatory mixing. They decried the notion that desegregation required, in addition to not keeping pupils out of any school because of race, the assignment of children because of their race to achieve a more even racial balance throughout the city's public schools.[29]

Yet they also knew that, because of the *Keyes* presumption, forced busing had been imposed on several other cities "when any evidence of past discrimination could be found, no matter how dated or isolated." They thought, in addition, that Chicago was "not going to reverse 25 years of accumulating federal case law on school desegregation." Consequently, when Chicago's turn in court was about to come, the school board accepted a consent decree that, it hoped, would get the Department of Justice off its case with a minimum of disruption to the public schools.[30]

Some of the school board's optimism derived from its understanding that Robert L. Green, a black dean at Michigan State University, would serve as the chief consultant in developing a new desegregation plan. Generally regarded as a liberal in the school-desegregation field, Green was a competent scholar with a quiet demeanor. He was also a man who was more concerned with improving the quality of public education than with achieving racial balance. He said that teachers should set high standards for students, that parents must become involved in the learning process, and that desegregation offered the opportunity to achieve "widespread school reform at one shot." Because of Robert L. Green, wrote Casey Banas, the education editor of the *Chicago Tribune*, "Chicago has an excellent opportunity to improve its public schools."[31]

Green feared that the federal courts would withhold approval if his plan either rejected busing or allowed for the continuation of predominantly white neighborhood schools. Therefore, to make sure that whites made up no more than 65 percent of the enrollment at any school, Green proposed the forced busing of some 24,500 students (as compared with 114,000 who would have been bused under the plan the Carter administration had proposed).[32]

Green's plan came in for criticism from blacks like Herbert Martin, the executive director of the Chicago branch of the NAACP, who declared, "It does not go far enough." Martin asked, "How do they justify schools remaining 65 percent white when whites constitute only 18 percent of the school population?" Saying that racial isolation should be ended by requiring that every public school in Chicago must have a majority of "minority" pupils, Martin either disregarded the likelihood of white flight or preferred an enrollment that would be almost all-black.[33]

Green's plan was also criticized by whites who favored neighborhood schools. "I don't think it's good for children," Mayor Byrne said, and Alderman Pucinski confessed that he had "some problems." Green's plan allowed more than 200 schools to remain almost all-black even as it prescribed that no school could be more than 65 percent white. Pucinski asked, "Where is it written in the great book that they can have 200 schools with only black children and not have any school more than 65 percent white?"[34]

Considering the demographics and the case law on school desegregation, Green's proposals were moderate and restrained. The plan also called for twenty-three magnet schools and thirty-five magnet programs to promote desegregation. Some prospective magnets would be high schools that specialized in science or the performing arts; others were elementary schools that would be converted into "scholastic academies" where principals would have the authority to expel unruly students and parents would sign a contract agreeing to abide by school rules on homework, discipline, and dress code. In addition, Green called for expensive new programs at schools that, because of the preponderance of black students, would remain almost all-black even after "desegregation."[35]

Most moderates supported Green's plan, not because they thought it was preferable to neighborhood schools but because they feared that something even more damaging might be imposed by a federal judge. Yet such a position, while arguably a sound legal strategy, had no political appeal. With integrationists and partisans of neighborhood schools both taking exception to the amount of mandatary reassignment that Green had proposed, the school board rejected Green's plan in April 1981. Alderman Pucinski expressed the view of many white critics when he said, "We'll take our chances with the Reagan administration."[36]

Pucinski's faith was not misplaced. In cooperation with Reynolds and his deputies, the school board in Chicago prepared a 276-page plan for submission to District Judge Milton I. Shadur. The strategy was to promote voluntary mixing, largely by emphasizing educational programs designed to appeal to children of all races, and thereby avoiding mandatory measures that required busing. Reynolds predicted that this "first urban *voluntary* desegregation remedy" would lead to "a greater degree of desegregation in Chicago than could have been accomplished under a mandatory busing plan."[37]

The revised plan kept Robert Green's proposal for "scholastic academies"—with added provisions that parents would be required to visit the schools regularly, and teachers to visit the students' homes. The new plan increased the number of magnet schools that would specialize in a particular area—with the state superintendent of education predicting that the schools "would be so good that suburban students would bang on the doors to get in." Thr revised plan also retained Green's emphasis on establishing special programs at schools where the enrollment remained disproportionately black.[38]

The new plan promised that by 1983 whites would make up no more than 70 percent of the enrollment at any public school, but, departing from the approach favored by both the Carter administration and Robert Green, the new plan disavowed forced busing. It proposed to rely entirely on voluntary measures, with Reynolds reiterating that it would "produce more desegregation, and stable desegregation at that, than a mandatory busing program."[39]

Integrationists were irate. Roger Fox of the Urban League said that the plan did not go far enough to remedy the history of segregation in Chicago. Gary Orfield, then a professor at the University of Chicago, lamented that the plan left too many blacks racially "isolated." "It is really not much of a desegregation plan at all," Orfield said. "All it will accomplish, perhaps, is to increase the number of minority students in those schools which are still virtually all white on the city's Northwest and Southwest sides." Thomas Atkins of the NAACP said it was "a white appeasement plan," with "the message" that segregationists should "just stall and stall and wait long enough until you get your friends in the Justice Department, and then kill affirmative action and desegregation."[40]

Because of this criticism, the school board and the Civil Rights Division must have felt trepidation when their plan was presented to District Judge Shadur. Before President Carter appointed him to the bench, Shadur had been one of the organizers of the Lawyers' Committee for Civil Rights. In the 1960s he had worked for civil rights legislation in Illinois under the aegis of the American Jewish Congress. In the 1970s he had filed an amicus brief in support of the leaders of the Black Panther Party. He had also been one of the lead lawyers in a controversial lawsuit that demanded the construction of public housing in prosperous white neighborhoods.[41]

Nevertheless, Judge Shadur found for Reynolds and the school board on every disputed point. Their plan was "not only adequate to pass constitutional muster," Shadur wrote; it was "reasoned and reasonable."[42]

Shadur's rationale corresponded with Reynolds's legal arguments. Reynolds rejected the position of the NAACP, which demanded "racial balance in all schools" or, as a fallback, "a mandatory minimum percentage of black enrollment for all schools." He also eschewed the rhetoric of the Carter administration, which had asserted that racial imbalance was "educationally disadvantageous to all students" and that all would benefit from "the greatest practicable reduction in racial isolation."[43]

Instead, Reynolds focused on the amount of integration that could reasonably be achieved in view of an enrollment that by 1983 was only 16 percent white, seeking to increase racial mixing through the lure of magnet schools and innovative programs rather than by the coercion of forced busing. He acknowledged that a number of schools would inevitably remain almost all-black, but said little could be done about that except to upgrade the quality of education in those schools. He insisted that the forced dispersion of whites in predominantly black schools would not produce more racial interaction than voluntary measures but, rather, would stimulate white flight. He reminded the court that the racial composition of the Chicago schools did not and would not depend solely on decisions by the school board or the U.S. government, as, in the United States, parents were still free to decide what was best for their children.[44]

Judge Shadur agreed. He admitted that "concerns as to white flight" could not be allowed "to impair constitutional rights," and he understood that many civil rights activists thought it was unconscionable for the Chicago school system, "with fewer than 20% of its students white, [to] view a school as 'integrated' if it drew as many as 70% of its students from that small white pool." But Shadur was convinced that an even dispersion of whites would cause an exodus that would damage the prospects for any sort of integration. Given the overwhelming majority of blacks in Chicago, Shadur observed, the purpose of desegregation had changed. The objective was no longer to break down the isolation of blacks and mix them with whites; it was to ensure that whatever whites remained in the system mixed with minority children.[45]

For a while after Shadur approved the Reynolds-Chicago plan, all seemed to work well. In November 1983 the school board achieved its goal of having minorities make up at least 30 percent of the enrollment in every school. Achievement test scores rose, with average scores in the magnet schools exceeding the national average and scores in other schools improving even as they lagged the national norms. A few thousand students left private and parochial schools to enroll in magnet schools, and the number of white students dropped at a slower rate than at any time since the 1960s. "The student enrollment decline has virtually halted and 'white flight' has subsided," school superintendent Ruth B. Love said in 1984. "I feel we have a growing confidence in our school system."[46]

The editors of Chicago's leading newspaper sang the praises of the plan. The magnet schools were "accomplishing what they were intended to do," the *Tribune* declared. "They have lured students of all racial and ethnic groups into voluntarily integrated schools without the whip of court-ordered busing." Many public schools admittedly remained almost all-black; but the small number of whites precluded any other possibility, and the editors commended the school board for working conscientiously to upgrade the quality of education "in schools that remain racially isolated."[47]

Even critics of the magnet plan, such as education writer Casey Banas, conceded that the magnets provided "a superior and integrated education." In 1983 the overall enrollment in Chicago's magnet schools was 17 percent Hispanic, 27 percent white, and 52 percent black.[48]

Within a few years, however, the initial optimism was dashed. In 1988, when U.S. Secretary of Education William Bennett called Chicago's schools "the nation's worst," no leading local official challenged him. An alarming 45 percent of the students did not graduate from high school, and only 7 percent of those who were in high school scored above the national average in reading. Meanwhile, the proportion of whites in the total student enrollment declined to 12 percent.[49]

Poverty and a tangle of social problems were partially responsible for the situation. But attention to socioeconomic factors should not obscure other important considerations. In 1988 school superintendent Manfred Byrd ascribed the problems to "underfunding," but that was doubtful in view of the fact that Chicago, with an annual expenditure of $4,672 per pupil, was spending more than thirty-one of the fifty largest school systems in the nation, and $600 more than the statewide average in Illinois.[50]

Reynolds thought a bloated educational bureaucracy deserved some of the blame for the problems in Chicago. Between 1976 and 1986, as total student enrollment declined by 18 percent, the number of employees providing *support services* increased by 47 percent, and the number of teachers assigned to administrative work in the central and district offices rose by 30 percent. By 1988, when 420,000 students were enrolled in the public schools, the school board employed approximately 3,300 people in the central and district offices, while the Catholic schools of Chicago managed to educate more than 160,000 students with only 32 central office administrators. It seemed to Reynolds that there would be no significant improvement in the public schools unless the bureaucracy was cut drastically.[51]

Reynolds's criticism of the bureaucracy was muted since it did not involve legal issues. The same cannot be said about another dispute that pitted Reynolds against a former ally, Judge Shadur, a dispute revolving around the meaning of a provision of the consent decree that the Carter administration and the Chicago school board had negotiated in 1980. Paragraph 15.1 provided that "[e]ach party is obligated to make every good faith effort to find and provide every available form of financial resources adequate for the implementation of the desegregation plan."

The school board said this provision required the federal government to pay for a substantial portion of the expenses related to desegregation—that is, some of the expenses incurred in starting the magnets; in supplementing educational programs in the schools that remained disproportionately black; and in giving workshops, seminars, and courses to help teachers and administrators deal with the academic, social, and disciplinary problems that went with integration.[52]

In 1983 the school board asked Judge Shadur to find that the consent decree required the federal government to pay for desegregation expenses that the board did not have the wherewithal to cover. "This is different from a school system's hoping the federal government will give it money," an attorney for the school board stated. "We have a contract with the federal government under the consent decree; we have done our part, and they haven't done theirs." An associate superintendent explained that Chicago was "concerned because even though our plan seems to fit so well with what the Reagan administration wants [no forced busing] and is touted throughout the nation as the way to do it, we still don't have any federal money for it."[53]

Judge Shadur agreed. He calculated that Chicago had spent $120 million on the desegregation plan, while the U.S. Government had provided only $9 million. Shadur then ordered the Reagan administration to set aside $250 million to fund desegregation in Chicago for five years, beginning in 1983. He ordered the administration, in addition, to lobby Congress to provide additional funds for education.[54]

Shadur's anger was evident. Rather than take "affirmative step[s]...to find and provide adequate financing for the [desegregation] Plan," he complained, the Reagan administration had proposed spending cuts and even the abolition of the Department of Education. According to Shadur, these policies flouted the "contractual undertaking" of the United States He held that the Reagan administration had failed to consider "its obligations under the Consent Decree in general and under Section 15.1 in particular."[55]

Judge Shadur had kept his personal biases in check during the early stages of the litigation. As noted, he approved the Reynolds-Chicago plan to achieve desegregation through magnets and without forced busing, but after that, Shadur's liberal views came to the fore. When the Reagan administration appealed his orders to provide $250 million and to lobby Congress for additional money, Shadur said the administration had "willfully ignored the orders of this Court" and was acting in "bad faith." Because of this, Shadur held that the obligation of the U.S. government was no longer to be measured by the availability of funds, but by the "unmet needs" of the Chicago school board.[56]

When he went to the Seventh Circuit Court to contest Shadur's decision, Reynolds emphasized an important legal distinction: what did it mean,

Reynolds asked, when the United States promised "to find and provide every available financial resource adequate for the implementation of the desegregation plan"? Judge Shadur had said "available" was "simply a term of emphasis" or perhaps a tautology. "After all," Shadur wrote, "by definition 'unavailable' financial resources could not be provided." For Shadur, the language of the consent decree obliged the U.S. government to provide whatever was needed to pay for desegregation in Chicago. By way of contrast, Reynolds said that *available* was a term of limitation, and the United States was obliged to provide Chicago, as it had already done, only with a fair portion of the funds that Congress had made "available" for desegregation. His position was that the consent decree had not obligated the United States to provide funds, but only to assist Chicago in locating funds that Congress appropriated for school districts that were undergoing desegregation.[57]

Reynolds reminded the court of appeals that the U.S. government had been the plaintiff against Chicago, alleging that Chicago's schools were being operated in violation of the Constitution. No claim had been made against the United States, and if the case had gone to trial, Reynolds pointed out, a court could not have entered any judgment against the United States. It was not credible to assume, as Judge Shadur had done, that the government had ineptly written a blank check or had "bargain[ed] away the constitutional prerogatives of the President to recommend legislation to Congress." He stated that when it accepted the consent decree, the government had no intention of giving either the district judge or the school board the power to dictate public policy. From the start, Reynolds said, the government's position had been that while the school board would qualify for some federal program assistance, the Constitution required the board to bear the responsibility for desegregating its schools.[58]

There was much more in Reynolds's legal briefs and oral arguments. He waxed on about Judge Shadur's disregard for "the fundamental doctrine of Separation of Powers." He said Shadur's orders were "an unprecedented intrusion" into functions the Constitution assigned to the chief executive and to the Congress. He complained that Shadur had "usurped" powers that did not properly belong to the judiciary.[59]

Reynolds carried the day. On 30 November 1984, a unanimous panel of judges from the Seventh Circuit Court found for the government on every important point. Judge Shadur's opinion and order were vacated and, in an unusual move, the appellate court ordered that a new judge should take over the case. If Reynolds had a trophy case in his office, it would contain the scalp of Milton I. Shadur.[60]

Thus *Chicago* was a triumph for Reynolds. He persuaded the Chicago school board, the local district court, and the Seventh Circuit Court of Appeals to reject mandatory reassignments and to embrace magnets and choice as a better way to achieve school desegregation. He also protected the prerogatives of the president and beat back an effort to saddle the U.S. government with expenses that previously had devolved on local authorities. Unfortunately, things did not end so well for the public schools of Chicago, which remained among the worst in the United States.

Notes

1. WBR, Statement to House Judiciary Committee, 19 November 1981, WBR Papers; *U.S. News* (27 May 1991): 58, 60.
2. Seattle School District v. State of Washington, 473 F.Supp. 996 (1979), 1006; Rex E. Lee and William Bradford Reynolds, Brief for the United States, State of Washington v. Seattle School District, 4-5, Supreme Court Library.
3. Seattle School District v. State of Washington, 473 F.Supp. 996 (1979); 633 F.2d 1338 (1980).
4. Rex E. Lee and William Bradford Reynolds, Memorandum for the United States, State of Washington v. Seattle School District, Supreme Court Library; Lee and Reynolds, Brief for the United States, ibid.
5. Seattle School District v. State of Washington, 473 F.Supp. 996 (1979), 1009; Rex E. Lee and William Bradford Reynolds, Brief for the United States, State of Washington v. Seattle School District, 7, Supreme Court Library.
6. Washington v. Seattle School District, 458 U.S. 457 (1982); 1985 Senate Hearings, 251; *New Republic* (11 October 1982): 16–19; Norman C. Amaker, *Civil Rights and the Reagan Administration* (Washington: The Urban Institute Press, 1988), 35–36.
7. Davis v. East Baton Rouge, 721 F.2d 1425 (1983), 1429; *New Orleans Times Picayune*, 12 January 1981,15:1.
8. Davis v. East Baton Rouge, 398 F.Supp. 1013 (1975); 570 F.2d 1260 (1978), 1263.
9. East Baton Rouge v. Davis, 287 F.2d 380 (1961), 381; Davis v. East Baton Rouge, 219 F.Supp. 876 (1963); 398 F.Supp. 1013 (1975), 1018.
10. United States v. Jefferson County Board of Education, 372 F.2d 836 (1966), 846–47, 846–47 n.5.
11. Ibid.
12. U.S. v. Jefferson County Board of Education, 380 F.2d 385 (1967), 410–11; Davis v. East Baton Rouge, 570 F.2d 1260 (1978), 1261.
13. Davis. v. East Baton Rouge, 514 F.Supp. 869 (1981), 873.
14. Ibid., 886; 721 F.2d 1425 (1983).
15. John F. Ward, quoted in *New Orleans Times Picayune*, 23 May 1981, 12.1.
16. Davis v. East Baton Rouge, 514 F.Supp. 869 (1981), 874, 871, 873; *New Orleans Times Picayune*, 5 May 1981, 1:1.
17. *New Orleans Times Picayune*, 28 June 1981, 32:1; 10 May 1981, 16:3; 26 May 1981, 14:1.
18. Davis v. East Baton Rouge, 721 F.2d 1425 (1983), 1437–38; *New Orleans Times Picayune*, 10 August 1982, 13:1; Swann v. Charlotte-Mecklenburg, 402 U.S. 1 (1971), 26, 31.
19. *New Orleans Times Picayune*, 10 August 1982, 13:1; 20 January 1983, 18:1; Davis v. East Baton Rouge, 721 F.2d 1425 (1983), 1434.

20. *New Orleans Times Picayune*, 20 January 1983, 18:1; 18 December 1982, 16:3.
21. *New Orleans Times Picayune*, 18 December 1982, 16:3; interview with Mike Carvin, 2 March 1983.

    Carvin and Reynolds's explanation differed from that of Professor Rossell. What really happened, she said, was that Reynolds was "bamboozled" by some of the "old style civil rights lawyers who opposed magnets and favored forced busing." In particular, she mentioned Franz Marshall, a black career attorney in the Civil Rights Division. Rossell said Marshall, after noting that a minority of the school board still opposed the magnet plan, convinced Reynolds that Judge Parker would not accept magnets unless the board was unanimous in its support for the plan. Interview with Christine Rossell, 24 March 1993.
22. *New Orleans Times Picayune*, 19 February 1983, 1:5.
23. Interview with Ken Sills, 24 March 1993.
24. Brown v. Board of Education, 347 U.S. 483 (1954), 494.
25. *Chicago Tribune*, 25 July 1984, 2:1.
26. *Chicago Tribune*, 7 January 1983, 2:3; Rex E. Lee and William Bradford Reynolds, Brief for the United States, U.S. v. Board of Education of Chicago, 5–7, Supreme Court Library.
27. *Chicago Tribune*, 23 February 1981, V, 2:1; 4 April 1981, 1:4; U.S. v. Board of Education of Chicago, 588 F.Supp. 132 (1984), 146.
28. *Chicago Tribune*, 5 April 1981, II, 4:1; U.S. v. Board of Education of Chicago, 717 F.2d 378 (1983), 380.
29. These views were also expressed in the editorials of the *Chicago Tribune*, 2 March 1981, 8:1; 5 April 1981, II, 4:1; 8 April 1981, VI, 2:1; 11 April 1981, III, 2:1.
30. *Chicago Tribune*, 11 April 1981, III, 2:1; 8 April 1981, VI, 2:1
31. Ibid., 14 January 1981, V, 2:6; 22 April 1981, 22:1.
32. Ibid., 3 April 1981, 1:6.
33. Ibid., 4 April 1981, 1:4.
34. Ibid., 3 April 1981, 1:6.
35. Ibid., 6 April 1981, 2:3; 12 December 1982, 14:1.
36. Ibid., 17 April 1981, 15:1; 7 April 1981, 1:2.
37. Ibid., 3 January 1982, 18:1; WBR, remarks to the House Judiciary Committee, 5 April 1982, WBR Papers.
38. *Chicago Tribune*, 3 January 1982, 18:1;; 1 February 1982, 9:4.
39. Ibid., 13 February 1982, 1:4.
40. Ibid., 7 January 1983, 2:1; 8 February 1983, 3:2; 12 January 1983, 19:1.
41. Ibid., 14 January 1983, 19:1.
42. U.S. v. Chicago Board of Education, 554 F.Supp. 912 (1983), 919.
43. Ibid., 923, 922; *Chicago Tribune*, 28 March 1981, 1:8.
44. *Chicago Tribune*, 8 January 1983, 1:6; WBR, Brief for the United States, U.S. v. Chicago Board of Education, case 80-C-5124, 1982, U.S. District Court, Chicago.
45. U.S. v. Chicago Board of Education, 554 F.Supp. 912 (1983), 920, 918, 921.
46. *Chicago Tribune*, 3 November 1983, III, 1:1; 10 November 1983, 30:1; 20 April 1984, 1:1; 7 August 1983, 1:1; 6 January 1984, 1:5.
47. Ibid., 25 July 1983, 1:12; 10 November 1983, 30:1; 8 January 1983, 1:6.
48. Ibid., 17 July 1983, 1:1.
49. *U.S. News* (8 January 1990): 31; *Phi Delta Kappan* (June 1989): 802–6; *Newsweek* (4 July 1988): 60.
50. *Newsweek* (4 July 1988): 60, 61.
51. *Phi Delta Kappan* (June 1989): 803; *Newsweek* (4 July 1981): 61.

52. U.S. v. Chicago Board of Education, 588 F.Supp. 132 (1984), 156–70 and passim.
53. Robert Howard and Ben Williams, quoted in *Chicago Tribune*, 2 June 1983, 1:2.
54. U.S. v. Chicago Board of Education, 567 F.Supp. 272 (1983), 290, 274, 283.
55. Ibid., 283, 282, 275.
56. U.S. v. Chicago Board of Education, 588 F.Supp. 132 (1984), 211, 238; Rex E. Lee and William Bradford Reynolds, Brief for the United States, U.S. v. Chicago Board of Education, 4–5, Supreme Court Library,.
57. U.S. v. Chicago Board of Education, 567 F.Supp 272 (1983), 282; William Bradford Reynolds, Brian K. Landsberg et al., Brief for the United States, U.S. v. Chicago Board of Education, 5, 17, 19–20, Supreme Court Library.
58. William Bradford Reynolds, Brian K. Landsberg et al., Brief for the United States, U.S. v. Chicago Board of Education, 1, 22 and passim, Supreme Court Library; Rex E. Lee and Reynolds, Brief for the United States, ibid., 25, 8.
59. Rex E. Lee and William Bradford Reynolds, Brief for the United States, U.S. v. Chicago Board of Education, 25–25a, Supreme Court Library.
60. U.S. v. Chicago Board of Education, 744 F.2d 1300 (1984), 1300.

18

Shaping a New Policy

In Seattle, Baton Rouge, and Chicago, William Bradford Reynolds pointed the Reagan administration away from forced busing. The features of the administration's program became clearer in Bakersfield, California, where Reynolds developed the administration's "blueprint for desegregation in the future," and in Yonkers, New York, where Reynolds presided over the most protracted school-desegregation lawsuit of the 1980s.[1]

I
White Flight and Magnets

White flight loomed large in Reynolds's thought. In the 1970s, integrationists had downplayed the gravity, and sometimes even the existence, of the phenomenon, but by 1980 the importance of white flight was generally acknowledged, although there was no consensus about the reasons for it.

Some observers said racism was responsible. As evidence, they mentioned that more than 50 percent of the nation's students were transported to school by bus, but only about 4 percent were bused to foster integration. "Given these figures, it is clear that busing is not the real issue," said David Tatel, a civil rights lawyer who had worked for the Carter administration. Jesse Jackson summed up the opinion of many African-Americans when he said that the target of white protest was "not the bus but us."[2]

By 1980 it was not fashionable to concede Jackson's point, but at one time some influential whites had admitted as much. They said integration was based on the assumption that skin color was no more important than the color of hair or eyes, and they feared that "the instinctive desire for the preservation of our race" would be suppressed if students were "imbued with this philosophy." The prominent South Carolina statesman James F. Byrnes warned that integration would "break down social barriers in the period of adolescence and ultimately bring about racial intermarriage." The journalist James J. Kilpatrick admonished that there was "nothing but disaster...in risking an accelerated intermingling of blood lines." Because he believed in the conservation of races, Kilpatrick was opposed to what he called "the coffee-colored compromise, a society in which every distinction of race has been blotted out by this principle of togetherness."[3]

But more was involved. There was less flight from integration in medium and small school districts than in large and distant ones where parents had less influence over the education of their children. There was also much more flight if the test scores of the black students were especially low or if the blacks came from the so-called underclass. In fact, after comparing the amount of flight with the students' test scores and social characteristics, one scholar, Christine H. Rossell, concluded that white parents were acting rationally. After comparing the cost of complying with court-ordered busing with the expense of moving or sending their children to private schools, they then chose the course "with the greatest benefit and least cost."[4]

Rossell's study suggested that the NAACP was on the mark when it entitled one of its pamphlets, *It's Not the Distance, "It's the Niggers."* The NAACP meant to imply that whites objected to busing for racial reasons. But in using the inflammatory epithet, the NAACP unintentionally acknowledged that many whites were especially worried about certain types of black students—students who were academically slow, physically intimidating, or so disruptive that teachers had to devote more time to discipline than to instruction.[5]

Desegregation led to real problems, but many people considered it an unpardonable faux pas to discuss the situation candidly. Even before he joined the Reagan administration, Reynolds knew that most books on education discreetly avoided topics that did not conform to the dogma of integrationists. This knowledge was reinforced by an incident that occurred in his own office.

In July 1981, one of Reynolds's deputies, Robert J. D'Agostino, wrote a memorandum that advised against pursuing a lawsuit in Yonkers. Citing statistics that indicated that blacks were disproportionately punished for disciplinary problems, lawyers in the Civil Rights Division planned to argue that blacks were being treated improperly. "Why improperly?" D'Agostino asked, going on to say that "blacks, because of their family, cultural and economic background, are more disruptive in the classroom on the average." At another point, D'Agostino questioned the civil rights lawyers' contention that a "disproportionate number" of blacks were steered into vocational programs, asking, "Disproportionate to their school achievement? Disproportionate to their needs?" D'Agostino said the civil rights lawyers were prisoners of an integrationist "mindset."[6]

D'Agostino's remarks were sensible. National statistics indicated that blacks were suspended from school twice as often as whites, but there was little evidence to support contentions that blacks were being treated unfairly. In general, white students were disciplined as frequently as blacks for truancy, cutting classes, and using drugs, but the overall suspension rate was greater for blacks because blacks were disproportionately punished for theft, fighting, and defiance. Blacks were also disproportionately overrepresented among students who were expelled after hearings that left little room for error or bias, with the proportion of interracial assaults committed by blacks especially high.[7]

Since black teenagers, on the average, scored about three grades below whites on standard tests of reading and mathematics, D'Agostino's comments on vocational training were also on the mark. From the early days of desegregation, critics had feared that teachers would adjust to an increased range of aptitudes by lowering standards. Problems could have been avoided if students were grouped by achievement, but, as noted previously, egalitarians often insisted that this amounted to resegregation. Many of them opposed ability grouping—some even said such grouping was unconstitutional—and told anxious parents that their children would be better off learning at their own individual pace or participating in cooperative projects and peer tutoring with "differently abled" peers.[8]

D'Agostino dismissed these reassurances. He thought all students—slow learners as well as those who were bright—needed to learn at a comfortable pace and to the level of their abilities. He also recognized that many parents, blacks as well as whites, had taken their children out of public schools because they regarded the reassurances as cant. In the city of Chicago, blacks operated forty-eight private schools and 46 percent of the students enrolled in the Catholic parochial schools were black. In Chicago, the *Tribune* observed, "[T]he flight from the public schools, often thought of as an exodus of whites afraid of desegregation, is not a white-only phenomenon after all." In Chicago, it was "bright flight."[9]

Although D'Agostino's memorandum was perceptive, it struck a raw nerve among career lawyers in the Civil Rights Division. More than 100 of them complained that the memo was insensitive if not racist. One attorney described D'Agostino's "general tone" as "an insult to black people worldwide"; another called it "outrageous and appalling"; while a third said the comments were "not appropriate characterizations for one who does civil rights work." To keep his staff in line, Reynolds publicly said the controversial memo had "understandably evoked criticism," and Reynolds made D'Agostino promise that in the future he would express his views "with a greater degree of sensitivity."[10]

L'affaire D'Agostino left a lasting impression. Reynolds learned that one could not speak candidly about some matters. Thereafter, while mentioning flight as a prime reason for the failure of forced busing, Reynolds was circumspect in explaining *why* so many parents were fleeing.

To stem the flight, Reynolds latched on to the idea of magnet schools. Some magnets had been around for years, although before they were used as a desegregation tool, they were usually called "specialty schools." Two famous examples were the Boston Latin School and the Bronx School of Science, where admission at each was by examination. Another example during the era of segregation was the all-black Dunbar High School, an academically oriented institution in an impoverished area of southeast Washington. Yet Dunbar drew its students from throughout the District of Columbia and was not a neighborhood school. For years, in fact, "it had been the pattern that most youngsters who *lived* near Dunbar did not *go* to Dunbar." Although admission was not based on test scores, Dunbar's reputation for academic toughness was sufficient to attract a high caliber of student.[11]

In the 1960s, additional magnet schools were established when progressives said that traditional schools—with their emphasis on structure, order, and control—destroyed the students' native curiosity and love of learning. In the 1970s and 1980s, the progressives acquired powerful allies as some government bureaucrats and federal judges seized on magnets as a way to integrate school systems without busing.

The bureaucrats and judges recognized that there was deep concern about the quality of integrated education. They heard parents basically saying, "I am for desegregating the schools, but I am more interested in my child having a good education." They knew that many parents would remove their children from public schools if they thought education was taking a back seat to social engineering.[12]

To stem defections to private, parochial, or suburban schools, integration-minded bureaucrats and judges allowed parents to have more say about where their children went to school and what they studied. They hoped, as one judge declared, that parents would "think twice...when there is a school...available with the special curriculum."[13]

Integrationists sometimes waxed rhapsodically about the value of racial interaction. They said public schools should do more than sort students and impart academic information—they should bring "all racial groups together in classrooms so that they will emerge from public schools as members of a socially unified community."[14]

But on other occasions the integrationist argument took on a harder edge. One lawyer wrote that the "primary propose" of the public schools was to "inculcate values," including "moral, political, and social ideas, attitudes, opinions and beliefs." The goal was to make sure that, whatever parents might think, children would be exposed to the "values and societal norms" of the dominant cultural elite. Other integrationists questioned the parents' right to determine the cultural setting for their children by their grouping themselves together in communities that were distinctive in terms of either racial or socioeconomic mix. They even questioned the parents' right to patronize private schools. One letter to the *New York Times* explained that "a parent's ignorance or bigotry is no reason to make the child suffer the loss of an integrated environment."[15]

But full integration could not be attained in the 1970s and 1980s. Too many middle-class parents feared the influence of the peer group and wanted above all to sequester their children from the pull of downward mobility. Despite reassurances, most parents did not think their children would benefit from mixing with youngsters who had different mores and low academic levels.

Therefore, some integrationists settled for magnet schools. By sanctioning schools that appealed to students with similar academic interests and cultural values, they tacitly allowed for both the concentration of middle-class youngsters and for the exclusion of the underclass. They made allowances for parents whose views were graphically expressed by one parent in Chicago.

> I would have done anything to get my child into a magnet school. That's the bottom line. You do what you have to for your kids. No one wants to send their kids to the neighborhood school. I've walked past the school enough, and I've heard enough. I know kids from the neighborhood who go there, and their parents are gang leaders. They have guns; they deal drugs; they have sex against their building, out in the open. I'm not interested in those kids being [my child's] playmates.[16]

Some integrationists felt guilty about the compromise, but the magnets allowed balanced racial interaction to occur in at least some schools. Since the proportion of blacks in most urban school districts was so large and the Supreme Court had set up barriers to interdistrict busing, magnets seemed to be the only way to achieve even a modicum of integration in many cities. By the 1980s, as Judge Milton I. Shadur had noted in Chicago, it was inevitable that most blacks would remain in mostly black schools, and the only "isolation" that integrationists could realistically hope to reduce was the isolation of whites. As one educator suggested:

> White America needs to realize that the coming generation is one-third minority...[Whites] must learn to be at ease with people of color, to consider them their equals (and in many specific contexts, such as supervisor and worker, their superiors).... White students raised in the isolation of all-white, or nearly all-white, small towns, suburbs, and city neighborhoods simply do not acquire the knowledge or attitudes that will allow them to participate constructively in the multiracial society they will face as adults. In short, for the good of the society, white children need to be in desegregated schools—or better yet, desegregated neighborhoods.[17]

Nevertheless, the magnets raised questions of equity. Although only one-quarter to one-third of all magnet schools selected students on the basis of grades and test scores, self selection was sufficient to give the schools a predominantly middle-class student body. Critics complained, however, that most children were left behind when the best teachers and the brightest students were attracted to magnet schools that were receiving extra financial resources. "What we've got is just another system of separate but unequal education," said Leon Finney, Jr., the chairman of a citizens' group in Chicago. "We have replaced racism with elitism and exchanged one segregated system for another."[18]

Worst of all, critics said, the magnets damaged the self-esteem of nonmagnet students. One parent complained that while her son attended "an elite [magnet] school," her daughter had to spend her days "at a school for throwaways.... She is in a school where all the kids have serious attendance and academic problems...[and] are totally isolated from kids who will stay in school and achieve." The parent said her daughter's "shame about herself, her classmates and her school are a problem."[19]

Some of the criticisms could be answered. One study calculated that on average magnets cost only 8 percent more than neighborhood schools. Another pointed out that magnets generally enrolled such a small proportion of the total student enrollment (only 8 percent in Chicago), that there were still plenty of good teachers and strong students in the neighborhood schools. Yet another study concluded that magnets were more effective in promoting desegregation than forced busing. Reynolds thought that, in general, the criticisms were a result of egalitarian ideology and not of familiarity with magnet programs. He said he had "yet to witness a situation...in which implementation of a comprehensive magnet program benefits but a few and is otherwise educationally draining on the system as a whole."[20]

Yet there was no gainsaying the fact that magnets could not accommodate all the students who wished to enroll. In Chicago there was an official lottery, with only 10 percent of the applicants actually gaining admission to a magnet school. Some people tried to improve their odds "by applying personal clout [or] by inventing nonexistent siblings and minority ancestors for their kids." Parents worked for the PTA, hoping that their child would become one of the three "principal's picks"—students each magnet principal was allowed to choose outside the lottery. "It's like everything else in Chicago," one mother said. "It comes down to who you know." One journalist reported that "for many middle-class families, there are only three schooling options: Finesse your way into a magnet, come up with the cash for private school tuition, or move to the suburbs."[21]

Reynolds was aware of all this. Nevertheless, he thought voluntary magnets produced more actual desegregation than coercion did. He also thought public schools would become stronger if they had to compete for students who could choose a school with a different emphasis or pedagogy. By incorporating choice and magnets, desegregation could be structured to benefit, rather than damage, the quality of public education.

Magnets, then, impressed Reynolds as the best solution to a complicated problem. They offered a way to comply with the Supreme Court's demand for feasible and workable affirmative steps to achieve the greatest possible degree of racial interaction. It was not enough to be opposed to forced busing, Reynolds reiterated. That was only "a starting point in developing just and sound policies to achieve the central aim of school desegregation"; it was necessary, in addition, to develop "a reasonable and meaningful alternative."[22]

Of course, Reynolds came in for criticism. The standard contention of the civil rights lobby—a view put forward in Thomas D. Barr's report for the Lawyer's Committee for Civil Rights—was that the Supreme Court had "made it clear that voluntary plans were inadequate to fulfill the promise of equal educational opportunity and should not be relied on." By opposing coercion and favoring voluntary magnets, Barr said, Reynolds manifested a "disregard" for "the indisputable law of the land."[23]

In point of fact, *murky* or *convoluted* would have described the jurisprudence of the Supreme Court more accurately than *indisputable.* In any case, the Court itself never ruled against magnets—not in Chicago and not in subsequent litigation that involved other school districts.

In his indictment of Reynolds, Barr called particular attention to a statement Reynolds made before the House Judiciary Committee: "We are not going to compel children who don't choose to have an integrated education to have one." Although the Supreme Court never explicitly required that affirmative steps must be compulsory, Barr cited Reynolds's statement as another indication of alleged disrespect for the law.[24]

Actually, Reynolds's comment was vulnerable to criticism from another direction in that Reynolds's statement was part of a litany to the effect that the Reagan administration was committed to the principle of nondiscrimination. It went along with assertions that "the use of race to justify treating individuals differently...can never be legitimate"; that "racial classifications are wrong—morally wrong"; that "our Constitution is color-blind."[25]

Yet when it came to school desegregation, Reynolds and the Reagan administration accepted some race-conscious policies that were designed to achieve a "better" racial mix. They rejected forced busing, to be sure, but in Baton Rouge and elsewhere they accepted affirmative "pairing," "clustering," and boundary adjustments. In Chicago and other cities they endorsed the use of racial quotas for allocating places in magnet schools. They did so because by the 1980s the jurisprudence of school desegregation had strayed so far from nondiscrimination that the idea of race neutrality had become an anachronism. Despite rhetoric rejecting race-conscious solutions, Reynolds accepted inoculations of racial consciousness as the only way to avoid a more thorough, coercive racialism.

II
Bakersfield (and Buffalo)

Bakersfield is situated about 110 miles north of Los Angeles at the southern end of one of the nation's most productive agricultural regions, the San Joaquin Valley. In addition to the ranching and farm families long resident in the valley, there were a number of white sharecroppers and laborers who settled there after the dust bowl migrations of the 1930s, and after World War II there was an influx of Chicanos. By 1982–83, the population of the city had increased to 115,000, and 18,000 students were enrolled in the public schools. Blacks made up 16 percent of the student body; whites, 36 percent; and Hispanics, 46 percent. The Bakersfield City School District served children from kindergarten through eighth grade, with high school students assigned to a separate countywide school district.

Although Bakersfield was a city of only medium size, the roots of its desegregation case were complex and tangled. Before and after *Brown*, students were assigned to neighborhood schools, and an unusually retentive administration had kept information on enrollment and attendance boundaries going back to the nineteenth century. In 1968 and 1969, when state and federal officials inquired about the ethnic and racial makeup of the city's schools, the local supervisor of information, Janice Blanton, naively thought the government would be favorably disposed if she "bent over backwards and supplied things they didn't even know we had." She shipped "hundreds and hundreds and hundreds of pounds of material back to Washington," information that was eventually used against Bakersfield. Later one federal agent told Blanton, "When I saw all those documents, I knew we could get you."[26]

As the population of Bakersfield expanded, the city built new schools whose enrollments were ethnically imbalanced as a succession of different groups clustered in, and gradually moved through, different neighborhoods. At the time most people thought there was nothing wrong with this, but in 1975 the Office of Education cut off federal funds for Bakersfield on the ground that the city had not complied with the Civil Rights Act of 1964. By then the office had reinterpreted the Act to require integration, so it really did not need the 111 days of hearings that were held to show that enrollments in Bakersfield were not ethnically balanced.[27]

The office said the local school authorities had done more than fail to keep pace with the evolving understanding of the Civil Rights Act. After analyzing the documents, the office pointed to instances where school attendance boundaries apparently were shifted to promote ethnic cohesion rather than mixing. Instead of taking affirmative action to promote the maximum feasible amount of racial interaction, the federal officials said, Bakersfield made it more difficult for the students of the city to mix in tri-ethnic classes. The bottom line, according to an administrative law judge, was that Bakersfield had intentionally built new schools and adjusted old attendance boundaries in order to separate black, Hispanic, and white students.[28]

Whatever the past situation may have been—and Bakersfield steadfastly insisted that it had never intentionally segregated the ethnic groups—the school district knew it would have to take affirmative steps before federal funds would be restored. Therefore, the district implemented a number of policies to produce more mixing. In 1977 a Task Force for the Reduction of Racial Isolation was established. In 1979 the ethnic balance in the upper grades was evened out by closing one of the city's four junior high schools and reassigning the students to the other three. In 1980 a similar policy was instituted for younger students, when three elementary schools were closed. In addition, by taking steps to disperse its programs for bilingual education and for mentally retarded students, Bakersfield dealt with two other matters that also contributed to ethnic imbalance.[29]

Yet these steps were not enough to satisfy the Carter administration. Before the federal funds could be restored, Carter's lawyers said, there had to be root-and-branch eradication of the vestiges of Bakersfield's old dual system. And that, they said, would require forced busing. When Bakersfield balked, the lawyers made plans for a lawsuit. However, Ronald Reagan became president before the litigation formally began.

Bakersfield opposed busing for the usual reasons: some people resented coercion; others objected to the principle of assigning students on the basis of race; still others said that since the city had not intentionally kept the ethnic groups apart, there was nothing remedial about busing for balance; and some feared that busing would lead to lower educational and disciplinary standards.

Whatever the reason, opposition was so widespread that school officials said that busing would be counterproductive. Instead of achieving a more even balance, they warned, busing would precipitate white flight. They noted that white enrollment was already declining, both in absolute numbers and as a percentage of the total. Even without busing, whites were gravitating toward the Panama-Buena School District, southwest of Bakersfield—where there was more open space, where the houses were newer, where there was an additional $1,000 a year in per pupil spending, and where 75 percent of the public school students were white.[30]

The five members of the school board, including the Hispanic and black members, unanimously favored a voluntary approach to integration. Lily

Nahama, the Japanese-American president of the board, declared that "forced busing would kill our community." It was necessary, she said, "to do this in a gentle manner, so that it will be acceptable to the community."[31]

Taking everything into account, the situation was conducive to the sort of desegregation that the Reagan administration favored. Thus, in what turned out to be the first school desegregation case initiated and concluded by the administration, Reynolds and the Bakersfield City School District negotiated a consent decree that District Judge Edward Dean Price approved in January 1984.

Under the decree, magnet programs were set up to attract whites to four predominantly black and Hispanic schools where whites had previously accounted for only 8 percent of the enrollment. At the same time, black and Hispanic students were urged to use a preexisting open enrollment program to transfer to two schools where the enrollment had been 80 percent white. Other provisions required the school district to spend $130,000 for a special reading program at five schools that would remain "racially isolated" and also to set up a program of "mini magnets" to enhance social awareness and racial harmony by having students visit predominantly other-ethnic schools about fifteen times a year. In addition, the school district promised that future decisions that touched on school construction, closings, or attendance boundaries would be made with an eye toward "further desegregation." The district promised to bring the racial ratio at each school within 20 percentage points of the systemwide racial ratio, and to do so within three years.[32]

What the consent decree omitted was as important as what it included. Without requiring mandatory reassignment of students, the Reagan administration had settled a controversy that had been simmering for more than a decade. Under Reynolds, the Civil Rights Division said that desegregation could be achieved through improved education and voluntary transfers and without resort to forced busing.

Unlike the Carter administration, which had also supported magnet schools but insisted that voluntary means of desegregation must be accompanied by compulsory measures, the Reagan administration would not go beyond voluntarism. Far from apologizing for any "retreat," Reynolds touted the Bakersfield plan as "a blueprint for desegregation in the future." Bakersfield's plan would become a model for the nation, Reynolds predicted, precisely because it did not rely on forced busing ("which does not work anywhere in a very meaningful way").[33]

The black member of the Bakersfield school board supported the plan, as did a former president of the local branch of the NAACP, but there was criticism from national civil rights leaders. Ralph Neas denounced the plan as inadequate, saying, "Magnet schools alone will not do the job." He added, "It seems once again that the Department of Justice is refusing to enforce effectively our civil rights laws."[34]

In testimony before the House Judiciary Committee, critics accused Reynolds of acting in "defiance of the judiciary." William L. Taylor said the Supreme Court had rejected freedom of choice, shifted the burden of desegregation away from parents and children, and had made it "abundantly clear that the remedy for...segregation...is the mandatory reassignment of students." Taylor added that the Court had said that voluntary measures could not be "the sole technique employed to desegregate a system," and he cited *Bakersfield* as an instance of Reynolds's disrespect for "the rule of law."[35]

Drew Days agreed. Reynolds's predecessor as assistant attorney general for civil rights said the Reagan administration was "not enforcing the law of school desegregation faithfully." Days wrote that the administration had rejected "the concept of a school board's affirmative duty to desegregate," and that it was "turning back the clock" to freedom of choice.[36]

Yet Days's and Taylor's comments missed the mark as legal analysis. Although the Supreme Court had charged local school boards with the affirmative duty to formulate desegregation plans that promised realistically to work, the Court had not required coercion. Bakersfield was willing to take affirmative steps that stopped short of forced busing, and the question as to whether voluntary measures would work there would be answered in due course.

Something else was responsible for the inflated criticism of *Bakersfield*. That something was *Buffalo*. Buffalo had been accused of gerrymandering attendance boundaries so as to keep a new junior high school predominantly white—an accusation that was similar to the charge that got Bakersfield in trouble. Unlike Bakersfield, however, Buffalo was found guilty in a federal court, and the judge, applying the *Keyes* presumption, demanded that the school board take affirmative steps to achieve racial balance throughout the city. The board tried to get by with voluntarism and magnets, but the judge insisted on a mandatory backup plan for children who did not voluntarily choose to attend racially balanced schools. Under the backup, laggards would be assigned to an integrated school outside their neighborhood for about half of their grade-school years. In addition, the school board was required to keep separate lists of prospective employees and to hire one black for each white until blacks made up the same percentage of teachers and administrators as they did of the overall population in the area.[37]

Critics said this "remedy" was disproportionate to the wrong, but many liberals regarded *Buffalo* as a prototype. The *New York Times*, which had mocked Reynolds with an editorial that characterized the Bakersfield plan as "a 'blueprint'...for segregation," published a front-page account that touted Buffalo's plan as "a national model of integration." An article in the *New*

Republic similarly praised *Buffalo* as an example of how to make a choice plan work.[38]

Partisans of *Buffalo* emphasized two points. One was the variety of magnets in Buffalo—including the largest Montessori school in the country, a science school with a curriculum built around zoo animals, and Traditional High (where there was mandatory nightly homework and a dress code). The other was the compulsory backup. According to journalist James Traub, "Truly 'voluntary' desegregation, that totem raised by the Reagan Administration, does not work." Traub observed, "Even in Buffalo, 15 percent of the students must be mandatorily reassigned to achieve the judge's criteria for racial balance." Yale law professor Paul Gewirtz similarly observed that one of the "lessons" of *Buffalo* was that magnets and choice "must be thoroughly intertwined with a mandatory program."[39]

Thus *Buffalo* and *Bakersfield* emerged as rival models. Neither plan included all that their architects would have preferred. If Reynolds had his way—that is, if the jurisprudence of the Supreme Court had not moved from nondiscrimination to affirmative action—there would have been no racial goals for the Bakersfield schools. If the civil rights lobby had its way, the desegregation area would have included the suburbs of Buffalo as well as the city, and all children would have been required to attend public schools. Within the limits of the practicable, however, *Bakersfield* and *Buffalo* represented polar opposites. *Bakersfield* held out the possibility of both freedom and desegregation. *Buffalo*, while coercive, stood for a sort of integration that, it was thought, just might win the support of middle-class parents.

Because the stakes were high, each side tried to discredit the other. Drew Days said that voluntarism had "proved ineffective in the past.... The weight of evidence [shows] that magnet school plans, standing alone, have proven inadequate to achieve meaningful desegregation." Another integrationist, William M. Gordon, went further. Without any qualifications about how magnets might promote desegregation if there was a mandatory backup, Gordon concluded that "magnet plans do not work as a remedy for school segregation."[40]

For his part, Reynolds struck out at the Buffalo plan when the case was on appeal to the Supreme Court. Although the high court eventually decided not to consider the case, Reynolds prepared a legal brief in which he argued that the court-ordered plan for hiring teachers and administrators was at odds with what the Supreme Court had said about racial quotas and preferences in *Stotts v. Memphis Firefighters*. Pennsylvania senator Arlen Specter was concerned about this and, according to Reynolds, promised to vote for Reynolds's confirmation as associate attorney general if Reynolds would change his position on *Buffalo*.

> Specter said that if I modified the position I had already taken in court—if I distinguished between permissible goals and impermissible quotas, for example—he would support me. I'll never forget it. I looked at Specter and said, "Senator, if changing a position that I have already stated in court is the price for your vote, I don't want your vote. It's not worth it. I think the position I took in court is the right position. I think it is legally compelled, and I will not change." Then I said I would regard this as a conversation that never took place. Specter got very tight-lipped. He gave me a cold, cold stare. He said, "I guess this meeting is over." I said, "I don't have any reason to continue it."[41]

Back in Bakersfield, local authorities encountered some problems. One involved the minimagnet cultural programs (where students visited predominantly other-ethnic schools about fifteen times a year); while they may have enhanced social awareness, they also pulled students out of classes and disrupted regular academic programs. Another problem concerned the bilingual centers, which posed a certain contrariety with dispersed integration. Also, students with low reading skills often refused to leave predominantly minority schools that had extra reading teachers and counselors. The local district judge observed that it was "anomalous in the extreme" for children to receive "a lower level of educational services as a direct result of [attending] a desegregated school."[42]

Despite the problems, the voluntary magnets attracted enough students to satisfy the terms of the consent decree, as in 1989 the district met the goal of having an enrollment at every public school that was within 20 percentage points of the districtwide ratio. The proportion of whites at the four schools with the largest proportion of minorities increased from 8 percent in 1983 to 21 percent in 1991, while the proportion of minority students at the most concentrated white school increased from 20 percent to 44 percent.[43]

The results with respect to academic achievement were less encouraging. Bakersfield's students, when compared with students elsewhere in California, ranked between the 19th and the 32d percentile, but school administrators had a point when they said that every district should be evaluated "on the basis of its own unique characteristics." When compared with other schools and school districts serving students with similar backgrounds, Bakersfield did better (with average scores between the 42d and 66th percentile).[44]

The effect of integration on race relations was more difficult to gauge. Integrationists sometimes said their goal was to promote interracial camaraderie, but official documents focused on numbers. Judges, federal bureaucrats, and public interest groups demanded a certain amount of racial mixing, and local authorities tried to survive by complying with these demands.

Most of the evidence on race relations is impressionistic. The numerous studies on the topic suggest that for every instance in which mixing leads to increased interracial friendship, there is another case of heightened racial tensions. In Bakersfield, as elsewhere, much depended on individual experiences. Some students complained about ethnic tensions, and many families that were new to the area settled in predominantly white suburbs outside the limits of the Bakersfield City School District. Other students formed friendships across ethnic lines, and there was little flight from the city. In the schools, there were problems with gangs, but some of the gangs were "actually mixed gangs, neighborhood gangs, as opposed to ethnic gangs."[45]

In a speech in 1984, Reynolds admitted that while it was "a bit too early to declare the magnet program a complete desegregation success," Bakersfield had achieved racial balance without setting the stage for other evils. The schools were integrated without instigating white flight or otherwise damaging the quality of public education. Considering everything, Reynolds thought Bakersfield justified the administration's decision to turn away from "the mandatory transportation feature" and to emphasize instead "expanded educational opportunities that attract students to the public school, not drive them away."[46]

III
Yonkers

In *Bakersfield*, the Reagan administration did not go far enough to satisfy most civil rights activists. The same cannot be said about *Yonkers*. In this latter instance, the administration developed an expansive definition of intentional discrimination and also took the unprecedented step of linking school and housing discrimination in the same case.

Yonkers is located in suburban and affluent Westchester County, immediately north of New York City. With a population of 195,331 in 1980, Yonkers was the fourth-largest city in the state of New York. Blacks made up 18.8 percent of the total population and 37 percent of the 21,683 students enrolled in the public schools. The neighborhoods in east and northwest Yonkers were quite nice, but the downtown area had fallen on hard times.[47]

The trouble in downtown Yonkers began after the largest employer there, the Alexander Smith Carpet Mills, closed its doors in 1950. Unemployed workers found it difficult to maintain or renovate their houses, and in 1970 the mayor reported that many people were "living in desperate, horrible conditions."[48]

Believing that "the best thing we could do" was to provide "safe, decent standard housing" for low-income people, city officials planned to build several subsidized housing projects. Since many people in the more well-to-do sections of east and northwest Yonkers complained that the projects would cause traffic problems and depress property values if they were located in their areas, the projects were built near downtown Yonkers in an area known as "Southwest," where there was no organized opposition to the construction and where community leaders even predicted that the projects would stimulate a redevelopment of the area. Although the city tried to persuade poor whites to live in the projects, from the outset more than 80 percent of the subsidized tenants were black. Over the years, while the population of east and northwest Yonkers remained overwhelmingly white, the proportion of whites in southwest Yonkers declined from 90 percent in 1960 to 60 percent in 1980.[49]

Except for a few students who were handicapped or had other special problems, no students were bused to schools in Yonkers. Instead, geographic boundaries were traced around the schools and the areas were kept sufficiently compact so that youngsters could walk to schools in their neighborhoods. Blacks and whites mixed in all of the city's thirty-six schools, but the racial balance in individual schools depended on the racial composition of the neighborhoods. In the twenty-five elementary schools, there was a wide range in the proportion of blacks from 1 percent at P.S. 9 to 98 percent at P.S. 6, with at least one school in every decile between. At the five high schools, the percentage of blacks also varied (from 2 to 9, 16, 47, and 62). People who subscribed to the perspective and definitions that had prevailed in the Supreme Court when *Brown* was decided, or in the Congress that enacted the Civil Rights Act of 1964, could view the Yonkers school system as a model of nondiscriminatory desegregation. Integrationists, however, regarded the racial imbalance as evidence of unconstitutional segregation.[50]

On 1 December 1980, after Jimmy Carter had been defeated for reelection but before he left office, the Civil Rights Division filed a lawsuit alleging that the city of Yonkers had segregated its public housing and that the board of education was operating a system of segregated schools. The case marked the first time that the Justice Department linked school and housing discrimination in one case.

The litigation dragged on for more than a decade and a summary can only cover some of the issues. Essentially, the Carter administration accused the city of intentionally discriminating against blacks by refusing to situate subsidized public housing in the middle-class, affluent, and overwhelmingly white areas of east Yonkers while, instead, building subsidized projects in the poorer southwest region. Carter's lawyers then charged the school board with compounding the discrimination by adhering to a neighborhood school policy and, in addition, accused the school board of discriminating with respect to vocational education and student discipline.

Yonkers was designed to expand the jurisprudence of school desegregation. In *Yonkers*, the Carter administration asked the courts to require the local school board to end a racial imbalance that allegedly had been caused by the city government's construction of public housing.[51]

The Carter administration also used *Yonkers* to develop a novel approach toward intentional discrimination. In a 1977 case known as *Village of Arlington Heights*, the Supreme Court had declared that "disproportionate impact" was "not the touchstone of an invidious racial discrimination" in housing cases, as "[p]roof of racially discriminatory intent or purpose is required to show a violation of the Equal Protection Clause." Yet Carter's lawyers maintained that a discriminatory purpose could be inferred if the foreseeable consequences of a policy impeded balanced mixing. They said the whites of east and northwest Yonkers were really thinking about race when they said they were concerned about traffic problems and property values. If there was a disproportionate "effect," Carter's lawyers said, there must have been a discriminatory "intent."[52]

After the Reagan administration came into office, Robert J. D'Agostino, as noted above, recommended against pursuing the *Yonkers* lawsuit. In a memorandum to Reynolds, D'Agostino noted that there was no extant law that required the building of low-income housing projects in affluent neighborhoods. D'Agostino said the Carter administration had resorted to disingenuous interpretation to require such a policy, and he further declared that *Yonkers* involved exactly the sort of legal activism that Ronald Reagan had criticized during the presidential campaign of 1980.[53]

Nevertheless, Reynolds allowed the case to proceed. Some critics wondered if he had not been captured by the career lawyers in the Civil Rights Division who were already at work on *Yonkers* before Reynolds took office. They pointed in particular to Josh Bogin, a young lawyer from New York, who, like Reynolds, was a litigator. Once Bogin took a position, he fought hard for it, and in *Yonkers* that meant fighting against D'Agostino within the Civil Rights Division as well as fighting against the city of Yonkers in the federal courts.

Bogin was furious when he learned of D'Agostino's memorandum. Bogin has said that he did not leak it; but after someone gave it to the *Washington Post*, civil rights activists and sympathizers responded with a fusillade of criticism that was calculated to force Reynolds to continue with the case.[54]

Yet there was possibly more to Reynolds's decision to proceed with *Yonkers*. Since Reynolds distrusted the career lawyers in the Civil Rights Division, it seems unlikely that they put one over on him. The decision was made at a time when Reynolds's handling of the *Bob Jones* tax exemption case had been criticized, and it is possible that Reynolds caved in before the prospect of more bad publicity in the liberal press. It may also be that Reynolds was persuaded by the argument that city officials and the school board in Yonkers had engaged in purposeful, intentional discrimination. Within the Justice Department, one lawyer said, "[A]lmost everybody agreed that *Yonkers* was an egregious case of intentional discrimination."[55]

When viewed superficially, it appears that Reynolds was right. In a 600-page opinion written after hearing testimony that ran to 14,000 pages of transcript, Judge Leonard B. Sand ruled for the Civil Rights Division on every important point. The city of Yonkers, Judge Sand held, had "illegally and intentionally" maintained segregated public schools and segregated public housing projects. On appeal, a panel of three judges from the Second Circuit Court unanimously affirmed Judge Sand's decision. The Civil Rights Division also won on most of the related questions that were appealed over the course of the next decade.[56]

Perhaps this should settle the question. Judge Sand's opinion has been described as a "'classic legal document,' significant not only because of its findings and conclusions but also for the way in which it was researched and presented." The opinion was so meticulous and comprehensive that it was almost certain to pass muster on appeal (where findings of fact are not to be set aside unless clearly erroneous and where the district judge is entitled to considerable deference in assessing the credibility of witnesses).[57]

Nevertheless, this writer doubts that many juries would have reached the same decision. In *Yonkers*, there was no direct evidence of racial discrimination against blacks. The lawyers for the Civil Rights Division, and Judge Sand as well, even conceded that there was "little evidence that the residents of the City's affluent areas expressly mentioned race as a reason for opposing subsidized housing in those areas." There were no "overtly racial statements by opponents of public housing."[58]

The critics of public housing said they wanted to preserve "the 'residential character' of single-family neighborhoods," to avoid congestion and traffic problems, and to maintain the value of their properties. But Josh Bogin and other lawyers from the Civil Rights Division convinced Judge Sand that "racial opposition was 'certainly...nothing anybody would put into words.'" They led Judge Sand to conclude that the proffered explanations were merely pretextual "'smokescreens' for underlying racial fears." One of their key witnesses, a former mayor of Yonkers, declared that in his opinion, race was "definitely" a factor in the opposition to subsidized housing. Another witness, the pastor of a church in Yonkers, said, "Basically this is out-and-out discrimination not only against negroes, but against lower-income whites as well." The civil rights lawyers also made much of a videotape of a community meeting where one white opponent of housing projects recalled how neighborhoods in the Bronx had been ruined after public housing projects were built there. The man concluded by saying, "I'm not a good speaker...but I think you get the idea"—an assertion that lawyers from the Civil Rights Division insisted was laden with racism.[59]

These statements constituted the only direct evidence cited in Judge Sand's lengthy opinion. Yet even if the statements were more clearly incriminating, it would not be fair to determine the nature of community opposition on the basis of the bigoted comments of a few citizens. Judge Sand was doubtlessly correct in writing that "many of those who lived in East Yonkers had moved there from the Bronx and other areas of New York City, and had expressed strong fears that subsidized housing would lead to the same 'deterioration' which they had sought to escape." But why did Judge Sand place the word *deterioration* in quotation marks, thereby implying that opponents really feared black people because they were black rather than the general degradation that often occurs in and near subsidized public housing projects?

Judge Sand and civil rights lawyer Bogin were New Yorkers. Bogin had lived in the city, while Sand lived on a 32-acre estate in the Pound Ridge area of northern Westchester county—an area that had no public housing. They knew that conditions in the Bronx had deteriorated; they knew that the environs of many subsidized housing projects had become disaster areas; but they had more sympathy for low-income blacks than for whites who fled the city to live in suburban Yonkers. Most of those whites lived in modest, middle-class homes, but Judge Sand thought these people were white trash. His opinion bristled with moral indignation.[60]

The civil rights lawyers, and later Judge Sand, maintained that the white people of Yonkers had devised an extraordinary antiblack conspiracy that went well beyond refusing to build public housing projects in affluent neighborhoods. The lawyers and the judge also found fault with the Yonkers school board for establishing entrance requirements for the city's trade and technical high schools. Because of these requirements, African-Americans (who constituted 37 percent of the districtwide enrollment at the time of the trial) made up only 11 percent of the students at the trade schools. Judge Sand conceded that "direct evidence of discriminatory intent is absent from the record," but nevertheless concluded that "this disproportionality is sufficient to support a finding of intentionally created segregation." In this instance, Judge Sand held, school officials intended to achieve the underrepresentation of blacks that they must have known would be the foreseeable consequence of using standard tests.[61]

Nor was this all. The civil rights lawyers and Judge Sand also noted that black students were disproportionately punished for what was called "aggressive or 'acting out' behavior." This was not because blacks misbehaved more frequently, the civil rights lawyers maintained, but because teachers were insensitive to differences in cultural styles. Judge Sand endorsed the testimony of witnesses who referred to the "inherent racism" of whites and emphasized the "'cultural differences' between minority children and the district's professional staff." Paradoxically, Judge Sand also endorsed the contention that school authorities were allowing so called bad actors to terrorize other students in the bathrooms and on the playgrounds as part of a plot to foment "resistance to desegregation" by reinforcing the perception that "the terms 'nigger' and 'retards' were interchangeable."[62]

Having found Yonkers guilty on several counts, Judge Sand proceeded to impose a remedy. First, he ordered Yonkers to begin construction of 200 low-income housing units in east Yonkers and to make plans for an additional 800 units. Then he imposed a school desegregation plan that was estimated to cost about $37 million. The plan adjusted attendance boundaries, closed some schools, built others, and created or expanded twenty magnet programs. The goal was to bring the racial ratio at regular schools to within 20 percentage points of the overall racial balance and to narrow the differential to 10 percentage points in the magnet schools.[63]

A lawyer for the NAACP characterized Judge Sand's school plan as "a total victory," and Justice Department officials were also pleased because the plan emphasized the importance of magnet schools.[64]

By closing some schools, dispersing students, and developing new magnets, the schools went a long way toward satisfying Judge Sand's numerical requirements. The rest of the distance was covered by the forced busing of a few thousand students, which displeased many parents. "I didn't ask for this," one angry white father declared as he waited with his children at a bus stop. "They used to go to School 16, one block from my house. Now [other children] take a bus here, while kids from here go by bus to other places." A black mother similarly complained that she wanted her eight-year old daughter to attend the same neighborhood school the mother had attended when she was a girl; but the daughter was bused across town because spaces in the nearby school were being reserved for white children.[65]

The court-appointed monitor of the desegregation plan insisted that the program was "good educational policy," but many citizens looked on with the wary eyes of parents who had seen things go wrong before. Some critics pointed to substantial and stubborn differences in the scores on standard achievement tests, where the average minority high school freshman in Yonkers scored three grade levels below the average for white students. Others warned that there would be increasing problems with discipline.[66]

The skepticism increased as events unfolded. Contemporaneous with Judge Sand's order, plainclothes police were assigned to Lincoln High School for the first time; and later, after a number of incidents involving weapons, metal detectors were installed at the entrances to all the high schools. Nevertheless, problems persisted, and in 1990 the police commissioner said there were at least nine youth gangs in Yonkers (including one female street gang along with gangs formed among Hispanic, black, Puerto Rican, Jamaican, Italian, and Albanian groups).[67]

Nor was much progress made in reducing the gap in academic performance. To address this continuing problem, school authorities in the early 1990s developed another plan with a proposed price tag of $170 million (an amount that made Judge Sand's $37-million plan seem small by comparison). Of that $170 million, 43 percent of the money was earmarked for upgrading the magnet programs and for reducing class size by hiring more teachers. The rest was to go for a curriculum that would teach students to tolerate and understand other cultures, for workshops on social interaction, and for more individualized instruction. The proposal led to further litigation that is yet to be resolved.[68]

Meanwhile, many white parents either moved elsewhere or sent their children to private schools. As a result, the number of white students in the Yonkers public schools declined from 13,840 (when the lawsuit began) to 6,671 in 1993.[69]

Most residents of Yonkers would have disputed the assessment of a NAACP lawyer who said it was "clear" that the school integration program was "largely successful." Yet integration fared better in the schools than in housing.[70]

There was an enormous public outcry against Judge Sand's order to build 200 (of an eventual 1,000) units of subsidized housing in east Yonkers. Homeowners said that by the 1980s even the most doctrinaire liberals should have recognized that new housing projects would create more problems than they solved. Responding to the public pressure, officials in Yonkers stymied Judge Sand for five years. Because members of the city council rejected necessary zoning changes, the first phase of court-ordered subsidized housing was not opened until 1992; and the case remained in litigation in 1995 as Yonkers continued to balk at the additional 800 units.[71]

Bakersfield and *Yonkers* are more than tales of two cities. They are stories of quite different approaches to school desegregation. Despite bad notices in the liberal press, *Bakersfield* was a success. The Reagan administration rejected forced busing and developed an affirmative plan that satisfied the courts' requirements for numerical mixing while avoiding white flight and other damage to the quality of education. Things did not go so well in *Yonkers*. There the administration won the case and propitiated the press. Yet, except for public relations, *Yonkers* was a disaster. It precipitated white flight and damaged neighborhood stability, and it did so for no sufficient reason.

Why did Reynolds allow this case to proceed? Part of the answer had to do with the institutional momentum that had built up after the Carter administration filed the case. Another part probably had to do with political calculations. Because the civil rights lobby and the major media were accusing Reynolds and the Reagan administration of abandoning the struggle for civil rights, there was the temptation to accept the assurance of lawyers who said the city of Yonkers really had segregated its public schools. In reaching this conclusion, Reynolds uncharacteristically allowed himself to be captured by career civil rights lawyers who themselves were captives of an integrationist mindset.

Notes

1. *New York Times*, 26 January 1984, 1:1.
2. Ibid., 18 July 1981, 15:1; 8 March 1982, 19:3.
3. Herbert Ravenal Sass, "Mixed Schools and Mixed Blood," *Atlantic Monthly* (November 1956): 45–49; *U.S News* (5 October 1956): 104; James J. Kilpatrick, *The Southern Case for School Segregation* (New York: Crowell-Collier, 1962), 52–53, 70–72; Stephen B. Oates, *Let the Trumpet Sound* (New York: Harper & Row, Publishers, 1982), 167.
4. *National Observer*, 7 June 1975; Christine H. Rossell, "Is It the Busing or the Blacks?" *Urban Affairs Quarterly* (September 1988): 138–48.
5. *It's Not the Distance: "It's the Niggers"* (New York: NAACP Legal Defense and Education Fund, Inc., 1972).
6. *Washington Post*, 10 September 1981, A17a.
7. Charles M. Achilles et al., "A Study of Issues Related to Discipline," 1982 report in files of Evans v. Buchanan, Civil Action 1816, U.S. District Court, Wilmington, Delaware. For more on the situation with respect to discipline, see Judith Lynne Hanna, *Disruptive School Behavior: Class, Race, and Culture* (New York: Holmes & Meier, 1988); and Raymond Wolters, *The Burden of Brown*, passim.
8. For the situation in Washington, D.C., where Judge J. Skelly Wright found that grouping students by ability was unconstitutional, see Raymond Wolters, *The Burden of Brown*, part 1.
9. *Chicago Tribune*, 4 January 1982, 4:4; 3 February 1982, 12:1; information provided by Brother Donald Houde, 4 August 1995.
10. *Washington Post*, 10 September 1981, A13d.
11. Thomas Sowell, "Black Excellence—The Case of Dunbar High School," *The Public Interest* (Spring 1974): 13, 3–6.
12. *Journal of Law and Education* (Spring 1989): 197; *New Republic* (13 April 1987): 17.
13. Hart v. Community School Board, 512 F.2d 37 (1975), 54.
14. Heather Latham, student paper, University of Delaware, Fall 1992.
15. Kevin Brown, "Termination of Public School Desegregation," *George Washington Law Review*, 58 (1990): 1164, 1110, 1113–14; Michael Laudor to *New York Times*, 2 November 1981, 22:3.
16. Marj Halperin, "The Lottery," *Chicago* (December 1988): 161.
17. U.S. v. Chicago Board of Education, 554 F.Supp. 912 (1983), 921; Mary Haywood Metz, "In Education, Magnets Attract Controversy," *National Education Association Journal* (January 1988): 55.

18. *U.S. News* (27 May 1991): 58; Janet R. Price and Jane R. Stern, "Magnet Schools as a Strategy for Integration and School Reform," *Yale Law and Policy Review*, 5 (1987): 293; *Chicago Tribune*, 17 July 1983, 1:1; 18 July 1983, 1:1.
19. *Yale Law and Policy Review*, 5 (1987): 291.
20. R. Blank, *Survey of Magnet Schools: Analyzing a Model for Quality Integrated Education* (Washington: U.S. Department of Education, 1983), 36; *Chicago Tribune*, 18 July 1983, 1:1; Julie A. Maloney, "Magnet Schools: An Attractive Desegregation Alternative," *Journal of Legislation*, 13 (1986): 48–71; WBR, remarks to Metropolitan Center for Educational Research, 13 September 1984, WBR Papers.
21. *Chicago* (December 1988): 159, 160, 161.
22. WBR, remarks to House Judiciary Committee, 19 November 1981, WBR Papers.
23. *1985 Senate Hearings*, 244, 239, 248.
24. Ibid., 245.
25. Ibid.; WBR, remarks at Amherst College, 29 April 1983, WBR Papers.
26. Janice Blanton, interview with Heather Latham, 16 November 1992.
27. "Chronology of Events," typescript provided by Bakersfield City School District.
28. Ibid.; *New York Times*, 12 February 1984, 28;1.
29. "Chronology of Events," typescript provided by Bakersfield City School District.
30. *Annual Report of the Bakersfield City School District*, 28 April 1992.
31. *New York Times*, 28 February 1984, 28:1.
32. Consent Decree, 25 January 1984, U.S. v. Bakersfield City School District, Case 84–39, U.S. District Court, Bakersfield; *Washington Post*, 26 January 1984, A1a.
33. *New York Times*, 26 January 1984, 1:1.
34. *Los Angeles Times*, 26 January 1984, 3:1.
35. *Hearings of the House Judiciary Committee*, 99th Congress, 1st Session (1985), 332, 329, 328.
36. Drew S. Days III, "Turning Back the Clock: The Reagan Administration and Civil Rights," *Harvard Civil Rights-Civil Liberties Law Review*, 19 (1984): 330, 326, 325.
37. Arthur v. Nyquist, 415 F.Supp. 904 (1976); 712 F.2d 809 (1983); 712 F.2d 816 (1983).
38. *New York Times*, 1 February 1984, 26:1; 13 May 1985, 1:5; *New Republic* (7 November 1983): 18–20.
39. *New Republic* (7 November 1983): 20; *Columbia Law Review*, 86 (May 1986): 768.
40. *Harvard Civil Rights-Civil Liberties Law Review*, 19 (1984): 317; *Journal of Law and Education*, 18 (Spring 1989): 202.
41. Interview with WBR, 13 November 1992. Specter denied making the statements. Arlen Specter to author, 2 February 1993.
42. Order of the Court, 5 September 1986, 7, 2, 4–5, 13, Civil Action CV-F-84-39-EDP, U.S. District Court, Bakersfield.
43. Order of the Court, 30 January 1990, Civil Action CV-F-84-39-EDP, U.S. District Court, Bakersfield; *Eighth Annual Report of the Bakersfield City School District* (28 April 1992): 4, 5, 36.
44. *Eighth Annual Report of the Bakersfield City School District*, 18.
45. Nancy St. John, *School Desegregation*, passim; Al Caetano, interview with Heather Latham, 12 November 1992.
46. WBR, Remarks to the Metropolitan Center for Educational Research, 13 September 1984, WBR Papers.

47. U.S. v. Yonkers, 624 F.Supp. 1276 (1985), 1289, 1291, 1383–85.
48. Ibid., 1290, 1329.
49. Ibid., 1339, 1337, 1289. 1291, 1383, 1315, 1327–42.
50. Ibid., 1381–85.
51. Drew S. Days, III, "School Desegregation Law in the 1980s," *Yale Law Journal*, 95 (1986): 1737–68, 1754.
52. Village of Arlington Heights, 429 U.S. 252 (1977), 165, 270.
53. *Washington Post*, 10 September 1981, A17a.
54. Interview with Josh Bogin, 6 July 1993; interview with Sarah Vanderwicken, 23 April 1993.
55. Interview with Brian Heffernan, 30 April 1993.
56. U.S. v. Yonkers, 624 F.Supp. 1276 (1985); 837 F.2d 1181 (1987).
57. *New York Times*, 24 November 1985, XXII, 1:6.
58. U.S. v. Yonkers, 624 F.Supp. 1276 (1985), 1315, 1311.
59. Ibid., 1311, 1315, 1288, 1303, 1362, 1363, 1303.
60. Paul Craig Roberts and Lawrence M. Stratton, *The New Color Line*, 52
61. U.S. v. Yonkers, 624 F. Supp 1276 (1985), 1451–53.
62. Ibid., 1457, 1459, 1455, 1456.
63. U.S. v. Yonkers, 635 F.Supp. 1538 (1986); *New York Times*, 15 May 1986, II, 3:1; 8 June 1986, XXII, 4:5; 13 June 1986, 34:1.
64. *New York Times*, 27 April 1986, XXII, 1:5; 15 May 1986, II, 3:1; 15 June 1986, XXII, 6:5; 28 September 1986, IV, 7:1.
65. Ibid., 25 September 1988, 1:2; 8 February 1987, XXII, 1:1; 29 May 1988, XXII, 1:2; 4 June 1986, 26:1; 9 September 1988, XXII, 1:2; 25 September 1988, 1:2.
66. Ibid., 29 May 1988, XII, 1:2; 25 September 1988, 1:2.
67. Ibid., 4 August 1985, XXII, 21:3; 19 June 1987, II, 4:1; 16 December 1990, XII–WC, 27:1.
68. Ibid., 25 September 1988, 1:2; interview with David Weinberger, 27 April 1993; interview with Laura Babcock, 27 April 1993.
69. Information provided by Laura Babcock, 27 April 1993.
70. *New York Times*, 9 August 1987, XXII, 1:5.
71. Ibid., 15 November 1987, XII, 10:4; 9 August 1987, XXII, 1:5; 21 August 1988, XXII, 1:4; 31 August 1988, II, 1:5; 10 September 1988, 32:4; 11 September 1988, 36:1; 11 September 1989, II, 3:5; 8 November 1989, II, 1:5; 9 November 1989, II, 13:1.

19

Gold Plated Desegregation

It is a canard to say that the Reagan administration did not pursue school desegregation, since, if there was evidence of intentional discrimination, the administration required local officials to take affirmative steps to achieve more racial mixing. Sometimes it did so even when the evidence of discrimination was weak. However, because of public opinion and white flight, the administration maintained that more racial interaction could be achieved if the emphasis was shifted away from forced busing and toward both magnet schools and voluntary transfers.

To attract transfer students, the new magnets had to offer alluring programs, and school officials soon realized that voluntary desegregation could be used to obtain facilities and programs they had long coveted. Most wanted to hire more teachers and to have smaller classes. They wanted more books for the libraries and better equipment for the laboratories. They wanted better cafeterias, bigger gymnasiums, and budgets that would allow teachers and administrators to attend more workshops and conferences. The problem was that most communities would not provide enough tax money.

When magnets became a popular technique for achieving school desegregation, school officials figured out how both to avoid problematical tax referendums and to tap directly into the public treasury. Since federal courts were empowered to remedy violations of the Constitution, the new facilities and programs could be required by order of the courts, and in this way, new spending could be undertaken without mustering support from taxpaying voters.

The ingenuity of school officials bordered on venality and initially took the Reagan administration by surprise. Eventually, however, William Bradford Reynolds insisted that courts should approve only those expenditures that were reasonably related to desegregation.

Some of Reynolds's erstwhile adversaries supported him on this point. One was Thomas I. Atkins, a black civil rights lawyer who had represented the NAACP in more than thirty school-desegregation cases and who had criticized Reynolds and the Justice Department for allowing thousands of black students to remain in almost all-black schools in Chicago. In that instance, instead of emphasizing the specter of white flight, Atkins said, the Reagan administration should have required the dispersion of the 16 percent white minority throughout the public schools of Chicago. When the district court approved the consent decree that Reynolds had worked out with the Chicago school board, Atkins condemned the judge for "put[ting] the official stamp of approval on a white appeasement plan."[1]

Nevertheless, Atkins took exception to some of the expenditures that other courts ordered in the name of desegregation. Thus he objected when a district judge in Buffalo directed the mayor and common council to accede to the local school board's request for an additional $7.4 million to implement desegregation. In this instance, Atkins said, the school board was using desegregation as a rationalization for spending that had nothing to do with desegregation. He accused board members of "pursuing their private agendas of unmet educational needs" while civil rights groups incurred the wrath of taxpayers "for the added financial burdens courts were imposing."[2]

This issue also became central to school desegregation litigation in St. Louis and Kansas City.

I
St. Louis

The roots of the school desegregation controversy in St. Louis went back beyond the 1950s. Prior to *Brown*, the Constitution of Missouri required that black and white pupils be educated in separate public schools. By 1956, however, most people thought the schools of St. Louis had been desegregated. With the aid of a plan developed by a high-level black administrator, all students were assigned, irrespective of race, to schools near their homes. At the time the term *desegregation* was not understood to require that black and white students must mix in proportionally balanced schools, and no such balance existed in St. Louis; but six of the city's seven previously all-white high schools had racially mixed enrollments, and about two-thirds of the elementary students attended interracial schools. A 1962 report to the U. S. Commission on Civil Rights praised the school board for "desegregat[ing] all its schools completely in the school years 1954–1955 and 1955–1956." For more than a decade, St. Louis was considered a model of desegregation that the rest of the nation might emulate.[3]

Subsequently, several factors combined to cause resegregation. In the 1950s and 1960s, many whites (and some blacks) purchased newer and more spacious homes in the suburbs of St. Louis. The trend was made possible by increased prosperity; it was facilitated by the construction of major highways, and it accelerated when substantial numbers of lower-class blacks moved into middle-class neighborhoods and schools. As a result, the proportion of black students in the public schools of St. Louis increased from 30 percent in 1950 to 73 percent in 1977. By then, there were so few white students remaining in the city that it would have been difficult to integrate all the schools. Between 1970 and 1975, St. Louis lost a larger proportion of its students—about 22 percent—than any large city in the country.[4]

The board of education said these trends were beyond its control. After a trial that lasted for thirteen weeks and covered 7,115 pages of transcript, the district court agreed. Judge James H. Meredith held that St. Louis had desegregated its schools in the 1950s and was not responsible for any subsequent resegregation. Judge Meredith said that in a growing, mobile society, school authorities were "[not] required to make year-by-year adjustments of the racial composition of student bodies once the affirmative duty to desegregate has been accomplished." He commended the school board for allowing student transfers, for establishing some magnet schools, for placing many blacks in high administrative positions, and for developing a plan that assured that 30 percent of the teachers at each school would be of the race that was in the minority at that particular school.[5]

After reviewing the evidence, the Eighth Circuit Court found, in 1980, that Judge Meredith was "clearly in error as to the constitutional requirements." According to the appellate court, the schools had never been properly desegregated in the 1950s. The court held that because the school board instituted a neighborhood school policy instead of exchanging blacks from north St. Louis with whites from south St. Louis, "the black schools remained predominantly black and the white schools remained predominantly white, with very few exceptions"—that is, the school board had ignored the imperative of integration.[6]

The rationale of the appellate court partook of *ex post facto*. Essentially, the court held that the integration mandates of the late 1960s and early 1970s—of *Green*, *Swann*, and *Keyes*—had implicitly been in effect in the 1950s. *Brown* had said that students must be assigned to school "on a nondiscriminatory basis," but the appellate court of 1980 understood *Brown* to have required all along "that students [must] be assigned 'differently because of their race.'" Because the school board had adhered to "'racially neutral' assignment plans," the court of appeals held that there had never been the proper sort of desegregation.[7]

The appellate judges also committed an error of logic. They noted that racial imbalance persisted after the school district converted to neighborhood schools, and then inferred "segregative intent" because they said the imbalance was "predictable," "inevitable," and "unquestionably foreseeable."[8]

Even the punctuation of the appellate court was open to question. By placing the term *neighborhood schools* in quotation marks, the judges implied that such schools were not truly neighborhood schools but part of a nefarious design to perpetuate segregation.[9]

Dubious as it was, the opinion of the Eighth Circuit Court became the law for St. Louis when the Supreme Court declined to review the case. The school board then proceeded in the early 1980s to implement a court-ordered plan called "the Orfield plan," which tried to minimize white flight by considering schools desegregated if blacks made up between 30 percent and 50 percent of the students. As a result, in a system that was already 80 percent black, all white students attended schools that were integrated but many blacks remained in schools that were almost all-black. The "black" schools were then compensated with extra money to cover the cost of especially small classes, additional remedial instruction, and programs that addressed "the motivational needs" of their students. The plan also called for the continuation of magnet schools and for voluntary transfers.[10]

The Orfield plan did not please some blacks, who wanted whites to be dispersed as a 20 percent minority in each school. Nor did it please most whites in St. Louis, who wanted the schools to be left as they were or, alternatively, for the city and suburban schools to be merged into one large and predominantly white metropolitan district. But the federal courts and the Department of Justice thought the Orfield plan held "the promise of providing 'the greatest possible degree of actual desegregation, taking into account the practicalities of the situation.'" Because whites made up only one-fifth of the students in the city's public schools, and many were expected to leave St. Louis if they were dispersed as a 20 percent minority in each school, the courts found that if the schools were integrated "by imposing an eighty/twenty ratio in each school, an all-black school system would probably result."[11]

By the 1980s full integration could be achieved only by dispersing blacks throughout the suburbs of St. Louis, but the Supreme Court's 1974 *Detroit* ruling seemed to block that. As noted previously, in *Detroit* the high court had said that "the scope of the remedy is determined by the nature and extent of the constitutional violation." It said outlying, suburban school districts could not be forced to merge with city school districts unless the suburban districts had been shown to have engaged in intentional racial discrimination—and during the St. Louis desegregation litigation of the 1970s, there had not even been allegations of discrimination by the suburban districts.[12]

Integrationists in St. Louis had been slow to recognize the dimensions of their problem. When they filed their lawsuit in 1972, they had alleged only that the city of St. Louis had failed to desegregate properly, and they had asked for remedies that would apply only in the city. It was not until several years later that integrationists belatedly alleged that the suburban districts had acted with "segregative intent" to create "a metropolitan-wide racially dual public education system." As a remedy, they then asked the courts to impose mandatory busing for racial balance throughout St. Louis and in more than twenty suburban school districts.[13]

The suburban districts denied the allegations, but shortly before the case was scheduled to go to trial in 1983, the integrationists and twenty-three suburban school districts settled their differences by agreeing to a consent decree that was approved by the local district court. The integrationists may have thought they did not have enough evidence to prove that there had been the sort of interdistrict violations that would justify forced busing throughout the region; the suburban residents may have feared that their schools would be merged into one large metropolitan district. After eleven years of expensive adversary trials, both sides were tired of litigation.

The consent decree provided that student volunteers would be transported by bus or taxi from predominantly black schools in St. Louis to predominantly white schools in the suburbs. Suburban students would also be afforded transportation to magnet schools in St. Louis. The goals of the settlement called for the suburban districts to increase their black enrollments to at least 15 percent and no more than 25 percent, while the city hoped to attract 2,500 white suburban students to its magnet schools.[14]

The Reagan administration initially favored the settlement. In the early months of Reagan's first term, before Reynolds was confirmed as assistant attorney general for civil rights, the Justice Department even proposed a novel program to encourage voluntary transfers. It asked the district court to require the state of Missouri to pay college tuition for pupils who voluntarily transferred to increase integration—with one semester of free tuition at the state's colleges in return for each year of participation in the transfer program.[15]

The initial response to the administration's proposal was favorable. One college chancellor praised the plan for "reward[ing] students for being good citizens. It says if you help us solve a social problem, we'll help with your education." A school board official said, "What a lovely, creative idea!" Even the pro-integration magazine *America*, while saying that voluntarism was not a satisfactory alternative to the "compulsory busing" that the administration was "backing away from," conceded that the transfer program was "worth testing" in St. Louis.[16]

Eventually, however, the Reagan administration withdrew its proposal because of harsh criticism from parents and students. Many whites felt betrayed and scoffed at William French Smith's legalistic distinction between voluntary incentives and forced busing. "It's like a bribe," one student declared. "A lot of people want to go to college but can't afford to do so and would have to agree to be bused to a school they might not want to go to in order to go to college." Others said the plan was "discriminatory" because white students from the city and black students from the suburbs could not participate. Still others thought it was unfair to youths from elsewhere in the state, whose hopes for limited scholarship money would be sacrificed for the benefit of "someone who occupied a seat on a bus."[17]

The provisions of the consent decree remained in force, but without the inducement of free tuition, few whites transferred to magnet schools in St. Louis. After five years, there were only 650 such transfers—a far cry from the goal of 2,500.[18]

The consent decree was more successful in steering black students to the suburbs. By 1988 all but two of the suburban school districts had reached the 15 percent minimum goal for black students, and six of the districts close to the city had been authorized to accept transfers beyond the 25 percent cap. With about 12,000 blacks from St. Louis attending schools in the suburbs, the number of city students who were attending almost all-black schools was reduced from 30,000 to 19,000.[19]

Integrationists praised the transfer program. One civil rights activist characterized it as "important" because it had "opened up so many opportunities for black children from the segregated city schools." A black youth recalled getting up at 4:30 in the morning to attend suburban Clayton High, where he was senior-class president, a member of the football and baseball teams, and the senior-prom king. He thought that the transfer program had "helped enrich a lot of people's lives." He said, "Neither the city blacks nor the suburban whites knew anything about each other. Teachers, students and even parents became more educated about other races. Their stereotypes changed quite a bit." The plan was so successful that other metropolitan areas copied parts of the program, although none tried anything that approached the scale of that used in St. Louis.[20]

Yet even in St. Louis there were problems. Jerome B. Jones, the superintendent of the city's schools, called the transfers "both a bane and a blessing." He explained that "the students with higher motivation and parents with higher aspirations have left the city." As a result, Jones said, the children remaining in the city schools lost the benefit of bright and hard-working role models. Between 1984 and 1994, the rate of graduation from St. Louis's public high schools plunged from 47 percent to 26 percent.[21]

Nor did all go smoothly in the suburbs. Reports of theft and violence in the suburban schools increased after the transfer program began, and at some schools tension between the transfer and residential students ran high. One high school junior at Parkway Central said there had been "culture shock" when the two groups were brought together because "the black kids and white kids had grown up differently." An official conceded that there were "socialization problems" because students were "being confronted with kids they haven't had to interact with before, and they don't always like it."[22]

In 1993 ten years after the transfer program began, *Newsweek* published an essay by a white high school junior. "I always notice one thing when I walk through the commons at my high school," Brian Jarvis wrote. "The whites are on one side of the room and the blacks are on the other." Jarvis wrote that he felt "uncomfortable" when he had to walk through the "black" side to get to class. It was not that he was threatened or harassed. The black students "just quietly ignore me and look in the other direction, and I do the same." Jarvis said he had "become friends with Vietnamese-Americans, Korean-Americans, Iranian-Americans, Indian-Americans, Russian-Americans and exchange students from France and Sweden." The only students who remained distant were the blacks, who made up 25 percent of the enrollment. Jarvis was not even able to maintain a friendship with a suburban black who had been a teammate in Little League and with whom he had bunked at summer camp. They usually said nothing when they saw each other, "except maybe a polite 'Hi' or 'Hey.'" It was "as if fate has kept us apart; though, more likely, it's peer pressure."[23]

Yet the biggest problem with school desegregation in St. Louis did not involve strained race relations or skimming the black "cream" from the city schools. It concerned money. The taxpayers of Missouri balked when faced with the expenses that desegregation entailed, but the courts then stepped in and ordered tax increases that solved the schools' financial problems. In the process, however, the judiciary traduced basic principles of equity and the constitutional doctrine of separation of powers.

The cost of desegregation in St. Louis was enormous. The additional expense of implementing the city-only plan was about $22 million a year. After the voluntary cross-district transfer program was implemented, there were additional expenses for transportation, capital improvements, preschool centers, and all-day kindergartens. More money was earmarked for "extracurricular activities," "curriculum development," "peer tutoring," "shared motivation," "role model experiences," "public relations," and "special parent-staff seminars." Still more was required for the employment of additional teachers (to reduce average class size to twenty students). In 1984 the district court estimated the extra annual expense for desegregation at about $15 million for St. Louis and $49 million for Missouri, with the costs "increas[ing] very substantially in future years." The state estimated that the annual cost of the desegregation plan would amount to "well over $100 [million]." The cost of all the desegregation programs amounted to about $1.5 billion over the course of thirteen years.[24]

To justify the expense, the district court used inflated legal language. Because the St. Louis Board of Education and the state of Missouri were "adjudged...constitutional violator[s]," they could be required "to remedy the deprivations [they] caused." Essentially, what the court said was that if the taxpayers would not voluntarily incur the expenses needed to eradicate the continuing effects of unconstitutional discrimination, they could be ordered to do so. It would be "anomalous," the Eighth Circuit Court explained, "to suggest that the district court has the power to disestablish a dual school system but does not have the power to fashion an appropriate remedy."[25]

But what was the offense? It was that the St. Louis board of education, after *Brown*, had merely "desegregated" its schools by converting to a neighborhood system with a few magnet schools and an affirmative policy for teachers and administrators. Then the state failed to warn the school board that *Brown* implicitly required the sort of integrative actions that would later be elucidated in *Green* and its progeny. The city school board and the state government were guilty of insufficient prescience. They did not know beforehand that the Supreme Court would later change the meaning of desegregation.[26]

As a former state attorney general who had been close to the litigation for a decade, Missouri's Republican governor John Ashcroft was outraged by what the courts were doing. He put up a spirited resistance in court and also made several trips to confer with members of the Reagan administration. During those trips he persuaded Reynolds to enter the case on the side of Missouri.

In the legal arguments they presented to the Eighth Circuit Court, Ashcroft and Reynolds noted, first, that the state of Missouri had not agreed to the so-called consent decree. In 1983 integrationists had settled their differences with the suburban school districts by agreeing to a plan that called for voluntary interdistrict transfers and several new or expanded enrichment programs. The integrationists, the suburban districts, and District Judge William Hungate further agreed that the state (that is, the taxpayers of Missouri) would be responsible for funding the provisions of the consent decree. But because the state government had not been a party to these proceedings, Ashcroft and Reynolds noted that the St. Louis case differed from a conventional desegregation lawsuit. The integrationists and the suburban school districts, parties that had been antagonists for years, had joined together in what amounted to a friendly suit to obtain money from the state treasury. Ashcroft and Reynolds complained that the state government had been denied its day in court. They said it was wrong to bill the cost of a consent decree to a party that had never given its assent.[27]

Ashcroft and Reynolds further noted that although Missouri had been found to have committed an intradistrict violation in St. Louis, there was no finding that the state had committed the sort of interdistrict violation that would justify requiring the state to fund an interdistrict remedy. Missouri's "unconstitutional" action was its failure to bus black and white children between north and south St. Louis in the 1950s. It had failed, in the words of the Eighth

Circuit Court, "to desegregate the schools on a system-wide basis, including the predominantly white schools of south St. Louis and the predominantly black schools of north St. Louis."[28]

Even if such inaction had been at odds with *Brown*, Ashcroft and Reynolds said, the remedy should not extend beyond St. Louis. The Supreme Court had told the lower federal courts *not* to impose school desegregation plans that were designed merely to achieve a socially desirable result. The high court said that the goal of desegregation was to correct the racial separation that had resulted from official discrimination, and that remedies could be imposed only on parties that had been found guilty of constitutional violations. It said court orders should be "tailor[ed]...to fit the nature and extent of the violation"; it said a proper remedy could "extend no farther than required by the nature and extent of [the] violation"; it said, "The controlling principle consistently expounded in our holdings is that the scope of the remedy is determined by the nature and extent of the constitutional violation"; and the Court had said, "Without an interdistrict violation, there is no constitutional wrong calling for an interdistrict remedy."[29]

Ashcroft and Reynolds argued, in addition, that the school districts of metropolitan St. Louis were using desegregation as an excuse for obtaining expensive new programs that were tangential to desegregation. They said the districts had requested, and the courts had approved, "funding for general educational improvements in the integrated schools which were unrelated to desegregation."[30]

Ashcroft and Reynolds conceded that courts could order more than the reassignment of students. For instance, to deal with the continuing effects of discrimination, it might be necessary to establish some training and orientation programs for teachers; or to achieve desegregation voluntarily, it was advisable to have some new programs and facilities. But Ashcroft and Reynolds said the array of new programs enumerated in the St. Louis consent decree were "only remotely related to desegregation." They said, for example, that on the record before the court, there was no justification for spending an extra $1.76 million for "Coordination of Instruction."[31]

Finally, Ashcroft and Reynolds pointed to the separation of powers. They recognized that the Supreme Court had upheld the judiciary's right to require the payment of taxes that were essential to protect constitutional rights. Despite the principle that all bills for raising revenue should originate with the people's elected representatives, a string of judicial interpretations had established that unelected judges could compel local governing bodies to appropriate money "to provide complete relief for those whose constitutional rights have been violated." Nevertheless, Ashcroft and Reynolds insisted that such orders should not be issued "routinely." They had to be tailored to the circumstances of each case, and in *St. Louis*, they said, the courts had "failed to make the findings" that should have been required to justify the order of spending that was imposed.[32]

As will be noted below, eleven years later the Supreme Court would endorse Ashcroft and Reynolds's arguments. In the meantime, however, they had only minimal effect. The Eighth Circuit Court scotched a few of the programs that Judge Hungate had approved in *St. Louis*, even as it allowed most of the new spending to stand. By a vote of 7–1, the appellate court brushed over the separation of powers and distinguished the voluntary interdistrict transfers in *St. Louis* from the coercive interdistrict busing plan that the Supreme Court had prohibited in *Detroit*. The Supreme Court then refused to review *St. Louis*, but the issues would not go away. They come up again in *Kansas City*.[33]

III
Kansas City

In *Brown II*, the implementation decision of 31 May 1955, the Supreme Court indicated that public school students should be assigned on the basis of their place of residence rather than on the basis of race. The Supreme Court considered two possibilities: whether, "within the limits set by normal geographic school districting, Negro children should be admitted *forthwith* to schools of their choice"; or whether the judiciary "in the exercise of its equity powers, [should] permit an effective *gradual* adjustment to be brought about." After deliberating, the Court gave the lower federal courts some leeway. It said they should consider what was "practicable" in light of local circumstances. It said they should "make a prompt and reasonable start" and then should proceed "with all deliberate speed," with the goal "to admit [students] to public schools on a racially nondiscriminatory basis."[34]

Three months later the Kansas City, Missouri School District (KCMSD) abolished its previous system of racial segregation and assigned all students, regardless of race, to nearby neighborhood schools. Because blacks and whites were clustered in different neighborhoods, adoption of the neighborhood school plan did not lead to balanced racial mixing. Integrationists later found fault with the policy, but at the time almost everyone thought the KCMSD had complied with *Brown*.[35]

Resegregation began immediately. There were 1,200 fewer white students in 1955 than there had been the year before, with two-thirds of the loss occurring among whites who had been assigned to schools in mostly black neighborhoods. With each year, more whites left Kansas City, and more blacks moved in.[36]

Witnesses before the local district court later spent several weeks expounding on the reasons for the demographic trends, but the root causes could not be identified with precision. White flight was influenced by affluence, the lure of suburbs, apprehension about lower academic standards and disruptive students, fear of crime, and a desire to live among other whites. The black in-migration was influenced by the greater availability of blue-collar industrial jobs in the city as well as by a preference for living near other blacks rather than as a small minority dispersed throughout the suburbs. By situating a disproportionate amount of low-income public housing in the city, by underwriting low-interest home mortgages in the suburbs, and by building roads, sewers, and the like, the government also made it easier for different groups to congregate in different areas.[37]

Whatever the reasons, the racial balance within the public schools of Kansas City shifted dramatically. When *Brown* was decided, blacks made up 18.9 percent of the 63,487 students in the KCMSD. Thirty years later, 67.7 percent of the 35,520 students remaining in the district were black. In 1984 whites made up 27 percent of the public school students in Kansas City and 93 percent of the students in eleven nearby suburban districts.[38]

Against this background, integrationists returned to court in 1977 and demanded that blacks should be spread evenly throughout Kansas City and its suburbs. They said that *Green* required balanced integration, and they called for forced busing as a way to remedy the spatial separation they said that government policies had caused. They said dispersion was "the only effective way to 'protect and preserve' the constitutional rights" of black students.[39]

District Judge Russell G. Clark found these arguments unconvincing. After hearing the plaintiffs' evidence, but before allowing the defense to proceed, Judge Clark dismissed the case against the suburban school districts. He held that even if everything the plaintiffs said was true, it would not prove that the suburban districts had committed the sort of interdistrict violation that the Supreme Court, in *Detroit*, had required as a precondition for ordering an interdistrict remedy. On appeal, a divided Eighth Circuit Court affirmed that the suburban districts were "not liable for interdistrict violation and may not be ordered to participate in interdistrict relief."[40]

By dismissing the case against the suburbs, the district and circuit courts ruled out the possibility of coercive metropolitan busing. That pleased then State Attorney General John Ashcroft, who hailed Judge Clark's decision as "a major victory for the suburban school boards in terms of autonomy for local school boards." It did not please integrationists who complained that the dismissal of the suburbs from the case "foreclosed the single opportunity by which 'effective' school desegregation could have been achieved."[41]

However, while ruling against the integrationists' demand for an interdistrict remedy, Judge Clark also held that the schools within Kansas City had never been properly desegregated. Therefore, Judge Clark held, the city could be required to do more—much more as it turned out—to achieve a greater degree of integration within the city itself. Like his judicial brethren in *St. Louis*, Judge Clark held that Kansas City had merely "desegregated" in the 1950s when it converted to a neighborhood school system. It had not anticipated the sort of substantial integration that *Brown* implicitly required and that the Supreme Court would later clarify in *Green* and *Swann*. Judge Clark found fault with the KCMSD for not moving beyond desegregation to achieve "mathematical racial balance in its schools."[42]

In addition to the KCMSD's "failure to do more" to achieve systemwide integration, Judge Clark found that racial imbalance "caused a...*reduction* in [black] student achievement." After listening to social scientists who testified for the plaintiffs, Clark concluded that predominantly black schools inculcated a "general attitude of inferiority among blacks" and "produce[d] low achievement." He said, in addition, that "this situation is correctable and that the schools in KCMSD, when provided with adequate resources, sufficient staff development, and proper teaching methods, can attain educational achievement results more in keeping with the national norms."[43]

Judge Clark's finding came as a surprise. By the 1980s, few credible social scientists believed there was any relation between integration and the academic performance of black students. Even in the late 1960s, when sociologist James S. Coleman first suggested that an integrated environment was the key to improving the performance of disadvantaged blacks, the view was never more than an hypothesis that, given the knowledge available at the time, could best be said not to have been erroneous. After further research, even Coleman admitted, in 1975, that it had been "wishful thinking" to believe that integration would lead to academic improvement. Thus it was extraordinary for Judge Clark to refurbish Coleman's old theory as a "finding of fact"—especially when the racial gap in test scores was not any greater in Kansas City than elsewhere.[44]

Nevertheless, in 1986 the Eighth Circuit Court upheld Judge Clark's finding that the KCMSD was responsible for academic retardation as well as for failing to achieve the proper sort of integration. It did so on the ground that an appellate court "[should] not reverse the district court's factual findings...unless they are clearly erroneous."[45]

This was a second turning point in the litigation. The first had been when the courts dismissed the case against the suburbs, thereby ensuring that any remedy would be limited to Kansas City; and the second was the holding that the failure to provide substantially balanced, predominantly white public schools deprived blacks of the constitutional right to an equal education. Together, these findings propelled *Kansas City* on a course that was uncharted and expensive.

In 1985 Judge Clark ordered the KCMSD to implement a three-year, $88 million program for "improving student achievement." In addition to $37 million for better school facilities, Clark called for an array of new programs. He ordered more kindergarten time for children who rated at or below the 45th percentile on the Kindergarten Inventory of Development Skills. He provided an expanded summer school and before- and after-school tutoring (because "additional learning time is a key component of any effort to improve the quality of education"). He demanded special stipends for teachers and staff members who attended seminars that discussed "the principles and goals of a desegregation plan" and the need for "a fair, equitable discipline program in a desegregated setting." To reduce class size, Judge Clark ordered the employment of 183 teachers. To prevent bright students from moving ahead of their peers, he called for greater use of the "mastery learning" approach to classroom management. To convince the community that these programs were needed as a remedy for discrimination, Judge Clark ordered the KCMSD to establish a "desegregation public relations program."[46]

Ambitious as it was, the $88 million plan of 1985 was only the first step. When the leaders of the KCMSD recognized that new programs and facilities could be required in the name of desegregation, they proposed additional expenditures which, in the words of the Eighth Circuit Court, were "concededly without parallel in any other school district in the country." At the behest of the KCMSD, in 1986 Judge Clark ordered that an additional $372 million be spent for capital improvements and for a comprehensive magnet plan. Unlike other school districts that had to patch and repair buildings, the KCMSD asked for (and Judge Clark ordered) new construction at a cost ranging from $61.80 to $95.70 per square foot. Unlike districts that offered a few magnet schools, the KCMSD proposed (and Judge Clark ordered) that all of the middle schools and high schools in the city, and one-half of the elementary schools, should become magnet schools. Special magnet programs were established in the foreign languages, the performing arts, and military science. There was a technical magnet high school that offered programs ranging from heating and air conditioning to cosmetology and robotics. The plan also included a twenty-five-acre farm and a twenty-five-acre wildland area for science study.[47]

To explain why Judge Clark required so many expensive programs necessarily involves a degree of speculation. By 1985 he had boxed himself in. Because he had dismissed the charges against the suburbs before finding that racial imbalance was responsible for the academic retardation of black students, Clark could not require interdistrict busing to obtain enough whites to solve the educational problem he had identified. If the requisite number of whites were to materialize, Clark therefore reasoned, there would have to be inducements. One lawyer praised the judge for ordering "a tremendous infusion of money into the schools." Another lawyer said the judge's plan "just may work," adding that "it may increase the attractiveness of the school system and make the urban center of our city a more attractive place to live and work."[48]

Judge Clark acknowledged that his "long term goal" was "to make available to all KCMSD students educational opportunities equal to or greater than those presently available in the average Kansas City, Missouri metropolitan suburban school district." He rejected proposals to repair or refurbish existing schools because he wanted new magnets that would be "so attractive that [they] would draw non-minority students from the private schools who have abandoned or avoided the KCMSD, and draw in additional non-minority students from the suburbs." He wanted "to regain some portion of the white students who fled the district," to "retain those who are still here," and to "redistribute the students within the KCMSD to achieve the maximum desegregation possible."[49]

The nature of the inducements was exemplified at Central High School. Once a solid fortress in an urban neighborhood, the old building was demolished in 1991 to make way for a new magnet with expensive equipment and an innovative curriculum. Adopting a modern version of the ancient Greek emphasis on a sound mind in a sound body, Central provided a computer for almost every student, emphasized courses in philosophy and foreign languages, and boasted athletic facilities that rivaled those of an Olympic Village. The field house had an indoor track, a fifty-meter swimming pool, whirlpool baths, indoor courts for handball and racquetball, and special rooms for wrestling and weight lifting. Central also had a model U.N. General Assembly that was wired for simultaneous translation in several languages.[50]

And Central was only one of seventeen magnet high schools in Kansas City. At other schools there were planetariums, greenhouses, and vivariums. There were radio and television studios with laboratories for editing and animation. There were movie-editing and screening rooms. There was a petting zoo, a 3,500-square-foot dust-free diesel-mechanics room, and a temperature-controlled art gallery.[51]

By 1992 the cost of the programs had amounted to a phenomenal $1.2 billion. The annual expenditure per student was $9,425—about 50 percent more than the average spent in the suburbs of Kansas City and three times the expense in some of Missouri's smaller school districts. According to Judge Clark, this was required to make amends for violating the Constitution. The violations, as noted previously, were (1) a failure to achieve substantially proportional racial enrollments throughout Kansas City in the late 1950s and afterwards; and (2) a failure to achieve substantially equal racial averages on standard student-achievement tests.[52]

Despite the new programs and facilities, there were widely reported problems with crime and discipline, and students in Kansas City continued to score below the average for big cities in most grades and subjects. John Alspaugh, a professor of education at the University of Missouri, reported that after six years there was "no improvement whatsoever in children's scores in standardised tests of reading and maths." Instead, the drop out rate increased every year and by 1993 stood at 60 percent. By 1993, in fact, students in Kansas City were further behind their peers in Missouri than they had been in 1987. Because of this, and perhaps because of racial prejudice as well, recruiters fell short of their goals for attracting out-of-district students. After five years, some 1,290 suburban students had transferred into the city, but in the meantime about 1,500 additional white students had left the KCMSD. Thus the racial ratio did not change appreciably.[53]

Some integrationists attributed the dearth of white transfers to racism. Author Jonathan Kozol said that if white parents opted for suburban or private schools over the "superior [public] schools" of Kansas City, it would prove that white flight occurred "not because of inferior schools or overcrowded classes, but because of simple bigotry." Kozol said, "If spending a billion dollars in Kansas City does not win back the white middle class, then we will discover something very evil about America."[54]

Whatever its cause, the paucity of transfers was an embarrassment. Despite a staff of eleven public relations officers and an annual budget of more than $1 million for brochures and advertisements, the KCMSD did not increase the proportion of whites in the district. Despite the attractive and well-equipped magnet schools, and despite an average annual expense of $3,717 for each student transported from the suburbs in a district-provided taxi, more whites continued to leave the KCMSD than to enter the district.[55]

The scarcity of white transfers created a problem because Judge Clark had fashioned an unusual quota arrangement. He had ordained that magnet schools must increase their proportion of white students by 2 percent a year until whites made up 40 percent of the total enrollment. Since whites made up only 25 percent of the resident students of Kansas City, the failure of the recruitment drive had the unintended effect of preventing about 3,000 black elementary-school students from filling magnet-school slots that remained vacant awaiting nonexistent white transfers.[56]

Many blacks had long regarded the emphasis on white "body counts" as implicitly demeaning. It was yet another insult when blacks were turned away from the new magnets. "We were hurting when we were segregated," one clergyman declared. "Now we're hurting when there's an attempt to desegregate." Jerald Hill, the president of the Kansas City-based Landmark Legal Foundation, asked authorities "to dust off the empty desks and open the classroom door to students who prefer to learn about statistics rather than simply to be treated as a statistic." It was "a strange twist of fate," Hill said, that "black students now find themselves again the victims of discriminatory treatment solely on the basis of the color of their skin."[57]

Some angry black and Hispanic parents responded by saying they were white on magnet school application forms. Others asked the state to pay for private schools. Because the desegregation plan had denied their children access to the new magnet schools, they argued that Judge Clark's plan was victimizing the children rather than removing the barriers of illegal discrimination. To remedy this wrong, they asked for vouchers to use at some fifty private schools that had agreed to take in 4,000 applicants from the KCMSD. One leader of the group was Judy Rivarde, a mother whose daughter had graduated from the public schools with good grades but such low ACT scores that she could not get into college. Mrs. Rivarde said she was afraid that her seven-year-old son Quentin would suffer the same fate if he was shut out of the new magnet schools.[58]

Judge Clark eventually dismissed Mrs. Rivarde's lawsuit, but in 1990 another angry group of taxpayers and government officials managed to take their case to the Supreme Court. By then the Reagan administration had passed into history. But in 1988, while he was still in office, Reynolds had prepared a legal brief that opposed the taxes that Judge Clark had imposed to pay for desegregation. The litigation before the Supreme Court concerned financial matters and the separation of powers.

By the 1980s the physical condition of many of Kansas City's public schools had deteriorated to the point where repairs would have been required even in the absence of desegregation. In one of his opinions, Judge Clark called attention to "inadequate lighting; peeling paint and crumbling plaster on ceilings, walls and corridors; loose tiles, torn floor coverings; odors resulting from unventilated restrooms with rotted, corroded toilet fixtures; [and] noisy class rooms due to lack of adequate acoustical treatment."[59]

Everyone agreed that the deterioration of the facilities was due to a policy that the KCMSD called "deferred maintenance," yet there was no agreement about the reason for the deferral. Judge Clark accepted the explanation of school officials who developed something of a conspiracy theory. As they saw it, whites in Kansas City had repeatedly voted against necessary taxes because most white children no longer attended the public schools. One school board member explained that the public schools "had lost voter support among majority white voters so completely that we were unable to meet our basic obligations." She said, "People don't want to pay higher taxes for schools where black children go. It's not 'their' kids."[60]

State officials, on the other hand, attributed the decrepit conditions to waste and mismanagement. They said that because student enrollments had declined by 50 percent since *Brown*, there was no need for higher taxes. Governor Ashcroft noted that even before Judge Clark devised his expensive plans, the amount spent per student in the KCMSD was already the seventeenth highest among 451 school districts in Missouri.[61]

Whatever the reason for the problems, it was clear that Judge Clark's new programs would require an enormous infusion of money. It was also clear that voters were not going to approve new taxes. Finally, in 1987, after Kansas Citians voted down proposals to raise taxes for school desegregation for the fourth time in nineteen months, Judge Clark ordered that real estate taxes be increased from $2.05 to $4 per $100 of assessed valuation. Clark also increased the state income tax of those who lived, worked, or operated businesses in the KCMSD from 6 percent to 7.5 percent. In addition, Clark reiterated an earlier holding that made the state government responsible for 75 percent of the costs of desegregation. On appeal, the Eighth Circuit Court set aside the income-tax surcharge but affirmed the other financial orders.[62]

In 1987, when Judge Clark imposed the new taxes, the United States was already well down the road of courts' ordering local governments to implement expensive new programs. In addition to school desegregation, courts had ordered states to build prisons and mental hospitals and to offer bilingual education. Nevertheless, Judge Clark's imposition of direct taxes touched off a furor. Taxpayers demanded that, pending appeal to the Supreme Court, the disputed levies should be placed in escrow accounts. "We did fight a Revolutionary War over the issue of taxation without representation," one man declared. Another characterized Judge Clark's orders as "real King George stuff." Many taxpayers expressed their ire by enclosing tea bags with their tax checks.[63]

In 1989 the Supreme Court agreed to decide whether Judge Clark had exceeded his constitutional authority. The Supreme Court limited its review, however, to the matter of judicial taxation. The Court said it would consider "the manner in which the remedy is to be funded" but rejected the state's argument that the abstract question of judicial authority could not properly be considered apart from the facts of the case. The high court refused to consider the state's argument that "the only reason that the court below needed to consider an unprecedented tax increase was the equally unprecedented [and excessive] cost of its remedial programs."[64]

The lawyers for Missouri soldiered on. They said the lower federal courts had implemented "an extravagant magnet remedy far beyond what is required to eliminate the vestiges of segregation." But the Supreme Court said that was beyond the limited scope of the review. Missouri said that the lower courts, after denying the existence of an interdistrict violation, had saddled taxpayers with responsibility for fancy schools that were intended to lure white youths back from the suburbs. But that was also beyond the boundary.[65]

The Supreme Court was interested in only one question, which each side tried to phrase to its advantage. The plaintiffs said the issue was whether a judge, after making a finding of discrimination, should have the power to protect the minority from the tyranny of the majority. The defendants said the question was whether District Judge Russell Clark, in the *Kansas City* lawsuit, had usurped authority and had unconstitutionally trammeled the rights of taxpayers and of the state government.

Missouri's lawyers made the best argument they could in the blinkered circumstances. They reminded the Supreme Court justices of the civics courses they had taken in high school—the ones that told about the separation of powers and the iniquity of taxation without representation. They noted that the constitutional provisions pertaining to the judiciary nowhere mentioned the word "tax" or anything that resembled it. They recalled Alexander Hamilton's assertion, in Federalist 78, that the judiciary had "no influence over either the sword or the purse." They quoted James Madison's words, in Federalist 48, that "the legislative department alone has access to the pockets of the people." They argued, in sum, that the Constitution denied judges the power of taxation.[66]

It was a powerful argument, one that persuaded the Supreme Court to conclude unanimously that Judge Clark had abused his discretion when he imposed the tax increase.[67]

But Missouri's victory was bittersweet because five members of the Supreme Court also held that judges have the authority to order local officials to raise taxes. Once courts have determined that there has been a violation of the Constitution, the majority ruled, judges can instruct local officials to do what is necessary to remedy the violation. Arthur A. Benson, a lawyer for the plaintiffs, hailed the decision as "a victory for civil rights litigants." He explained that the majority ruling affirmed "the principle that constitutional violations can and must be remedied, even if the remedy requires the constitutional violators to raise taxes, and whether or not their constituents are in favor of new taxes." David Tatel, another lawyer for the plaintiffs in *Kansas City*, praised the Supreme Court for reaffirming "that federal constitutional remedies do not depend on...the availability of money."[68]

Some editors were pleased with the Supreme Court's decision. After observing that "authorizing elected officials to levy a tax is vastly different from a judge imposing the tax himself," the *New York Times* praised the Court's majority for wisely upholding "the broad powers of federal judges to devise creative remedies for constitutional violations." The *St. Louis Post Dispatch* remarked that "when democracy fails, sometimes people have to pay." *Business Week* thought the Court's majority had manifested Solomonic wisdom in allowing Judge Clark "to order a financial remedy—but [refusing to permit him to] impose the taxes himself."[69]

Others accused the Supreme Court of making a distinction without a difference. The *National Review* said it was "disingenuous" for the Supreme Court to reproach Judge Clark "for having sought to impose the tax increase upon the city directly," but then authorize him to require elected officials "to enact the increase themselves." The Court thought it was maintaining "some semblance of representative government," but actually, the magazine said, it was perpetuating a "charade." "Better to have ventriloquists' dummies casting the votes than to reduce elected officials to such a role." In an editorial entitled "Judge George III," the *Wall Street Journal* dismissed the Court's decision as "simply too preposterous to survive for long," and added, "Kings did not ultimately succeed in taxing Americans without their consent, and neither will judges."[70]

Nor was opposition to the Supreme Court's opinion confined to conservatives. In a smoking editorial, the liberal *Washington Post* condemned "court-ordered taxation" and found it "very hard to understand how the Supreme Court could have refused to review the fantastic remedies ordered by the Kansas City judge." *Newsweek* warned that the nation's political system could be altered permanently if the Court's approval of judicial taxation caught on. "In an age where raising taxes is viewed by elected officials as hara-kiri," the magazine noted, "politicians now may have the perfect out: cut programs in those areas that are constitutionally mandated (schools, prisons, mental hospitals), wait for federal judicial enforcement that may dictate tax hikes, [and] then blame the judges."[71]

It is doubtful, however, that the decision of the Supreme Court will have much influence as precedent. By 1994, four of the five-justice majority had resigned, while all four of the justices who signed on to a spirited, and at times sarcastic, dissenting opinion remained on the Court. In the long run, the portion of the *Kansas City* litigation that pertained to taxes will probably be viewed as another byway in the Court's and the nation's difficult path to racial justice.[72]

The KCMSD, however, understood the decision of the Supreme Court as a signal to proceed with what it had been doing. In 1991 it hired a new superintendent of schools, a charismatic and innovative fifty-two-year-old administrator who had recently been forced to leave the superintendency of the Richmond, California, school district after questions about spending that outstripped revenue. Before that, he had been criticized for heavy spending in

Lake Travis, Texas, and for lapses in accounting in Montclair, New Jersey. With Walter L. Marks as superintendent, the taxpayers of Kansas City and of Missouri prepared for more spending and even higher taxes.[73]

True to form, in 1992 Superintendent Marks and the KCMSD asked Judge Clark to approve an ambitious ten-year plan to expand the magnet school system. Despite spending more than $1 billion for desegregation since 1986, Marks explained, there was still a long way to go to make the grade in student achievement. To continue with special programs for another ten years, Marks asked Judge Clark to provide the KCMSD with an additional $500 million. As Marks saw it, the expensive magnet programs had to be continued until the academic achievement of students in Kansas City reached the national norms on standard tests. To facilitate this eventuality, he also wanted a pay raise for teachers in the KCMSD.[74]

In April 1993 Judge Clark held that the Constitution required the continuation and expansion of magnet programs and a new pay raise for teachers. In explaining his decision, Clark repeated his legal rationale: because Kansas City had merely desegregated (rather than integrated) its students in the 1950s, it had failed to fulfill "its affirmative duty of disestablishing a dual school system"; and because of that failure, the academic achievement of black students had been depressed. Since academic retardation was a vestige of segregation, and since the Supreme Court had held that vestiges of segregation must be eradicated, Judge Clark ordered that magnet programs and judicial supervision of the KCMSD must continue until the academic achievement of black students improved substantially. A divided panel of judges from the Eighth Circuit Court then affirmed Judge Clark's orders because, according to the appellate judges, Clark's findings were not "clearly erroneous."[75]

Finally, in 1995, the Supreme Court repudiated Judge Clark. To do so, the Court took the unusual step of rehearing a case—and this time it reviewed *Kansas City* as a whole and not just the matter of the taxes and funding. The Court also ruled against the administration of President Bill Clinton which, after pointing to the low test scores, argued that Judge Clark's plan should continue because the local authorities had not yet done enough to desegregate their schools.[76]

In his opinion for the Court's majority, Chief Justice Rehnquist endorsed several of the points that John Ashcroft and William Bradford Reynolds had made when the *St. Louis* case was before the courts ten years earlier. While affirming that district courts should "eliminate to the extent practicable the vestiges of prior *de jure* segregation," Rehnquist brushed over the "clearly erroneous" standard and found that Judge Clark's order of a salary increase was "simply too far removed" and only remotely related to desegregation. Rehnquist also held that the performance of students on standard examinations was "clearly...not the appropriate test to be applied in determining whether a previously segregated district" had desegregated its schools.[77]

In *Kansas City*, the Supreme Court especially criticized Judge Clark for designing, and the Eighth Circuit Court of Appeals for approving, an interdistrict remedy to an intradistrict problem. The purpose of the Judge Clark's plan had been "to attract nonminority students from *outside* the KCMSD schools," but this *inter*district goal, the Court held, was beyond the scope of the *intra*district violation that Judge Clark had identified in the early stages of the lawsuit. Judge Clark had "devised a strategy to accomplish indirectly what [he] admittedly lacks the authority to mandate directly: the interdistrict transfer of students." In fact, the Court found, Clark's whole approach—the "pursuit of 'desegregative attractiveness'"—was beyond the scope of the lower courts' proper remedial authority.[78]

In a concurring opinion, Justice O'Connor stressed an important point. After noting that the low test scores and the pattern of ethnic concentration in different neighborhoods were due to "myriad factors...not readily corrected by judicial intervention," O'Connor said that school-desegregation remedies, like affirmative action plans, should be "narrowly tailored" to redress only the effects of past discrimination. O'Connor emphasized that the Supreme Court had found fault with Judge Clark's failure to specify "the incremental effect that segregation has had on minority student achievement." She noted that since Clark never identified the portion of the persisting achievement "gap" that should be attributed to segregation rather than to other factors, his remedial plan could not be "narrowly tailored."[79]

Like Chief Justice Rehnquist and Justice O'Connor, Justice Thomas rejected Judge Clark's use of the test scores. Thomas also thought the mandated increase in teachers' salaries was too tangential to pass muster as a remedy for illegal discrimination. He also agreed that much racial clustering was not due to discrimination but to "larger social forces [and] private decisions."[80]

Thomas made a number of additional points. He said he was "amaze[d]" that "courts are so willing to assume that anything that is predominantly black must be inferior"; that too many judges thought "that blacks cannot succeed without the benefit of the company of whites"; that they assumed that "blacks, when left on their own, cannot achieve"; and that their jurisprudence was "based upon a theory of black inferiority."[81]

As a black man, Thomas resented the insinuation "that black students cannot learn as well when surrounded by members of their own race as when they are in an integrated environment." He said that there was nothing wrong with "mere *de facto* segregation (unaccompanied by discriminatory inequalities in educational resources)." He insisted that "'racial isolation' itself is not a harm; only state-enforced segregation is. After all, if separation itself is a harm, and if integration therefore is the only way that blacks can receive a proper education, then there must be something inferior about blacks."[82]

Yet Thomas did not restrict his censure to lower courts. As Thomas saw it, the Supreme Court itself could not escape responsibility for the "misconception[s]" and "overreaching" of judges like Russell Clark. He felt that in *Green* and its progeny, the Supreme Court had misconstrued *Brown*. *Brown* had tied the wrong of segregation to official discrimination by government authorities, but in *Green* and other cases, the Supreme Court had strayed from the principle that government authorities must reject racial distinctions and "treat citizens as individuals, and not as members of racial, ethnic or religious groups." He noted that the Supreme Court itself had insinuated that the Constitution prohibited not racial discrimination but the disproportionate concentration of blacks; and that in the name of "desegregation," the Supreme Court had allowed many lower federal courts to impose "aggressive or extravagant" plans in pursuit of a better racial balance. The "judicial overreaching" that occurred in *Kansas City* was the result of the Supreme Court's own "approval of such extraordinary remedies in the past," he said. "The time has come," Justice Thomas insisted, for the Court "to put the genie back in the bottle."[83]

Justice Thomas also criticized the Supreme Court for having allowed lower courts, in the past, to trample upon "principles of federalism and the separation of powers and...to pursue other agendas unrelated to the narrow purpose of precisely remedying a constitutional harm."[84]

Agreeing with Thomas, the columnist George F. Will offered this assessment of *Kansas City*: "The road from *Brown* to this most recent school-related case—a case ostensibly about segregation but really about using racial patterns as pretexts for social engineering—has been winding and bumpy. The decision to restrain Judge Clark is one more sign that the nation is escaping from the intellectual dead end of solving social problems—including the most intractable ones, regarding race—by allowing judges to bend the Constitution to the service of their own political agenda."[85]

Notes

1. *Chicago Tribune*, 12 January 1983, 19:1.
2. Arthur v. Nyquist, 712 F.2d 809 (1983), 813.
3. Liddell v. Board of Education, 469 F.Supp 1304 (1979), 1313–18.
4. Ibid., 1318–22; *New York Times*, 23 September 1977, 20:1.
5. Liddell v. Board of Education, 469 F.Supp. 1304 (1979), 1361–62 and passim.
6. Adams v. U.S., 620 F.2d 1277 (1980), 1285, 1291, 1287.
7. Brown v. Board of Education, 349 U.S. 294 (1955), 300; Adams v. U.S., 620 F.2d 1277(1980), 1291, 1286, 1284, 1285.

8. Adams v. U.S., 620 F.2d 1277 (1980), 1287.
9. Ibid., 1284, 1285.
10. Liddell v. State of Missouri, 491 F.Supp. 351 (1980), 356; 731 F.2d 1294 (1984), 1303–04, 1312–13, 1299, 1301. The plan was named for its principal author, Professor Gary Orfield.
11. Ibid., 1304, 1306.
12. Milliken v. Bradley, 418 U.S. 717 (1974), 744, 745.
13. Liddell v. Board of Education, 567 F.Supp 1037(1983), 1042, 1059.
14. Ibid; Liddell v. State of Missouri, 731 F.2d 1294 (1984), 1305–09; *New York Times*, 8 June 1988, II, 4:1.
15. *New York Times*, 5 May 1981, 1:2; *Time* (18 May 1981): 77–78.
16. *Newsweek* (18 May 1981): 49; *Time* (18 May 1981): 77; *America*, (6 June 1981): 547.
17. *New York Times*, 8 May 1981, 16:1.
18. Ibid., 8 June 1988, II, 4:1.
19. Ibid.
20. David S. Tatel and Bryan Dean, quoted ibid.
21. Ibid.
22. Jennifer Ryan and Susan Uchitelle, quoted ibid.
23. *Newsweek* (3 May 1993): 14.
24. Liddell v. Board of Education, 491 F.Supp. 351 (1980), 357; 677 F.2d 626 (1982), 630; 567 F.Supp 1037 (1983), 1051; Liddell v. State of Missouri, 731 F.2d 1294 (1984), 1318, 1333, 1312, 1317, 1316; National Association for Neighborhood Schools, *Bulletin 68*, Summer 1993.
25. Liddell v. Board of Education, 567 F.Supp. 1037 (1983), 1052; Liddell v. State of Missouri, 731 F.2d (1294), 1321, 1311.
26. "The facts are that most schools in the heart of North St. Louis were black in 1954 and remain black today, and that most schools in South St. Louis were white in 1954 and remain white today. The Board of Education has simply never dealt with this overwhelming reality. If the Board had dealt with the problem in 1954–1956 and had implemented a plan for integrating the schools in North and South St. Louis, we would have a different case today. We would have to examine the question from an entirely different point of view." Adams v. U.S., 620 F.2d 1277 (1980), 1291. Also see Liddell v. State of Missouri, 731 F.2d 1294 (1984), 1328.
27. Ashcroft and Reynolds's arguments were generally congruent but were presented separately and differed on some points. Ashcroft's position was summarized in the court reports. For Reynolds's views, see the legal briefs that he, Charles J. Cooper, and Brian K. Landsberg prepared for *Liddell v. State of Missouri* and for *Liddell v. City of St. Louis*, Supreme Court Library.
28. Liddell v. State of Missouri, 731 F.2d 1294 (1984), 1328, 13302, 1304; William Bradford Reynolds, Charles J. Cooper, and Brian K. Landsberg, brief for Liddell v. State of Missouri, 10–11, Supreme Court Library.
29. Hills v. Gautreaux, 425 U.S. 284 (1976), 293–94; General Building Contractors v. Pennsylvania, 50 USLW 4975 (1982), 4981; *Milliken v. Bradley*, 418 U.S. 717 (1974), 744, 745.
30. Liddell v. State of Missouri, 731 F.2d 1295 (1984), 1315.
31. Ibid., 1315; William Bradford Reynolds, Charles J. Cooper, and Brian K. Landsberg, brief for Liddell v. State of Missouri, Supreme Court Library.

32. U.S. Constitution, Section 7, number 1; Griffin v. County School Board, 377 U.S. 281 (1964); Milliken v. Bradley, 433 U.S. 267 (1977); William Bradford Reynolds, Charles J. Cooper, and Brian K. Landsberg, brief for Liddell v. State of Missouri, 22–24, Supreme Court Library.
33. Missouri v. Jenkins, 63 LW 4486 (1995); Liddell v. State of Missouri, 731 F.2d 1294 (1984).
34. Brown v. Board of Education, 349 U.S. 294 (1955), 298 n.2, 300, 301, emphasis added.
35. Jenkins v. State of Missouri, 593 F.Supp. 1485 (1984), 1493.
36. Ibid., 1493.
37. Ibid., 1491.
38. Ibid., 1492, 1495; *New York Times*, 29 January 1985, 19:1.
39. Jenkins v. Missouri, 593 F.Supp. 1485 (1984), 1489; *New York Times*, 28 May 1977, 8:1; JoAnn Grozuczak Goedert, "The Future of Interdistrict School Desegregation," *Georgetown Law Journal*, 76 (1988): 1889–92; James S. Liebman, "Desegregating Politics," *Columbia Law Review*, 90 (1990): 1515–16 n.258.
40. Jenkins v. Missouri, 593 F.Supp. 1485 (1984), 1488; Jenkins By Agyei, 807 F.2d 657 (1986), 661.
41. *New York Times*, 3 April 1984, 26:3; JoAnn Grozuczak Goedert, "The Future of Interdistrict School Desegregation," *Georgetown Law Journal*, 76 (1988): 1894.
42. Jenkins v. Missouri, 593 F.Supp. 1485 (1984), 1492; Jenkins By Agyei, 807 F.2d 657 (1986), 706. The courts found particular fault with the KCMSD for acquiescing in the continuation of disproportionately black schools in the southeast corridor of Kansas City.
43. Jenkins v. Missouri, 593 F.Supp. 1485 (1984), 1492; Order of the Court, 15 June 1985 (emphasis in original), quoted in Brief for Respondents, 2, Missouri v. Jenkins, Supreme Court Library; Jenkins v. Missouri, 639 F.Supp 19 (1985), 24.
44. *National Observer*, 7 June 1975.
45. Jenkins By Agyei, 807 F.2d 657 (1986), 666.
46. Jenkins v. Missouri, 639 F.Supp. 19 (1985), 25, 41, 43–44, 31, 35, 30; Missouri v. Jenkins, 495 U.S. 33 (1990), 38. As noted in Chapter 16, mastery learning diverted fast learners into nonacademic "enrichment," while slow learners received extra instruction in academic subjects.
47. Jenkins By Agyei, 855 F.2d 1295 (1988), 1318–19; Missouri v. Jenkins, 495 U.S. 33 (1990), 60–61.
48. William Taylor and Richard King, quoted in *New York Times*, 16 November 1986, 32:1; 17 September 1987, 20:1.
49. Jenkins By Agyei, 855 F.2d 1295 (1988), 1302.
50. *New York Times*, 10 October 1989, 25:1; John C. Danforth, "The Earl F. Nelson Memorial Lecture," *Missouri Law Review*, 56 (1991): 246.
51. Missouri v. Jenkins, 495 U.S. 33 (1990), 77.
52. *New York Times*, 25 September 1991, II, 6:1; National Association for Neighborhood Schools, *Bulletin 67*, April 1993. The Supreme Court later stated that "per-pupil costs within the [suburban school districts], excluding capital costs, range from $2,854 to $5,956; per pupil costs within the KCMSD, excluding capital costs, are $9,412." Missouri v. Jenkins, 63 LW 4486 (1995), 4494.

    As will be noted below, Judge Clark required the state of Missouri to pay for three-quarters of the expense for desegregation, and beginning in 1991 funds were transferred from other schools around the state to pay for desegregation in Kansas City. "The rest of the state is mad as hell," said assistant attorney general Michael J. Fields. "Some districts are going bankrupt, firing English and math teachers, and then they look over here and see these Taj Mahal buildings." *Washington Post*, 11 April 1992, A1a.

53. *Kansas City Star*, 18 May 1993, A1; 27 February 1993, C1; 10 August 1992, A1; Alspaugh, as paraphrased by *The Economist*, 28 August 1993, 24. There was at least one other reason for the dearth of transfers: most suburbanites were pleased with their school districts. This, at least, was the conclusion sociologist David Armor reached after polling 1,495 parents of school-age children in Kansas City and its suburbs. See *Kansas City Star*, 27 February 1993, C1.
54. *Washington Post*, 11 April 1992, A1a.
55. *National Review* (15 September 1989): 28–29; *Newsweek* (31 July 1990): 56; *Kansas City Star*, 18 May 1993, A1. Some students were bused in from the suburbs, at an average annual cost of $1,655.
56. Richard Nadler and Tom Donelson, "Affirmative Reaction," *National Review* (15 September 1989): 28–29; *Newsweek* (31 July 1990): 56; *New York Times*, 3 August 1989, 14:4.
57. Rev. Emmanuel Cleaver, quoted in *Newsweek* (31 July 1990): 56; *National Review* (15 September 1989): 29.
58. Ibid.; *New York Times*, 3 August 1989, 14:4.
59. Jenkins v. Missouri, 672 F.Supp. 400 (1984), 403.
60. Ibid., 403; Jenkins By Agyei, 855 F.2d 1295 (1988), 1305; statement of Sue Fulson, *Hearings before the Senate Judiciary Committee*, 101st Congress, 2nd Session, 19 June 1990, 62; *St. Louis Post Dispatch*, 23 September 1987, 1:1.
61. *St. Louis Post Dispatch*, 23 September 1987, 6:1.
62. Jenkins v. Missouri, 672 F.Supp. 400 (1987); Jenkins By Agyei, 855 F.2d 1295 (1988); *St. Louis Post Dispatch*, 27 September 1987, 1:1; 20 August 1988, 1:1.
63. *Wall Street Journal*, 2 October 1989, 1:1; Michael Fields, quoted ibid; Bill Waris, quoted in *Newsweek* (12 October 1987): 98.
64. Missouri v. Jenkins, 495 U.S. 33 (1990), 53, 79–80.
65. Ibid., 53; John Ashcroft to Paul Simon, 17 July 1990, in *Hearings of the Senate Judiciary Committee*, 101st Congress, 2d Session, 19 June 1990, 171–76; *New York Times*, 20 April 1990, 32:1.
66. Jacob E. Cooke, ed., *The Federalist* (Middletown: Wesleyan University Press, 1961), 523, 334; *Washington Post*, 20 April 1990, A26a; *Wall Street Journal*, 2 October 1989, 1:1.
67. Missouri v. Jenkins, 495 U.S. 33 (1990), 34, 50–52.
68. *New York Times*, 19 April 1990, 22:1; *Los Angeles Times*, 19 April 1990, 20:1.
69. *New York Times*, 6 November 1989, 22:1; 20 April 1990, 32:1; *St. Louis Post Dispatch*, 20 April 1990, 20:1; *Business Week* (14 May 1990): 166.
70. *National Review* (14 May 1990): 18–19; *Wall Street Journal*, 23 April 1990, 14:1.
71. *Washington Post*, 20 April 1990, A26a; *Newsweek* (30 April 1990): 62.
72. The majority opinion was written by Justice White, who was joined by Justices Blackmun, Brennan, Marshall and Stevens. The dissenting opinion was written by Justice Kennedy and joined by Chief Justice Rehnquist and Justices O'Connor and Scalia.
73. *New York Times*, 8 May 1991, II, 7:1.
74. *Kansas City Star*, 27 February 1993, C1; 18 May 1993, A1; Missouri v. Jenkins, 63 USLW 4486 (1995), 4488 n.2.
75. Jenkins By Agyei, 11 F.3d 755 (1993); 13 F.3d 1171 (1993); 23 F.3d 1297 (1994); Missouri v. Jenkins, 63 LW 4486 (1995), 4488–89, 4499.

76. For a summary of Clinton's position, see *New York Times*, 24 November 1994, II, 16:4.
77. Missouri v. Jenkins, 63 USLW 4486 (1995), 4491, 4494. The decision of the Court was 5–4, but the dissenting justices focused on technical procedural points. They noted the irregularity of the Court's hearing the same case a second time. They also noted that despite the Supreme Court's longstanding insistence that it was "a court of law...rather than a court for correction of errors in factfinding," the Court had rejected the "findings" of Judge Clark—findings that had been "endorsed by the Court of Appeals." They said the court had departed "from the practices that produce informed adjudication." Only Justice Ruth Bader Ginsburg, in a separate dissent, suggested that she personally believed the previous decisions were correct. Ibid., 4512, 4512, 4516.
78. Ibid., 4492.
79. Ibid., 4498, 4494.
80. Ibid., 4498, 4499.
81. Ibid., 4498, 4499, 4500.
82. Ibid., 4500.
83. Ibid., 4500, 4501.
84. Ibid., 4498, 4502–5.
85. *Newsweek* (26 June 1995): 66.

20

Light at the End of the Tunnel?

In 1981 Ronald Reagan asked William Bradford Reynolds to find a better approach to school desegregation than compulsory busing. The centerpiece of Reynolds's alternative plan turned out to be magnet schools and other curriculum-enhancement programs that were designed to induce families to choose an integrated education. At the outset, however, Reynolds expected to give the new approach what he called "prospective application only." He did not propose to challenge busing plans that were already in effect, as the public, Reynolds said, would not be well served "by reopening wounds." He also noted that the law generally recognized a special interest in the finality of judgments, saying "that interest is particularly strong in the area of school desegregation."[1]

Yet it was inevitable that local school districts eventually would ask to be released from busing decrees. For a generation, the Supreme Court had emphasized that the courts' jurisdiction over desegregating districts should be only temporary. *Brown* said the district courts should "retain jurisdiction" during the "period of transition" between segregation and desegregation. *Swann* said, "[A]t some point, these school authorities and others like them should have achieved full compliance with this Court's decision," at which point "further intervention by a district court should not be necessary" unless there was proof of additional acts of intentional discrimination.[2]

The principle that court-ordered plans should be enforced only until segregation and its effects were eliminated was consistent with, and really mandated by, a standard maxim of equity law—the idea that "the nature of the violation determines the scope of the remedy." When a court-ordered remedy has accomplished its purpose—that is, when the unconstitutional condition has been remedied—the jurisdiction of the court should cease. Otherwise, the judiciary would improperly usurp the responsibilities of others.[3]

In addition, many people were eager to regain local control over their schools; and they thought Reynolds was guilty of a certain contrariety when he said court ordered busing was a failed experiment that should not be imposed in new places, but one that should not be challenged in areas where it was already in effect.

Thus, despite Reynolds's initial reluctance, it was not possible to avoid the question of when desegregation orders should be lifted. In 1985 former Solicitor General Rex E. Lee identified the termination of court orders as "the most important unresolved issue in the school desegregation area." The key questions were, When, and on what showing, should the governance of school systems be restored to elected officials? Under what conditions, if any, should court-ordered busing yield to local preferences for neighborhood schools? Reynolds played an important role in shaping the answers to these questions, doing so in litigation that arose in Norfolk and Oklahoma City.[4]

I
Norfolk

Unlike St. Louis and Kansas City, Norfolk did not move speedily to desegregate its public schools after *Brown*. Instead, for five years Virginia's largest city was caught up in a state policy that refused to countenance even token desegregation.

The policy was known as "massive resistance," and it received its greatest support in rural counties where the percentage of blacks in the student population ranged upward from about 50 percent. Some segregationists admitted that schools could be desegregated effectively in areas where blacks made up only a small proportion of the total population. But they said that "the problem of integrating, say, 57 Negro students in Dickenson County with 6,460 white students in Dickenson County is one thing. The problem of integrating 1,500 white students and 1,800 Negro students in Prince Edward County is quite another."[5]

Other segregationists said that by the fourth grade, white students as a group were two years ahead of blacks on standard tests of academic skills, and the gap doubled by the time the children were in high school. It followed, one said, that "if we are ordered to carry out horizontal integration, that is, to combine white and Negro pupils according to their present grade, the teacher who now has an aptitude range of three years among white pupils in one classroom will find a range of five to six years in a mixed class." Referring to statistics on illegitimacy and venereal disease, segregationists said the races also had different sexual mores. One white school superintendent bluntly declared, "Sexual promiscuity is what [whites] fear most." A white father said, "[M]ost blacks were so far behind our children academically and differed in mores and cultural attainment. There was nothing good that our children could gain from interaction in school with blacks."[6]

Responding to such sentiment, Virginia's state legislature declared that segregation was essential to the maintenance of high standards. To prevent "incalculable harm to the public schools...and the disruption of education," the legislature resurrected the doctrine of "interposition" that James Madison and Thomas Jefferson had outlined in the Virginia and Kentucky Resolves of 1798. Essentially, the legislature said that if the federal government exercised powers not authorized by the Constitution, a state government had the right to interpose its authority between the federal government and the citizens of the state. The disputed federal mandate then would become a nullity in the state unless the Constitution was amended to provide explicitly for the policy that was in question. According to the logic of interposition, alleged usurpations could be checked and suspended pending appeal to the people of the other states. In the absence of an amendment to the Constitution, the Virginia legislature insisted, states should retain the authority to operate segregated schools.[7]

Members of the legislature said the right to interpose could be inferred from the nature of the Constitution and its system of checks and balances. They further provided that the governor of Virginia should withhold state funds from any local district that voluntarily mixed the races in its public schools. They feared that the mostly black counties would be placed in an indefensible position if other areas complied with *Brown*.[8]

Yet local leaders in Norfolk did not regard desegregation with alarm and thought a school board could require desegregating black students to establish their qualifications by passing certain tests. Besides, since the black population was disproportionately concentrated in certain parts of Norfolk, they thought that conversion to a nondiscriminatory neighborhood school system would not lead to much racial mixing.[9]

Because of the state legislature's policy, however, Norfolk and other local communities were not allowed to desegregate their schools. In 1958, when Norfolk and two other cities admitted some blacks to previously all-white schools, Governor Lindsey Almond withdrew state funds and schools had to be closed. This touched off a reaction throughout the urban and suburban areas of Virginia, where most whites saw no need to maintain segregation. Similar opinions were also prevalent in the counties of the Shenandoah Valley and in the Appalachian Mountains, where the proportion of black residents was quite small.[10]

The opponents of massive resistance joined together in the state legislature, and eventually the legislators rescinded interposition and adopted a freedom-of-choice plan that allowed local communities to assign pupils without regard to segregation. Massive resistance ended in 1959 when twenty-one black students entered previously all white schools in Norfolk and Arlington, but the problems of the Norfolk school board were only beginning.

Initially, District Judge Walter Hoffman allowed the school board to limit desegregation to black children who made a good showing in an interview and scored well on standard tests. However, when the pupil-placement board routinely denied most of the applications of blacks who wished to attend racially mixed schools, Judge Hoffman struck down what he called "the unconstitutional application of a law which is constitutional on its face." The placement board professed to be concerned with character and academic qualifications, but Judge Hoffman found that "the race of the child [was] the controlling factor wherever a child of one race seeks admission to a school solely or predominantly attended by children of the opposite race." Despite *Brown*, Judge Hoffman said, "The melody of massive resistance lingers on."[11]

After the pupil-placement program was declared invalid, new members were elected to the school board and, according to Judge Hoffman, Norfolk made "great strides" toward desegregation. The board began by dividing the city into five attendance areas and by requiring all students, regardless of race, to attend a school in their district. This did not lead to racially balanced mixing, but by 1967 about 3,000 blacks were attending schools that previously had been all white. In addition, approximately 133 teachers were working at schools attended predominantly by students of a different race.[12]

This did not satisfy the NAACP. It demanded that the racial ratio of the faculty in each school should be about the same as the citywide ratio, and it proposed to give students in the predominantly black Area IV an option that would not be available to students elsewhere in Norfolk—the freedom to choose a school outside the district of their residence. In addition, the NAACP challenged a plan to build a new Booker T. Washington Senior High School in Area IV.[13]

This was too much for Judge Hoffman. In the past he had agreed with the arguments of the NAACP and had entered orders accordingly. Now, however, the judge wrote that the NAACP had "changed" so much that there was a question as to whether it was arguing "in good faith for the class that it represents." Judge Hoffman felt certain that the leaders of the NAACP, in opposing construction of a new school in a black neighborhood, were out of touch with most blacks in Norfolk. He also thought the assignment of teachers to reflect a citywide racial ratio would violate the Civil Rights Act because it would constitute "racial balance as distinguished from desegregation." He held, in addition, that it would be an impermissible form of racial discrimination to allow residents of black neighborhoods to attend schools outside their district while denying that choice to students who lived elsewhere in Norfolk.[14]

But the NAACP's proposals found favor with the judges of the Fourth Circuit Court, who reversed Judge Hoffman on every key point. In 1968 the circuit court said that the teaching staffs in Norfolk's schools should be racially balanced. The circuit court also required the school board, before beginning construction of new schools, to "determine whether the new school is located to perpetuate segregation."[15]

One year later, after the Supreme Court's decision in *Green,* the NAACP and the Civil Rights Division returned to court and argued that good-faith implementation of the governing constitutional principles required that students must be racially balanced in each school throughout Norfolk. Judge Hoffman characterized their argument as "saying that the only solution is 'bussing' (sometimes referred to as 'busing')."[16]

The Norfolk school board disputed this interpretation and warned that busing would precipitate a massive flight of middle-class families. The school board also prepared an extraordinary document to explain what it called the "optimal" approach to desegregation. With citations to sociologist James S. Coleman and to urban demographer Karl Taeuber, and with supporting testimony from Harvard professor Thomas Pettigrew, the school board maintained that "children of all backgrounds tend to do better in schools with a predominant middle-class milieu." The board further said that since most whites in Norfolk were middle class, and most blacks were not, it was necessary to have a majority white enrollment if a school was to have a predominantly middle-class atmosphere. The board argued, therefore, that the best situation for effective desegregation was one in which blacks made up about 30 percent of the total number of students. They felt that in such an environment blacks could escape the effects of being socialized in a lower-class black culture without suffering at the same time from psychological isolation.[17]

In Norfolk, where 43 percent of the 56,000 students were black, the optimal-mix theory meant that about one-third of the black students would have to remain in predominantly black schools. However, the school board proposed to stagger attendance assignments so that each child would spend "at least a substantial number of years...in an *optimally* desegregated school." It also proposed an array of compensatory educational programs for "any predominantly Negro school which may result from the limits of the number of available white middle class children."[18]

This satisfied Judge Hoffman. "The good faith of the School Board cannot be questioned," he wrote. He further predicted that if "social class climate" was not considered, "the beneficial results of desegregation will never be achieved and the educational system will collapse." Citing the testimony of Professor Pettigrew, whom he described as a "racial integrationist" and "undoubtedly the most outstanding and knowledgeable person in the field of sociology and race relations as related to education," Judge Hoffman warned that "unless an intelligent approach is made to the problem of desegregation from a social class standpoint—and not solely through the mixing of racial bodies—desegregation will be a complete failure." Rejecting the argument that *Green* required racial balancing in each school, Judge Hoffman approved Norfolk's plan for "optimal" desegregation.[19]

A divided panel of judges from the Fourth Circuit Court reversed Judge Hoffman's decision. The problem with the Norfolk plan, the circuit court decided, was that it allowed for too many schools that were almost all-black, and that it did not compel enough white children to attend schools in black neighborhoods.[20]

In a separate concurring opinion, Judges Simon Sobeloff and Harrison L. Winter insisted that "constitutional rights...cannot be made to depend on an appraisal of the 'reasonableness' of desegregating." While acknowledging that *Brown* had been concerned with equal educational opportunity, Judges Sobeloff and Winter said the principal holding of *Brown* was that segregation was unconstitutional because it implied that blacks were "inferior and not to be associated with." The purpose of desegregation was to end this sort of "living insult." Yet, they said, the optimal-mix theory suggested that whites were "a precious resource" and that black children would be improved by associating with their betters. This theory might be camouflaged in terms of socioeconomic class and the necessity of creating a middle-class milieu, Judges Sobeloff and Winter said, but it rested essentially on the generalization that, "educationally speaking, white pupils are somehow better or more desirable than black pupils."[21]

The Fourth Circuit Court also rejected Norfolk's system of geographical districting, with Sobeloff and Winter characterizing the "'neighborhood school' concept" as a "shibboleth" and "an impediment to the performance of the duty to desegregate." The circuit court ordered the Norfolk school board to use "all techniques for desegregation, including pairing or grouping of schools, noncontiguous attendance zones, restructuring of grade levels, and the transportation of pupils."[22]

Thus busing came to Norfolk. In 1971 the school board developed a plan that included the pairing and clustering of schools as well as widespread mandatory cross-town busing. Thousands of white students were assigned to schools in mostly black neighborhoods and, as a result, between 1971 and 1975 none of the more than sixty schools in the city was over 90 percent black, and only three were more than 70 percent black.[23]

Then, in 1975, the district court dismissed the case after holding that "all issues in this action have been disposed of." According to Judge John McKenzie, the judge who imposed busing in 1971 after taking over the case from Judge Walter Hoffman, the school board had "satisfied its affirmative duty to desegregate."[24]

Judge McKenzie also ruled in 1975 that the public school system in Norfolk had become "unitary." At one time this term was used to describe school districts that operated only one set of schools (unlike "dual" systems that had separate schools for blacks and whites); but by the 1970s *unitary* was a legal term to describe formerly dual systems that had taken whatever steps were needed to create "a unitary system in which racial discrimination would be eliminated root and branch." It meant that a school district had complied with six criteria the Supreme Court mentioned in *Green*: it was not enough for a formerly dual system to eliminate racially identifiable patterns of student enrollment; it must also eradicate the vestiges of past segregation with respect to "faculty, staff, transportation, extracurricular activities and facilities."[25]

In declaring that the schools of Norfolk had become "unitary," Judge McKenzie was saying that the school board had satisfied the six indicia of *Green*. There was no question about the transportation, facilities, and extracurricular activities, and by 1975 Norfolk had achieved compliance in the other areas as well. Three of the seven members of the school board were black, as was the school superintendent and two of the three regional assistant superintendents; and 41 percent of the principals and 44 percent of the faculty were black. As Judge McKenzie put it, "[T]he Norfolk School Board is an integrated body, the Norfolk school administration is racially balanced, the racial composition of the faculty and staff is mixed, and the overwhelming majority of school children of both races...attend schools whose student bodies are racially mixed." Because "racial discrimination through official action has been eliminated from the school system," Judge McKenzie wrote, "the Norfolk school system is now 'unitary.'"[26]

The plaintiffs represented by the NAACP did not challenge the finding of "unitariness." Instead, they expressed satisfaction with the way things had worked out. They noted that there was more racial interaction than there would have been without busing, and they said there were beneficial academic effects. They said scores on standard tests improved during the 1970s, and that the gap between the average achievement of blacks and whites had narrowed appreciably.[27]

Nevertheless, many parents of both races thought the quality of public education had declined. Some thought the tests were a poor index of quality. Others were skeptical because they knew how test scores could be manipulated. Elsewhere, there were well-documented instances where school districts, in an effort to increase public confidence in integrated schools, boosted scores by teaching to the tests, only to see the scores plummet when a different test was given.[28]

Enrollment figures were testimony to the prevailing skepticism. During the decade after busing began in 1971, Norfolk's overall population declined by 11 percent and school enrollments plunged 37 percent. The white population of the city declined by 24 percent, but white student enrollment in the public schools went down 52 percent. In 1970, 57 percent of the school district's 56,830 students had been white; but by 1980 the overall enrollment had declined to 36,643 students, 57 percent of whom were black. Among those leaving the city were two of the principal lawyers who had demanded busing for racial balance. While they maintained their law offices in Norfolk, they sold their homes and moved beyond the city limits to Virginia Beach, a 95 percent-white community where children attended public schools that were predominantly middle class (or even higher).[29]

So many people departed that Norfolk lost the distinction of being Virginia's most-populous city. As that honor passed to adjoining Virginia Beach, the economic health of Norfolk deteriorated and property values declined. Realtors observed that newcomers to the area brushed past their Norfolk house listings in favor of suburban school districts. "They've heard [about busing] long before they arrive here," one real estate agent said. "It's been a definite detriment to the housing market, especially for families with young children."[30]

Busing thus precipitated three sorts of middle-class flight. Some families moved away, others sent their children to private schools, and still others decided not to move into Norfolk. Overall, the white enrollment in the city's public schools declined from 32,586 in 1971 to 13,327 in 1983. A declining white birthrate was partly responsible, but knowledgeable observers attributed much of the loss to rejection of forced busing.[31]

The Norfolk school board continued busing for eight years after Judge McKenzie's finding of "unitariness." Faced with the prospect of resegregation, however, in 1983 the board proposed to end cross-town busing in the elementary grades and to return to a system of neighborhood schools. For years the board had considered schools "racially identifiable" as black if the enrollment was more than 70 percent black, and by 1977 it had reduced the number of such schools to one. Yet, because of the loss of white students, by 1982 the number of such schools had increased to seven, and a consultant warned that if forced busing continued, the overall proportion of black students would increase to 75 percent by 1987. Beyond that lay the possibility that Norfolk's school system might become 90 percent black, as were the systems in Baltimore and Washington, or 86 percent black as in Richmond, thereby making it impossible to achieve integration.[32]

The school board recognized that middle-class flight could not be used as an excuse to resist or evade desegregation; but it said that there was an important distinction between using the defense of white flight as a pretext to avoid integration and dealing realistically with practical problems. Since integration could not be achieved without white students, steps had to be taken to retain the support of at least some middle-class whites.[33]

To stop the flight, the school board proposed to return to neighborhood elementary schools. To show its good faith, it also proposed to gerrymander the school attendance areas to foster the maximum feasible amount of racial interaction; and it provided a majority-to-minority transfer program that allowed any student to transfer away from a school in which his or her race made up more than 70 percent of the student body. The board hoped that a return to neighborhood schools would also turn around plummeting parental support for the schools (one indication of which was a decline in PTA membership from about 20,000 before busing to a mere 3,500).[34]

Integrationists complained that the school board's proposal would lead to "retrogression." They said it would create six elementary schools that would be at least 70 percent white and twelve that would be at least 70 percent black. Depending on how many blacks chose the majority-to-minority transfer option, it was possible that some schools would become 95 percent black. Integrationists said the policy was illegal because it was animated by a discriminatory intent that could be inferred from the disproportionate impact.[35]

Yet when integrationists challenged the school board's plan in the district court, Judge McKenzie ruled against them. Because the public schools of Norfolk had achieved "unitary" status in 1975, McKenzie held, the burden of proof shifted from the school board to the plaintiffs, who were required to show that the school board's proposal resulted from an intent to discriminate on the basis of race. Judge McKenzie then held that the plaintiffs had "failed to satisfy their burden" in that they "failed to show that the Board intended to use this Proposed Plan as a subterfuge for a deliberate attempt to discriminate on the basis of race."[36]

Judge McKenzie admitted that disproportionate impact was "not irrelevant," but said the Supreme Court had made it clear that such impact was "not the sole touchstone of an invidious racial discrimination." Courts were obliged to consider all the evidence, and Judge McKenzie concluded that the school board's stated justifications were not "mere pretexts." He found, on the contrary, that the primary objective of the board was to make integration possible by stemming white flight and by increasing parental involvement in school affairs. He characterized the proposed plan as "a reasonable, voluntary attempt on the part of the School Board to ensure that the school system retains the greatest degree of integration over the long term."[37]

Civil rights activists were alarmed. They said Judge McKenzie's logic would have "enormous and sweeping impact" and would amount to "a charter for the resegregation of the public schools." It would reverse decades of "painstakingly built progress," NAACP lawyer Julius Chambers declared. It would return the jurisprudence of desegregation "to the time of *Brown*."[38]

To prevent the allegedly dire consequences, the activists appealed to the Fourth Circuit Court. They continued to argue that a racially discriminatory purpose could be inferred because the proposed neighborhood school plan would lead to a greater degree of racial separation than had existed under busing. They said, in addition, that the school board was wrong to consider white flight. Since the Constitution should not bend to the popular will, they said, white flight was not a valid reason for failing to maintain racial balance.[39]

Integrationists also copied a page from the book the Civil Rights Division had used in *Yonkers*. They noted that the schools that would have the highest proportion of black students were located near government-subsidized housing. They said that because housing authorities had replaced slums with modern housing projects for low-income people, and because the projects were occupied almost exclusively by blacks, the government was responsible for the pattern of residential clustering. They then argued that the Norfolk school board should be required to remedy the separation by taking affirmative steps to ensure balanced racial mixing in the schools.[40]

Integrationists also made spirited arguments outside the courtroom. Instead of describing the good-faith efforts of a local school board, they characterized Norfolk's return to neighborhood schools as "the culmination of decades of resistance to *Brown*" and said that "the retrogression plan" revived "the effects of past discrimination."[41]

Articles in law reviews lamented that "decades of litigation [would] have been for nothing" if school boards were allowed to abandon racial balance. They said "a broader definition of unitariness" was needed—one that would require the maintenance as well as the establishment of racially balanced schools. They said judges like John McKenzie had forgotten "the legacy that made *Brown* and subsequent school desegregation decisions necessary." "To ensure that the promise of *Brown* is not thwarted in the final hour," they asked the courts of appeal "to prevent the reestablishment of a resegregated system."[42]

For integrationists, it was not enough for school boards to correct the amount of separation caused by previous school policies. To foster "a desirable sense of community" among the nation's "sociologically diverse and multi-ethnic peoples," they wanted courts to require racial balance indefinitely. In the interest of intellectual honesty, some integrationists proposed to scrap the "corrective" explanation the courts had developed for desegregation. Others said that would not be necessary, since "corrective ideas can insist upon a great deal." "If judicial remedial efforts are really justified so long as any harmful effects of discrimination persist," Yale law professor Paul Gewirtz wrote, "there is the possibility that remedies might continue almost indefinitely.... As a society we will probably never completely free ourselves from our racial history; the impinging past will always be with us."[43]

In the 1960s and 1970s, similar legal arguments, buttressed by the preponderance of elite opinion, had usually carried the day. On more than one occasion the Fourth Circuit Court had rebuffed district judges for allowing local officials too much leeway. Many observers expected that once again the appellate court would set aside the decision of a district judge and endorse the integrationist arguments; that to save "the Soul of *Brown*," the circuit judges would again prohibit "retrogression" plans and would hold that the maintenance of racial balance was an essential precondition for a declaration of "unitariness."[44]

It did not turn out that way. Instead, the Fourth Circuit Court affirmed Judge McKenzie's rulings and expanded on his logic. The circuit court might have done this even if the Reagan administration had not challenged the opinion that prevailed in the law reviews. Perhaps it was inevitable that because of the *corrective* rationale for desegregation, courts eventually would insist that the remedy for discrimination must be transitory and congruent with the violation; perhaps the constitutional separation of powers ordained that in time courts would emphasize the importance of local control; or perhaps civil rights activists precipitated a backlash when they argued that judicial control of the public schools should continue indefinitely.

The Fourth Circuit Court (and eventually the Supreme Court) held that school districts could end court-ordered busing after they attained unitary status. To use an old metaphor, they gave local school boards a glimpse of "light at the end of the tunnel." They showed them how they could get federal judges off their case. In doing so, they endorsed a spirited argument that Reynolds made for the Reagan administration and in support of the Norfolk school board.

As Reynolds assessed the case, the key question was how and when court supervision should yield to local control. The answer for Norfolk depended on whether the district court had properly held that the school system was unitary; and whether it was proper, after a finding of unitariness, to shift the burden to the plaintiffs to show that the school board's neighborhood plan was motivated by racially discriminatory intent.[45]

Reynolds insisted that the finding of unitariness was warranted, as the evidence in the case was so strong that even the NAACP and its clients had not challenged the finding in 1975. Besides, Reynolds said, District Judge McKenzie had complied scrupulously with a framework the Supreme Court had set up for resolving questions of unitariness. In *Green* the Court had mentioned six discrete areas that had to be cleansed of the vestiges of past unconstitutional segregation before a school system should be declared unitary. In addition to requiring "desegregation" in student enrollments and in the assignment of faculty and staff, the Court had called for equity in facilities, transportation, and extracurricular activities. Reynolds said these criteria were the touchstones for determining whether a dual system had been dismantled.[46]

In making this argument, Reynolds parted company with many civil rights activists. They said there were "'surface' vestiges [of segregation] that are amenable to relatively swift remedial action." These were the *Green* factors. However, in addition, they said, there were "'underlying' vestiges" that would take generations to correct. These included racial clustering in different neighborhoods and the performance of black students "on standardized tests, drop out rates, graduation rates and the percentage of students attending [college] and undertaking full-time employment." Until racial disparities in these areas were eliminated, they said, the underlying vestiges of past discrimination would not have been eradicated. They said that even if black youngsters attended racially balanced schools, their academic performance would be depressed because their home environments would have been shaped by parents and grandparents who had not enjoyed the advantages of integrated education.[47]

These themes were sounded frequently in the law reviews. Thus one author insisted that "a number of factors in addition to the *Green* factors...should be considered by courts in determining whether unitary status has been achieved." Another warned that "inattention toward long-term, underlying vestiges of state-imposed segregation" would lead to "premature termination of desegregation remedies." Yet another counseled courts to display "patience" and not to approve plans that would "reinstate the effects of past discrimination."[48]

Reynolds agreed that school districts should not be allowed to revive the vestiges of past discrimination, but he said that the "vestiges" should be defined in terms of the six *Green* factors and not with respect to "ever changing notions of what 'effects' must be remedied." He regarded some of the alleged vestiges of school discrimination as "meritless." He said that "residential segregation exists in almost every major urban area in the country and is caused primarily by 'social, economic and demographic forces for which no school board is responsible.'" He thought the root cause of the poor academic performance of many blacks was not known, but that the effect of past school segregation, if any, was slight when compared to social, economic, and cultural factors.[49]

The "sole obligation" of school boards, Reynolds said, was "to eliminate racial discrimination in the public schools." He noted that the Supreme Court had declared that this was "a large task and one that should not be retarded by efforts to achieve broader purposes lying beyond the jurisdiction of school authorities." He emphasized that the integrationist gospel of underlying vestiges had not found favor in the Supreme Court. To the contrary, as noted previously, the justices had said that federal courts were not at liberty to use their powers merely to achieve socially desirable ends. They were required "to tailor 'the scope of the remedy' to fit 'the nature and extent of the... violation'"; and once a school board had fully and faithfully implemented an appropriately tailored court order, the court's authority to direct the operations of the local schools should end.[50]

Reynolds emphasized that *Brown* and *Swann* had conceived of judicial supervision as transitory and that a 1976 case, *Pasadena v. Spangler*, had established a framework for determining when a district court should declare a school system unitary. In Pasadena local officials had implemented a court ordered plan for racial balance but appealed the judge's insistence that a correct racial balance must be maintained indefinitely. ("At least during my lifetime," the judge declared, there must be "no majority of any minority in any school in Pasadena.") On appeal, the Supreme Court vacated the "no majority" portion of the judge's order. The Court held that there was no need to maintain racial balance in the face of demographic changes, and that once the effects of prior discrimination by the school district had been corrected, local officials could not be required to ensure "that the racial mix desired by the court was maintained in perpetuity."[51]

What this meant, Reynolds said, was that school officials should not be required to correct racial imbalance they did not cause, and that once a school board had implemented an appropriate remedial plan, the vestiges of discrimination had been eradicated. Further, he said, there was no need to maintain racial balance for the sake of racial balance. School districts should not be required to combat the personal preferences of individual parents or the force of social, economic, and demographic trends.[52]

Just as the Supreme Court's *Detroit* case of 1974 had established *geographic* limitations on court-ordered integration (no interdistrict busing unless there was interdistrict discrimination), *Pasadena* made clear that there were *temporal* limitations. Consequently, the Reagan Justice Department settled several cases by providing that school districts would be declared unitary after three years of implementing an appropriate desegregation plan. Reynolds believed this was the best way to balance *Green*'s demand for affirmative steps with the competing interests of local control and color-blindness.[53]

Reynolds said there was only one circumstance that justified the continuation of a busing plan. After a school district had implemented an appropriate court-ordered plan, he said, busing should continue if a return to neighborhood schools was prompted by a discriminatory purpose. He insisted, however, that the burden of proof should be placed on those who challenged the action. Integrationists complained that it was "unreasonable" and "virtually impossible" to show that the dismantlement of busing was not done for nonracial reasons, but Reynolds argued that without shifting the burden of proof, a declaration of unitariness would be "meaningless."[54]

Finally, Reynolds applied the coup de grace. He said the argument that a school board must continue to avoid policies that increased racial imbalance amounted to "an assertion that there is a constitutional right to attend racially balanced schools." But in *Swann* (and later in *Detroit* and *Pasadena*) the Supreme Court expressly held that there was no constitutional right to any particular degree of racial balance or mixing. The Court also said that "past discrimination cannot, in the manner of original sin, condemn governmental action that is not itself unlawful." After redeeming themselves, Reynolds said, local officials should be allowed to manage their affairs. He said, "That a school board once practiced racial discrimination in the operation of its schools cannot forever serve to condemn otherwise legitimate educational decisions."[55]

NAACP lawyers said Reynolds's argument was "outrageous," but in 1986 a panel of three judges from the Fourth Circuit Court unanimously agreed with Reynolds on every point, even repeating the theological imagery. The Supreme Court then declined to review the case, thereby allowing the decision of the Fourth Circuit Court to stand.[56]

Reynolds regarded the courts' decisions as a major turning point in the history of school desegregation. He said the Fourth Circuit Court and the Supreme Court had done more than simply let Norfolk off the hook. Because there were similar situations in "many, many other school districts around the country," Reynolds predicted that *Norfolk* would be "a model for the future and for other school districts to follow." He let it be known that the Reagan Justice Department would assist other school boards that wanted to regain local control for color-blind policies.[57]

That was just what integrationists feared. They said there would be "a very general resegregation of the public schools" if districts could be freed from the legal taint of their past by complying with desegregation decrees for a few years. James M. Nabrit III of the NAACP Legal Defense and Education Fund issued a warning to any districts that were tempted to emulate Norfolk: "We want [them] to know that we will furnish...lawyers.... They ought to know that we are going to be in there fighting."[58]

The NAACP did more than fight. In 1986, in a case from Oklahoma City, the NAACP persuaded the Tenth Circuit Court to take a different approach toward similar issues. Then, for five years, the Supreme Court let the Oklahoma ruling stand. The mixed signals left both sides guessing as to the justices' thinking on the basic questions.

II
Oklahoma City

There was no massive resistance in Oklahoma. In 1955 the school board of Oklahoma City accepted *Brown*, abolished segregation, and assigned students to neighborhood schools. Since most blacks lived in the east and southeast portions of the city, this did not lead to balanced racial interaction. Nevertheless, for years the school board insisted that it had attained "complete desegregation."[59]

Yet even before *Green*, during the years when most federal judges still distinguished between desegregation and integration, civil rights activists took exception to the Oklahoma City plan. They did so because it was common for homes in the northern and western portions of Oklahoma City to have restrictive covenants that prohibited ownership by people of the "Negro race." Although these covenants were not enforced in the courts after 1948, they remained a barrier to black mobility.[60]

In addition, the school board allowed students to transfer if they did not like their neighborhood school. Often transfers had nothing to do with race, stemming instead from lack of social acceptance or difficulties with particular teachers or coaches, but the school board also allowed transfers if a student was unhappy attending a school where his or her race was in the minority. In fact, there were so many such transfers that the program was sometimes called a "minority to majority" plan.[61]

Minority-to-majority worked against racial mixing, and in 1963 the Supreme Court laid the policy to rest on the ground that the Constitution banned assignments that were based in whole or in part upon racial considerations. The Oklahoma City school board then disavowed minority-to-majority but continued to permit transfers for "other valid, good faith reasons"—a practice that turned out to accommodate most students who did not wish to attend a school where their race was in the minority. One principal explained,

> The interest of the child must be considered in the granting of special transfers.... If the child is unhappy in a situation, his unhappiness is not going to make a contribution to his learning experience, and if he is unhappy then he should be permitted to seek a place where he can be happy.[62]

Yet the transfer policy was not administered impartially, and in 1961 a black dentist named A. L. Dowell sued when officials looked askance at his son Robert's request to transfer from the all-black Frederick Douglass High School to the predominantly white Northeast High School. The school board approved the request, but only on condition that the boy enroll in an electronics course. As described by the principal at Northeast, the course was so difficult that the youngster was "discouraged to the point of distraction." When the school refused the boy's request to be excused from the course, Robert enrolled at a Catholic high school and his father went to court.[63]

The ensuing trial established that ninety-eight white students who lived in the Douglass area had been allowed to transfer to Northeast without any scholastic course requirements. Believing that this amounted to unlawful discrimination, District Judge Luther L. Bohanon then ordered that Robert Dowell be admitted to Northeast High without any conditions.[64]

Judge Bohanon also concluded that the treatment of Robert Dowell was part of a larger pattern of illegality. The school board argued that it had "no affirmative duty" to increase the percentage of pupils who attended racially mixed schools; but, although *Green* would not be handed down for several years, Judge Bohanon thought otherwise.[65]

In 1961, only 1,203 of Oklahoma City's 10,142 black students went to school with white students, and by 1965 only 2,500 black students attended racially mixed schools. The assignment of teachers was also skewed (but not so disproportionately). Surely, Judge Bohanon wrote, *Brown* required more than this sort of "nonintegration." In 1963 he held that "vigorous, affirmative measures" were required to achieve "meaningful" school integration. Instead of the erstwhile "minority to majority" transfer plan, he required the school board to adopt a "majority to minority" policy whereby students who were assigned to schools where their race was in the majority would be entitled to transfer to schools where their race was in the minority. In general, Judge Bohanon found that the school board "had not acted in good faith in its efforts to 'integrate' the schools."[66]

In 1967 a divided panel of three judges from the Tenth Circuit Court affirmed, with the dissenting judge, Jean S. Breitenstein, writing that there was "nothing in the Fourteenth Amendment that compels integration." For Breitenstein, "discrimination" involved "the denial of equal rights," while "integration" required "compulsory association." He said that the Supreme Court's prohibition of "classifications based on race" should apply to "majority to minority" transfers as well as to "minority to majority," and that it should also apply to faculty assignments.[67]

After the Supreme Court's ruling in *Green*, it was clear that it was Judge Bohanon, and not Judge Breitenstein, who was in tune with the developing judicial trend. In response to continued prodding from Judge Bohanon, in 1969 the school board developed what was called the "Comprehensive Plan," under which each high school would be a home base for students in its attendance area and would also serve as a magnet center in areas such as mathematics, science, social studies, and foreign languages. Each student would take elementary courses and satisfy basic requirements in his or her home base, but all advanced work would be done at a specialty school.[68]

Judge Bohanon praised the plan. He said the concentration of equipment for a special content area would make for greater efficiency; that assembling teachers in a particular discipline would provide intellectual depth and excitement; and that the cumulation of courses would make it easier to offer "special compensatory programs for students with academically deficient backgrounds and advanced courses for students with particular interests."[69]

Most importantly, Judge Bohanon held, the magnet plan would facilitate integration. By ensuring that all students would be "exposed on a regular basis to students from all ethnic groups," it would "play a positive role in the evolution of...emotionally and socially fit citizens." Traditionally, schools had been charged with responsibility for teaching academic subjects, but Judge Bohanon thought it was also important to give students "the experience of functioning in a multi-ethnic situation similar to that of the larger society." He said that "extensive contact with other children at an early stage" was "indispensable" if youngsters were "to become inculcated with a meaningful understanding of the essentials of our democratic way of life."[70]

It turned out, though, that most students preferred to take all their courses at the same school. The school board then allowed more classes in the neighborhood schools, and by 1972 integration was stymied. Only 12 percent of the students participated in an interchange, most of whom were high-achieving whites who enrolled in advanced elective courses. Judge Bohanon did not conceal his dismay when he described the situation that had resulted from accommodating student preferences and from disparities in academic achievement.

> Stripped of the beautiful adjectives and the meaningless promises used to obstruct its true intent and effect, the current...Plan is simply a "freedom of choice" plan. It does not work and will not work to desegregate the schools.... Typically at Douglass, a black high school, large numbers of white students arrive at the school and sit in white classrooms with few blacks. The converse situation occurs as groups from a school with predominantly black enrollment are transferred to a school with a predominantly white enrollment, and upon arrival, sit in a class as a unit or with only two or three white students.[71]

Yet Judge Bohanon was not dissuaded. When the Comprehensive Plan of 1969 failed to produce the desired amount of racial mixing, he turned to a standard busing plan that was prepared by John A. Finger, a professor at Rhode Island College. Formally known as "A New Plan of Unification for the Oklahoma City Public School System," local residents generally called it "the Finger Plan." It remained in place for thirteen years.[72]

Under the Finger Plan, attendance zones for the city's middle and high schools were gerrymandered so that racial enrollments were balanced. In the elementary grades a similar balance was achieved by busing blacks into white areas during the first four grades and whites into black neighborhoods for the fifth grade. A special feature allowed elementary students to escape busing and to attend school close to home if they lived in neighborhoods where the racial ratio came within 15 percentage points of the citywide average.[73]

After the school board had implemented the Finger Plan for five years, it filed a Motion to Close Case on the grounds that it "[had] eliminated all vestiges of state imposed racial discrimination" and was "operating a unitary school system." After holding a hearing in 1977, Judge Bohanon entered an Order Terminating Case. He held that the school board had operated the Finger Plan "properly" and had established a "unitary system."[74]

The school board continued with the Finger Plan for another eight years, but in 1985 it eliminated busing and assigned elementary students to neighborhood schools. It did so for reasons that ostensibly differed from those that led Norfolk to the same decision.[75]

The overall enrollment in the public schools of Oklahoma City declined from 74,000 when busing began in 1972 to 39,000 in 1984, with white enrollment plunging from 61,000 to 20,000. The percentage of white students dropped from 83 to 47, while the percentage of blacks increased from 17 to 40. The loss of students caused some concern, but in making the case for a return to neighborhood schools, the Oklahoma City school board emphasized other considerations.[76]

In Oklahoma City seven census tracts on the eastern side of the city had remained predominantly black from the 1950s through the 1980s, a condition that led some observers to maintain that the city was still segregated. At the same time, however, the percentage of all blacks in the metropolitan area who lived in the seven census tracts declined from 84 percent to 16.8 percent. The bulk of the black migration was from the east and southeast to central Oklahoma City, but by the 1980s some blacks were living in every part of the metropolitan area. Finis Welch of UCLA reported that when it came to the decline in the amount of residential segregation, Oklahoma City ranked 8th among 125 metropolitan areas.[77]

Integrationists favored dispersion, but many rank-and-file blacks complained that their neighborhoods suffered when prosperous and educated blacks departed. The inner city lost the leadership and influence of blacks who were upwardly mobile, and it also suffered in a more concrete way. As blacks moved into white areas, the special feature of the Finger Plan kicked in: children in the newly integrated areas were exempted from busing and their districts were allowed to have neighborhood schools. The provision had originally been conceived as a way to induce and reward integration, but by the 1980s, blacks in east and southeast Oklahoma City said it was "inequitable and oppressive," because it meant that their children had to be bused additional distances to reach predominantly white schools, and also that some of the fifth-grade centers in predominantly black areas had to be closed.[78]

The closing of schools in black neighborhoods gave rise to second thoughts about busing, and there was also dismay because integration had not brought the expected educational benefits. In responding to demands for civil rights, it seemed, school leaders had lost sight of academics; they had focused on race relations almost to the exclusion of traditional education. James Traub, a journalist with pronounced liberal leanings, reported that in Oklahoma City "children in the late seventies and early eighties were faring worse with every year they stayed in school: elementary students who scored above the national average on achievement tests were becoming below-average high school students."[79]

By way of contrast, in the nearby but separate school district of Millwood, a formerly all-white suburban area that had become a middle-class black enclave, academic scores were improving. Many blacks in Oklahoma City mentioned Millwood with undisguised envy, and Russell Perry, the publisher of a local black newspaper, said that "eighty percent of black parents would send their children to Millwood if they could find a way."[80]

Thus when the school board of Oklahoma City proposed to return to neighborhood schools, it encountered little resistance from black parents. When authorities in Norfolk had made their similar proposal, there had been a sharp split in the black community, but in Oklahoma City the great majority of blacks thought the hardships that busing entailed outweighed the alleged benefits. In court, the NAACP demanded the continuation of busing, but it did so without much support from the black community.[81]

Perhaps because so many blacks opposed busing, Judge Bohanon allowed Oklahoma City to return to neighborhood schools. In years past, few district judges had been more reliably pro-integration. In the 1960s Judge Bohanon had imposed affirmative obligations in advance of *Green*, and in the 1970s he required busing to maximize racial mixing. He wrote about the importance of having the schools inculcate values and prepare students for democratic interaction in a multiethnic society, but in the 1980s Bohanon sided with the school board against the NAACP.[82]

In explaining his decisions of the 1980s, Bohanon reiterated the arguments that Reynolds had developed for *Norfolk*. He noted that the schools of Oklahoma City had been declared "unitary" in 1977, and said "that once a school system has become unitary, the task of a supervising federal court is concluded." He rejected the argument that school districts must *maintain* the sort of racial balance they had to achieve in order to become unitary. "Once successful desegregation has occurred and a school system has achieved unitary status," Bohanon said, "'the system-wide racial ratio may thereafter change from time to time as a result of non-discriminatory' actions."[83]

Bohanon acknowledged that a school system could forfeit unitariness by intentionally engaging in additional discrimination, but he said the burden of proof in such cases rested on the plaintiffs. In *Oklahoma City*, the NAACP said the intent to discriminate could be inferred because the return to neighborhood schools had the *effect* of increasing racial imbalance in some schools, but Bohanon found that the school board's proposal was motivated by "legitimate, non-discriminatory" reasons.[84]

Bohanon held that the return to neighborhood schools was prompted "primarily" by a desire to end the inconvenience of long bus rides. In addition, the school board was trying to boost scores. The board rejected the argument "that young black students cannot achieve academically in schools which are not racially balanced," and instead emphasized a correlation between the achievement of students and parental involvement in the schools. Bohanon candidly admitted that after he ordered the Finger busing plan, membership in the PTA had declined from 26,582 to 1,377, and he held that a desire to turn this situation around constituted yet another nondiscriminatory reason for a return to neighborhood schools.[85]

In 1989 a divided panel of three judges from the Tenth Circuit Court reversed Bohanon's decision. This came as a surprise because, after grappling with the case for twenty-six years, Luther Bohanon probably exceeded all others in knowledge of the situation in Oklahoma City, and because the findings of a trial judge are supposed to be set aside only if they are clearly erroneous. When, as here, there was more than one plausible interpretation of the evidence, Bohanon's findings could not be clearly erroneous.

The Tenth Circuit Court eluded *clearly erroneous* by holding that, as a matter of law, the school board still had the "heavy burden" of proving that its actions were not motivated by a racially discriminatory purpose. Despite the "unitary" finding of 1977, the circuit court said, the burden remained with the school board. After reallocating the burden, the circuit court then held that the NAACP's witnesses had done enough to prevent the school board from proving a negative. The board had not shown beyond question that it had no discriminatory purpose when it returned to neighborhood schools.[86]

The Tenth Circuit Court also said that once racial imbalance had been dismantled it should "remain dismantled." To preserve its unitary status, "a system with a history of segregation" had to "maintain" the policies that led to unitariness. Otherwise, it said, "minority citizens [would] have no assurance of any but short-term and pyrrhic victories." The court declared, "It is well to remember, that the course we are running is a long one."[87]

In developing its approach, the Tenth Circuit Court drew on precedents from commercial law. The court briefly mentioned the landmarks of school desegregation law—*Brown*, *Green*, *Swann*, and other cases—but it relied on a different set of cases, ones with names like *Safeway Stores*, *Thermodynamics, Inc.*, and *United States v. Swift & Co.* In these cases, which involved allegations of unfair business practices, courts had entered orders that were intended to be permanent, and in which, "compliance alone [was not] the basis for modifying or dissolving an injunction." In these cases, injunctions were to be modified only if there were "dramatic changes in conditions unforeseen at the time of the decree." And it was these cases, the Tenth Circuit Court held, that should set the standard for school-desegregation cases. "We take the simple position that an injunctive order entered in a school desegregation case has the same attributes as any other injunctive order issued by a federal court."[88]

In reaching its decision, the Tenth Circuit Court rebuffed the Reagan administration. In briefing and arguing *Oklahoma City*, Reynolds reiterated the points he had made in *Norfolk*. Citing *Brown*, *Swann*, *Green*, and *Pasadena*, he said that court-ordered desegregation plans were "intended to be temporary measures" that should be implemented "*only* until segregation and its effects have been eliminated." He said the Supreme Court had made it clear that unitary status should be awarded to districts that implemented an appropriate court-ordered desegregation plan. Once unitariness had been achieved, he said, "there was no longer the predicate for judicial supervision," and judges would "improperly usurp local authority" if they imposed their orders "beyond the time necessary to remedy the unconstitutional condition." After unitary status had been achieved, Reynolds argued, court supervision could be reinstated only if the plaintiffs carried the burden of proving there had been additional acts of intentional discrimination. Reynolds emphasized that the Supreme Court had admonished that school-desegregation cases were not vehicles for general social change, but had the limited objective of desegregating school systems.[89]

Judge Bohanon had agreed with Reynolds's points. So had District Judge McKenzie and a unanimous panel from the Fourth Circuit Court in *Norfolk*. But a divided panel of the Tenth Circuit Court decided otherwise. In Virginia and the other states of the Fourth Circuit, school boards that achieved unitary status were allowed to return to neighborhood school systems; but in Oklahoma City the school board was required to maintain its system of race-based student assignments and busing until the neighborhoods of the city were fully integrated. By the end of the 1980s, different appellate courts had developed different standards for terminating court-ordered busing.

III
The Supreme Court

To the surprise of some legal experts, in 1986 the Supreme Court declined to review the *Oklahoma City* case. The justices recognized that when it came to the questions of when and how school districts could go about dismantling court-ordered desegregation plans, the courts of appeal were interpreting the requirements of the equal protection clause differently. But the justices accepted the inconsistency as a price that had to be paid to avoid a premature decision. It was not until 1991 that the high court addressed the questions.

In the meantime, several appellate courts endorsed the approach the Fourth Circuit Court had taken in *Norfolk*. In a case from Boston, the First Circuit Court held that once a school district had achieved unitary status, local authorities should be free to act as long as they did not engage in intentional discrimination. This was also the view of the Fifth Circuit Court, which, in deciding a case from Austin, Texas, criticized the Tenth Circuit for "den[ying] meaning to unitariness by failing ever to end judicial superintendence of the schools." The Ninth and Eleventh Circuit Courts chimed in with similar opinions, and even in the Tenth Circuit, another panel of judges stated that a school desegregation decree should "terminate once the district is declared unitary."[90]

In the law reviews, however, a contrary trend emerged. Here the Tenth Circuit Court's decision in *Oklahoma City* was widely praised. If courts did not make sure that integration was *maintained* as well as achieved, one author stated, "the net accomplishments" of desegregation would be "minimal." Another wrote that if schools were allowed to "revert" or "retrogress" toward racially imbalanced neighborhood schools, the courts would have wrought only a "sanitized form of apartheid." Yet another said, "*Brown* and its progeny [might] become a mere footnote in legal history" if courts did not ensure that integration "has been once and for all achieved." Another said the Supreme Court "could not possibly have intended to impose a remedy...which would practically vanish once a particular school system has been declared unitary."[91]

In 1991, after allowing the questions to percolate for five years, the Supreme Court finally rendered its judgment on *Oklahoma City*. By a vote of 5–3, the Court held that school systems that once practiced racial discrimination should be released from court ordered busing if they had complied with court orders and had taken all "practicable" steps to eliminate the vestiges of their former discrimination. In his opinion for the Court, Chief Justice Rehnquist said federal court supervision of local school systems had always been "intended as a temporary measure to remedy past discrimination" and was not meant "to operate in perpetuity."[92]

The Supreme Court held that the Tenth Circuit Court had been "mistaken" to rely on precedents from commercial law, saying that in commercial cases, injunctions were intended to be permanent because of "the continuing danger of unlawful restraints on trade." But the Court held that when it came to school desegregation, *Brown*, *Green* and other opinions of the Court had emphasized that judicial supervision would be required only during the "transition" until the public schools were "freed of racial discrimination." Once that was accomplished, the Court said, the constitutional provisions respecting the separation of powers required a restoration of "local control over the education of children."[93]

In reaching its decision, the Court rejected the NAACP's argument that the vestiges of discrimination would not be removed as long as the pattern of residential settlement was racially imbalanced. The Court said it was impermissibly "Draconian" for lower courts to consign repentant school boards "to judicial tutelage for the indefinite future." It reiterated the importance of eliminating "as far as practicable" the vestiges of segregation, but it indicated that the matter of residential concentration "was the result of private decisionmaking and economics, and that it was too attenuated to be a vestige of former school segregation."[94]

In *Oklahoma City*, the Court also ignored the NAACP's argument that the vestiges of segregation would not be eliminated, and therefore unitary status should not be awarded until a school district had achieved proportionality among all groups in student achievement, college attendance, and job placement. The Court held that a school district was "entitled to a rather precise statement of its obligations under a desegregation decree," and since the district judge had not identified academic retardation as a vestige of segregation, it was too late in the day to require proportional performance on tests or other measures of achievement.[95]

The Court's opinion in *Oklahoma City* prompted a spirited dissent from Justice Marshall. Joined by Justices Blackmun and Stevens, Marshall complained that "the majority today suggests that 13 years of desegregation was enough." Marshall agreed that the commercial cases did not establish the proper standard for judging school desegregation, but he "strongly disagree[d] with the majority...on what must be shown to demonstrate that a [desegregation] decree's purposes have been fully realized." Marshall complained that the Court had backed away from "lasting integration," acquiesced in "the reemergence of racial separation," and no longer insisted on "preserving an integrated school system."[96]

Oklahoma City was a triumph for partisans of local control and neighborhood schools. "This is bad news," said integration stalwart William L. Taylor. On the other side, Reynolds's former deputy Charles J. Cooper praised the Supreme Court for holding that schools were not required to deal with conditions that were beyond their reach. "This is a major victory," said Cooper, who represented the Oklahoma City school board when the case was before the Supreme Court.[97]

Some aspects of the Court's opinion invited further litigation. The Court had rejected the NAACP's arguments because District Judge Bohanon had not identified academic retardation as a vestige of segregation, and because Judge

Bohanon had found that the residential pattern in Oklahoma City resulted from "private decisionmaking and economics"—which led integrationists to hope that they might prevail on another day before a different district judge.[98]

In 1992, however, the Supreme Court again emphasized that judicial supervision of public education should be temporary and should last only until local authorities had eliminated the effects of discrimination to the extent practicable. In a case involving the largest school district in the state of Georgia, the DeKalb County School System, the Eleventh Circuit Court had ordered massive busing to create racially balanced schools in a suburban area where, because of residential clustering, 50 percent of the black students attended schools that were more than 90 percent black, and 27 percent of the white students attended schools that were more than 90 percent white. Despite the imbalance, and despite a history of segregation prior to 1969, the Supreme Court set aside the decision of the Eleventh Circuit Court, decided against the NAACP, and allowed for neighborhood schools.[99]

Since *DeKalb* arose after the Reagan administration left office, the details of the case need not detain us here. Suffice to say that in his opinion for a unanimous Court, Justice Kennedy reiterated several of the themes that Reynolds had developed when he was litigating the cases from Norfolk and Oklahoma City. Justice Kennedy emphasized that "federal judicial supervision of local school systems was intended as a 'temporary measure'," that "local autonomy of school districts is a vital national tradition," and that "the ultimate objective" was "to return school districts to the control of local authorities." Kennedy further disavowed the argument that school districts must make affirmative efforts until residential integration has been achieved. He stated, instead, that judges would exceed their proper limits if they went beyond remedying discrimination in the schools and tried to shape general social conditions. If the judiciary tried to counteract demographic shifts, Kennedy explained, the local school districts would be subjected to "ongoing and never-ending supervision by the courts."[100]

It was clear by 1992 that the jurisprudence of the Supreme Court had shifted decisively. In the late 1960s and early 1970s the Court had called for root-and-branch eradication of the last vestiges of segregation, but in *Oklahoma City* and *DeKalb* the Court settled for correcting the remnants of segregation "to the extent practicable." The Court still required desegregation, but it drew away from requirements that would entail judicial supervision for the foreseeable future. To balance the conflicting requirements of desegregation and local control over education, the Court held that local districts that had complied with a court-ordered desegregation plan should be declared "unitary" and should be released from judicial supervision even if a return to neighborhood schools would lead to a retrogression from the racial balance that the district had to attain to qualify for unitary status.

Then in 1995, the Court removed any lingering doubt about the change in direction. In the *Kansas City* case discussed in chapter 19, the Court ignored the "clearly erroneous" standard and set aside some of the factual findings of an integrationist district judge. It said that courts should not use racial scores on examinations to determine whether a school system had achieved unitary status. It said that many of the problems and conditions that integrationists had taken exception to were "simply too far removed" to be considered vestiges of discrimination.[101]

Some integrationists conceded defeat. "I do think [*DeKalb*] is a retreat from *Brown*...and from the decisions that gave it content," said William L. Taylor. Christopher A. Hansen of the ACLU, who had worked for black plaintiffs in several desegregation lawsuits, predicted with dismay that the Supreme Court's ruling would prompt many other school districts to seek independence from court control. A more upbeat Rex Lee declared, "The very general effect is going to be greater discretion [for] school boards...so long as they act in good faith."[102]

Notes

1. WBR statement before Subcommittee on Civil and Constitutional Rights, House Judiciary Committee, 19 November 1981, WBR Papers.
2. Brown v. Board of Education, 349 U.S. 294 (1955), 301; Swann v. Charlotte-Mecklenburg, 402 U.S. 1 (1971), 31–32.
3. Swann v. Charlotte-Mecklenburg, 402 U.S. 1 (1971), 16.
4. *New York Times*, 4 November 1985, 1:1.
5. Statement of James J. Kilpatrick, *Richmond News Leader*, 8 June 1954.
6. T. J. McIlwaine, quoted in *New Republic* (10 October 1955): 14; interview with Robert T. Taylor, 23 July 1979; Raymond Wolters, *The Burden of Brown*, 83–84, 86.
7. Senate Joint Resolution No. 3 (generally referred to as the "interposition resolution"), quoted in Adkins v. School Board, 148 F.Supp. 430 (1957), 434–35.
8. For an excellent account of "massive resistance" in Virginia, see James W. Ely, *The Crisis of Conservative Virginia* (Knoxville: University of Tennessee Press, 1976). For another good account, see J. Harvie Wilkinson III, *Harry Byrd and the Changing Face of Virginia Politics* (Charlottesville: University Press of Virginia, 1968).
9. The Supreme Court had authorized such tests in Shuttlesworth v. Birmingham Board of Education, 358 U.S. 101 (1958).
10. Norfolk v. Beckett, 260 F.2d 18 (1958); Beckett v. Norfolk, 181 F.Supp. 870 (1959).
11. Beckett v. Norfolk, 181 F.Supp. 870 (1959); 185 F.Supp. 459 (1959), 462.
12. Beckett v. Norfolk, 269 F.Supp. 118 (1967), 122 (extrapolating from the enrollment in the senior high schools), 139.
13. Ibid., 138, 124–28.
14. Ibid., 139 and passim.
15. Brewer v. Norfolk, 307 F.2d 37 (1968), 42.

16. Beckett v. Norfolk, 302 F.Supp. 18 (1969), 21.
17. Beckett v. Norfolk, 308 F.Supp. 1274 (1969), 1280 and passim.
18. Ibid., 1282.
19. Beckett v. Norfolk, 269 F.Supp. 118 (1967); 306 F.Supp. 1274 (1969), 1306, 1284.
20. Brewer v. Norfolk, 434 F.2d 408 (1970).
21. Ibid., 414; Brunson v. Board of Trustees, 429 F.2d 820 (1970), 823–27.
22. Brewer v. Norfolk, 434 F.2d 408 (1970), 414; Adams v. School District 5, 444 F.2d 99 (1971), 101.
23. William Bradford Reynolds, Charles J. Cooper, and Michael Carvin, Brief for the United States, Riddick v. Norfolk, 3, case 84-7412, Fourth Circuit Court of Appeals, Richmond (cited hereafter as Riddick brief).
24. The order of 1975 was not published, but a substantial portion of it is included in Riddick By Riddick, 627 F.Supp. 814 (1984), 818–19.
25. Ibid.; Green v. New Kent County, 391 U.S. 430 (1968), 435, 439, 442.
26. Riddick brief, 7.
27. *Education Digest* (November 1983): 42–43.
28. For examples from Fairfax, Virginia, and Cleveland, Ohio, see *Washington Post*, 14 March 1989, B5a, and *Time* (13 July 1981): 56.
29. Riddick By Riddick, 784 F.2d 521 (1986), 525; *Washington Post*, 9 February 1986, D1a; *New York Times*, 8 February 1986, 32:1; Beckett v. Norfolk, 308 F.Supp. 1274 (1969), 1287 n.26.
30. Joan Gifford, quoted in *Washington Post*, 9 February 1986, D1a.
31. Riddick By Riddick, 627 F.Supp. 814(1984), 817, 822.
32. Riddick By Riddick, 784 F.2d 521 (1986), 526, 528; 627 F.Supp. 814 (1984), 822.
33. Riddick By Riddick, 784 F.2d (1986), 539.
34. Riddick By Riddick, 627 F.Supp. 814 (1984), 817–18, 824.
35. *Louisiana Law Review*, 48 (1988): 790; Riddick By Riddick, 784 F.2d 521 (1986), 527; 627 F.Supp. 814 (1984), 820.
36. Riddick By Riddick, 627 F.Supp. 814 (1984), 820, 821, 823.
37. Ibid., 820, 824, 822.
38. *New York Times*, 17 June 1986, 20:1; 8 February 1986, 32:1; *Black Enterprise* (May 1986): 18.
39. Riddick By Riddick, 784 F.2d (1986), 539; *Phi Delta Kappan* (May 1986): 679–80.
40. Riddick By Riddick, 627 F.Supp. 814 (1984), 825–26; 784 F.2d 521 (1986), 538.
41. *Louisiana Law Review*, 48 (1988), 801, 813.
42. *Case Western Reserve Law Review*, 37 (1986): 57, 70; *North Carolina Law Review*, 65 (1987): 643, 634; *Oklahoma Law Review*, 40 (1987): 557.
43. *Journal of Legal Commentary*, 6 (1991): 312, 311; *Columbia Law Review*, 86 (1986): 782, 796.
44. *North Carolina Law Review*, 70 (1992): 615.
45. Riddick brief, 1.
46. Ibid., 12, 27–32.
47. *Columbia Law Review*, 87 (1987): 799; *George Washington Law Review*, 58 (1990): 1142.
48. *George Washington Law Review*, 58 (1990): 1162; *Columbia Law Review*, 87 (1987): 794; *Louisiana Law Review*, 48 (1988): 838, 839.

49. Riddick brief, 32, 33, 36.
50. Ibid., 33, 20; Swann v. Charlotte-Mecklenburg, 402 U.S. 1 (1971), 22; Hills v. Gautreaux, 425 U.S. 284 (1976), 293–94.
51. Pasadena v. Spangler, 427 U.S. 424 (1976), 433, 436.
52. Riddick brief, passim; *Louisiana Law Review*, 48 (1988): 818.
53. Riddick brief, 26; *Columbia Law Review*, 86 (1986): 791, 797.
54. Riddick brief, 37–41; *Missouri Law Review*, 56 (1991), 1155.
55. Riddick brief, 37, 41; Swann v. Charlotte Mecklenburg, 402 U.S. 1 (1971), 24–25; Mobile v. Bolden, 446 U.S. 55 (1980), 74.
56. *New York Times*, 7 December 1984, 18:6; Riddick By Riddick, 784 F.2d 521 (1986), 538 and passim; Riddick v. Norfolk, 107 S.Ct. (1986), 420.
57. *Washington Post*, 17 June 1986, A1d; *New York Times*, 9 November 1986, IV, 7:3.
58. *Washington Post*, 31 May 1986, Bf3; 4 November 1986, A1d.
59. Dowell v. Oklahoma City, 219 F.Supp. 427 (1963), 430–31, 434.
60. Ibid., 433.
61. Ibid., 440–41; Dowell v. Oklahoma City, 244 F.Supp. 971 (1965), 974.
62. Goss v. Board of Education, 373 U.S. 683 (1963); Oklahoma City v. Dowell, 375 F.2d 158 (1967), 162; Laderle J. Scott, quoted in Dowell v. Oklahoma City, 219 F.Supp. 427 (1963), 438.
63. Dowell v. Oklahoma City, 219 F.Supp. 427 (1963), 436, 439.
64. Ibid., 439, 427, 447.
65. Dowell v. Oklahoma City, 244 F.Supp. 971 (1965), 975.
66. Dowell v. Oklahoma City, 219 F.Supp. 427 (1963), 437, 440, 447; Oklahoma City v. Dowell, 375 F.2d 158 (1967), 163, 164, 161; Dowell v. Oklahoma City, 244 F.Supp. 971 (1965), 978, 977.
67. Oklahoma City v. Dowell, 375 F.2d 158 (1967), 169–70.
68. Dowell v. Oklahoma City, 307 F.Supp. 583 (1970), 586–89.
69. Ibid., 660–61.
70. Ibid., 599; Dowell v. Oklahoma City, 219 F.Supp. 427 (1963), 441.
71. Dowell v. Oklahoma City, 338 F.Supp. 1256 (1972), 1262–63 n.4, 1263–64, 1264.
72. Ibid., 1267–71; Dowell v. Oklahoma City, 465 F.2d 1012 (1972), 1014.
73. Dowell v. Oklahoma City, 606 F.Supp. 1548 (1985), 1550.
74. Ibid., 1550–51.
75. Dowell v. Oklahoma City, 677 F.Supp. 1503 (1987), 1505.
76. Dowell v. Oklahoma City, 677 F.Supp. 971 (1965), 975; 890 F.2d 1483 (1989), 1525; 677 F.Supp. 1503 (1987), 1509.
77. Dowell v. Oklahoma City, 677 F.Supp. 1503 (1987), 1507, 1508.
78. Ibid., 1515, 1514.
79. *Atlantic* (September 1991): 30.
80. Ibid., 30.
81. Ibid., 30–31; *Washington Post*, 8 February 1986, A11a.
82. For a biography, see Jace Weaver, *Then to the Rock Let Me Fly: Luther Bohanon and Judicial Activism* (Norman: University of Oklahoma Press, 1993).
83. Dowell v. Oklahoma City, 606 F.Supp. 1548 (1985), 1555–56; 677 F.Supp. 1503 (1987), 1518.
84. Dowell v. Oklahoma City, 677 F.Supp. 1503 (1987), 1516, 1517.
85. Ibid., 1516, 1523, 1516–17.

86. Dowell v. Oklahoma City, 890 F.2d 1483 (1989), 1493, 1493–1501, 1519. Professors Robert Crain, Gordon Foster, and Yale Rubin were three of the expert witnesses for the NAACP.
87. Ibid., 1499, 1493, 1499 n.41, 1505.
88. Ibid., 1491, 1490.
89. William Bradford Reynolds, Roger Clegg, David K. Flynn and Mark L. Gross, Brief for the United States, Dowell v. Oklahoma City, 5, 7, 13–14 and passim, Case 88-1067, Tenth Circuit Court of Appeals, Denver.
90. Morgan v. Nucci, 831 F.2d 313 (1st Cir. 1987); U.S. v. Overton, 834 F.2d 117 (5th Cir., 1987), 1175, 1176, 1177; Spangler v. Pasadena, 611 F.2d 1239 (9th Cir., 1979); NAACP v. Duval County, 883 F.2d 945 (11th Cir., 1990), 669.
91. *Hastings Constitutional Law Quarterly*, 14 (1986): 45, 71; *Louisiana Law Review*, 48 (1988): 789; *Yale Law Journal*, 95 (1986): 1768; *Missouri Law Review*, 56 (1991): 1156; *Oklahoma Law Review*, 40 (1987): 557; *Case Western Reserve Law Review*, 37 (1986): 43. Also see *Dickenson Law Review*, 92 (1988): 437–60; *North Carolina Law Review*, 65 (1987): 617–44; and *Columbia Law Review*, 87 (1987), 794–816.
92. Oklahoma City v. Dowell, 111 S.Ct. 630 (1991), 637, 638.
93. Ibid., 636, 637.
94. Ibid., 638, 638 n.2. In legal language, "attenuated" means that a vestige is too remote or weak to warrant judicial action.
95. Ibid.
96. Ibid., 639, 641–42, 643.
97. *Washington Post*, 16 January 1991, A1a.
98. Oklahoma City v. Dowell, 111 S.Ct. 630 (1991), 638, 638 n.2.
99. Freeman v. Pitts, 60 USLW 4286 (1992).
100. Ibid., 4292, 4294.
101. Missouri v. Jenkins, 63 USLW 4486 (1995), 4512–13, 4494–95.
102. *New York Times*, 1 April 1992, 1:5; *Washington Post*, 1 April 1992, A1e. Lee handled the appeal for DeKalb County when the case was before the Supreme Court.

21

Conclusion to Part III

When the Supreme Court decided the *Brown* case in 1954, desegregation was necessary for the nation's foreign relations and in light of emerging moral values. By the second half of the twentieth century, most Americans subscribed to the nondiscrimination principle—the idea that the government should not discriminate against citizens on the basis of race.

But the *Green* opinion of 1968 involved a different principle. *Brown* required that segregated school systems be disestablished, in the sense that the assignment of children to particular schools should not depend on race; but *Green* required school officials to consider race and to take affirmative steps to achieve more racial interaction than would be achieved by racially neutral methods.

The Supreme Court meant well when it required local school districts to consider race in order to increase integration. Martin Luther King was assassinated on the day after the Supreme Court heard the oral arguments in *Green*, and the nation experienced one of its worst periods of racial rioting during the weeks when the justices considered the case. Once again, it must have seemed, the time had arrived for decisive judicial leadership.

In the end, however, *Green* and its progeny damaged public education. As noted in the preceding chapters, *Green* paved the way for a number of dubious educational "reforms." In the wake of integration, many schools turned away from grouping students by achievement and placed the full range of students in the same class. New educational practices were implemented—mainstreaming, heterogeneous grouping, peer tutoring, cooperative learning, mastery learning. For a quarter of a century, disadvantaged students were *in* and gifted student were *out*. Instead of making special efforts to advance high achieving students, special programs were implemented for slow learners. At the same time, many teachers, principals, and school districts turned away from traditional disciplinary policies that had been used to control adolescent misbehavior. They did so because enforcement of the policies had a disparate impact on black students.

As a result there was some convergence in SAT scores—with those at the bottom of the distribution improving their scores by about 50 points while the scores of students in the top 10 percent plummeted. "In 1972, 17,560 college-bound seniors scored 700 or higher on the SAT-Verbal. In 1993, only 10,407 scored 700 or higher on the Verbal—a drop of 41 percent in the raw number of students scoring 700 and over, despite the larger raw number of students taking the test in 1993 compared to 1972."[1]

Green also led to an increase in middle-class flight from the public schools. Many of the fleeing parents had not objected when their children attended racially mixed schools in their neighborhoods. But they complained about assigning children on the basis of race and took exception to the misbehavior and academic standards of lower-class students. As sociologist James S. Coleman has noted, "School integration is just not stable where the proportion of blacks in the district is very large." During the decade after court ordered busing plans were implemented, middle-class enrollment generally declined by about 50 percent.[2]

In formulating the Reagan administration's approach to school desegregation, William Bradford Reynolds took cognizance of two main points: one was the massive middle-class flight from racially balanced integration and especially from forced busing; the other was the law as set forth in *Green* and its progeny. Reynolds recognized that because of *Green*, it would not be possible to pursue color-blind policies. The law required affirmative steps to increase racial integration. However, because of widespread opposition to coercive integration, Reynolds argued that voluntary measures such as magnet schools would produce more actual integration than court-ordered busing.

The courts accepted Reynolds's argument, and during the 1980s, voluntary programs that emphasized magnet schools became the preferred and most frequent method for promoting integration. There were few new instances of 1970s-style forced busing.

Then Reynolds developed a blueprint for ending forced busing in school districts that had previously been subjected to court orders. In the *Oklahoma City* and *DeKalb* decisions of 1991 and 1992, the Supreme Court endorsed Reynolds's plan. The Court held that *unitary status* could be awarded once a formerly segregated school district had complied with a court-ordered desegregation plan. After unitary status had been awarded, the Court declared, local authorities should be freed from court-ordered busing as long as they did not engage in intentional discrimination. The Court said that judicial supervision of local schools was warranted only during the transition period when public schools were cleansing themselves of discrimination and its effects— and it defined the effects of discrimination more narrowly than integrationists would have liked. The Court also said that judges exceeded their authority if they went beyond remedying discrimination and tried to counteract demographic trends and social conditions.

The journalist Nat Henthoff complained that the Supreme Court had placed its seal of approval on "educational apartheid." It was a grave mistake, Henthoff insisted, for the Court to have decided that school districts were under no obligation to remedy the racial imbalance that resulted from demographic patterns and socioeconomic considerations.[3]

Other integrationists continued to point to what they said were persistent remnants of discrimination. They noted that blacks generally did poorly according to nearly every yardstick of academic achievement—test scores, suspensions, assignments to special education, drop-out rates. They said most schools had never achieved true desegregation, and they insisted that court-ordered integration plans should remain in force until the last vestiges of discrimination had been eliminated "root and branch."

In fact, in the early 1990s, integrationists moved toward a new definition of *desegregation*. Initially, at the time of *Brown*, desegregation had been understood to require color-blind nondiscrimination. Later, with *Green* and its progeny, desegregation required affirmative racial assignments to achieve a substantial amount of racial interaction. Then, in the 1990s, integrationists maintained that desegregation required judges to maintain supervision of the public schools until local school districts achieved equality of outcome with respect to discipline, academic performance, and participation in extracurricular activities.[4]

In its *Kansas City* decision of 1995, however, the Supreme Court rejected this definition and approach. The Court said that school districts were not responsible for remedying problems that were not caused by the schools, and that school authorities were required only to eliminate the traces of their own discrimination "to the extent practicable."[5]

By the mid-1990s, the direction of the law was clear. After the *Oklahoma City* decision of 1991 and the *DeKalb* decision of 1992, several courts terminated their desegregation orders, and this trend should accelerate after the *Kansas City* decision of 1995. Some probusing lawyers have conceded defeat, while William Bradford Reynolds derived satisfaction from knowing that he had played a role in persuading the federal courts to change the jurisprudence of school desegregation.

Nevertheless, busing for integration will not end quickly. In many local jurisdictions, probusing forces have become institutionalized and are prepared to resist those who insist that the government should neither classify nor treat citizens on the basis of their race or ancestry. Battalions of bureaucrats have found employment because of forced busing, and these bureaucrats will fight to protect their jobs and programs even after the courts no longer require busing for racial integration.

The situation in New Castle County, Delaware, provides a good example of the general pattern. When busing for racially balanced integration began in 1978, thousands of middle-class students left the public schools, but many "progressive" bureaucrats moved in. Ninety-eight people were hired to work full-time as human relations specialists, and many of them eventually gravitated into school administration. Superintendents and principals were chosen after they gave assurances that busing for racial balance could be structured to boost the achievement and self-confidence of slow students. Others were employed to organize multicultural sensitivity seminars or summer workshops and retreats. Regular teachers then received extra money to attend sessions that purported to improve the teachers' ability to resolve conflicts with disruptive students whose values supposedly differed from their own. Some workshops and seminars recommended "empathetic listening" as a means for effecting "behavior modification." Others dealt with "values clarification," "action planning," and "consultation skills." Still others addressed the need for "non-arbitrary and nondiscriminatory discipline" and for counseling black students to enroll in advanced academic courses.[6]

This was only the beginning. As the probusing editors of the *Wilmington News Journal* conceded, "[A] lot of empire building occurred in school systems during desegregation." Eventually, the "desegregated" schools even established special offices in the black and Hispanic neighborhoods for what were called "parent/student advocates" and "intervention specialists." One of their jobs was to rush to the schools and defend the interests of minority students, if the students got into trouble with a teacher or building administrator. Arrangements were also made so that blacks and Hispanics who did not make a passing score on the teacher certification exam could still be employed as teachers if they made "comparable scores" on other tests.[7]

Meanwhile, central school authorities made it difficult to suspend disruptive students. They required teachers to fill out long forms and to list witnesses to alleged infractions, and they candidly acknowledged that they were piling on the paper work because they wanted to discourage teachers from suspending unruly students. They did so because black students were being suspended more frequently than whites, and because the school administrators attributed this frequency not to misbehavior on the part of the students but to insensitivity and discrimination by the teachers. The problem, the administrators implied, was that middle-class teachers often did not understand or sympathize with the style of lower-class black students.[8]

Some administrators went to extremes in explaining this approach. In courtroom testimony, one of them said that disciplinary codes were intended to "sooth suburban parents" by controlling "black boys." She further declared that "when one group expresses its frustration by fighting and another group does not, it's unfair to make a rule that disciplines only the fighters."[9]

One supporter of court-ordered forced busing confessed that he was "utterly baffled" by this argument. He recalled that "in the '30s and '40s, long before I learned to deal with my temper, I'd slug someone at the drop of an insult." He continued to do so until he learned that he might be hit back or even suspended from school. It never occurred to him that he might have been "a victim of cultural bias against violence in school."[10]

In suggesting that school officials ought to be even-handed in punishing both the slugger and the slugger's victim, the probusing witness probably damaged her cause. Her statements bordered on the ridiculous.

Of course the failure of progressive reforms in general, and of court-ordered busing in particular, does not mean it is impossible for poor children to do well in school. The experience of many Catholic schools proves the contrary. So does the experience of many successful public schools. Schools can make a difference. The problem is that progressive educators gravitate toward schools that are under court-ordered integration plans. Then they implement reforms that are actually counter-productive. Instead of insisting on order, homework, and tried-and-true educational methods, the progressives implement approaches that make things worse for many students. Instead of supporting the teachers, many progressives blame the teachers for being narrow minded, middle class, and insensitive to the multicultural style of students who are disruptive or inattentive to schoolwork. Instead of expelling unruly students, they send the teachers away for reeducation in sensitivity workshops.

It is hard to imagine a greater disservice to the black community, as well as to others, than the institutionalization of support for both troublemakers and inattentive youths who have disrupted the education of their fellow students. There were many problems with forced busing: it was based on a strained interpretation of the equal protection clause; it did not lead to better education or improved race relations; it stimulated middle-class flight from the public schools; and, perhaps worst of all, it led the federal judiciary into a mesalliance with dubious trends in progressive education.

Notes

1. Donald M. Stewart to *New York Times*, 5 November 1994, 22:4 (reporting that "since 1976 the average scores of African-Americans have risen 20 points on [the SAT] verbal and 34 on math"; Richard Herrnstein and Charles Murray, *The Bell Curve*, 428; Daniel Singal, "The Other Crisis in Our Schools," *Atlantic* (November 1991): 59–74; David Armor, "Why is Black Educational Achievement Rising?" *The Public Interest*, 108 (Summer 1992): 65–80.

2. *National Observer,* 7 June 1975, 1.
3. *Village Voice*, 31 May 1994, 22.
4. The *Kansas City* litigation discussed in chapter 19 illustrated this trend. Another example was *Evans v. Buchanan*, the Delaware desegregation case. For more on this case, see my article, "The Consent Order as Sweetheart Deal," *Temple Political and Civil Rights Law Review* 4 (Spring 1995): 271–299.
5. Missouri v. Jenkins, 63 USLW 4486 (1995).
6. Raymond Wolters, *The Burden of Brown*, 229–30; Evans v. Buchanan, 447 F.Supp. 982 (1977), 1014–17; Billy E. Ross, "Training: The Key to Successful School Desegregation," in Dennis C. Carey, ed., *The Politics of Metropolitan School Reorganization* (typescript in University of Delaware Library); Jeffrey A. Raffel, *The Politics of School Desegregation: The Metropolitan Remedy in Delaware*, 80.
7. *Wilmington News Journal*, 4 January 1994; Consent Order, Evans v. Buchanan, 28 November 1993, Nos. 56-CV-1816-1822, MMS, 31, 33, 27, U.S. District Court, Wilmington.
8. Interview with Lisa Bullock, 5 March 1982; Raymond Wolters, *The Burden of Brown*, 245–46.
9. Gloria Grantham, quoted in *Wilmington News Journal*, 30 December 1994.
10. Ralph Moyed, "Even-Handed Discipline Code is Empty-Headed," *Sunday News Journal*, 15 January 1995.

Appendix
The *Bob Jones* Case

Although this is a long book, much more could be said about the civil rights policies of the Reagan administration. While dealing with voting rights, affirmative action, and school desegregation, William Bradford Reynolds and the Civil Rights Division also developed important new initiatives and policies with respect to housing discrimination, the desegregation of higher education, and the criminal prosecution of individuals and groups that were violating the civil rights of others. Each of these areas could be the subject of a separate monograph.

Since more remains to be written about the administration's civil rights policies, readers may be surprised by an appendix that deals primarily with taxes, religious freedom, and the separation of powers. However, when some of my liberal friends heard that I was writing a book that would be generally supportive of Ronald Reagan's civil rights policies, they asked What about *Bob Jones*? How can you defend what the administration did in that case? Doesn't that prove that Reagan was a racist?.

Because *Bob Jones* did much to shape the public's perception of Reagan's record on civil rights, it deserves mention and discussion in this book.

* * *

The *Bob Jones* case revolved around whether Bob Jones University, a racially discriminatory Christian school in Greenville, South Carolina, was eligible for tax-exempt status.

The two points at issue were (1) Should the U.S. Government forbear from collecting taxes on money that was contributed to the university? and (2) Should contributors be allowed to deduct the amount of their contribution from their taxable income?

The language of the relevant tax law indicated that organizations that were established for any one of several enumerated purposes should be tax exempt. Section 501(c)(3) of the Internal Revenue Code stated that organizations would not be liable for taxes if they were operated for religious, charitable, scientific, literary, or educational purposes, or to foster amateur sports competition or for the prevention of cruelty to children or animals. As an educational institution, Bob Jones University had enjoyed tax-exempt status from its founding in 1927 until 1 December 1970.[1]

On that date the Internal Revenue Service (IRS) withdrew the tax exemption. The turnabout came as a result of a Mississippi lawsuit that challenged the constitutionality of giving tax exemptions to schools that discriminated against blacks. In response to court-ordered integration of the public schools, many all-white private schools were established—so many that the prospects for successful school integration were damaged. In the Mississippi case, black plaintiffs said that tax deductibility for contributions had made it easier for the organizers of the private schools to raise money at the crucial juncture when new schools were being built. They said, in addition, that it was unconstitutional for the federal government to "frustrate" school integration by giving "substantial and significant support to the segregated private school pattern." They argued that one of the central issues of public policy involved the mandate of the Constitution, as interpreted by the Supreme Court in *Brown*. They said that mandate required the federal government to pursue and suppress, and certainly not to encourage, segregation.[2]

Before the Mississippi case went to trial, the IRS, in response to orders from President Richard Nixon, changed its course and announced that it would no longer give tax exemptions to private schools that practiced racial discrimination. Daniel Patrick Moynihan, a member of Nixon's staff at the time, later said the change came about because Nixon accepted the constitutional rationale the plaintiffs had prepared for the case.[3]

A more cynical explanation is also possible. Nixon initially rejected the advice of Robert Finch, a cabinet member who wanted to take away the tax exemptions of racially discriminatory schools. Nixon noted that the tax law authorized exemptions for schools and said nothing about racial policies. Besides, Nixon said, "whites in Mississippi can't send their kids to schools that are 90 percent black; they've got to set up private schools." He instructed his domestic advisor, John Erlichman, to "tell Finch to stay out of this. Tell him to do the right thing for a change."[4]

Nixon changed his mind after another staff member, Bryce Harlow, warned that criticism from the liberal press and from civil rights organizations would be costly in the midterm congressional elections and would detract from Nixon's ability to pursue important initiatives in foreign policy. After hearing that the administration would suffer politically, Nixon ordered IRS commissioner Randolph Thrower to change the policy and to deny tax exemptions to racially discriminatory schools.[5]

In changing the policy, however, the IRS did not embrace the constitutional argument that *Brown* required the government to deny all benefits to private institutions that practiced racial discrimination. *Brown* had required the desegregation of public schools and could be used against private institutions only if the benefits derived from tax exemption were equated with substantial and significant support from the government. But the Supreme Court, in *Walz v. Tax Commission* (1970), had held that a tax exemption amounted only to restraint from demanding private financial support for the government, not a flow of assistance or revenues from the government to the exempt organizations. Therefore, the IRS had to find a different rationale to justify reversing its policy.[6]

The IRS devised an explanation that involved a reinterpretation of the word *charitable*. Commissioner Thrower acknowledged that the relevant law provided tax-exempt status for organizations that were religious, charitable, scientific, literary, or educational; but Thrower explained that the IRS had reinterpreted the word *charitable* in a legal sense rather than in the ordinary meaning of benevolence to the poor and suffering. Under the common law, Thrower said, organizations did not merit classification as *charitable* unless they served the general welfare, were beneficial to the community, and were not operated in a way that was contrary to public policy. Thrower then ruled that to qualify for a tax exemption, a school would have to be charitable as well as educational.[7]

Thrower recognized that the reinterpretation was based on a shaky legal foundation. For seventy-five years the IRS and the federal courts had interpreted the word *charitable* in its customary sense. Indeed, it was an axiom of construction that bureaucrats and courts should generally assign to words, and to grammatical formulations, their ordinary meaning. By using the disjunctive *or*, instead of the conjunctive *and*, Congress had indicated that tax exemptions were to be given to organizations that were operated for any one of several designated purposes. The distinct references indicated that Congress intended that tax exemptions should be given to institutions that were "religious" or "educational" or "charitable."[8]

But Nixon had asked the IRS to adjust the law to the requirements of changing times; and Commissioner Thrower and the IRS proposed to do this by allowing tax exemptions only to those educational institutions that were also charitable in the common-law sense. After 1970, it was not enough for a school to be an educational institution. To qualify for tax exemption, the IRS decided, schools had to be charitable in the sense that they served the general welfare, were beneficial to the community, and did not operate in a way that was contrary to public policy. Since both the Supreme Court and Congress had indicated that racial discrimination in education violated a fundamental public policy, the IRS canceled the tax-exempt status of Bob Jones University and of other schools that openly discriminated against blacks.[9]

A three-judge district court upheld the IRS's new interpretation of the tax law, and the Supreme Court summarily affirmed the decision of the district court. Some journalists and lawyers said that should have settled the matter.

The *New York Times* observed that "in America's legal system the law comprises not only statutes but also the judicial constructions and explanations thereof." In the case of institutions that practiced racial discrimination, the *Times* explained,

> the judicial explanations have been as follows: Congress granted tax exemptions to schools, churches, charities, nonprofit social enterprises and animal rescue leagues because they help the country in ways different from, but generally in harmony with the way the Government spends tax money. They are thus entitled to tax exemptions because they promote public policy.
>
> Tax exemptions...are meant for institutions that advance the public good in some way: racist schools violate everything America stands for and frustrate the tax-supported commitment to integrated education.
>
> Federal tax law simply does not allow an exemption "unless the school...has a racially nondiscriminatory policy as to students."[10]

Others noted, however, that the Supreme Court had never really grappled with the question. They said the key points at issue had not been resolved because summary affirmances traditionally have little precedential value, and the special circumstances of the Mississippi lawsuit made the summary affirmance of no binding significance. The Supreme Court observed that because the IRS had switched its position before the trial and sided with the black plaintiffs who were suing the IRS, the case "lack[ed] the precedential weight of a case involving a truly adversary controversy."[11]

Regardless of the legal merits, Bob Jones University lost its tax exempt status in 1970. It did so because it openly and admittedly practiced racial discrimination. Until 1971 nonwhites were denied admission to the university. For a few years after that they were admitted, but only if they were married or had been employed at the school for at least four years. Beginning in 1976, unmarried nonwhite students were allowed to enroll, but racial discrimination persisted because the university promulgated a disciplinary rule that prohibited interracial dating and marriage. In 1981 the university reported that about a dozen of its 6,300 students were "yellow and black."[12]

Making an already complicated situation even more perplexing, Bob Jones defended its discriminatory policy on religious grounds. It said that God intended for the races to remain separate, and in court it pointed to specific biblical passages that could be interpreted to this effect. The district judge held that these convictions were "genuine religious beliefs." The university had originally denied admission to all nonwhites, and later prohibited unmarried blacks and Asians, as the best means of prohibiting interracial dating and marriage. After the Supreme Court affirmed in 1976 that it was unconstitutional for private schools to deny admission because of race, Bob Jones revised its policy to permit unmarried blacks and Asians to matriculate; but it continued to insist that its prohibition of interracial dating and marriage was doctrinally required.[13]

The trial court held that Bob Jones's prohibition of interracial dating and marriage was based on a religious conviction, and the court also found that the university was essentially a religious institution. Judge Robert F. Chapman observed that "the cornerstone" of the institution was "Christian religious indoctrination, not isolated academics" with the overriding goals "to teach the principles of the Bible and [to] train Christian character." Every class began with a prayer. Every teacher was required to be a born-again Christian who could testify to at least one saving experience with Jesus Christ. Students were not allowed to dance, smoke tobacco, or play cards, and were expected to eschew questionable music and movies.[14]

Despite the religious complication, in 1977 the IRS sued Bob Jones University for $489,679 in unpaid taxes. The university paid a small portion of this amount and then sued for reimbursement. In 1978 the district court ruled in favor of the university, on the grounds that the IRS had abridged the constitutionally guaranteed right to free exercise of religion, and also that it had misconstrued the tax law. In 1980, by a vote of 2–1, the Fourth Circuit Court of Appeals reversed the district court on both points. In 1981, the Supreme Court agreed to hear the case.[15]

When the case had been before the Fourth Circuit Court, the Carter administration had argued in support of the IRS, and at first it appeared that the Reagan administration would do likewise. In fact, in September 1981, Lawrence G. Wallace, the deputy solicitor general, filed a brief in the Supreme Court stating that he intended to argue against tax exemptions for Bob Jones, but then a cry of alarm was sounded in the office of one of the junior lawyers in the Department of Justice, Bruce Fein. In a three-page memorandum, Fein, an associate deputy attorney general, contended that the legal doctrines of the IRS and of the solicitor general were inconsistent with Ronald Reagan's campaign promise to appoint judges and bureaucrats who would interpret the law as Congress had intended.[16]

Fein's memorandum impressed the second-ranking official in the justice department, Deputy Attorney General Edward C. Schmults, who thought the *public policy* doctrine that the IRS had devised was "contrary to the statutory language." Schmults thought it was a mistake to leave the tax-exempt status of private schools "to the sole discretion of the Internal Revenue Service based on its independent view at the moment of national policy goals." Schmults said, "It is for Congress to make national public policy by the enactment of laws."[17]

Schmults believed that the Nixon administration, "when confronted with the politically explosive issue in 1970,...succumbed to the pressure of public opinion and had allowed the IRS to proceed down a path that was politically palatable but legally unjustified." Schmults said that he was "offended...by the racially discriminatory practices of Bob Jones University," but he also insisted that "we cannot allow our strong disagreement with such policies to dissuade us from coming to grips with the hard legal issue that is presented." It was important to oppose racial discrimination, Schmults said, but "the combat [should] be waged within the letter and spirit of the law as determined by Congress, not outside the law or in disregard of the federal statutes on the books."[18]

Reynolds became acquainted with *Bob Jones* at about the same time as Schmults, in December 1981. After reading the brief that the deputy solicitor general had prepared in opposition to Bob Jones, Reynolds walked over to Schmults's office and said, "Ed, I just read the brief that the SG [solicitor general] wants to file in *Bob Jones*. I think there's a lot of mischief in it. It's very unpersuasive.... Do we really want to file this, given all our pronouncements about federal intrusiveness and separation of powers?"[19]

Schmults then asked that the case be reviewed by the Department of Treasury, in which the IRS was housed. The deputy secretary, R. T. McNamar, initially knew little about *Bob Jones*, but he was an attorney and welcomed the change of pace that came with considering a nonfinancial question. Together with Peter Wallison, the general counsel at Treasury, McNamar read widely on the subject, "taking the unusual step of going back...to read all of the majority and dissenting opinions in the district court and court of appeals rulings in *Bob Jones*" and a number of other tax-exemption cases.[20]

As a result of this review, McNamar and Wallison, like Fein, Schmults and Reynolds before them, concluded that the public-policy theory of the IRS was in conflict with Ronald Reagan's belief that unelected bureaucrats and judges should not make policy. "That is what this matter is all about," McNamar said. "Should administrators and executors of the law be free to define public policy in the absence of legislative authority duly enacted by Congress?" To McNamar it was clear: "The answer is no."[21]

McNamar also noted that the rationale of the IRS was difficult to limit and could lead to other decisions that would not be well advised. Since it was "clearly national policy" for the United States to become self-sufficient in energy, McNamar observed, a consistent application of the public-policy doctrine would require the IRS to revoke the tax exemptions of organizations, like the Sierra Club, that discouraged domestic energy production. McNamar recognized that such revocation was not in the offing, but that only confirmed his belief that the doctrine of *public policy* led to government not by laws but by the changing whims of IRS bureaucrats.[22]

Other members of the Reagan administration shared McNamar's concern about allowing IRS to define public policy. Schmults mentioned that there were laws and public policy statements against discrimination on the basis of sex. "My wife went to Wellesley," he said. "If we support [the rationale of the IRS],...why couldn't the IRS commissioner take away the tax exemptions of Wellesley, Smith, Bryn Mawr, and other single-sex schools?"[23]

Reynolds shared this concern and warned that the ramifications of the IRS's approach might be particularly troublesome for religious organizations. "What about churches that favor nuclear disarmament?" he asked. "What about churches that are opposed to war or to military conscription?" "They are at odds with public policy. Should IRS have the independent authority to revoke their tax exemptions?"[24]

When posed within the councils of the Reagan administration, these questions seemed theoretical, if not rhetorical. But several of the nation's churches regarded the matter as one of such practical importance that they filed legal briefs in support of Bob Jones University. Lawyers for the American Baptist Churches asserted that racism was "wrong and that [Bob Jones's] reading of what the Bible teaches about human relations is faulty." Nevertheless, their brief said, "the wrongness of racism cannot be the real issue in this case.... The very existence of a religious organization is at stake."[25]

Attorneys for the General Conference of the Mennonite Church also expressed their disagreement "with Bob Jones University's interpretation of Scripture...[and] with the policy of forbidding inter-racial dating." But the Mennonites recognized that their own religious pacifism and support for draft resisters "could easily be seen by the IRS as violating 'public policy.'" If that happened, the Mennonites said, many church programs would be brought to "a screeching halt" because "in this enlightened day and age a religious organization can be more easily destroyed by taxation than by burning at the stake."[26]

Other groups made similar points. Lawyers for the Amish said the public-policy doctrine evoked "memories of decrees of many another sovereign... seeking to force...conformity to the will of the state." Attorneys for the (Mormon) Church of Jesus Christ of Latter-Day Saints insisted that religious activities would be "imperiled" if IRS officials had the "power to grant or deny the lifeline of tax exemption based on what they choose to call 'public policy' irrespective of authorization by Congress." Because the question of tax exemption impinged on the free exercise of religion, the Mormons said, policies should not be left to implication but should be "clearly and affirmatively expressed" in statutes.[27]

Arguments such as these had some influence on Reynolds. In 1981 more than 106,000 nonprofit organizations were classified as tax exempt, and Reynolds found it impossible to believe that all or even most of these organizations were promoting public policy. He knew, rather, that they received favorable treatment because the nation's tradition of limited government worked against public action in many areas and because the exempt organizations were perceived as contributing to the diversity of a vigorous, pluralist society.[28]

But Reynolds did not subscribe completely to the arguments about pluralism and diversity. The Supreme Court, he noted, had frequently distinguished between religious belief (which was protected by the free exercise clause of the First Amendment) and religiously based practices (which could be constrained to serve important secular interests). In one case the Court held that the government's concern for public order and morality justified the criminalization of Mormon polygamy (which the Court equated not with the practices of the Old Testament patriarchs but with "human sacrifices" and "a wife...burn[ing] herself upon the funeral pile of her dead husband"). In another case, the Court held that a religiously based opposition to medical care did not counterbalance the state's compelling need to require inoculation against smallpox. In a third case, the Court ruled that religion could not be used as a justification for making children work in violation of child labor laws.[29]

There were some contrary cases such as *Wisconsin v. Yoder* (1972), where the Supreme Court excused Amish children from state requirements for compulsory education. But Reynolds thought the Court had indicated that in cases involving religious practice (as distinguished from religious belief), there should be a balancing process that would sanction restrictions that served an important government interest if those restrictions imposed only an indirect burden on the exercise of religion. In the *Bob Jones* case, Reynolds wrote, the IRS policy ("despite...claims to the contrary") placed only an "indirect and limited burden...upon [the] right to free religious belief or exercise." Reynolds conceded that parents had a constitutionally protected right to have their children educated in schools that fostered a *belief* in racial separation, but he insisted that "the first Amendment does not protect a school's *practice* of racial discrimination."[30]

Reynolds also differed from *Bob Jones* and its supporters on another important point. Some of the legal briefs and one of the federal judges who had previously considered the case had noted that some forms of racial discrimination were not at odds with public policy. In the *Bakke* case, the Supreme Court had reversed a lower-court order that prohibited the consideration of race when it came to admitting students to a medical school at the University of California; instead, while ruling against racial quotas, the Court permitted discrimination in the interest of diversity. And, as noted in several of this book's chapters, in other cases the Court also bent the rule against racial discrimination to sanction *benign* discrimination. Meanwhile, the civil rights lobby demanded even more in the way of affirmative racial preferences.[31]

Against this background, it was hard to argue that there was a public policy against all forms of racial discrimination. Especially when it came to "such intimate and private matters as the selection of a spouse," Amherst College professor Hadley Arkes noted, "even...liberals of the largest nature" had reservations. Thus the *New York Review of Books*, which never would have published advertisements for employment with an expression of preference for workers of a particular race, could regularly run personal advertisements that sanctioned racial discrimination in the choice of partners for dates and marriage (e.g., "'SWM seeks SWF.' Translation: single *white* male seeks single *white* female").[32]

The national consensus against racial discrimination did not extend to the choice of partners. If it did, the *New York Review* should not have retained its second-class mailing privileges while Bob Jones lost its exemption from taxes. The university, it seemed, had not received the same tolerance as others who discriminated on the same grounds because the university was, as Judge Hiram E. Widener noted when the case was before the Fourth Circuit Court, "a small, isolated, religious organization, not affiliated with a larger denomination" and without friends or influence in Washington.[33]

Reynolds did not mention these points in the legal briefs and memoranda he prepared on the *Bob Jones* case. For Reynolds, as for the other members of the administration who worked on the case, the controlling issue was whether Congress, when it enacted Section 501(c)(3) of the tax law, intended to authorize the IRS to revoke the tax-exempt status of otherwise qualified organizations whose practices were at odds with what the IRS deemed to be public policy. After considering the language of the law (with its separate enumeration of tax-exempt categories and its use of the disjunctive *or*), and after reviewing the legislative history (in a nine-page memorandum and in a fifty-two-page legal brief), Reynolds came to the conclusion that Congress had not intended to deny tax-exempt status to racially discriminatory private schools. "This is not to suggest that Congress cannot legislate in such a manner," Reynolds wrote, "but only that it thus far has not done so."[34]

A second question concerned whether the rationale of the IRS could be narrowed in a way that would allow the IRS to deny tax exemptions to racially discriminatory schools without endorsing a broader principle that would give IRS the authority to punish other organizations. To address this concern, Deputy Solicitor General Wallace revised the argument he had made before the Fourth Circuit Court (and that he planned to present to the Supreme Court). After studying Wallace's revised brief, however, Reynolds, Schmults, and McNamar found that it still did not resolve their problems with the public-policy doctrine.[35]

By the end of 1981, this is how things stood. Early in December of that year, as noted above, Bruce Fein, a young lawyer in the Department of Justice, had warned Deputy Attorney General Edward Schmults that the government's position on the *Bob Jones* case was at odds with the separation of powers and with Ronald Reagan's campaign rhetoric. Schmults's initial belief, that Fein was right on both points, was then reinforced when Schmults referred the matter to R. T. McNamar and Peter Wallison of the Treasury Department and to William Bradford Reynolds of the Civil Rights Division. However, Attorney General William French Smith did not become involved in the case until January, when he returned from California where he had been spending the Christmas holidays.

To learn more about the case, Smith read a number of the documents, court opinions, and legal briefs. Then he presided at a two and one-half hour meeting on 6 January 1982. The meeting began with Wallace explaining why he thought the government should continue to support the position of the IRS. Reynolds then summarized his views, and the meeting was opened for discussion.[36]

Wallace emphasized that a divided Fourth Circuit Court had endorsed the rationale of the IRS. He said that taxpayers were continually devising "schemes" to give them "some form of tax advantage" and argued that the IRS "inevitably" had to apply the law to situations "that Congress might not have specifically anticipated." Besides, Wallace observed, there were two safeguards against IRS abuses: "judicial review, or, if Congress is dissatisfied with a rule adopted by the [IRS], it can amend the statute." By refusing to do so, Wallace argued, Congress had acquiesced in the interpretation of the IRS.[37]

In response, Reynolds argued that any effort to understand a law should begin with the words of the statute to be construed and then proceed to an examination of the legislative history. Since 1894, Reynolds noted, the language had remained largely intact, always separately enumerating *educational* and *charitable*. Reynolds said that Congress could have changed the law, but as then Justice Rehnquist has written, the Supreme Court itself had repeatedly held that "congressional inaction is of virtually no weight in determining legislative intent." This was especially the case, Reynolds indicated, with respect to the tax law, which Congress frequently modifies. In 1976, he pointed out, Congress denied tax-exempt status to social clubs that had racially discriminatory policy statements—an action that indicated that if Congress wanted to change the policy with respect to racially discriminatory schools, it knew how to do so.[38]

Shortly after the meeting, Attorney General Smith informed the White House that he had decided in favor of Reynolds's position. Within the administration, the overwhelming concern had been with the separation of powers and with developing a position that was sound, principled, and legally correct. Ted Olson, a lawyer who supported the IRS during the meeting with Smith, recalled that there had been almost no mention of how the public would respond to a reversal of the IRS's position. At one point Olson said,

"This is going to be an extraordinarily controversial and unpopular decision. We're going to be called racists. Let's step back for a moment and think about this before we go ahead. I don't think we're going to be vindicated in the Court, and it's going to be extremely unpleasant in the process, so why are we doing it?" Well, nobody as much as blinked. The inference I drew from that was that people thought the merits of their position would stand on their own, or that they simply did not appreciate the magnitude of the storm on the horizon.[39]

This is not to say that the *Bob Jones* lawyers were political innocents. Ronald Reagan's opposition to intrusive bureaucratic regulations was well known, and during the presidential campaign of 1980 Reagan had taken particular exception to the way the IRS had escalated its campaign against private schools in 1978 and 1979. At that time the IRS had ruled that private schools would lose their tax exemptions if they were established within a few years of court-ordered integration, and if the percentage of minority students in the school was less than one-fifth of the percentage of minority children in the community. To regain its exemption, a school would have to do more than promise not to discriminate; it would have to rebut the appearance of discrimination by implementing affirmative action policies that IRS bureaucrats would draw up with respect to admission and scholarships.[40]

The 1980 Republican party platform promised to "halt the unconstitutional regulatory vendetta launched by Mr. Carter's IRS commissioner against independent schools." One of Reagan's position papers on education stated that he would oppose "the IRS' attempt to remove the tax exempt status of private schools by administrative fiat."[41]

Reagan found plenty of company in criticizing the proposed IRS policy of 1978–79. Several churches said their schools (and seminaries) could not satisfy the IRS because, although they did not discriminate, very few members of minority groups belonged to their congregations. Within six months, the IRS received 150,000 letters criticizing the proposed policy—more than it ever received on any subject.

In addition, scores of witnesses gave volumes of testimony in hearings before the House and Senate. Many members of Congress expressed concern over the IRS defining acceptable public policy, criticized the use of statistics to infer discrimination, and condemned the requirement of quotas or other affirmative preferences to qualify for a tax exemption. Finally, in 1979, Congress enacted the Ashbrook-Dornan amendment, which prevented the IRS from denying tax exemption to any school unless the denial had been in effect prior to 22 August 1978. Because Ashbrook-Dornan was phrased prospectively, it did not apply to schools like Bob Jones that had previously lost their tax exemption, but the passage of the amendment indicated that many members of Congress thought the IRS should not deny tax exemptions unless this was clearly the intention of the legislature.[42]

Administration officials were aware of this history. They knew that the "vendetta" against private schools had caused many of Carter's erstwhile supporters to vote for Reagan in 1980. They knew that Reagan had emphasized the importance of the separation of powers and had been critical of policy making by unelected bureaucrats. In proposing to restore tax-exempt status to Bob Jones University, these officials assumed that they were carrying out the policies of the president, and in this sense political considerations were present throughout the debate over *Bob Jones*.

But contrary to what some politicians and journalists would say, there is almost no evidence of a more mundane sort of political calculation. Democratic Senator Daniel Patrick Moynihan declared that the administration's policy had been crafted "to placate two Senators and one Congressman." Tom Wicker told readers of the *New York Times* to "never mind the sophistical [legal] explanation being offered"; the administration's policy was a sop to "conservative movers and shakers like Senator Strom Thurmond and Representative Trent Lott of Mississippi." Anthony Lewis pulled out the rhetorical stops, writing that he had never heard "anything more preposterous, lame, cynical or outrageous than what Ronald Reagan had to say about 'the law' and racist schools"; the administration's arguments were an "afterthought" to camouflage a policy that had been designed to please racists who had voted for Reagan.[43]

To support their argument, Wicker and Lewis mentioned that Congressman Lott had sent letters on behalf of Bob Jones to the president and other officials. "The last time I read the Constitution," Lott wrote, "it provided that the *Congress* is to make the laws—not appointed officials." As summarized in the president's log of congressional mail, Lott was urging Reagan to "intervene in this case"; in response, in the margin of the log, Reagan wrote, "I think we should."[44]

Upon receiving a written note from the president, a White House aide usually prepared a position paper for members of the senior staff. In this instance, however, the notation remained unnoticed in the files until a junior aide in the office, William Gribbin, sent a copy to Congressman Lott and saw to it that some members of the White House staff were aware of the matter. Eventually Lott's letters, and Reagan's notation, would be published, leading some to conclude that the turnabout in government policy came in response to pressure from Lott.[45]

In point of fact, however, no one in the White House did anything to initiate a change in policy. The change was instigated by Treasury and Justice officials who developed their policy independently. With the exception of

Edward Schmults, those in charge of the Bob Jones policy knew nothing about the president's notation. Schmults wondered "how the hell" Lott got the notation "out of the White House," but beyond that "didn't pay any attention to it, send it around, or mention it to anyone. I already felt the president's position was pretty clearly staked out from the campaign."[46]

Schmults, Reynolds, and the others who worked on the *Bob Jones* case insisted that neither Lott nor any other politician influenced the development of their legal position. On the contrary, they said, they opposed the IRS despite recognizing that their position would be politically unpopular. They noted that Peter Wallison, in one strikingly prescient memorandum, had warned that the administration would suffer politically if it supported Bob Jones. Wallison predicted that the media would disregard the legal argument "that the tax laws are not the proper vehicle for pursuing racial discrimination," and that the liberal press would raise an "outcry" and would interpret the new policy "as a statement by the administration that overtly discriminatory practices are not objectionable." Thus, Wallison concluded, "a change in the administration's support for the [IRS] in the *Bob Jones* case could be very troublesome—with the political benefits heavily outweighed by the political liabilities."[47]

Despite recognizing that their new policy would be politically controversial, the administration's lawyers decided that, in good conscience, they could no longer support the rationale of the IRS. Fred Fielding, the legal counsel to the president, recalled that they developed a new policy because they thought it was "the right thing to do." R. T. McNamar said he felt "like the little kid in the crowd who had to stand up and say, 'The emperor [the IRS] has no clothes.'" Reynolds said that he recognized "that a reversal would likely produce an adverse reaction, but there never was a question...that that aspect of the equation should influence the legal call."[48]

But that is not the way the *Bob Jones* case was presented in the media. With the exception of the *Wall Street Journal*, the newspapers with national reputations condemned the administration. This was reflected in headlines that appeared in the days immediately after the new policy was announced on 8 January 1992. The *New York Times* characterized the policy as "Tax Exempt Hate." The *Boston Globe* said that the administration was "Subsidizing Discrimination." The *Los Angeles Times* called it "The Rewarding of Bias." The *Washington Post* depicted the president as "Ronald Crow." Benjamin Hooks of the NAACP said that the policy reversal "panders and appeals to the worst instinct of racism in America." Democratic party chairman Charles T. Manatt said that the Reagan administration had "effectively made every American taxpayer a forced contributor to segregationist schools."[49]

Administration lawyers complained that the media either offered no explanation of why the administration had changed its policy, or suggested that the administration was racist or racially insensitive. Peter Wallison recalled that he knew there would be trouble when reporters at a press conference "regarded all this discussion about Sec. 501(c)(3) and the common law definition of charity as silly lawyers' talk." Instead of inquiring about the legal points, he said, the reporters kept asking: "Did the White House direct you [to change the IRS policy]?" "Are you saying that the administration favors racial discrimination in private schools?" Wallison concluded that the reporters wanted to sell newspapers and regarded a story about separation of powers and the abuse of administrative discretion as "a great big yawn." Wallison said, "I was trotting out some [legal] principle that they weren't the least bit interested in, and they were talking about how great it was to catch the administration with its pants down."[50]

Reynolds offered a less charitable view of the media. As he saw it, most of the reporters at the leading newspapers were liberals who slanted their news coverage to favor the Democratic party. Especially when it came to civil rights questions, he said, "the grand liberal press" could be expected to do this.[51]

The administration's lawyers also received a lot of flak from members of the White House, especially from Deputy Chief of Staff Michael Deaver, whose background had been in public relations. Deaver had little patience when Edwin Meese told him, "You should do what is right, regardless of what the perceptions were.... We came here to chart new legal policy and you just don't give up selling your case because the *Washington Post* and a bunch of liberals in the NAACP take you on."[52]

As Deaver sized up the situation, "once the public perception turned sour the President was being hurt by it, [and] we had to address that instead of going over the hill with the flag flying." David Gergen, an assistant to the president for communications, agreed. "We had to avoid the charge that we were bigoted," Gergen said. "If your administration is perceived as racist, you can't exist. You can't govern in that situation."[53]

To turn things around, Deaver arranged for Reagan to meet with two black members of the administration: Thaddeus A. Garrett, Jr., a domestic affairs advisor to Vice-President Bush, and Melvin Bradley, a junior staffer in the Office of Policy Development. Garrett and Bradley told Reagan that many blacks regarded the legal arguments as a smoke screen concocted by officials who were either bigots or insensitive to the problem of racism. According to Deaver, Garrett and Bradley "were the first people who discussed the issue with [Reagan] from something other than a legal standpoint and he was very moved by their accounts." In fact, Deaver reported, "the President was astounded.... He turned to me and said, 'We can't let this stand. We have to do something.'"[54]

At this point the administration could not plausibly retreat from the legal position that the IRS lacked the authority to deny tax exemptions. However,

Deaver and others in the White House persuaded the president to call for *legislation* to outlaw exemptions for schools and other institutions that discriminated racially. On 12 January 1982, only four days after the policy change had been announced, Reagan modified the government's position. He repeated that "agencies [such as IRS] should not be allowed to govern by administrative fiat," but Reagan also emphasized that he was "unalterably opposed to racial discrimination in any form." In addition, the president said, "I believe the right thing to do on this issue is to enact legislation which will prohibit tax exemptions for organizations that discriminate on the basis of race."[55]

The liberal press looked askance at Reagan's call for legislation. One article in the *New York Times* said it was "an abrupt policy change prompted by his advisers' warnings that he was being viewed as a racist." Another article characterized Reagan's proposal as "contortionist politics forced by serious miscalculation." Reporters at a press briefing suggested that Reagan was trying to silence the "political uproar" and avoid a "political disaster."[56]

Since the administration had underestimated the extent of the "uproar," the questions about motives were inevitable, but there was no inconsistency between the 8 January announcement of a new legal position and the 12 January call for legislation. Reagan was simply saying that he thought Congress should give the IRS the authority to deny tax exemptions to discriminatory institutions.

A few weeks earlier, when the new legal position was still being discussed, officials at Treasury and Justice had considered the possibility of asking for legislation, but there was a problem of timing. Bruce Fein had flagged the *Bob Jones* case on 7 December, only one week before the administration was supposed to file its brief with the Supreme Court. The administration received a postponement until 8 January, but that meant the discussion of the case and the preparation of new briefs had to be done in only one month. Those who worked on the case assumed that legislation eventually would be prepared; they remembered "sitting around the table and people saying, in passing, 'if legislation is proposed, we can just endorse it.'" R. T. McNamar suggested that the administration should have its own legislation ready when the new legal policy was announced, but he failed to follow through because of the pressure of dealing with Polish debts (along with *Bob Jones* and the Christmas holidays). Reynolds, who at the time was also involved with complex voting rights cases, later said, "There was a definite feeling, given the pressure, [that] it would have taken a superhuman effort to draft legislation.... We felt the legislative program could be a follow-on, instead of tightly married to our filing of the case."[57]

In retrospect, McNamar considered it a major gaffe, for which he took "full personal responsibility," not to have had a legislative proposal ready on

8 January. Even Reynolds acknowledged "in hindsight" that it would have been politically expedient if the first public announcements had contained "more verbiage...about how we deplored racial discrimination." But Reynolds's choice of language indicated that he was more comfortable with legal analysis than with public relations. For Reynolds, the need was to explain the legal reasons that made the administration change its position in a case that was already before the Supreme Court. For him, it was of secondary importance to craft legislation or press releases to deal with what he called the "hue and cry."[58]

But a more adept presentation of the case probably would not have made any difference. Even if the Reagan administration had announced the new IRS policy with a simultaneous call for legislation, civil rights leaders, Democratic politicians, and liberal journalists would not have laid off. They thought the administration was wrong on *Bob Jones*, and they sensed that it was vulnerable.

Critics made two major points. First, they said that neither Reagan nor his staff understood "the symbolic and actual importance of what they were doing"; they were "subsidizing racism"; they were sending "a dangerous signal conferring respectability and moral legitimacy on positions quite properly considered abhorrent."[59]

A second criticism took issue with Reagan's statement that there was "no basis in law" for denying tax exemptions to discriminatory schools. At first the *New York Times* insisted that the problem was that the administration had chosen to disregard "the law already on the books." Later the *Times* acknowledged that "the tax laws do not specify in so many words that racially discriminatory schools should not get exemptions." Nevertheless, the *Times* noted that "well-reasoned lower court rulings long ago found that purpose in the law."[60]

Times columnist Anthony Lewis explained that since 1970 the IRS had framed its policy "in light of court decisions saying what the law was." Harvard law professor Bernard Wolfman similarly maintained that the IRS had "followed court decrees" and had done "no more than the law *required* it to do." Ralph Spritzer, another law professor, reiterated that "the federal courts...have not merely ruled that there is statutory authority for denying tax benefits to racist institutions and their contributors; they have held that provisions of the Internal Revenue Code require their denial." The Lawyers Committee for Civil Rights Under Law accused the Reagan administration of "contemptuous disregard" for court orders.[61]

Because they thought the law already denied exemptions to Bob Jones as well as similar institutions, and because they said that "the only lawlessness here is that demonstrated by [the] administration," most liberal critics opposed the passage of a new law. They said that "would lend credence to Mr. Reagan's claim that he had some legal basis for trying to kill an eleven-year old Internal Revenue Service regulation on tax exemptions." Besides, given the bad press Reagan was receiving, Democrats were, as Anthony Lewis noted, "inclined to do nothing, leaving the administration to twist slowly, slowly in the wind."[62]

But the law was not settled because the Supreme Court had never ruled on the tax-exemption issue, and in these circumstances, the question was bound to go before the justices. When it did, Reynolds argued the case for the administration, saying that there was "no evidence that [Congress] intended to delegate broad authority to the IRS." Congress had not yet passed legislation, Reynolds said, to "tak[e] away tax exempt status from a school that racially discriminates."[63]

When *Bob Jones* was before the Supreme Court, the Court invited the prominent black attorney and former cabinet member William T. Coleman to defend the policy of the IRS. Coleman maintained that since *Brown* there had been "a fundamental national policy...condemning racial discrimination in education." Consequently, Coleman said, it was unconstitutional for the government to support "any arrangement" that fostered discrimination. For that reason, he said, the IRS correctly decided in 1970 "that private schools practicing racial discrimination are not entitled to tax-exempt status."[64]

Coleman acknowledged that the tax law did not specifically mention discriminatory schools, but he argued that the IRS had understood the will of Congress. After all, Congress knew about the policy and acquiesced, for a decade, in the interpretation of the IRS, and by refraining from overruling the policy of the IRS, Coleman said, Congress implicitly ratified that policy. In the brief he submitted to the Court, Coleman wrote: "Congress has been fully aware of the IRS decision on this issue since the day it was made, and has repeatedly refused to alter the IRS ruling."[65]

In what the press described as "the most dramatic moment" of the oral argument, Justice Powell asked Coleman, "Is there any limiting principle to the right of the IRS to determine public policy?" If the Court ruled for the IRS, Powell wanted to know, would the IRS then be free to move against single-sex schools or against churches that harbored illegal aliens? Coleman then assured Powell that racial discrimination was in a class by itself historically. "We didn't fight a Civil War over sex discrimination," Coleman said.[66]

Reynolds was not persuaded by Coleman's arguments, as Coleman had not made any points that Deputy Solicitor General Wallace had not mentioned within the councils of the Reagan administration. But Reynolds's opinion no longer mattered. The case was before the Supreme Court and, by a vote of 8–1, the justices ruled in favor of Coleman and the IRS.

Writing for the Court's majority, Chief Justice Burger said that after *Brown* and the congressional debates over the civil rights laws, there undoubtedly was a fundamental public policy against racial discrimination in education. Burger conceded that "nonaction by Congress is not often a useful guide," but because Congress was well aware of the policy at issue in *Bob Jones*, this case did not involve an ordinary claim of legislative acquiescence. In this instance, the Court held, Congress' failure to act amounted to an endorsement of the IRS policy.[67]

Brushing aside the argument that tax exemptions had been intended to limit the influence of governmental orthodoxy and to promote diversity in a pluralistic society, Burger said that the purpose was to reinforce a common community conscience. Exemptions had been granted in accord with the common-law standard of charity—"to encourage the development of private institutions that serve a useful public purpose or supplement or take the place of public institutions of some kind."[68]

Justice Rehnquist dissented, and Justice Powell, while concurring in the judgment, did not agree with the Court's explanation of the purpose of tax exemptions. But most journalists, even some who usually are suspicious of conformity and favorably disposed toward dissenters, expressed few reservations. Anthony Lewis wrote that the chief justice's "magisterial" opinion had "demolished the legal arguments made by the Reagan lawyers," that it proved that the administration's real motives were political, and that the change in policy was a payoff to people who had supported Reagan in 1980.[69]

Most of the media concurred, and Lewis's view may well become the textbook truth about *Bob Jones*. Perhaps not, however. David Whitman, the author of a good scholarly monograph on the case, has criticized the media for assuming that the administration's arguments were camouflage for bigotry and politics. Instead, Whitman concluded that the administration "took the actions it did...because of its conservative philosophy and views on statutory construction." The liberal line on *Bob Jones* has also fared poorly in the law reviews. In 1985 Dirk Roggeveen, a law clerk in the Department of Justice, reported that only eight of thirty-one law review articles were supportive of the Supreme Court's opinion (with eighteen critical of the Court and five taking no position). Virginia law professor Paul B. Stephan represented the majority point of view when he wrote that the *Bob Jones* Court had "strained the limits of credible interpretation."[70]

For his part, Reynolds acknowledged that the administration "didn't handle [the *Bob Jones* case] as well as we could have from a public relations standpoint." Reynolds belatedly recognized that it was naive to have expected the media to understand that *Bob Jones* was about the separation of powers and was not a civil rights case. Reynolds also recognized that the Reagan administration "paid a high price for *Bob Jones*." Because of it, critics would characterize other administration policies as *racist.* "Sometimes they didn't even use the word," Reynolds said. "They could just say, 'It's another *Bob Jones* case.'"[71]

Nevertheless, even after the passage of ten years, Reynolds thought it would have been unconscionable to have ducked the case. He recognized that "the rest of the administration, if they had the opportunity to revisit *Bob Jones,* would say, Hell no," but Reynolds still thought they had done the right thing.

> Even though we lost 8 to 1, I believe to this day that the position we took is the legally correct position. I think it was important that somebody said to the Supreme Court, *We are not going to assign policy-making functions to an agency like the IRS without having Congress weigh in on it one way or the other.* That to me is a fundamental proposition in our scheme of constitutional government.[72]

Notes

1. 26 U.S.C. 501(c)(3); Bob Jones University v. U.S., 461 U.S. 574, 481. Section 501(c)(3) also gave tax-exempt status to organizations whose purpose involved "testing for public safety."
2. Green v. Kennedy, 309 F.Supp. 1127 (1970), 1137, 1134.
3. Statement of Daniel Patrick Moynihan, *Hearings of the Senate Finance Committee,* Legislation to Deny Tax Exemptions to Racially Discriminatory Schools, 97th Congress, 2nd Session, February 1982, 238–40 (cited hereafter as 1982 Senate Finance Hearings).
4. David Whitman, *Ronald Reagan and Tax Exemptions for Racist Schools* (Cambridge: Center for Press, Politics and Public Policy at the Kennedy School of Government, Harvard University, 1984), 7–8; John Erlichman, *Witness to Power* (New York: Simon and Schuster, 1983), 224.
5. David Whitman, *Ronald Reagan and Tax Exemptions for Racist Schools,* 7–8.
6. Walz v. Tax Commission, 387 U.S. 664 (1970).
7. Statement of Randolph W. Thrower, before the Senate Select Committee on Equal Educational Opportunity, 91st Congress, 2nd Session, 12 August 1970, 1995; Green v. Connally, 330 F.Supp. 1150 (1971), 1156–64.
8. See Reiter v. Sonotone Corporation, 442 U.S. 330 (1979), 339 ("Canons of construction ordinarily suggest that terms connected by a disjunctive be given separate meanings, unless the context dictates otherwise").
9. Ibid. The new IRS ruling (71-447) declared that when Congress provided exemptions for religious, charitable, or educational organizations, it "intended to express the basic common law concept [of 'charity'].... All charitable trusts, educational or otherwise, are subject to the requirement that the purpose of the trust may not be illegal or contrary to public policy."
10. Green v. Connally, 330 F.Supp 1150 (1971); 404 U.S. 997 (1971); *New York Times,* 13 February 1982, 24:1; 5 February 1982, 30:1; 14 January 1982, 22:1.
11. Statement of Edward C. Schmults, *1982 Senate Finance Hearings,* 207; Bob Jones University v. Simon, 416 U.S. 725 (1974), 740 n.11.
12. Bob Jones University v. U.S., 461 U.S. 574 (1983), 580–81; Laurence I. Barrett, *Gambling With History: Reagan in the White House,* 418.

13. Bob Jones University v. U.S., 468 F.Supp. 890 (1978), 894; McCrary v. Runyon, 427 U.S. 160 (1976).
14. Bob Jones University v. U.S., 468 F.Supp. 890 (1978), 894.
15. Ibid.; 639 F.2d 147 (1980). On appeal to the Supreme Court, the *Bob Jones* case was consolidated with a second case that concerned the Goldsboro (N.C.) Christian Schools. By policy, the Goldsboro schools refused to admit black students.
16. *1982 Senate Finance Hearings*, 59–61.
17. David Whitman, *Ronald Reagan and Tax Exemptions for Racist Schools*, 32; *1982 Senate Finance Hearings*, 200, 199.
18. *1982 Senate Finance Hearings*, 238, 201.
19. David Whitman, *Ronald Reagan and Tax Exemptions for Racist Schools*, 31.
20. Ibid., 32.
21. *1982 Senate Finance Hearings*, 222.
22. Ibid., 242, 222.
23. David Whitman, *Ronald Reagan and Tax Exemptions for Racist Schools*, 34.
24. Interview with William Bradford Reynolds, 11 January 1991.
25. Amicus Curiae Brief for the American Baptist Churches in the U.S.A., 14, Bob Jones University v. U.S., Supreme Court Library.
26. Brief of Amicus Curiae, General Conference Mennonite Church, 1, 4, 3, 5, Bob Jones University v. U.S., Supreme Court Library.
27. Brief of Amicus Curiae, National Committee for Amish Religious Freedom, 4, Bob Jones University v. U. S., Supreme Court Library; Memorandum of Amicus Curiae, Church of Jesus Christ of Latter-Day Saints, 11, 14, ibid.
28. Interview with William Bradford Reynolds, 11 January 1991; concurring opinion of Justice Powell, Bob Jones University v. U.S., 461 U.S. 574 (1983), 608–9. On this point Reynolds and Powell agreed with comments that Justice Brennan made in Walz v. Tax Commission, 397 U.S. 664 (1970), 713: "Government grants exemptions to religious organizations because they uniquely contribute to the pluralism of American society by their religious activities. Government may properly include religious institutions among the variety of private, non-profit groups that receive tax exemptions, for each group contributes to the diversity of association, view point, and enterprise essential to a vigorous pluralistic society."
29. William Bradford Reynolds, et al., Brief for the United States, 45–50, Bob Jones University v. U.S., Supreme Court Library. Reynolds was referring to Reynolds v. United States, 98 U.S. 244 (1978); Jacobson v. Massachusetts, 197 U.S. 11 (1905); and Prince v. Commonwealth of Massachusetts, 321 U.S. 158 (1944).
30. Ibid., 45–50; Wisconsin v. Yoder, 406 U.S. 205 (1972).
31. Amicus Curiae Brief of Congressman Trent Lott, Bob Jones University v. U.S., 18, Supreme Court Library; Bob Jones University v. U.S., 639 F.2d 147 (1980), 163–64; University of California v. Bakke, 438 U.S. 265 (1978).
32. *National Review* (24 June 1991): 26–27.
33. Ibid.; Bob Jones University v. U.S., 639 F.2d 147 (1980), 157.
34. William Bradford Reynolds to William French Smith, 5 January 1982, WBR Papers; Reynolds et al., Brief for the United States, Bob Jones University v. U.S., 12 and passim, Supreme Court Library.
35. David Whitman, *Ronald Reagan and Tax Exemptions for Racist Schools*, 44.
36. Chronology of the *Bob Jones* Case, WBR Papers.
37. David Whitman, *Ronald Reagan and Tax Exemptions for Racist Schools*, 49–50.

38. Ibid., 51; Bob Jones University v. U.S., 461 U.S. 574 (1983), 601, 620–21.
39. David Whitman, *Ronald Reagan and Tax Exemptions for Racist Schools*, 53, 51–52.
40. Ibid., 21; IRS news release (IR-2027), 21 August 1978.
41. Donald Bruce Johnson, *National Party Platforms of 1980* (Urbana: University of Illinois Press, 1982), 184; Reagan-Bush Committee, Statement on Education, reprinted in *1982 Senate Finance Hearings*, 62–63.
42. See *Hearings before the Subcommittee on Oversight of the House Committee on Ways and Means*, Tax Exempt Status of Private Schools, 96th Congress, 1st Session (1979). The Ashbrook and Dornan amendments were passed in 1979, 1980, and 1981 as riders to the appropriations act for the Treasury Department. After 1981, there was no longer a need for such riders because, as Reynolds noted, there was not even "a remote possibility" that the Reagan administration would return to the IRS policies of 1978 and 1979. *New York Times*, 4 June 1983, II, 16:1.
43. *1982 Senate Finance Hearings*, 248; *New York Times*, 12 January 1982, 15:5; 19 January 1982, 27:1; 21 January 1982, 23:1.
44. Chronology of the *Bob Jones* case, WBR Papers; Trent Lott to Rex Lee, 30 October 1991, *1982 Senate Finance Hearings*, 51–52; Reagan's handwritten notation, reprinted in *1982 Senate Finance Hearings*, 71, 73; David Whitman, *Ronald Reagan and Tax Exemptions for Racist Schools*, 37.
45. David Whitman, *Ronald Reagan and Tax Exemptions for Racist Schools*, 37–39.
46. Ibid., 40–41.
47. Peter J. Wallison to Donald Regan (thru R. T. McNamar), 22 December 1981, *1982 Senate Finance Hearings*, 74–76.
48. David Whitman, *Ronald Reagan and Tax Exemptions for Racist Schools*, 46, 33; *1982 Senate Finance Hearings*, 248; Lincoln Caplan, *The Tenth Justice*, 84.

    After the administration's lawyers had decided on the legal position, the political ramifications were discussed at additional meetings with White House Counsel Fielding, with Chief of Staff James Baker, and with Presidential Counselor Edwin Meese. President Reagan was not present at the discussions but was informed of the impending change. When a storm of criticism erupted, some officials told the press that Reagan had not been fully briefed and had not understood the full significance of *Bob Jones*. CBS News reported that "senior White House aides are saying...that the President was blind-sided, that he was totally unaware of the potentially severe political backlash." But at a televised news conference Reagan took responsibility for the *Bob Jones* policy: "I'm the originator of the whole thing...What we were trying to correct was a procedure that we thought had no basis in law, that the Internal Revenue Service had actually formed a social law and was enforcing that social law. And we think that that's a bad precedent and it's a bad thing to do.... I didn't anticipate that it was going to be misinterpreted as it was." David Whitman, *Ronald Reagan and Tax Exemptions for Racist Schools*, 45, 94, 102–3; Transcript of CBS "Evening News with Dan Rather," 12 January 1982, 6; *New York Times*, 20 January 1982, 20:1.
49. *New York Times*, 12 January 1982, 14:1; 10 January 1982, 1:4; *Los Angeles Times*, 12 January 1982, II, 4:1; David Whitman, *Ronald Reagan and Tax Exemptions for Racist Schools*, 67, 66.
50. David Whitman, *Ronald Reagan and Tax Exemptions for Racist Schools*, 62, 80, 63.

51. Ibid., 80–81. Reynolds essentially anticipated the thesis of social scientists S. Robert Lichter, Stanley Rothman, and Linda S. Lichter, who reported that "across four elections [from 1964 through 1976], the Democratic margin among elite journalists was 30 to 50 percent greater than among the entire electorate. Less than 20 percent of the journalists supported a Republican candidate in any of the four elections." To illustrate how political bias was reflected in the media, Lichter, Rothman, and Lichter presented a content analysis of press coverage of three major issues (busing for integration, the safety of nuclear power, and the role of the oil industry in the energy crisis). *The Media Elite* (Bathesda: Adler & Adler, 1986).
52. David Whitman, *Ronald Reagan and Tax Exemptions for Racist Schools*, 72–73.
53. Ibid., 73, 85.
54. Laurence I. Barrett, *Gambling With History*, 415–16. Deaver later said, "One of the reasons we got into this mess was that the only people Ronald Reagan had talked to about the issue [before the decision was announced on 8 January 1982] were lawyers. So far as I am concerned, lawyers are not real 'people.' They live in their own world. That was one reason the President was so moved when he finally got to talk with some of the blacks on his staff who didn't discuss the issue from a legal standpoint." David Whitman, *Ronald Reagan and Tax Exemptions for Racist Schools*, 86.
55. *New York Times,* 13 January 1982, 1:6.
56. Ibid., 13 January 1982, 1:6; 17 January 1982, IV, 4:3.
57. David Whitman, *Ronald Reagan and Tax Exemptions for Racist Schools*, 35–36, 60.
58. Ibid.; *New Republic* (25 January 1988): 11.
59. Tom Wicker, "Subsidizing Racism," *New York Times*, 12 January 1982, 15:5; Robert M. Cover, "Court Has High Aim, Bad Plan on Bias," *New York Times*, 11 July 1983, 15:1.
60. *New York Times*, 21 January 1982, 20:5; 5 February 1982, 30:1; 26 February 1982, 1:1; 28 February 1982, IV, 18:1.
61. Ibid., 21 January 1982, 23:1; 19 January 1982, 27:1; 25 January 1982, 30:4; 14 January 1982, 10:4.
62. Ibid., 5 February 1982, 30:1; 8 February 1982, 19:1.
63. *Los Angeles Times*, 13 October 1982, 17:1; *New York Times*, 12 February 1982, 20:3.
64. Because the Reagan administration refused to argue the position the Government had taken in the courts below, the Supreme Court had to appoint another attorney—Coleman—in order to have an adversary proceeding. William T. Coleman, Jr., Brief of Amicus Curiae in Support of U.S. 6, Bob Jones University v. U.S., Supreme Court Library.
65. Ibid., 8; *New York Times*, 22 October 1982, 16:3.
66. *Los Angeles Times*, 13 October 1982, 17:1; *New York Times*, 25 October 1982, 18:1.
67. Bob Jones University v. U.S., 461 U.S. 574 (1983), 600.
68. Ibid., 588.
69. *New York Times*, 26 May 1983, 27:5.
70. David Whitman, *Ronald Reagan and Tax Exemptions for Racist Schools*, 79; Paul B. Stephan III, "Bob Jones University v. United States: Public Policy in Search of Tax Policy," *Supreme Court Review* (1983): 35.
71. *New Republic* (25 January 1988): 11. Interview with William Bradford Reynolds, 11 January 1991.
72. Interview with William Bradford Reynolds, 11 January 1991.

Index